When War Passed This Way

By

W. P. Conrad and Ted Alexander

A GREENCASTLE BICENTENNIAL PUBLICATION

IN COOPERATION WITH THE
LILIAN S. BESORE MEMORIAL LIBRARY
Greencastle, PA

WHITE MANE BOOKS
SHIPPENSBURG, PENNSYLVANIA

The acid-free paper used in this book meets the guidelines for permanence and durability of the Committee on Production Guidelines for Book Longevity of the Council on Library Resources.

For a complete list of available publications
please write
White Mane Books
Division of White Mane Publishing Company, Inc.
P.O. Box 708
Shippensburg, PA 17257-0708 USA

**Published as a feature of the
Greencastle Bicentennial in cooperation
with the Lilian S. Besore Library.**

1st Printing, 1982
2nd Printing, Revised 1987
3rd Printing, 2016

LIBRARY OF CONGRESS

Library of Congress Cataloging-in-Publication Data

Conrad, W. P.
        When war passed this way / by W.P. Conrad, Ted Alexander.
            p.   cm.
        Reprint. Originally published: Greencastle, PA : Lilian S.S.
Besore Memorial Library, 1982.
        Includes bibliographical references and indexes.
        ISBN-13: 978-0-942597-02-8
        ISBN-10: 0-942597-02-8 : $24.95
            1. Greencastle Region (Pa.)--History.   2. Cumberland Valley (Md.
and Pa.)--History--Civil War, 1861-1865.   I. Alexander, Ted.
II. Title.
F159.G78C63   1987
974.8'44--dc 19

PRINTED IN THE UNITED STATES OF AMERICA

TABLE OF CONTENTS

INTRODUCTION

When War Passed This Way was an expression used by people of Pennsylvania's southcentral region to explain the Confederate invasion of 1863. It is used as the title of this account of the Civil War's impact on those who lived in this part of the Commonwealth during the four tragic years of hostilities and the decades that followed. However, the story's central theme is mainly found in the experiences of those who lived in the Greencastle-Antrim community during this period.

This project has evolved from approximately five years of research into records of the United States Army Military History Institute, the National Archives, the Library of Congress, Pennsylvania's State Library and Archives, private and public libraries, Grand Army of the Republic records, files of National Military Parks, newspapers of the war and post-war years, letters and diaries from both public and private collections, records of both Northern and Southern historical societies, and countless interviews with older residents whose early family members lived during the Civil War and through the decades that followed.

We wish to thank the following staff members of the U.S. Army Military History Institute for their contributions: Dr. Richard J. Sommers, archivist historian, who provided continuous guidance and advice concerning resource materials; Michael J. Winey, curator, who furnished valuable information concerning Pennsylvania troops and photographs from the library's extensive collection; Randy Hackenburg, the assistant curator; and John Slonaker, chief librarian.

Of equal importance was the help of Michael Musick at the Old Army and Navy Branch, National Archives, who provided materials concerning the U.S. Signal Corps and information from military and pension records and Paul T. Heffron, acting chief of the Manuscript Division-Library of Congress, who made possible a review of the Hotchkiss and Ewell papers.

Mr. and Mrs. George H. Bricker, of the Philip Schaff Library — Lancaster Theological Seminary, contributed the Charles Hartman Diary while Diane M. Telian, manuscript librarian at the Historical Society of Pennsylvania in Philadelphia, provided access to the Patterson-Cadwalader collection.

The staff of the Pennsylvania State Library made available many issues of area newspapers that covered Civil War developments in the south-central region of the state. Invaluable help and encouragement came from John Frye, director of the Western Maryland Room of the Washington County Free Library.

Local libraries furnished an abundance of material. Research help by the following is appreciated — Jane Schleicher, chief librarian at the Chambersburg Coyle Library; Eleanor Giltinan, reference librarian for the Conococheague District Library; Victoria Weiner, head librarian, and Louise Mowen, assistant librarian, at Greencastle's Lilian S. Besore Memorial Library; and Elizabeth J. Cooper of the Fenwick Library of Mercersburg. The files of Waynesboro's early newspapers at the Record Herald office contributed greatly to the project.

Special recognition must be given to the Frank L. Carbaugh Legion Post of Greencastle for making available local G.A.R. records and artifacts and to John Craig and William Moore for their interest and help. Another source was the Franklin County Office of Veterans Affairs. Through this agency's director, Robert Meck, burial lists of the area's Civil War veterans were provided. We, also, wish to thank Thomas Bohon for his help in editing the manuscript for historical accuracy.

All of these resource institutions and persons, along with others too numerous to mention, provided necessary background information to develop the story. In addition, we wish to thank the artist, Mark Noe, for his illustrations and the use of art subjects he produced for Greencastle's First National Gallery of History. Decorative Arts of Hagerstown's Valley Mall provided excellent restorations of old photographs used to further illustrate the text.

The seemingly endless typing and re-typing that eventually resulted in a final manuscript came only through the dedicated endurance of Jane C. Alexander. Her help in preparing the material that constitutes this segment of Pennsylvania's history is greatly appreciated.

W. P. Conrad and Ted Alexander

MAP OF
FRANKLIN
COUNTY PA
Scale 3 miles to the inch

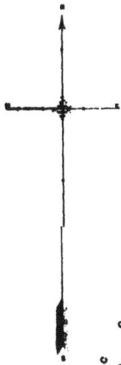

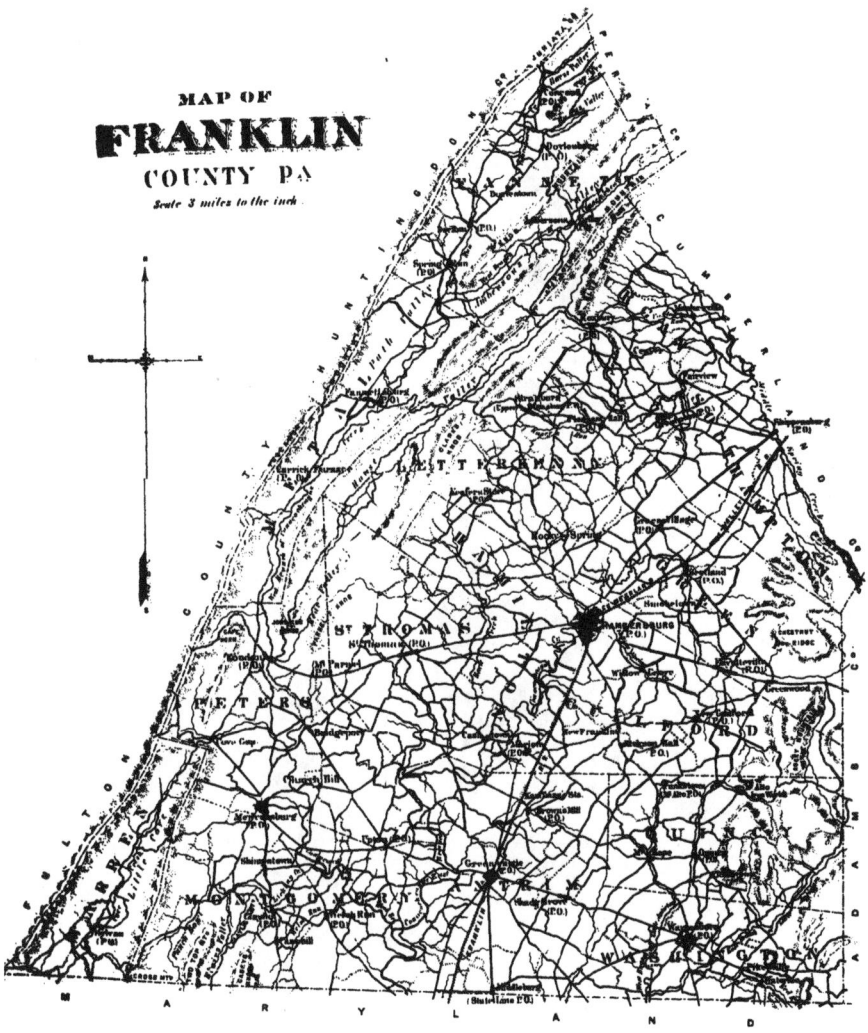

CHAPTER I

PEACE BEFORE A TROUBLED TIME

This is a story of how the Civil War touched the lives of those who lived in the southern part of Pennsylvania's broad, fertile Cumberland Valley. It was through this southcentral part of the state that Franklin County became a virtual corridor for armies of both the North and South as they moved against each other for strategic advantages throughout the four year struggle. In the center of this passageway lay the small town of Greencastle and its neighbor Antrim Township. This rural community, bordering on the Old Line State of Maryland, was the centerpiece of a trail of events which wove a wartime web that ensnared all who lived then and through the years that followed.

Greencastle and Antrim are names that came from Northern Ireland, home country of the Scotch-Irish who first settled in the region. These pioneer people migrated into and acquired land holdings in the frontier part of the Penns' colony as early as 1740. A century later the population consisted of descendants of these early families and sons or grandsons of German immigrants who had fled from the Rhineland to settle in the area just prior to and after the Revolution. Also living in both town and country were several hundred Negroes. Some were free men as the result of Pennsylvania law. Others had been liberated at the death of their masters, while some were descendants of fugitives from the upper South.

By 1860 Greencastle was home to approximately 1,300 people while 3,400 lived on the farms and in the villages of Antrim. Villages, large enough to have post offices, were Browns Mill, a little less than three miles north of Greencastle; Shady Grove, about three miles to the east; and Middleburg, also called Muttontown, five miles to the south, just north of the Maryland line. There were two growing hamlets, one in the southwest corner of the township to be known later as Coseytown and the other, called Clay Hill, two miles to the east of Browns Mill.

The town, founded in 1782 by John Allison, a first generation American of Scotch-Irish descent, was the center of community life. In 1805 Greencastle was separated from the township when the General Assembly declared it to have borough status. Over the next half century its importance as a market place and nucleus for social relationships between its residents and the rural people was well established. Here were the shops of skilled craftsmen, retail stores, commission merchants, and wholesale businesses. It was a place where surplus grain, fruit, vegetables, butter, eggs, and other produce could be sold. Here, too, were hotels with dining halls, saloons, and facilities for overnight lodging. In the town could be found doctors, dentists, apothecary merchants, and when death came to a loved one there were undertakers skilled in crafting coffins for final interment.

Greencastle lay on a comparatively level terrain between sloping ridges to the east and hill country beyond its western border. Its two main thoroughfares were Carlisle Street, a north-south route, and Baltimore Street which followed an east-west course. Where they crossed in the middle of the town the open space was known as Center

GREENCASTLE

Scale 300 Feet to the Inch

(Adaptation of 1868 …)

ATLAS OF FRANKLIN COUNTY   POMEROY AND BEERS
THE TOWN DURING THE WAR

Square which everyone called the Diamond. Four side streets, named for their direction from the main ones, completed the original plan. Eventually North Street became Madison, East was named Washington, South became Franklin and West was known as Jefferson Street. By 1850 the borough's boundaries had expanded to a point where three additional streets were required. These came to be known as East Second, South Second, and West Second Streets. Ten years later there were 231 families living along these thoroughfares. Some lived in one or two storied log houses or framed structures covered with weatherboard siding. Unlike Antrim, there were few stone dwellings. However, more affluent people lived in brick homes generally located along the two principal streets.

Nearly all families had a stable for a cow or more if they could afford them. These were essential for a regular supply of milk, butter, and cheese. A horse and buggy or carriage might also be housed in the stable if the family was rich enough for such luxuries. Every household depended on its back lot for raising food. Both renters and property owners had their vegetable gardens and a variety of fruit trees, berry bushes, or grape arbors. No one was without a potato patch that also yielded turnips later in the season. Everybody had chickens and few were without hogs to be butchered when cold weather came in the late fall or early winter days. Open grazing of cattle and pigs was still allowed but owners were liable for damages if they trespassed on neighboring properties.

BESORE LIBRARY COLLECTION   BY MICHAEL CONRAD
EARLY LOG HOUSE STILL SERVING AS A DWELLING

Homes were built close to the front property lines. Where there were side yards they were enclosed with white washed picket fences. Shade trees, most often maples, elms, or poplars, lined the streets and board walks or brick pavements could be found in front of most homes along the main thoroughfares. However, the families living away from the center of town knew only foot paths to separate their properties from the edges of the streets.

Many townspeople owned and operated their own businesses, but most families were supported by the father and older sons working at establishments engaged in retail or wholesale merchandising or manufacturing. There were many craftsmen, as late as 1860, still engaged in the time honored arts of making shoes, boots, or hats. Others could fashion, to the customer's needs, what was required in the way of clocks or various kinds of household furniture. Weavers worked at making carpets, shawls, blankets, or coverlets and there were tailors practicing their trade in little shops along the town's main streets. Yet, as each year passed such artisans could feel the competition from stores where similar factory made commodities were sold.

Work could be found in the building trades or in the town brick yards. There were butchers, pump makers, blacksmiths, tinsmiths, coppersmiths, coopers, shingle makers, and sawyers. There was a tannery as well as several wagon, coach, and buggy shops. Foundries molded parts for farm equipment, stoves or fireplaces. They produced household laundry irons, cookware such as pots, kettles, skillets, bake ovens, griddles, waffle irons, and other articles needed in every kitchen. A copper and brass foundry made kettles, candle sticks, fireplace fixtures, bed warmers, building trim, lock parts, buttons, and other kinds of hardware. There were firms that manufactured farm equipment and tools including wheelbarrows, plows, harrows, grain drills, mechanical threshers, grain cradles, hay forks, rakes, sickles, and scythes. Nearby farms and mills also provided employment for workers who lived in the town.

Most women were occupied with their household duties. However, some made a living as dressmakers or milliners while others worked in homes of well-to-do families as cooks and general housekeepers. Negro women were also employed as cooks and house workers while their men often served the same families as drivers, stablemen, and gardners. Many blacks, both men and women, found employment in the town's hotels.

Retail establishments played important roles in the economic life of Greencastle and its rural area. General stores carried a full array of merchandise - dry goods, groceries, hardware, dishware, boots, shoes, and an extensive line of items called notions. By 1860 specialty stores had come into local retail business life. One sold nothing but groceries and another specialized in clothing like fancy coats, skirts, hose, gloves, suspenders, shirts, and many varieties of cloth for home dressmaking. There was a shop that limited its sales to hats, caps, boots and shoes.

Hardware stores advertised building and housekeeping items like oils, paints, putty, window glass, hinges, locks, screws and nails. Table and pocket cutlery, tubs, buckets, churns, ropes, brushes, gunpowder and lead were also available. One such business carried a complete line of "beautiful coffin trimmings." Another shop offered the latest tinware made of extra heavy metal with great "savings" to its customers.

There were commission merchants, also known as factors, who supplied a service to those with produce or merchandise to be shipped to city markets. These businessmen, for a percentage of the sales, found the best prices available for the sellers in Baltimore or Philadelphia. [1]

In 1860 the business leaders of Greencastle were generally merchants and owners of larger shops engaged in producing farm equipment and building needs. Prominent merchants at this time included J. W. Barr, John Bert, John Goetz, Jacob Hostetter, A. L. Irvin, Jacob Pensinger, H. P. Prather, Wesley Rhodes, T. S. Riley, John Rowe, Daniel Snively, John Spielman, and George W. Ziegler. Principal commission merchants were Addison Imbrie, A. K. Schaffert, and Jacob Smith. Imbrie, along with John Bradley, J. B. Crowell, W. H. Davison, Edwin Emerson, and Franklin Keller were manufacturers who operated foundries and steampowered shops that made grain drills, hay rakes, door and window frames. Charles Hartman and Nicholas Martin were the town's principal blacksmiths; Christian Hoover was its brick maker; and Andrew Stiffle its tanner. Henry Walter owned the marble works, Archibald Logue ran a freight service, and Samuel Stoner operated an omnibus line between Greencastle and Waynesboro. General David and Jeremiah Detrich plus Augustus Shirey were the town's undertakers. The only newspaper, a weekly called "The Pilot", was owned and published by James W. McCrory. [2]

There were three hotels to accommodate travelers as well as local people. At this time hostelries were recognized as community centers for public meetings, polling places at election times, and where farmers could hold sales of livestock or used equipment. They also were important as news gathering centers since travelers often brought news from the outside world that supplemented stories found in city newspapers or the local weekly. The Union Hotel, oldest of the three, was owned by Major Joseph Hollar. It was on the southwest corner of the Diamond. Several doors away from the train depot on North Carlisle Street stood the Franklin House operated by Daniel Foreman. The newest, established in 1859, was the Antrim House located on the northeast corner of the East and Baltimore Street intersection. Its owner was Thomas Pawling, a descendant of the family who had operated the earliest tavern in this part of Pennsylvania.

Stores, shops, factories, foundries and all other businesses brought profits to owners and wages to workers. Side by side they both labored for as long as twelve hours daily with Sunday as the day for rest. Wages ranged from fifty cents to a dollar a day according to the type of labor. The standard of living in 1860 varied little from that of the earlier years of the century. Beef sold for as little as seven cents a pound. Veal and pork were six cents for a like amount. Butter could be bought for as little as twelve cents and lard for six cents a pound. Fresh oysters from the Chesapeake Bay sold for thirty five cents a quart. Molasses cost sixty cents a gallon and a barrel of flour came to five dollars. Horse owners had to pay thirty three cents for a bushel of corn and thirty five for oats. Tobacco sold for twenty five cents a pound and a quart of whiskey could be bought for eighteen cents.

Rents for homes ranged from two to four dollars a month, while a substantial dwelling could be built at costs ranging from seven hundred to a thousand dollars. The more luxurious homes of the wealthy families would have cost five to six times this amount. Furniture made by local cabinet and chair makers was crafted from lumber furnished by area saw mills. Pine, poplar, hickory, were used for less expensive pieces while walnut, cherry, and maple were fashioned into more elaborate furnishings. [3]

Few families used coal for heating or cooking. Firewood, which sold for $1.50 a cord, was the most popular fuel for heating homes in the winter months. Food was prepared on wood or coal burning cook stoves. Water for the families came from cisterns or barrels that collected rainwater drained from roofs of houses. Some had wells and there were public wells in various parts of the town. Equipped with wooden pumps, these provided water to travelers as well as nearby families when their home supply was diminished. The wells also served as a major source of water for fighting fires.

Fires were a constant menace. Although there was a firefighting brigade, the only equipment was a hand pumper that had been bought in 1828. When a place caught fire this piece was used to throw water on adjoining buildings to keep the fire from spreading. Men and boys, along with women at times, helped fight conflagrations by forming bucket lines which ran from the nearest well to the fire. Nearly every home had a leather bucket for this purpose and when an alarm was sounded neighbors came to help fight the blaze by this primitive method. Except for the hand pumper, this bucket brigade method was used to fight fires in rural places too. Since most buildings were widely scattered in the country the danger of extensive loss was not as great as in the town.

As in the colonial period, candles or lard oil lamps were still used for lighting homes during the evening and early morning hours. The town had a few street lights which also used lard oil. These gave sparse illumination at street and alley crossings along the main streets. However, for practically everybody, lighting ones way outside the home was a personal responsibility. Moonlit nights presented little difficulty but in the dark of the moon it was well advised to light the way by hand carried lanterns. [4]

BESORE LIBRARY COLLECTION   EARLY PHOTOGRAPH
GREENCASTLE FROM CENTER SQUARE-SOUTH ON CARLISLE STREET
C1870

At the dawning of each day traffic began. Coach drivers, freight wagoners, drovers, and all others who had journeys to finish were on their way and the streets came alive with townspeople going to their businesses or places of employment. Those who left town for other destinations could travel north on the Harrisburg Pike. Such a journey could lead to Chambersburg, Shippensburg, Carlisle, and the state capital. To the south a poorly kept public road ran, by way of Middleburg, to Hagerstown, Maryland. This route went through Greencastle on Carlisle Street and south of the borough limits it veered slightly to the east to follow its southerly course. Travelers could also approach the road from East Street which eventually joined it beyond the town's southern edge.

A second route into Maryland was another turnpike constructed by local investors to provide farmers and businessmen of Franklin County access to the Chesapeake and Ohio Canal at Williamsport. Here they could take their grain, potatoes, or other produce for shipment to markets along the canal or on to the nation's capital. The limited supply of coal used locally came from barges hauling this fuel from Cumberland, a receiving station for coal mined in western Virginia and southwest Pennsylvania. The road was called the Greencastle and Maryland Line Turnpike and Plank Road. South of the borough it joined the Hagerstown Road as it left town by forming a diagonal junction or fork with this highway. (*In modern times the Harrisburg Pike became known as U.S. Route 11 and the Turnpike and Plank Road was designated as an alternate Route 11.*)

Turnpikes such as these used the latest road construction technique developed by the Scotch engineer, John Loudon McAdam. They were built of broken stones of uniform size with raised centers to allow for drainage into run-off gutters at each side, a method that provided roads capable of supporting the heaviet kinds of traffic known at that time.

By 1860 the Cumberland Valley and Franklin railroads had become an important part of the valley's north-south transportation system. In 1859 the Cumberland Valley Company had leased the Franklin system which ran between Chambersburg and Hagerstown. Improvements followed and by 1862 the entire line was owned by the Cumberland Valley Company. Running from Harrisburg to Hagerstown, it provided both passenger and a limited freight service.

Through Greencastle the tracks ran down the center of Carlisle Street with a woodyard and water station at the northern end, a passenger depot in a store room north of the Diamond, and freight warehouses just beyond the town's southern boundary. Local business leaders gradually began to use the line since its connections at Harrisburg with the Pennsylvania Railroad represented improved opportunities for buying or selling commodities in a greater number of markets.

Despite the railroad's value to the local economy, the most important avenue of commerce was the toll road that connected Pittsburgh with Baltimore, the closest port city to the local area. Franklin County's portion of this throughfare was the Waynesburg *(Waynes-*

boro), Greencastle and Mercersburg Turnpike Company. *(Currently part of Pa. Route 16.)* Running through the town on Baltimore Street, it was a busy route generally filled with horse drawn wagons hauling grain, flour, bacon, potatoes, and other commodities from inland Pennsylvania to the Maryland city. Return trips brought to the merchants of towns and villages along its way such merchandise as molasses, coffee, tea, saltfish, oysters, drygoods, boots, shoes and other city products. The turnpike also accomodated drovers with their herds of sheep, cattle, hogs, and even geese or turkeys being driven to the city markets. [5]

By 1860 Baltimore was the principal port not only for Maryland but for southern Pennsylvania, northern Virginia, and it had become important to Ohio as well after 1853 when the Baltimore and Ohio Railroad was completed to Wheeling on the Ohio River. Pennsylvania was a major source of wheat for the city's flour mills, yet in 1857 the city exported 270,557 barrels of flour that had been milled in the Keystone State. Most of the port's trade was with South America and in return it received hides for leather making and coffee. The city also served as a major port for the southern states. For example, in 1860, 35,000 bales of cotton were shipped to Baltimore's textile firms to be processed into fabrics for sale in Maryland and Pennsylvania. This brief picture of Baltimore's commerce shows how important the city must have been to people living in the Greencastle-Antrim area and in other towns of south-central Pennsylvania. [6]

These major avenues of commerce were supplemented by a network of side or back roads connecting neighborhoods with each other and the entire rural area with the town. Dusty in dry weather, filled with deep ruts, and sometimes impassable in rainy periods or during the winter or spring thaws, they nevertheless knitted the entire area into one economic and social entity. The country roads provided access also to rural sections of Maryland and their villages or towns. Antrim had over 110 miles of public roadways, the most of any township in the county. Other municipalities possessed similar systems and it was possible, through this labyrinth of routes, to get to the county seat and other towns without using the main turnpikes for one single mile.

Most roads traversed local streams at fordings. There were two exceptions. One was a five arch bridge a mile west of Greencastle that spanned the Conococheague Creek, the township's western boundary. This was built when the turnpike was constructed. Several miles down stream there was a covered wooden bridge which crossed a road connecting the village of Upton, in Peters Township, with the turnpike to Williamsport. It was near Martin's Mill, an important grist and saw mill serving people of the western parts of Antrim Township.

Leaving Greencastle in any direction, by turnpike or back road, travelers would encounter open fields interspersed with stretches of timberland covered with hard and soft wood trees, brush, bushes, and occasional varieties of wild fruit trees. There were two kinds of arable land, legacies of an ancient geologic age when this portion of the continent was the floor of a vast, endless, shallow sea. One kind was limestone found in the central and eastern parts of the township. It was a loamy soil accounting for the many prosperous farm lands of the area. To the west on the hills that stretched along the Conococheague was a slatey or shale like soil of lesser quality. Here the fields required liberal rainfall or crops suffered. This region was generally referred to as the pine hills a tribute to the profusion of evergreens that often dotted their crests, sloping sides, and ravines.

Most of the people who farmed these lands were of German origin. At least eighty percent of the families were known as Pennsylvania Dutch. These sturdy, frugal, hard working and highly religious people had provided the community with farmers and skilled craftsmen for at least three generations prior to the Civil War. The remaining Scotch-Irish, descendants of the early settlers, still farmed the lands their ancestors had secured from the Penn proprietors. Many of their places were operated by tenant laborers or hired hands while the owners managed and directed them. Although the Scotch-Irish did not dominate the agriculture of this era, they nevertheless were leaders in improving farm management with the latest equipment or newest methods to bring better crop yields.[7]

Most rural families lived in log houses, some covered with clapboard siding, or in limestone homes erected during the post-Revolution period. Others possessed newer dwellings constructed of brick from the town's brick yards. With holdings as large as three hundred acres or as small as ten they labored from dawn to dusk through most of the spring, summer and fall seasons.

Large families were a necessity and it was not unusual to find from twelve to fifteen children in their homes. When old enough, girls helped their mothers with the many household responsibilities, while boys labored in the fields and wood lots or around the farm buildings along with their fathers.

A common practice at the time was for poor people with large families to hire their children to farmers. Girls provided extra hands for the wives while the boys worked as farm laborers. Papers were signed by the father to bind his child over to the farmer for a given period of time. In return the farmers paid the father, at the end of each year's bondage, an agreed upon sum of money. Children as young as twelve years of age were hired out in this manner and their parents received as little as fifty cents a week or a year's pay of twenty-six dollars for their child's labors.

Most girls and boys who were a part of this bondage system had few complaints. They lived better, in most cases, than in their own homes. Although they were expected to work for their keep, they ate their meals with the family, slept in the home, attended school, went to church with the host family, and often entered into social gatherings along with their erstwhile parents, and their children. Tales of cruelty in this system were not unheard of but few children were abused. Laws provided for penalties if masters mistreated their wards. However, in general, the relationship between the bonded girls or boys and their masters was mutually helpful. Many children who were a part of this system became successful farmers or business leaders in later years.[8]

Hired hands, found in the villages or Greencastle, were available for wages as low as fifty cents a day. Many men and boys from the Negro families living in Antrim also worked on nearby farms. During peak work periods a time honored custom was for neighbors to help each other.

Plows drawn by two horses required a single driver and on larger holdings several teams were needed for the fall and spring plowing. Spiked harrows were used to level the furrows for the seeding that followed. Grain was planted either by hand or on larger farms by horse drawn mechanical drills. Some farmers used reapers but most of the wheat, oats, rye, buckwheat, or barley was harvested manually with grain cradles and threshed with wooden flails or mechanical threshers powered by two horse treadmills. Hay was mowed with scythes, raked into windrows and, after curing, gathered and stacked or stored in the hay lofts of the commodious barns for which Pennsylvania was noted. Corn was cut with sickles or specially designed knives, stacked in shocks to be husked at a later time, and eventually stored in cribs adjacent to the barns. In addition to these basic crops, potatoes were grown for home consumption and for town or city markets. Hops were produced for breweries in the county and Philadelphia or Baltimore. Honey was another profitable farm product while flax was raised for making linen and linseed oil.

Raising livestock was essential to every farm operation. Farm animals provided manure to fertilize the fields, hides for leather, and wool for clothing. But most importantly they were a primary source of food. Cattle supplied milk, butter, and cheese; a steady supply of beef; and cash when sold to livestock dealers or local butchers. Sheep were raised mostly for wool and occasionally for food. Hogs, slaughtered in the fall and winter, gave every household a year long supply of lard, cured and smoked hams, bacon, sausage, as well as butchering time delicacies - such as souse, panhaus, pudding, tenderloin, stuffed hog maws, and a host of fresh pork cuts for frying and roasting. Chickens, turkeys, geese, and ducks comprised the poultry that became main dishes for the dining table. Eggs, essential to most meals, were also a source of income. Earnings from egg sales usually went to the housewives for what was called "pin money."

Another profitable business was found in the uncleared lands of the farms. Here could be found wood for fuel, fencing, and lumber. Cutting cordwood for home use and sale to villagers or townspeople became a highly gainful business. Fuel wood customers could be found not only in the homes but among the merchants, shop owners, and professional people. The railroad was in constant need of this fuel for their locomotives. Lumber was also sold for building construction and to places where wooden pumps, tools, shingles, furniture, barrels and many other miscellanous products were manufactured.

No farm was without a vegetable garden or berry patch, while arbors filled with grapes and orchards with apple, peach, cherry, pear, or plum trees were in abundance. A variety of vegetables and fruit brought gustatory delight with their freshness, as savory dishes prepared when they were first picked, and through the rest of the year through various kinds of preservation. Most of these foods could be retained for months by pickling, drying, and canning processes. Some fruits and berries were converted into jellies and preserves while cool cellars kept potatoes and apples, along with kegs of sauerkraut and crocks of fresh lard. These basements with their earthen floors were also repositories for jars of preserved fruits and vegetables plus jugs of wine and brandies made from the farm's fruits and berries. They were also storage places for apple butter, vinegar, and cider pressed from the family supply of apples during the later months of every autumn. Such farm living came as close to self sufficiency as humanly possible. Except for those necessities purchased at the nearest general store the soil was the basic source of most family needs.

ATLAS OF FRANKLIN COUNTY   POMEROY AND BEERS
ANTRIM — AS IT WAS C1868

Leading farmers of the community were such men as Nathan H. Brumbaugh, Andrew and James Davison, Archibald Fleming, Joseph Hade, John and Lazarus Kennedy, Andrew J. McLanahan, James Mitchell, Gideon Rahauser, Jacob Shook, Jacob Stover, David Strite, and A. B. Wingerd. There were four Snivelys, all prominent in the affairs of the area - Benjamin, Joseph, Samuel and Melchi, who founded the village of Shady Grove. George W. Brumbaugh and John Ruthrauff farmed and also dealt in livestock.[9]

The fields of the countryside also provided wild food for both farm and non-farm people. Springtime yielded an abundance of field greens. Dandelion, dock, poke weed, landcress, wild asparagus, and butter leaf were delicacies in the early weeks of each growing season. Fields and meadow lands offered a variety of wild plants for making tea, for use as beverages or medicinal purposes. These included peppermint, catnip, spearmint, boneset, and one, with a rich promise, called life everlasting. Chicory was used too as a beverage when combined with coffee. Spring fed streams were places to find watercress and along their banks were stalks of calmus.

The woods also abounded with food. Here were mushrooms and other forms of edible fungi. Roots and bark from young sassafras trees along fence rows or in wooded areas were used for making tea. Walnut, chestnut, hickory nut, and shell bark trees yielded their harvests every autumn.

A generous supply of game provided meat for many families. Muzzle loading shotguns and rifles were the principal tools for killing animals of the field and woods. Trapping small game was a common practice. Deer were available in valley and mountain woodlands. However, the quarry most accessible included rabbits, squirrels, ground hogs, possums, and muskrats. One man who lived on the southwest edge of town in the 1850's once boasted that he could go into the woods back of his house and shoot enough squirrels for a meal before breakfast. Game birds such as wild turkeys, ducks, geese, pigeons, doves, and bobwhites were in abundance as hunters killed them for food for their family tables.

Sportsmen fished the smaller streams and creeks with rod and line but those who depended on the waterways for food used more effective methods. They gathered fish with nets or seines, by gigging, and with baited hooks on under water lines that stretched across creeks, bank to bank. These were set at night and the catch of fish or eels gathered each morning. Turtles were taken from their nests under creek banks and frogs were hunted throughout the warm weather months.

Although there were early game laws by this time they were rarely enforced. For most people interested in hunting or fishing they knew no seasons or limits. Abundance of game and fish provided many poorer families, especially those who lived in the hill country near the Conococheague, with a year round supply of food. Few persons imagined, in 1860, that this would ever end.[10]

Rural residents not engaged in farming worked at a variety of other occupations or in businesses of their own. The most prominent was milling. Powered by water from dams fed by small streams or sluices along the creek, there were at least thirteen such operations in various parts of the township. North of Greencastle could be found three grist mills along Muddy Run. Owned by J. M. Brown, Mathias Kisecker, and A. B. Rankin, they produced flour, corn meal, and livestock feed. Kisecker also operated a saw mill.

FIRST NATIONAL GALLERY OF HISTORY   MARK TWAIN NOE
KISECKER MILL

Near the northern edge of the borough, Isaac Ilgenfritz owned a woolen mill that got its power from a stream originating at Moss Spring. Beyond the western limits of the town stood a grist and bone mill. Both, owned by Addison Imbrie and A. K. Schafhirt, were powered by a stream from McCauley's Spring. The bone mill made meal from pulverized bones to be used as fertilizer.

A profusion of mills could be found in southwestern Antrim. Along the creek there was one owned by Samuel and Nathaniel

Martin and a fulling mill, that processed flax, was the property of Jacob Sites. Near the Turnpike leading to Williamsport, Robert Johnston ran a grist mill and the only commercial distillery in the community. Below this operation were two more mills operated by the Henkell and Whorley families. Near Middleburg and in the Marsh neighborhood of eastern Antrim were saw mills run by Samuel Shindle and C. D. Lesher.

Millers made their living from shares of flour or meal processed for the farmers.They received what was called a toll or an eighth of what was ground as their portion. The woolen mill owner took his share of the wool brought to be carded and woven, and sawmillers were either paid given amounts or they retained a portion of the lumber for themselves.[11]

Country stores, found in Antrim's villages and at other strategic points, such as crossroads, were important to all rural families. Here they could buy drygoods, agriculture implements, coffee, salt, patent medicines, tobacco, gun powder and lead, shoes, and many other items that were essential to rural living. A barrel of whiskey was usually available for retail purposes and occasional drams for customers to promote their goodwill and increased sales which may have followed. Rural stores also sold the text books used in the township schools. Barter was a recognized system of exchange by all storekeepers. Farmers brought such produce as eggs, butter, grain, bees wax, feathers, tallow, hides, or whiskey to exchange for the merchandise they needed. The stores were also favorite places for loafing by both farmers and villagers. Here, too, were congregating points for political speeches and the arguments that followed. At times they were used as polling places. When a community became large enough to qualify for postal service it usually was the general store that became the post office. In most cases this was true if the storekeeper was of the right political persuasion.

By 1860 Middleburg was the only Antrim village to have a tavern. This hostelry, owned by Jacob Brumbaugh, was on the southeast corner of the square along, what the villagers called, the Hagerstown Pike. It accommodated travelers including teamsters and drovers doing business in Hagerstown or points beyond. Another tavern, operated by the Wilhelm family, was patronized by Antrim people living in the western part of the township. It was in Upton, a village along the Waynesburg, Greencastle, and Mercersburg Turnpike, in Peters Township.[12]

Blacksmith shops could be found in villages and at other points along rural roadways. As in the town, craftsmen plied their trades in shops near their homes. Some of the artisans were skilled in making wagons, and coaches, while others produced plows, harrows, grain cradles, and wooden shaking forks or hay rakes. Coopers made barrels for farmers, millers, and those who needed to store whiskey, cider, vinegar, lard oil, and other commodities in their homes or places of business.

As in most small town-rural communities, organized religion played an important part in many people's lives. Their houses of worship were found in both Greencastle and Antrim. Some rural families attended church in the town while there were townspeople who belonged to congregations in the country. Churches of German origin - Reformed, Lutheran, Mennonite, Dunkard, United Brethren - formed the great majority. A lone Presbyterian place of worship in Greencastle served its Scotch-Irish parishioners on West Baltimore Street. By 1860 Methodists had a church on South Carlisle Street and Negro families attended their little sanctuary near the southern edge of the town. The German Reformeds and Lutherans formed a union church in Greencastle following the Revolution. They worshipped in a log structure on South Carlisle Street, but by 1860 the Reformeds had moved to a new edifice on East Baltimore Street and the Lutherans to one on North East Street.

By 1860 Antrim people had places for worship in Middleburg and Browns Mill. A combined Reformed and Lutheran church, constructed of stone, served the many German families of the Middleburg region while another building accommodated a Methodist congregation. Although there were many Mennonites living in the township as early as 1790, they did not have a house of worship until 1830. At this time they constructed a church in Browns Mill. Most other plain sects held services in the homes of members living in Antrim or places of worship in adjoining townships or across the Mason-Dixon line in Maryland.

Most congregations had grave yards near their churches. In Greencastle there were three exceptions. The Reformeds still used the burial place at the site of their early church. Presbyterians still buried at Moss Spring where their original church had stood and the Methodist cemetery was on South Washington Street on the present public school site. In addition to church grave yards many rural people had burial plots on portions of their farms.

Lutherans, Reformeds, Mennonites, and other plain sects conducted services through the early years of the century solely in German. However, by 1860, most congregations had gone to the use of English. In some instances an arrangement prevailed where the

German language was used once a month. This was to satisfy the older parishioners who still believed they communicated best with their Maker in the language of their forefathers.

Although churches were concerned with early efforts to educate the community's children, by 1860 education was a public responsibility. Pennsylvania's School Law of 1854 gave improved state subsidies and with monies raised by local taxes, schools became an important part of community life. [13]

In Antrim there were twenty one-room school houses, all except one, constructed of brick or logs. The exception was a stone building at Browns Mill. Greencastle had four one-room buildings located in different parts of the town. Of the twenty-five teachers in these houses of learning, sixteen were men who earned salaries of $35.00 per month in Antrim and $33.00 in Greencastle. Women teacher salaries ranged from $25.00 to $30.00. Schools were in session four months a year with the term usually beginning in October. Teaching for men was considered part-time employment since schools were in session when farm work was at a minimum. Subjects taught included spelling, reading, grammar, geography and arithmetic. For most children this was the only formal education they ever received and since attendance was not compulsory, many passed through childhood with little or no formal training.

More affluent families sent their daughters to private "select" schools in the town where they received training in academic subjects, etiquette, sewing, and knitting. Board and room were provided for those who came from the township or nearby towns. Young men from such homes also attended private schools. Some were students at the Chambersburg Academy while others attended such institutions in Greencastle. At mid century an academy was operated by Clarke and James McDowell, the county's first school superintendent. By 1860 James had died and the school was run by the surviving brother. Here boys were taught not only rudimentary subjects, but higher mathematics and foreign languages. Obviously the teachers in these schools were better educated than those of the public system. They were at least graduates of preparatory schools or in some cases possessed college degrees.

Although limited, the education girls and boys received was better than that of their parents. The public one-room schools provided the basics and many by their own efforts, succeeded in acquiring greater knowledge through reading and improving their skills. Those with the training of select schools and academies had advantages not known to those from lower income families, but in many instances a lack of academic training was no hindrance to eventual success as farmers, craftsmen, merchants, and businessmen. [14]

Sickness was a constant problem and everyone relied heavily on home remedies for treating common ailments. Yet the ravages of disease and lack of simple sanitary precautions brought untold loss of life especially among children and mothers who died from complications during or following childbirth. Diphtheria, measles, smallpox, cholera, scarlet fever, typhoid, pneumonia, and whooping cough were common killers. People died from consumption, now known as tuberculosis, and acute indigestion which in most cases would be diagnosed today as heart failure. Farm and shop accidents often resulted in death from infections that followed.

During this mid-nineteenth century era even the best educated and most skilled physicians had to practice their arts within the restraints of medical knowledge of the day. These limits, plus the meager education of the general public in matters related to health, gave people in 1860 a life expectancy far less than that of modern times. National statistics for this era show that women had a life span of 40.5 years and for men it was 38.3 years. High levels of death among children accounted for the low life expectancy statistics. In fact, many men and women lived to advanced ages having survived the perils of infancy and later years of childhood.

Local doctors who practiced medicine during this era included such men as William Grubb, James King Davison, Charles Michaels, Adam Carl, George D. Carl, Edwin D. Rankin, Cephas Wingerd, and George R. Kauffman. All except Dr. Grubb, who studied under the renowned physician, Dr. John McCellan, were graduates of medical colleges in Pennsylvania or Maryland.

People depended largely on home remedies concocted from herbs commonly found in the area or drugs purchased in local drug stores. In 1860 Dr. Adam Carl and his son, William, conducted a pharmacy, where these could be purchased. Grocery and general stores also carried patent medicines which were advertised to possess cures for most every ailment known to man. [15]

Despite the ever present shadow of death or high rate of illness and a daily existence, filled with long hours of labor, there were compensating moments for relaxation. There was a social side to·life enjoyed by both young and old. The most prominent weekly event was going to church and then get-to-gethers for Sunday meals where members of the family gathered around a groaning table heaped with culinary efforts of the housewife or family cook. This could be at the home of parents, grandparents, aunts and uncles, or perhaps cousins. Beyond these weekly gatherings there were other occasions for recreation and fun and frolic. One simple and popular pastime was the custom of "neighboring". The latch string was always out for visiting neighbors. At times, an entire family would go to the home of a friend or relative after supper. The hostess would have gingerbread or doughnuts and cider for the evening's refreshments. While older family members talked of crops, politics, or the most recent gossip, the children played games. Also, singing by both young and old was part of the evening's fun. When bedtime came, the women collected the household's bedding and spread it on the parlor floor for the visitors. After a night's sleep and hearty breakfast, the guests would depart for their homes with promises of reciprocating the hospitality of the previous evening.

People who lived on farms, as well as those of the villages or borough, extracted pleasure from many work related activities such as quilting bees, corn husking parties, and times when friends came together to help make cider and apple butter, at harvest time, when barns were raised, or at butcherings. Public auctions, weddings, and funerals also brought people together for socializing. Contests among the men and boys of the community included competitions in marksmanship, wood cutting, horse pulling or racing, grain cradling, and mowing hay. The fall and winter months brought town and country people together at events like singing schools, public debates, and spelling bees usually held in the nearest one-room school. Hayrides and dances were popular and during snow periods sledding, skating, and sleighing parties were common pastimes.

Few holidays were celebrated. The principal ones, Christmas and Easter, always called for special observances. Christmas was the occasion for caroling parties, family feasting, and giving toys and inexpensive gifts to children. Easter was a more solemn kind of observance. Some churches celebrated this day of consecration with the communion sacrament. Plain sects, such as the Mennonites, observed the sacrament by holding Love Feasts in their houses of worship.

A New Year's Eve custom was belsnickeling, when revelers dressed in outlandish costumes, called on homes in their neighborhoods. The new year was ushered in at mid-night with discharging pistols, muskets, and rifles. New Year's Day was a time for visiting neighbors and friends to offer good wishes for the coming year and to drink a glass of wine or whiskey. Needless to say that after several visits there was an unusual amount of befuddlement in many parts of the community.

Independence Day or the Fourth of July was usually observed with special programs accompanied by bon fires, exploding fireworks, and discharging muskets or rifles. In rural areas observance of this holiday with elaborate programs was seldom found, but explosive noises dominated the day.

Two customs, distinctly of German origin, were the observance of Grundsaudaad or groundhog day and Fastnacht. Groundhog day was said to foretell the weather, a matter of great importance to farmers. If there was sunshine on February 2 the woodchuck or groundhog would see his shadow and return to his winter hibernation, thus predicting six more weeks of winter weather. In Germany the Tuesday before Ash Wednesday was celebrated with carnivals and feasting before the long fast of the Lenten season. Although their Palatine forefathers had discarded the gaiety of this Shrove Tuesday, the custom among Pennsylvania Germans was to bake and eat doughnuts to symbolize the feast before the six weeks of self denial. Observance of other holidays such as St. Valentine's Day, April Fool's Day, and Halloween called for no special celebrations. The first day of April and Halloween were for the pranksters while St. Valentine's was for lovers.

Traveling tent shows or small circus troupes visited the area from time to time and an occasional concert by the Chambersburg band was usually well attended by young and old from both town and country.

Finally it must be remembered that the town and village taverns or hotels continued to be centers of conviviality. These establishments were gathering places for enjoying good food and drink. They provided an atmosphere of relaxation from daily cares where stimulating conversation, heated arguments, and occasional brawls were commonplace. Barrooms were sanctuaries for men only and drunkenness was widespread, especially on Saturday nights. Controls over excessive drinking were apparently limited to restraints put upon husbands by their wives and frequent arrests made by town or township constables for drunken and disorderly conduct. (*Arresting disorderly citizens, serving legal papers on debtors, and enforcing local ordinances seem to have been the principal responsibilities of these law enforcers. By 1860, records show that other law breakers consisted mainly of those accused of larcencies and assaults. Major crimes such as arson, burglary, robbery, or murder were extremely rare.*)

Among those who fought the evils of alcohol it was argued that much of the lawlessness that did prevail would be reduced if the sale of spiritous and malt liquors was prohibited. This argument, along with the known danger to health and the relationship of drinking to poverty were instrumental in bringing the temperance movement into Franklin County. As early as 1837 newspapers told of local chapters of the Sons of Temperance being formed. Yet, by mid-century little had been accomplished. Except for the numerous pledges to forsake the "cup of iniquity" and occasional temperance rallies, the movement showed limited success.[16] By 1860 the National Hotel, Franklin and Antrim House, along with the Brumbaugh tavern in Middleburg, were still in business serving the community as havens where worldly cares could be forgotten and the conviviality induced by whiskey, rum, wine, cider, and beer continued as always.

So it was that the people of Greencastle and Antrim Township lived in 1860. It was a time of seeming prosperity with improved transportation that brought distant markets closer to the community. Gradual improvement of agricultural methods meant better use of the fertile lands and more abundant harvests. Few people realized, at the time, that the coming of steam operated machines would eventually free manufacturing from the limits of water power. It was a time that marked the beginning of the end of the ancient crafts and the pride that accompanied the workmanship of their practitioners.

Yet the traditions of the past, among the Scotch-Irish and German people of both town and township, still dominated the pattern of community life. Hard work with limited diversions, respect for family living, concern for education, reliance on neighbors for help in troubled times, and an unshakable confidence in the watchful eye of a merciful Divine Providence — these were the essential beliefs that carried all from the cradle to the grave.

This limited description of the Greencastle-Antrim community attempts to provide a picture of how its people lived in the last full year of peace the nation would know over the next four years. As 1860 ended, the news of Southern plans for secession were not too alarming. Only South Carolina, by then, had taken this step and attempts were constantly being made to cool the indignation among slave state leaders, an indignation that had been growing ever since the election of Abraham Lincoln nearly two months before. Yet, as the new year dawned, few Northerners believed that all of this Southern hostility would lead to a full scale war. Most certainly few could have known in 1860 that it was the last year of peace before a troubled time for all America.

What Greencastle or Antrim resident could have known that the future would bring to this little town and its countryside an almost constant pattern of enemy raids or rumors of impending raids, threatened invasions, or actual invasion? Few, if any, would have foreseen that their community would become a vital ink in a communication system that would run the length of the Cumberland Valley to the state's leaders in Harrisburg. Who could have known that Greencastle and its rural countryside would become a military staging area with armed camps at times virtually surroundig the town?

Above all, no one could have foretold the immeasurable heartache that families suffered when they saw their men and boys leave for service in the Federal forces. Nor could they have known of a future filled with sorrow that would come from messages of loved ones killed on distant battle fields or wounded and lying in some hospital far from home.

CHAPTER II

SEEDS OF WAR

War came in 1861 but its causes had their foundation in America's earliest colonial period when the first seeds of Negro slavery were planted in the Virginia Colony. In 1619 a Dutch trader sold twenty blacks to work with indentured laborers, their white counterparts. They were not referred to as slaves then but in time there developed, throughout the colonies, a gradual dependence on Negroes who could be bought and sold like any other property.

Over the next two centuries black slaves became the very foundation of the South's economy while in the North their economic importance gradually vanished. By 1850 this institution had created a profound moral question for the nation and the Southerners' insistence on extending it into the western territories transformed slavery into a serious political and economic concern as well.

Not all Negroes were slaves for there were sizable numbers of free blacks in many parts of the nation. The census of 1860 showed Pennsylvania with nearly 60,000 free blacks. States like Maryland had almost 84,000, and Virginia 58,000 and in the rest of the South there were probably 130,000 blacks who could be called free men. Yet the same census showed only sixty-four slaves in the North while below the Mason-Dixon Line and Ohio River there were 3,953,760 Negroes in bondage.

The elimination of slavery in Pennsylvania was a slow process that developed after the Revolution and through the early decades of the nineteenth century. Although the Keystone State was the first to legislate a gradual end to slavery the rest of the North acted more slowly. Not until 1805 could it be said that every northern state had made some provision for eventual emancipation.

The story of Pennsylvania's involvement with slavery began as early as 1661 when a Dutch governor along the Delaware announced that none would be allowed in his jurisdiction. William Penn owned slaves, yet in 1700, he urged Quakers to take a stand against holding men in bondage. At his death, in 1718, all of his blacks were freed by the terms of his will. Despite this early evidence of opposition, the practice grew in most parts of the colony. In 1750 there were as many as 11,000 black bondsmen in Pennsylvania, but by 1780, the number had been reduced to 6,000. Most of these were domestic servants with less than ten percent working on farms. The census of 1790 listed 3,737. Ten years later there were 1,706 and by 1840 only forty Negroes were still in bondage. This gradual elimination was due to the anti slave legislation of 1780.

In 1779 the Supreme Executive Council of Pennsylvania recommended to the State Assembly a plan for the gradual emancipation of slaves and the next year this proposal was given the force of law. It provided that on or before July 4, 1827 all adult slaves were to be liberated. Children born before that date were to be freed when they reached the age of twenty-one. The law also provided that Negro slaves coming into the state were to be set free.

One of Antrim's sons, James McLene, a member of the Executive Council, favored this legislation. McLene lived in the Browns Mill community and was a political leader throughout most of his adult life. He served in the Continental Congress and in 1777 was Speaker of the State Assembly. He was active in the movement to establish Franklin County and from 1790 to 1794 served in the U.S. House of Representatives. After this McLene returned to Browns Mill and at his death in 1806 he was acting as a Justice of the Peace in the township.

Through Greencastle's and Antrim's early years those who owned slaves were generally Scotch-Irish. Few German farmers had them, not only for moral or religious reasons, but it was more economical to work their lands themselves. The national census of 1790 showed 330 slaves in Franklin County and every decade that followed saw a steady decline until in 1850 there was none. The last sale of slaves in the state took place in 1829 on a farm near Guilford Springs just a few miles from Antrim's northern border. [1]

Pennsylvania's experience in banning slavery was repeated in other northern states. This was prompted by the fact that such labor was not suitable for economic reasons and of equal importance was the growing opposition to it on religious and humanitarian grounds. The first organization to call for the abolition of slavery throughout America was founded in Philadelphia in 1775 and when the Civil War came it was still functioning and known across the land as the "Pennsylvania Society."

During the early years of the nineteenth century abolitionists were constantly showing, by petitions to Congress, by public meetings, and through anti-slavery newspapers, their determination to end slavery throughout the south. Most hoped this could be accomplished by federal legislation. However, radical elements called for more drastic measures. One was to establish a plan to help slaves escape to freedom. Admittedly, this was of primary benefit to those who lived in the Upper South. It came to be known as the Underground Railroad, an organized network for moving fugitive Negroes from one hiding place to another through Pennsylvania and New York to Canada. Similar operations were conducted in Ohio, Indiana, and Illinois. Leaders of the system, praised its effectiveness in freeing thousands of Negroes. However, recent studies suggest that such claims were probably exaggerated and that the system was not as effective as claimed by its proponents. The most prominent organization responsible for most of this operation in Pennsylvania was the Philadelphia Vigilance Committee. Records show this group was able to free only about a hundred fugitives a year. There are strong indications that more fugitives gained freedom through their own efforts and not by the planned escape routes offered by the underground system.

One account tells of three slaves leaving their owner who lived near Hedgesville, Virginia. This is about seven miles northwest of Martinsburg. They walked to Greenville in Pennsylvania and took a train as part of their escape plan. This undoubtedly was Greencastle which was approximately twenty-five miles from Hedgesville. To get to Greenville, in Mercer County, would have meant walking over 250 miles where there was no railroad. It is not known whether these blacks were ever captured or if they eventually got to Canada.

Whatever ways of escape were used, there were concerned whites who helped runaways but in most cases it was the colored people living in the North who helped their black brothers and sisters get to the freedom land beyond the northern border. In Franklin County there were abolitionists who aided fugitives as they passed through this part of the state. Many of the routes were through the mountains on either side of the Shenandoah and Cumberland valleys, yet tradition holds that several homes in the Greencastle-Antrim area served as hiding places for those fleeing to Canada.[2]

Prior to 1850 there were few dangers in helping runaways, but with the passage of the Fugitive Slave Act the practice became more precarious. The force of federal law was now back of those looking for escaped slaves. Under this legislation anyone helping fugitives was subject to both fine and imprisonment. However, enforcement of the law was often dependent on local courts. Franklin County's record of cases dealing with runaways shows the courts generally ruled to uphold the federal law.

Throughout the free states there were men in the business of catching fugitive blacks and returning them to their owners. Newspapers were constantly printing advertisements of owners looking for their property and these men were avid readers of the daily and weekly journals. Here they could find descriptions of runaways and the rewards offered for their capture. One account tells of a Chambersburg constable, John Grove, assisting in the capture of two fugitives from Winchester and receiving a reward of $600 from the owner.

With the force of federal law, slave catchers became more active in apprehending fugitives. Two of Franklin County's most notorious men of this stripe were Clagget Fitzhugh and Daniel Logan. They, along with their associates, were despised by all who opposed slavery. During the Civil War these men became active in the Confederate cause serving as informers and agents who helped Southern raiding parties as they came into this part of the state.[3]

In the meantime the extremists of the anti-slavery movement continued their work. Just as the Nat Turner affair, in the 1830's, was applauded by abolitionists, the fugitive slave resistance of 1851 at Christiana in Lancaster County was greeted with equal enthusiasm. Frederick Douglass, the noted anti-slavery advocate, called the Christiana uprising a "battle for liberty." When Edward Gorsuch and a posse attempted to recover several slaves who had escaped from his farm in Baltimore County, Maryland, they were met by a band of fifteen to twenty ex-slaves headed by their black leader, William Parker. In the fighting that followed, Gorsuch was killed and his son, Dickinson, wounded. Eventually all of the Negroes, except Parker and three others who escaped to Canada, were captured and tried in state and federal courts. A verdict of not guilty in a federal district court, sitting in Independence Hall, freed them and their Quaker neighbors who had befriended the blacks. This was a direct blow to the Fugitive Slave Law and the anti-slavery forces saw the verdict as a victory for their cause.[4]

After the Christiana incident the nation's torment continued. Abolitionist settlers were attacked in the Kansas Territory by pro-slavery bands from Missouri. In 1856 John Brown and his four sons came to Osawatomi, Kansas to establish a defense force for the little town of Lawrence. From there he led raids into nearby pro-slavery settlements. In one, at Pottawatomie Creek, five men were killed in cold blood and retaliation followed, with a reign of terror sweeping through Kansas. One of Brown's boys was killed and the abolitionist, along with his remaining sons, returned to the East.

These incidents were deplored in both North and South but the greatest blow to the anti-slavery cause came when the Supreme Court, in its 1857 Dred Scott decision, declared Congress to have no power to prevent slavery in any territory.

In the meantime the Republican Party had been formed in 1854. One of its purposes was to oppose the extension of slavery into the western territories. Free labor advocates, western farmers, and remnants of the weakened Whig party, along with northern business and industrial leaders formed the nucleus of this new political force. Abolitionists naturally leaned toward the Republican cause. When its first national convention was held at Philadelphia in June of 1856 one of Franklin County's delegates was George W. Ziegler, a Republican leader from Greencastle. [5] In November the party's nominee, John C. Fremont, was defeated for the presidency by James Buchanan of Pennsylvania, a native of the Mercersburg region. Despite this defeat, the new party continued to grow in strength as opposition to the Dred Scott decision gained momentum. Then in 1859, the name of John Brown once again flashed across the conscience of the nation.

This time the abolitionist leader had concocted what appeared to be a foolhardy plan to capture the arsenal at Harpers Ferry in Virginia. From there he planned to distribute weapons to black leaders for full scale slave uprisings throughout the state. Brown's plot began in Pennsylvania with Chambersburg as his base of operations. Here he assembled his little army and weapons for the raid. Ever loyal to their father and the cause he represented, his remaining sons, Oliver, Owen, and Watson were part of the army. During June and July Brown stayed at the Union Hotel in Greencastle and the Brumbaugh Tavern at Middleburg at times when he was traveling from the county seat to the Kennedy farm in Maryland - the point from which the raid would begin. There were four black abolitionists in the group. One of these, Osborne Anderson, met his leader at Middleburg on the night of September 24. Brown had been waiting there to transport him to the farm by wagon and they drove through the night, reaching their destination the next morning. Anderson was the last of the twenty Brown had assembled and three weeks later, in the late evening hours of October 16, his army began its mission, doomed to become another episode in the sorry tragedy that was unfolding.

When news of the attack spread into Virginia and Maryland, militia units were immediately dispatched to the scene. There followed sporadic fighting with losses on both sides. During the next twenty four hours Brown and his men were surrounded with all avenues of escape closed. In the meantime United State Marines, led by Col. Robert E. Lee, arrived and in the forenoon of October 18, Colonel Lee directed his aide, Lt. J. E. B. Stuart, to ready his men for an assault on the engine house where Brown and his followers had barricaded themselves. After a fruitless attempt to talk them into surrendering, twelve Marines stormed their stronghold. Within three minutes the fighting was over. Throughout this futile affair five citizens and one Marine had been killed. The abolitionist lost nine men, including his sons, Oliver and Watson. Four of the abolitionists, along with their leader, were captured.

Seven of Brown's army, who had been assigned to guard weapons in a nearby school house, got away. After hiding until nightfall they worked their way to the South Mountain and over the next several days, by following the mountain's rugged roads and trails, they found themselves in Pennsylvania. John E. Cook was one of the escaping party. When they got to the Mont Alto region, in Franklin County, he volunteered to go to the village for food. As he made his way down the mountain he was apprehended by David and Daniel Bumbaugh, iron furnace workers, and within hours the abolitionist was a captive of Clagett Fitzhugh and Daniel Logan. They took their prisoner to Chambersburg on October 25, just a week after the raid had been suppressed. In the county seat Cook was tried and found to be one of Brown's collaborators. For the capture Fitzhugh and Logan received a $1,000 reward, part of which they shared with their collaborators, the Bumbaughs. Albert Hazlett, another of Brown's men, was captured in Carlisle several days later. Both he and Cook were returned to Charles Town and held with the other prisoners. The remaining five, including Owen Brown, were never caught. One of these was Osborne Anderson, the black who had met Brown a month before at Middleburg. Anderson later wrote his experiences which told of his relationship with Brown and the part he played in the illfated escapade.

On October 31, John Brown was found guilty of treason against the Commonwealth of Virginia and on December 2, 1859 he was hanged. Six days later his funeral was held at North Elba near Lake Placid in New York where the eulogy was delivered by America's leading anti-slavery orator, Wendell Phillips. His eloquence enshrouded the fallen leader with a mantle of martyrdom. Through Brown's death the abolition cause was now stronger than when he lived. [6]

Over the next several months Brown's fellow captives met the same fate as their leader. Although the death of the fiery abolitionist and his collaborators brought a sense of relief to some Southerners, his plan to arm slaves and turn them against their masters sent waves of anger and revulsion throughout the South. In this scheme they saw a gathering storm, a storm that could eventually engulf them in a flood that might sweep away the very way of life they had known for generations. The John Brown plot was, in the minds of many, not only the work of abolitionists, but a scheme of the Republicans to bring slave holders to their knees. Both Republicans and abolitionists were balanced out as equals on the scale of hatred with which the Harpers Ferry event was weighed and a chorus of cries for secession was heard throughout the Southland.

In the North the martyred Brown became a rallying symbol for the most radical abolitionists as the song, "John Brown's Body", echoed across the land above the Mason-Dixon Line. "His soul is marching on" became a phrase that stirred even those who had never been a part of the anti-slavery movement and more people began to question the nation's future if slavery were to spread into the lands west of the Mississippi.

Although leaders of the Republican Party vehemently denied any connection with the Harpers Ferry plot they certainly were not above taking comfort in realizing the potential political strength the ghost of the fallen hero could generate. As the presidential election of 1860 was not far away party leaders began to see the possibility of victory. Although William Seward of New York was mentioned most as the logical choice for the party's nomination, a new name had come to focus in the minds of many Republicans. The name was Abraham Lincoln, of Illinois. His clear and concise views on the nation's future were beginning to appeal to many, not only in the West, but in the East where Republicanism was stronger. His debates with Stephen Douglas in 1858 during the campaign for the Untied States Senate had caught the attention of party leaders all over the North. Although Lincoln lost this election he began to speak at rallies in other parts of the country and his star continued to rise. One of his most important opportunities came on February 27, 1860 with an address at the Cooper Union in New York. Here he impressed his audience and the press with an appeal for sectional conciliation, calling for a strong spirit of nationhood. He repudiated the John Brown outrage and other radical views in this highly acclaimed speech.

In May of 1860 the Republicans met in Chicago to select their candidate. Their platform insisted, among other things, that it was the right of Congress to prohibit the spread of slavery into the western territories and that the Dred Scott decision was unjustified. On May 18 the choice for the presidential candidate was made. Andrew Curtin, of Bellefonte, and Alexander K. McClure, of

Chambersburg, played important roles in getting the Pennsylvania delegation to support the candidacy of Abraham Lincoln who was nominated on the third ballot. Later his running mate, Hannibal Hamlin of Maine, was chosen and in several months the campaign was in full swing all over the nation.[7]

The Democrats split into Southern and Northern factions. A Southern segment, meeting in Charleston, South Carolina, nominated John C. Breckinridge, Buchanan's vice president, for the presidency. He was from Kentucky and his running mate was Joseph Lane of Oregon. Northern Democrats nominated Stephen A. Douglas from Illinois and H. V. Johnson of Georgia. A fourth political group, known as the Union Party, met in Baltimore to choose John Bell and Edward Everett as nominees.

All aspirants declared their devotion to the Union, yet Douglas accused those Southerners favoring disunion to be supporters of Breckinridge. Since it was the custom of the day, Lincoln did no campaigning, but his fellow Republicans, by political rallies and through newspapers favorable to them, did the work of rallying support for their standard bearer. They said little of slavery where it was an established part of the economic system. They stressed the prospect of free land in the territories and opposition to extending slavery into them. Many abolitionists deserted Lincoln and his party for not coming out more strongly against slavery.

Douglas was the only candidate to travel through the North,

speaking against the evils of Republicanism. He still hoped for a compromise solution to the slavery question. Bell would hold the Union together at any cost while Breckinridge continued to support the right of the people to determine whether a state would be slave or free. This view was the pro-Southern position, a view around which growing numbers of those favoring secession were rallying.

Pennsylvania held an election for state offices in October of 1860 and the result was a sweeping victory for the Republicans. Andrew Curtin was elected governor and the party gained majorities in both houses of the Assembly. Some older local residents might have remembered that Andrew Gregg Curtin was the grandson of Andrew Gregg, a one time United States Senator. Senator Gregg, in turn, was the grandson of Major General James Potter, of Revolutionary War fame, who grew to manhood in the Browns Mill community of Antrim Township. Potter's wife, Mary Patterson Chambers, of the county seat's founding family, was the newly elected governor's great grandmother.

Franklin County's voters apparently were not too impressed with Curtin's ties to the home area, but they did give him a narrow victory, with 3,692 votes, over his opponent, Henry Foster, who received 3,267. A. K. McClure and George W. Ziegler, from Greencastle, were leading supporters of the Republican candidate. John Rowe, a businessman and strong Democrat from Greencastle, worked throughout the county for Foster's election. Rowe was well known in Democratic circles, having been elected Surveyor General in 1856 when his party still dominated the state. McClure, through his work for the Republican cause, served the new governor in different capacities. His most notable leadership came as Adjutant General during the war, when he was in charge of raising troop quotas through both volunteer and conscription campaigns. [8]

The Keystone State's October election indicated its political climate had changed from Democrat to Republican. This was certainly a portent of things to come in the November presidental election. Since the majority of electoral votes were in the northern states, if Pennsylvania's October result was any barometer, the Republican candidate would surely be the next president.

This prediction held true for, on November 6, the voters of the nation elected Abraham Lincoln to be their next president. When the news spread through the country there was jubilation among the Republicans and dismay among the Northern Democrats. Fear, anger, and a sense of calamity gripped most of the South. Cries calling for secession grew as pro-slavery leaders predicted the end of their way of life once the "nigger loving" Republicans took office.

Lincoln had won a majority in the electoral college, but his popular vote was only 1,866,452. Since his opponents had received a total of 2,815,617 votes, the Republican candidate was elected by only forty percent of the voters. He would be a minority president. New Jersey split its vote between Lincoln and Douglas. All others above the Mason-Dixon line and the Ohio River plus California and Oregon went for Lincoln. Breckinridge won the Deep South along with Delaware and Maryland. Douglas and Bell shared the remaining states.

In Pennsylvania Lincoln garnered 268,036 votes to 179,871 for the other candidates. Franklin County gave the Republican nominee 4,151 while 1,636 were cast for Breckinridge. Douglas received 796 and only 83 went to Bell. The voters of Greencastle and Antrim favored Lincoln with 488 votes and Breckinridge followed with 263. Douglas received 152 and not one vote was given to Bell. Putting the opposition votes together (415) it can be seen that Lincoln had a majority of only seventy-three. The Republican cause had not been excessively embraced by the community's electorate. This brought some comfort to the diehard Breckinridge Democrats who were concentrated in parts of Antrim, especially in the Middleburg area.

Of interest, also, to local citizens was the outcome in Maryland. Of the 92,441 votes cast, Lincoln received only 2,204. To Greencastle and Antrim Township people, the voting pattern of their next door neighbors in Washington County was of special concern. Here the returns gave 2,567 to Bell, 2,475 to Breckinridge, 283 to Douglas, and only ninety-five votes for Lincoln. These Maryland results reflected a strong anti-Republican feeling and this was of some concern to the Greencastle-Antrim farmers and business leaders. Their economic life depended greatly on Baltimore and the western Maryland area around Hagerstown. As tensions resulting from the election grew, what would the Marylanders do about the question of secession? This was of no little concern to those who lived just north of the Mason-Dixon Line. [9]

However, as the weeks passed, this concern became miniscule when compared to the problems facing the nation. The certainty of Republican control of the executive functions of the federal government added more fuel to the fires of secession. There was no longer any question in the minds of the political leaders of the Deep South about the future. To them Lincoln's election spelled doom to plans for extending slavery. No longer was the doctrine of states' rights a philosophic matter. Reality dictated that little attention would be given the rights of Southern states and the very institution of slavery would be in jeopardy once the Republican president took office. It was in the seven lower Southern states, that over 200,000 slave owners lived and where over half of the 3,900,000 blacks of the South were in bondage. With the value of the average slave set at $800 it is not difficult to understand the astronomical amount of money at stake in such an uncertain political climate. Clear cut decisions, uncluttered by political or moral overtones, were needed and they were not long in coming.

The first move was made by South Carolina. On December 20 representatives from all parts of the state gathered at Charleston to decide the issue that had grown over the previous two decades. They had reached a point of no-return. The ultimate states' right would now be exercised. By unanimous vote of the 169 delegates, they passed a solemn ordinance that their "State's union with the United States of America is hereby dissolved."

Despite pleas from moderate Southern politicians and leaders in the North the secessions continued. By February 1, 1861 the seven lower states — Alabama, Florida, Georgia, Louisiana, Mississippi, South Carolina and Texas — had left the Union. Three days later representatives of these states met in Montgomery, Alabama. A constitution was adopted and the Confederate States of America became reality. Jefferson Davis of Mississippi was named president of the new nation. [10]

Northern leaders continued to assure the seceded states that if they reconsidered they would not be deprived of their slaves. President Buchanan agreed that states could not secede but felt he had no power to prevent them from leaving the Union. Yet, he did nothing to stop the Southerners from seizing forts, military supplies, and funds of the federal government. In this climate of national helplessness few who urged a compromised settlement were given much attention.

On March 4, 1861 Abraham Lincoln was inaugurated as the sixteenth President of the United States. His inaugural message was one of conciliation. He appealed to the patriotism of the South. He assured their people that the North had no intention of interfering with the rights of the Southern states. Beyond holding federal property and collecting taxes he would leave them in peace. His offer of understanding and appeasment in trying to hold the nation together was the last attempt to mend the shattered Union, but it failed.

Unlike Buchanan, Lincoln took steps to hold federal forts, including Fort Sumter located in Charleston's harbor. On April 12,

1861 Confederate forces began shelling the South Carolina fort and the following day its garrison surrendered. Two days later the President declared the seceded states, by this act, had violated national laws. The die was cast and the Civil War had begun. Lincoln called for 75,000 volunteers to serve for three months. A wave of patriotism engulfed the North and the Confederacy countered with plans to raise an army of 100,000. The final acts of secession came when Virginia, Arkansas, Tennessee, and North Carolina left the Union. On May 21 the decision was made to move the Confederate capital to Richmond, Virginia. With the loss of representatives and senators from the seceded states, the Republican Party now controlled the federal government. Slave states that eventually stayed with the Union were Kentucky, Maryland, Delaware, and Missouri.

The news of Fort Sumter's fall and Lincoln's call for volunteers swept through Pennsylvania like a drought fed prairie fire. Down the Cumberland Valley telegraph lines spread the President's message to the towns and villages. Patriotic rallies were hurriedly organized and liberty poles, carrying the Stars and Stripes, were erected on practically every diamond or center square. A great demand developed, almost over night, for material to make flags and buntings. Merchants found a ready sale for badges, shields, and other devices containing the national colors or patriotic mottoes for people to show their loyalty to the Union.

Community leaders spoke out against the rebellion, calling for a united effort to defend the country. "The Union must be preserved" was the theme of speech makers as crowds of home folks roared their approval. Jacob Hoke, a prominent Chambersburg merchant and chronicler of wartime events in Franklin County, noted the fervor with which the people were embracing the President's acts to save the nation. He also made a very practical observation - "If Virginia adopted the ordinance of secession (*which it did on April 17*), the seat of war would be right along our border; and being in the great Cumberland Valley which extended away down through Maryland and Virginia into Tennessee, armies of both contending parties would doubtless pass through our town."

Hoke's prediction was considered reckless but time and events proved him to be correct. If Maryland decided to ally itself with the Confederacy, which many Pennsylvanian's feared, the prediction would have been more ominous. It was not until after elections in November that this border state decided not to secede.

Area newspapers promoted the recruitment of men by featuring stories of the improved pay for military service. With free board and room, plus a guaranteed income of thirteen dollars a month, one area paper commented — "Many a young man out of employment would jump at the chance of making so good a salary." Another incentive was a kind of local protection fund raised to help families whose sons or fathers enlisted. In the Greencastle area a list of subscribers to such a project contained the names of sixty-seven businessmen and farmers who subscribed more than $3,000 for this purpose. The money was to assist families who needed financial help while their breadwinners were serving their country. Chambersburg was said to have raised "several" thousand dollars in support of a similar fund.[11]

During the week of April 15 volunteers began coming into the county seat to join the men being recruited by Captain Charles Campbell who had been commissioned to organize an artillery company. Such activity was being duplicated all over the state. The fervor in answering the President's call was being channelled into an organized recruiting plan, developed by Governor Curtin. On the night of April 12 the Legislature enacted a law to reorganize the militia. The next day the Governor went to Washington to offer aid and assistance to the federal military authorities and on April 15 Curtin telegraphed Eli Slifer, Secretary of the Commonwealth, saying, "Accept all military organizations offered. Our services will be required immediately." On the same day Colonel A. K. McClure wired Slifer telling him he had met with the President, the President's military advisor, General Winfield Scott, and Senator Simon Cameron. Pennsylvania was to furnish 14,000 men and that two regiments were wanted within three days.

As the call spread "patriots from every valley and hillside in Pennsylvania were pouring in their offers of services." Provisions were developed to care for the volunteers and offers to advance money came from financial institutions all over the state. Enthusiasm for volunteering was so intense that within a matter of days the state had met Mr. Lincoln's call for fourteen regiments, which was later reduced to thirteen. The service of thirty additional regiments had to be refused. The Commonwealth was prepared to furnish more than half of the 75,000 the President had called to defend the nation.

It was in such an atmosphere that Campbell's recruits assembled in Chambersburg. In all, 205 men enlisted in this first unit from the county. On Friday, April 19, these troops, known as the Chambers Artillery, left for Harrisburg where, after being assigned to an encampment, known as Camp Curtin, they were formed into three companies and attached to the 2nd Regiment Pennsylvania Volunteers as infantrymen.

Company A was commanded by Captain Peter B. Housum with a staff of officers from Chambersburg. Fifty-six of its members were from the county seat while the remainder were from Greenvillage, New Franklin, Waynesboro, Fayetteville, Caledonia, Newville, and McConnellsburg.

Captain John Doebler led Company B. He and his staff also were from Chambersburg. This unit consisted of county men from Chambersburg, Quincy, Newville, Scotland, Greenwood, Fayetteville, Mercersburg, McConnellsburg, Loudon, and Strasburg. Two of its volunteers were from York and Lancaster counties. Two were not Pennsylvanians. Julius Ladd was from New York and the other was really far from home. He was John Swuninski of Poland.

The third outfit was Company C led by Captain J. G. Elder of St. Thomas. Its largest contingent consisted of thirty-six men from Greencastle, of which seven were commissioned and non-commissioned officers serving on Elder's staff. Other enlistees were from Waynesboro, St. Thomas, Marion, Upton, Mercersburg, Chambersburg, Cashtown, and Loudon. Two were from Gettysburg and two others lived in Leitersburg, Maryland. [12] *(Appendix I)*

This kind of enthusiasm continued until the true dimensions of the conflict gradually came into focus. With the first successes of Confederate forces the dreams of an early end to hostilities began disappearing. The idea that this was a "breakfast war" was soon forgotten and eventually the volunteers came to understand the ineptness of their leaders. As they began to see that politicians were great talkers who promised much but delivered little, their innocence continued to evaporate. Inadequate arms or equipment and poor quality clothing, shelter, and food led to a feeling that too many were profiting from the war at the expense of those who did the fighting and the dying.

Within a year the early "rally round the flag spirit" had all but disappeared and bounties became popular as a way to encourage enlistments. This was followed by the Federal Militia Act, and eventually there came a national draft whereby the government placed its long finger on young men to serve. This law eliminated the various governors as the principal agents for raising the armies needed to prosecute the war. The draft law, enacted in March, 1863, brought men into the federal armies for a period of three years. Yet, it preserved the practice of allowing volunteering and for the draftees to hire substitutes or to pay $300 for exemptions. Cries of "rich man's war" were heard throughout the North and riots protesting compulsory service occurred in practically every state - the most notorious being the July riots in New York City.

Through all of the various means of raising armed forces there still remained a deep seated loyalty to the concept of the United States of America. Despite the turmoil of protest armies continued to be filled with men willing to fight for the preservation of their nation and the war continued. For four years the struggle would go forward. Over 2,770,000 men fought to keep the nation whole and Pennsylvania provided 362,000 of its sons for this cause.

In the spring time of 1861 few could have seen the enormity of the war the nation faced. This was true in both the North and the South. Yet this confrontation could have been predicted. For at least four decades it had been postponed by a series of compromises. But, within the high pitch of radicalism found in both the slave and free states war had become inevitable.

The seeds of the Southern way of life, supported by a system of human bondage — planted in the soil of Virginia over two centuries before, had now blossomed into the death giving poison of armed conflict. America was at war with itself. How this struggle touched a small town - rural part of Pennsylvania is the story which will unfold on the pages that follow.

CHAPTER III

THE FIRST CAMPAIGN

On the very day Franklin County's Chambers' Artillery left for Harrisburg, April 19, 1861, five companies of Pennsylvania troops, some in civilian clothes, entered the relatively unprotected city of Washington. People poked fun at this motley body of soldiers and for weeks they were called the "Ragged Army From Pennsylvania." The only other regular troops near the capital were about 400 Marines and fifty-six officers and men at the city arsenal. Several volunteer militia companies lived in the District of Columbia, but their reliability was uncertain since many were said to be secessionist sympathizers.

Pennsylvania's troops had reached the capital by way of Baltimore, where they were forced to make their way through angry pro-Southern mobs. The following day, violence became widespread when the 6th Massachusetts and a unit from the Keystone State moved through the port city. Both were attacked leaving four soldiers and twelve citizens killed, while thirty-six servicemen and an unknown number of Baltimorians were injured. The Pennsylvania troops were especially vulnerable because they were not only without uniforms but, more importantly, they were without weapons to defend themselves! [1]

This unrest and violence in the city which was linked to southern Pennsylvania's economic life sent shock waves throughout the Cumberland Valley. To add to the anxiety caused by the Baltimore riots, the United States Arsenal at Harpers Ferry was burned and abandoned on April 18, leaving it to the mercy of Virginia troops who were able to salvage a generous amount of weapons and other military equipment for their own use.

The next day the forty-five man garrison, that had left Harpers Ferry, marched into Hagerstown. When they discovered the train had just left for Chambersburg, the officer in charge hired wagons and carriages to continue their flight northward. By noon they had reached Greencastle and that evening Chambersburg became their bivouac area for the night. Citizens along their route found little comfort in seeing regular army men in full retreat just five days after the war had started. [2]

This was not the last heavy traffic from Maryland. Secessionists in the eastern parts of Maryland had destroyed bridges along the Northern Central and Philadelphia, Wilmington, Baltimore railroads causing a complete cessation of all rail travel from eastern Maryland into the Philadelphia area. Hundreds of Northerners who had been sojourning in the South could not get home by these normal eastern routes. The same was true of Southerners attempting to get to their homes in Virginia or further south. This situation resulted in heavy passenger loads for the Franklin and Cumberland Valley line. People coming north could get to Frederick from Washington by train and by stage to Hagerstown. There they could take a train to Harrisburg and for those going south the procedure was reversed.

Jacob Hoke, in his "Reminiscences," told of seeing the Massachusetts political leader, Caleb Cushing, enroute northward on April 20 and the same day he saw the Russian minister as he made his way to New York. Hoke also wrote that on a train to Greencastle two men, "whose features were distinctively Southern," were spotted. Each carried a Sharps rifle and "had in charge several large chests which they guarded with great care." He could not say whether the chests contained money or percussion caps, which the South needed desperately. Since there were no military regulations, at the time, that would authorize officials to investigate the alleged Southerners, they passed out of Pennsylvania with whatever it was that they were guarding so closely. Newspaper accounts during the next month constantly mentioned the stampede from Baltimore and other parts of Maryland. Each day the valley's railway coaches were filled with people fleeing into Pennsylvania. [3]

Although neighboring western Maryland was largely pro-Union, there were some slave holders living there and many were Southern sympathizers. The editor of the Hagerstown Mail favored secession and in Frederick one of its prominent young attorneys, Bradley Johnson, raised a company to fight for the South. Since the state had not yet decided to remain in the Union the fear of it going into the Confederacy was everywhere. Added to this suspense was the dread of invasion from Virginia which was just ten miles from the Mason-Dixon Line. Such a state of affairs naturally kept Pennsylvanians of the southern counties in constant anxiety, sometimes bordering on paranoia. This mood rose and fell throughout the war with each Union defeat in nearby Virginia or with any report of suspicious looking horsemen crossing the Potomac River.

As far into the state as Harrisburg, people were not immune to these anxieties. On April 23 a rumor spread through the capital that water in its reservoir had been poisoned by Southern spies. Guards were placed around the basin and a vigilance committee was formed to protect the city.

When Virginia's troops occupied Harpers Ferry, reports began circulating that Rebel forces were planning raids into Pennsylvania's border towns. Hanover Village in York County, on April 23, braced itself for an attack from an army moving out of Maryland. The alert came when, from the south, a cloud of dust along a road leading to the village, was detected. The army turned out to be a large group of Negroes hurrying northward as they fled from their masters. They were seeking sanctuary in Pennsylvania.

It was these same runaways who caused panic in Carlisle the next day. A rider arrived there from Hanover with the frightening information that a large Rebel force was on its way to attack the military post in that town. Alarm bells sounded all over the place. Fife and drum units began calling out the three rifle companies of the home guard and everybody was terrified. Women and children wept as people prepared to flee. The excitement began to subside after several hours passed and no invaders appeared. Scouts who had gone to check the "invading force" began returning with the same story of the previous day in York County. The band of ex-slaves was approaching Carlisle as they continued their flight. [4]

Cumberland County's seat of government had known violence even before war had come. There was a belligerent pro-Southern element there and during the 1860 election campaign, fights occurred frequently between pro and anti-slavery elements. This antagonism continued as Southern sympathizers molested soldiers from the U.S. Army garrison stationed there. On February 28 a soldier was killed during one of these confrontations. [5]

In the latter part of April, Chambersburg braced itself for an attack from Maryland. Franklin County's residents were urged to collect arms for the defense of the county seat. A news report told of "great excitement among the people near the state line." Business and farm work ceased as the people anxiously waited the course of "forthcoming events," yet nothing happened. In fact the Waynesboro newspaper of April 26 proclaimed — "Old Glory Flies Again." The story went on to tell of railway passengers from Hagerstown reporting a sudden change in sentiment in "that section of Maryland in favor of the Union." There is no explanation for this exhibition of pro-Union sympathy, but it did not explain away the known presence of secessionists in that area. [6]

Although some comfort came with this indication of pro-Union sentiment in Washington County, anxieties continued in southern Pennsylvania. On May 31 a party of woodcutters was fired on by a gang of alleged "Pennsylvania Secessionists" near Shade Gap. The Chambersburg Dispatch advised its readers that all such "Northern traitors should be shot down like dogs." The fire eating editor of this journal, George H. Merklein, appeared to be the county's leading alarmist. He was an associate of A. K. McClure, who considered him to be an outstanding composer of editorials. Merklein did not live to see the Union preserved. He died October 14, 1863.[7]

Another worry developed later in the summer of 1861 when it was reported that "large quantities of merchandise" were being sent by wagons from Baltimore to Virginia on a daily basis over the turnpike which ran from the port city to Emmitsburg, through Waynesboro, and Greencastle. The terminal point along this toll road was said to be Greencastle and from here the wagons supposedly went to Hancock, Maryland, by way of the Williamsport toll road. Where the toll road intersected the National Pike the wagons would then travel westward to Hancock. Here the supplies were ferried across the Potomac on flat boats or rafts to the Virginia side.

Again the Chambersburg Dispatch offered its advice by calling on the people of Waynesboro, Greencastle, and Mercersburg to form committees to check suspicious looking wagons. The paper argued — "A loyal man, engaged in honest legitimate trade, will not be offended at such inspections." This brought on another period of fear and suspicion. People began seeing Southerners under every bed — wagon bed that is. Some avid patriots took it upon themselves to report suspect wagoners. A few arrests were made, but the parties were freed when suspicions proved to be unfounded.[8]

A real scare did come to Greencastle during the night of August 21 when a warehouse, belonging to David Oaks and James Austin, was set afire. The main building and adjoining sheds, containing 350 barrels of flour, along with groceries, salt, and coal burned to the ground. It was immediately assumed that this was the work of secessionists. The morning following the fire saw the formation of a posse and by afternoon three suspects were captured. A hearing was held that evening at the local magistrate's office. Tom Pawling, owner of the Antrim House and a super patriot, brought a rope to the hearing for the immediate dispensation of justice but he was overruled when the magistrate bound the prisoners over to the county for trial.

A clearer picture of the crime developed at the subsequent court proceedings. It was learned that the arsonists were members of a gang of renegade Union soldiers led by an ex-soldier and former Philadelphia fireman. They had broken into the warehouse office where they blew the safe from which money, amounting to sixty dollars, was taken. To cover the burglary, they then proceeded to fire the buildings. As the town's church bells sounded an alarm they hurried away but returned to watch the blaze. Strangers among the crowd of onlookers aroused suspicions and led to the eventual capture of three of the culprits. Although the conflagration was clearly not the work of secessionists, the Chambersburg's Dispatch editor once more called on citizens to arm themselves and arrest "every suspicious stranger that may be found prowling about."[9]

Apprehension about a possible invasion was not just limited to the people of Franklin County and those who lived in the Cumberland Valley. In fact the nation's newspapers also exhibited a constant alarm. The Detroit Daily Tribune in its edition of May 25 carried a dispatch that reported, "Beyond doubt 9,500 Confederate troops are posted between Point of Rocks and Williamsport on the Potomac. Among them are 300 Cherokees. Apprehensions prevail of an invasion of Cumberland Valley from Virginia. Great damage will be done."

Three days later the Detriot paper again mentioned troops being readied at Harpers Ferry. " . . . There are also three hundred Cherokees with tomahawks, scalping knives and rifles; they are from North Carolina and Georgia . . . Great apprehension prevails in the Cumberland Valley of invasion from Virginia. Ten thousand head of cattle and five thousand horses could be seized . . . A forward movement of Virginia may be expected at any moment."

Other national newspapers reported the presence of over 1,000 "blood thirsty Indians" at Harpers Ferry. It was said the Rebels were preparing to strike across the border and that the redskins would serve as special raiding parties to pillage the Pennsylvania countryside. Again, these reports proved to be false. Reporters had mistaken a group of tanned Mississippians who had been assigned to the Harpers Ferry encampment. For lack of better headgear they wore skull caps and bandanas around their heads, giving the appearance of Indians. [10] *(Throughout the war Indians did serve on both sides. However, their only known appearance as soldiers in Pennsylvania came in 1863. During the Gettysburg Campaign Company H, of the 12th South Carolina infantry, passed through the county and contained many soldiers from the Catawba tribe).*

It should be noted that Harpers Ferry, at this time, was commanded by a Virginia colonel named Thomas Jonathan Jackson, who, within a few months, would come to be known as "Stonewall". Jackson's first wife had maternal roots in Antrim Township. Her name was Eleanor Junkin whose grandmother was Eleanor Cochran who lived with George Brown's family during the colonial period. Brown and his bother Thomas operated the mill along Muddy Run which gave its name to the settlement in that part of the township.

After the Revolution Eleanor Cochran married Joseph Junkin, a veteran of the war. The couple had fourteen children - ten sons and four daughters. One of the sons, George, was the father of the daughter who married Jackson. At the time of the marriage Dr. George Junkin was president of Washington College in Lexington, Virginia. This again demonstrated the blood relationships and cultural ties that the Cumberland Valley's people had with those who lived in the Shenandoah country. [11]

During this period of turmoil, plans went forward for the defense of the nation's capital and approaches to it. The General in Chief of the United States Army was the seventy-five year old Winfield Scott, a veteran of both the War of 1812 and Mexican War. He was a Virginian who remained loyal to the Union but because of age and poor health, he had no plans to actively serve in the field. However, he was one of the few men around Lincoln who foresaw the need to prepare for a major military effort.

Scott's immediate concern was to improve Washington's defenses as fast as possible. One of his first moves was to call on Robert Patterson, a Pennsylvanian who had served as a colonel in the War of 1812 and a major-general in the war with Mexico, as Scott's second in command. This sixty-nine year old veteran was commissioned a major general again and placed in command of a military district comprising the states of Delaware, Maryland, and Pennsylvania and the District of Columbia. Now it was up to Patterson to organize the three month troops being raised and to get as many of them as possible into the capital's defenses.

By April 27, Patterson's initial assignment was reduced when Colonel Joseph Mansfield, a veteran of the Mexican War, was given command of Washington, D.C. and part of northern Maryland. Benjamin Butler, a political appointee from Massachusetts, was given the area between Washington and Annapolis to administer, leaving Patterson Pennsylvania and Delaware to command. He then shifted his headquarters to Philadelphia where he concerned himself with the pressing job of organizing and forwarding regiments to Washington and Baltimore. [12]

By this time Harrisburg had become an important center of military activity, where volunteers kept pouring in daily. The city, of 16,000 residents, was soon overrun by enlistees and visitors. Despite the creation of Camp Curtin there was a deplorable lack of accommodations. By April 24 about 7,000 young men, mostly from the Lebanon and Cumberland valleys, had come to Harrisburg and the overflow from Camp Curtin was housed in churches of the city. It was during this time the 2nd Regiment of Pennsylvania Volunteers, to which the Chambers Artillery had been assigned, was organized.

On Saturday, April 21, the 2nd Regiment left Harrisburg, by rail, to go to Washington. At Cockeysville, Maryland they found the railroad bridge destroyed. The unit was then ordered back to York where it remained until June 1 when it was sent to Chambersburg to become part of an army being assembled there by General Patterson. This order came as General Scott recognized the danger that was developing with a concentration of Confederate forces at Harpers Ferry and in the Shenandoah Valley under the command of General Joseph E. Johnston. [13]

A threat to Washington seemed to be imminent when it was learned that an army of 18,000 Southerners, under General P. G. T. Beauregard, was gathering at Manassas Junction, a rail center just twenty miles southwest of the city. If Federal forces were to move against Beauregard, Patterson's army would be needed to pin down Johnston's to prevent it from joining the Confederates threatening the capital. To do this the general planned a concentration of regiments in southern Franklin County capable of covering any operation which might develop in Maryland as far east as Frederick and to the west as far as Cumberland.

The army would gather at Chambersburg where it would be drilled and shaped into a fighting force. Then from both the county seat and Greencastle it could advance beyond Hagerstown to threaten Harpers Ferry. Another diversionary force could then move to Cumberland if necessary. The strategy was designed to draw Johnston into a confrontation or get around his army to prevent its retreat from the Shenandoah country. Either course was to keep Johnston's force from joining Beauregard at Manassas. It is important to remember that the forces assembling in Franklin County were an army in name only and although the plans against the enemy seemed logical it would certainly require a miracle to implement them.

To understand this requires a review of the state of preparedness in 1861. There were two forms of military organizations in the country - the regular army, consisting of about 16,000 men, mostly scattered throughout the west, and state military organizations known as the militia. In time of war the President could call the militia units to serve the nation only through the state governors.

This system of mobilizing manpower had its origin in the Revolution and under federal law, passed in 1795, the President was empowered to call out the militia whenever the laws of the United States were opposed in any state. This authority was used by President Lincoln in his call of April 15, 1861.

Pennsylvania's militia law of 1814 placed all able bodied men between the ages of eighteen and forty five on call for a term of not less than seven years. Every male of military age was required to serve in a company which had to have a minimum of three days training every year. Companies were to contain a hundred men although in practice their size varied from sixty to over a hundred. These basic units were then formed into regiments usually consisting of 1,000 soldiers. After 1849, when a law was passed to make the three day training non-mandatory, most companies virtually disappeared. Eligible men, by paying a fifty cent tax, were excused from this responsibility. [14]

Although the traditional militia program became a haphazard operation, volunteer companies, filled with public spirited and patriotic young men, continued to be active in various parts of the Commonwealth. Their members looked on soldiering as a romantic adventure and drilled on a frequent schedule. They had their own specially designed uniforms which they proudly displayed in parades and drill competitions.

Some of these units were part of a proud tradition with roots traceable to the Revolution. One was the 1st Troop, Philadelphia City Cavalry, formed in 1774 as a troop of light cavalry and filled with the cream of Philadelphia's society. This company was Washington's body guard during the Revolution and served with distinction in the War of 1812. On April 15, 1861, in response to Lincoln's call, they were among the first to offer their services to Governor Curtin. Eventually the Philadelphians were assigned to the United States Cavalry stationed at Carlisle and commanded by Colonel George H. Thomas. [15]

After the Revolution the Greencastle-Antrim area maintained a form of military tradition with its own special companies. In the War of 1812 the Antrim Greens fought at Chippewa and served in the defense of Baltimore. In 1847 a company which included men from the rest of the county was with the army throughout the Mexican War. General David Detrick was a leader in the state militia for thirty-nine years until his retirement in 1859. He was also the town's leading undertaker who, throughout the Civil War, had the sad duty of burying many of the area's sons who died defending the Union. [16]

Path Valley had a volunteer company known as the Washington Blues. It was a disciplined and well drilled unit whose muster rolls showed a membership of over a hundred men. When news of Fort Sumter came to the valley, seventy-seven of its men responded to the first call in April, 1861. Two men from Antrim joined the Blues when they assembled in Chambersburg to be led to Harrisburg by the captain of their choice, Samuel Walker.

Other early volunteer companies from Franklin County included such units as the Union Volunteers and Franklin Volunteers of Chambersburg, the Concord Light Infantry, and the Mercersburg Rifles. They all took part in the War of 1812. However, through the years of peace that followed there was a decline in enthusiasm for soldiering. This was especially true in southern Pennsylvania's rural sections where farming required most of the time with little to spare for marching and drilling. Religious convictions opposing the taking of arms also worked against the concept. [17]

However, when war came volunteer companies were the first to respond. Prior to hostilities there were about 500 such units in the state averaging about forty men per company. In all, Governor Curtin had at his disposal an aggregate of nearly 20,000 uniformed troops. The potential militia force of eligible males in the state would have been around 355,000 men. [18]

This was the manpower situation in 1861 as Patterson planned his campaign against the Confederates. The initial enthusiasm showed no shortage of men willing to fight. However, with the exception of a few regular army units and some elite volunteer companies, they had little or no military experience. Furthermore, the troops needed weapons, clothing, shelter and food.

In Pennsylvania, available arms were in the hands of the volunteer companies. An inventory of these weapons showed 12,080 muskets, 4,706 rifles, 2,809 cavalry swords and sabers, 3,147 pistols, and sixty-nine bronze cannons. Out of this collection the only usable pieces were about 2,500 muskets, 1,200 rifles, and 500 swords. The rest were too old, too heavy, or too impaired. [19]

On May 8 the Secretary of War announced that the national government would equip all state troops mustered into the federal forces. Clothing, however, was in short supply and the states were advised to furnish uniforms for which they eventually would be reimbursed. The promptness with which the War Department armed the men was of a very slow variety, however.

Regiments eventually stationed at Chambersburg and later at Greencastle had a varied array of weapons with different calibers. The 4th Connecticut Infantry had 1842 muskets and the 1st Rhode Island regiment had two different types of rifles. However, Colt revolvers were also part of their weaponry. Men of the 1st Pennsylvania Regiment were armed with old style muskets and twelve rounds of ball cartridges which had to be carried in their pockets since they had been issued no cartridge boxes. The 20th Pennsylvania was given unserviceable muskets which were replaced later with those of the rifled variety. Some regiments possessed at least three different calibered guns and it was not until June 26 that an attempt was made to determine how many rounds of ammunition were in the various companies.

The variety of arms was also matched by the varied types of uniforms. Some of Pennsylvania's troops were still in civilian clothes and this was true of Patterson's men. They had been issued uniforms which in a few days had fallen to pieces, the result of shoddy material used by profit hungry manufacturers. One soldier, when at Chambersburg, wrote home to tell his parents that they were likely to remain there for sometime "as the Government Inspector inspected the clothing of our regiment and condemned it, telling us to remain where we are till supplied with better". The 9th Pennsylvania, while at Greencastle, was issued inferior outfits and in other instances shoes, issued by the government, totally disintegrated after several weeks — the product of another profiteer. It was not long before local papers commented on the scandalous way these men were being clothed and shod. The story was taken up by city newspapers who demanded an investigation. Governor Curtin launched an inquiry into the matter. He refused to pay for the faulty uniforms and later issues were of a greatly improved quality. [20]

The Civil War has often been called the war between "the Blue and the Gray." However, throughout the first year of conflict many Northern militia units were clothed in gray uniforms, a tradition which went back to the war of 1812. Pennsylvania was no exception. Contracts for uniforms were let quickly and clothiers filled them with cloth most available. Often this was gray. One company in Patterson's army was McMullens Independent Rangers. Its men wore dark gray uniforms with white havelocks, linen or cotton cloth which hung from the caps to give protection against the sun, similar to those used by the French Foreign Legion. The 4th Connecticut had gray uniforms with felt hats of the same color. Later in September of 1861 an effort was made in Greencastle to raise a company of volunteers to be called the "Grays." Similar uniforms were found in other encampments and in contrast some Southern troops, during the early months of the war, wore blue outfits. However, by the end of the year most opposing forces were using blue and gray to identify their armies. Yet there were some Union units in gray uniforms as late as 1863. After the Battle of Gettysburg, some Pennsylvania and New York militia regiments, operating in the Waynesboro-Greencastle area wore gray outfits.

The 20th Pennsylvania Regiment, which eventually camped at Greencastle, was clothed in the old United States light blue jackets and pants, the style worn in the Mexican War. This uniform was of excellent quality and did not require replacement during the regiment's term of service. General Patterson personally favored these outfits and it was through his efforts that enough were secured for these men. The 1st Rhode Island Regiment was dressed in a unique uniform outfit of loose blue blouses, gray trousers, and broad brimmed black hats. Each man, also carried a large red blanket strapped across his back. A slit in the center of each blanket changed it into a Mexican style poncho that could be worn as a cloak over the shoulders. [21]

Since France set the trend for military fashion during this era, another popular dress of militia companies from many states was the Zouave outfit. It consisted of a short jacket, baggy trousers — usually red, white leggings and a fez, turban, or kepi as the head piece. This style was of French origin and went back to their wars in North Africa as early as 1830. The outfit became popular in France and later it was introduced into America by Elmer Ellsworth, a Chicago law clerk and friend of the Lincoln family. The Ellsworth Zouave Cadets, formed in 1859 by the clerk and a French fencing master, became a popular attraction in the midwest. Their close order drill performance won such acclaim that they toured the East in 1860 and their flashy dress captured the fancy of Americans at a time when many volunteer companies were being formed. When war came there were Zouave regiments and companies in both the Confederate and Federal armies, but as the war progressed most were abandoned. Yet, as late as 1862, two New York and two Pennsylvania infantry regiments combined to form a Zouave Brigade in the Army of the Potomac. *(After Lincoln's inauguration, Ellsworth was a frequent visitor in the White House and was killed May 24, 1861, at Alexandria when he attempted to remove a Confederate flag from a tavern.)*

New York and Pennsylvania furnished most Zouave units to the Union forces. One of these was the 23rd Pennsylvania Regiment, popularly known as Birney's Zouaves from Philadelphia. *(This regiment wore a modified Zouave uniform with kepi, and dark blue short jacket and pants)*. It was part of Patterson's army which later trained at Greencastle. During the time Birney's men were there the troops were reviewed by the division commander, Major General Cadwalader. They impressed him so much that he wrote to Governor Curtin asking that they be re-organized and mustered in for three year service.

This craze hit Greencastle in August, 1861 when William Shorb and G. H. Miller were chosen to lead "a volunteer company of Zouaves, ... whose services are to be tendered to the government for three years or during the war". There were forty three names on the roll, "ready to do, dare, and die, if need be, to maintain unbroken the Union of our States and unsullied the Flag of our Fathers". Beyond the initial enrollment, there is no record of further progress. In October, 1861 it was announced that Chambersburg was forming such a company. Like the Greencastle effort the plans never materialized. Apparently the stolid, conservative Dutchmen who lived in Franklin County would not exhibit themselves in such costumes. They would have been "zu fein" — too fancy. [22]

Although the dress of most Union troops generally became uniform, some units maintained their own style of apparel throughout the conflict. One example of this individuality was found in the 126th Infantry Regiment from Franklin County that served from August 1862 to May 1863. The uniform was blue but the coat style was similar to that of the cavalry - short waist length jacket. Photographs also indicate the headgear to be a short brimmed hat, rather than the usual kepi worn by most Northern soldiers.

With their various kinds of uniforms the first troops began coming to Chambersburg in late April. In addition to the camp at the Fairgrounds, west of the borough, another was established on the Eberley farm east of the town. It was soon occupied with the men quartered in hastily built wooden huts and camp meeting tents furnished by some of the local churches. After these were filled the soldiers were housed in the Court House or in town and rural homes, while some were forced to sleep in the open. [23]

This meager force, of approximately 3,000 men, was the only evidence of an army in Franklin County for about a month. The men spent their days in drill or marching into town for parade demonstrations. On May 15, on one of these occasions, the ladies of the town presented the 7th and 8th Regiments with a "handsome" flag. This same day Governor Curtin visited the county seat to review his troops. [24]

Exposure brought an epidemic of "spotted fever" causing

widespread sickness and many deaths. It began after a spell of rainy weather and a freak storm on May 3 which blanketed the area with four to five inches of snow. A hospital was established in the Mansion House on the corner of the Diamond and East Market Street and the ladies of the town prepared food for the invalids. As the epidemic grew another hospital was set up in Franklin Hall, the town's commercial and entertainment center, located on the northeastern corner of the Diamond. This problem continued through the summer with hundreds of men hospitalized at times. Newspapers reported as many as two and three military burials a week.[25]

Other difficulties developed to cause concern among town authorities, the county sheriff, and military leaders. The rate of crime rose sharply with greater incidents of robbery, thievery, assaults, and increased drunkeness. Prostitutes became a problem as they, along with other camp followers such as gamblers and confidence men, began making their appearance.

A robbery of a man and his lady at one of the town's hotels was committed by four soldiers. The criminals were never arrested and a chorus of protest came from the newspapers. One editor commented — "Such conduct should call down the indignation of every true soldier. It will lead to serious results if carried on much further. Soldiers, as well as civilians, must learn to respect the laws, if not, must abide the consequences of their violation."[26]

Court proceedings for the Quarter Session in August, which covered the preceding three months, included a case where soldiers were accused of murdering a black resident of Chambersburg. Other cases included such violations as assault and battery, malicious mischief, larceny, and burglary. One editor commented on the rise in crime by saying, "The Criminal Docket was larger than it has been for several years. Almost every grade of crime was before the court."[27]

When military authorities were provided evidence of unsoldier like behavior, the culprits were disciplined by being placed in a guard house. The court house cellar was used for such detention purposes. More obstreperous men were bound by ropes and placed in a separate part of the cellar.

Others were drummed out of the service and sent home. This happened on several occasions. One example occurred on June 13 when three Rhode Islanders were given this punishment. The Chambersburg Dispatch reported the incident with the comment that this was the way to serve them, "they will not act like men, send them home disgraced. A few samples of that kind would have the effect of restraining others, and our volunteers will prove to be really and truly soldiers." [28] There is no way of knowing the immediate reaction to such comments. Future events would seem to indicate the editor's advice fell on the deaf ears.

Despite all the problems it appears that Pennsylvania's volunteers were given ample rations. The Commissary General's Report for the period covering April 19 to November 4, 1861 shows that $210,722.67 was spent for food. This expenditure covered the cost of beef, pork, groceries, bread, potatoes, flour, salt, sugar, etc. used in the camps, while $18,881.00 was paid to home owners for boarding troops. Between June 3 and July 23 the camps around Greencastle received over 23,000 pounds of food plus 417 gallons of vinegar, 600 pounds of soap and 400 pounds of candles. The report indicates that after November 4 the "subsistance of the volunteers of Pennsylvania was assumed by the Federal Government." [29]

On Tuesday, May 28, Chambersburg's people were excited to see the 2nd Pennsylvania Regiment arrive from York. This regiment contained the Chambers Artillery volunteers who had gone to Harrisburg in April. Along with them was the 3rd Pennsylvania and the two units were marched from the train station to a camp west of town. This came to be known as Camp Givens, named for Major James Givens of the 2nd Regiment.

Within a week's time 8,000 men moved into the county seat. In addition to Camp Givens other camps were located on the grounds of A. K. McClure, north of town; the farm of Christian Bitner, south of town; and another along the Harrisburg Pike beyond the Conococheague Creek. Men were also quartered in the Court House, several churches, and other public buildings. [30]

If Patterson's forces were not up to military expectations they did have well known officers. Major General George Cadwalader, a lawyer and Mexican War veteran, would command the 1st Division. He was from an old Philadelphia family and stayed with the state military establishment throughout the war. When it ended he was Commander of the Department of Pennsylvania.

Colonel George H. Thomas, head of the 1st Brigade, was a regular army officer. Although a Virginian, he cast his lot with the Union and eventually gained fame as "The Rock of Chickamauga" in 1863 and led his troops to victory at Nashville in 1864.

Captain Abner Doubleday, who had been at Fort Sumter when it fell, commanded a battery of guns. He later proved his competency, as a general, at Gettysburg. Although his role as the founder of baseball has been discounted he is still remembered as the author of "Reminiscence of Fort Sumter" and "Chancellorsville and Gettysburg", two authoritative volumes on these phases of the war.

Colonel Ambrose E. Burnside commanded the 1st Rhode Island Regiment. His invention of a breech loading carbine in 1856 was a valuable contribution to the Union cause. He later gained fame at the Battle of Antietam and was commander of the Army of the Potomac at the disasterous Battle of Fredericksburg. Little did the people of Franklin County realize, when they first saw Burnside, that he would be responsible for sending many of their sons to death a year and a half later.

Prior to going to Chambersburg, Patterson informed General Scott of his plans to move against Joseph Johnston's Confederate forces at Harpers Ferry. He told the General-in-Chief he would lose no time. "All the troops are anxious to be on the move and see their foe — a desire which shall soon be gratified," [31] — surely a case of extreme overconfidence.

Fitz John Porter, the assitant Adjutant General, also notified General W. H. Keim, who was in charge at Chambersburg, of the commanding general's plans. Keim was directed to organize the

CAMP SLIFER

MARCH OF TROOPS

FROM CHAMBERSBURG

HARPER'S WEEKLY   PATTERSON'S ARMY IN CHAMBERSBURG   JUNE 29, 1861 various regiments for "instant movement" to face the enemy. Porter was with Patterson when he came to Chambersburg on Sunday, June 2, accompanied by McMullen's Independent Rangers, a company from Philadelphia. Little did they know what they would find. [32]

The commander, with his entourage, was met at the railroad station by his staff and a large body of soldiers. There followed a grand parade over the town's streets to the "delight of many" but to the dismay of the religious minded people of the borough. Such violation of the Sabbath was uncalled for and Jacob Hoke indicated that history showed many examples of leaders coming to no good end when such divine prohibition had been ignored. [33]

Despite local misgivings about desecrating the Sabbath, Patterson came with the confidence of one having faithfully served his nation as a conqueror in Mexico and humility was not becoming to the assignment he had been given. Sunday or not, he was the commander of an army that had grown to 18,000 men and he was about to embark on a campaign to help bring the rebellion to a swift conclusion.

After several days of troop inspections it must be assumed that the commanding general began to have misgivings about the readiness of the men he was to lead to war. Fitz John Porter indicated his displeasure with the quality of the army when he wrote, "Our volunteers are as green as green can be. Marching is their forte if they have a drum or a band. They cannot form a square, yet of those I have seen, they think themselves perfect." Because of their awkwardness some of these "green troops" had serious accidents resulting in injuries and in one instance a private of the 11th Pennsylvania was killed by the accidental discharge of a comrade's musket. To overcome these difficulties, orders were given to all officers that drill had to be increased and a more disciplined atmosphere was to prevail throughout all encampments. [34]   As the Commanding General came to realize the inadequacies of his poorly trained and ill equipped army his plans continued, but at a slower pace. General Scott ordered him to delay his advance until he received reinforcements of regular artillery and infantry.

By now the army was· divided into two divisions, the first commanded by Cadwalader and the second by Keim. (see *Appendix II*), On June 7, part of the 1st Division's 1st Brigade, commanded by Colonel Thomas, moved into Greencastle. Thomas was cautioned to move with care. Porter forwarded a communique to him with specific orders not to go further until the entire army was prepared "to sustain the advance." [35]   At the head of Thomas's column were four companies of the 2nd U.S. Cavalry. This regiment had been organized in 1855 by the then Secretary of War, Jefferson Davis. Although generally led by Southern officers, many of the enlisted men were immigrants from Germany and Ireland. The regiment had spent the previous five years in Texas fighting Indians and Mexican bandits. Although a Virginian, Thomas remained loyal to his regiment and flag, while many fellow officers from the unit, including Albert Sidney Johnston, E. Kirby Smith, John Bell Hood and Robert E. Lee had cast their lot with the Confederacy. [36] Attached to the 2nd Cavalry was the eighty-eight man company of The 1st Troop, Philadelphia City Cavalry. The 21st Pennsylvania Infantry, a Philadelphia based volunteer unit composed mostly of Germans, the 23rd Pennsylvania *(Birney's Zouaves)*, the gray clad company of McMullen's Rangers, and a company of the 8th U.S. Infantry, made up Thomas's Infantry. Also, in this advance column were two companies of the 1st U.S. Artillery, the "Heroes of Ft. Sumter," commanded by Captain Abner Doubleday. Greencastle was soon filled with troops.

One resident recalled — "the whole town turned out to do them honor...citizens brought food of every description including hot coffee to the soldiers along the streets and public highway." Doubleday confirmed this hospitality in an article written after the war — "Our march through Pennsylvania was a continuous ovation. Flowers, fruits and delicacies of all kinds were showered upon us, and the hearts of the people seemed over-flowing with gratitude for the very little we had been able to accomplish." [37]

Within the next few days the rest of Cadwalader's 1st Division moved into the Greencastle area. Their first encampment, Camp Wingerd, was located just south of the town on the farm of A. B. Wingerd where there was open meadow land. A plentiful supply of water came from a stream originating at a spring located on the Jacob Stover farm, east of Greencastle. *(Part of this farm now serves the school district as a Center for Environmental Studies).* North of the town another camp was near Rankin's Mill in a "beautiful grove of oak and cedar of some thirty acres" with its water supply coming from Muddy Run. This site was called Camp Meredith in honor of a popular regimental leader, Colonel Sullivan A. Meredith of the 10th Pennsylvania Volunteers. On the farm of John B. Witmer, the Moss Spring area was another popular camp ground. [38]

On June 8 the army's leader received another message from General Scott telling him to move with caution. He reminded Patterson:

"I have said that we must sustain no reserve; but this is

not enough, a check or a drawn battle would be a victory to the enemy, filling his heart with joy, his ranks with men, and his magazines with voluntary contributions.

Take your measures, therefore, circumspectly; make a good use of your engineers and other experienced staff officers and generals, and attempt nothing without a clear prospect of success, as you will find the enemy strongly posted and not inferior to you in numbers." [39]

Dated June 9, a letter expressed the general's "mortification" at being informed of large numbers of stragglers, many in a drunken condition, some "far in advance of the column and many of them miles in the rear." Needless to say the units around Greencastle continued to be busily engaged in company and battalion drill. [40]

Weekends brought visitors from nearby towns including many from Hagerstown and Washington County. Among those who had come through the area from below the Mason-Dixon Line several weeks earlier was a horse doctor. He rode into the various camps on an ungainly type of horse with saddle bags filled with remedies for spasms and ringbone. There is no information available to know what kind of business success he achieved, but it was later disclosed that the "doctor" was non-other than Turner Ashby, a scout and cavalry commander, assigned to Colonel Jackson's troops at Harpers Ferry. Ashby went as far as Chambersburg and although he may have sold no horse medicine it was said, "he returned with an immense amount of information." [41]

Many of the men attended services in the Greencastle churches. One soldier wrote that he had dinner with the Rev. Bridenbaugh, the local Lutheran pastor. Inviting soldiers for a meal was a common practice which continued throughout the war. For Sunday afternoon recreation some went to the Conococheague Creek, west of town, for swimming and fishing. Others obtained passes to "ride the cars" to Chambersburg to visit friends in town or in regiments still stationed there. [42]

Not all Greencastle residents provided free food. The local newspaper of June 20 carried an article headed "A Patriot" - "We are very sorry to note it, but such conduct deserves a puff. One of our farmers, we are told, in the kindness of his heart, gave to our poorly fed soldiers, bread, onions, and butter at the following charges: a cent a piece for onions, 25 cents a pound for butter, and 50 cents for a loaf of bread. We are told he got his reward. His garden was stripped the same night. We have heard of men who would steal cents from dead men's eyes, and have no doubt he is a near relative of them." [43]

(The only comparison available, to indicate the exhorbitant prices charged by the farmer, was in the price of butter. Market reports of the time show butter selling for as low as eight cents a pound.)

No doubt the camps at Greencastle did not escape the enticements offered soldiers at Chambersburg, such as prostitution and gambling, much to the consternation of those townspeople who, from birth, had been nurtured on strict Protestant principles of morality. Drunkeness continued to be a problem and in one instance charges were preferred against Major John Wynkoop of the 6th Pennsylvania Regiment. He was accused of being drunk continuously since the regiment left Philadelphia in April. Fellow officers testified that he was "not safe or reliable". The charges were later dropped since his commanding officer felt they ". . . were made in bad motive and as his services are much needed." The fact that officers were now quarreling among themselves did little, however, to improve the morale of the troops. [44]

Many of the men had come to expect harassment from time to time by certain civilians, but on June 6, a picket stationed near the town, experienced such treatment in a most dangerous manner. Someone shot at him. "The ball tore his overcoat and both legs of his pantaloons, just grazing the flesh and producing a slight abrasion of

57

the skin. The person who fired, was in citizen's dress and was hotly pursued, but finally escaped." Such experiences occurred throughout the summer and as troops moved toward Hagerstown, they would increase. Although the secessionist spirit had been dampened in Western Maryland, there were those who would never accept any one, even soldiers, associated with that "Republican" down in the White House. [45]

On Tuesday, June 11, the 1st Rhode Island Regiment and battery, commanded by Colonel Burnside, entered Greencastle. The regiment was accompanied by former Governor Elisha Dyer of Providence and later in the week Governor William Sprague joined his troops. Certain equipment brought by the new arrivals created excitement throughout the camps. The Rhode Islanders had with them a large observation balloon which was to "be used to obtain views of the position and movements of the enemy".

There was no evidence that the balloon was used in this campaign. There remains, however, a description of the Rhode Island encampment while at Greencastle. The regiment's chaplain, Augustus Woodbury, painted a verbal picture of it in the regimental history — "Now we are fairly 'under canvas' and there is no one of us but looks back, with feelings of liveliest gratification, to the time of our encampment on the southern border of Pennsylvania. The weather was of the deliciously balmy temperature of early June. The days were clear, and the soft light of a young moon shone down at night among the trees that shaded our encampment. The air was fragrant with the fresh clover and the new mown hay. The wide-spreading wheat fields were robed in their richest colors. The distant mountains were outlined by the Western sky, and were transfigured in the glory of each sunset hour. Through all, was breathing the spirit of a loyal, a patriotic, a thrifty, hospitable, and generous people." [46]

Major General George Cadwalader arrived in Greencastle on June 12 to assume command of the 1st Division as it prepared to move against the enemy. Patterson was still proceeding slowly. A message to Army Headquarters at Washington advised that office of Cadwalader's arrival, but the army's snail like advance was blamed on lack of transportation. However, the commander expected to be established in Hagerstown within three days.

Assistant Adjutant General Porter, on behalf of his commander, issued an order to all officers concerning the anticipated advance into Maryland. Dated June 12, it specified routes the various units would take and the places for establishing camp sites. The 1st Brigade, under Colonel Thomas, was to move to Williamsport by the turnpike from Greencastle. It would camp near the town, "but far enough from the river to be free from the enemy's shot". By the same route, the 4th Brigade, commanded by Colonel D. S. Miles, would follow and camp along the stream back of them. (*This would have been along the Conococheague Creek.*) By using the Hagerstown Road, the 3rd Brigade, under General E. C. Williams, was ordered to march to and establish a camp at Sharpsburg. General G. C Wyncoop would take the 2nd to Hagerstown by rail and then march east on the Frederick turnpike to the vicinity of Funkstown while the 5th Brigade, headed by General J. S. Negley, also would go by rail to Hagerstown and deploy along the road to Williamsport.

Each brigade was ordered "to post guards and sentinels so as to secure a continuous line from camp to camp, and place its pickets far enough in advance and on the flanks to secure against surprise." Such an arrangement created a web-like military structure which extended in three directions encompassing the towns of Funkstown, Sharpsburg, and Williamsport with Hagerstown serving as the center. The 5th Brigade was, also, assigned the responsibility to guard store houses, hospitals, etc. in Hagerstown. A final admonition was delivered — "The men must be kept in camp ready at all times for instant action, and be drilled in the school of the company and regiment." [47]

Upon reading his instructions, and possibly after seeing the nature of the army he commanded, General Cadwalader wrote to headquarters. His message had a familiar ring. He expressed the same timidity as that of his commander about further forward movements and declared he would make no move by "exposing any detachment to the chance of injury or disaster." One of Cadwalader's first considerations was the men's health. On June 14 he ordered his senior medical officer to establish a hospital in Greencastle. He directed Surgeon William H. Saggart of the 10th Pennsylvania Regiment to take charge of the hospital which was to be a building rented for this purpose.

The next day, June 15, at approximately 6 a.m. the troops began their march into Maryland. It was hot and the road extremely dusty. One soldier wrote that there had been no rain for quite awhile. Before many miles, men began fainting and hundreds fell by the wayside. When passing through Middleburg they welcomed the cool water, from the village wells, that residents brought to the edge of the road. Barrels and buckets of water were there to quench the thirsts, and tubs, constantly being refilled, were used to cool burning and grimy feet.

While the men from Greencastle camps were trudging along the roads into Maryland, some of the 2nd Division from Chambersburg were riding in style and comfort to Hagerstown on Cumberland Valley railroad cars. The remainder were forced to march much to their consternation. They found little sympathy from the Greencastle soldiers. However, those who arrived in Hagerstown left the train only to find themselves moving toward Harpers Ferry on foot. As they neared their objective the men could see huge columns of smoke billowing skyward through a gap in the distant mountains. The place was being abandoned by the Rebels. After intelligence reports verified this, Cadwalader was ordered to cross the Potomac at Williamsport and march southward into Virginia to counter any northerly move Johnston's army might make. [48]

This contingent proceeded cautiously down the Virginia side of the river and occupied the Falling Waters area. Just weeks before, Cadwalader learned, the region had been infested with Southern troops and people living on the Maryland side were frequently fired at by the Rebels. Canal operators were happy to see the army at Williamsport since nearly a hundred coal barges were massed there, their owners afraid to continue to the District of Columbia for fear of this kind of harassment. [49]

From Falling Waters, Cadwalader sent advance forces towards Martinsburg and General Patterson was elated with what seemed to be a Confederate retreat. Then everything changed. Washington authorities ordered Burnside's Rhode Islanders and the regular army troops to report to Irvin McDowell's force assembling for its march into Nothern Virginia to destroy Confederate forces concentrated at Manassas. Since these regulars formed the backbone of his army, Patterson panicked and Cadwalader was ordered to bring his men back over the river into the safety of Maryland. All leaders on both sides during this early phase of hostilities could have panicked. Patterson was not the only commander of green troops. His opponent had a force just as green and numerically smaller. It was also true that the armies facing each other at Manassas were filled with untried volunteers.

For two weeks the campaign remained inactive. Excessive heat made lengthy marches unbearable. Hospitals at Hagerstown and Greencastle were filled with victims of both heat and fatigue. However, during this interval, Company B of the 2nd Pennsylvania Regiment, one of the Franklin County units, discovered a cache of weapons in a tavern at Funkstown. It was assumed that these were to be used by Rebel partisans when needed. [50]

By now Johnston's forces were entrenching themselves near Winchester. With each passing day, time was running out for Patterson. His army, by mid-July, would begin to evaporate since enlistments would then be expiring. Calling in vain for reinforcements, he decided to go into action again.

MAJOR GENERAL ROBERT PATTERSON   U.S.A.M.H.I.   MAJOR GENERAL GEORGE CADWALADER

On July 2, Cadwalader's division, led by Patterson's son-in-law, John Abercrombie, began fording the river at Williamsport and started marching down the Shenandoah Valley. What followed has come to be called the "Battle of Falling Waters." It was a brief, forty-five minute skirmish where the undisciplined troops on both sides began to run from each other. One Confederate soldier, when confronted by an officer who wanted to know why he was running, replied — "Because I can't fly!" Company I of the 15th Pennsylvania managed to be captured almost single handed by a young Virginia cavalry colonel named James Ewell Brown Stuart.

The casualties proved to be light in comparison to battles of the future but since it was one of the war's early encounters it did gain recognition at the time. The Federals suffered four killed, sixteen wounded, and forty-nine captured. The Southern forces, commanded by Thomas Jackson, reported twenty wounded with none killed or captured.

Jackson withdrew his brigade and the next day Patterson triumphantly marched into Martinsburg. His forces, by now, were reduced to approximately 13,000 having lost many of his army through reassignments, sickness, and desertion. In the town the Confederates had left forty-eight wrecked locomotives and cars, a burned out depot, and torn up tracks. One instance of resistance occurred on July 4 when drunken soldiers began looting houses in Martinsburg and its vicinity. One of the homes entered by an inebriated Pennsylvanian was owned by Benjamin R. Boyd. The only members of the family there were the wife, Mary, and her seventeen year old daughter, Belle. The father was serving in Johnston's forces at the time. When the soldier became abusive and used "offensive language" in the presence of the ladies, Miss Boyd drew a revolver from her dress and killed him. Federal authorities did nothing about the incident. In fact they seemed to admire the young lady for her courage under such trying circumstances. Belle Boyd went on to become a spy for General Jackson and a heroic legend of the Civil War era.

Although the destroyed rail facilities and equipment indicated a retreat by Johnston, Patterson called a halt, claiming lack of supplies for the delay. The army lay in Martinsburg for a week while he tried to come to a decision. During this time the commander asked for reinforcements and General Scott wired immediately to tell him he had dispatched four New York regiments to his command. This contingent was reported to have passed through Greencastle on July 7 enroute to Martinsburg. Upon arrival they were to join what was to be an advance on Winchester. However, the newly arrived men were too exhausted to continue marching and another delay ensued. Finally the army did move up the valley as far as Bunker Hill, about eight miles south of Martinsburg. Here the advance stopped. [51]

The cautious Patterson now turned to his staff for a council of war. All of his ten subordinates argued against a move on Winchester. Supplies and transportation were insufficient and it was argued that the army could not live off the land, a case of doubtful reasoning since they were in the most fertile region of Virginia which had been supplying Johnston's men for several months. John Newton, the army's chief engineer, urged an eastward movement toward Charles Town, a suggestion which won unanimous approval from the brigade leaders. Under these circumstances the general, remembering Scott's constant concern for caution, accepted the advice of his staff and two days later, July 17, the army from Pennsylvania marched into Charles Town.

While all these delays and changes of strategy were taking place in the Shenandoah Valley, General McDowell's forces had begun moving toward Manassas. By July 18 his 30,500 man army was at Centerville, well within striking distance of Beauregard's force of approximately 20,000. When Confederate authorities learned of the oncoming Federals they ordered Johnston to come to the aid of Beauregard. The Rebel leader, knowing of Patterson's withdrawal to

Charles Town, responded immediately. A message from Richmond had reached him at midnight, July 17, and within hours his men were on their way across the valley, over the mountains at Ashby Gap, to Piedmont. By rail they continued towards Manassas and on July 20 Jackson's brigade arrived at midday. The remainder of Johnston's army was there the next morning. This is said to be the first time, in military history, that rail transportation was used to achieve strategic mobility.

On Sunday, July 21, the first Battle of Bull Run or Manassas resulted in a complete rout of McDowell's forces. Although both the Union and Southern soldiers were untried in battle and there was confusion on both sides, the arrival of Johnston's forces was instrumental in bringing victory to the Confederacy. The presence of Jackson's brigade holding a position against the enemy inspired General Barnard Bee to call to his South Carolinians and exclaim, "Look! There is Jackson standing like a stonewall. Rally behind the Virginians." Thus the sobriquet, "Stonewall" was born, a nickname still spoken with reverence by many Virginians.

Two days after the debacle at Manassas, Patterson read in a newspaper of his relief from command with an honorable discharge. His failure to hold Johnston in the Shenandoah had contributed substantially to McDowells' defeat. As he returned to Philadelphia he passed through Greencastle and Chambersburg on a regular passenger coach with few people recognizing him. (*A court of inquiry requested by the humiliated officer was denied but he constantly maintained his failure was due to Scott's shortcomings.*) [52]

During the time Patterson's army was involved with its campaign, recruiting in Franklin County never ceased. In May the 1st Pennsylvania Artillery was mustered into Federal service for a three year term. Battery A, led by Hesikiah Easton, was composed entirely of Franklin Countians.

Another company from the county was raised and on June 22 Captain William Dixon led his men to Harrisburg to become Company D of the 6th Pennsylvania Reserves. Among its soldiers from Greencastle was First Sergeant Joseph A. Davison who later rose to the rank of lieutenant-colonel. After being armed at Camp Curtin the regiment returned to a camp near Greencastle named for Colonel Charles J. Biddle, son of the noted financier Nicholas Biddle. On July 22, under the command of Major Samuel Harshbarger, the regiment was ordered to Washington to help defend the city. By rail the men were rushed to Harrisburg and from there to Baltimore. As they marched along the streets to board a train bound for the capital, a private from Company E slipped on the pavement and fell. His musket accidentally discharged, wounding Sergeant William Kriner in the leg. The men panicked, not knowing the cause of the shooting. They feared another altercation with secessionists was about to happen, and began readying their muskets to protect themselves. With great difficulty the troops were kept from firing into crowds along the way and after officers explained the accidental shooting the men were mollified. The regiment then proceeded to the capital where they were mustered into the federal service. The next several months were spent in manning Washington's defenses. [53]

After Patterson's dismissal General Nathaniel P. Banks was given command of the Federal forces in the Shenandoah region. Yet, fears generated by the loss at Manassas, led to another wave of apprehension among the people living above the Mason-Dixon line. The residents of the Cumberland Valley were especially worried. What if Banks was overwhelmed?

On July 26, a public meeting was held in Greencastle to recruit more men. Similar meetings were held in other parts of the county and within the next several weeks about two hundred volunteers were gathered into companies from the various towns and rural areas. A company of cavalry left Chambersburg on August 16 for Harrisburg. The unit, consisting of only fifty-nine men, was to be filled by recruits from towns along the rail line. Led by Captain George Stitzel, a Mexican War veteran, the men marched to the depot in the county seat in a parade headed by the local Brass Band. Over 400 friends and relatives had assembled to bid them goodbye. These Franklin countians were later assigned to Company D of the 11th Pennsylvania Cavalry. Stitzel became a lieutenant-colonel and the unit served the Union for three years. [54]

John R. Stickell, of Antrim Township, was authorized by state officials to begin an enlistment campaign to raise as many as two companies in Franklin County. A schedule of his recruiting visits to county towns and villages was published in area newspapers on August 30. The Chambersburg Dispatch urged the young men of the county to flock to the recruiting agent, Mr. Stickell, to "show their devotion to their country". With patriotic fervor the paper referred to the holy war "to prevent the overthrow of one of the mildest and least oppressive Governments in the world, and the establishment upon its ruins the most hateful that could be concocted in the brain of the veriest despot."

An earlier edition of the same journal warned its readers of a growing secessionist movement in the county. The editor cited actions of federal grand juries which questioned the right of certain news-papers to print anti-Union articles. Specifically the Chambersburg editor warned residents of the Orrstown community to be aware of someone subscribing to thirty-two copies of a pro-Southern paper called the "Day Book." His warning ended by asking, "Who is the traitor in Orrstown that takes such an active part in obtaining circulation for a paper the teachings of which are so utterly treasonable as to merit a presentment by the Grand Jury to the U.S. Court?" [55]

All through the summer of 1861 people of Antrim and nearby townships could hear the booming of cannon in the Shenandoah country as skirmishes between contending forces continued across the Potomac in Virginia. Another development which caused uneasiness came from seeing or hearing of the stream of refugees fleeing out of Virginia by way of the Shenandoah into Maryland and the Keystone State. These were people who refused to take the oath of allegiance to the Confederate States of America. Nearly a thousand were said to be living in Washington County, Maryland. [56]

Amid all of these scares the Chambersburg Dispatch reached the conclusion that if the Rebels did overcome Federal forces to the south of the county, there would most certainly be an invasion. The paper's efforts to arouse citizens to enlist and to move against traitors was topped by a call in the September 3 edition; ". . . one half the villages of the State could be surprised and sacked by an enemy at any moment. Let every citizen be the owner of a musket or rifle. These are the effective weapons of war, and if the population at large possesses them each home will be an armory, and every township invincible. . ." Fortunately this kind of advice was never considered seriously. The cost in lives and property would have been disasterous if such opposition had been mounted by civilians against invading soldiers. [57]

Although the Shenandoah became an avenue for incursions into Pennsylvania at later times nothing developed in 1861. The fears that existed among Franklin countians never materialized during the first year of war, but Pennsylvanians living along the southern border did welcome the events which took place in that portion of Virginia west of its Great Valley. As early as June 11, 1861 pro-Union delegates met in Wheeling to organize what eventually became West Virginia, a state whose northern border touched Pennsylvania's western counties. Its eastern section was only twenty miles from Antrim Township.

During the spring of 1861 Major General George B. McClellan had moved troops into this part of Virginia to control the strategically important Baltimore and Ohio Railroad. Most of the mountain people were pro-Union and welcomed McClellan's forces. Yet those who were pro-Southern formed bands of marauders who spread terror throughout the area.

By late summer the Cincinnati Times reported that the struggle between these secessionist forces and the Union troops created a danger to all western Virginia. The bands of Southern sympathizers had degenerated into assassins. "They are committing murders daily, lying in ambush for that purpose. Not only the Union volunteers, but their own neighbors, who peaceably and quietly sustain the cause of the Union, are victims of their malice and blood thirsty hate. They steal upon our pickets and murder them. They shoot down their neighbors, daytime and at night and burn their property to ashes." To combat these Rebel "bushwhackers" Captain John P. Baggs organized an anti-guerilla force called "Snake Hunters." Along with McClellan's men, the "Snake Hunters" eventually stopped this harassment and halted further damage to the Baltimore and Ohio for the time being. Throughout the war this fighting remained what might be termed a "stand off."

Similar pro-Southern partisan units were formed in Western Maryland. These and their counterparts from the mountains of western Virginia would form the nucleus for forces which eventually conducted raids into Maryland and southern Pennsylvania. Individuals from these units also formed gangs of horse thieves who found a ready market for their stolen animals in the Shenandoah. In additon, Union deserters banded together to share in the same business. Colonel John D. Imboden of the Army of Nothern Virginia welcomed these men which he referred to as "partisan rangers". "It is only men I want" he proclaimed "men who will pull a trigger on a Yankee with as much alacrity as they would be a mad dog..." [58]

As the year reached its final months, life in the Greencastle-Antrim area began to return to normal. Despite the fears of spring and summer, each passing day brought more relaxation from the terror of earlier months, but men were still going off to war. In September a company from the area joined the 87th Pennsylvania Regiment and in October the 77th Pennsylvania was organized in Pittsburgh with one full company and parts of three others from Franklin County. [59]

Thursday, September 26, was set aside throughout the North as a day of "humiliation, prayer, and fasting." Appropriate services were held in most churches of the county to recognize this occasion. Two weeks later the President authorized General Scott to suspend the writ of habeas corpus between Maine and the District of Columbia when necessary to combat suspected subversion. The North was moving towards a military state in order to prosecute the war.

Through the summer and early fall months, questions concerning the role Maryland would play in the war still plagued Pennsylvanians along the Mason-Dixon Line. This was a prime concern of the Federal authorities. Since the state practically surrounded the capital city, to have it secede was unthinkable. Fortunately Maryland's governor, Thomas Hicks, opposed secession. Early victories of the Confederates influenced the national government to impose greater military controls over the state. Evidence of sympathy for the South was suppressed by seizure of property, suppression of newspapers, and the arrest of known secessionists. Military rule by Federal troops, headed by B. F. Butler, was imposed on the people. In November, elections were held for state offices including the governorship. Political leaders who favored secession were arrested and jailed. For the election Maryland soldiers were furloughed to go home and cast their ballots for the pro-Union gubernatorial candidate, Augustus W. Bradford. Provost Marshalls were posted near polling places to arrest suspected pro-Southerners before they could vote. Needless to say, Bradford was elected. Maryland was saved for the Union and from then on many who believed in the Southern cause left their homes to live in the Confederacy. [60]

Winfield Scott resigned on November 1 and George Brinton McClellan, who had succeeded Irvin McDowell, as head of the army, was named General-In-Chief of the Union forces. As the year ended, General Banks was still controlling the northern part of the Shenandoah - a comfort to all who lived in Pennsylvania's southern border country.

CHAPTER IV

A FULL YEAR OF WAR

The winter of 1861-62 was one of the cruelest of the century. Despite frigid weather and heavy snows some Confederates were not content to stay indoors or near their campfires. In early January Stonewall Jackson moved into the mountain country of western Virginia. Known as the Romney campaign it was designed to disrupt the Baltimore and Ohio Railroad's operations, cripple commerce on the Chesapeake and Ohio Canal, and draw Federal troops out of the Shenandoah.

Part of the plan was to destroy Dam Five of the canal, a reservoir used to maintain proper water levels in locks west of Williamsport. Jackson's men were able to demolish a small section, but it was restored several days after the raid. This portion of the canal was important to farmers of Montgomery and Peters Townships since many shipped farm produce from the Clearspring, Maryland area where Dam Five was located. On January 4, after dispersing several small Union forces, the Confederates were opposite Hancock, Md., along the Virginia side of the Potomac. Jackson sent Turner Ashby across the river, under a flag of truce, with a message for the Federals stationed there. They were told to evacuate or he would begin shelling the place. It was hoped that the Union force would either surrender or retreat.

When the mandate was ignored Rebel cannon began their bombardment. There followed an artillery duel between the two forces and sounds of the firing could be heard as far away as Greencastle and Antrim Township, a distance of approximately twenty-five miles. However, Jackson's men ran into another adversary - the weather. Already hampered by heavy snow lying on the ground it began snowing again, deepening the layer to six inches. The Confederates finally withdrew. Five days later Jackson and his men moved back into Romney. Stonewall evidently decided his men had enough of the winter for awhile. Here they made camp and did not undertake another campaign until the weather moderated. [1]

In March Jackson began moving back into the southern part of the Shenandoah. Followed closely by Union forces under Nathaniel Banks, the Federals occupied Winchester on March 12. This success was part of a general spring offensive by the Northern army to take Richmond. The major operation called for George B. McClellan to move his army, under naval protection to the York-James Peninsula and move on the Southern capital. Then as the army sailed from Alexandria with confidence in ultimate victory, Federal leaders began to see the peril the nation's capital faced because so much of the Army of the Potomac was on its way to Richmond and few soldiers were left to guard the city. Suppose the Rebels unleashed a surprise attack from out of the Shenandoah Valley?

On March 23 Jackson struck a Union force, headed by General James Shields, at Kernstown below Winchester. The Confederates were outnumbered and eventually retreated into the southern part of the valley, but this action was enough to pin down the Federals and demonstrated the vulnerability of the Union if the Southerners had prevailed over Shields.

President Lincoln then decided to make Washington more secure. He reinforced Harpers Ferry to bring greater strength into the Shenandoah region and instead of sending additional troops to McClellan he used them to strengthen the defenses in and near Washington. These were moves that brought relief to those who lived along Pennsylvania's southern border. Fear of Rebels breaking across the Potomac into Maryland and Fulton or Franklin counties had been constant ever since the people of the area heard the shelling of Hancock back in January.

Farmers of Antrim were into their spring planting with hopes for better prices in 1862. The previous year had been a bad one for grain sales, but since the war's end was not in sight demands would surely increase. All over the North people were talking about higher farm prices. One thing was certainly true - there would be less farm workers. As calls for soldiers increased fewer men were left to work. This meant longer hours in the fields and more work for the women and boys or girls.

There was a growing demand for more wool since the North could no longer get cotton and more sheep were being raised as prices continued to rise. Yet farmers were constantly complaining of dogs attacking their flocks. A. B. Wingerd was said to have lost sixty-seven head in March to these roving predators. [2]

Another means of overcoming the cotton shortage was to encourage farmers to plant more flax and hemp. Growing flax was nothing new. It had been a popular crop since colonial days. From it producers could get linseed oil, feed for cattle, and fibers for making linens. However, growing hemp was a new undertaking in the Greencastle area. The stalks, when matured, were from six to ten feet tall. In late summer the crop was cut and allowed to lie on the ground where over several week's time the bulky portions of the stalks would rot away leaving only the fibers. These were separated by a "hemp rake," allowed to dry, and then twisted into rope or twine or woven into a rough cloth for making burlap used for bagging. The fabric was then made into sacks for storing or shipping flour, meal, grain, salt, etc. Attempts were made to combine flax and hemp fibers to produce a cottonized thread for weaving purposes but this proved to be impractical.

Sugar and molasses were in short supply and farmers were encouraged to raise sorghum to produce syrup which became a sweetener for family use. Reports indicated that as many as 300 gallons of the syrup could be produced from one acre of sorghum. The plant grew to heights of over eight feet and could be cultivated and harvested with no more labor than that required for producing corn. Christian E. Lesher, whose mill was located in the Marsh district of Antrim, went into the syrup making business. Farmers would bring their sorghum to the mill where it was crushed and the juice boiled down to produce a thick syrup. The fibers of the stalks could, also, be used as feed for cattle.

Greencastle's dealers and manufacturers of farm equipment saw in the labor shortage prospects for increased sales. Grain drills, mechanical threshers, reapers, hayrakes and wagons would be needed in ever increasing numbers as the war continued. Manufacturers continued to look for ways to improve production. In June it was reported that Jacob Wister, a millwright living in Greencastle, had found a way to improve flour production. It was called a "universal knocker." Bolting cloth, through which flour was sifted, could be kept cleaner with this new device allowing more flour to separate from the bran. Chambersburg's Valley Spirit claimed, "A miller who has tried Wister's improvement says his gain is ... from four to six pounds of flour on the barrel." As the war progressed this invention was a valuable asset to the milling businss. In 1860 flour sold for five dollars a barrel but through the war years it reached prices as high as seven dollars.

The need for gun stocks prompted sawmill operators in the North to go into this kind of manufacturing. Mathias Kisecker went into the business of producing walnut stocks for the makers of muskets and rifles used by the Federal forces, while other sawmills prospered as the demand for lumber increased for the manufacturing of farm equipment. The Ilgingritz mill also wove blankets for a company having a contract with the army. [3]

Another sign of the war's impact came when, in June Clarke McDowell announced he was closing his academy. War pressures had brought a decline in interest for the school's services. It would never open again, but others would take its place. Public schools held their sessions as usual. [4]

Elections were held on April 2 in Antrim, supervisors — Jonathan Stickell, John Stover, and John Wallech, were elected. School directors — Henry Stine, John Grove, and Jacob Shook, were also chosen. Henry Baltzley was elected constable; Lemuel Snively, township clerk; Henry Ditch, assessor; and Melchi Snively, justice of the peace. In Greencastle fewer offices were filled. John Rowe was chosen as justice of the peace; David Hawbecker was elected constable; Jacob Zuck, assessor; and two school directors, James McLanahan and William Kreps, were also elected. [5]

JOSEPH HENSON HOUSE   HOME OF JACOB SHOOK   BY MICHAEL CONRAD

News of the Battle of Shiloh, fought on April 6 and 7, reached the county near the end of that week. It was learned that tremendous losses were incurred by both sides. Estimates of 23,000 Southern and Northern men killed, wounded, or missing made this encounter the bloodiest ever fought on the North American continent to that time. Later reports told of the 77th Regiment of Pennsylvania Infantry being at Shiloh. This was of interest to Franklin Countians because Colonel Frederick Stumbaugh, who had been with the 2nd Pennsylvania Volunteers under Patterson, commanded the 77th and

Peter Housum, served as second in command. Company A was composed entirely of veterans of the earlier Volunteer Regiment which included men from Greencastle-Antrim. This unit led the final charge against the Confederates in this struggle. Editions of the Chambersburg Dispatch for the next three weeks carried letters from men who took part in the battle. They also contained notices of countians who were killed or died from wounds. It was the only Pennsylvania regiment to participate in the battle. In the final charge on the second day, the 77th, with Company A in the lead, took many prisoners, including the commander of a Confederate regiment. But Shiloh was only the beginning, for the 77th would continue fighting in the war's western theater until the end.[6]

The Peninsular Campaign continued through April, May, and June while the nation watched and waited as the battles were reported. Numerous outfits from Franklin County were with McClellan in this attempt to capture Richmond. The 6th Pennsylvania Reserves with its company of countians was used primarily for rear guard duty. Another county unit, Company K of the 12th Pennsylvania Reserves, saw front line action in the Seven Days' Battle.

Hesekiah Easton, leader of Battery A of the 1st Pennsylvania Artillery lost his life at Gaines Mill on June 27 when his guns ran out of ammunition. As advancing Confederates called for the battery to surrender, Easton cried, "No. We never surrender." The volley that followed killed him, but in the melee that ensued most of his men escaped capture. Second Lieutenant Jacob Detrich, a cousin of General David Detrich of Greencastle, was also attached to this battery. When Easton fell, Detrich took command but was wounded by minie balls penetrating his left arm. In addition to the men who survived, only twelve of the battery's famous forty-eight gray horses were rescued. Easton's own mount, which Detrich was able to ride out of the battle, had to be destroyed because of excessive wounds.

The 11th Cavalry of Pennsylvania, containing the company raised in Franklin County in October, 1861, also saw service in this fighting. Lieutenant Colonel George Stitzel and Major John Nimmon, both of Chambersburg, served on the regiment's staff. Other countians with the state's 107th Regiment were with McClellan in Virginia.

While both the western and eastern campaigns were in progress, men from the Greencastle area, with the 97th Regiment of Pennsylvania, were serving in a sea borne expedition that captured Fort Pulaski near Savannah. The regiment continued to be involved in operations along the Carolina and Florida coasts until Spring of 1864. [7]

Although McClellan's army fought its way to within sight of Richmond, in the end it failed to take the city. There followed a series of battles, beginning June 25, and the Southerners gradually pushed the Union forces away from their capital city. After the Seven Days' Battles, climaxed by a terrible battle at Malvern Hill, the Federal Army disengaged and retreated to Harrison's Landing on the James River. Of more than 100,000 men taken to the Virginia Peninsula, some 15,000 were now dead, wounded, or missing.

Malvern Hill was McClellan's last important engagement on the Peninsula. He had failed and Lincoln decided to try a new general. John Pope was given charge of an army to insure Washington against attack. It was to operate in central Virginia and the Shenandoah. Henry Halleck, named General in Chief of Union Armies on August 4, ordered McClellan to bring his forces back to support Pope who was preparing to move against the Rebels southwest of Washington.

On July 17, the President, sensing an emergency as the Peninsular Campaign was ending without Union victory, signed into law a measure which came to be known as the "Draft of 1862." It placed in readiness the nation's men, between the ages of eighteen and forty-five, to serve in the militia for nine months. States would be given quotas which each governor was responsible for raising. As part of the apparatus for implementing this militia act, Governor Curtin named commissioners in the counties to act as agents to call up men for military service. Donald R. Wunderlich, a Greencastle commission merchant, was given this job for Franklin County. [8]

The first nine months unit raised locally under the new law was the 126th Regiment. It consisted of two and a half companies from Juniata and Fulton while seven and a half were from Franklin. When this regiment was mustered into the service in August it became the largest body of troops ever raised in the county at any single enlistment time. Until August there had been few recruitments. The 107th Regiment, of which Company K was from the county, had been organized at Harrisburg on March 5 and the 2nd Pennsylvania Heavy Artillery which was formed earlier in January at Philadelphia included some countians. [9]

Robert E. Lee was given command of the Confederate forces after General Joseph Johnston was wounded on May 31. When McClellan's army was brought back to Washington, Lee began developing plans to invade the North. At the same time a Rebel invasion of Union held

Kentucky, under Generals Braxton Bragg and Kirby Smith, was to take place. This proved to be the only time the South conducted an all out offensive on both Eastern and Western fronts simultaneously.

Pope's forces met Lee's at Manassas on August 29 and there followed another federal debacle. As the defeated army staggered back to Washington, the capital once more lay in fear of being overrun by the Rebels. Pope had failed and on September 2 McClellan was reinstated. Two days later Lee's Army of Northern Virginia crossed the Potomac into Maryland.

Confederate morale had never been higher. Forcing McClellan from the Peninsula and defeating Pope's army provided a confidence never experienced before. If hopes became reality the war would soon be over. A successful invasion could punish the North and avenge the suffering Virginia had been through for nearly a year and a half. Maryland could be brought into the Confederacy and the yoke of its Northern oppressors lifted. From Maryland an advance into Pennsylvania could result in destroying both the Baltimore and Ohio and the Pennsylvania railroads. Destruction of the Susquehanna River bridges could end future movement of troops into Virginia by way of the Cumberland Valley. A swing to the east might mean the capture of Philadelphia or the taking of Baltimore. Either outcome would end the use of this corridor for moving men and supplies to the capital. Washington would be isolated and brought to its knees through a strongly enforced seige. Finally, with such glowing promises of success, England and France would accept the Confederacy as a legitimate state and victory would be guaranteed.

On September 4 Lee's army entered Frederick and by the next day his men were camped around the town. As they marched through the western Maryland countryside they found divided sentiment. The welcome they expected was not all that enthusiastic. The soldiers, under strict orders to behave themselves, caused little or no property damage and only minor instances of misbehavior towards the citizens. What the Marylanders saw in Lee's forces led to little confidence that these men comprised an army of liberation. They appeared to be ill fed to the point of starvation. One Virginia veteran told of troops living on green corn and apples through most of the campaign. A fourth of the army was without shoes and most were clothed in varying degrees of raggedness. Many wore a variety of military clothing and civilian dress. Lee had reported to Jefferson Davis his need for shoes and uniforms and one of the secondary objectives of the invasion was to find shoes. It was estimated that, at least 40,000 pairs were needed. Yet as his forces progressed through Maryland they were able to secure a mere 1,700 pairs.

Nearly starved, nearly naked, nearly shoeless, this was the Army of Northern Virginia. But it was a fighting force that had taken on heavy odds before and to these men the odds were pretty good that they could keep on winning battles.

While the Confederates were occupying Frederick and setting up camps near the town, Captain W. T. Faithful, of the 1st Maryland Regiment of the Potomac Home Brigade, carefully assembled the sick and wounded Federal troops of the area. After securing enough transportation for his men, he quietly moved them to Harpers Ferry and sent what supplies he could to Pennsylvania.

Meanwhile along Pennsylvania's southern border panic was spreading. Many families from Hagerstown and as far away as Clearspring were either fleeing into Franklin County or sending their valuables to friends there. Anxieties also gripped the people north of the state line. Chambersburg's bank sent its money supply to Harrisburg. Home guard units were gathering in the towns and business places closed at five o'clock each evening to free men for drill exercises. When word reached the border towns that Lee had left Frederick, on September 10, tensions heightened. Guard units from all over the county were ordered to march to Chambersburg. State emergency forces were promised and were to be sent into the area as soon as they could be assembled. [10]

Before leaving Frederick, Lee and Jackson studied maps of Pennsylvania and General Jackson asked for and carefully perused those of Franklin County. As the Rebels moved along the National Road towards Boonsboro it was a foregone conclusion of most of the men that within days they would be well into Pennsylvania's Cumberland Valley. The Confederate's plan was to use Hagerstown as a base of operations. It was the southern terminus of the railroad which ran to Harrisburg. Good wagon roads led from that part of Maryland deep into Pennsylvania. Reports of militia moving towards Hagerstown, at first, concerned General Lee but he learned from his scouts that only a few enemy pickets were in the Greencastle-Chambersburg area. [11]

A body of Confederate cavalry entered Hagerstown around 9 a.m. on September 11. By noon they were sending patrols and measures were immediately taken to prevent stores and supplies from being shipped into Pennsylvania. These cavalrymen were under the command of Lt. Colonel Luke Turnan Brien. He was from an old Maryland family with roots in Frederick and Washington counties. Several years prior to the war he and his wife bought a farm near Middleburg, so he was very familiar with many of the backroads. That afternoon the mayor, cashier of the bank, sheriff, and other loyal citi-

zens of Hagerstown arrived in Greencastle. As news of the Rebel occupation spread through Franklin County, farmers began taking their livestock to counties of central Pennsylvania or to hiding places in the creek hills and mountain valleys, while merchants began hiding their store goods. Governor Curtin, in a telegram to President Lincoln, stated . . . . "The people of Greencastle expect a dash on that place this afternoon" *(Sept. 11, 1862 3:30 p.m.)* In Greencastle the Rev. Edward Briedenbaugh, reported that on Saturday night, September 13, a battery of Federal artillery caused a commotion as it passed through the town on its way from Hagerstown and that all churches except his were closed the next day. However, his attendance was small, yet "good concerning the circumstances." [12]

Chambersburg's "Valley Spirit," of September 10, carried news that Commissioner Wunderlich would be in the county that week to supervise drafting of militiamen. Handbills had been distributed to show the time and places where he would conduct his business. Friday, September 12, was set for Greencastle. The commissioner would be at Mrs. Hollar's place on West Baltimore Street to meet with men from Greencastle-Antrim and "that part of Montgomery and Peters townships which voted in Greencastle." The purpose of his visit was to meet those enrolled who "seek exemption" from militia service. His records indicated that 832 men, living in the district, were eligible for this duty. [13]

Governor Curtin kept the Federal military authorities constantly informed as news came to him from the Cumberland Valley. He sent an expert telegrapher, William W. Wilson, to Greencastle to act as a dispatcher of intelligence reports brought to him by scouts of Pennsylvania's 15th Cavalry which had been ordered into the region. Wilson carried a portable telegraph and used a railway hand car to travel between Greencastle and the Maryland line. When news arrived he would tap the wires along the tracks and relay his information to the governor's headquarters in Harrisburg. [14]

The 15th had its origin in October, 1861 when William J. Palmer, personal secretary of J. Edgar Thomson, President of the Pennsylvania Railroad, organized it as the Anderson Troop to serve as a bodyguard for General Robert Anderson of Fort Sumter fame, who commanded the Army of the Ohio at Louisville, Kentucky. During August of 1862 Palmer returned to his home state to conduct an enlistment campaign. Within two weeks enough men were recruited to form a regiment. It was then officially designated as the 15th Pennsylvania Volunteer Cavalry, mustered into service on August 22, 1862 at Carlisle. Before the unit could be issued horses, Lee invaded Maryland and the regiment was broken into detachments for various kinds of duty. Palmer, under the circumstances could do little as regimental commander, so two hundred men were assigned to him to engage in reconnaissance missions beyond Franklin County's southern border. After receiving uniforms, blankets, revolvers, ammunition, and three days rations, this force was divided into four companies. On September 9 the men left Carlisle and after traveling down the valley by train they arrived in Greencastle at four o'clock that afternoon. Sleeping quarters were provided in one of the warehouses south of the town.

COLONEL WILLIAM PALMER   U.S.A.M.H.I.

The next morning townspeople came out in force with breakfast for the cavalrymen. Orders were issued by the state which empowered the troopers to impress horses for the time the 15th would be in the area. One of the men assigned to this duty was accompanied by Jacob Shook, a farmer with strong pro-union sympathies. At times Shook explained the difficulty in finding horses on certain farms because the owners were "Breckenridge Democrats" who did not favor the war. A camp was made on the Shook farm that lay near Greencastle along the road to Leitersburg, Maryland. It had ample space in an open field through which a shaded brook ran from an ever flowing spring on the adjacent farm owned by Jacob Stover.

By evening about 150 horses were found and Colonel Palmer, with twenty mounted men, left camp at nightfall to go beyond the Maryland border on an intelligence gathering mission. When approaching Middleburg, someone along the way told them it was Muttontown and from then on this was the name the cavalrymen used. Palmer left most of his men in the village area but he and Private John Jackson moved south through the enemy lines. Dressed as farmers they spent the following day talking to Southern soldiers and civilians in and around Hagerstown. On Friday, September 12, the spies returned with information for Harrisburg. At a pre-arranged meeting place he met telegrapher Wilson near a warehouse along the railroad in what is today known as Mason-Dixon. *(That morning Wilson and two assistants had a narrow escape. While eating breakfast at a farm house near Middleburg, a Confederate cavalry patrol appeared, driving them off and eating his breakfast.)* From here Wilson relayed Palmer's first report to Curtin's headquarters. He described his sources of information and the numbers of wagons and Rebels he had seen. Everything he saw indicated the Confederates were not on a mere raid but were planning to invade the state. Their army was well disciplined, not disturbing any of the Maryland people or their property. He thought when Lee entered Pennsylvania his policy "may be to treat the non-combatants roughly," in regards to "the matter of property."

For nearly a week the 15th continued to scout the entire southern Franklin County area. At times they picked up deserters from Lee's forces and secured information about troop movements. Their presence also gave an illusion of more federal forces along the border than there really were, no doubt a factor in discouraging the Confederate cavalry from crossing the state line in force. On the same day Colonel Palmer went through the Rebel lines, a squad was sent on a mission towards Waynesboro. Reports persisted that Confederates were in the Shady Grove area. Upon arriving in the village they learned of enemy horsemen being seen several miles south of the turnpike that connected Greencastle and Waynesboro. Yet, all remained quiet as an outpost was manned through the night. Other posts were established along the road between Chambersburg and Waynesboro and in the Quincy community. Despite rumors, no Rebel forces were encountered. [15]

While the 15th was engaged in scouting the enemy, Wilson remained in Greencastle. Flying an American flag over his hand-car, and with two soldiers from the 15th cavalry attached to him, he was able to continue reporting to Curtin's office. Later he relayed information which seemed to show a change in Confederate plans. His informants reported movement of the enemy at Williamsport and that they were crossing the river into Virginia. It was later learned that those troops were marching towards Harpers Ferry to help in fighting expected there. Governor Curtin sent the intelligence the 15th gathered to Washington and its importance was reflected in subsequent moves made by the Federal forces which, under McClellan, were cautiously pursuing the Rebel army through Maryland.[16]

Part of Lee's strategy was to capture Harpers Ferry. This would enable him to shift his supply lines into the Shenandoah. Jackson, with six divisions, was assigned to do this. As the Confederates approached the town, on September 13, the leader of 12,000 men stationed there, Colonel Dixon S. Miles, decided his position was untenable. Rebel forces seemed to be on all sides. Escape was impossible and surrender was the only sensible course to follow.

A Union cavalry leader had other plans. Although the Federal position appeared to be hopeless, he argued that cavalry troops could escape. Colonel Benjamin "Grimes" Davis of the 8th New York Cavalry was the author of the plan and although Miles first objected he eventually consented to let the men try. Another officer, Lieutenant Colonel Hasbrouck Davis, of the 12th Illinois Cavalry helped complete the details. Aside from those two regiments, other units involved were the 7th Squadron Rhode Island Cavalry, 1st Maryland *(Companies H and I)* and the 1st Regiment Potomac Home Brigade Cavalry *(Coles Battalion).*

At eight o'clock on the evening of September 14 the horsemen began assembling. Major Augustus Corliss, of the Rhode Island outfit, told his men that by morning they would either be "in Pennsylvania, on the way to Richmond, or in Hell." Nor comforting words with such odds spelled out so forcefully, but the Potomac was crossed on a pontoon bridge to the Maryland shore without incident. With local guides directing them along narrow roads, over streams, through wooded areas, and across ravines, they were able to skirt Confederate camps of the immediate area with few mishaps. On one occasion the force ran into Rebel pickets. Gunfire was exchanged but the horsemen were able to escape in a northerly direction. Near Sharpsburg they ran into another enemy outpost. When asked to identify themselves, a reply rang out — "Friends of the Union." The Confederates began firing but failed to hit anyone as they escaped. Nothing, yet, had changed their course, which was still headed north and at one point they were obliged to dash through a bivouac area where the enemy lay sleeping.

Eventually the cavalry reached St. James where a halt was ordered to rest the horses. Within thirty minutes the journey continued through a wooded area along a road to Williamsport. One of the forward riders came back with word of a Rebel wagon train headed for Virginia. When the Union horsemen came up to the train "Grimes" Davis, a native of Alabama and a former resident of Mississippi, called out in his best southern drawl and ordered the train to change its direction. It did and with dawn fast approaching the wagons were soon on their way, at double speed, toward Pennsylvania.

As the early light of morning provided clearer recognition, one teamster asked one of their new comrades the name of his regiment. He was told he belonged to the 8th New York. "The hell you say," was the amazed reply. Within seconds the teamsters knew they were captives traveling north in the Cumberland Valley. One driver tried to free the horses from his wagon. Another, hauling ammunition, attempted to set his afire. Some refused to move their teams. When it was made clear that anyone attempting to stop the train would be shot, the journey continued with increased speed. Around nine o'clock on the morning of September 15 the train of about sixty wagons and an "army" of horsemen were seen on the tollroad coming toward Greencastle. [17]

At first townspeople thought the borough was being invaded, but when the truth was discovered they crowded the streets to greet the cavalrymen and curse the captives. Even housewives, standing along the street with their children, urged them to yell at the "damned Rebels." Some of the more genteel ladies of the town, however, showed their charitable dispositions by bringing bread and water to the prisoners. One of Palmer's men described the captured Confederates as a "sorry looking set, ragged and dirty, without uniforms, and some without shoes. One I saw on horseback with a spur buckled to his barefoot." He talked with several prisoners from Georgia who told him they were tired of the war.

Many of the teamsters were slaves and they were freed upon reaching Greencastle. It is quite probable that some stayed in the area to work on farms and found homes with ex-slaves who lived in the township. Others went on north and their fate remains unknown. By this time there were several hundred blacks in the Greencastle area who had fled from Maryland and Virginia after the war started. Some of the men, when colored troops were permitted, fought in the Federal army.

The most angry tirade was reserved for Clagget Fitzhugh, the slave catcher, who had earned the hatred of Franklin Countians for the role he played in capturing John Cook of John Brown's army. Fitzhugh had apparently left the county when the Confederates came to Maryland. His services, as a scout, were accepted and he was serving the wagon train as a guide when captured. As he limped through the streets, cries — "Hang him," "Down with the traitor," and "Kill him," — greeted the sunburned, dirty, and scared Fitzhugh. Some of the townspeople made a rush to seize him, but he was quickly put under heavy guard and rushed off to confinement for his own protection.

In addition to the wagons filled with ammunition, some reports told of a herd of beef cattle being part of the captured spoils. Estimates of as high as 200 captives were also reported. Upon arrival in the town, the captors turned everything over to the 15th Cavalry. Prisoners were jailed and all captured material was sent to Chambersburg to be turned over to the quartermaster stationed there. The next day the captives were sent to Harrisburg. News of all these events of September 15 was sent to Harrisburg by William Wilson who was still on the job operating from his mobile office.

The heroes of the hour, the wagon train captors, were overwhelmed by the generosity shown them. They told how they were treated earlier in southern Antrim when farm people gathered along the road to hand them fruit, cakes, and pies. Now in Greencastle most households were open to the officers and men where once again they were fed. To those who had gone into camp sites near the town, wagons filled with food were taken to them. One New Yorker, Pvt. Henry Norton, later wrote that the provisions included almost everything anyone could eat. "They . . . told us to help ourselves, and we had a good square meal and some left over for another time. The boys thought that soldiering wasn't bad after all." [18]

After a night's rest, the feeding continued the next morning. One Illinois officer was told by the owner of a large farm near Greencastle that he had served a hundred breakfasts that morning. Samuel Pettengill of the Rhode Island cavalry told how the men, camped on the Jacob Shook farm, had no cooking utensils, but during the time they were in the Greencastle area he and his comrades were "boarded around" in the neighborhood so as not to impose too great a burden on any particular household. The story of their escape and journey through enemy lines was an "open sesame" to the well provisioned homes and barns of the farmers where ample food was available to both men and their horses. This was a unit made up largely of college students from Dartmouth and Norwich and nicknamed the "college cavaliers." Although their enlistments had expired by now, instead of going home they volunteered to remain in service until the invasion threat was over. They became part of McClellan's reserve forces south of Hagerstown, but having only a sparse ration of hardtack, no cooking utensils, or opportunity to forage for food — "strong reasons existed for a return to Greencastle." Prior to returning home the men stopped off in Greencastle to say goodbye to friends and enjoy the good cooking of the local people. [19]

On the day the town welcomed the captors of the Confederate wagons, a trainload of Pennsylvania emergency militiamen arrived. Eventually as many as 10.000 would move into the area to occupy the campsites used the year before by Patterson's army. Governor Curtin had finally pried General John F. Reynolds loose from McClellan's staff. He had insisted that this Pennsylvanian was the man needed to organize and lead the state's militia to protect his homeland from the ravages of the oncoming Rebels. The militia was composed of all classes, generally older men, clergymen with their church members, judges, lawyers, merchants, mechanics, clerks, and farmers. Curtin had been forced to ask for these temporary volunteers since the Federal Government, fearing for the safety of Washington, and thinking the Army of the Potomac to be outnumbered, would not spare any regular troops for the state's defense. Reynolds was assured the militia would make a creditable fighting force.

The governor's enthusiasm for calling "the state's citizens to give their full measure of devotion" was not as eagerly accepted by these undisciplined men, now called to defend the state. Reynolds knew this and did not want to leave his forces which were in pursuit of Lee, but he was a soldier and when ordered he obeyed. Despite objections from McClellan and members of his staff, the President ordered Reynolds to proceed to Harrisburg. Lincoln could not risk offending a governor who had done so much to help prosecute the war. On September 13 Reynolds left his men at Ridgeville, (Ringgold), Maryland.

U.S.A.M.H.I.   CARLISLE, PA.
MAJOR GENERAL JOHN F. REYNOLDS

The general arrived in Harrisburg the next day and found the disorderly mob he suspected would be waiting there. Arms, equipment, and most of all, organization, were needed. To expect much training was beyond hope. On September 15, Reynolds reached Chambersburg where he found more confusion. Transportation was the worst bottleneck. Someone was needed to unscramble the problems arising from getting troops down the valley's railroad and return with empty cars over the line's single track for reloading. Finally a private, named Joseph D. Potts, was found who knew something about railroading. He was a militiaman from Williamsport, but as a civilian, the general manager of the Philadelphia and Erie Railroad. With his experience the traffic was soon straightened out and the next day more state troops rolled into the county seat. Upon arriving they were hurried off the cars into churches and every other available building.

The whole experience continued to exasperate General Reynolds unmercifully. Here he was in Chambersburg, with reports coming in of fighting in nearby Maryland. He had left a real army that would soon face the enemy in a major engagement, while he was plagued with questions about saddles and oats for Palmer's cavalry; an artillery officer's concern for cups and kettles; for special treatment for the governor's political friends; and a host of other minor details.[20]

Finally the general left all these matters to lesser officers and went to Hagerstown. If he was exasperated, the militiamen were not filled with unbounded happiness either. Henry F. Charles, from Port Treverton, recorded his impressions of the service. He came to the state capital the day Reynolds arrived, only Henry came as a private. When his company got to Harrisburg the men were marched to Camp Curtin. They stood around awhile and then the outfit was sent to the Pennsylvania Depot. Here they received their first and only meal of the day — dry bread, cold ham, and a tin of coffee. From the depot they were sent to the capital yard, and when night came they were ordered into the capital building. "We did not sleep much as the boys were singing and dancing just as if they were at some great frolic."

Henry and his comrades had no uniforms. "We were a mooly crowd . . . I had a braided cloth coat, satin vest, big black silk necktie, graded calf boots and the rest were dressed equally as good and some much better." Each man was given cartridges, a Harpers Ferry musket with bayonet, a haversack, and a canteen. The ammunition was to be carried in the haversack since there were no cartridge boxes. After being assigned to Company D, 18th Regiment, his unit was placed on a Cumberland Valley train the next morning. When they got near Greencastle the railroad was blocked with cars. Here there was trouble with a regiment that did not want to serve. "Their colonel disembarked them and had them fall in formation to cross the state line. They said they had only enlisted for state duty. Then he gave the command — 'Every damn coward step in front,' not a man had the courage to step out so he gave the command to return to the cars. He was a Dutch colonel and with this example there was no trouble with the other regiments." [21]

This experience was repeated many times as Reynolds moved his poor army towards Maryland. He knew the governor was coming and maybe his presence would inspire the men to get going. After the news of fighting at South Mountain the general was sure a decisive engagement with Lee would not be long in coming. Although doubtful of the effectiveness of his force, Reynolds nevertheless wanted to be ready if needed. The troops were given forty rounds of ammunition and three day's rations. A message was sent to Harrisburg to tell the governor he was taking his men to join McClellan, "if such a thing is possible." This phrase betrayed Reynold's feelings, for he had just heard from Chambersburg that "large numbers" of the troops refused to set foot south of the state line. [22]

While Reynolds was involved with the Pennsylvania Emergency Militia and the captured wagon train was bringing excitement to the town of Greencastle, far greater events were transpiring in nearby Maryland. On the day the militia's commander left the Army of the Potomac its advance units met Lee's rear guard in the mountains west of Frederick. Fighting began the next morning, September 14, and continued until nightfall. The Pennsylvania Reserves, *(Reynold's old command)* led by General George G. Meade, helped force the Rebels to withdraw. Thus ended the Battle of South Mountain. On September 15, the Harpers Ferry garrison of some 12,000 Federal troops surrendered to Stonewall Jackson.

The stage was now set for the final act of Lee's campaign. The news of Jackson's success at Harpers Ferry convinced the Southern leader to make his stand at Sharpsburg, a small village fifteen miles south of Hagerstown. At hand were only 19,000 men but when Stonewall's force joined him he would have an army of nearly 40,000.

As long lines of blue clad divisions poured over South Mountain and into the valley, the Confederates knew they now must face McClellan's Army of the Potomac, a force nearly three times the size of theirs. With his back to the river, Lee remained confident. He felt he could take advantage of every cautious move, every mistake his adversary was capable of making.

There followed, on September 17, what has been called the "bloodiest single day of the war." The carnage began in the haze of early morning and continued on through the day until late afternoon. When night came over 26,000 men lay dead or wounded on the farmlands near Antietam Creek. Through the next day both armies held their fire. Neither side made a move against the other and by evening

Lee's generals convinced him to leave the field of battle. Through the night that followed, the Army of Northern Virginia quietly crossed the Potomac into the safety of its native state.

Many considered the battle a draw. However, Lee's hopes and dreams, so high just two weeks before, now lay dead along with the broken bodies of men left behind. Nowhere in the North was there greater joy than in Pennsylvania and in the Cumberland Valley a gigantic sense of relief spread all the way to Harrisburg.

Although the Confederates were no longer a threat, John F. Reynolds still seethed. He had been able to get only a meager part of his "army" into the vicinity of Hagerstown. A generous estimate would be no more than 2,500 men. *(After the battle, Reynolds did move about 7,000 militiamen toward Williamsport)* Despite Governor Curtin's appearance, the fighting spirit of the volunteers was still limited to what they insisted was their responsibility — "To defend the state against invasion." Alexander McClure admitted later that no officer could have coaxed the militia into action against Lee's veterans. He described the few who did go with Reynolds as "little better than a demoralized mob."

The threat to Pennsylvania was over and on September 25 Governor Curtin declared the emergency no longer existed. Now the militia could go home and railroad officials were given the monumental task of getting the men out of Franklin County. Again chaos prevailed as officers began issuing transportation orders without proper authorization. On one occasion a Reading regiment was ordered out at two o'clock in the morning to board a north bound train. When they got to the station there was no train and they just sat and waited. The Reading Dutchmen sat all day as they watched train after train, loaded with other troops, ride past them. When a battery of artillery was ordered to board the cars no one could find it. Deserters who had been jailed could not be found. While the troops were taken up the valley to Harrisburg, freight trains kept hauling military materials back down the line to supply an army that was on its way home. Officials had neglected to stop shipments and supplies just kept piling up at Hagerstown and warehouses along the way. Eventually all of these problems were unsnarled and order once more prevailed as normal service returned to the Cumberland Valley line.

General Reynolds was dismissed with high praise from Governor Curtin. He was now permitted to join McClellan again. When the militia's commander left his "army" he thanked just one colonel, Harry McCormick, and his brigade of four regiments. This was the only complete unit to venture into Maryland. The rest he ignored. A few of his staff he wished well but beyond these expressions of gratitude the record remains silent. Reynolds wrote to his sister, informing her that he was leaving Chambersburg *(September 26)* to join General McClellan. He had dispersed all the militia to their homes "which they were so exceedingly anxious to defend, only they preferred to wait until the enemy actually reached their own door steps before they encountered him."

One Harrisburg paper, the "Patriot," noted that Reynolds had reserved praise for just "one brigade." An editorial was critical of the volunteers "who have heretofore lived the life of luxurious ease, never having slept on anything harder than a feather bed until now." Their lack of discipline had enabled them to "rob hen roosts, break open spring houses, wander away from camp without permission, and hunt squirrels with their muskets." [23]

Many families in the Greencastle-Antrim area would have supported the charges of the "Patriot." A few unidentified militiamen, however, received high praise from local patriots. A farmer, living along the Harrisburg Pike north of Greencastle, thought he could insure his property against damage when he took his family and livestock to the mountains. He left a message on his front door — "We are neutral, neither for the North or the South." The Confederates never got to his doorstep but members of the Pennsylvania militia did. After reading the plea of neutrality, they burst into the farm home and ransacked the place. This action is probably the closest these men got to upholding the honor of the state. Here was a farmer too cowardly to fight and protect his home. They showed him. [24]

Of course the emergency soldiers suffered no battle casualties but one unfortunate accident did occur. A train filled with the 20th Militia Regiment, on returning to Harrisburg collided with one passing in the opposite direction. Four men were killed and thirty injured — a tragic end to this episode in the state's history. [25]

Despite the ignoble behavior of its militia, Pennsylvania's sons did contribute to the victory at Antietam. Its soldiers were in nearly every division that fought in this battle. General George Meade's division, with the exception of one regular army artilley battery, was made up of men from the Keystone State. Its casualties amounted to 569 men killed, wounded or missing and this was after losing 399 of its force at South Mountain. Andrew Humphreys's Division, which included eight regiments of Pennsylvanians, arrived on the scene September 18 to become part of the troops held in reserve.

Franklin County men at Antietam included members of the

130th Pennsylvania Volunteer Infantry led by Colonel Henry Zinn. This unit was part of General William French's division which was in the assault on the Confederate center at Bloody Lane. Private Henry White, of Zinn's infantry, who later lived in Greencastle, was taken prisoner, escaped, then recaptured. However, in the disarray of battle, White made his way safely back into his lines again. He continued on active duty and fought at Fredericksburg and Chancellorsville. Company K of the 12th Pennsylvania Reserves, comprised of Franklin Countians, served in Meade's 3rd Division. It took part in the early morning fighting against General John B. Hood's noted Texas Brigade when the furious struggle in the Cornfield occurred. This part of the battle also saw Battery A of the 1st Artillery giving support to Joseph Hooker's First Corps. The battery was Captain Hezekiah Easton's former command. At Antietam it was led by Lieutenant John Simpson.

Company K of the 107th Infantry, all from Franklin, also fought with Hooker's Corps. It was part of the only Pennsylvania regiment in a brigade of New Yorkers commanded by General Abraham Duryea. These men had the distinction of being in all the major battles — Cedar Mountain, Second Bull Run, and Turner's Gap — prior to Antietam. Lieutenant Colonel James Mac Thompson, of Chambersburg, commanded the regiment when it, too, took part in the Cornfield fight against troops of Stonewall Jackson. Company D, of the 6th Reserves, led by William Dixon of St. Thomas, saw action at South Mountain and than at Antietam. This was Lieutenant Joseph Davison's outfit. He had contracted a fever while on the Peninsula and was recuperating at this time.[26]

The 15th Cavalry, whose men were still in the Greencastle area, served constantly on scouting missions and Colonel William Palmer led a small force of the cavalrymen into the Antietam conflict. During the fighting they were stationed back of the line of battle to prevent stragglers from passing to the rear. Palmer's men also assisted in caring for the wounded who were carried to barns and other improvised hospitals used by the surgeons. One detachment accompanied artillery into the Dunkard Church area where the heaviest fighting took place. Fred Anspach, of Company D, wrote of being at the church. "I had a splended view of the battlefield; saw the charges of the infantry and the batteries giving and receiving a hot fire. In the rear and close to a barn was a field hospital filled with wounded. The surgeons were at work, with coats off and sleeves rolled up, and the barn doors were used for tables on which were placed those receiving attention."

After Lee retreated into Virginia, Palmer under orders from McClellan, went on a mission to determine the enemy's movements.

He was not ordered to go beyond the river but since he could learn little from the Maryland side he crossed the Potomac to get to the rear of the Confederate forces. The cavalryman had two civilians with him; one a "cool, courageous blacksmith" and the other a "patriotic parson." All three were dressed in civilian clothes. The colonel believed he might learn the true situation of Lee's army and if he found it to be in a critical condition "the war might be ended then and there."

Palmer did learn several things. The first was that J.E.B. Stuart was preparing for a raid into Pennsylvania. He also discovered the enemy cavalry patrolled the Virginia side of the river very carefully and within hours he learned he was a prisoner of war. Without sensing their presence, Palmer rode right into the arms of a Rebel patrol. Along with the blacksmith, the colonel was handed over to General William Pendleton, Lee's Chief of Artillery. The parson escaped and brought to McClellan the news of Stuart's plans and the rest of the sad story. Both prisoners were held as spies who, if found guilty, would be subject to the death penalty. Palmer and his associate insisted they were engineers employed by the Chesapeake and Ohio Canal Company. Their story must have been convincing since they were not executed. Instead the captives were sent to Richmond where they remained in prison for four months before being freed.

With their leader gone, the 15th came back to Greencastle and returned their horses to the owners. By train they went to Carlisle where the unit was reorganized. On November 7 the regiment was shipped by rail to Louisville, Kentucky and a month later became part of the Army of the Cumberland, led by General William Rosecrans. [27]

Throughout the period prior to and during the Battle of Antietam the business life of Greencastle's area almost came to a standstill. Editor James McCrory explained why, for nearly a month, his newspaper was not published. The issue prior to the campaign in Maryland, September 9, was the last until October 7 when he renewed publication. "Our readers may wonder why our appearance has been delayed so long. The want of help, the general suspension of business, and the alarming state of our national affairs will, we trust, form our apology." "The Pilot," in its October 7 edition, told of business resuming and how the railroad cars were filled with persons going over to Maryland to visit the battlefield. "Guns, cannon balls, swords, and other relics have been carried off in large numbers. Some, too, for the melancholy purpose of looking for the grave of a son or brother." [28]

Women of Greencastle, like those of other towns and villages throughout the Commonwealth, had organized a local chapter of the Ladies Aid Society. They scraped lint, rolled bandages, made compresses, and collected linen for the military hospitals in Hagerstown and Chambersburg. In the county seat hundreds of injured men were housed in Franklin Hall, the school building next to the county jail, and the town's Academy building. William Heyser, a prominent Chambersburg businessman, recorded in his diary the visits he made to the hospitals. He told of going to the Academy, where 100 men with amputated arms and legs were hospitalized, and to the school at the jail "to offer a little help some way." Death was always near and Heyser tells of reading the Masonic service at burials of fellow Masons who died in Chambersburg's hospitals. Trains continued to pass through the town carrying deceased victims of Antietam to their final resting places in other parts of Pennsylvania or New York. He wrote of the sad spectacle of funerals for men from Chambersburg. "Every day we hear the sad strains of martial music as the hearses pass carrying the dead from some distant battlefield to be buried at their home. The hearses are draped with flags and the procesion partly military." [29]

As the county recovered from all the anxieties that surrounded Lee's possible attempt to invade the state its people were threatened once again in early October. While the Army of the Potomac waited in the Sharpsburg area, the Army of Nothern Virginia was waiting on the other side of the nearby Potomac in the Shenandoah Valley. McClellan's army was still a capable fighting force but Lee needed time to re-build his. To secure this time he had to isolate the Federal army by cutting as many of its supply routes as possible. He still did not know of McClellan's plans and if he were to regain mobility he needed horses. The Southern leader, after several days of consultation, decided on a plan to fulfill his needs. Colonel John Imboden was directed to take his cavalry toward Cumberland and attempt to disrupt traffic on both the Baltimore and Ohio rail line and the Chesapeake and Ohio Canal. J.E.B. Stuart was ordered into the Cumberland Valley to disable its railroads, gather information, and secure as many horses as possible.

Early on October 9 Stuart's force, of about 1,800 cavalrymen, began moving up the valley towards the Potomac. About four o'clock the next morning they reached the river at McCoy's Ford, a few miles west of Clearspring. An advance party started across the mist covered stream and upon reaching the Pennsylvania shore ran into Union pickets. Since there were not enough Federal soldiers in the area, Captain Thomas Logan, who headed the picket force, stayed in hiding to learn of the Rebel plans. Within minutes he knew. Stuart was going in the direction of Mercersburg. Eventually McClellan knew the Confederates were in Pennsylvania. Colonel Palmer's agent, the parson, had brought information about the very thing that was happening. This was why Federal troops had been sent to guard the river crossings, but Stuart had carried it off despite the precautions.

Through a light rain, the invaders reached Mercersburg by noon. Eventually the full force arrived and squads were sent into the countryside to gather horses. Most farmers lost from two to five but the Hoke farm, north of the town, yielded eighteen head. Storekeepers were forced to sell whatever the men wanted and accept payment with Confederate money. Stuart then headed for Chambersburg in what was, by now, a pouring rain. With the party were seven prisoners taken from the Mercersburg area - Perry Rice, Daniel Shaffer, Charles Louderbaugh, John McDowell, George Rupley, George Steiger and Joseph Winger, Claylick's postmaster. In St. Thomas they picked up William Conner.

By this time Union forces had been set in motion to trap the Rebels. General William Averell, who had moved west to counter Imboden, was ordered to come back and follow Stuart. General William Franklin started towards Chambersburg with a body of men along the road from Hagerstown to Greencastle. William Brook's brigade and the 12th Illinois Cavalry, headed by Hasbrouck Davis, was also sent to pursue the Rebel force.

Governor Curtin became excited about the safety of his state and the telegraph lines from Harrisburg to Washington once more were filled with demands for men to protect Pennsylvania. The last word the war office heard from the governor was that the Rebels had taken Chambersburg. This was around eight o'clock that evening. By then Stuart was in the town and the telegraph lines were cut - one of the first acts of any occuppying force. Chambersburg had been surrendered to the invaders under terms agreed to by A. K. McClure. The rebels assured him that private property and the people would not be molested. They would take only what they needed.

The town was placed under martial law while enemy details searched for military stores and horses. One squad was sent to destroy a railroad bridge that spanned the Conococheague Creek at Scotland, a village north of Chambersburg, but the mission had to be aborted. The bridge was made of iron. It could not be chopped down or burned. Enough explosives were not available to blow it up so the rail line at that point remained intact.

Stuart spent the night at the town's best hotel, the Franklin House, while many of his officers visited A. K. McClure's farm home north of the town. They stayed and talked, drank his coffee, smoked his tobacco, and continued talking all through the night. Breakfast was served to about 100 officers and men the next morning.

Before daybreak, around four o'clock, bugle calls sounded through the cool, damp morning's darkness. It had stopped raining and as the men assembled on the town's square they appeared in uniforms taken during the night from warehouses filled with military stores. In the early hours of October 11 General Stuart and his long blue clad line began riding out of the county seat toward Gettysburg. A rear guard, headed by Colonel W. C. Butler, remained behind. Before the colonel and his men left, warehouses, the depot, and machine shops were ablaze. Torches had fired large quantities of clothing, blankets, ammunition, guns, and other supplies. Railroad tracks were torn up and several cars set afire. Butler's men took all the hats and shoes they could carry as they left to join the main column.

HARPER'S WEEKLY 11/1/1862   REBELS EXCHANGING UNIFORMS IN CHAMBERSBURG   THEODORE DAVIS

As the Rebels moved eastward, squads were sent into the many farms along the turnpike to take more horses. They left Franklin County as they moved over the mountains on their way to the village of Cashtown. With them were approximately 1,000 horses but only four of the civilian prisoners. The others were paroled while in Chambersburg. Remaining were Rice, Shaffer, Winger and Conner who eventually found themselves in Richmond's Libby Prison. Perry Rice died there but the others were exchanged after two month's imprisonment. When Stuart reached Cashtown he turned south. Orders came down the line. They would close ranks and there would be no more scouting for livestock. When they entered Maryland near Emmitsburg the column was five miles long and on its way home.

All through southern Pennsylvania and the Maryland area east of South Mountain Federal troops were looking for Stuart. Several times they almost trapped him but by luck, bravado, and tactical skill he brought his men south, past Frederick and eventually to a place not far from where the Monocacy flows into the Potomac. They were near Poolesville, about twenty miles below Frederick, and not more than six from the Potomac. Here advance units ran into a sizable Union force led by General Alfred Pleasonton. The Federals lost time because they assumed the blue coated horsemen to be on their side. When the truth was learned from rifle fire that greeted them, Pleasonton's forces lost more time getting their artillery in place. The outcome was more luck for the Rebels. They escaped across the Potomac. It started raining again. The river rose and Jeb Stuart with his men were back in Virginia. His cavalry had covered 130 miles in three days with the loss of one man wounded and two missing.[30]

Intelligence, horses, hats, boots, clothing, and some arms were brought back to the Southern army. Left behind were broken rail and telegraph lines, burned buildings and their contents, but most of all, demoralized citizens in Pennsylvania and humiliated leaders of the Army of the Potomac.

The parson, who succeeded in getting back to safety after Palmer and the blacksmith were captured, became an example of how innocent people could be arrested and jailed on mere suspicion. His name was I. J. Stine, a minister, who lived in the Shippensburg area.

On September 24, 1862 President Lincoln had issued a proclamation which provided that persons guilty of disloyal practices would be subject to martial law. The right of habeas corpus could be suspended in order to enforce the provisions of his proclamation. Thousands of persons were imprisoned by this decision and I. J. Stine was one of them. A few days after the Battle of Antietam the parson was arrested on the charge of "betraying Colonel Palmer into Rebel captivity." The next day, on appeal to Governor Curtin, he was honorably discharged and released.

However, on October 23, the preacher was "decoyed" away from his family and at Newport, in Perry County, he was arrested by Federal officers and taken to Philadelphia. Here Stine was placed in the Moyamensing Prison. Two days later he was transferred to Fort Delaware and held on charges of treason. There were three specific accusations. One was that Stine plotted to have Governor Curtin captured when he was in Hagerstown after Antietam. Another, that he helped lead Stuart's cavalry into Pennsylvania and it was again charged that he had betrayed Palmer. The first two charges, Stine emphatically denied. Palmer was still a prisoner in Rebel hands and the minister remained silent on this count. He said nothing for fear the Confederates might learn the truth of the colonel's mission in Virginia.

Information held by military authorities enabled them to claim that Curtin narrowly missed capture when Rebel cavalry dashed through Hagerstown. From certain remarks "which fell from their lips," the horsemen were evidently in search of him. The governor was said to have escaped only a few hours before the enemy made their run through the town. They claimed that all of the kidnapping plans had been arranged by Stine. His accusers also said he was present when Stuart came into Chambersburg on October 10.

Local newspapers began looking into the charges. They found abundant evidence to show Stine was innocent on the first two counts. Greencastle's "Pilot" reported on November 4 - "Now we know from reliable persons, who were in Hagerstown at the time mentioned that no 'rebel cavalry' dashed into the place; nor, indeed have there been any 'rebel cavalry' in Hagerstown since the day of the battle." Shippensburg's paper, "The Press," reported the Rev. D. H. Focht could prove Stine was in New Bloomfield "from the 7th to the 10th and on Friday the 10th at ten o'clock he left to go to Shippensburg, by way of Newport and Harrisburg — a distance of nearly eighty miles on the way, but to the north of Chambersburg." He could not have been in the county seat when Stuart was there.

State officials and prominent citizens came to the defense of the accused man. A. K. McClure, on November 8, wrote to the prisoner that he had been collecting facts and testimony. He told him "In a very short time I will be able to present the matter so clearly that your discharge cannot be a matter of doubt." John Rowe, of Greencastle, also assured Stine, in early November, that he knew he was innocent and that Governor Curtin would give the matter his attention. The Rev. Henry Baker, of the Newville Lutheran Church, claimed that he was in Chambersburg at the time of "great raid." He was in frequent conversations with some of Stuart's men and no doubt someone mistook him for Stine.

Eventually Stine was released in February from Fort Delaware but not until Palmer had safely returned from his imprisonment. This was on January 7, 1863. The colonel's explanation of his arrest by

Stuart's patrol evidently gave the Secretary of War, Edwin M. Stanton, cause to issue him a "parole of honor." He returned to find his family homeless; his wife distraught from his imprisonment and grieving over the loss of their baby while he was confined; and to make matters worse, he had lost his pastorate. His was a high price to pay. Treated as a common criminal, sent to prison without trial, and released only upon the word of the Secretary of War, Stine's case demonstrated how unfounded rumors could lead to denial of justice. If he had any consolation it came from the fact that his friends did work to set him free. Others in similar predicaments did not have this comfort. Some died in prisons while others remained in captivity until the war ended. [31]

After Antietam there was no let up in calling men into the service or getting volunteers for special units. In early October, Lieutenant Benjamin F. Winger, along with Adam Ferguson and Daniel Henry were in the Cumberland Valley lining up recruits for the 2nd Pennsylvania Heavy Artillery which was then stationed in the defenses of Washington. It so happened that these recruiters came to Chambersburg on October 10, the evening Stuart and his force came to town. It was dark yet somehow Ferguson was captured while Winger and Henry escaped detection. They were able to secure civilian clothes and remained incognito during the rest of the Confederate occupation. Winger was the son of Joseph Winger, the Claylick postmaster, who had been taken hostage the day before. After the Rebel raiders left Chambersburg, Lieutenant Winger and his remaining associate continued their recruitment efforts. In the end 167 men were signed to join the heavy artillery unit — many of them from the Greencastle area. [32]

HENSON COLLECTION
PVT. NICHOLAS GREENAWALT

In November a call came for more nine month militiamen. The 158th Regiment was organized in Chambersburg with five companies from the county and the rest from Cumberland and Fulton. This unit spent most of its time in North Carolina on guard duty. Another unit organized in November was the 16th Cavalry Regiment. Company H, consisting of 203 officers and men, was from the county. Most of its three year service was spent in campaigns against Confederates in Virginia until the war's end. The last call of the year included Company A of the 165th. Raised in Gettysburg on December 6, the unit served for nine months in Virginia helping with guard duty and repulsing Rebel raids in and around Norfolk. [33]

The President's displeasure with McClellan's unwillingness to press on with the job of defeating the Confederates started rumors of a forthcoming change of command for the Army of the Potomac. Although McClellan began moving his army into Virginia on October 26, by the end of the month he had made little progress. There were some minor skirmishes in the Blue Ridge mountains where, at Snicker's Gap, Franklin County's men, of the 126th, were campaigning. Finally on November 5 McClellan was replaced by General Ambrose Burnside. Five days later the general, who failed to follow his advantages after Antietam, left his troops. This ended the military career of "Little Mac" the nickname his army had affectionately given him. The majority of his men thought he was a soldier's general.

Despite the anxieties and sorrows, as the first full year of warfare approached an end, the North was experiencing a prosperity never known before. Economic growth was true for the Cumberland Valley as well as other parts of the Union. Chambersburg's William Heyser on November 4, wrote, "Business is good at the bank, we declared a five percent dividend on the past six month's business. The stock is ten dollars above par. We have a surplus of $42,000." The only other lending institution in the county, Waynesboro's Savings Fund Society, was also reported to be prospering. [34]

Storekeepers, hotel keepers, and other businss men were said to be making more money than ever. This was especially true of the warehouse owners in Chambersburg, Greencastle, and Hagerstown who had as clients both state and federal quartermaster departments. During Lee's Maryland invasion state militia authorities contracted for warehouse space to hold military supplies such as tents, blankets, knapsacks, cooking equipment, uniforms, and munitions. The only loss reported by the state's Quartermaster General, R. C. Hale, was that of 330 blankets "which should have been delivered at Greencastle, but were carried by the railroad to Hagerstown, where they were taken...by the United States for use of the wounded in hospitals near Sharpsburg." By the end of the year some of the warehouses were still filled with military supplies. [35]

Farmers could see the war's effect on grain sales. Between

January and December, wheat prices had risen from a dollar fifty to a dollar and seventy-five cents. Corn rose from sixty-eight cents to ninety-five while barley made the biggest leap. It had nearly doubled — eighty cents a bushel to a dollar fifty-five. Breweries were the chief buyers of barley as beer and ale consumption reached all time highs. Wool prices were also climbing. Before the war a pound of wool was worth between forty-five and fifty cents but by 1862 it rose to as much as seventy-five cents a pound. Farmers were banding together to protect themselves against dog packs. A nationwide sheep growers association would soon demand government protection and compensation for sheep destroyed by dogs.

Farm machine sales also boomed as the supply of farm laborers decreased. The county had seen over fifteen hundred of its men leave for military duty during the year and improved farming methods had to follow if farmers were to stay in business. Reapers and mowers were used more than before the war and the most popular new equipment was the mechanical hayrake. Called a sulky rake, it had removable curved teeth of springy steel which gathered timothy, clover, or alfalfa into windrows where it could be baled or stacked in less time than before. Hay prices were increasing because so many horses were used by the army. Hay sold for ten dollars a ton in 1860 but as the war progressed the price quadrupled. Another development brought increased reliance on artificial fertilizer. Usually consisting of combinations of ground bone, lime, phosphate, sand, quano, and night soil, it gained wide acceptance during the early war years. Increased farm prices led to a greater use of soil improving compounds and dealers began carrying fertilizer in addition to farm tools and machinery. Wages for farm labor rose to as much as a dollar a day while skilled workers ranged between a dollar seventy-five and two dollars. In other parts of the country a day's pay went as high as three dollars. Living costs, however, out striped higher incomes and the average family was little better off than before the war boom started. [36]

Amidst such prosperity, in a war torn nation, Thanksgiving services were held in the area's churches on November 27. They were well attended. Prayers for a speedy end to the war and for the safety of men in the the armed forces provided a common theme for all congregations. Heyser wrote in his diary that this was the time of year that everyone changes his living habits. With the coming of cold weather families come closer together but the great war "casts a gloom over all." Thanksgiving was a way people could mark this beginning of a new season.

As December followed, fears of invasion lessened. Families were receiving letters from their men and boys scattered over the war's many theaters of action. Most of the letters, however, came from soldiers in the Army of the Potomac in the Fredericksburg, Virginia area. Many Pennsylvania's soldiers were there as they faced Lee's forces across the Rappahannock. During the week of December 15 news of a terrible battle fought the week before at Fredericksburg reached the Cumberland Valley and as casualty reports became known, hundreds of families in the Valley and other parts of the state were in mourning or anxiously waiting, not knowing if their wounded sons or husbands would live or die.

It would be a hard Christmas for the nearly 300 families of Greencastle and its countryside whose fathers or sons were in the armed forces. Yet, where there were children the sorrows of the year had to be forgotten, at least for a time, in order to bring some cheer to them. Area newspapers carried advertisements telling of recently arrived ingredients for baking holiday cakes and cookies - raisins, currants, almonds, citron, figs, lemons, etc. Newly arrived fruit included cranberries, apples, pineapples, and brandied cherries.

A variety of toys including India Rubber balls, dominoes, checkers, flags, drums, and skates were available. Advertisements suggested pocket Bibles, testaments, hymn books, and diaries as suitable gifts for men in the service. Another item, promoted in city newspapers, was a badge for soldiers that showed their name and service unit. These were very practical gifts since the government issued no identification tags to the men. City journals also carried advertisements for playing cards, army watches, tool chests, and, for the ladies, Grover and Baker's highest premium sewing machines. For the entire family enjoyment there were musical boxes in which revolving metal cylinders played as many as thirty-six tunes — a real luxury item with prices ranging from $275 to $450.

As usual Christmas Eve services were held in town and rural churches. The familiar hymns of promised peace and goodwill were sung with prayers for the men and boys down at Fredericksburg and in other camps, the wounded in Washington and Baltimore hospitals, and for families of the dead now lying in Virginia's war torn soil. Candles glowed in the windows of town and country homes as groups of neighbors with their children came by to sing familiar carols. Cookies and cider were available to all as they moved through the neighborhood with their songs of joy and hope.

Christmas Day, 1862, was sunny yet very cold with thick layers of ice on mill dams, the creek, and farm ponds. From morning to night the day would be spent in a similar manner throughout the area. A typical Christmas day in rural Antrim would go like this: As the family awakened at an early morning hour, both mother and father got the fires started in both kitchen and parlor. The doors were opened in the dining room located between these rooms to have it warm by noon, while older boys and girls got dressed. The father and older sons would then go to the barn to care for the livestock, while mother and daughters started breakfast and began preparing food for the noonday feast.

Eventually there would be cries of delight from the younger ones as they gathered their gifts from under the festooned pine or cedar tree in the far corner of the parlor. Near mid-morning the first arrivals usually made their appearance and others followed until in-laws, grandparents, and maybe a spinser aunt or batchelor uncle were in the house. The visiting men and boys unhitched their teams in a yard fronting a stable where the horses could be housed for the day. Meanwhile, more gifts for the children were distributed as the mother and daughters continued preparing the biggest meal of the year.

By noon tables for young and old would be filled with mountains of food. After a prayer by the head of the house the eating began. There would be beef, ham, oysters, turkey, and vegetables galore, along with mashed potatoes and oceans of gravy. Separate tables piled high with edibles accommodated the children while adults ate at a dining table with every available extension used to maximize its size. Desserts of canned and spiced fruits, along with nut bread, fruit cake or a variety of pies, usually topped off the dinner which could last as long as two hours — filling everyone beyond all measurable human capacity.

As the tables were cleared the task of washing cookware and dishes followed. The men usually went to the stables to feed and water the horses, while the children played indoors or out — some going to skate on a nearby pond. Chewing tobacco or smoking cigars was enjoyed by the men as they stayed out of the way until the dining room was cleared.

Adults could finally settle down in the parlor or dining area. The remainder of the day would be spent in talking about the war, politics, farm business, or the latest gossip, but most of all, much effort had to be expended in trying to stay awake despite the clamor of children at play with their newly acquired toys. Late afternoon goodbyes eventually came as the visitors hitched their teams to buggies or surries and, with everyone aboard, their homeward journey began. There followed snacks of leftovers for those who needed any evening meal. Going to bed followed as the hallway's grandfather clock accounted for the lateness of the evening hour. It was all over for another year.

One week later the old year was ushered out and the new one welcomed in. At midnight, and despite ordinances prohibiting loud noises from explosives like firecrackers, torpedos, and guns of many varieties, 1863 was serenaded as usual. Belsnicklers were out in full force and homes were open for refreshments. The next morning the custom of serving drinks to well wishers started and continued through the day. Those who followed an old custom would have pork and sauerkraut for the first mid-day meal of the new year. This would have been dinner. The evening meal was always called supper.

Some people remembered, also, that his was the day the Emancipation Proclamation went into effect. Mr. Lincoln had established this after the Union success at Antietam. The war was now a crusade to break the chains of human bondage in those states that had seceded. Julia Ward Howe had composed the "Battle Hymn of the Republic" back in February of 1862. It now became the anthem for this crusade. "Let us die to make men free, while God is marching on" was a phrase to stir the hearts and minds of the nation into realizing the Proclamation's promise. It became a slogan for the remainder of the war. John Brown's soul was still marching across the land.

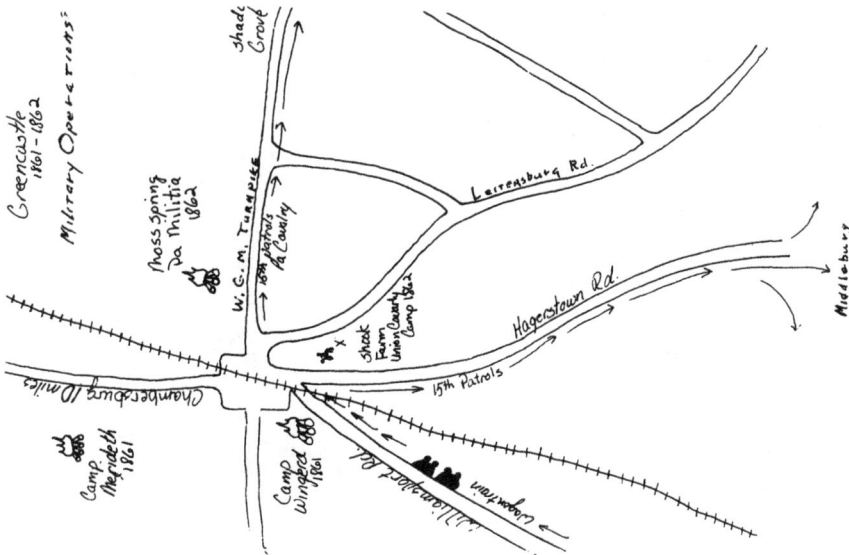

BY MELODY MENTZER — ANDREW BARBAZANES

CHAPTER V

FRANKLIN'S FIRST NINE MONTH SOLDIERS

When the Army of the Potomac, under George B. McClellan, failed to take Richmond and the Peninsula Campaign of 1862 became a complete disaster, fear of a Confederate advance on Washington prompted President Lincoln to issue a nationwide call for volunteers. On July 17 the Commander-in-Chief was authorized to accept the services of 300,000 men, including 100,000 for a limited service of nine months. Within three weeks the 126th Regiment was organized as part of Pennsylvania's response to this appeal.

The regiment was recruited in Franklin, Fulton, and Juniata counties. Companies A, D, and G were from Chambersburg, B consisted of Antrim Township and Fulton County men, C was from Mercersburg, and Waynesboro furnished E Company. Path Valley

GEO. COLBY — CO. K   U.S.A.M.H.I. — CARLISLE, PA   JOHN PFOUTZ — CO. A MUSICIAN

and St. Thomas provided Company H and Greencastle's Company K completed the roster from Franklin County. Companies F and I were from Juniata.

This unit of volunteers, consisting largely of men and boys from Franklin County, was regarded as its most singular contribution to the war effort. It was a unit to which local people could point with pride. Its leadership was drawn totally from Franklin. Colonel James G. Elder, the commanding officer, was from St. Thomas. Lieutenant Colonel D. Watson Rowe and Major James Austin were Greencastle men. The regiment's Adjutant was John Stewart of Chambersburg and T. Jefferson Nill, from Waynesboro, was the Quartermaster.

On August 7 the Franklin County companies assembled in Chambersburg to be transported by train to Harrisburg. Prior to leaving their home towns and villages they had said farewell to families and friends. Each man carried with him a New Testament given by churches of the home area. The Presbyterians of Greencastle gave the soldiers a small pocket size book containing passages of scripture, prayers, the commandments, verses of well known hymns and advice for their moral and physical health. Some brought sewing kits and had box lunches prepared for the first day's journey on the road to war. [1]

CONRAD FAMILY COLLECTION
GEORGE MISSAVY'S BLOOD
STAINED PRESBYTERIAN BOOK

By August 10 the various companies assembled at Harrisburg's Camp Curtin. Here they were supplied with arms, clothing, and necessary camp equipment. On the 15th, just five days after the last of the regiment's 984 recruits had arrived, they were ordered to the front. Late that afternoon the men were marched to the railroad yards, loaded on coal cars, and hauled through the night to Washington. Arriving at 4 a.m. the next day they immediately became a part of the forces defending the city. Confederates under Robert E. Lee's command were said to be moving from Richmond in the direction of the nation's capital. [2] Later in the day the regiment was moved into the vicinity of Alexandria. Here it was joined with other Pennsylvania units — the 91st, 129th and the 134th regiments to form a brigade headed by General Erastus B. Tyler.

By August 23, 1862 the Rebels
had continued their thrust toward
the capital and Mr. Lincoln placed
the army to oppose them in General John Pope's hands. Fighting
began on the 29th and Lieutenant
Colonel Rowe was ordered to take
six of his companies and a section
of artillery to a bridge spanning
Bull Run. However, before he could
assemble his forces the armies
were already engaged in what was
to be called the second Battle of
Manassas. Rowe and his untried
men never got to the bridge. It had
been overrun by the enemy and

COL. D. WATSON ROWE   BESORE COLLECTION

his orders were countermanded. Rowe's wide eyed recruits watched in
dismay as Pope's demoralized army passed in full retreat with long
lines of walking wounded, bewildered stragglers, and hospital wagons
filled with badly maimed soldiers hurrying back to the safety of the
capital. The battle at Bull Run had been lost. Greencastle's Company
K was sent to help guard and care for the wounded at a hospital near
Fairfax Station. Within the week the whole Union army was back in
Washington preparing entrenchments to defend the city.

On the following Sunday, September 7, services for the brigade
were held in the evening with the Rev. Samuel J. Niccolls as the
minister. He was from the Chambersburg Falling Spring Church
which had given him leave to serve the brigade as its chaplain. At the
very hour the service was being held the Army of Northern Virginia had crossed the Potomac into Maryland and was in the vicinity
of Frederick.

During the following week the men learned of the dismissal of
Major James Austin for taking sick leave without permission.
Although he was in the hands of a Washington physician, his failure
to follow military orders had resulted in a summary dismissal. Further investigation of the incident revealed medical reasons for his
absence and his rank was restored. However, within several days the
Major resigned his commission. The incident gave all the men a
greater concern for military regulations. Even officers had to follow
orders, though sometimes they did not make sense even to the average private. Although Austin was vindicated there were others of
lesser rank who left the brigade and never did return. Some men
were not physically able to stand the forced marches and other rigors

of military life. Others simply rebelled against the discipline of army life. Solicitude for family, impatience with the monotony of the service, and panic on the eve of battle were other causes for desertion.

Regarding the 126th record, a review of its roster reveals that throughout the nine months enlistment there were thirty-two desertions. Twenty-three came within the first three months of service, before the regiment had seen combat. This total was three percent of the regiment, less than half of the state's desertion experience. Throughout the war Pennsylvania's forces suffered a seven percent rate of desertion. Greencastle-Antrim residents were pleased to know that their Company K had no deserters and there were only three from Company B, the Fulton-Antrim unit.

News of Lee's invasion of Maryland began to come to the men through letters or hometown newspapers the following week and they conveyed the excitement and fears of their families living along the state's southern border. Tales of farmers taking their livestock to hiding places and the arrival of militia units at Chambersburg, Greencastle, and Waynesboro emphasized the concern Pennsylvanians had for their safety. Would the invasion stop in Maryland or move northward into the home country?

After Pope's loss at Manassas the President called on General McClellan once again and Federal forces were immediately ordered to oppose the invaders. Tyler's men started from Washington on September 14 and by evening they had marched through Rockville. By the 16th the brigade reached the Monocacy River. Here they learned that a battle at Antietam Creek had already begun. While at the Monocacy, the two brigades P. H. Allabach's and Tyler's became a part of the division commanded by General Andrew Humphreys.

On September 17 the march continued. Moving through Frederick, where crowds lined the streets to greet them they tramped all night through the Middletown Valley, up the long slope of South Mountain and down towards Sharpsburg. By eight o'clock the next morning the division arrived at the field of battle where they were placed in reserve. Humphreys's division of six thousand men waited all day but the fighting was finished. During the following night Lee's army crossed the Potomac into the safety of Virginia.[3]

When the brigade went into camp they crossed the Antietam by the arched stone bridge now named for General Burnside. As the men approached the encampment near the southern end of the battlefield they saw many dead Confederates. The Southern corpses were piled around a disabled artillery battery. One cannoneer apparently had been eating apples at the moment of death. His pockets were filled to overflowing with red tinted fruit. His leg had been severed and his comrades had placed the remains of the appendage under his head to serve as a pillow. Within a matter of days burial squads removed the fallen bodies of both sides and the soil along the Antietam Creek became a resting place for the nearly 5,000 dead of both sides.[4]

Here is where Tyler's brigade went into what seemed to be a permanent encampment. The days were spent in drill followed by more of the same. The 126th was not far from home. Less than twenty miles to the north lay Fulton and Franklin Counties and throughout the stay near Sharpsburg hundreds of visitors came to see their soldier friends and relatives. Baskets filled with home delicacies brought welcomed relief from the daily rations the men had come to accept as the routine diet of all soldiers. Ladies from Waynesboro visited their company and presented the men with a specially decorated banner. On another occasion State Colors were presented to the brigade and their division was honored with a review by the President. [5]

William Groninger from I Company told of the day Mr. Lincoln came to visit the army. It was on October 3 and when the men saw the President with his stovepipe hat they became embarrassingly aware of his awkward appearance. Sitting astride his horse, during the review, the Commander-in-Chief's legs seemed to touch the ground whereas McClellan's ease in the saddle was a thing to admire. Groninger described the occasion as another example of the time honored military tradition of "hurry up and wait." They had gone out to be reviewed early in the morning, but the President and McClellan did not appear until late afternoon. [6]

On October 16 the division made a reconnaisance into Virginia after crossing the Potomac below Sheperdstown. Within three days the men were back in camp. Here they spent the time in more drill, parading, and guard duty. Two weeks later, on October 30, movement began again and the division crossed the river below Harpers Ferry into Virginia's Loudon County. On November 2 they marched to the Blue Ridge Mountains and at Snicker's Gap the men were able to look out across the Great Valley known as the Shenandoah. As Franklin County's soldiers drank in the beauty before them, some must have thought of home. Their own valley lay just to the north, an extension of the quiet scene that streched out below. While in this mountain country the weather grew cold, but the chilling discomfort was offset by the luxury of living off the farms of Virginia's Blue Ridge people. Veal and mutton became a part of each day's meals. Eventually this had to end and Humphreys's men were brought down from the mountain heights into the vicinity of Warrenton.

Here they remained while rumors circulated of an impending "shake up" in the army's command. Finally word came that McClellan was to be removed. Ambrose Burnside was to be the new leader of the Army of the Potomac. On Monday, November 10, the troops stood in line for two hours while McClellan's farewell address was read and then "he left us and went to New York." Two days later the V Corps was once again called to hear the farewell message of their commander, Fitzjohn Porter, who had been replaced by Joseph Hooker. Burnside's first move was to reorganize the army from six corps to three "Grand Divisions." *(Each consisting of two corps)* On the following Sunday, November 16, Hooker reviewed Humphreys's division, of which the 126th was still a part. It was said that the men were impressed with their commander whose nickname was "Fighting Joe." That evening the Rev. Nicolls preached his farewell sermon to Tyler's brigade. A number of chaplains followed but none stayed for any length of time.

Within the following week the division marched to Falmouth on the Rappahannock River northeast of the town of Fredericksburg. This operation covered a distance of forty miles and by November 20 the entire Army of the Potomac stood across the river facing Fredericksburg. Earlier units could have crossed the Rappahannock at several usuable fordings but by the time the entire army arrived heavy rains had brought the water to bank level. Now the high water decreed that control of Fredericksburg would be determined only by force of arms. General Lee, who had deduced Burnside's plan, quickly moved General James Longstreet's corps from Culpepper Court House to occupy positions in and behind the town. On November 26 Lee sent word to Stonewall Jackson, encamped at Winchester, to bring his troops to Fredericksburg. Jackson and his men were 150 miles away, and twelve days later they were entrenched on the hills west of the town. By December 1 the two armies were fully placed, ready to see who would control Fredericksburg.

During this manueuvering the men of the Elder's regiment found themselves short of rations and with the ever increasing cold weather their tents provided meager comfort. Eventually they learned to reinforce their shelters with log walls and carefully erected chimneys. With such improved quarters, Falmouth seemed to take on the appearance of a village ready for a long winter's seige. It was to this encampment that three officers, left back at Antietam because of sickness, returned. They were Captain Reed and Lieutenant Cook of

Chamberburg's Company D and Lieutenant Hornbaker from Company C of Mercersburg. These were popular leaders and the men welcomed them with warm enthusiasm.

Within several days the soldiers had the opportunity to welcome something they had not seen for a long time — namely their army pay. Privates received $36.40, their wages for exactly two months and twenty-four days. They had not been paid since mid-September and the sight of money even at the meager rate of $13.00 per month was a boost to everyone's morale. Many of the men could now send a goodly portion home to their families. Others would find how to spend theirs in ways long known to soldiers. [7]

One of Chambersburg's soldiers, Private Philip Welsh of Company A, wrote to his mother concerning the regiment's morale. The short rations were due to knee deep mud through which supply trains could not travel. At one time the men were without food for a day and a half. He told of their spirits deteriorating — "Some of the boys are very tired of it" and "They curse the Union, the government, and everything else." Although the tardy pay helped the morale of some, the griping continued. His letter ended, "The Rebels have still got possession of Fredericksburg — some say they are there in force, others say not, but I suppose we will all know in a few days." These were direfully prophetic words, for within two weeks young Welch and all others in General Burnside's army would know the force they faced. [8]

During the first week of December the commanding general devised a plan to dislodge Lee's forces from their defenses on the high ground back of Fredericksburg. The two most strategic hills of this terrain, Taylor's and Marye's, were together, known as Marye's Heights, located about a quarter mile to the rear of the town. Most of Burnside's staff felt the enemy's position to be impregnable, but their leader insisted on his plan to cross the Rappahannock and attack Lee from two directions. Generals Edwin Sumner and Joseph Hooker were to use their divisions to dislodge the Confederates from the hills beyond the town while William Franklin was to move his forces against the Rebels from the south. Despite heated protestations from officers who saw a bloodbath facing their men, Burnside continued to insist that the North's superior numbers could easily conquer Lee's army. The veteran soldier from Pennsylvania, Major General Darius N. Couch, referred to the plan as a "rash undertaking."

Finally orders came for the attack to begin on December 11 during its early morning hours. It would be dark and when the time came, Burnside's men were favored by a heavy fog that reached the edge of the Rappahannock. Around five o'clock engineers began laying pontoon bridges across the river. Noise from the moving boats aroused enemy pickets stationed in the town and within minutes sharpshooters began taking their toll of those unable to return from the water's edge into the safety of the fog. Although riflemen returned the enemy's fire their efforts produced no relief. The next tactic was to unleash a barrage of artillery fire to level the buildings sheltering the sharpshooters, but when the guns stopped, the Southerners once more began cutting down the engineers with unerring accuracy.

Attempts to continue the work ceased while volunteers from Michigan, Massachusetts, and New York regiments assembled to cross the river to try and establish a bridgehead. When ready, they crawled to the water's edge, jumped into pontoons, and paddled across the water under heavy enemy fire. Within minutes they reached the other side and were able to secure the bridgehead after losing one man killed and several wounded. With their fire power concentrated on the sharpshooters, the engineers were able to place their first bridge. As more men poured over the pontoons, fighting continued through the streets of the town forcing the Confederate riflemen to gradually withdraw. By evening four crossings had been established and during the night another was completed. The Union forces were now capable of moving into Fredericksburg to position themselves for the execution of Burnside's plan.

While all of this was happening the 126th started moving from Falmouth towards Fredericksburg. The brigade broke camp at four o'clock on the morning of December 11 and moved to a field about two miles from the river. The next day they were ordered to march to a pine woods, a mile closer to the town. Here Tyler and his men waited. They could hear the cannon booming as the enemy's artillery kept trying to destroy the pontoons while Union batteries attempted to silence the Rebel guns. Then they heard bands playing to bolster the spirits of long lines of men streaming across the floating bridges. When night fell they saw the lighted sky over Fredericksburg. It seemed as though the whole town was afire and as smoke billowed upward and across the water sharp white flashes were seen through the smoke. This was from the artillery duel that continued on through the darkness of the late evening hours.

Rumors began trickling back to the men. They learned of the citizens of Fredericksburg fleeing into the countryside and how Northern troops continued forcing the enemy through the streets until the town was cleared of Rebels. Other tales described the pillaging that followed. As tobacco warehouses were sighted the Northern troops soon emptied them. Houses were robbed of every valuable item that could be carried away. Stories persisted that some had taken sewing machines and even pianos across the river to be sent home. Furniture, chinaware, statuary, glassware, stoves, clothing, and valuable pictures were demolished. The Bank of Virginia had its safe blown open but only its records were found. Libraries were ransacked and their volumes strewn through the streets. Wine cellars were discovered and the contents of casks and bottles quickly consumed. One description tells of articles of silver — pitchers, tableware, lamps, and jewelry — being taken to add to the personal wealth of the pilferers. This plundering by Federal soldiers in Fredericksburg set a precedent for later destruction in the Shenandoah Valley and provided the South ample reason for retaliation in the months to come. [9]

In the pre-dawn darkness of the next day, December 13, fog once more covered the entire area. Flickering camp fires dotted the countryside as men began making hot coffee to accompany their breakfasts of hard tack. About ten o'clock the mists started clearing and sounds of battle began to roll across the heavens south of Tyler's encampment. This was the beginning of the day that would reveal the strength of the enemy lying in wait beyond the town of Fredericksburg.

The noise of musket and cannon fire came from George G. Meade's Pennsylvanians as they attempted to dislodge Confederate forces on the wooded hills southwest of the town. Through the rest of the morning and until late afternoon the battle continued. Yet, in the end the Northerners were forced to withdraw to safety near the river. Here they could see their dead scattered among the wounded whose cries were heard all through the night that followed.

While the action to the south was taking place other Union troops were being massed in the town to storm Lee's forces entrenched on Marye's Heights. These men were from Sumner's and Hooker's divisions. Through the afternoon they stormed the Rebel ramparts on the hill and each wave was slaughtered by withering musket and artillery fire of the enemy. Finally Andrew Humphreys received word to bring his untried Pennsylvanians into the battle. These were the nine month troops that included Tyler's men. It would be their first combat experience. The long term enlistees, the veterans, had little confidence in them. However, Humphreys had drilled and disciplined them to a point where he believed they would not falter.

Tyler's brigade was ordered to cross the river on the upper pontoon bridge. From this point the unit turned left to march into the center of the town. It was getting late, but at three thirty o'clock the brigade was sent to the western edge of Fredericksburg and out into a low meadow where the men could see blazing cannon on the hill they knew as Marye's Heights. They also saw a low stone fence that ran parallel to the high crest where the artillery was located. This fence appeared to be halfway up the incline and from it deadly fire of musketry kept mowing down the long lines of Union infantry attempting to overrun it.

In the meadow Tyler and his men waited as Confederate and Union batteries lobbed their shells over them and into each other. Before long they noticed several enemy guns being turned in their direction. As shell after shell began falling among them they sprawled close to the ground, the only protection available. Torn earth and mangled bodies were thrown into the air as the cannonading continued, yet no orders came to move from this place of carnage.

For nearly a half hour the shelling continued and then the brigade was ordered to move to the left of their position. From here they were to start the final drive to dislodge the Rebels from their stone fence barricade. Throughout the day all attempts had failed and the remnants of these efforts lay dead or wounded in front of the wall. Closer to town rows of able bodied men were hugging the ground, too scared to retreat any further. They were waiting until darkness before returning to their lines.

As rapidly as possible, for it was growing late, the assault columns were formed. The first line contained the 134th and 129th.

STONE WALL AT MARYE'S HEIGHTS   BESORE COLLECTION   A.C. REDWOOD

Eight paces to the rear the second column contained the 126th and the 91st — all Pennsylvanians commanded by General Humphreys. While the troops took their positions an artillery duel provided a prelude for this last assault and as daylight began fading orders came to fix bayonets. There would be no firing and halting to reload. *(In the earlier assaults, as Union regiments halted to return fire and reload, their ranks had been decimated by the continuous enemy fire.)* This would be a race of cold steel against the musket fire of the enemy. The Northern leaders had not yet learned after a full day's fight, that the stone fence fronted a sunken road running parallel to it. Here several lines of infantry, in relative safety, could take turns firing and reloading. This accounted for the almost constant fire the Federal columns had faced throughout the day.

Down the lines came the order — "Officers, twelve paces to the front." Bugles sounded and then, with cheer after cheer, the men began moving out across the slope that rose towards the stone wall. As they moved through the open field there lay the lines of men who had failed in the previous assaults, the able bodied infantry waiting to get to safety. Whether they were afraid of being run over by Tyler's infantry with its officers on horseback no one knew, but they began rising from the ground. They began calling for the attackers to halt and with violent gestures kept pointing to the rear. This disarranged the oncoming lines and broke the momentum of the charge, but the columns passed through and over them.

Colonel Elder led the right side of his regiment around a brick house that lay ahead while Lieutenant Colonel Rowe's Companies H and K went around the other side. Rowe's men had a clear field ahead while Elder's were impeded by fences that had to be broken through. Beyond the house the lines merged and firing from the entrenched enemy intensified. It became a sheet of flame as the men charged ahead. Rebel cannon began throwing shrapnel into the oncoming lines but their momentum carried the men still closer to the wall.

Then everything became a nightmare. The men lying to the rear began firing at the enemy through the lines ahead of them. The soldiers with Elder and Rowe stopped for they were now getting fire from the rear. Bullets were now coming from both front and back. In the excitement they stopped to load their muskets to begin firing at the entrenched enemy line. This was the fatal misake. The bayonet charge was finished. To stop and reload and fire again meant mounting casualties. Officers attempting to reform the lines, to carry them to the stonewall, were soon struck down. Elder's left thigh was severely shattered, Tyler was struck in the chest with shrapnel and Humphreys, after losing his horse, continued on foot trying to reform the men. Six line officers were hit and carried from the field. More and more soldiers kept falling as their feeble fire against the enemy proved to be pitifully futile.

Then darkness covered the field and the call to retreat was sounded. As the survivors came straggling down from the higher ground they sought refuge in and back of the brick house at the foot of the hill. About nine o'clock the brigade was withdrawn and rested in the streets of the town. The weather had turned bitter cold and the men, who had discarded their blankets prior to battle, now huddled quietly together for body warmth. They could hear the cries of the wounded as stretcher bearers carried them to ambulances. The dead lay silent and the muskets, rifles, and artillery too were quiet — resting for the coming dawn.

The next day was Sunday and the regiment's men were assigned to picket duty. On Tuesday the message came that the Union forces were to retreat back across the river. Rowe had been placed in command of the regiment with the rank of Colonel, and as his men approached a bridge to re-cross the river they found it had been cut away. Hurriedly they ran to another only to see it beginning to float out into the current. Fortunately there were engineers nearby who retrieved the pontoons and swung them back to the west bank of the Rappahannock. The 126th was the last Northern regiment to leave Fredericksburg. It had been detailed to cover the humiliating retreat of Ambrose Burnside's Grand Army back to Falmouth. [10]

Philip Welsh, of Company A, wrote to his mother four days after leaving Fredericksburg. His first hand account of the battle and its aftermath provides a vivid picture of what he and his comrades in the 126th experienced.

Camp near Fredericksburg, Va.
Dec. 19, 1862

"My dear Mother —

I suppose you have heard before this time that our regiment was in the Battle of Fredericksburg and that Uncle Thomas was wounded. George wrote a letter to you yesterday giving you an account of the battle and of our desperate charge. So you need not expect much of a letter from me this time. You have no idea what an awful thing it is to be in a battle and what awful sights we witnessed on the battlefield. I will try and give you an account of myself after we crossed the river. We crossed the Rappahannock River about 2½ Saturday. We had scarcely got across until the shells commenced to whiz around us.

We double-quicked up several streets and stopped there about ½ hour to put our knapsacks in some empty store rooms. We left there and went out toward the field of action. We did a great deal of dodging when the shells would burst near us but they commenced to come too fast for us, so we filed off in one of the streets and got behind the houses. We did not have to stay there very long until orders came for us to go forward. We got out on the pike and went about ¼ of a mile and turned into a kind of a swamp on the right of the road. Our brigade was crowded up as close to each other as possibly could get — we all laid down in the mud never thinking what a dangerous position we were in until we saw 4 or 5 Rebels push a cannon out from behind a large earth work and fire a shell at us. It struck in the 91st Reg't knocking off Major Todd's leg and wounding several others. The next shot they sent struck in our company killing 3 and wounding 2. Poor Dave Washabaugh (Emma Washabaugh's brother) had his head torn off. The other 2 that were killed was Abram Reitzel and Frank McGlaughlin. I shall never forget that time if I live one hundred years. It was the most horrible thing that ever I saw. They fired 2 or 3 rounds more, we had to get out of that as quick as we could. We crossed the pike to get out of range of the guns but in crossing the sharp shooters commenced to pick our men off. Lieut. Fortescue of Co. G was shot through the head and was killed instantly. We then formed a line of battle right in front of a Rebel battery under cover of a small hill — we were ordered to fix bayonet — I knew then that we were to make a charge on the Rebel battery. The bullets and shells were flying around us like hail. Col. Elder rode up and down our line telling us to stand to our posts. Gen. Humphreys ordered all the officers to the front, and then the bugle sounded the charge; we charged about 300 or 400 yards. We passed over two lines of battle, which confused our men very much. First the man on my right fell and then the man on my left. I could see them falling all around — every place I looked I saw poor fellows lying around dead or wounded. Before we made the charge we had orders not to fire until order to do so, but some of the fellows commenced to fire — I did not know what in the world to do. There was a continuous roar of musketry and artillery. The Rebels were behind a stone fence, so we could see nothing but the flashing of their guns. I got down on my knees and loaded and fired as fast as I possibly could, we did not stay under their murderous fire very long but skedaddled back to our starting place. I did not know that Uncle Thomas was hurt until George told me. I had lost sight of George and him both. I did not see George until I came off the field. In coming off the field I overtook Captain Doebler *(Captain John Doebler of Company A)* — he could scarcely get along. I asked him if he was shot, he told me he was. I took his arm and almost dragged him along. I do honestly believe some of the bullets was not more than one inch off of my face. I was expecting to fall every minute. Our company suffered more than any other in the division — we had 14 wounded in the charge, 3 killed and 1 wounded in the meadow, making 18 in all. After our brigade was formed we were marched into town and laid in the mud until about 2 o'clock next morning when we were again marched out on the field — we stayed there until about daylight and again went to town. We laid in a graveyard two days under their fire. The shells were flying over us all the time, but did no damage except a piece of one went into a knapsack which I had my feet against. On Monday night, after we had gone to bed we got orders to get up as quietly as we could and get into line. We were marched down to the edge of town to plant a battery. After we were through we went on picket about 2½ miles to the left — we stayed there all night in the rain. Next morning one of Tyler's Aids came out as fast a his horse could go, and told us to run for our lives — he said if we did not get out of that we would be cut to pieces in less than 5 minutes. I was so sick I could scarcely get along but with hard scratching I managed to get along with the rest. We double quicked all the way until we got to the Pontoon Bridge. I was almost dead. I had made up my mind that if the Rebs would come on us I would not run another step. Our regiment was the last one to cross over the river — it covered the retreat of the whole army. Early in the morning one of our drummers asked Gen. Tyler where the 126th was — he said they were lost that nobody knew where they were. I will have to stop writing for my fingers are so cold I can scarcely hold the pencil. I commenced this letter on the 19th and to day is the 21st — it is very cold here. I will try and write another letter in a few days if the weather gets warmer — we are all well here at present — Uncle John will get his discharge in a few days. George got a letter from Pap the other day. We never got that money that was sent to us. Give my love to all and write soon.

> Your affectionate Son [11]
> Phil"

When news of Fredericksburg reached the hometowns and villages of the men of the 126th a wave of sorrow spread across the entire region. In later years a Greencastle resident recalled that when the news came, "It was the saddest day in the history of the town." The regiment's losses amounted to thirty killed and forty-six wounded. At the time of the battle estimates were higher because of uncertainties with identifications. The total casualties in Tyler's brigade amounted to 1,000 dead, wounded, and missing. [12]

In the 126th, Company A of Chambersburg suffered the highest loss with eight killed and nine wounded. The Fulton-Antrim Company lost two men killed while five were wounded. Mercersburg's unit had two killed and four wounded. Chambersburg's other companies D and G, suffered three killed and seven wounded. Two were dead, two were missing, and one wounded in the Waynesboro Company. Juniata's losses were one killed, eight wounded. The Path Valley-St. Thomas Company had two killed, one taken prisoner, and nine wounded. Among the latter was the Regiment's commanding officer, James Elder. Next to Chambersburg's A Company, Greencastle's K suffered the most. Seven were killed and seven wounded.

Greencastle-Antrim men who died at Fredericksburg were Adam Bert, George Byers, James Mitchell, George Shook, Charles Shirey, Henry Spidell and Joseph Shatzer, all of Company K. Henry Strickler, John H. Logue, John Detrich, David Appenzellar, George Alexander, James Moorehead, Cyrus Baughman, Henry Ruthrauff, and Jacob Swisher were the severely wounded. The home town newspaper, "The Pilot," carried many tributes to the fallen heroes and a poem dedicated to the valor of these men appeared in the February 23 edition.[13] *(See Appendix III)*

Charles Hartman, Superintendent of the Reformed Sunday School, kept a diary in which he told of soldiers who had been members of his classes. He remembered Adam Bert, Charlie Shirey, and George Shook as young men he had once taught. His notes indicate that Rhode Island men found young Shook when they were searching for one of their own with the same name. Hartman wrote, "The testament that Rev. Rebaugh gave him was the means by which he was found. His mother showed me and keeps it as a treasure in memory of her dear boy. She has my sympathy." [14]

When Mr. Lincoln heard of the outcome at Fredericksburg he suffered a severe depression which lasted for days. To hear how Burnside lost 12,600 men when he outnumbered Lee's forces nearly two to one was unbelieveable. The President had announced his Emancipation Proclamation on September 23 to become effective January 1, 1863. This step was taken after the victory at Antietam. Now, after such a devastating defeat, the threat of freeing slaves in the seceded states seemed to have a hollow ring. Criticism was heaped on Lincoln for having given an incompetent, such as Burnside, the command. As stories of the general ignoring advice of his staff officers came to the Cabinet's attention, pressures mounted to have him removed.

Within the week following the battle Tyler's men returned to their pine woods camp site. While here a truce was established to allow both sides to bury their dead. One man from each company was chosen for the detail. When the men returned at night, after digging graves all day, they told of working along side Confederates engaged in the same gruesome duty. When the work was completed the soldiers parted on good terms. Rebels and Yankees shook hands and left to take up the tools of war once more. It is doubtful that these men ever saw one another again, although their units would meet in future skirmishes or full scale battles. Yet for that one brief moment in December of 1862 they simply knew each other as fellow Americans hiding the awful evidence of this tragic madness.

However, in one of war's many ironies, these same Confederates, who had killed so many Franklin countians at Marye's Heights, would be in their Pennsylvania county within less than seven months. The Southerners behind the stone wall would be part of General Lee's invading army of 1863. They consisted of men from the infantry brigades of Generals Robert Ransom from North Carolina and Lafayette McLaws of Georgia. Artillery on the Heights was under the command of Colonel E. Porter Alexander of Georgia. These men marched through Antrim Township and Greencastle in June the following year on their way to Gettysburg.

By Christmas Eve Tyler's men were back in the camp near Falmouth. Here they were given an extra ration of whiskey and as a special treat, dried apples. Such generosity was soon forgotten when, on Christmas Day, rations returned to normal. Those with extra cash could celebrate more lavishly if near sutler wagons or a brigade slaughter house where, on the side, butchers might bargain away such delicacies as tripe, head cheese, or special cuts of beef.

Through the early part of January the regiment remained in camp where it continued drilling and attempted to escape the bitter winter weather by making their huts more airtight. In the meantime General Burnside decided that the best strategy was to keep on the offensive. His plan was to move the army up the Rappahannock, hoping to make a crossing that would permit him to flank Lee's army, still at Fredericksburg. If possible he could drive southeast and cut the Confederate communications with Richmond. Although Burnside's subordinates viewed the plan as impractical, because of weather conditions, the general persisted.

On Monday, January 19, the various units of the Army of the Potomac assembled to hear a message from the commanding general, concerning plans for eventual victory over the enemy. It was read to the men and upon completion three cheers, proposed by the officers, were very faintly given. The next day the army was to begin its glorious campaign — doomed from the beginning and ending ingloriously in what was later called "The Mud March."

At half past two in the afternoon, the next day, the 126th marched out of camp with an army of 130,000 men, artillery, and wagon trains. This was the beginning of the attempt to cross the river to get Lee once and for all. As Tyler's brigade moved from its camp the rains began. It continued to pour all through the night with frequent high winds. The men became drenched while the roadway became a veritable quagmire. Lieutenant George Welsh, of Company A, *(Phillip Welsh's brother)* in a letter to his mother, described the ordeal. An excerpt follows:

"We marched about 2½ o'clock & bivouacked about 2 miles from camp. The weather was very cold — during the night the weather moderated and commenced raining. We started about 8 in the morning and made about 4 miles till noon when we halted for the day, the rain still falling pretty steadily. On Thursday, the whole division was put to making corduroy road. *(Placing logs on the road beds to make them more passable.)* The roads having become almost impassable — wagon trains, pontoon trains and artillery all stuck in the mud. You may well imagine what the roads were like when I inform you that army wagons required 12, 14 and some as high as 16 mules and horses to move them from their mirey beds — in many cases they had to be unloaded, and several barrels of whiskey falling into the hands of the soldiers produced the usual effects of indulgence in the ardent. Such a scene I do not wish to witness again. Friday was spent in completing roads and on Saturday morning we turned our faces back to camp — where we arrived about noon. Truly 'Man proposes but God disposes.' It is the impression in camp that no movement will be made soon. It is said that winter is now only fairly setting in and that from this time till the latter part of April there is rain every few days, which renders the movements of a large body of troops impossible. The weather is still unsettled."

Michael D. Reymer, a member of Company K, had been detached in September to serve as one of the Provost Guards at V Corps Headquarters. From time to time he wrote letters to the Greencastle newspapers. The February 10 edition carried his account of the "Mud March." Part of his letter contained these observations. "We caught up with the army in the evening. It had halted because it could not advance. We never wish again to see the Army of the Potomac in a plight, such as we saw it this evening. Stationary cannons were everywhere visible. We saw sixteen horses attached to one in the vain endeavor to extricate it. Four more additional quadrupeds of the long eared species were attached, and then, by very much yelling, more lashing and not a small amount of army profanity, it was eventually drawn out. This is only one of many similar scenes. Stalled teams were numberless. Many wagons were tongueless, and not a few in possession of only three wheels. Just before we turned in for the night we saw a squad of artillerists appropriating several convenient dead horses in the capacity of a bridge, the better to facilitate the passage of their pieces over a low place. the scheme was successful. It rained all day. On Thursday morning we were ordered back to our old camp again. It was still raining, and had been all night. About ten o'clock we commenced our journey . . . The whole army was ordered back on Thursday, but in consequence of the impossibility of the roads, its progress was slow. The pioneer corps was increased by large appointments pro tempore, as much of the way had necessarily to be well corduroyed before they could succeed in bringing back the cannon. All obstacles, however, were successively surmounted, and the boys once more occupy their old quarters." [15]

After returning to camp the men learned that President Lincoln had removed Burnside and Joseph Hooker was ordered to replace him. For the next three months the time was spent in drilling. A system of furloughs was started and the men took turns at going home for brief visits.

Tyler's brigade was moved to a camp several miles west of Falmouth where there were better supplies of wood and water. For three months the army stayed at the Falmouth site. During this time several events were noted. The brigade raised money to buy their commanding officer a young horse. It was a thoroughbred, bought in Ohio, described as "pure white and superbly beautiful." During the stay at Falmouth, Governor Curtin visited the Pennsylvania units and assured them of his admiration and that of the people of the state. A Swiss officer, General Polerdi, came and reviewed various divisions of the army. The men welcomed these visits by dignitaries since they served to relieve the tedium of the day to day routine.

Another pay day arrived in April and the Greencastle newspaper noted this event in its April 28 edition. The editor praised the soldiers of Companies K and B for their frugality and their sense of responsibility to their families. The payment brought the regiment's payroll up to March 1 and would probably be the last until the term of enlistment expired in May. Company K's men sent home $5,105 and the local enlistees of Company B forwarded $1,919 to their families. "This money ($7,024) was consigned to W. A. Reid who has paid over the larger part of it to the families and friends of the soldiers." The news item ended with the comment — "The boys have done very well in sending home so large an amount of money. It is highly creditable to them." [16]

In early April the President, with his wife and son, Tad, plus friends and his staff came to Falmouth. The party traveled by boat to Aquia Landing, a village on the Lower Potomac, and from there, by freight train, they rode through a snow storm to get to the army's base camp. Mr Lincoln and his family lived in a large tent throughout their five day stay. During the visit the Commander-In-Chief reviewed Hooker's Army of the Potomac. All references to Burnside's Grand Divisions or Grand Army had disappeared. The President seemed to be extremely impressed with what he saw. He was especially pleased with the cavalry which was now organized as a separate corps under General George Stoneman.

The new leader of this army boasted of its prowess and his plans to capture Richmond. It was observed that Mr. Lincoln seemed skeptical, and considered Hooker's cocky spirit as reminiscent of McClellan. The capture of Richmond held a lower priority in the President's mind. Defeating Lee's army was always Lincoln's chief concern. Hopefully, both objectives could be accomplished with so many men.

April 27 was the day orders came down from headquarters that the army was to begin its spring offensive. Three corps were to move up the east bank of the Rappahannock. At suitable fordings the troops would cross and march well beyond both the Rappahannock and Rapidan rivers. They would then march southward to get to the rear of Lee's army at Fredericksburg. While this movement was taking place, two corps were left near the town to move against the enemy if the opportunity arose. This was to hold them in their defensive positions. The Army of the Potomac had two remaining corps to be held in reserve. Stoneman's cavalry of 10,000 horsemen was to precede the army as it moved up the Rappahannock. From the north the cavalry would then sweep south, behind the Southerners, cutting all lines of communication between Richmond and Fredericksburg. They were to destroy railroads and canals, block roads, and prevent supplies from reaching Lee's army.

Hooker's plan was excellent and with a total force of 134,000 compared to Lee's 60,000, the strategy seemed certain to bring victory. The outcome, of course, depended on every part of the plan being executed properly. Yet it possessed several weaknesses. There was the failure of Hooker to appreciate the mastery of military strategy possessed by Robert E. Lee. The terrain was unfamiliar and this, combined with bad weather could be disasterous to the Federals. Finally there was the character of "Fighting Joe." Did he have the heart to fight to win?

Stoneman failed to carry out his assignment. Heavy rain, unfamiliarity with the terrain, and a decision to split his forces into small units, brought only minimal effectiveness. Lee first learned from J.E.B. Stuart's cavalry of Hooker's advance down into what Virginians called the Wilderness. This was heavy wooded terrain, thick bush and scrub country with meandering streams, deep gullies, and occasional swamp areas. The Southern leader, who knew the Wilderness country much better than his enemy, then developed a plan to trap the boastful Joseph Hooker.

Lee left Jubal Early with 10,000 men to hold the positions at Fredericksburg. With his remaining troops he began moving westward towards Chancellorsville, named for the Chancellor House which stood at forks in the road leading to Fredericksburg. The main artery was the Orange Turnpike which ran to Richmond. Near the Chancellor House two routes forked from the toll road. The River Road branched from the main highway in a northeastern direction. The Plank Road went to the southeast. It was along these routes that Hooker was moving his forces toward's Fredericksburg.

During the night of Friday, May 1, Lee stationed 17,000 men west of Fredericksburg to confront Hooker's advancing columns while Stonewall Jackson, with 26,000 moved westward on roads to the south of Chancellorsville. Federal leaders assumed this movement to be a hurried retreat of the Rebels attempting to get to Richmond before Union forces cut them off. However, by late afternoon Jackson's purpose proved to be quite different. His men began moving against the Northerners stationed west of Chancellorsville. He had outflanked Hooker's forces. With ferocious determination Stonewall's men attacked Oliver Howard's and Henry Slocum's XI and XII Corps from the west. Through the brush and dense undergrowth they steadily advanced, defeating all who dared oppose them. The Union forces were crushed and fled in a confused retreat back towards Chancellorsville.

While all this was happening, Humphreys's Division, including Tyler's Brigade, which was with the force moving towards Fredericksburg, became part of a retreat the commanding general ordered when news of Jackson's success reached him. The next day the division was moved to a high bluff, known as Scott's Dam, north of Chancellorsville. While here rumor came down the line that Stonewall Jackson had been wounded by fire from his own men the night before. *(His death, eight days later, brought an immeasurable loss to the Confederacy and one which General Lee could never replace.)* [17]

Tyler's Pennsylvanians waited and on Sunday morning, May 3, the brigade was ordered from the high ground and hurried along the road where Howard's forces had been shattered by Jackson's men. It was in this area the 126th learned that General Alfred Pleasonton's cavalry, including the 17th Pennsylvania Cavalry Regiment, had helped keep the enemy from complete victory. Company G of this regiment had been recruited in Franklin County the previous fall and some of its members were well known to men from the Antrim, Chambersburg, Mercersburg, and Waynesboro communities. [18] As Tyler's troops continued their march, about thirty men seized the opportunity to drop out among the survivors of the XI Corps and Colonel Rowe had the rolls called. Only 490 responded. However, there was no time left to search for malingering soldiers as the regiment was ordered into the line of battle on the right of General William French's 3rd Division of the II Corps.

Except from the north, Confederates practically surrounded the Army of the Potomac. They were massed around Chancellorsville like a roughly shaped horse shoe. Rebel forces lay to the west, south, and east with units to the west in positions ranging from a quarter to a half mile away and the others as much as a mile from the Federal lines. Before long it was learned that the enemy was concentrating its troops for an assault from the west. In short time the fighting began with Tyler's men on the extreme right of the Union line. The 126th was virtually "in the air" and subject to a possible flanking movement that could be disasterous.

General J.E.B. Stuart was now in command of the Southerners, having taken Jackson's place the night before. His apparent objective was to push his men against Tyler's unprotected right flank and beyond. Screened from the enemy's view, the Rebels worked their way through the dense woods and brush with occasional bursts of musket fire. As his troops returned fire against the unseen enemy, Rowe soon realized they would eventually run out of ammunition. He sent his Sergeant Major, George Ziegler, to tell Tyler of his predicament. There was no reply and Major Robert Bronson followed with the same message. Eventually Rowe, himself, went to see the general. When he explained the situation, Tyler was not impressed. His order was to continue firing, telling Rowe "your men are doing excellently." Within an hour the brigade's ammunition was exhausted and the men were forced to take cartridges off the dead and wounded to supply themselves. While this was happening the enemy kept pressing forward. As each minute passed it became clear that unless ammunition soon arrived the line would be overrun. Word finally came that no cartridges were available, that the line was to retire when its ammunition was exhausted. [19]

What followed was unbelievable chaos. Stuart's forces poured in all along the front. From the right and rear they came, killing and maiming and capturing hundreds who could not escape into the thick woods. Lieutenant Clay McCauley, of Chambersburg's Company C, years later, told of the predicament the 126th was in. "The fight went on. So continuous had been the firing, that the underbrush at our front was literally cut down at about waist height. Gradually I saw one after another of our men cease firing. Ammunition was exhausted. We called for supplies. None were to be had. Something had gone wrong. The men began to feel it. As our firing slackened I noticed a foreboding disorder on our right. Then a feeling of suspense and doubt seemed to thrill along the line. About that time I felt a blow on my right side, as if I had been struck by a heavy hammer. A spent ball had hit me, the effects of which I felt for a year thereafter. The disorder, changing into tumult, came near and nearer. At last it swept in upon the company next to mine. Then it struck my own company's right. The companies, rising in successive ranks from the ground, the men with questioning looks at one another, started at first slowly and then rapidly backward. It was not a panic. It was a rather disorderly falling back of almost helpless men, from a coming danger they felt themselves powerless to resist. They were good soldiers. They had led in the boldest and farthest charge made by the Union forces up Marye's Heights at Fredericksburg, the preceding December . . . But what can men do when without ammunition they see the line of which they form part steadily backing away from some oncoming force? A wave rolling backward on a curving beach does not more steadily sweep broken on its way than did the retreat of our battle line from right to left that Sunday morning. The rebels, discovering that our ammunition was exhausted, had charged upon us, striking our extreme right. . .

"What then happened to me a letter written not long afterwards describes in these words: 'Soon I found myself alone. I saw that I must run or be killed. I started to run, but after a few steps my scabbard caught between my legs and threw me down upon my face. Up again, I tried to break through the bushes, but the bullets were whizzing around at a terrible rate. I fell again, and was so exhausted I could go no farther. I crawled alongside one of the wounded. In a moment the rebels were on me.' I remember well, now, that poor mangled fellow, at whose side I was. Seeing me he had begged for water. I was about to give him my canteen, when, looking up, I discovered the rebels rapidly coming through the brush. Those moments are now more like the memory of some dreadful dream. Instinctively I started to rise. But, as I rose, I saw a rebel skirmisher take a sudden and not very agreeable interest in me. With a jerk he brought his musket to a direct aim. I was his mark. Probably you understand just what it is to look into a loaded gun, whose hammer is up and whose trigger is under the finger of a man who would just as soon pull as not. Under the circumstances, naturally, I remained just where I was, in a half-risen posture. For several seconds I looked into the muzzle of that advancing musket. I saw, as in a mist, many moving men, and heard the noise of their rush. But my brain was concentrated on that one advancing figure. He came upon me swifter than I can write of him. When within a few paces, down came the gun to a charge, and with the bayonet at my breast he yelled out, 'You ____ ____ of ____ a ____' give me that sword.' While he spoke the rebel line came up. It passed with a rush. Two regiments deep they were. I afterwards learned that the Sixth and Fifth Alabamas were at our immediate front. My captor, a big, tawny-bearded fellow, noticing that I was but a boy, changed his manner at once as I gave him my sword. Seeing that I did not rise, he asked me if I was hurt. 'I do not know,' I replied. I added, 'Get me out of this as quick as you can.' I suddenly remembered that just beyond where we had entered the tangle, in the open space, were batteries, about forty guns, planted in a crescent and bearing on the woods. I thought that our line would fall back to those batteries and rally there. I was sure, too, that as soon as the rebels should appear at the edge of the woods, something would happen. I had no desire to be killed by grape, canister, shell or anything else from our own guns. I therefore urged our retreat into the rebel lines as quickly as possible. My new acquaintance from Alabama agreed with me. He put a strong arm under my shoulders and, half carrying me, started for the rear. I cannot tell how far we had gone — perhaps it was a hundred yards — when the expected something happened. It seemed as if a tornado out of a clear sky had, all at once, burst upon that forest. We had just reached a breastwork and where there was quite a deep hole. With the first crash, into that hole we fell. For about ten minutes a roaring torrent of iron plunged through the air above us. We were almost covered by fallen tree-limbs and branches. The noise was horrible. Gradually the devastating stream ceased, but as it slackened back came the rebel crowd all in disorder. . . Back with the retreating rebels we two scrambled towards the farther rear. Soon the rebels halted under the shouts of their officers. I was carried on to where I at length met General Rhodes, to whom I surrendered and by whom I was sent still farther back. Our way lay over one of the plank roads so much spoken of in connection with the fight. On this the struggle of the day and night before had been severest: Our own and the rebel dead by the score lay side by side there. Twice batteries plunged by us, the hoofs of the horses and the carriage-wheels crushing and mutilating the dead bodies of friend and foe. Along the roadside were gathered hundreds of wounded of both armies. Their only shelter from the blazing sun was blankets stretched over them and held in place by the closed hammers of four muskets, the muskets reversed and struck upright by their bayonets into the ground. It was a sickening march. Rebel reserves passed us, hurrying to the front on double-quick. Supplies of ammunition were being carried forward. Farther on, we reached what I was told had been the front line of the 'Yankee' breastworks. At that point was a house filled with and surrounded by wounded and dying from the hapless 11th Corps. Many evidences of a fearful struggle were visible there. Leaving these, we soon were inside the original rebel position. I was delivered over to an officer and made one more of a large crowd of our own men already gathered there. At last, then, the morning's horror was past. I threw myself upon the ground, physically exhausted, a discouraged, miserable prisoner of war." [20]

McCauley's story continued to tell of his eventual imprisonment in Libby Prison at Richmond. He was a lucky man for within two weeks he became part of a prisoner exchange. By the time the regiment was mustered out, the lieutenant was back with his company.

While MacCauley and his comrades were being overrun the remaining troops were able to retreat to an open space in the rear. Here they found refuge back of an artillery battery which raked Stuart's lines with grape and cannister forcing them to melt back into the shadows of the forest. When reinforcements from John F. Reynold's I Corps came forward, Tyler's men retired to the safety of a wooded area away from the fighting. Here the survivors had their spirits revived. They learned that Sedgewick's Corps had finally dislodged Lee's forces at Fredericksburg. But, hopes for victory in this sector were later shattered when Confederate divisions led by Generals Anderson, McLaws, and Early trapped the Federals at Salem Church and drove them back across the Rappahannock.

Hooker's last chance of victory had ended and on May 5 the Army of the Potomac once more, standing in defeat, began its withdrawal. In a driving, torrential rain Tyler's men waited. There was no food, since the commissary stores had been burned. There was no shelter since all tents had been discarded earlier. The soldiers lay or sat all night long, waiting for an order to move. Finally, at daylight the next morning, they were told to begin marching toward the Rappahannock. While the 126th waited to cross, the Pennsylvania Cavalry's Assistant Surgeon, Dr. Henry G. Chritzman, helped to treat the wounded of the regiment. Young Chritzman had studied under Dr. William Grubb of Greencastle before attending the Pennsylvania Medical College and was well known by both Greencastle and Antrim men. [21]

All through the forenoon the swollen river was crossed on pontoon bridges at a place called United States Ford and after a march of twelve miles through the ever present Virginia mud, the exhausted troops reached their old camps in and around Falmouth. Fredericksburg, then Chancellorsville — the Rappahannock seemed to be a river of shattered dreams, shattered hopes for a victory that would destroy Lee's army.

The 126th suffered seventy one casualties — forty eight wounded, ten taken prisoner, four missing, and nine killed. Company H of Path Valley and St. Thomas had the greatest number of losses with nine wounded, two killed and four missing. Mercersburg's unit lost eleven wounded, one killed, and one missing. Juniata's Company I had three dead and eight wounded or missing. Chambersburg's three companies had none killed but their wounded or missing totalled fourteen. Company I of Juniata lost nine through wounds or missing in action. The Antrim-Fulton company lost eight — one killed and seven wounded and missing. Greencastle's Company K had two killed, two wounded, and one taken prisoner. [22]

Federal losses at Chancellorsville amounted to 17,278 killed, wounded, and missing while the Confederates suffered 12,821 casualties. Although losing twenty two percent of their army, they still had won a great victory. (Military authorities called Lee's victory a "masterpiece" and it is still studied as a nearly perfect example of strategy.)

Lincoln was with a newspaper friend, Noah Brooks, when the news finally reached the White House. "My God!" he exclaimed. "What will the country say? What will the country say?" Within days Lincoln and his Chief of Staff Halleck set out for Falmouth to learn, firsthand, of the army's condition. Hospital ships passed them on their way to Washington, yet through the rainy weather the President sailed on to see what had happened. At the camp he found the army intact, morale low, and Hooker's corps commanders complaining of the blunders that led to their defeat. Upon his return to the capital, the President faced renewed complaints of his conduct of the war and demands that Hooker be fired. This he could not bring himself to do. He felt the man deserved a second chance.

Some generals had doubted Hooker's ability from the beginning. Among these were George G. Meade and Darius N. Couch, leaders of Pennsylvania troops. Meade quarrelled with his commander, but stayed. Couch tried to get others to go with him to see Lincoln. When this failed he notified the President that he could no longer serve under Hooker and asked to be relieved of his command. After his release, Couch returned to Pennsylvania to join the staff of Governor Curtin as head of the state's home guard forces.

When accounts of the Chancellorsville battle reached Pennsylvania its people were dismayed. There was some relief in the Franklin, Fulton, and Juniata counties when it was learned that their regiment had not suffered as it had at Fredericksburg. Yet, when the lists of casualties began reaching the towns and rural sections a pall of sorrow once more cast itself over homes of the deceased. The Greencastle area's dead included Jonathan Bowman, George Missavy, and Simon Rupley. William Snively had been taken prisoner and the wounded were identified as George Brunner, M. W. Kisecker, Lieutenant J. Gilmore Rowe, and William Rupert. Christian Hager was listed as missing in action, but later found his way back to his outfit.

Greencastle's May 12 issue of "The Pilot" published the news of Chancellorsville by saying — "The general gloom which pervaded the community was deepened still more by news from the Army of the Potomac. Great anxiety was manifested to know how our soldiers came out of the battle. And here we must say, we are all very much indebted to the kindness and promptness of our gentlemanly operator, in furnishing us with all the intelligence from the army which he was allowed to communicat.e *(This refers to the telegrapher stationed at the line's office on West Baltimore Street in a small building located near where the Martin Insurance business now stands.)* From dispatches, private letters, and published lists in the New York Herald we make out the following casualties." The list which followed was identical to the Official Record with only a few exceptions. Jonathan Bowman was listed as missing in the news account when in fact it was later determined he had been killed. Several men were reported wounded but the Official Records failed to verify this information.

The paper also carried tributes to two of the community's dead heroes. Simon Rupley and George Missavy, with an explanation that they were not killed instantly, but died in a few hours from their wounds and that their bodies were buried "on the other side of the river." Rupley was described as "one of our most useful citizens. At the time of his enlistment he was extremely engaged in various kinds of business. Not only his friends, but the town will also feel his loss."

"Missavy was a hard working, industrious young man. In battle he was steady and unyielding, never wavering, never unduly excited.

Truly the brave have fallen! Their virtues are too well known to require the services of our humble pen." [23]   *(See Appendix IV)*

Charles Hartman noted the loss of two more of his Sunday School boys, Simon Rupley and George Missavy. Their deaths at a time when they looked forward to coming home made the tragedy still more painful. Missavy's death presented his family not only intense grief but extreme anxiety concerning the future of the father, John. He was still serving in the ranks of Company B, and although within weeks he should be coming home, he could be killed or wounded in the time that remained. Although the enlistment of both a father and son in the same unit was not uncommon, it was a singularly trying fact of life for the Missavy family. Their's was a poor household, where the mother, Catherine, was left at home with four younger daughters ranging from two to eleven, and three older girls, who worked as hirelings in farm homes.

After John Missavy and Catherine Walck were married in 1842, the couple lived as tenants on various farms until 1860 when they moved to a rented house on West North Street. From this home both the father and son worked as hired hands on farms in the township. At the outbreak of war, George, who was eighteen years of age, enlisted as a three month volunteer in Company C of the 2nd Pennsylvania Volunteers. In 1862 both the son and father, who was forty two years old, became part of the 126th Regiment. George was assigned to Company K as a corporal and John was a private in the Fulton-Antrim Company. Each received fifty dollar bonuses which they left at home and when they were paid during the enlistment period most of their earnings were sent back to the family. [24]

As the early days of May passed, the tension of waiting to see the survivors of the 126th mounted. All over the county hundreds of mothers, fathers, brothers, sisters, friends, and sweethearts began to count the days. On Saturday, May 9, a meeting was held at the Railway Ticket Office to make arrangements for Greencastle's reception of the nine month soldiers. J. C. McLanahan announced that he had received a message from Lieutenant J. Gilmore Rowe saying the regiment would start for home on May 8 and those assembled were reminded that immediate action was necessary. A committee of twelve, headed by Dr. E. D. Rankin, was appointed to begin planning the homecoming. Henry P. Prather was named to head a temporary organization to raise necessary funds. Addison Imbrie and William McNulty were to serve as vice-chairmen while William Reid was the secretary.

Rowe's message concerning the date for the regiment's departure was off schedule by four days — May 12 was when final preparations were made for leaving the Falmouth camp. The men spent this last day visiting other regiments and saying goodbye to those they had soldiered with over the months since the previous August. At six o'clock the next morning they were hauled by rail to Aquia's Landing where a ship, the "Warner", waited to carry the troops to Washington. Upon arriving in the capital, the men marched to the Soldier's Rest to spend the night. On the 14th they boarded a train to Baltimore and from there, through the night, they continued their homeward journey.

At seven o'clock the train pulled into the Harrisburg station. Home was only fifty to sixty miles away and with drums beating and flags flying, the 126th marched across the city to Camp Curtin. Here was where the venture started. Here was where it would end. For several days the men were free to enjoy themselves in town or in the camp. Some adventurous spirits spent the time visiting bars and other places of amusement in town while others stayed in camp. Waiting accompanied by more waiting was familiar to all the men. It took four days to complete the papers required for the mustering out process. Finally on Wednesday, May 20, 1863, the 126th was dismissed from military duty. Paid in full and with their discharges in pocket the men started home.

Greencastle had sent a special committee to escort the local heroes home. Just as the train started leaving the Harrisburg station the telegraph line flashed word to the home town. When the news hit the telegrapher's office, boys were ready to run the message to the town churches and sextons began pealing the bells. All over town they rang. Home, home, they were coming home. The joyous cacophony lasted for at least half an hour.

When word came they had left Chambersburg, after the ceremonies there, bells all over town began to ring. Again, church bells, dinner bells, school bells, all kinds of bells sounded the gladness. At about 2 p.m. the train pulled into North Carlisle Street and stopped at the water station. Here the soldiers from Greencastle, as well as those from Mercersburg and Waynesboro, disembarked to take their places in the procession that had been planned.

Down North Carlisle the parade began moving as mounted marshalls led the way with the band blaring its martial airs. Then came the veterans of the War of 1812, the Mexican War, and those who had served earlier in the Civil War. These were followed by the reception committee and the town authorities. Finally there came the newest veterans of the 126th, followed by family, friends, and little boys from everywhere. The line of march took the procession over practically every street in town. All along the route flags hung from windows while huge banners stretched across the streets near the Diamond. Signs of "Welcome Home" fluttered all along the route and houses were festooned with large bouquets of flowers and wreaths of evergreen.

Finally the parade ended on the Diamond where a formal ceremony was to take place. A temporary stage had been erected on the north eastern corner of the Square. It, too, was decorated with patriotic colors and the upper frame work held a large banner carrying an inscription, "Fredericksburg" and "Chancellorsville." Above it was a wreath encircled sign saying, "Welcome Home." From the stand a speech of welcome by the Rev. Edward Briedenbaugh was "eagerly received and loudly applauded." Major Robert Bronson, leader of the

Mercersburg Company, proposed "Three cheers for the good people of Greencastle." Colonel Rowe proposed three cheers for the B, C, E, and K companies and then "said goodbye to the boys who had so long marched with him." The exercises concluded with a prayer by the Rev. T. G. Apple of the Reformed congregation.

Store rooms on the Square had been cleared and in them were tables filled with food waiting for the men of the four companies. All this had been arranged by the ladies of the town and township. Not only had they brought the food, they had also decorated the rooms and tables for this happy occasion. Through the afternoon the festivities continued and in the early evening hours "conveyances from Waynesboro and Mercersburg arrived to take their veterans home." Archibald Logue, the local baggagemaster, had carefully transported the baggage from the depot and all belongings of the men had been meticulously tagged, waiting for their departure. [25]

When the Mercersburg men approached their home town they were met by a vast assemblage of citizens and escorted into town. "A piece of music, composed for the occasion, was sung by the fair ladies and gentlemen of the place from the balcony of Murphy's Hotel. The Rev. Dr. Thomas Creigh delivered an address of welcome."

Waynesboro's soldiers were welcomed on their arrival about seven o'clock that evening. They were escorted into the town by a welcoming committee and addresses were given by the Rev. Dr. Dorsey and the Rev. Kester. The Waynesboro "Record" stated that the officers and men "look well and are in good spirits." It was announced by the town's newspaper that a dinner would be served the men of Company E on Wednesday, June 3, in the grove upon the farm of George Jane near town. The affair "will be conducted under the auspices of the Union League." [26]

Local soldiers gradually found the way to their homes in town and Antrim families began taking their husbands and sons to their places. As shadows fell across the countryside the day ended. As long as they lived, the soldiers and the home folks would never forget this glorious day of homecoming.

Of the 146 men who left the Greencastle-Antrim community in August of 1862, 115 returned on May 20, 1863. Many would re-enlist in later calls. Others stayed to go back to their business, shop, or farm employment. Of the thirty-one that did not come home, ten lay in graves at Fredericksburg and Chancellorsville. Some of the wounded were still in military hospitals, although most from the first battle had been home for some time. This was also true of those released earlier because of sickness or disabilities.

All were home or accounted for, but the war would go on and the people of the Greencastle-Antrim community had not heard the end of battle casualty reports nor the torment such news brought. Nor had they seen the last homecoming. More would be returning over the months ahead. More grief, more gladness were still a part of the future.

CHAPTER VI

THE INVASION

As the 126th was celebrating its homecoming, Robert E. Lee, in consultation with Jefferson Davis, was developing plans for another advance into the North. Confederate victories at Fredericksburg and Chancellorsville brought a wave of dissatisfaction for the war throughout the North and these triumphs had whetted Southern appetites for another try to gain one great victory beyond the Mason-Dixon line. Hopes still lingered for English and French recognition of the Confederacy and the capture of Harrisburg, Philadelphia or Baltimore might achieve such recognition. A Southern victory in the North could also ease the seige at Vicksburg and prolong this city's control of the Mississippi River.

The first hint of trouble from the Rebels came on June 15 when large numbers of Negro men, women, and children came streaming out of Maryland over Antrim's roads and through Greencastle. These were contrabands or blacks freed through the Emancipation Act. They were hurrying northward into the safety of Pennsylvania.

The frightened refugees were followed in mid-morning by a wagon train, racing wildly through the town. A remnant of General Robert Milroy's army, it was escaping from General Richard Ewell's men who had trapped the Union forces at Winchester. The panic stricken teamsters and their out-riders had lost many horses and wagons in their hasty flight, leaving the road from Williamsport to Hagerstown and up to Greencastle strewn with broken wagons and dead or exhausted horses.

Milroy's men, rushing through the town towards Chambersburg, left the impression that Confederates were right on their heels and town and country people began to ready themselves for the approaching enemy. Merchants started packing their goods to be taken into hiding. Farm animals were driven to areas where they would be safe from detection. Housewives began emptying their homes of furniture, bedding, and clothes before Rebels came to burn their places. Noon came and a detachment of the 1st New York Cavalry Regiment, led by Captain William Boyd, arrived from Williamsport. This was the wagon train's rear guard. Boyd assured everyone that the Rebels were at least twenty miles away and the panic began to subside.

However, about six o'clock that evening, a Greencastle man identified as James Shirey, a veteran of the 126th Volunteers, rode into Greencastle with important news. He had just encountered the enemy near the state line along the Williamsport toll road. Shirey said he talked to officers and men of the invading force and after telling them he lived in the area he was allowed to take a by-road that led to Middleburg. Along the way he ran into several Union cavalrymen and a railroad telegraph operator. Although not identified, this probably was William Wilson, the telegrapher who had played such an important role in the campaign of 1862. After sending a message to Harrisburg to tell of the impending invasion, the telegrapher and horsemen hurried to Chambersburg. [1]

Shortly after Shirey arrived General Albert Jenkins's cavalry dashed into the town. It was learned later that the Rebel invasion of Greencastle was not a rash undertaking. The Confederate leader, thinking there were Union forces in the area, divided his brigade to attack the town. Lieutenant Hermann Schuricht, in his diary, tells how his 14th Virginia Cavalry Regiment — with "pistols and muskets in hand, traversing ditches and fences, we charged and took the town. The Federal cavalry escaped and only one lieutenant was captured. After destroying the railroad depot, and cutting the telegraph wires, the brigade took up its advance to Chambersburg, Pa."[2] *(The railroad water tower was also burned.)*

While occupying Greencastle, Jenkins's men commenced searching stables for horses. The local paper reported, that the people suffered from confusion and fear, not wanting to believe it was a real invasion. "We were confident then that it was only a raid for plunder." Jenkins left a small body of men in Greencastle before leaving for Chambersburg but along the way there was skirmishing with the 1st New York cavalry. This delay held up the invaders and it was eleven o'clock that evening before they entered the county seat.

The next day's city papers reported Lee's army to be in Pennsylvania. Headlines of the Philadelphia Inquirer declared, with unbridled exaggeration, that Greencastle had been "sacked and burned." The Jenkins force became an army of 5,000 infantry, cavalry, and artillery. The water tower and warehouse fire had ballooned into a conflagration engulfing this entire town and showed "a determination on the part of the Rebels to burn, plunder, and destroy our cities."[3]

Actually Jenkins's cavalry consisted of 1,500 men described as a collection of farmboys, mechanics, and shopkeepers from the Shenandoah Valley and the mountains of western Virginia. They were the grandsons and great grandsons of the German and Scotch-

Irish pioneers who had migrated from the Cumberland Valley into the Great Valley of Virginia during the colonial and post Revolution periods. Many had served with Turner Ashby in the 1861 and 1862 operations of Stonewall Jackson. They came out of Virginia on a variety of horses including some captured from the Federal cavalry — still carrying the U.S. brand.

These lean, lank, dark tanned men, clothed in a host of different uniforms, were the antithesis of everything known about correct military attire. A few wore the standard Confederate gray but most were dressed in coarse textured homespun, tattered and torn, but so grimy that one had to guess the original color. Others had Union cavalry and infantry jackets or coats. The men's pants of all shades — black, brown, grey, and blue — were generally tucked into knee high cavalry boots or roughly cobbled brown leather shoes.

The Reverend Dr. Philip Schaff, head of Mercersburg's Marshall College, said, "The Rebels were poorly and miscellaneously dressed and equipped with pistols, rifles, and sabers, hard looking and full of fight, some noble, but also some stupid and semi-savage faces." They truly were fierce looking men. Beyond the weapons Dr. Schaff described, many carried shotguns or braces of revolvers in their belts. Others had Colt pistols tucked in saddle holsters in addition to other arms. As many as possible carried the English short Enfield rifle, an accurate and popular weapon with many Southern soldiers. Beside the saber, common to most cavalry units, some carried Bowie knives tucked in their belts or left hanging from their hips.[4]

Their fierce demeanor was further enhanced by their headgear. Covering their long, matted hair, usually of shoulder length, were straw or gray and black slouch hats adorned with feathers and plumes of many colors. Beards, sometimes extending to their waists, completes the description of this body of horsemen — the first military representatives of the Confederacy to come to the Cumberland Valley in the invasion of 1863.

Often referred to as Jenkins's Mounted Infantry, they lacked the ability, experience and discipline of Jeb Stuart's cavalry. For example, they lacked the training which allowed Stuart's men to make organized mounted saber charges. Jenkins's troops, with their heavy rifles, were more adapted to getting to the scene of combat, dismounting and fighting as infantry. Hit and run tactics and bushwhacking was another one of their talents. Since J.E.B. Stuart was covering Lee's right flank, the Jenkins's mission was to scout ahead for the oncoming invaders.

Albert Jenkins came from the mountain country of western Virginia. He was a graduate of Jefferson College at Canonsburg, Pennsylvania and the Harvard School of Law. Prior to the war he served two terms in Congress and was active in the politics of his home country. As a military leader Jenkins was said to be unreliable and lacked administrative ability. Because of these weaknesses, Lee had assigned him to "Old Dick" Ewell who in turn placed him under the highly disciplined wing of General Robert E. Rodes.[5]

LT. GEN. RICHARD S. EWELL   BESORE COLLECTION   BRIG. GEN. ALBERT G. JENKINS

These fierce looking, heavily armed horsemen were the first Confederate invaders the people of Antrim and Greencastle saw. Less than a year before many had lined the streets to jeer and curse captive Rebels as they marched through the town, but on June 15, 1863 they were quiet — very quiet. The wheel of fortune had turned and not a word of ridicule was heard throughout the hour or so that the visitors occupied the community.

Jenkins spent two days *(June 16-17)* in the county seat. The first night he stayed at Colonel A. K. McClure's home, however, the Colonel was absent, having taken a quick leave when he heard enemy forces were in Greencastle. Aside from being a prominent Republican politician, McClure had served as Curtin's assistant adjutant general in 1862, and had been active in recruiting troops from Franklin County. He also headed a loose knit intelligence network which operated along the Maryland border. It was from one of these operations that he learned of Confederate plans to arrest and imprison him. Thus, the reason for his hasty retreat. The rest of the time, Jenkins made the Montgomery House his headquarters. While in Chambersburg the town's citizens were ordered to turn over all privately owned firearms. A collection of good, bad, and indifferent guns followed and after sorting the lot, the invaders kept usable pieces and broke the rest on the courthouse steps.

Foraging parties, sent into the surrounding country, collected not only horses and cattle. Jacob Hoke recorded his reaction to another type of foraging — capturing Negroes to be taken back to Virginia. "These poor creatures — those of them who had not fled upon the approach of the foe — sought concealment in the growing wheat fields about the town. Into these the cavalrymen rode in search of their prey and many were caught — some after a desperate chase and being fired at." Many of these blacks were born and raised on free soil, but the Southerners ignored pleas of such freemen. In some cases whites intervened and secured the release of those where proof could be given that they had been life long residents of the community.

Storekeepers were forced to sell merchandise for Confederate notes or shinplasters "issued by the city of Richmond and other southern corporations." Fortunately many shopkeepers had hidden most of their stock and little was left for sale. The most important military accomplishments of the cavalry were to wreck the telegraph lines between Hagerstown and Chambersburg and to destroy the railroad bridge at Scotland. This was done with torpedoes or cans of black powder, explosives that Stuart, the year before, did not have when his attempt failed. [6]

While the main cavalry force was in Chambersburg the detachment, left in Greencastle, tried to keep order and confiscate merchandise where it could be found. George Bert who had just opened a shoe and boot shop had little stock since his sales consisted of custom-made footwear. However, one of the Rebels approached him near his shop on East Baltimore Street. Seeing the boots Bert wore, he said, "Hello there mister. Let me try on those boots." George complied. The soldier, after seeing they fit, left his wornout shoes and rode away to join his fellow troopers. [7]

Several of the pickets, while having breakfast, "at a public house," were taken prisoner by local citizens. They were speedily conducted to Waynesboro and imprisoned. The same day, a messenger on his way from Jenkins to General Rodes, whose division was at Williamsport, was captured by Greencastle civilians. He also was sent to Waynesboro. The captured dispatch stated that Yankees had come up the road from Shippensburg towards Chambersburg and that he, Jenkins, had fallen back into the town. Apparently the Rebel leader was losing his nerve since the only Federal forces in the area were small detachments of the 1st New York and loyal Maryland cavalry units.

On the afternoon of June 16 from thirty to forty Negro women and children, made captive at Chambersburg, were brought to Greencastle in wagons bound for Virginia. In charge of this small caravan was a Southern chaplain and four soldiers. As they came through the town a crowd of citizens surprised them. The guards were disarmed, traces were cut — allowing the horses to run into the country, and the chaplain and his men taken to Waynesboro.

Capturing the enemy by local citizens required unusual courage and records seem to indicate that this practice was limited to Greencastle. Tradition holds that these forays against the invaders were inspired by the hot tempered, Union advocate, Tom Pawling. Owner of the town's Antrim House, Pawling had gained a reputation for his impulsive and violent behavior in putting down disorders in his barroom. "Old Tom knew how to handle such trouble makers," his cronies would have said.

But, before long clearer thinking prevailed. More reasonable people began to see the hazards the community faced if such acts continued. Strong retaliatory measures would most certainly be taken when the enemy arrived in force. Town authorities began to make arrangements to have the captured Confederates returned from Waynesboro. This action came none too soon for a body of the Jenkins cavalry, led by Colonel M. J. Ferguson, arrived in Greencastle that evening. The officer heard of the incidents and was satisfied with the steps taken to return the prisoners. He promised there would be no punitive action if the men were brought back. [8]

The next day Jenkins withdrew his men from the county seat. This was prompted by what was thought to be an army approaching from the direction of Shippensburg. Rebel pickets, stationed on Shirk's Hill, to the north of the town, saw through the early morning mists a line of Union cavalry moving slowly down the Harrisburg Pike. As visibility improved, the pickets could see what appeared to be a mass of soldiers to the rear of the horsemen — at least a brigade marching to the relief of Chambersburg. A messenger was dispatched to General Jenkins and preparations were immediately made for an orderly withdrawal. By noon the entire Confederate force was on its way to Greencastle.

What the Rebels took for an army was a crowd of several hundred curious residents of Greenvillage and neighboring communities who were on their way to get a good look at the occupiers of Chambersburg. Just as they might have gone to a circus or carnival, they were anxious to see these unusual looking men dressed in all kinds of uniforms. They wanted to see the long hair and beards of the men from Virginia.

Word of this episode leaked back to Rodes who, in turn, saw that Ewell got to know about it. Eventually General Lee heard the story, but he still needed the cavalry leader and no disciplinary action was taken. However, he told Ewell to place one of his staff officers with Jenkins if he felt this was necessary. [9]

When Jenkins returned to Greencastle, the town's citizens who had gone to retrieve the captured Rebels had just returned with only the chaplain, his soldiers, and drivers. The others had been taken to Gettysburg. As soon as he arrived the chaplain began making demands on the town. The slaves were his property. He demanded $50,000 to cover his losses. When he found no response to this demand, he reduced the ransom to $25,000. Several leading citizens explained in unequivocal terms that no one in Greencastle was going to engage in the slave trade, and that he need not expect one cent by way of indemnity. Swearing vengeance, the chaplain gave the people two hours to raise the money or the torch would be set to the town.

There was no such amount of ready cash available in town or township and people began to remove valuables from houses, offices, and stores. The ultimatum's time came and went. Despite volumes of profanity and blustering condemnation of the town's residents the fires were never set. Firmness of purpose and lack of funds obviously saved the day. [10]

"The Mercersburg Journal" of July 17, 1863 resumed publication after being closed for nearly a month. The editor's review of events covering the invasion and Gettysburg's aftermath included a story of a group of the Negroes who had been freed at Greencastle. "Several miles on this side of Greencastle, toward evening, we passed 13 of these rescued contrabands of whom 3 were adults and the balance children...on their way down to give themselves up, having heard that the town was threatened with burning. Long before they got there, however, their hard masters had left." Such loyalty to the town they associated with their freedom would certainly have pleased people like Tom Pawling and his associates. Fortunately these fugitives did not have to relinquish their freedom. There is no record to show their fate in other raids that continued throughout the invasion.

That evening the main body of the Jenkins force moved back toward Middleburg with large numbers of horses, wagons, and other plunder. However, from their camps along the Mason-Dixon line the leaders sent foraging parties toward both mountains. One detachment, under Colonel Ferguson, went to Mercersburg and over the Cove Mountain into Fulton County. Upon reaching McConnellsburg shortly after dawn on the 18th, its stores and shops were visited and purchases made with Confederate scrip. Twelve thousand dollars worth of cattle, 120 horses, and several Negro boys were taken from the farms of the area. As the Rebels left the town its streets were littered with old shoes, boots, and hats discarded for better ones "bought" in McConnellsburg. Returning through Mercersburg, this community was spared for the time being. The enemy had taken so much from Fulton County that they had little room for additional loot nor time to scour the countryside for more cattle and horses or Negroes.

Another band of foragers, sent to Waynesboro, crossed South Mountain and penetrated Adams County as far as Fairfield. In this area they ran into pickets of the Philadelphia City Troop and Bell's cavalry of Gettysburg. This stopped further seizures in that region, but the party returned to camp with large numbers of livestock and much merchandise.

Both raids brought additional blacks to be returned to Virginia. No one can estimate the numbers of Negroes who suffered this fate, for the practice continued throughout the time Lee's army was in Pennsylvania. Entire Negro families were seized in the Mercersburg area and on several occasions Confederate officers helped release such captives, because they, too, were heartsick when they saw this happening.

Beyond the cavalry units involved in the foraging business, there were irregular guerilla bands from the mountains of western Virginia who worked along the fringes of the regular army. Their enterprise included - taking horses, cattle, store goods, household valuables, and Negroes. Upon returning to Virginia they sold their merchandise for personal profit. [11]

Greencastle residents began to feel more secure when the Rebels seemed to be going back into Maryland to stay. They were wrong. On the morning of June 18 a gang of railroad workers pumped their way into town on a hand car. They had been sent to repair the telegraph lines destroyed by the invaders. About ten o'clock a sudden dash of horsemen from the Jenkins camps to the south resulted in capturing the work crew and their means of transportation. However, within an hour, they were released. [12]

Although some farm people were able to hide their horses, cattle, and sheep in the creek hills, the mountains, or as far away as Lebanon or Lancaster counties, it is estimated that the value of livestock, including horses, taken by Jenkins amounted to approximately $250,000. The direct financial loss was compounded by the timing of the raid. It had come at a time when farmers were about to harvest their wheat. The loss of horses meant that most of the grain would simply lie and rot in the fields. Some, whose principal wealth was in livestock, went bankrupt. Yet, this was just the beginning. The confiscation of farm animals and merchandise would continue for two more weeks. Stories of local farmers losing their animals during these raids were frequently heard for years following the war.

On one occasion a small boy was playing in his front yard as several horsemen were passing. "Hello sonny, where's your daddy?" The youngster replied, "Oh, he's in the cellar with his horses." The horsemen were Rebel foragers. Finis. [13]

John Royer owned a farm a mile west of Middleburg. While trying to hide his horses, he was surprised to see several Confederates waiting at the end of his lane. They not only acquired his horses but they spied a smoke house filled with hams, sides of bacon, and sausages. After collecting this larder, Royer was carefully paid in full with currency of the Confederacy. [14]

BESORE COLLECTION   McDOWELL'S BLACKSMITH SHOP

Where the old Waynesboro road crosses the one to Hagerstown, in the Hollowell area of the township, stood the McDowell blacksmith shop. It had been operated by brothers, John and Henry McDowell, since the early 1800's. Famous throughout the district, they served not only local farmers but those who traveled through the area.

During the invasion, Rebels helped themselves to equipment they needed and when it was all over the shop was stripped of everything. [15]

Just west of the Conococheague, in Montgomery township, the "Pinefield" area was hard hit. Lazarus Kennedy, whose farm lay where the east and west branches of the creek meet, lost all of his horses and much farm equipment. He also was made a prisoner, but released before being taken into Maryland. The school house at "Pinefield" served as a collection station. Daniel and George Garling were made prisoners and turned over to an officer at the school building. When asked their father's name the Confederate was surprised to learn it was John Garling, a man he had done business with before the war. The boys were dismissed and told to hurry home. [16]

Adam Zarger, as a child, lived in the Antrim Grove area. When Rebels were taking their cattle, his mother pleaded to let her keep a favorite heifer. Finally the officer in charge relented and allowed her to keep it. Overwhelmed with relief, Adam shared his mother's joy as the enemy left. The Zarger horses had been hidden in a huge house cellar, but when news came that more Rebels were coming the family decided to load their belongings on their biggest farm wagon and start towards Shippensburg. As they left the home place, Adam's dog became excited, ran under the wagon, and was killed. After this, who cared whether the Rebels came or went. They could have taken the heifer for all Adam cared. His dog was dead. [17]

This period produced for the Confederates ample horses to replace their worn out mounts plus cattle and sheep, to feed the oncoming army, and a variety of other materials that would sustain the men as they moved towards Pennsylvania - clothing, hats, boots, shoes, cloth, blankets, and cooking equipment.

The uncanny way enemy foragers found hidden cattle and horses gave rise to rumors that local Southern sympathizers were serving as informers: "They found thickets, dales, and secret places which few of our people could find without being shown," said the Greencastle editor. [18] Adherents of Breckinridge, now called "Copperheads," stood in fear of being called spies or collaborators. Yet, there were no reports of arrests. The people of 1863 were puzzled and through the years following the war the mystery was never solved.

As the livestock and horses were being sent into the Shenandoah Valley, the Greencastle area served as the funneling point for most of this traffic. By the end of the invasion the town's streets and Antrim's roads were gashed with deep ruts. They turned into veritable streams when rains came and, worse yet, became cesspools of rotten vegatation and animal waste causing much concern about possible health hazards for the community.

One observer noted that the road to Williamsport, where Rodes's division camped, was crowded with wagons, horses, and droves of cattle and sheep going south from Greencastle. Despite the pleasure derived from getting better rations, equipment, and clothing, some cavalrymen were disappointed. The horses brought back from Maryland and Pennsylvania proved "utterly unserviceable and seemingly have as little taste or talent for war as their fat Dutch proprietors." Mennonites and Dunkards had followed the ways of peace for generations. Could anyone expect more than quiescent dispositions in their horses? Another interesting commentary came from General Rodes. He complained that all of the horses seized by Jenkins's men were "rarely accounted for." This observation gives further credence to the claim that many of the foragers were in business for themselves.

The extent of the seizures in southern Pennsylvania can be seen in accounts written by firsthand observers. A soldier of John B. Gordon's Georgia brigade wrote that he saw, at a big horse shoe bend in the Shenandoah River near Mt. Jackson, Virginia, two to three thousand acres of bottom and filled with cattle and sheep. Upon inquiry one of the herdsmen told him that approximately 26,000 head of cattle and 22,000 head of sheep taken in Maryland and Pennsylvania were gathered there. A Confederate surgeon wrote that thousands of cattle were gathered in Pennsylvania, "enough to feed our army till cold weather." [19]

These losses brought financial ruin to many people but from the Confederate point of view the people of the Keystone state were only being paid back for the two years Virginia's people suffered from ravages of invasion by Union armies. The stories coming out of the western theater of war also told of ways Federal troops were vandalizing parts of Tennessee and Mississippi. Raids in Pennsylvania resulted in losses but not the destruction of property suffered by the people of the South. Futhermore, in most cases the Northerners were paid for what was taken in Confederate money or given receipts for later payment. There are no records to show that Federal soldiers paid Southern people for their losses. War was what William Tecumseh Sherman said it was.

Although southern Pennsylvania's people lost property, beyond taking civilians captive, there were few instances of persons being physically harmed. The invaders were under strict orders against violating persons and property. Nothing was to be taken unless paid for or regulations made specifying the kind and quantity of the property received. Also, receipts were to be issued for all that was taken.

In Franklin County there was only one instance of a civilian being killed. In the Marion community a band of Rebels became intoxicated after raiding a farmer's wine cellar. They approached the Henry Hege farm and demanded his money. A drunken soldier threatened to kill him but better judgement prevailed when one of his comrades persuaded him to let Hege go. Isaac Strite was not as fortunate as his neighbor. When drunken Rebels came to his place, he gave them money. Another group came and demanded more cash. When he told them he had no more they killed him. After burying him in a manure pile, the murderers quickly left the area. There is no record to indicate whether the killers were ever apprehended. This is the only known murder of a civilian by the invaders. However, on July 3 a band of Rebel foragers was surprised by three Union scouts in Mercersburg. The skirmish that followed resulted in the capture of one Confederate and the death of another who was buried in the Presbyterian graveyard. In the Fort Loudon area, two Confederate stragglers were captured when found looting a building. They were led out of the village and shot by several recently discharged veterans. The bodies were hastily buried in the village cemetery. [20]

For three days Greencastle was relatively quiet, but in the early morning hours of June 22 Colonel Ferguson and his men returned. "The Pilot" reported systematic pillaging of the town's stores and great quantitites of goods destroyed. The editor mentioned nothing of receipts or offers of payment. Since many merchants had sent most of their stock to friends in Lancaster County, or in some cases, to homes of town or rural customers, they escaped bankruptcy. Warehouses were looted and their contents loaded on wagons to be taken back to the main army. [21]

Jenkins had returned and it was then the people learned, without doubt, that the Rebels were invading Pennsylvania. They had seen only horseback riders prior to this day, but now they knew what lay ahead, for after the cavalry came Robert Rodes's Division of Ewell's Corps. Rodes and his troops had left Hagerstown that morning. After two days of hard rain, the weather cleared and as the sunshine brightened the Rebels' spirits they marched toward Middleburg. These were not the ragged long haired, dirty soldiers people had seen during the previous week. When they arrived in Greencastle its citizens witnessed the first of what seemed to be an unending line of gray and butternut clad veterans. Rodes's division was composed of disciplined regiments that had been fighting for two years.

One onlooker described them - "Knapsacks and the whole personal kit was in order. Arms were at every man's command. A significant touch to neatness was a toothbrush at hatband or buttonhole. The officers uniforms were of light gray cloth, the garniture a brilliant gold galloon, the privates' a dark gray with a few martial frills." This division had spent the early part of the previous week at Williamsport where their free time was spent in swimming, fishing, and resting along the banks of the Potomac. They appeared to be a "fit, well fed, well conditioned army." [22] No one should have questioned the fact that they were well fed. These troops were the first to consume a portion of the cattle, sheep, and other provisions Jenkins had been sending back to the troops coming out of Virginia.

Unlike the Rebels that had appeared in Maryland in September of 1862, most of the invaders were well clothed and shod. Over the months since that ill fated invasion, mills of the Carolinas and Georgia had been busily engaged in making military uniforms. The men of Rodes's division were from North Carolina, Alabama, and Georgia. They had benefited from the proximity of these factories. However, gray cloth usually associated with the South was missing in other divisions of Lee's army. The blockade had forced weavers to use a brownish-yellow vegetable dye called "butternut" and eventually this became a color often used for Confederate uniforms.

The shortage of shoes that constantly plagued the South was temporarily eased during the winter of 1862-63. Several thousand men had been furloughed to make shoes and by the spring of 1863 the Army of Northern Virginia was fairly well shod. However, the invasion of Pennsylvania resulted in acquiring far less footwear than had been anticipated. When the campaign was over the need for shoes and boots became a problem once more. Little improvement came through the remainder of the war. [23]

Better clothed, better shod, and better fed, the first of Lee's forces were in Pennsylvania and over the next week sounds of a marching army would be heard night and day, as it moved through the countryside, villages, and towns of the Cumberland Valley.

Governor Curtin had anticipated the invasion when Jenkins first appeared. His pleas for Federal troops were dismissed with the suggestion that state troops be raised to defend the valley and approaches to Harrisburg. Federal forces under Hooker were maneuvering to prevent Lee's army from turning out of the Shenandoah Valley towards Washington.

Eventually through efforts of the Governor and General Darius N. Couch, now serving as Commander of the Department of the Susquehanna, emergency militia regiments and batteries assembled in Harrisburg. Despite the immediate danger to the state, only 8,000 men responded to its defense. By August 1 some 37,000 had answered the call but in the crisis of late June the Commonwealth's men of militia age, as in 1862, showed an indifferent brand of patriotism. However, 12,000 New York militia came to Harrisburg and with expressed contempt for the Pennsylvanians they joined in manning the fortifications erected to defend the approaches to Harrisburg on the western side of the Susquehanna. Entrenchments were built in Marysville, Lemoyne, Bridgeport, Oysters Point, and other areas of the Camp Hill region. One important development was the use of colored troops and black railroad workers who performed much of the work in constructing the fortifications. At first Governor Curtin was reluctant to use black troops but when authorized by Secretary of War, Edward Stanton, Negro volunteers were accepted. [24]

General Couch was not content to rely totally on the fortified approaches to Harrisburg. He decided to send troops down the Valley to delay the Confederate advance. Washington was urging this action so as to give Hooker's army time to catch Lee's forces. Another important reason was to repair the railroad bridge at Scotland and restore telegraph lines as far south as possible. Chosen to lead this mission was General Joseph Knipe, of Harrisburg, a veteran of the Mexican War. His brigade eventually consisted of 800 New Yorkers; a battery of naval guns from the Philadelphia Naval Yard; an Invalid Company, composed of wounded veterans who could perform only limited service; and Captain William Boyd's Company C of the 1st New York cavalry, which, after escorting Milroy's train to Harrisburg, had been on scouting duty in the Valley. It was Boyd's men who reported Rebel movements to authorities in Harrisburg throughout the early phases of the invasion.

On June 20 Knipe and his force traveled by rail to Shippensburg and the next day came into the Chambersburg area after the bridge at Scotland had been repaired. When word of Rebel forces advancing out of Maryland was received, hastily constructed entrenchments were manned along roads leading from Chambersburg to Waynesboro and Greencastle. [25]

As Rodes's division came into the Greencastle area, during the morning hours of June 22, Jenkins was ordered to form an advance detail north of the town. Sensing a possible ambush, Jenkins instructed Captain J. A. Wilson (Company I, 14th Virginia Cavalry) to move slowly up the Chambersburg Road, but if he ran into any Federals along the way he and his men were to retreat in a manner that would create an impression of panic. Jenkins would have his main body waiting in the wheatfields along the road near the Archibald Fleming home where Fleming's son, William, lived with his family and managed the farm.

Further up the road in the Kiesecker Mill area the Jenkins cavalrymen ran into two of Boyd's men at a blacksmith shop having their mounts' shoes tightened. While in the process of taking them captive the Rebels saw a body of cavalry approaching at full speed. The captain's force quickly retreated towards Greencastle. As they passed the Fleming property they saw Jenkins's horses grazing along the railroad and Wilson knew his brigade was waiting, hidden in the ripened wheat on both sides of the road.

REBEL AMBUSH AT THE FLEMING FARM   SKETCH BY MARK T. NOE

While this action was developing, advance units of the Rodes division were frantically deploying a force of nearly 8,000 men along the hill to the northwest of the town. In this area, presently occupied by the Sunnyway Foods Store and the Baumgardner housing development, cannon were unlimbered. In later years it was said that one of the cannoneers was Thomas Miller, a former resident of Greencastle. Several years before the war he and his family had moved into Virginia and now, as part of Rodes's division, he was preparing for battle on very familiar ground. Earlier that morning the Rebels had been led to believe that a large army was moving toward Greencastle. This information came from D. K. Appenzellar, a local veteran of the 126th, who was taken into custody. When the Confederates learned he had been in Chambersburg the previous week they questioned him about troop movements there. The captive quickly obliged by telling his questioners that Couch was there with an army of 20,000 men.

Actually, the force the Rebels faced consisted of thirty five cav-

144

alrymen headed by William Boyd. As the horsemen approached the Fleming home he and his men reined their mounts to a slower pace. When the officer suspected a possible ambush ahead the troopers halted. On the hill near Greencastle Boyd could see men pulling into position what appeared to be artillery caissons. Carefully the Federals gathered behind the house while their leader continued to study what was happening on the road near the town.

For some unexplained reason several men slowly rode from the rear of the house to the front along the pike. Suddenly rifle fire from the wheat field enveloped them and two men fell. The remaining ones took cover and, as heavy enemy fire continued, Boyd and his force made a quick withdrawal toward Chambersburg.

During the intense flurry of rifle fire members of the Fleming family huddled in corners of their home to protect themselves from the bullets crashing through the windows. When the fighting subsided, Fleming's daughter, Mary, rushed out the front door to the nearest fallen soldier but he was dead. Then she hurried to the other cavalrymen. He was wounded in the leg and after Mary helped him stem the bleeding he crawled to a culvert under the railroad tracks opposite the Fleming home.

The dead man was William H. Rihl. Shot through the head, he had died instantly. After Boyd's men left, a squad of Confederates buried the body in a shallow grave near the spot where he fell. Before burying him they removed his cap, belt, shoes, and metal coat buttons. Several days later a group of Greencastle people disinterred the body, placed it in a coffin, and accompanied by a "large concourse of citizens," the soldier was interred in the town's Lutheran graveyard. *(In 1886 the local G.A.R. Post buried Rihl's remains in a grave where he fell and marked it with a suitable monument - a tribute to the first Union soldier killed on Pennsylvania soil.)*

The wounded man, Sergeant Milton Cafferty, had made friends with the Ilginfritz family and Dr. George Carl at the time the Milroy wagon train was in the Greencastle area. Upon receiving permission from the Confederates, the sergeant was moved to the Ilginfritz home near the northern limits of Greencastle. Here he was treated by Dr. Carl and cared for by the women of the household. Cafferty remained in Greencastle until mid-July. When able to walk, the Ilginfritz men

ALEXANDER COLLECTION
DR. GEORGE CARL

dressed him in civilian clothes to disguise him during the remainder of the invasion and, upon complete recovery, he returned to his regiment to serve until war's end. By then he had risen to the rank of captain. [26]

William H. Rihl was born in Philadelphia in 1843. At the time he entered the service he was eighteen years of age, five feet six inches tall, of light complexion, with blue eyes, and dark hair. He joined the cavalry company of Captain William H. Boyd in mid-July of 1861. All of this company's recruits were from the Philadelphia area and on July 22, 1861 Boyd and his men arrived in Washington during the hectic days following the Union defeat at the first Battle of Manassas.

The company was immediately sent to patrol the countryside south of Washington, but it was August 18 before the men saw action in a skirmish near Mount Vernon. In early September the company was attached, as B, to the 1st New York "Lincoln" Cavalry headed by Colonel Andrew McReynolds. For the remainder of the war the regiment served in Maryland, Virginia, and Pennsylvania.

This New York outfit served in the Peninsular campaign as a reconnaisance force. During Lee's invasion of Maryland, in 1862, its assignment was to harass and strike the enemy wherever possible. This resulted in skirmishes at Front Royal, Smithfield, Bunker Hill, Leetown, Winchester, Sheperdstown, and Martinsburg.

After accompanying Milroy's ammunition train from Winchester into Pennsylvania, the 1st New York performed scouting missions through out the weeks of Lee's invasion. Between June 16 and July 23 its various units engaged the Confederates in skirmishes at Hancock, Greencastle, Shippensburg, Harpers Ferry, Cashtown, Carlisle, Kingston, Keedysville, McConnellsburg, Bendersville, Falling Waters, Cranston, Frederick, Cunningham's Cross Roads (Cearfoss), Waynesboro, Waterloo, Williamsport, Sharpsburg, and Martinsburg. This list shows the Lincoln Cavalry to have been in running battles with enemy units during the invasion and along the line of retreat from Gettysburg.

Throughout the time these cavalrymen were in the Greencastle area they suffered other casualties beyond the killing of Rihl and wounding of Cafferty. On July 3 Gustav Suthermeister was captured in the town and two days later, in skirmishes along the Williamsport turnpike, John Schmidt and Alexander McMillian were killed. Schmidt lost his life in an engagement near the Mason-Dixon line while McMillian was shot at Cunningham's Crossroads.

The Lincoln Cavalry fought through the remainder of the conflict, in the Shenandoah Valley and the mountain country of western Virginia. It took part in the defeat of McCausland's forces after the burning of Chambersburg and the battles that eventually led to Federal control of the Valley. As the war came to an end the regiment was at Appomattox Court House when General Lee surrendered to Ulysses S. Grant, April 9, 1865. [27]

After losing Rihl and Cafferty, Boyd returned to Chambersburg and told General Knipe of the encounter near Greencastle. He informed the commanding officer that the Rebel force was of at least division strength but he had no way of knowing whether it was advancing. Knipe immediately sent additional men to the south of Chambersburg while he and his staff ventured down the road towards Marion to study the terrain of that area. During this reconnaisance, A. J. Schaff of Chambersburg, was stopped as he came from Greencastle. Knipe learned that he had seen the skirmish at Flemings. When asked if other roads could be used by the enemy to advance on Chambersburg, Schaff told the general of the Warm Spring and Grindstone Hill roads that might easily be used. Knipe immediately saw that he was in an untenable position.

Upon returning to the county seat the general gave orders to abandon the town. Chaos followed as Chambersburg's protectors rushed to the rail station, leaving cannon, other weapons, tents, clothing, and rations where they had been camping. There was little order in the evacuation, but home guard units did salvage some of the cannons and put them on cars before the train left for Carlisle.

Several hundred men received their orders too late. They became lost in the streets of Chambersburg and upon arriving at the station found no train. On foot these soldiers got to Scotland but the train had passed on to Shippensburg. They resumed their march to that town, arriving at two o'clock in the morning. Still there was no train, but by commandeering wagons, buggies, and carts, the totally exhausted men finally got to Carlisle. The company of invalids was left stranded in Chambersburg. Knipe had neglected to see to their transportation, but they eventually found safety in York.

Knipe's force was the last military group to use the railroad during the invasion period. By June 30, the shops in Chambersburg were totally demolished and the tracks from Chambersburg to the north as far as Scotland and south to Marion were completely destroyed. Piles of cross ties, telegraph poles, and fence rails were set afire. The rails were then placed on the fires and when red hot they were twisted or bent so as to make them totally unusable.

Jacob Hoke reported that after the departure of Knipe's army the camp site was quickly visited by certain elements of the local citizenry — "Many persons went to the abandoned camp and helped themselves to what they pleased of clothing and other articles. The next morning some of the citizens went out . . . and brought in tents and other things which yet remained, among which were sardines and other delicacies rather suited to a sociable picnic than the stern realities of war."

The only heroes of this experience seem to have been the home guard members who salvaged the cannon left behind and a conscientious citizen, Abram Metz. This gentleman loaded his one horse wagon with "pantaloons, blouses, blankets, buckets, camp kettles, pistols, etc., which he hauled down to Shippensburg where the train was lying over, and delivered them to their panic stricken owners." Mr. Metz's reward came as he returned to Chambersburg. Along the way he ran into a Confederate advance party which relieved him of his horse. [28]

On the day Rihl was killed Charles Hartman became involved with members of Rodes's division when he and other prominent Greencastle men were forced to help capture Negroes. While he was forced into this unhappy task other members of town council were being held as hostages. At the time G. H. Davison was chief burgess while the other councilmen were Jeremiah Detrick, W. W. Fleming, John Wilhelm, and A. K. Weir.

Hartman's diary of June 22 contains the following account — "One of the exciting features of the day was the scouring of the fields about town and searching of houses for negroes. These poor creatures, those of them who had not fled upon the approach of the foe, concealed in wheat fields about the town. Cavalrymen rode in search of them and many of them were caught after a desperate chase and being fired at. In some cases the negroes were rescued from the guards. Squire Kaufman and Tom Pauling did this and if they had been caught the rebels would have killed them. I was one of the town council. We were marched all day in the hot sun and dusty roads through the town and country. Heavy demands made upon us for salt, meat, onions and such. Also bridles and saddles, harness. The town council was held till their demands complied with. This was the hardest day in all my life. I never was the same strong man afterwards. I was marched till I was worn out. Andrew Stiffel they gave an old nag to ride, but then Dr. J. K. Davison, Wesley Rhodes and myself told the officers that they had the wrong man. This was an innocent citizen, a tanner by trade. They were after Sam Stickel, the man that had interfered with their wagons. They told Stiffel to rest on my porch at the pump awhile. They mounted their horses again and left without him. They would have taken him to Richmond prison if we would not plead for him." [29]

During the remaining hours of the day Rodes's division continued passing through the town. Among the infantry was the 53rd North Carolina Regiment. As these men marched along Carlisle Street a Private Leon recorded several observations — "The people seemed downhearted, and showed their hatred to us by their glum looks and silence, and I am willing to swear that no prayers will be offered in this town for us poor, ragged rebels."

Another "Tar heel" said that he was impressed with the fat lands and magnificent barns, but missed his favorite home landscape. He wrote, "Their quantity of land is so limited, that they haven't the woodland to spare for groves, but have a small yard without trees." This observation reflects the frugal life found among the area's town and farm people. Land was not wasted. As much soil as possible was used for crop production and their homes would never match the plantation type homes of the South. Long driveways, through groves of ancient trees, leading to spacious mansions, were few and far between in Pennsylvania's Cumberland Valley. [30]

A Negro servant's conversation with a local farm wife was also recorded. She suggested that he run away from the officer he served and stay in Pennsylvania as a free man. "Are you treated well?" she asked. "I live as I wish," was the slave's courteous and prompt reply. "And if I did not, I think I couldn't better myself by stopping here. This is a beautiful country, but it doesn't come up to home in my eyes." [31]

Many commissioned officers had body servants who looked after their personal needs. Such an attendant cooked, mended and laundered clothes, and maintained clean and orderly quarters for his master. After battles he would search the area if he failed to return. If he found him wounded he would bind up his wounds or if killed, bury him and mark the grave when the battle was far from home. Such slaves possessed a loyalty not seen among the blacks who fled into Pennsylvania prior to and during the war. Their lives had not known such a style of living.

When Rodes arrived in Greencastle he made his headquarters at the J. S. Loose home east of town. It was located along the turnpike to Waynesboro where the Grindstone Hill road joined the toll road. Part of the division camped in fields of the Loose farm. Upon his arrival Rodes appointed Colonel Edward Willis of the 12th Georgia Regiment to act as provost marshall. Willis was given a detachment to maintain order. "The Pilot's" editor said, "To the guards from this regiment and to the officers and men credit must be given for the good order maintained." [32]

General Rodes wrote — "At Greencastle the orders of General Lee regulating the conduct of troops and officers of all departments whilst in the enemy's country were received, but they had, in substance, been anticipated by orders, first from division and then from corps headquarters. The conduct of the troops of this division was entirely in accordance with those orders, and challenged the admiration of their commanding officers, whilst it astonished the people along the line of march. These latter, very generally, expected to be treated by us with the wanton cruelty generally exhibited by their troops when they are upon our soil. As a general rule, they apparently expected to see their homes burned down, and all their property carried off or destroyed." [33]

Rodes was referring to Lee's orders to treat civilians humanely. Prior to issuing them, Lee had told General Issac Trimble, a Marylander, that he "had received letters from many prominent men in the South urging retaliatory acts while in the enemy's country, on property etc. for ravages and destruction on Southern homes." Lee then asked Trimble, "What do you think should be our treatment of people in Pennsylvania?" Trimble replied "General, I haver never thought wanton destruction of property of noncombatants in an enemy's country advanced any cause...our aims are higher than to make war on defenseless citizens or women and children." General Lee replied - "These are my own views, I cannot hope that heaven will prosper our cause when we are violating its laws. I shall, therefore, carry on the war in Pennsylvania without offending the sanction of a high civilization and of Christianity." [34]

On the night of June 22 Rodes received a message to report to General Ewell's headquarters at Beaver Creek, located between Boonsboro and Hagerstown. Here he met with his commanding officer and General Jubal Early. The divisions headed by General Edward Johnson and Early had finally reached Ewell and a major part of Lee's army was now ready for its thrust into Pennsylvania. Ewell, along with Rodes, came to Greencastle the next day. Again a search for supplies began and orders were repeated that everything was to be paid for with Confederate money or receipts given to guarantee future payment. Major J. A. Harmon, the Commissary and Quartermaster with Rodes, demanded Greencastle's authorities to collect the following articles: 100 saddles, 100 bridles, and twelve pistols. The order was to be met by two o'clock that afternoon. [35]

ALEXANDER COLLECTION
WILLIAM DETRICK,
A CHILD WHO WITNESSED
THE INVASION

This was followed by another requisition for onions, sauerkraut, potatoes, radishes, and other food items. If the demand was not met within a given time houses would be searched and stripped of all provisions. Greencastle's major response was in the onion category. The people came from all directions with buckets, bags, and baskets filled with onions. They wanted onions. They got onions. Since the new crop had not been harvested it must be assumed that the generosity of the townspeople was prompted by practical reasons. They simply cleaned out old onions to ready their bins for those due in August. Whenever food was requisitioned the Confedertes constantly asked for onions and sauerkraut. It was explained that both were antiscorbotics and were made part of the men's diet to prevent scurvy. [36]

Another levy required the delivery of 2,000 pounds of lead, 1,000 pounds of leather, 100 pistols, twelve boxes of tin, and 200 curry combs and brushes. The Chief of the Topographical Engineers, Jedidiah Hotchkiss, also demanded two Franklin County maps. [37]

These demands were so heavy that the borough's council found, with the exception of onions, them impossible to meet and made little or no effort to satisfy them. However, on their own, the Rebels did secure some saddles, bridles and a considerable amount of leather which they removed from Andrew Stiffel's tannery. The local paper estimated Stiffel's loss to have been $2,000. George W. Ziegler's general store yielded assorted items including curry combs, bolts of webbing, gun leggings, lanterns, saddle nails, draw chains, buckles, rivets, screws, handsaws, paddocks, butcher knives, hog and sheep skins, frying pans, locks, axles, brace kits, nails, hinges, and scythes. The value of this collections was $342.52. With a receipt, an order guaranteeing future payment, the merchandise was hauled away. Undertakers General David Detrich and his brother, Jeremiah, by the nature of their profession were expert wood workers. Accordingly they were ordered to make a field desk for the Adjutant General of the division. [38]

Soldiers tried to buy food and meals from farm and town families. Private Leon of the 53rd North Carolina commented on this problem. "Tom Tiotter and myself went out to buy something to eat, but when we came to a house, they would close their doors in our faces, or let us knock and not open. We got the ear of one or two ladies, and after proving to them that we were not wild animals nor thieves, they gave us what we wanted, but would not take pay for anything."[39]

Leon was a private but when it came to officers, they were treated differently. Hotchkiss, the topographic engineer, wrote in his diary, "The people were much surprised to see us, but manifested no hostility - quietly submitting to our rules. The day was quite pleasant. Judge Wilson and several others of us dined at a Pennsylvania House." There is no identification of the family who was host to the Southern gentlemen, but his diary indicates this happened while in Greencastle. His benefactors could have lived in the town or on one of the nearby farms. [40]

During the afternoon of June 23, part of Rodes's division advanced towards Chambersburg and camped overnight near Marion. As their men marched up the Harrisburg Pike some of them visited the home of Jacob and Elizabeth Grove along the road in the Kesecker Mill area. After eating all of Mrs. Grove's bread they ransacked the cellar but found nothing to their tastes. In retaliation they emptied their vinegar barrels and crocks of curdled milk. Later in the day a contingent unlimbered cannon to engage Union soldiers seen, from a distance, on the Grove farm. Fortunately for the family there was no battle. The Rebels had mistaken fifteen year old Benjamin and Jacob, aged twelve, sons of the Groves, for Federals. The boys were wearing blue shirts and trousers as they worked near the barn. [41]

Further along the road another farmer, Henry Hege, told of the continuous stream of men passing his home. "...they commenced passing early, and passed all day - regiment after regiment - one wagon after another. A great many came to our house for something to eat...We had our house locked all the time and when they wanted bread, we gave it out at the door and locked it again. Some of the Rebels got cross on our hands and wanted to break our house open, but we talked kind to them, and I passed some jokes with them and all was right." [42]

Officers were not too concerned about their men approaching civilians for food but in parts of Antrim some homeowners, who were reluctant to share their food, had few qualms about giving whiskey or hard cider to the soldiers. Although saloons were closed and the sale of alcoholic beverages prohibited by Confederate authorities, it was impossible to control dispensing liquor by individuals.

To this day descendants of Robert Johnston, whose distillery was two miles south of Greencastle along the Williamsport Turnpike, tell how Johnston's whiskey helped bring defeat to the Confederates at Gettysburg. Since the people of Antrim and Greencastle were partial to Johnston liquor this was the brand they gave to the invaders and their excessive imbibing caused hangovers which made too many Rebel soldiers incapable of functioning properly when they arrived at the battlefield. This exaggerated claim was made in jest after the invasion by Robert Johnston, but it remains as part of the family folklore even unto the third and fourth generations.

People living in the invasion's path were beginning to see, on a more intimate basis, the Southern soldier. Before this time, men on horseback, combing the countryside and towns for horses, cattle, Negroes, animal feed, flour, harness, store merchandise, and other items were coming and going. Now the stream of infantry, artillery, and horse drawn wagons seemed to be unending. Men dropping out of the line of march and going to homes for food and other contraband was a common practice. Town and country people were now talking to the invaders and incident after incident disclosed reactions from both the invaders and the local residents - some friendly and others quite the opposite.

Taking chickens, geese, ducks, pigs, smoke house delicacies, honey, butter, cheese, and other edibles was common. Stripping cherry trees, filled with many ripened varieties, was the cause of much dismay and anger on the part of housewives who had planned to can or preserve this fruit. One Confederate wrote home that the reaction of housewives upon seeing their trees picked clean, was often quite vituperative. Colonel Clement A. Evans wrote in his diary of the "rough and profane language of the Pennsylvania belles." He suggested that, prior to coming into Pennsylvania, he never knew women could swear as proficiently as men. [43]

Another kind of pilfering produced a scarcity of men's hats for some time after the invasion. Many Rebel soldiers had headgear that had seen better days. Hats with broken rims, filled with holes, and in general disarray were constantly being exchanged for those worn by men along the line of march. The soldiers would dart from their ranks, remove a gentlemen's hat, and leave theirs in exchange.

Henry Strickler, of Greencastle, who had lost his left arm at Fredericksburg had been discharged from the Findlay Hospital in Washington on April 27, just two months before the invasion. His home was on North Carlisle Street and while standing along the curb during the passage of one regiment he was approached by a Confederate staring fondly at his new hat. Quickly Strickler removed it and firmly told the soldier, "You took my arm at Fredericksburg, but I'll be damned if you'll take my hat." Seeing his empty coat sleeve the Southerner stepped back into the line of march, and without answering continued towards his fate at Gettysburg. [44]

After a search for more horses in the Chambersburg area, detachments of Jenkins's cavalry returned to Greencastle with animals to be sent to the rear for the oncoming army. These men were sorely in need of rest. They had been in the Valley for over a week with little respite from their labors and that day their work had been more hazardous than usual. They were attacked several times in the Caledonia area. Mountain men in this region had hastily organized gangs to take pot shots at the enemy and then retreat into the heavy forests where they could hide, but when the Confederates appeared in greater numbers this kind of "bushwacking" eventually ended. [45]

As Rodes's men moved out of Greencastle they were followed by the division led by General Edward Johnson. As these men passed through the borough, townspeople saw Stewart's Brigade which included the 1st Maryland Battalion. Some local citizens may have remembered that when the war started this was a unit organized by Bradley Johnson, a prominent lawyer from Frederick. The division also contained hundreds of men who spoke a strange language. It was a foreign tongue, and as they passed along Carlisle Street their talk made no sense to the people on the sidewalks. These were soldiers from the colorful Nicholls Louisiana Brigade consisting of Creole and Cajun fighters speaking a dialectic mixture of French and Spanish.

Johnson's troops also contained the noted Stonewall Brigade - soldiers who had been with Thomas Jackson, under his direct command or as part of larger units he led, until his death at Chancellorsville. The brigade was composed of men from the Shenandoah, many with family bloodlines running back into the very valley they were now invading. A review of this unit's rolls showed the majority were farmers and skilled craftsmen or merchants. Nine percent were college graduates, some having attended institutions in Pennsylvania. [46]

At the time Rodes and Johnson were marching through Greencastle, Jubel Early's division had moved out of Maryland along roads leading to Waynesboro, and by way of Quincy to the Philadelphia Turnpike in the vicinity of Greenwood. This screening movement along South Mountain was designed to protect the main body of Confederates from Federal attack.

Ewell ordered Early to proceed to Gettysburg and York to destroy the Northern Central Railroad and the Wrightsville Bridge which spanned the Susquehanna. This expedition proved to be a very profitable venture. At Caledonia the Rebels destroyed an iron works owned by Thaddeus Stevens; at Gettysburg they discovered a shoe factory; and at York they found a town ready to surrender and provide them with supplies (*165 barrels of flour or 28,000 pounds of bread, 3,500 pounds of sugar, 1,200 pounds of salt, 1,650 pounds of coffee, 300 gallons of molasses, 21,000 pounds of bacon or pork, or 32,000 pounds of fresh beef, plus 28,000 in United States currency;*) after obtaining supplies at York, the Rebels found that the state militia had destroyed the Wrightsville Bridge by setting it afire. While all of this was taking place, events were happening which forced Ewell to recall Early. Lee's army might be running into trouble and Early was ordered to rejoin Ewell at Carlisle.

On the invading army's western flank General George H. Steuart moved his brigade (*June 24th*) along the ranges of the North Mountain. Although his territory was not as populous as that of Jubal Early's, Steuart's men made raids on Mercersburg where hams, bacon, molasses, flor, and sugar were "purchased." Crossing the mountain at Cove Gap the Confederates ran into home guard units which opposed them ineffectively. While in the McConnellsburg area, foraging resulted in taking more horses and cattle back to the main army. Moving on to Chambersburg by way of Fort Loudon two stragglers from the brigade were killed by civilians. [47]

Samuel Firebaugh, one of Steuart's men, had not been impressed with Greencastle. He described it as a "pretty hard looking place" as opposed to Mercersburg which he pictured "as a very pretty place." Firebaugh was delighted with Fulton County where he "got plenty of apple butter and butter to eat." [48]

For two days the main body of Ewell's Corps continued to pass through Greencastle and Antrim. To accommodate this enormous amount of traffic, engineers dismantled fences along the roads to allow the infantry to walk along the edges of the fields while cavalry, wagons, caissons, artillery, and staff officers used the roadways. Fence posts and rails were piled at convenient places to provide fuel for camp fires and cooking.

Richard S. Ewell was no stranger to the Commonwealth. After graduation from West Point he worked as a civil engineer for the Columbia Railroad of Pennsylvania and prior to the war he was stationed at the Carlisle Barracks for a time. He had lost a leg at the Second Battle of Manassas, but upon his recovery, continued to serve. When accompanying his troops he either rode in a carriage or on horseback secured by straps to his mount. He was a close friend of General Jackson and was now in command of many of the men who had fought with Stonewall. Nicknamed "Old Baldy" he was nervous, eccentric, and a confirmed agnostic. However, his association with Jackson was said to have changed his views on religion and turned him to the Christian faith.

Ewell's forces continued moving through the Antrim and Greencastle area as late as June 25. Jed Hotchkiss, in a letter to his wife, said, "We started from Greencastle at an early hour and went to Chambersburg." Then he listed all the store items he purchased there for his wife and with confidence he ended his letter - "I hope to get home in due time if we stop short of New York." Greencastle's editor noted that when Ewell passed through the town on June 24 he was "seated in a carriage closely examining a map. He appeared pale and delicate." [49]

On the morning of June 24 General Ewell entered Chamberburg. Setting up headquarters at the Franklin Hotel, he issued orders prohibiting the sale of liquor and requisitioning mattesses to be used at a hospital to be located at the King Street school. He also met with his staff to advise them about further requisitions and troop movements for the next several days. Later Ewell continued his journey northward, following the divisions that had preceded him. By June 27 he was in Carlisle. He and his officers visited old friends they had known when stationed at the Barracks. The commanding general took extra precautions to see that no damage came to Dickinson College. On Sunday, June 28, two worship services were held at the Barracks. Other services were conducted by chaplains of the various units camped about the town. A committee of ministers called on

Ewell to ask if he objected to including the usual prayer for the President of the United States. "Certainly not" retorted the commander, "Pray for him. I'm sure he needs it." [50]

About the time Ewell arrived in Carlisle, James Longstreet's Corps was crossing the Potomac. Over the next several days his divisions moved through Maryland and into Pennsylvania. With Longstreet was General Robert E. Lee and as he and his officers rode through Middleburg they were greeted warmly by some of its residents. At the David and Mary Martin farm, just north of the village, Lee stopped to quench his thirst at a wooden pump which stood in the Martin's front yard. Alice, a five year old daughter, was given the honor of pumping water for the commanding general. *(This pump still stands along Route 11.)* Although not documented, local tradition holds that Lee camped at the Dunkard Church in the Bushtown area for a time. This was located about two miles north of Middleburg.

BESORE COLLECTION
MARTIN FARM PUMP
by MICHAEL CONRAD

The first of Longstreet's Corps entered Greencastle just as the last of the II Corps was leaving. This was a division led by a romantic looking officer who wore his black hair in perfumed ringlets. His name was George E. Pickett, a medium sized man, dressed in a well fitting uniform and carrying an elegant riding whip as he rode with his men up North Carlisle Street. When Pickett's men reached the house of James Harris *(where the Citizens Bank now stands)* Dolly, his teenage daughter, came to the front porch and waved an American flag at the Confederates while calling them traitors. Pickett rose in his stirrups, lifted his hat in a salute to the girl and the men laughingly followed their commander in this act of Southern chivalry. Dolly, when faced with such gallantry, called to the passing soldiers that if she had a Confederate flag she would wave it too. As Pickett and his men passed on, the drama of this incident was enhanced by the division's band playing "Dixie" when it marched by the Harris home. Greencastle now had its own version of what would be called, at a later time, the "Barbara Fritchie" legend. [51] *(See Appendix IV)*

During the next several days thousands of Confederates would march through Greencastle. Their camps occupied many of the areas where Union troops camped in 1861 and 1862. The Williamsport Turnpike was the main avenue most of the regiments used. Compared to the Hagerstown Pike it was not as dusty in dry weather nor as muddy when it rained and during this time there was an over abundance of rain.

As Kershaw's Brigade of Longstreet's Corps crossed the state line, some members of one of the "plain sects" apparently thought, since all recent Northern military efforts had failed to stop the Rebels, they would prevail upon "divine intervention." The historian of this South Carolina brigade described the incident - "In passing through Pennsylania, many curious characters were found among the quaint old Quaker settlers, who viewed the army of Lee not with 'fear' or 'trembling' but more in wonder and Christian abhorrence. When the front of the column came to the line dividing Pennsylvania and Maryland, it was met by a delegation of those rigorously righteous old Quakers who, stepping in the middle of the road, commanded as in the name of God, 'So far thou canst go, but no farther.' After performing this seemingly command of God in accordance with their faith, a total abhorrence to war and bloodshed, they returned to their homes perfectly satisfied. It is needless to say the commander of Lee's 2nd Corps paid little heed to the command of the pious Quakers." Since there was none living in the area, the historian must have mistaken Mennonites or Dunkards for members of this sect. [52]

By June 26 Greencastle and its nearby rural areas were filled to overflowing with enemy troops. There were camps south of the town along both the Hagerstown and Williamsport roads. They were camped at Rankins Mill, along the Harrisburg Pike, and at Moss Spring. To the east the Loose, Stover, and Shook farms also were used..

General A. P. Hill led part of his Corps through the town in an early morning rain, which, at times, came down in torrents. As this contingent marched along Carlisle Street few spectators were on the sidewalks. They did, however, continue observing, from doorways and windows, the lines of drenched soldiers. Yet, no one recognized General Lee as he and his staff passed through. The local newspaper makes no reference to the leader of the invasion. Because the commanding general had no reason to linger in Greencastle during a continuing downpour he came and left without fanfare. One soldier did describe Lee, "when on a march, to have the appearance of an old plain farmer." On June 26 Robert E. Lee was probably dressed in all the rain gear at his disposal thus making him more unrecognizable. [53]

By ten o'clock General Lee was in Chambersburg. The rain was less intense by then for he was easily recognized by Jacob Hoke and some of his associates. When the commander entered the public square he was met by General Hill. The two rode a short distance from their staffs and after a brief conference, Lee and his officers went out the turnpike toward Gettysburg. Hoke noted that a large part of Hill's division had already headed east and now Lee was going in that direction. This apparent change in troop movement could mean that Baltimore and Washington were now threatened. Since the telegraph lines to Harrisburg had been destroyed, Jacob Hoke and other Chambersburg leaders had been secretly sending important news to the capital by men who volunteered for this duty. One of these messengers was Benjanin S. Huber. He was assigned to take the information concerning this change of Confederate plans. On foot and later on horseback, Huber make his way to Roxbury, then across the mountains into Perry County. At Newport he caught a passenger train of the Pennsylvania Line to Harrisburg. Upon arriving in the capital at three o'clock on the morning of Saturday, June 27, Huber met Colonel D. Watson Rowe of Greencastle. When he told Rowe his message, the Colonel conducted him to the capital where his information was given to Governor Curtin and General Couch. By noon this vital pieces of intelligence was known to military authorities in Washington. [54]

Meanwhile Confederate troops kept swarming into southern Pennsylvania. Letters and diaries tell of the soldiers' reactions. One officer of the 2nd Virginia Cavalry recorded - "I crossed Mason's and Dixon's Line today and am now some five or six miles within the boundaries of the Keystone State, surrounded by enemies and black looks, Dutchmen, and big barns." [55]

As the remainder of Pickett's division entered the state on the 26th one of his men described the Middleburg area — "We passed the line — this afternoon near a small village named *Middletown* on the maps but called Muttontown by the natives - though for what reason I could not ascertain. It is easy to see however, that Muttontown is altogether appropriate for the demeanor of many of the inhabitants is sheepish in the extreme!" His observations continued, "Strange to say we met with a more marked exhibition of welcome at this Pennsylvania town than in any portion of Maryland. I saw fully a dozen miniature Confederate flags waving from windows, while all along the streets were ladies waving handkerchiefs and scarfs from the piazzas and upper windows! Can it be that these people are sincere? Or, are these demonstrations merely a part of Dutch cunning to placate the oft-pictured, wild, cantankerous, ravenous Reb of whom so many lies are told that simple people believe him a monster of cruelty? Possibly tho', these are Democratic families that have been persecuted and harassed by their abolition neighbors until they really welcome the advent of our army as a relief. Of course, we have little knowledge of the real feelings of the people." [56]

On the afternoon of the 27th, as the last of Pickett's soldiers left town, Major Horace W. Jones, the Division's Quartermaster, called on George W. Ziegler's store to purchase eighty-two gallons of molasses at sixty-five cents a gallon and a barrel of mackerel for ten dollars. Jones, for the moment, lost track of his geographic bearings. When writing out the receipt for the purchase he wrote Greencastle, Md., but upon remembering where he was he simply scratched out "Md." and substituted "Pa." The quartermaster noted on the receipt that Ziegler had refused the Confederate money offered in payment. Upon realizing the merchant's apparent generosity, he then "purchased" a dozen bottles of writing fluid. [57]

One of the men of the division wrote of the curious and timid way the people of Greencastle looked at the Rebels as they passed through the town. "Here and there a group would surround some tall, gaunt, sunburnt Georgian, Texan, or Misissippian whose slouched hat and butternut covered shoulders were fully 'head and shoulders' taller than the amazed citizens, who would swaller with avidity the Confederates' mighty yarns about the 'two hundred and twenty-six thousand more of us coming on behind.' " [58]

Actually the size of Lee's army that passed through Greencastle was more like 50,000. Although the total number of Confederates in the invasion, numbered over 70,000, most of the cavalry was to the east of the South Mountains. Early's Division and part of Hill's Corps came through Franklin County by way of Waynesboro. Aside from the numbers of soldiers, hundreds of horse drawn wagons, over two hundred cannons, and other equipment moved through the town. To pull all of these vehicles, four and six horse teams were generally used. Several thousand horses passed through Antrim and Greencastle.

On Friday, June 26, through sporadic rains, Longstreet's Artillery Reserve inched its way through Greencastle. With caissons and wagons accompanying the guns they marched out the Brown's Mill road into the fields northeast of the town. This artillery, which would lay down the barrage before Pickett's charge at Gettysburg, camped at Moss Spring. One of these Batteries was the Washington Artillery of New Orleans. Lieutenant William M. Owen, an officer in this unit, upon entering Antrim, made this observation - "On the 26th we marched, in a drizzling rain, to Hagerstown and on to Greencastle, Pa. The farmers apparently did not know a war was going on. General Lee's orders are positive against any appropriation of private property, even chickens, milk and butter were sacred. (*Note: This latecomer would soon learn how sacred this order had been to those who had preceded him.*) Sergeant Ellis was detected by the officer of the day with a pair of fat geese; but he convinced the lieutenant that it was 'all on the square,' and that he had paid for them; we believe the officer dined with him that day. We established headquarters for the night at a very fine farmhouse, and were well entertained by the hospitable occupants, man and wife. The couple were German, and were employed at one hundred dollars a year to attend to the farm in the absence of the owners. Upon taking leave of our hosts in the morning we handed them two silver half-dollar pieces, which they received with expressions of surprise and delight. Hans said, 'Johanna, put dis silber mit der due-bit piece dot you got last Christmas. Py jimminy, dis war is big luck for some peebles!' "[59]

Some Rebel soldiers would find a measure of congeniality among the Pennsylvania Dutch if they were able to "Sprechen sie Deutsch." These were the Southerners of German orgin. Some were descendants of early settlers in the Shenandoah country and the Carolinas, while others were German immigrants of recent years. Names like Bonebrake, Burkheimer, Eshleman, Eckhardt, Heefner, Schmidt, Schnader, Wingert, etc., were often found on rosters of Confederate regiments. The commander of the Washington Artillery was Major B. F. Eshleman. One North Carolinian who came from a Moravian settlement in his state made friends with a German speaking lady in Greencastle. They found something in common when speaking Deutsch and he later told of the good food they shared during the visit. [60]

All through Friday and through Sunday, (*June 27 and 28*), the rains continued as Longstreet's Corps kept marching through Greencastle and at night the countryside was lit up with their camp fires. "The Pilot" described the corps as the "largest and most destructive set of men" that came through the community during the entire invasion. Hood's Texas Brigade came upon several barrels of whiskey after crossing the Potomac. It had been found near Hagerstown and brought to Williamsport where, upon emerging from the river, each man was given a gill of liquor. Those who did not imbibe gave their portions to others who professed to have no qualms about such matters. Within thirty minutes half of the outfit was thoroughly intoxicated. John Stevens, who remained sober, said that he saw more fellow Texans drunk in Williamsport than he ever saw in his entire life. "They were drunk all over - through and through, up and down, side, edge, and bottom, fore and aft, sideways and edgeways... He never had heard such cussing and swearing, laughing, crying, or yelling. The sober boys were kept busy keeping the drunks from killing each other and when many finally "passed out" they were dumped into wagons or ambulances and hauled toward Pennsylvania through the rest of the day. Some became lost, many not seen for as long as fifteen hours. When these 'hungover' stragglers later reached their commands, Stevens wrote,..."they were quite sober, but their eyes looked like two burnt holes in a blanket." J. M. Polk, of the 4th Texas, vowed, "I don't suppose the oldest man living in America ever saw as many men drunk at any one time." However, regardless of their condition the brigade finally got into Pennsylvania. In later years, veterans of this outfit bragged of a feat never performed by any other fighting unit during the war. "They had breakfast in Virginia, lunch in the state of Maryland, supper in Pennsylvania, and slept that night in the state of intoxication."[61]

Hood's Division went into camp just south of Greencastle on the evening of June 26th, and Company K of the 5th Texas was detailed to guard General Hood's Headquarters. Hood and his staff pitched their tents and parked their wagons in the front yard of a "palatial" home a short distance from town. Numerous outbuildings and well-tended gardens and orchards surrounded the mansion. Hood personally addressed the company when it reported to him for duty. "Boys, you are now on enemy's soil; stack your arms and do pretty much as you please...stay close by and prevent any stranger from coming here to kill me, and establish your camp here by my tent." That was all the encouragement the Texans needed. Hastily stacking arms as ordered, the company scattered in all directions over-running the summer kitchen, smoke house, spring house, garden, and poultry yards. Private John Stevens claimed that within five minutes of stacking their weapons, the spring house, the gardens and the poultry yard were, "as empty as last year's bird nest." The abundant yield from the spring house included a tub of fresh hog meat, ten to fifteen pounds of butter and ten to fifteen gallons of milk. From the garden which had just reached its prime growth, not a single thing was left "that could be eaten, cooked or raw." Nearly 300 chickens, ducks, and turkeys were gathered from the poultry yards.

The chickens and other fowl made such a loud commotion, with their cackling that the lady of the house, who with the arrival of Hood was now staying in one of the upper story rooms, was alerted. She pleaded with the general to call off his hungry men but to no avail. According to Private Stevens, Hood confessed that his troops were partial to chicken and reminded her that the "Yankees had killed every chicken and nearly everything else in Virginia and that the North ought to have a little teaching what war means."

The next "victims" of the men from the Lone Star State were three large, rich, bee gums. The nice sealed comb was extracted from the gums into a wash tub, bread tray and large tin pan that had been "borrowed" from the complaining matron of the house. The containers of honey were brought to the campfires where the soldiers, squatting

162

"shoe mouth deep" in feathers, were busily engaged in roasting the results of the evening's raid. After a delicious dinner of well-cooked duck, chicken, and turkey, accompanied by assorted fresh green vegetables, washed down with cool milk, and topped off with rich, golden honey, the guardians of General Hood soon drifted off to a deep sleep. Stevens readily admitted "of all the eating that you ever saw a lot of men do, I reckon we done it there that night." [62]

The next morning, June 27, with regimental bands blaring, the Texans resumed their march. They passed through Greencastle and continued toward Chambersburg. Most were impressed with the beautiful country — green hills, neatly kept orchards, grain rich fields, and fat livestock. Many of the roads were macadamized, a far cry from the dusty, deep-rutted dirt roads they had known in Virginia. They found the houses and barns were sturdily built and neatly kept. What most impressed the Texans was the condition of the barns. John Stevens wrote that the barns and farms were very neat and clean and "appeared to be models." John West, in a letter written June 29, 1863, admitted that he had "not seen a barn in the last three days that was not more substantially and carefully built and fitted out than any house, . . . in the country of Texas." The barns, he said, "were positively more tastily built than two-thirds of the houses in Waco." [63]

Another Texan, J. B. Polley, described his experiences in the Greencastle area. "Just after crossing the boundary line into Pennsylvania, I went to a farmhouse in sight of the road and inquired if the owner of it had any bacon for sale. Answered in the affirmative, I asked the price and was told 'fifteen cents a pound.' Reflecting that in Virginia the price was two dollars for the same quantity, and bacon almost impossible to buy at that, I determined to lay in a good supply. So selecting from his well-filled smoke house two sides which weighed exactly eighty pounds, and were streaked with lean and fat in exactly the right proportion to be exceedingly toothsome, I tied them together with a piece of old rope and, throwing them across the loins of my horse, handed the farmer a twenty dollar Confederate bill. 'Oh!' said he, as he took it gingerly between thumb and forefinger and eyed it as if suspicious that it were unclean, 'I can't pass this kind of money here in Pennsylvania.' 'Yes, indeed you can, my dear sir,' said I, speaking with the fervor of absolute conviction. 'Can't you see from the army passing by that we intend to take possession of this little neck of the woods? You will need our money to pay taxes and for many other purposes, and you had better begin to get hold of it.' 'But I can't change this bill, for I haven't got any of the same kind,' he whined. 'Oh! that's a small matter,' said I; 'just give me greenbacks — I ain't afraid of them.' 'I'll see what I can do,' he answered, after a moment's hesitation, and walked into the house. In less than a minute I heard the shrill voice of an angry woman scolding vigorously and, guessing that the farmer was encountering opposition that might interfere with the trade, deemed it prudent to mount my steed and be prepared for emergencies. I had scarcely settled myself in the saddle when the farmer appeared and, extending the bill toward me, said: 'Here, Mister, give me back that ar bacon and take your money — I can't make the change, for I haint got eight dollars in the house.' Fully equal to the imperative demands of the occasion, I resolved not to suffer such a pitiful trifle as eight dollars of Confederate money to spoil a good trade, and, assuming the most lordly Southern air of which I was capable, said: 'Then just keep the change, sir,' touched my weather beaten hat with the politeness of a Chesterfield and, giving free rein to my horse, soon overtook a wagon and unloaded my prize into it."

Polley told of another encounter with a local family — "An old Dunkard gave us such an early breakfast next morning that when at noon we halted before a large and elegant mansion, surrounded by beautiful grounds, we were as hungry as bears. It fell to my lot to ask for entertainment, and, dismounting, I rapped gently at the front door. Waiting a reasonable time and hearing no sound from within, I rapped again a little more vigorously than before, and after another interval of absolute quiet, a third time. Then a well preserved lady of fifty opened the door and, her face as white as a sheet, looked silently at me. Raising my hat in acknowledgement of her presence, I stated my errand. Not a word fell from her lips until she had first looked at me from head to foot and then glanced in the direction of my companions; then she said in a tremulous voice: 'You are rebels, are you not?' 'That is what you call us, madam, I suppose, but we call ourselves Confederates,' I explained. 'Orders have been published,' said she, 'prohibiting citizens from giving any aid or comfort to the Confederates.' 'I shall regret very much, Madam,' I rejoined, 'to have the orders obeyed in our particular case, for in that event we will have to ask elsewhere for food, and we are quite hungry, I assure you.' 'That alters the case,' she replied quickly, smiling for the first time, 'the Bible commands us to feed the hungry, and it is of higher authority than the orders of man. Ask your friends in — I will give you dinner.'

"To make a long story short, within half an hour, eight Confederates sat around a long table in a spacious dining room, eating huge slices of light bread, cold ham, corned beef and roast mutton, interspersed liberally with sweet pickles, jam, jelly and apple butter, drinking genuine coffee and the richest of milk, and, between sups and bites, chatting as merrily with our hostess, her three handsome daughters and an old gentleman whom the girls called Uncle John . .

"We sat there fully three hours; then Capt. Mills suggested departure, and, calling me to one side, quietly dropped a treasured five dollar gold piece into my hand, saying in a low voice: 'Here, Joe, pay for our dinner with this. They have been too kind to us to be offered Confederate money.' Turning to the hostess, I offered the coin and asked if it would satisfy her for her trouble. 'Yes, sir, it would were I willing to accept pay,' said she, drawing back rather indignantly. 'But I am not. We have heard horrible stories of the treatment we might expect from Confederates, but if all are gentlemen like yourselves, I will make them as welcome to my house and table as you have been.'" [64]

Captain W. C. Ward, in 1900, wrote of his memories of the invasion. At the time he was a private in Company G, 4th Alabama Regiment of the brigade commanded by General Evander M. Law. These Alabama troops were, also, part of Hood's division. "When the division reached a point just south of Greencastle, Pa., the men were halted and went into camp. Guns were stacked, and every preparation made for a good night. Near the bivouac there was a large spring, affording abundance of water for the weary soldiers. Many of the men went into the country foraging, returning-some, with chickens; some with honey; some, with butter and whatever else that was edible on which their hands could be laid. It was quite dark and while the spring could be found, its topography could not be well observed. A member of Company K, from Scottsboro, Ala., going to the spring with his camp kettle for water, reached out into the spring and filled his kettle; but as he was thin from light diet, in drawing the full kettle toward him, he staggered, and his cap, saturated with the dirt and perspiration of a long service, fell into the water and disappeared from his sight. He returned to the camp capless. Shortly afterwards Jack Stewart, a tall member of Company G, six feet six inches high, and of the thickness of a fishing pole, went to the same spring with his kettle to procure water. Reaching out the full length of his arm, he drew in his kettle filled with water. Returning to the bivouac, he put the ration of beef for his mess into the kettle, and left it to boil over a slow fire, while the men, tired out, dropped off to sleep. Next morning at daybreak we were aroused to hastily prepare for the onward march into the land of our enemies. As rapidly as it could be done, the boiled meat was taken from the kettles and fairly divided among each mess. As this process was going on, there was heard a guttural muttering from Jack Stewart, expressive of intense disgust and disappointment. It was: '_____ _____ _____ boys! Just look here!' All eyes were turned on Jack Stewart. The fingers of his left hand were spread out in his right. He held a forked stick, on which was suspended the well-boiled cap of Company K. The broth in the kettle was well colored with the dirt and perspiration of the cap,

165

and the mass in the kettle was disgusting. Poor Jack and his mess-mates had to go without meat."

Ward told of going through the town. "We were a joyous crowd. Marching rapidly northward, we soon entered Greencastle. Leaning over a fence that inclosed a cottage was a man with two ladies. They appeared to be absorbed looking at us; and while we were looking a man of Company K, bareheaded, his shock of hair waving in the sun-light, went rapidly up to where the man and the ladies were standing. Not a word spoke he, not a motion made he, until he was within arm's length of the man; and then, without bow or other recognition of their presence, he simply lifted the man's hat and transferred it to his own head. The last we saw of that man and his companions he was scratching his naked head and the women were laughing at him. We were a merry lot. Entering the one long street of Greencastle, we found the people not at all afraid of us, as might have been expected. John Young, a private of Company I, of Huntsville, Ala., a man so bow-legged that he took in all sides of the street, remembering the wrongs that Huntsville had suffered at the hands of the Yankees, went up to an old gentleman standing in the presence of some ladies at the foot of a stairway that ascended immediately from the street, and lifted from the gentleman's head a beautiful new felt hat, at the same time carelessly dropping his own well-worn Confederate wool covering. The old gentleman seemed dazed. Rubbing his hands through his thin hair, he realized the situation, and was overheard to say: 'I really believe that soldier has taken my hat.'

"While going through Greencastle, the fife and drum of the Forty-eighth Alabama Regiment played 'The Bonnie Blue Flag.' The doors of the houses were all closed, but there was evidence of life in the upper stories. Back in the shadow of one of the upper rooms, while the fife was screaming out, I saw a young woman singing with all her might, and with great seriousness, 'The Bonnie Blue Flag," keeping perfect time, from the motion of her lips, with the drum band."[65]

A. J. C. Fremantle, a British military observer, accompanying General Lee and his army, entered this description of Hood's Texans in his diary — "They carry less than any other troops, many of them have only got an old piece of carpet or rug as baggage, many have dis-carded their shoes in the mud, all are ragged and dirty, but full of good humor and confidence in themselves and in their general, Hood." The Englishman was with General Lafayette McLaws who headed a division from South Carolina, Georgia, and Mississippi. When this part of the army entered Greencastle, on June 28, Fremantle "found all the houses and windows shut up, the natives in their Sunday clothes, standing at their doors regarding the troops in a very unfriendly manner. I saw no straggling into the houses, nor were any of the inhabitants disturbed or annoyed by the soldiers. Sentries were placed at the doors of many of the best houses, to prevent any officer or soldier from getting in on any pretense."[66]

Despite Fremantle's observations, Rebels were still visiting homes to seek food. Mrs. Sarah Hade, who lived on North Carlisle Street, met a group of Confederates at her front door. They asked for something to eat and she agreed to feed them but informed them she had a butcher knife and would not hesitate to use it if they got rambunctious. With thanks they ate her food and left unscathed. The knife, however, was still in Mrs. Hade's hand when they said good-bye. [67]

Townspeople noticed that when McLaw's men marched through Greencastle there were twenty to thirty slaves behind each regiment. These were servants of the officers. In addition to the slaves, unarmed men carrying stretchers brought up the rear. On their hats they wore red badges, an insignia showing they were members of the ambulance corps. Along with this division rumbled over eighty supply wagons. *(It was also noted that many a Rebel wore knapsacks bearing the names Massachusetts, Vermont, New Jersey and other Union regiments to which they originally belonged.)* [68]

Upon entering the town's Diamond, McLaws was disturbed when he saw a Liberty Pole that had been erected when the war first started. Although other officers were not offended by this symbol of local patriotism, he was outraged. He ordered some of his South Carolina troops to cut it down. Perhaps his wrath had been prompted by the manner in which local women taunted his men. In a letter to his wife, McLaws wrote that the young women of the town had scoffed at his soldiers. He contrasted them unfavorably to "southern gentlemen and ladies." These troops eventually moved on and the last major body of Lee's army to pass through Greencastle was the cavalry brigade of General Fitzhugh Lee, a nephew of the commanding general. [69]

As the Army of Northern Virginia, with little opposition, moved through southern Pennsylvania, Joseph Hooker's Army of the Potomac was following a northerly route out of Virginia and through the Maryland towns of Frederick, Mechanicsville, and Emmitsburg.

Leading the army's advance into Pennsylvania was General John F. Reynolds with many regiments from the Keystone State. Another Pennsylvanian, General George G. Meade, received the unexpected responsibility of commanding these Federal forces when Joseph Hooker was relieved of his command. On June 28 Meade assumed this leadership role and within three days his men would be desperately fighting with Confederates at Gettysburg.

By Monday, June 29, the divisions of McLaws and Hood had moved to Chambersburg and on to the Fayetteville area. Longstreet's other division, led by General Pickett, was northeast of Chambersburg. Hill's Corps was in the South Mountain region — one division east of the range at Cashtown and two others between Fayetteville and Caledonia. Ewell's Corps, with the exception of Early's Division, which was returning from York, lay between Shippensburg and Carlisle. This was as close as Ewell's main force got to Harrisburg. His cavalry, under Jenkins, however, had been within four miles of the defenses along the Susquehanna.

Stuart was in the Union Mills region of Maryland, north of Westminster and General John Imboden, who had been sent into western Virginia and Pennsylvania to disrupt canal and rail routes, had moved back east through McConnellsburg. On June 29 his cavalry was in Mercersburg, getting ready to move to Chambersburg. The day before, a part of his force had been attacked in Fulton County by Federals consisting of a body of 1st New York cavalry and militiamen from Mount Union. Two Confederates were killed while thirty two were captured. [70]

By this time Robert E. Lee had ordered Ewell to start moving from Carlisle towards Gettysburg. His wagon train had been sent back to Chambersburg and headed east. Longstreet's men had cut across country to Fayetteville and were marching toward Cashtown. It was now apparent to observers in Chambersburg that Southern forces were being concentrated in the Gettysburg area. On June 30 another messenger, Stephen Pomeroy, was sent to deliver this information to Governor Curtin. Across the fields north of Chambersburg to Roxbury and then over the mountains to Path Valley, by walking and then by horseback, Pomeroy reached Port Royal. Here he was stopped by a military picket, but after explaining his mission, he was taken to a telegraph office and some time during the early morning hours of July 1 the message was sent to Harrisburg. State officials relayed the information to Washington and General Meade was notified by Secretary Stanton — "between midnight and seven o'clock the morning of July 1, that Lee had pulled his troops back from Harrisburg and Carlisle to the vicinity of Chambersburg and was apparently concentrating east of the mountains." [71]

General Lee was still in Franklin County on July 1 and from his headquarters at Greenwood he dispatched a message to Imboden. The commander was about to move on towards Gettysburg, but his instructions stressed the importance of sending all remaining forces arriving in Chambersburg to Gettysburg. To protect his rear, Lee ordered Imboden to "throw out pickets on the roads to Shippensburg, New Guilford, Chambersburg, and Greencastle . . . to turn off all persons seeking the army by the direct road from Greencastle to Greenwood. It will be necessary for you to have your men well together and always on the alert, and to pay strict attention to the safety of the trains, which are for the present placed under your charge and upon the safety of which the operations of this army depends."

When Lee wrote this message he was aware of the approaching federal forces. Accordingly, he would need complete freedom to deal with problems that lay ahead. Imboden was his insurance against any distraction from the rear. [72]

On this very day advance units of both armies ran into each other, but the main forces were still marching. Tens of thousands of young Americans were only a day or two away from the tragic destiny awaiting them at Gettysburg.

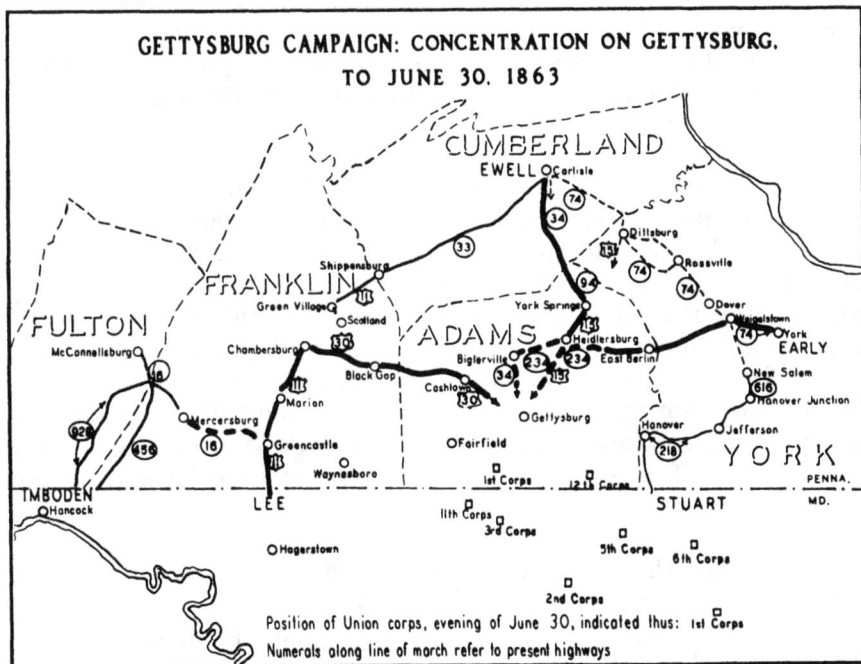

GETTYSBURG CAMPAIGN: CONCENTRATION ON GETTYSBURG. TO JUNE 30. 1863

Position of Union corps, evening of June 30, indicated thus: 1st Corps
Numerals along line of march refer to present highways

THE PENNSYLVANIA HISTORICAL AND MUSEUM COMMISSION   HARRISBURG, PA.

CHAPTER VII

ULRIC DAHLGREN

While the two armies were struggling against each other at Gettysburg the Confederate line of communication continued to run through Franklin County into Maryland and Virginia. Greencastle people frequently saw squads of Southerners going north or south — to and from General Lee and stations in the Shenandoah that had telegraph connections with Richmond. During this period a young Union cavalry officer, named Ulric Dahlgren, played an important role in the historic events taking place at that time. He was a twenty one year old Pennsylvanian who had recently joined the Union cavalry.

Ulric's father, John A. Dahlgren, an admiral, was sometimes called the "Father of Modern Naval Ordnance." He was the inventor of the Dahlgren gun, a rifled cannon used in naval warfare. Both the Merrimac and the Monitor were armed with this type of ordnance. In 1861 Dahlgren was given command of the Washington Navy Yard when its earlier head, Franklin Buchanan, defected to the Confederacy and eventually commanded the Merrimac. The admiral, in 1863, was the leader of the South Atlantic Blockading Squadron, a responsibility he held until the end of hostilities. He also was a personal friend of Lincoln.

With such paternal connections, Ulric Dahlgren had little difficulty receiving a commission when he entered the armed forces. Secretary Stanton had an above average interest in the young man and personally saw to his appointment as a captain — a somewhat higher rank than ordinarily given so young a soldier. Although his background might have suggested a safe desk job in the military establishment, young Dahlgren was set on being a cavalryman. Despite his training in both civil engineering and law, the excitement of military horsemanship appealed to him more than the engineering corps, the staff duty he had been performing since he entered the service.

Until the Civil War the cavalry had little popularity among fighting men. "Whoever heard of a dead cavalryman?" was a satiric question often asked by men of the infantry and artillery. This was their way of showing contempt for the men on horseback. In the early months of the war the Union cavalry was no match for Confederate horse soldiers. The Southerners' superior horsemanship could not be matched by "farm and city boys" on Union horses. This led to further disdain for the mounted fighters.

In 1863 this attitude began to change. Hooker's move to establish a Cavalry Corps under George Stoneman and the subsequent achievements of this command after Chancellorsville began to increase the popularity of the cavalry. Prior to this organizational change, various army commanders had fragmented the cavalry assigned to them. They were mostly used as detachments for guard and escort duties.

One of the engagements that brought increased esteem to the men on horses came on June 9, 1863. On this day Federal cavalry fought Jeb Stuart's men at Brandy Station, one of the engagements that served as a prelude to Lee's eventual invasion of the North. Although infantry were on the field of battle, Brandy Station was predominately a cavalry fight. The 1st New Jersey made six regimental charges and the 6th Pennsylvania Cavalry fought continuously for twelve hours. Names like John Buford and David Gregg were being heralded as meritorious leaders although they were cavalry officers.

There was no clear cut victory but the cavalry came out of Brandy Station with greater prestige than it had ever known. Of interest to Greencastle residents was the news that one of the officers who captured the Rebel wagon train in 1862 was killed in this battle. "Grimes" Davis lost his life while leading one of the charges against Stuart's men. He was one of nearly a thousand Union men killed, wounded or captured in the fighting. After Brandy Station fewer remarks were heard about the fighting capabilities of Federal cavalrymen and before the Civil War ended the United States Cavalry was a prestigious part of the nation's military establishment. Names like Philip Sheridan, Judson Kilpatrick, George Custer, Wesley Merritt, and Alfred Pleasonton would be well known throughout the North and South.

As the invasion of 1863 moved out of the Shenandoah and into the Cumberland Valley, Union cavalry units of General Pleasonton were following a parallel route along the eastern slopes of Blue Ridge and South Mountains. Among these was a reconnaissance party led by Ulric Dahlgren. Pleasonton had given the captain a sergeant and fifteen men. However, the squad he eventually led consisted of only ten men, with four scouts, and a Sergeant Kline. Since the sergeant was from the 3rd Indiana Cavalry it is assumed that Dahlgren's entire command came from this regiment. [1]

By July 1 Dahlgren's party had reached the Maryland village of

Funkstown. Here they met two men, James C. Moorehead and Thomas Cunningham, both veterans of the 126th Pennsylvania Infantry and native sons of the Greencastle community. As the Greencastle men saw the horsemen approaching *(Dahlgren's force was disguised in civilian clothes)* something about the orderliness of their approach caused Cunningham to say to his companion, "I'll bet five dollars they are Union men."

Dahlgren heard the remark and asked, "How can you tell Union men from rebels?" The answer from Cunningham was simple enough, — "We are Union soldiers and ought to know." There followed a conversation concerning Rebel forces and their strength in the immediate area. When Dahlgren learned that Lee's army was well beyond Hagerstown, he asked if the men could accompany his party that far. Moorehead told the captain his home was in Hagerstown but he originally came from Greencastle and that he was well acquainted with the roads of southern Pennsylvania. The young officer had never heard of Greencastle but when he learned it was in Pennsylvania he decided to venture that far.

Moorehead went with the troopers into Hagerstown to inform his family of the proposed mission and from there, by back roads, the party came to the country home of Rev. Isaac Shank northeast of Middleburg. Here they ate supper and fed their horses. Since it was still daylight, Dahlgren decided to go on. The group rode north on a narrow country lane until they came to the road that ran from Greencastle to Leitersburg. Here the horsemen turned toward Greencastle and when they reached a wooded area owned by John Detrich the captain decided this was a suitable place to camp until morning.[2]

At daylight Moorehead rode into the town to talk to friends about recent Confederate activity in the area. He learned that major troop movements had ended several days before and that only occasional squads of Rebels had been passing through the town since then. Moorehead's friends were not aware of a raid the day before in Mercersburg. John Mosby, the Confederate partisan ranger, had been there and his force of eighty men had looted a store and robbed several citizens at gun point. They also captured several free Negroes whom they took with them as they headed towards Greencastle.[3]

If Moorehead had known about Mosby, his report would not have been so eagerly accepted when he returned to the camp. Dahlgren decided to move on and having discarded their civilian dress, the men now, in their Union uniforms, rode up the road to East Street. Here they turned and continued as far as the Antrim House. Moorehead was given three men to scout the roads south of town while Dahlgren waited.

TOM PAWLINGS ANTRIM HOUSE

Within minutes the whole town knew Union troops were in Greencastle. People streamed out of houses, shops, stores, and hotels to see the blue coated cavalrymen. Not since June 15, when Boyd and his men had passed through, had they seen friendly soldiers. Cheer after cheer greeted Dahlgren and his men.

Soon Moorehead returned to tell the captain he had spotted a squad of Southerners on the Williamsport road headed toward Greencastle. He estimated the Rebels to be at least a half mile from town. Dahlgren immediately ordered all residents off the streets and placed his men in position on the Diamond. He then rode back to the Reformed Church on East Baltimore Street, climbed into its bell tower, and scanned the countryside with his spy glass to determine whether Confederates were on any other roads. There was none. *(Mosby had apparently moved back into Virginia after leaving Mercersburg).* The Union leader saw only the enemy detachment Moorehead had reported and he was confident he could surprise and capture them.

The captain gathered his little force into the southeast corner of the Diamond and waited. As the Southerners passed the Joshua Yous store, located about seventy five feet from where the Federals were waiting, Dahlgren ordered his men to round the corner. With drawn sabers and horses at full speed they charged into the oncoming Rebels who were overcome within minutes.

An eyewitness, Abraham Mupert, described the encounter. "They *(Dahlgren's men)* did not fire a shot, but some shots were fired by some rebel soldiers who were in the rear. Two bullets . . . struck the Carl house . . . and the marks are to be seen to this day."

173

Twenty-two foot soldiers and two mounted couriers were made prisoners. Two bags, containing mail, were taken to the side of the street, cut open, and the contents scattered on the sidewalk near Prather's store on the southwest corner of the Diamond near the Union Hotel. They contained letters, but nothing of military value. When the captain noticed a valise tied to a courier's saddle, and the courier's extreme nervousness, he removed it and to his surprise, found a dispatch from Richmond to General Lee.

Immediately Dahlgren and his men, along with the prisoners, left Greencastle and started toward Waynesboro. He directed several of his squad to barricade the road on the hill east of town near John Ruthrauff's home. *(The Oak's property next to the Besore Library.)* Across the highway they piled a wagon, hay ladders, and bales of straw and hay to serve as a temporary hindrance to pursuers if any came. The detachment remained until they were certain no Rebels were following. Eventually they left to join the main body near Shady Grove.

Several of the Union horsemen, along with Moorehead, were assigned to march the prisoners to Emmitsburg, while Dahlgren and the remainder of his men hurried on to Gettysburg. After the captives were turned over to proper officers, Moorehead returned to Hagers town where he continued scouting for the army in Maryland and Virginia. [4]

Captain Dahlgren arrived at Meade's headquarters near midnight. The Confederate dispatch proved to be a reply to one General Lee had sent to Richmond on June 23. At that time the Southern commander suggested to President Davis that Beauregard move his army of 30,000 men to Culpepper Court House, a strategy he thought could trick Union leaders into believing an attack on Washington was imminent. At the time Joseph Hooker's army was still in Virginia. It is apparent that Lee hoped such a move would force Hooker to defend Washington and give him greater freedom of movement as he continued to carry the invasion into Pennsylvania. With the Union forces concentrating on Beauregard the Army of Northern Virginia might then accomplish its mission.

Dahlgren had brought a vital piece of information. The captured dispatch, now in General Meade's hands, was dated June 29. Over the signature of Samuel Cooper, the Adjutant General of the Confederate States Army, Lee was informed, on behalf of President Davis, that Richmond was threatened by a Federal force of approximately 30,000 men assembled on the Peninsula. The message ended — ". . . we must look chiefly to the protection of the capital; in doing this we may be obliged to hazard something at other points. You can easily estimate our strength here and I would suggest for your consideration, whether in this state of things you might not be able to spare a portion of your force to protect your line of communication against attempted raids by the enemy." Instead of helping him, Cooper was asking Lee to help relieve the threat Richmond faced.

Meade now knew that Lee could expect no reinforcements. This was undoubtedly an important piece of intelligence and for years there were many who claimed that Dahlgren's captured message turned the tide at Gettysburg. The most persistent story claimed that Meade was about to leave the field of battle during the night of July 2 but decided to stay and continue fighting after reading the captured dispatch. It was said ". . . the General had been consulting with his corps commanders, and had resolved to withdraw his army to Pipe Creek, the position that had been previously selected by General Warren, his chief of engineers, and in pursuance of that plan was then engaged in retiring his heaviest pieces of artillery from the front. A perusal of the dispatch captured and presented by Dahlgren wrought a sudden change in Meade's plans and the artillery was quickly ordered back to the positions from which it has been withdrawn, and the Federal army made ready to recommence the battle on the following morning." [5]

Although there is no official documentation to support this story, it persisted and the importance of the captured message became exaggerated. Whether true, partially true, or false, it is a fact that Ulric Dahlgren's raid was a morale booster for the cavalry and it certainly brought joy to the people of Greencastle. One Greencastle citizen described this joy — "If a band of angels had come down, they would not have been more unexpected. I may probably add, not so welcome. It required only a few minutes to apprise the town of their presence and all Greencastle seemed to be on the street. Hats flew into the air. Cheer followed cheer. Even the old and most staid ministers, everybody was ready to bid them welcome and some wept for joy. Their leader, the gallant Dahlgren, though a mere youth, had the entire confidence of his men and handled them with ease and skill." [6]

The capture of the dispatch brought into focus the weakness of the line of communications between Lee and Richmond. Beyond failure to guard against interception of such an important message was the fact that it was not a coded communication. Colonel E. P. Alexander, who commanded a portion of Longstreet's artillery at Gettysburg, was highly critical of the way this message was sent. "How careless it is to send valuable information around without putting it in cipher." This was his criticism at a later time. Alexander, who was in Greencastle and camped at Moss Spring just the week before, was qualified to make such a judgement. Prior to the war he had helped develop the "wig wag" communications system which was used by both the Confederate and Union Signal Corps.[7]

The Confederate Adjutant General, Cooper, failed to codify this important message. There probably would be more such dispatches and with the blessings of his superiors, Dahlgren was encouraged to go out and find more. He left camp on the morning of the decisive day at Gettysburg, Friday, July 3, and hurried back to Emmitsburg where he found a brigade of cavalry led by General Wesley Merritt. The general gave him a hundred men from the 6th Pennsylvania Cavalry to continue his scouting. *(This detail came from a select volunteer regiment. Led by Richard H. Rush, it was organized in Philadelphia in 1861 and during the unit's early months of service it was trained as a lancer regiment. With the lance they were drilled to form mass charges into enemy lines, a style of combat used in European armies. Improved weaponry of the Civil War with its increased fire power made such a tactic highly impractical. Furthermore the rough, wooded terrain of parts of the nation limited this outdated style of warfare, and by the time these men were assigned to Dahlgren, the lances were no longer a part of their fighting equipment. They were, however, a specially picked detail led by a Captain Treichel.)*

In late afternoon, July 3, the troopers left Emmitsburg and got as far as Ridgeville *(Ringold, Md.)* where they established a camp for the night. During the early morning hours of the next day the command headed for Greencastle. At dawn they were approaching the town when, to the captain's surprise, he was met by a body of mounted civilians. Headed by Tom Pawling, the men were armed with shotguns and carried axes as additional weapons.

Before entering Greencastle one of Pawling's scouts came with news that Confederate cavalry were in the town. Dahlgren did not turn back and after a quick consultation with Treichel the band of soldiers and civilians charged into Greencastle. The Confederates quickly began a hasty retreat by way of South Carlisle Street and out the Williamsport Turnpike. There followed a running battle through Antrim Township with sporadic fighting in separate encounters that continued for several miles into Maryland.[8]

The most detailed story of one of these encounters comes from McHenry Howard who was part of a band of Rebels chased back into Williamsport that day. He had been in Martinsburg on July 2 and the next morning went on to Williamsport where he joined a body of men from various commands returning to join Lee's forces. Two officers, a captain and a lieutenant, were in charge of this group of thirty to forty men. Everyone was in good spirits since the word had come from the front that Lee was marching on Baltimore.

After leaving Williamsport they rode until dark and camped in a recently harvested wheat field. Before bedding down for the night a squad of Confederates hurried by, reporting they had been attacked and had lost a wagon eight or nine miles back near Greencastle. The next morning, July 4, Howard's group came within a mile of the

borough when "we heard a shot and then met a mail carrier galloping down the road, who reported that he had been attacked while passing through the town."

A party of six, including Howard, formed an advance group and went into Greencastle which "seemed sullenly quiet, doors and windows closed and nobody on the street." When they got to the square they suddenly found themselves under fire and cavalry came dashing down on them. Shots were exchanged and the sound of crashing panes could be heard as they turned and fled. The Confederates made a fast exit and hurried back to their main body. With the Union force pressing hard they retreated as fast as their horses could carry them. After running for two miles, Howard tried to rein in his mare but each time this happened bullets came "pretty thick and I let her run again." There was so much dust that the shooting was wild and after another two or three miles the Federals discontinued the pursuit.

By this time scattered members of the group had come together, but the officers had disappeared. Probably mingled with the men, they had decided to abandon the command to Howard who then took responsibility for getting to Williamsport as quickly as possible. They continued down the turnpike for about half an hour and upon reaching a rise in the road they saw Union cavalry ahead. This force had evidently taken a side road and had come onto the pike ahead of them. There were "twelve or fifteen, just in front and jogging quietly, unconscious of our approach."

Howard continued, "We immediately fired on and charged them

and after returning a few shots, they broke and ran, soon turning off the road, one after another, and scampering across the fields. Just before we charged, I had fired my pistol at a man who tumbled from his horse, but of course somebody else's bullet may have struck him. Him we picked up and put on his horse, and carried on with us and also another whom we captured." The injured man had a scalp wound which was not considered serious. The entire group eventually reached Williamsport. Howard concluded his story by saying, "So much for my twenty hours in Maryland and Pennsylvania and also for my only cavalry experience. I had fired but the one shot . . . and this was one of the only two shots I fired during the war. I should add that in this little campaign we had three men captured — at Greencastle — and one wounded, who got off." [9]

Another encounter on July 4 resulted in the death of one of Dahlgren's scouts. George Wardman had been captured by a party of Confederates three miles south of Greencastle on the toll road near the John P. Hade farm. When Wardman tendered his saber to the leader, he handed it to him point first — a flagrant violation of military courtesy and a move that could have endangered the intended recipient. In retaliation the officer shot and killed him.

The next day two soldiers of the 1st New York Cavalry were killed along this same road. They were John Schmidt and Alexander McMillian. All three bodies were brought back to Greencastle. Schmidt and McMillian were interred in the Lutheran cemetery and Wardman in the Methodist graveyard. When a school house was built on the Methodist burying grounds after the war the remains were taken to the Cedar Hill cemetery and placed in a plot reserved by the local Grand Army of the Republic Post. [10]

The local newspaper reported that when Dahlgren appeared again on July 4 he attempted to capture another mail carrier but did not succeed due to the over eagerness of one of his men. The Howard incident was described by the newspaper in this manner: " . . . about fifty of the Southern Cavalry came down South Carlisle Street, demanding to see the town authorities, but just before they reached the square, the Federal soldiers *(seventeen in number)* made a dash and drove them out in splendid style, capturing a considerable number. Though the shots whistled in close proximity to our ears, the citizens remained on the street to witness the result." [11]

It would seem that there were different groups fighting at different times throughout that day along the Williamsport turnpike. Accounts differ but records of casualties are so varied that it is impossible to establish a clear understanding of all that happened. A regimental history of the 6th Pennsylvania claims the capture of eighty four prisoners with one Union casualty. Lieutenant Morrow received a slight wound when he suffered a fall at the time his horse was shot from under him. However, the capture of so many Rebels seems to be an exaggeration when compared to the other records. Jacob Hoke reported seventeen infantrymen and seven horsemen captured and several Confederates wounded. He also said, "The Union forces . . . escaped without injury or loss."[12]

Dahlgren's own diary reveals little about the fighting. He wrote — "Saturday, July 4 — started at 2 a.m. Attacked Jenkin's cavalry in Greencastle. Whiteford captured Paymaster." When the fighting was finished, Dahlgren noted — "Passed the 4th in Greencastle. The enemy's communications entirely destroyed. Remained in the town all day, feeling proud of our work. Citizens very uneasy about our being there." Apparently, once again, local residents feared some sort of retaliation when the Confederates returned in force.[13]

The next day, through torrential rains, Lee's army was returning, but there was little time for retribution since the Southerners were hurrying to get a train of ambulances and supply wagons back into Virginia as quickly as possible. They had lost at Gettysburg.

Dahlgren and his men were still in the area, harassing the retreating Rebels at every opportunity. Later in the day they made their way toward Boonsboro. Enroute he heard that Judson Kilpatrick's cavalry was fighting another part of Lee's retreating army near Smithsburg. Early Monday morning, July 6, Dahlgren entered Boonsboro where he found Kilpatrick preparing to march toward Hagerstown. The general knew of the wagon train's route that had moved through Greencastle the day before and of the path a major part of Lee's army was following along roads south of Waynesboro. Dahlgren felt the train might be intercepted in the Hagerstown area. Along with the men who accompanied him from Greencastle plus a detachment of the 18th Pennsylvania Cavalry, led by a Captain Lindsay, they headed for Hagerstown as part of Kilpatrick's force.

Before reaching the town they ran into enemy pickets who were driven off. Kilpatrick had just made his dispositions for a full attack when he discovered he was about to face the head of an enemy force consisting of infantry, cavalry, and artillery. Discretion being the better part of valor, orders were given to recall his various detachments, but it was too late for the men with Dahlgren and Lindsay. When these two leaders and their men entered Hagerstown they rode toward Potomac Street. The main portion of the party turned to the right to move on to Center Square, but Dahlgren and Lindsay went to the left in pursuit of five Confederates. One of the Rebels taking aim at Lindsay fired and killed him. Dahlgren, with raised saber, rushed the man and cut him down. Pushing on, the Federal horsemen were soon enveloped in a shower of bullets coming from all directions. They kept firing at points where the enemy seemed to be hiding with little or no effectiveness. Dahlgren and several of his men were wounded, and some were killed. Finally the only course left was to get out as quickly as possible. A retreat was sounded and the cavalrymen left Hagerstown as fast as their horses could carry them. Beyond the town's limits Dahlgren fell from his horse. In the excitement he failed to realize the extent of his wound. A bullet had penetrated his right leg and his foot was severely mangled. The loss of blood had exhausted him. Fortunately he was still alive as men carried him to an ambulance where he stayed through the night. He had regained consciousness and his note book contained — "Foot not very painful. Slept well."

The next day he was driven to Boonsboro where a surgeon removed bone fragments from the wound. Ulric noted, "Foot easy and comfortable. Slept well." The following day he was taken to Frederick but his notes begin to show concern. Although the record said, "Foot easy, no fever," he was told "the foot had better come off."[14]

Finally the wounded Dahlgren was placed on a coach of the rail line to Washington. After dark, on July 9, his car reached the city's depot. From here he was carried by litter to his parents' home where for the first time since he was wounded he knew the luxury of a soft bed. Over the next several days friends and relatives visited the young soldier. President Lincoln called and sat with him offering words of encouragement. Secretary Stanton came along with prominent members of Congress and the military establishment. His father was not home. He was at sea with his fleet enforcing the blockade of the Confederacy.

Despite the best attention medical officers could provide, Dahlgren's foot would not heal. He was growing weaker and could no longer have visitors. His condition reached a point where all traffic in front of the house was prohibited and a soldier was placed at the front door to prevent anyone but medical personnel from entering. Finally the decision was made to amputate. The operation was a success and after three days all danger had passed. Within the next several weeks, with the help of crutches, Ulric was mobile once again. His spirits were lifted when he was shown a document signed by the President. It was a commission naming him a colonel of cavalry in the United States Army.

After the leg was amputated a decision had to be made. What was to be done with the severed limb? It could not be buried just anywhere. With the summer's intense heat it would have been indelicate to transport it to the family plot in Philadelphia. Preserving the appendage in alcohol could be an embarrassment while the rightful owner remained alive. Then an officer in the Navy Department found a solution to the problem.

Commodore Andrew A. Harwood, Superintendent of the Washington Navy Yard and an old friend of Admiral Dahlgren, provided the answer. It so happened that a gun foundry was being erected in the yard. Its cornerstone was about to be laid and like all cornerstones it contained the usual hollow compartment for depositing documents and other memorabilia as a record of the time for posterity. This opening could become the sepulcher for the detached member of Ulric's body.

There followed what could be described as an unusual, grotesque ceremony. It might even be termed a macabre rite. A black horse drawn hearse carried the "deceased" leg to the Navy Yard. The procession included a company of Marines, some sailors, while a party of officials formed a guard of honor. Amid the metallic noises and odors of the Yard, the clatter of horse drawn carts and wagons over its cobbled streets, and the constant noise of men at work, the ritual proceeded. A casket, designed to hold the leg, and swathed in black, the small coffin was placed in the cornerstone which was then sealed. At a later time a facing on the stone carried this inscription — "Within this wall is deposited the leg of Col. Ulric Dahlgren, U.S.V. Wounded July 6th, 1863, while skirmishing in the streets of Hagerstown, with the Rebels after the Battle of Gettysburgh."

Years later the facing was removed but the tomb was empty. No casket, no flag, no bones, nothing was there and no explanation has ever been found. Apparently no one was interested enough to try to find the answer to the vacant crypt. [15]

By mid February of 1864 Colonel Ulric Dahlgren was back in action. His mobility was now improved by a wooden leg strapped to the remainder of his right limb. At Brandy Station he learned of a plan to liberate Union prisoners held in the Belle Island and Libby prisons at Richmond. The raid was to be led by General Kilpatrick. Ulric approached the general with hopes of taking part in this expedition. Kilpatrick remembered his fighting spirit and assigned him to lead a body of 500 picked men to spearhead the operation, while the general led the main contingent of 3,000 horsemen supported by six pieces of artillery.

By eleven o'clock on the night of February 24 the entire force crossed the Rapidan River at Ely's Ford after driving Rebel outposts from the area. The following day, when they reached Spotsylvania, Kilpatrick headed toward Richmond with the main body, while Dahlgren took his smaller force toward Goochland, thirty miles northwest of the Confederate capital. During the evening of the day the Federal forces were deployed, the War Department at Richmond learned of the oncoming enemy. Immediately infantry and artillery units were placed to guard approaches to the city while a cavalry force, under Wade Hampton, was dispatched to intercept the invaders.

Kilpatrick's and Dahlgren's forces were scheduled to make their assaults simultaneously the following day. As Dahlgren's command moved through the Virginia countryside they left a trail of burning mills, houses, and farm buildings. Heavy rains held up the advance and the time schedule became uncoordinated. Kilpatrick approached the Richmond redoubts on March 1 on time, but the enemy was too strongly entrenched. Since the other part of his force, under Dahlgren, was not where it was supposed to be and the Confederates were giving more resistance than expected, the commanding general withdrew.

In the meantime, Dahlgren reached Goochland on March 1 and split his small force. Captain J. F. Mitchell, of the New York 2nd Cavalry, with a hundred men, was sent down the James River's north bank to dash into Richmond. Colonel Dahlgren took the remaining cavalry to a point where he expected to ford the river and move on Richmond from the south. A young Negro, Martin Robinson, serving as Dahlgren's guide, by mistake or on purpose, directed the cavalry force to a fording that was impossible to use. This created more delay and the impetuous Dahlgren, thinking the guide had betrayed him, hanged him for what he thought was an act of treachery.

That afternoon, around three o'clock, Mitchell joined Dahlgren and despite heavy resistance the Federals moved within two and a half miles of Richmond. By then it was night and they withdrew after suffering heavy losses. The night was cold, rainy, and dark. Like blind strangers in a foreign land, the group lost its way and became separated. Eventually, by morning, Mitchell got his men back to Kilpatrick but Dahlgren, with approximately a hundred cavalry, was discovered and followed by a body of Virginia cavalry led by Lieutenant James Pollard. In the King and Queen Court House area Pollard set an ambush and at about eleven o'clock on the night of March 2 Dahlgren and his troopers ran into the trap. Escape was impossible and the fight that followed ended in death for many and capture for the remainder. The young colonel was not one of the captives. A charge of buckshot hurled him from his mount and the twenty year old Dahlgren lay dead in the mud along a road leading to the court house.

There followed a controversy that was never resolved. A thirteen year old boy, William Littlepage, searching for valuables on the dead bodies, came to Dahlgren. He took his watch, some papers, and a notebook. In the papers were orders plus, what appeared to be, instructions for killing Jefferson Davis and members of his cabinet. Confederate leaders claimed them to be authentic but Federal authorities denied their authenticity, saying they had been planted on Dahlgren's body to be purposely found. Kilpatrick denied any knowledge of an assassination plot, yet General Lee agreed the instructions were genuine. If they were valid and assassination was one of the expedition's objectives then the Civil War had degenerated into absolute total warfare. His friends pointed to Dahlgren's unblemished character and his devotion to a code of civilized soldiering. Throughout the Union the official explanation was generally accepted.

ALEXANDER COLLECTION
COL. ULRIC DAHLGREN

The South saw nothing but the evil faces of Lincoln and Stanton back of a diabolic plot which could never be forgotten. Dahlgren's wooden leg was displayed in a Richmond store window for a while and later it was fitted to the leg of John Ballard, one of Mosby's Rangers. The captured papers eventually became part of the National Archives collection. [16]

During the post-war years Greencastle's people continued to see Ulric Dahlgren as their special hero. South Second Street was renamed to become Dahlgren Street. The Knights of Pythias honored him by giving his name to its local lodge and the first Grand Army of the Republic organization in the town was known as the Dahlgren Post.

As late as 1917, over fifty years after his death, William Wilhelm, Esq., of Pottsville, at an Old Home Week gathering, proposed that a monument be erected to Dahlgren's memory. He suggested the memorial be placed on Greencastle's Center Square. Mr. Wilhelm spoke for more than an hour, giving a review of the hero's life with details of his wartime exploits in the local area. At intervals during the address three poems about Dahlgren were recited by Misses Ada Phillippy, Helen Fisher, and Zourie Speilman, An account of this ceremony appeared in the August 9, 1917 edition of the "Echo Pilot" and its editor, William Patton, agreed with the idea of a monument — "Undoubtedly Col. Dahlgren's memory should be perpetuated in Greencastle in some formal way and it would be highly appropriate that this should be done through the Old Home Week organization."

The memorial was never erected. If there was an organized effort to continue such a project there is no evidence. The nation was involved in World War I and the chief community concern was directed towards the local war effort. A monument could wait. In this case it was forgotten. However, where Dahlgren's force was stationed, prior to its charge on July 2, 1863, there stands a plaque. Placed in the corner of the public square by the Pennsylvania Historical and Museum Commission it remains as the only recognition of this incident.

One of the town's most avid admirers of Dahlgren was Dr. Franklin A. Bushey, a veteran who had served as a surgeon in the 4th Pennsylvania Cavalry. Dr. Bushey was one of the leading members of the local G.A.R. Post and a faithful organizer of Memorial Day programs. Fifty seven years after Dahlgren's death he wrote an article for the local newspaper, C. C. Kauffman's "Progressive News." In it he described the exploits of the young Federal officer in and near Greencastle during and after the Battle of Gettysburg. The article also contains a glowing tribute to Thomas Pawling. "Mr. Pawling was so sincere for his love for the Union, that his acts brought him into conflict with Confederates during the Gettysburg Campaign and his life, on two occasions, was placed in imminent peril, and from which his cool and daring audacity alone rescued him."

Bushey's writing so impressed Dahlgren's mother, Madeleine Vinton Dahlgren, that she wrote to thank him for taking an interest in preserving the "record of Ulric's deeds." Her letter, appearing in the March 11, 1921 issue of the "Progressive News," closed with a tribute to her son — "There is no name more maligned, more defamed, by the rebel spirit of the South than his. It is a portion of the glorious heritage he has left his family that he was so bitterly hated by the enemies of his country." [17]

Admiral Dahlgren had died in 1870. Yet when his widow wrote to Dr. Bushey she was still living in the family residence in Washington, but her heart was in the rugged beauty of the South Mountains near Boonsboro. Here she had erected a summer home some years after her husband's death. In addition she built a chapel of native stone in which a special section served as a cryptorium where she hoped her children and grand children would some day be entombed. Mrs. Dahlgren had been married to G. E. Stoddard and there were children to both marriages.

The last known local reference to the Dahlgren family appeared in the March 10, 1955 edition of the Hagerstown Morning Herald. The paper carried a feature article which told of vandals desecrating and ransacking the chapel. Remains had been removed in the ghoulish search for valuables of in a mad spirit of vandalism. At that time the only living person connected with the family was Josiah Piece, a son-in-law of Madeliene Dahlgren. He and he alone was the owner of the chapel, since he was the only heir with a legal interest in this "lonely portion of the Dahlgren estate."

Ulric's body was never placed in the cryptorium. Following the war his remains were taken from the lonely grave near Richmond where he was buried after the skirmish on March 2, 1864. From there the body was moved to the family plot in the West Laurel Hill Cemetery of Phiadelphia where it remains to this day. [18]

The Dahlgren name is still remembered but the remembrance is for Ulric's father. He is part of the nation's naval history. Admiral John A. Dahlgren continues to be mentioned in text books studied at the United States Naval Academy and Dahlgren Hall perpetuates his memory. One of the largest structures on the Academy's campus, it houses the school's weapons department. Its huge floor is still used for athletics, as an auditorium, and as the locale for social events including the traditional "Farewell Ball" held at every graduation during June Week. [19]

But what of the Admiral's son? This blond haired youth whose young life was so filled with the promise of greatness is seldom remembered anywhere. But for one small town where a street carries his name and a plaque marks an incident in his brief career, Ulric Dahlgren is lost in the vast expanse of a war involving millions of soldiers. Yet, in Greencastle, except for its Civil War enthusiasts, the name is unknown to most of the citizens. The street and the marker on Center Square mean little to the people living there.

Ulric Dahlgren's star rose and fell in a period of less than a year. His family and friends knew and loved him. They and the Greencastle people of 1863 remembered him the rest of their lives for he was their hero. He had brought the first glimpse of freedom to their town after three weeks of Rebel control.

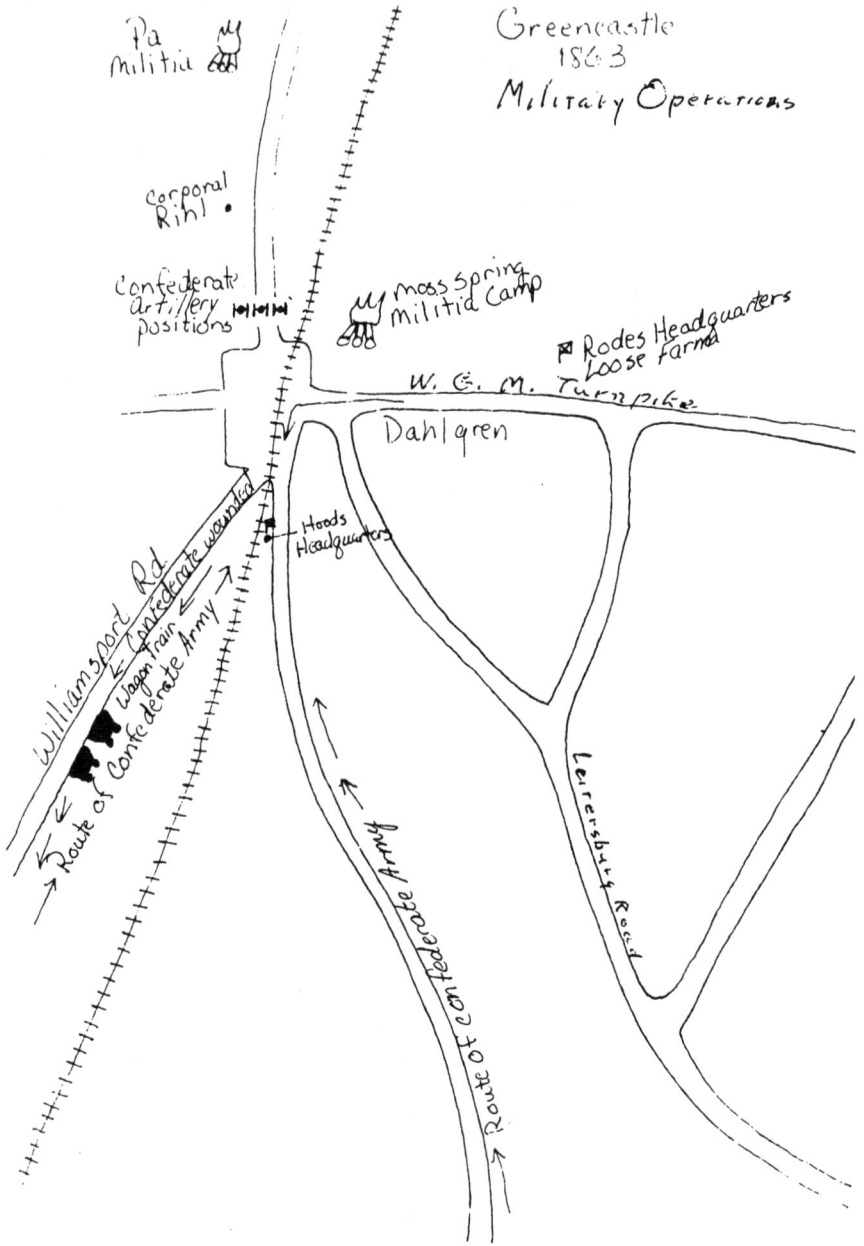

Greencastle 1863
Military Operations

Pa militia
corporal Rihl
Confederate artillery positions
moss spring militia camp
Rodes Headquarters Loose farm
W. G. M. Turnpike
Dahlgren
Hoods Headquarters
Williamsport Rd.
Confederate wounded
Wagon train
Route of Confederate Army
Route of confederate Army
Leitersburg Road

BY MELODY MENTZER AND ANDREW BARBAZANES Middleburg

CHAPTER VIII

RETREAT FROM GETTYSBURG

For three days they fought at Gettysburg but Lee's men could not dislodge Meade's blue clad forces entrenched in the hills near the town. It was the bloodiest battle ever fought in the western hemisphere and when it was over 50,000 Americans were killed, wounded or missing. *(Of the Army of Northern Virginia that passed through Franklin County the preceding fortnight, 3,903 lay dead, 14,735 were wounded while 5,425 were missing. Federal casualties were less, but only slightly, for when the fighting ceased on July 3 the days that followed revealed 3,155 lost lives, 14,529 wounded, and 5,365 captured or missing.)*

Within the next week Greencastle's people would hear that John Fulton Reynolds, the Union general who had been embarassed by the state's militia the year before, was killed in the early hours of the first day's fighting. They would hear of the struggle at Little Round Top where the 6th Pennsylvania Reserves helped keep Longstreet's men from capturing the hill that secured the Union's left flank. Company D of the 6th was from Franklin County and men from the Greencastle area were there as part of Joseph A. Davison's command. They would also learn that Company K of the 107th Pennsylvania Infantry was part of this gigantic struggle and that the 17th Pennsylvania Cavalry fought in the first day's fighting along the Cashtown Road. Both units contained soldiers from the local area.[1]

George B. Snively, of Shady Grove, was a member of Company G of the 17th Pennsylvania Cavalry. While at Gettysburg he served as a mounted orderly who delivered messages to various division headquarters. On one mission his horse was shot from under him. His was one of thousands of horses lost during the three days of fighting.[2]

The third day of battle began in the early morning hours just prior to daybreak when Union artillery began shelling Confederate forces, threatening the right flank of Meade's defenses on Culp's Hill. The fighting that followed continued throughout the morning until the Rebel attackers finally withdrew. Then just after one o'clock Confederate batteries of E. P. Alexander began pounding the center of the Federal defenses along Cemetery Ridge - a prelude to the heroic assault of Pickett's division and portions of A. P. Hill's command. Union cannon answered the Confederate barrage with all the guns at their disposal.

There followed an artillery duel which lasted for nearly two hours. The din of this engagement created havoc with the horses. Henry Cordell of Antrim Township was one of the men assigned to attend the artillery's horses during the battle. As the sounds of roaring cannon and exploding shells approached a pitch of tumltuousness unlike anything ever heard before, the frightened animals broke their tethers, and stampeded into the countryside east of Gettysburg. It took hours to recover the frightened beasts and this episode was the most enduring memory of the battle for Cordell. [3]

Despite the three days of battle with its thunderous roar of cannon fire the people of Franklin County were ignorant of the terrible fighting that was taking place at Gettysburg. Jacob Hoke noted, "Although but twenty-five miles from Gettsyburg, the inhabitants of Chambersburg were scarecely aware that a great battle was being fought...A few of our citizens, who resided upon the outskirts of the town, heard the sound of the guns. These sounds, however, were very indistinct. The large majority of our people did not hear them at all." [4]

The Reverend Thomas G. Apple, pastor of Greencastle's Reformed Church wrote, "We knew nothing of the Battle of Gettysburg while it was going on." Antietam's battle sounds carried as far as Greencastle and from time to time throughout the war the noise of cannon fire in skirmishes along the Potomac could be detected by local residents. But, not a soul in the town had even an inkling of this engagement. [5]

Not knowing that such a nearby battle had taken place was a puzzle to everyone. Yet, Gettysburg, the greatest battle ever fought in America, while not audible in the county, was heard over a hundred miles away in western Pennsylvania. This phenomenon was verified by the Rev. Cyrus Cort, who later served as a minister to the Greencastle and Middleburg Reformed churches. He and a companion heard the battle sounds in Westmoreland County - a hundred and forty miles west of Gettysburg.

Since prevailing air currents run from west to east, how Gettysburg's sounds could be heard at such a distance to the west was a mystery to Jacob Hoke and he could not rest until an explanation was found. As late as 1884 he was seeking the answer and eventually Spencer F. Baird, Secretary of the Smithsonian Institute, provided a solution which was verified by A. B. Johnson, Chief Clerk of the United States Light House Board.

Research by Joseph Henry, Director of the Smithsonian Institute, at an earlier time, revealed that "Sound moving with the wind is re-fracted down toward the earth, while moving against the wind it is refracted upward and passes over the head of the (*nearby*) observer." Professor Henry cited instances of the same phenomenon occuring at the battles of Seven Pines and Gaines' Mill in June of 1862.[6]

Franklin County people may not have heard the sound of battle but by July 5 they learned first hand that one had been fought. This was the day the wagon train, carrying thousands of Confederate wounded, streamed across the mountain and down through the valley. General John D. Imboden was in charge of this procession of horror as it passed over Adams and Franklin counties' mud bound roads making its way to the Potomac River.

Imboden, in later years, described the beginning of this agonizing postlude of battle. "It was a warm summer night; there were few camp fires, and the weary soldiers were lying in groups on the luxuri-ant grass of the beautiful meadows, discussing the events of the day, speculating on the morrow or watching that our horses did not strag-gle off while browsing. About eleven o'clock a horseman came to summon me to General Lee. I promptly mounted and accompanied by Lieutenant George W. McPhail, an aide on my staff, and guided by the courier who brought the message, rode about two miles toward Gettysburg to where half a dozen small tents were pointed out, a little way from the roadside to our left, as General Lee's headquarters for the night. On inquiry I found that he was not there, but had gone to the headquarters of General A.P. Hill, about half a mile nearer to Gettysburg. When we reached the place indicated, a single flickering candle, visible from the road through the open front of a common wall-tent, exposed to view Generals Lee and Hill seated on camp stools with a map spread upon their knees. Dismounting, I approach-ed on foot. After exchanging the ordinary salutations General Lee directed me to go back to his headquarters and wait for him. I did so, but he did not make his appearance until about one o'clock, when he came riding alone, at a slow walk, and evidently wrapped in profound thought.

"When he arrived there was not even a sentinel on duty at his tent, and no one of his staff was awake. The moon was high in the clear sky and the silent scene was unusually vivid. As he approached and saw us lying on the grass under a tree, he spoke, reined in his jaded horse, and essayed to dismount. The effort to do so betrayed so much physical exhaustion that I hurriedly rose and stepped forward to assist him, but before I reached his side he had succeeded in alighting, and threw his arm across the saddle to rest, and fixing his eyes upon the ground leaned in silence and almost motionless upon his equally weary horse,...The moon shone full upon his massive features and revealed an expression of sadness that I had never before seen upon his face...."

Lee's staff came soon and Imboden was given his orders. The commander said, "We must now return to Virginia. As many of our poor wounded as possible must be taken home. I have sent for you, because, your men and horses are fresh and in good condition, to guard and conduct our train back to Virginia. The duty will be arduous, responsible, and dangerous, for I am afraid you will be harassed by the enemy's cavalry."

Imboden told Lee he had 2,100 well mounted men, including McClanahan's six-gun battery of horse artillery. He was assured that other artillery would be available and that although there was a shortage of ammunition, the convoy could expect a shipment which was on its way from Winchester to Williamsport. The route of the train was then outlined. "You will recross the mountain by the Chambersburg road and then proceed to Williamsport by any route you deem best, and without a halt till you reach the river. Rest there long enough to feed the animals; then ford the river, and do not halt again till you reach Winchester, where I will again communicate with you."

The next morning, July 4, Imboden learned the wagons, ambulances, and wounded could not be collected to form the train until later in the afternoon. Additional artillery arrived and when ready to move, the convoy would be escorted by the cavalrymen and a total of twenty-three artillery pieces. Fitzhugh Lee's cavalry would follow as a rear guard force.

Shortly after noon a furious rain started. It fell in blinding sheets quickly overflowing the meadow lands and streams swept away fences plus military debris lying in their wake. During this continuing downpour hundreds of

wagons, ambulances and artillery carriages were assembled in the fields along the road to Cashtown — "in one confused and apparently inextricable mass." As the storm continued, the wounded men lying on the bare boards of the wagons were drenched. Attempts to cover the wagons with canvas brought no protection and the horses and mules, blinded by the wind and water, became unmanageable. Thunder, with accompanying flashes of lightening made communicating orders almost impossible and if understood, difficult to execute.

Finally, about four o'clock, the column began to move toward Cashtown and from there to ascend the mountain. All night long, through the never ending storm, the procession moved out of the various Confederate camps at Gettysburg taking the wounded with the best chances for survival and leaving the remainder to be cared for in Union hospitals. As the line of wagons moved westward it was estimated to be approximately seventeen miles long and at quarter mile intervals squads of cavalrymen and artillery batteries accompanied the procession. Orders had been given to abandon wagons if they became disabled. Nothing was to interfere with the constant forward thrust of the train.

Various accounts tell of the terrible agonies of the wounded. All along the line their cries were constant - "God, why can't I die." - "My God, have mercy and kill me." - "Stop, for God's sake take me out and let me die by the road." - "I'm dying. My poor wife and children. What will become of them?" Others constantly moaned. Some prayed while others cursed and swore. Most of these maimed soldiers had been without food for thirty-six hours. Few had straw to lie on and the jolting of the wagons further increased their agonies. Beside the wounded carried by the wagons there were those with head, arm, or shoulder wounds who were forced to walk in the procession through the incessant downpour. Imboden said, "During that one night I realized more of the horrors of war than I had in all the preceding years." [7]

Norvel Baker, of the 18th Viginia Cavalry, was one of the men who guarded the train. His diary told of this terrible assignment. "Twas an awful night, it rained all night, one thunder storm after another. The rain fell in sheets and vivid flashes of lightning and so dark we could not see our hand an inch from our eyes when there was no lightning. The roar of the waters and heavy bursting thunder, the cries of the wounded and dying soldiers made it awful." [8]

All night long officers encouraged the drivers to keep going. Darkness gave them safety because Federal forces would hesitate to attack in the blackness of the night for fear of killing their own men.

Imboden was certain that when day broke his command would be harassed by Union cavalry. His aim was to get as far as possible under night's cover. Instead of going into Chambersburg after reaching the western side of the mountain the train left the turnpike at Greenwood and turned south on the road to a hamlet called New Guilford. From there the column moved westward to Marion. Upon reaching this village the Confederates took a left turn and followed the road to Greencastle. By daybreak this cross country route found the head of the train in Greencastle and Imboden knew he was just fifteen miles from the Potomac where safety lay on the other side of the river. Yet, the tail end of the train was still far back along the roads of Franklin County. It is estimated that as the front wagons reached Greencastle the train stretched back as far as the Caledonia area where the last of the convoy was still descending the mountain.

Eye witnesses along the route estimated the number of wounded to be as many as twelve thousand. They saw broken wagons and dead or dying soldiers in or near the useless vehicles. Barns and houses along the road were converted into improvised hospitals. At places, where wagons were ditched or teams stalled, the train took to the fields, and since the rain was still falling, wheels sank to the axles in the soft earth. Drivers cursed and whipped their horses to get out of the mud and many more vehicles had to be abandoned. In addition to lost wagons, roads were strewn with caissons and an occasional cannon. Dead soldiers were removed from the wagons and thrown along the roadside thus freeing space for the wounded lying in stalled vehicles. Beyond all these difficulties the retreating train had little or no food. Imboden recalled that the only food in the convoy consisted of a few loads of flour and some cattle and sheep, most taken the previous week in the county. However, the need to get to Williamsport as fast as possible left little time for feeding anyone.[9]

Jacob Snyder, whose farm in the New Franklin area bordered the train's pathway, described how he first heard the rumbling of passing wagons during the night. He went to the front door of his home and within fifteen minutes the hallway and front yard were filled with walking wounded, begging for water and dressings for their wounds. Snyder later went to his barn where he found soldiers taking cattle. Some were saved, however, when he closed the barnyard gate. The Rebels left without protesting. In talking to the men he learned of the battle. Yet, some of his visitors assured him - "They were only going back to get more ammunition and would return and clean out the Yankees." Snyder's son, Milton, told of squads of Confederates burying discarded bodies along the road and how some of the wounded were left in the fields. "I shall never forget those ghastly wounds, those thousands of faces dusky with powder."[10]

Henry Hege, whose farm lay along the retreat, wrote, "Their wagon train was about fifty-six hours passing and nearly all hauling wounded. Some would groan at every jerk the wagon made. All those that were just slightly wounded had to walk. I saw some walking that were shot in the arms, some shoulders, some in the face. Oh, it looked awful as their wounds were not dressed yet. Their wounds looked all black and blue." [11]

Henry Omwake, whose home was in the Clay Hill community related how he heard the rumbling noise of the train at his home that Sunday in July and that he and several friends hurried over to Brown's Mill. Here they could see the passage of the long line of wagons along the Chambersburg road. He told how Rebel foragers went over the countryside along the retreat route to gather horses or mules and carriages or spring wagons to replace wagons that had to be discarded, and there were herds of cattle and sheep that formed a part of the long procession. Omwake saw disabled wagons stocked full of guns which were set afire and as the guns heated the charges exploded. Other firearms were destroyed by bending the barrels between spokes of wheels. No usuable weapon was left to fall into enemy hands. [12]

A Greencastle resident, J. C. Smith, also wrote of the walking wounded. The scene he described ran from early Sunday morning on through the day. "Those wounded in the arms or shoulders would tear away the garment and expose the wounded part. Such arms - swollen to twice or thrice their natural size - red and antry. When they came to a pump, one would place his wounded member under the spout while another would pump cold water on the sore. Then he would do a like service to his comrade. Thus the pumps were going all that day." The last of the train came through the town near sundown on Monday evening, July 6 and "there ended our connection with the Southern Confederacy." [13]

Years later David Shook told of Greencastle people during the second night of the train's passage, capturing its horses and cattle. "As cattle passed by I saw many turned into alleys. Horses tied behind wagons had their halters cut, and were led away unobserved. Many horses, too, gave out here and were left...I captured a fine bay horse, hid him in the barn, fed him well and felt proud of my possession. A few days later a citizen of Greencastle came to the barn, recognized his horse, proved him, and took him away. The Confederates had taken this horse on their way to Gettysburg...Many persons threw taunts at the retreating foe...'Have you been to Philadelphia already?' 'Did you meet the Pennsylvania militia down there?' 'Did you get enough of Meade over there?' " One officer called one of the questioners "an impudent puppy." [14]

Some of the Confederates who came through Greencastle recorded their experiences at a later time. One, identified only as Leinback, a musician in the marching band of the 26th North Carolina infantry, remembered how only a week or so before he and his friends had passed this way with high hopes for victory. He contrasted the jubilant and proud eagerness then with their return. How different in defeat and humiliation was the homebound march. It was filled with pangs of hunger and pain as they slowly trudged along the muddy streets and roads.

Impelled by hunger, he describes their first "acts of depredation" prior to leaving Pennsylvania on the outskirts of Greencastle - "We scarcely had anything to eat. Amongst us we had a few small pieces of silver money. We had poor success in buying or begging anything along the road. We came to one house where, for our money, a women gave us some small slices of bread not nearly its value. This kind of 'raised our dander,' and some of the boys, going around the house, found the cellar door unlocked. That was all we wanted to know. While we were negotiating in front of the house, the rest went into the cellar and appropriated what we could find. Our stomachs and canteens relieved the milk crocks of their contents, a dish of cold meat was quickly transferred to haversacks, other portable edibles also, while Dan, the scamp, walked off with a ham bone on which there was some meat, which he and I divided when we got behind the barn." [15]

ALEXANDER COLLECTION   CONFEDERATE AMBULANCE TRAIN

Another Southerner commented on his feelings when going through Greencastle: "...where we had so lately flaunted our banners with proud enthusiasm, we found the citizens grouped on the streets, eagerly discussing the news from Gettysburg and illy concealing their exultation over the retreat, if not defeat, of our army. This feeling, of course was perfectly legitimate and natural but I felt like cursing some of the cowardly time servers who had so cringingly welcomed us upon our advance." [16]

At one point during the first night of the retreat, a section of the line containing four or five wagons, reached Marion and the drivers did not know how to get to Greencastle. They were told to take a right turn at the next road. They did and eventually found themselves in Chambersburg. When the convoy arrived in the county seat the wounded were taken to the King Street (*School*) hospital. Jacob Hoke told of seeing a Confederate whose arm had been amputated close to the shoulder. He was standing on the pavement talking to some of the local residents. When asked what all the wounded meant, he replied, "It means that Uncle Robert has got a hell of a whipping." Others denied this, but there was little doubt that they were victims of a terrible battle. Hoke described the wounds as "Filthy, bloody, with wounds undressed and swarming with vermion, and almost famished for food and water, they presented such a sight as I hope I may never see again be called upon to witness." After being taken into the hospital their wounds were dressed and food supplied. "These arrangements a few of the citizens kept up until the ensuing Friday, when General D. N. Couch, reached here, and relieved us of our charge." [17]

The agonizing plight of the wounded during the retreat was further aggravated by attacks during the daylight hours of the journey. Imboden told of these beginning when the head of the column reached Greencastle. "Here our apprehended troubles began. After the advance - 18th Virginia Cavalry - had passed perhaps a mile beyond the town, the citizens to the number of thirty or forty attacked the train with axes, cutting the spokes out of ten or a dozen wheels and dropping the wagons in the streets. The moment I heard of it I sent back a detachment of cavalry to capture every citizen who had engaged in this work and treat them as prisoners of war. This stopped the trouble there, but the Union cavalry began to swarm down upon us from the fields and cross roads, making their attacks in small bodies, and striking the column when there were few or no guards and thus creating great confusion." [18]

Norvel Baker, of the 18th Virginia, reported how he and his comrades had traveled all night and at daylight his squad was near the head of the column at Greencastle. "...and a few miles south of this town, the enemy attacked the train. The guard at this part of the train was not strong enough and we were ordered back. The wagoners had jammed the road full of wagons, so we had to take to the fields by the sides of the road. We went on the run and got there to find the enemy having their way, but some of our boys were coming from the other end of the train, and we soon got their teams together again and moved on to Williamsport, Md." [19]

The early opposition in and near Greencastle, described by Imboden and Baker, undoubtedly came from a sizable force of horsemen from the 6th Pennsylania Cavalry and Tom Pawling's squad of Greencastle men. The regiment's historian recorded this event - "On the 5th one of their scouts reported the movement of the train, strongly guarded on the Williamsport and Chambersburg road, about three miles from their bivouac of the night previous. The command was moved near to the road and lay concealed until about 300 wagons had passed, when, the forces being divided between Lieutenants Morow and Herkness, they charged to the front and rear of the train at the same time. With the assistance of citizens (*Pawling's men*) they destroyed 130 wagons and ran the horses off to the woods, captured two iron guns and 200 prisoners. The strong infantry guard of the train soon appeared in overwhelming numbers, and a severe fight ensued, in which we lost nearly all the prisoners we had previously taken, and a number of our own men captured. Lieutenant Herkness received a severe sabre cut and was taken prisoner. Our men fled to the woods and were scattered in small squads during the night. They rendezvoused at Waynesboro, Pa. on the following morning, they succeeded in bringing to Waynesboro about thirty prisoners." [20]

It is apparent that these squads of Union cavalry continued their "hit and run" tactics throughout the day in the rain that continued through Sunday night. The following day was cloudy but heavy rains returned on Tuesday. Until the last of the train moved on into Maryland, Thomas Pawling's squad worked with the cavalry in disabling wagons at opportune times. At one point, south of Greencastle, Imboden was nearly captured, but J. H. McLanahan's Virginia Horse Battery came in time to drive away the Union force with several rounds of cannister. [21]

Much of Milroy's cavalry which escaped from Winchester in mid June were concentrated in the Bloody Run (Everett) part of Western Pennsylvania, under the command of Colonel Lewis B. Pierce. A body of emergency militia was also part of this force. On July 3, General Couch ordered Pierce to move into the Cumberland Valley to harass Lee's rear. Pierce was in McConnellsburg on the evening of the 5th when a messenger brought word of the Confederate retreat. Hearing this the Colonel sent a body of 200 select cavalrymen of the 1st New York and the 12th Pennsylvania Cavalry, under Captain Abram Jones of the New York regiment, to intercept the enemy. Near Cunningham's Crossroads *(Cearfoss)* the force attacked the wagon guards, thinly scattered along the line. A running skirmish followed and the Federals captured a hundred wagons, three pieces of artillery, and 500 prisoners. Pierce reported the enemy loss to be "considerable" while his command lost only one killed and three wounded. The prisoners and wagons were brought back to Mercersburg by way of the Hagerstown road that ran through Welsh Run. Arriving in Mercersburg, the wounded were placed in Seminary buildings and other improvised hospitals where they were treated by local physicians. [22]

Dr. George Carl, in an interview years later, described one of his experiences during this time. He was still treating Sergeant Cafferty's wound received in the fighting at the Fleming farm on June 22. "Another wounded soldier whom I recall in particular as a patient was a South Carolinian who was shot through the lung during Lee's retreat." The Confederate was obviously one of the men guarding the hospital train and was wounded in a skirmish along the Chambersburg road. Members of the Kiesecker family apparently found the wounded soldier and removed him to the barn on their farm north of Greencastle. Dr. Carl recalled, "I was sent for to attend him. When I looked into the barn the first thing I asked was whether he hoped to return to the South?" He replied, "I will." He was a magnificent specimen of manhood and his wound was not necessarily fatal. After dressing his wound he was carried on South with the retreating army and I never heard whether he recovered or not." [23]

According to Greencastle's newspaper not all the action against the retreating Confederates was launched by Union soldiers and Pawling's partisans. "The Pilot" reported in its July 28 edition — "We are told that during the retreat of the Rebels, one young lady, a resident of Antrim Township made three of the 'chivalry' dismount and give up their horses. Her father had lost all his stock by Jenkin's gang. Such instances of female heroism as the foregoing are not numerous now-a-days." [24]

While Jones's men hit the Rebels at Cunningham's Crossroads, the rear guard of Imboden's column was struck by part of Colonel J. Irvin Gregg's cavalry brigade near Caledonia. Gregg's force was from the Army of the Potomac and included the 16th Pennsylvania Cavalry. Company H of this regiment had been raised in Franklin County. One detachment from this company, under Sergeant John F. Metz of

Marion, was detailed to take the advance and harass the retreating Confederates. Within the next two days Metz's detachment fought numerous skirmishes between South Mountain and Greencastle, capturing many prisoners and several enemy cannon. [25]

Henry Omwake described events of Monday forenoon, July 6, when a body of several thousand Confederate cavalry came into the Clay Hill area. These men were under Fitzhugh Lee's command and were guarding the rear of the wagon train: . . . "a body of four or five thousand cavalry, apparently unhurt by fighting, came in two divisions, one by the route over which the train of wounded had gone, the other by way of Clay Hill, past our home. Persons living at the turn of the road were advised to get away to one side, as an attack by Union cavalry was anticipated; however, they passed by unmolested; emptying every house of bread and milk as they went. On all the high hills vedettes were posted; several of these, when the order was given to fall in line after the main body had passed, spied the only two horses in the neighborhood, hid in a thicket some distance to one side. They ordered the horses brought out, and the one, being lame, was turned over to its owner, while the other, which belonged to me, they took with them. This was the last demonstration by the Southern army in this region. After this body of cavalry had passed, there was no more sight of 'secesh,' save the few wounded left at points along the road." [26]

When Fitzhugh Lee and his cavalry reached Greencastle he demanded to see the town's authorities to make requisitions for supplies, but knowing Union cavalrymen were not far behind, he took no time to "hunt up the Council." Nobody seemed to know who any of the town's officials were. No one knew the name of the chief burgess. They could not recall the councilmen's names. He declared the town to be the strangest place he ever saw. Upon learning nothing from the citizens, the Rebel leader did discover the road that led to Williamsport. It was the quickest way to get to Imboden and little time was lost in heading down the turnpike. [27]

When Imboden finally reached Williamsport with most of the train, on the afternoon of the 5th, he took possession of the town; converted it into a gigantic hospital for the thousands of wounded; and directed all its families to begin cooking for the disabled men. Surgeons who accompanied the train immediately started to work, while the dead, not left along the line of march, were buried in fields near the town.

A swollen river prevented passage into Virginia. The Potomac was more than ten feet above its fording level and the continuing rainy weather made a crossing unlikely for some time. However, two small ferry boats were found and made ready to carry the walking wounded across. After their wounds were dressed and they were fed the boats began taking them to safety. From Virginia's side their journey continued along the road to Winchester.

On Monday afternoon, July 6, Imboden successfully repulsed the Union cavalry division of General John Buford, which had arrived via Frederick. Meanwhile, elements of Union General Judson Kilpatrick's cavalry division were busily engaged in fighting the Confederates in and around Hagerstown.

The main body of Meade's army moved parallel to Lee's on a route east of the South Mountain range via Emmitsburg and Frederick. They eventually crossed the mountains at Turners and Cramptons Gap, then moved upon Lee at Hagerstown and Williamsport. All this happened as Federal cavalry harassed the Rebel wagon convoys. Other Union forces in the area played a limited supporting role in the pursuit of Lee. Approximately 8,000 men from General B. F. Kelley's Department of West Virginia were moved to Hancock, Maryland but saw no action. In addition, about 6,500 men were brought up from Washington to hold Maryland Heights and guard the South Mountain passes. Among these units was the 158th Pennsylvania Drafted Militia. These men had left Franklin County in November of 1862 and were now within a month of the end of their enlistment period. Nearly a whole company was from the Greencastle-Antrim community. [28]

While Imboden was taking his train to Williamsport, the main' body of Lee's army was following another course leading to the same destination. At the head of this retreating force was another wagon train carrying more wounded, ammunition, and much of the booty taken during the invasion. The British observer, Colonel James Fremantle, recorded this description in his diary: "Wagons, horses, mules, and cattle captured in Pennsylvania, the solid advantages of this campaign, have been passing slowly along this road . . . Those taken by Ewell are particularly admired." This second wagon train left Gettysburg the night of July 4, after Imboden had started his trek across the Cashtown mountain. In heavy rain it followed the road south to Fairfield and from that village took a short western route over the Maria Furnace Road and came out on the toll road east of Monterey. *(The infantry corps of Longstreet, Hill and Ewell followed.)*

While the wagon train rumbled across the mountain, Kilpatrick's cavalry division, reinforced by Huey's brigade, of Gregg's division, moved from Emmittsburg up to Monterey Pass to strike the retreating Confederates. Dr. Henry G. Chritzman, of the Greencastle

community and a surgeon attached to Huey's command, told of this action — "July 4th, we moved to Emmitsburg and reported to Kilpatrick; moved same evening to intercept Ewell's wagon-train which was reported to be near Monterey Springs. The brigade moved rapidly up the mountain-road, striking Ewell's wagon-train about three o'clock in the morning of July 5th, in the midst of a furious thunder storm, whilst on its retreat from Gettysburg.

'At once there rose so wild a yell
Within that dark and narrow dell,
As if all the fiends from heaven that fell,
Had pealed in the banner cry of hell.'

This, combined with the Plutonic darkness made it one of the nights long to be remembered. When we came up with the wagon-train, Federal and Confederate cavalry, wagons, ambulances, drivers and mules became a confused mass of pursued and pursuing demons whose shouts and carbine shots, mingled with the lightning's red glare and the thunder's crash, made it appear as if we were in the infernal regions. Especially so as the cries of the wounded often rose high above the din of the conflicting forces.

"Frequently a driver would be shot or leave his mule team, when the unrestrained animals would rush wildly down the narrow road, and in many instances the wagons with the mules attached would be found at daylight at the bottom of some deep ravine crushed to pieces, with the mules dead or dying. It was a fearful ride suiting well the fearless intrepidity of our daring commander. A Confederate brigade, then a long train of wagons and ambulances, then our brigade in the center, with Ewell's corps in our rear, going down that narrow mountain road upon the principle of the devil take the hindmost, — you have Kilpatrick's dash across Monterey Pass.

"The result of this brilliant movement was the capture of a large number of wagons, ambulances, and mules with fifteen hundred prisoners. The brigade reached the foot of the mountain about daylight; leaving the Baltimore pike where it turns toward Waynesborough, the column moved on to Smithsburg, Maryland, where the wagons and ambulances were burned. The command rested at this place during the day. As the shades of evening drew nigh we were treated to a compliment of shot and shell by Stuart, who appeared at Raven Rock Gap, above the little village. Soon our battery got into position, when Stuart was compelled to retire; our brigade taking up the line of march for Boonsborough, where it arrived about midnight without further interruption." [29]

This was the largest military engagement in the history of Franklin County. Years later, a county historian summarized the local reaction to this event — "Citizens along the line from Rouzerville to Leitersburg remember very vividly the pyrotechnic display of July 4 and 5, 1863, made by the burning of rebel wagons thoroughly supplied with the pork and flour of Pennsylvania farmers; but in the future they prefer to have their celebrations under the direction of men pursuing peaceful callings." [30]

The fighting continued and the next day Kilpatrick reported to his commander, General Alfred Pleasanton, that his forces had captured one entire regiment, most of its officers and one battle flag. Clearer understanding of the skirmishing followed several weeks later when Kilpatrick reported the destruction of Ewell's train with the exception of eight forges, thirty wagons, and a few ambulances carrying Rebel officers. His report went on to say — "At 9 a.m. on the 5 the command reached Smithsburg with 1,360 prisoners, one battle flag, and a large number of horses and mules, several hundred of the enemy's wounded being left upon the field. We lost five killed, . . . ten wounded, and twenty-eight missing."

Kilpatrick·was often prone to exaggerate his reports and this is illustrated by the wide discrepancies of Union, Confederate and local civilian testimony on the number of wagons, ambulances and prisoners captured by the Union cavalry. *(See Appendix V)* Whatever the correct numbers may have been this was only part of the Army of Northern Virginia's wagon train. General Lee acknowledged in a report the capture of a number of wagons and ambulances, "but they succeeded in reaching Williampsort without serious loss." [31]

Lee's three infantry corps followed the wagons. the black, rain laced night of July 4 saw the army slogging along the mud filled road to Fairfield. By July 6th the troops were following parallel routes to Hagerstown via Smithsburg and Leitersburg. Longstreet's Corps led the way into Hagerstown and on to the Potomac. On the 7th the rear guard of the army, Ewell's Corps, arrived and set up camps north and east of the town. Part of this corps would remain in these camps until the 10th. Fighting continued in and around Hagerstown.

Captain William Boyd, with a detachment of the 1st New York, told of how he visited Greencastle on the morning of July 9 then headed south on the Williamsport Road, turning left on the Line Road to Middleburg. Here, along the state line, his force gave chase to a group of Rebel foragers in wagons and "had a skirmish with some 80 infantry." Boyd reported: "We drove them, but were unable to get the wagons, as it was within 1 mile of their camp. We retraced our steps to Middleburg . . . While at Middleburg I learned that Lee's head-quarters were on the pike between Hagerstown and Williamsport . . ." Boyd returned to Chambersburg that day, but other detachments of the regiment remained in and around Greencastle, under the command of Major Alonzo Adams. [32]

Meanwhile Lee was making preparations to meet a possible on-slaught from Meade's infantry steadily moving toward Hagerstown from the east. Although the wounded and prisoners were being ferried across the swollen Potomac, high water prevented any kind of crossing for the large numbers of infantry, artillery, and wagons. All that could be done was wait and prepare. By the morning of July 12 the Confederates had nearly completed a strong line of fortifications nearly eight miles long. The river formed the base for this rough tri-angular system that stretched between the Falling Waters and Wil-liamsport fords. The southern or right flank of the triangle ran from Marsh Run near the Falling Waters crossing to an apex at St. James and from this point the northern side followed a course back to the Conococheague north of Williamsport. In addition, strong inner defenses were put up at Falling Waters and Williamsport to cover the river crossings. One Confederate officer declared this whole system of earthworks formidable enough to withstand a month's siege.

A pontoon bridge at Falling Waters, destroyed by Union cavalry on July 3, was reconstructed with timbers taken from dismantled warehouses used by the canal company. All along the lines a Rebel force of some 50,000 waited to fight off an oncoming Union army of approximately 86,000. They waited but hoped the river would soon subside enough to let them get to safety in the Old Dominion.

President Lincoln, upon hearing of Vicksburg's surrender on July 4, was exuberant. Immediately he sent this news to Meade. If he would finish off Lee's army the war would soon end. But Meade was not anxious to move quickly against an enemy who appeared to be so firmly entrenched. His superiority of numbers was not quite as mean-ingful when measured against the advantage Lee possessed. His army was well fortified, and like a wounded animal, it would fight ferociously until the very end if necessary. The Union commander no doubt dreaded a repeat of Fredericksburg.

On Sunday, July 12, a staff decision opposed attacking the Con-federates. However, if General Meade was to move despite his officers' reluctance, time was running out. By July 13 the river was gradually receding and Lee's engineers decided it could be forded. The commander, on hearing this, waited no longer. His army could now escape.

During the night Ewell's men, in water up to their armpits, waded across the river at Williamsport. Longstreet and Hill used the pontoon bridge at Falling Waters to take the artillery, wagons, and some infantry to the Virginia side. Here other foot soldiers made their way to the homeland's safety by the water route. It was said the tallest men formed two lines from shore to shore with their guns interlocked to mark a strong and stable lane across the river. Through this passage, the rest of the men waded in water up to their necks to the safety of the far shore.

The crossings were not free from peril. Heavy rain made visibility difficult — some wagons had to be abandoned while others were lost in the rushing waters. Ammunition became soaked and rendered useless. Ewell's men lost their shoes — said to be as many as 8,000 pairs. Bonfires were lit on both sides of the fording points but despite these beacons some men were swept down stream before they found places to climb from the river. The only Union attack during the crossings came from Kilpatrick's cavalry who discovered the retreat in the early morning hours and after this foray was driven away the withdrawal continued without further major interference. [33]

Meanwhile, a brigade of cavalry under the command of Colonel Andrew T. McReynolds, *(the remnants of Milroy's force, including the 1st New York)*, gathered at Greencastle and from there moved into Maryland. Up to this time most of these troops had fought in small detachments harassing the enemy, capturing prisoners and wagons. [34]

Be nine o'clock the next morning, July 14, practically all of the Confederates were in Virginia. General Lee crossed the Potomac on the pontoon bridge before Longstreet and Hill got their men across. It was the last time, as the head of the Army of Northern Virginia, he would ever travel that way again.

Harsh judgements, by the President, the cabinet, military officials, congressmen, northern newspapers and the general public, fell on George Meade. But the fact remained — he had, with little prior notice, taken command of the Union army and turned back the invaders. Northern cities, including the capital of the United States targeted by Lee's invading army, had been saved. The war would go on and all the criticism of the victor at Gettysburg would not alter this salient fact. More killing, more suffering, and more sorrow filled homes would continue for nearly two more years, but for the time being all was quiet along the Potomac.

A postscript to this point in history concerns a group of Franklin County men who had gone to Hagerstown after Imboden's wagon train left Pennsylvania. This body of curious citizens hoped they would be able to witness the final destruction of Lee's forces in that area. They didn't. Instead most of them were made prisoner and taken by the Confederates into Virginia.

On July 6, Dr. George R. Kauffman, of Brown's Mill, along with thirteen men from Chambersburg, followed the retreating Rebels to Hagerstown hoping to witness what they thought would be another large battle. They walked from the county seat to Middleburg where they remained overnight. The next morning their trip continued along the Cumberland Valley Railroad line. A short distance from Hagerstown they ran into Confederates but were allowed to pass on to the town. Yet, they found no battle. There were plenty of enemy soldiers all over the place, but the only Federal troops in the area were about 5,000 prisoners who had been brought from Gettysburg by General Pickett and his men.

Eventually nine of the battle seekers were taken prisoner. Four had short stays at Libby and Castle Thunder prisons in Richmond before being returned to the North. Two returned in August of 1864 while those that remained — J. Porter Brown, D. M. Eiker, and Kauffman wound up in the Salisbury Military Prison in North Carolina.

The story of their escape and harrowing experiences while traveling northward through North Carolina, Tennessee, Kentucky and Ohio before reaching Pittsburgh is one of Franklin County's best epics of the Civil War. These three curious men who had left for Hagerstown on July 6, 1863 did not return to Chambersburg until April 8, 1865. After one year, eight months, and eight days, by way of Richmond, Salisbury, Knoxville, Cincinnatti, and Pittsburgh, they finally reached their homes — arriving just in time to hear of Lee's surrender the next day. They never did get to see a battle.[35]

Over the next several weeks Confederate prisoners were herded through the streets of Greencastle on their way to northern prisons. The local newspaper reported that, during this same period, Rebel deserters were also seen coming through the town having left their army after its successful crossing into Virginia. General Couch, also, reported the capture of approximately 1,300 enemy soldiers who, after the fighting at Gettysburg, were in the South Mountains making their way through the forests, attempting to escape to Canada. [36]

Pennsylvania's emergency militia, raised to protect the state capital and stay the advancing Confederates back in June, continued to play a limited role during the Gettysburg campaign and the retreat of the Army of Northern Virginia. General William F. Smith's division, which included the New York militia sent to defend the approaches to Harrisburg, had crossed South Mountain at Mount Holly Springs enroute to Gettysburg only to learn that the battle was over. One regiment was sent to police the battlefield but the main body was diverted through Pine Grove Furnace and Caledonia, re-entering the Cumberland Valley to meet Meade's army at Hagerstown. Another division, headed by Napoleon Jackson Tecumseh Dana, under orders from General Couch, moved straight down the Valley toward Chambersburg and Greencastle. Here he was replaced by General Fitz Henry Warren.

On July 8, State Adjutant General Lorenzo Thomas informed Secretary of War Stanton that these forces were headed south to join with Pierce and move on the enemy's rear. President Lincoln, who was anxiously waiting for the Pennsylvania troops to strike and discouraged by their slowness, responded: "Your dispatch of this morning. . . is before me. The force you speak of will be of no imaginable service if they cannot go forward with more expedition. Lee is now passing the Potomac faster than the forces, you mention, are passing Carlisle. Forces now beyond Carlisle, to be assigned to regiments at Harrisburg and the united forces again to join Pierce somewhere and the whole to move down the Cumberland Valley, will in my unprofessional opinion, be quite as likely to capture 'the man in the moon' as any part of Lee's army." [37]

Mr. Lincoln's memory of the Pennsylvania emergency soldiers' "eagerness" to fight under General Reynold's leadership, the year before, probably reinforced his feeling that their haste to get close to General Lee's army would be a very calculated type of hurriedness. Events seemed to support the President's assessment. By July 8 Smith's division was at Waynesboro. Many of the New York Militia wore grey. One regiment, the 23rd, cut patches of white cloth into Greek crosses which they sewed on their jackets as a distinguishing mark less they be mistaken for Confederates. Early on the morning of the 10th, the 23rd and 71st New York regiments moved out on reconnaissance along the Greencastle Pike for about three miles. From the high terrain east of Shady Grove it was determined that the distant view over much of southern Cumberland Valley revealed no Confederates. This should have brought relief to these warriors, but the regimental history of the 23rd reported the major concern was the heat: . . "our men were fairly roasted in a sizzling heat from which there was no shelter." [38]

COMPANY F — 23rd NEW YORK MILITIA   CARLISLE, PA

As Couch's force came into the southern part of the Valley they numbered over 26,000 men — at Waynesboro 7,600 with Smith; under Dana at Chambersburg, 12,000; and at Mercersburg, 6,700 with Pierce. Although impressive looking on paper the fact remained that most of these men were emergency troops no more anxious for battle experience than those volunteers who had been in this part of the state during the Battle of Antietam. Therefore, the only major contribution of Couch's force, as they slowly crept forward against no opposition, was the constriction of the area over which Confederate foraging parties could roam — making Lee's position more uncomfortable.

General Meade, remembering the frustration and discontent of General Reynolds in September of 1862, could place little reliance on their willingness to enter combat. They were untrained and had few supplies with practically no means of procuring them. General Smith admitted he had entered the campaign with no wagons or quartermasters, who would have been responsible for finding supplies. On the 12th Smith's troops left Waynesboro, going by way of Leitersburg to join Meade at Hagerstown. One of his regiments, the Philadelphia Blue Reserves, assisted Kilpatrick's cavalry in a skirmish near Hagerstown, losing one man killed and nine wounded. This minor affair represented the extent of any fighting done by the emergency troops in cooperation with the main body of the Army of the Potomac during Lee's retreat. [39]

On July 13 General Couch informed Meade that 12,000 of his troops were near Greencastle and ready to move. The next day Lee escaped into Virginia and the commanding general declined the offer. It may have been just as well since these militiamen suffered from the same problems found in Smith's command. They were short of supplies and the condition of the road south of Chambersburg was described as "not in condition to haul any great amount of supplies." As a result these emergency forces camped around Greencastle until the end of July. [40]

James McCrory, the Greencastle editor, in his July 28 edition, showered these soldiers with such enthusiastic praise that his readers must have thought he believed they were responsible for Lee's decisive defeat and retreat. "Scarcely had the foot of a rebel pressed the State's soil, ere the people of Pennsylvania responded to the call of the Governor and men forsook their profitable employment, neglected their business, left their comfortable homes, and shouldered a gun. Such are the men we have amongst us and they deserve the greatest credit for their promptness with which they marched to the defense of the State. A finer looking set of men cannot be found, than those who, at different times during the past two weeks have marched through our streets. That they will fight was demonstrated at Hagerstown. . . " [41]

McCrory's glorification of the militia and the prospect of having them in the community was not shared by everyone. In fact many remembered the ineffectiveness of these kinds of soldiers the year before and of Knipe's forces in June. William Heyser of Chambersburg probably reflected the feelings of most frugal and practical minded people when he noted "How ironic, now we have plenty of troops around and not needed, before, in our hour of need, there were none." On July 10 he wrote, "Some troops came in this morning and moved towards Greencastle. About 3,000 passed through Mercersburg . . . Tonight General Couch arrived mid much cheering. The speeches they give are politically slanted and do nothing toward ending the war . . ." Heyser also complained of soldiers idling about the town and doing nothing but lying on cellar doors and door steps. He was outraged at the indecent behavior of many girls — "bareheaded, mingling with the crowd and a number of them hanging on the arms of strange soldiers." To many like Heyser the presence of so many troops was wasteful and only added unnecessary costs. Since the people of Franklin County had suffered enough personal loss from the invasion — losses that most likely would be borne by property owners with little hope for any kind of help from the government, to have 12,000 men all around the town doing little or nothing was downright shameful. [42]

Those men at Greencastle were stationed at camps used before by both Federal and Confederate troops. They were at Rankin's Mill and in a wooded area on lands owned by John Tobias near the southern edge of the town. *(See Appendix VI)*. "The Pilot" reported — "A splendid band is attached to Colonel Campbell's regiment and the woods often ring with excellent music." Men led by Colonel Brisbane were at Moss Spring. Mr. McCrory ended his encomium with the statement that although the town was host to nearly 12,000 men, "The Provost Guard keep excellent order, and our town is almost as quiet as of old." A separate news item provided a partial explanation for the excellent order and quiet town. The Provost Marshall had directed that all liquor in the borough be destroyed. No one could get a drink, not even the hotels' regular barroom customers. [43]

General Meade's attitude towards the emergency militia continued to be somewhat negative and no doubt he expressed his feelings to General Couch. On July 23 Couch ordered Smith to get the remainder of his troops out of Hagerstown and fall back to Greencastle if "the mutinous state" of some of his men could not be corrected. Whether order was restored is not reported but a few days later some of General Smith's regiments were sent back to Greencastle. If these were the units containing the mutineers their discontent would not likely disappear when they discovered the town to be without social lubricants. [44]

Apparently not all those encamped in the area were happy about their treatment by local inhabitants. At least one soldier reported his discontent to his home town newspaper, Easton's "Daily Express." Despite the popular belief that the state's soldiers were welcomed with open arms and plied with free victuals, this man told of exhorbitant charges for food by some people in Greencastle. "Allow me to say, all the bread this regiment *(38th)* got, we paid a big price for. I will give you the prices. Half loaf of bread, 25 cents; pies, 25 cents; and nothing free of charge. At Greencastle everything is double. We can scarcely get a postage stamp." He also said that any quantity of Confederate money was selling at 25 cents per dollar. [45]

In the August 4 edition of "The Pilot," the editor rebutted these accusations and defended his constituents by recalling the times Greencastle people welcomed troops with enthusiasm and generous helpings of a variety of refreshments. ". . . the people of this community are noted for their kindness and hospitality extended to the Union soldiers. That they may have not done as much as usual for them, last month, is owing to the straitened circumstances of our people. Still a great deal was given . . . I saw hundreds at a time, fed on the Public Square, and I know the people in the country were equally liberal. The prices given above are extortionate, but this was not the regular prices among citizens and farmers . . . "It may be, some unprincipled persons asked the prices . . . quoted. If so, they deserve the lasting contempt of all good citizens." As for the postage stamps, the local editor pointed out that everyone suffered from a breakdown in postal service. The invasion had interrupted this governmental function as well as many other normal peacetime activities. The sale of Confederate money at twenty-five cents to the dollar was denied. There was no explanation of what the going rate might have been. [46]

That some of the emergency soldiers must have been satisfied with their stay in Greencastle was reflected in another item in the August 4 issue. "The splendid band attached to the 39th P. V. Militia visited town last Monday evening." They first serenaded the commanding officer, General Fitz Henry Warren, whose headquarters were in a building on the southeast corner of the Square. *(This was the property of the Eachus family — now owned by Mrs. Joseph Shoemaker)* After the concert honoring the general, the musicians visited other public places and "discoursed such excellent music, as is not often heard here."

By Thursday, July 30, the camps around Greencastle were emptying. The last contingent to leave was the men of Nagle's Brigade who had been in the Tobias woods. The outfit's musicians played a stirring march as its members marched out Carlisle Street towards Chambersburg the day before. For two weeks various units had been leaving. Philadelphia's troops left on Saturday and during this time those who had been stationed at Hagerstown passed through the town to the county seat. Unlike the "Boys of '62," who rode the trains, these men had to march as far as Chambersburg before rail transportation was available. The line had been temporarily repaired that far but it would be several weeks before it was sufficiently rebuilt to allow traffic to get to Hagerstown. [47]

One of Brisbane's men, John T. Lewis, Jr., of the Philadelphia Greys wrote of the encampment at Moss Spring. His diary also told of the regiment's departure to Harrisburg — a typical experience for all those who were in camps near Greencastle. The Greys were ordered to leave Hagerstown on July 20. Before the march to Greencastle, all prisoners able to walk were collected to be escorted northward. When the Greys left Hagerstown at noon they had approximately fifty captives accompanied by two platoons. They apparently left Hagerstown by the road to Cunningham's Cross Roads and up the Williamsport Turnpike because they did not arrive in camp until six o'clock. Lewis explained, "There is a road of about eleven miles but we came another."

When Lewis and his comrades arrived in Greencastle they were relieved of further responsibility for the prisoners. He described the Moss Spring locale — "The camp was a splended one and in a woods at the head of a fine . . . magnificient spring . . . It was the same camp that the regiment had when out in the raid of last fall. It was called Camp Rest."

The following day was spent in loafing, reading, and sleeping. But on Wednesday the men were drilled in the morning and a dress parade was held in the afternoon. "We still had some eatables left from what we had at Hagerstown and we got some things from Greencastle." On Thursday the diary reported that a Mr. Drayton received a furlough to go to Philadelphia to request of city council a twenty-five dollar bounty for each of the men. Apparently the Greys had not received the same enlistment payment as other outfits.

On Friday, July 24, young Lewis was detailed for guard duty and when relieved he began to feel ill. The next morning when reveille sounded at the early hour of two o'clock, he knew the brigade was getting ready to leave camp. Despite lack of sleep and continued sickness he forced himself to fall into the line of march to Chambersburg. He got "about halfway" along the road and had to fall out while his regiment passed on. After a period of rest a Dr. Darrach came along and helped carry some of his gear and eventually he was able to join his unit which was resting along the way. Finally he and his fellow soldiers reached Chambersburg, marching the entire distance through a heavy rain.

On Sunday, July 26, the men were ordered to Harrisburg and at six o'clock that evening they boarded cars described as "barren . . . with boards up the sides and the middle for seats..." Each car held about thirty persons and when filled to capacity the remaining sold-

U.S.A.M.H.I.   CARLISLE, PA.
PVT. THOMAS SPARKS — PHILA. GRAY RES.

210

iers sat on the car tops to ride up the valley. In the early morning hours of the next day the Philadelphia Greys boarded another train and by twelve noon John T. Lewis, Jr. and his comrades were home again. Incidently, they did get the twenty-five dollar bonus from the city council. Mr Drayton's mission had not been in vain. [48]

Sarah Hade's home seemed to be a magnet for soldiers. During the invasion she fed hungry Confederates and during the stay of the militia she nursed one of Pennsylvania's soldiers who became ill. In a letter dated August 6, 1863, H. W. Pinkerton wrote to Mrs. Hade to thank her for this kindness. In part he told her — ". . . We are all safe home again although I am not enjoying good health since I arrived in Harrisburg. But hope I shall speedily be restored to my former health. . ." Pinkerton, who lived at Tremont in Schuylkill County, recognized the difficult period the local residents had been through when he wrote, ". . . hoping this may find you and your family in good health and that you may never have to witness another scene as you people of Cumberland Valley have witnessed in the last few weeks." [49]

The departure of the militia marked an end to this eventful episode in the lives of the community's people. It was an experience that no one could forget and for several generations beyond that time their recollections would continue to be repeated. James McCrory, in an editorial marking the year's end, said, "This year will be remembered forever by us, if for no other reason, on account of the grand invasion of Pennsylvania — and the occupation of our town by the Confederates for several weeks. Such a sight as Greencastle saw in June and July, she will never see again. So long as one house stands to mark the site of this town; so long will incidents of the invasion under Lee — relating to this neighborhood — be told by the fireside. In far off western homes many years from now, old men, who are the young men of today, will release to wondering grandchildren the moving accidents which befell them here in 1863, when Greencastle was in the Southern Confederacy." [50]

CHAPTER IX

BEFORE AND AFTER THE INVASION

The story of 1863 cannot be limited to accounts of the invasion and its peripheries. What happened before and after this period was also a part of the chronicle of events that affected the lives of people in the community. Since copies of the town's newspaper were available for the year, much of this chapter could rightfully be called - 1863: Through the Eyes of the Editor. Greencastle's and Antrim's experiences mirrored those of most people in other parts of the county. News of lost or crippled lives from the various fighting fronts brought a constant stream of sorrow to homes throughout the area. Although January and February found less action along the battle lines, the war's tempo increased as another springtime's moderate weather gradually appeared in parts of the South. "The Pilot" carried letters from soldiers and military reports telling of increased hostilities in these regions.

The one most important developement to affect the lives of more than a few families was the passage of the Federal Draft Act by Congress and the President's approval on March 3, 1863. This legislation called for drafting men between the ages of twenty and forty-five with exemptions for the physically or mentally unfit and for men with dependents. Certain classes of state and federal officials were also exempt. The charge that the law favored the rich came from a provision which allowed drafted men to hire substitutes or pay three hundred dollars to be exempted from serving.

Although there was much opposition to the draft law in parts of the North, including sections of Pennsylvania, there is little evidence of any major opposition in Franklin County. William Heyser noted that the draft was "disturbing everyone." His farmer was distressed because it would take all the men, leaving women to run everything. The editor of "The Pilot" objected to the law because it had no provision for exempting newly married men. He used the Scriptures to express this reservation - "When a man hath taken a new wife, he shall not go out to war; neither shall he be charged with any new business; but he shall be free at home one year and shall cheer up his wife which he has taken." - Deuteronomy - 24:5. Since there was little evidence of frivolity in this newspaper, under James McCrory's editorship, it can only be assumed that the scripture was sincerely used to express his views. How this stand on taking young men from their brides was greeted by the general public is unknown, but the law was never amended to meet the scriptural requirement cited by the editor. [1]

Provisions of the law enabled federal officials to establish quotas for each state. At the state level quotas were then set for counties which were translated into numbers of men to be raised in local muncipalities. The law also established bounties which would be paid to those who volunteered for duty in outfits of their choice. Volunteers were counted so as to reduce the number of men called by the draft. Local communities in order to encourage voluntary enlistments also raised money to be used for local bounties. When the deadline for enlistments passed and local quotas had not been met, the remainder was raised through the draft process.

During the late winter and spring months no special volunteer units were raised in the area. However, later news accounts told of men enlisting in old or newly formed regiments. Several hundred soldiers from the local area were still in units raised the previous year and most of them were in regions that would see more action before they saw the home town again.

The enthusiastic concern for the welfare of soldiers' families at the beginning of the war cooled off as hostilities continued. Forgotten were earlier assurances given to volunteers that their wives and children would never suffer. Initially local communities raised funds to help such families that came upon hard times. Yet by March of 1863 a committee representing Franklin County was established to bring help to such households. George W. Ziegler was one of this Relief Board's members. The board, apparently with no tax money to dispense, existed solely to urge citizens to provide food, clothing, and fire wood or money for necessities to help such indigent families.[2]

Another program, instituted by Governor Curtin, was praised by one soldier in a letter to "The Pilot." He complimented the governor for instituting a system to permit sick and wounded to be sent to their homes where they could "have their wives, mothers, and sisters take care of them and make them comfortable so that their afflictions would be made but a small burden while, if they would have lain in some open hospital and perhaps under the charge of some worthless surgeon *(of which we have too many)*, they might have been buried."[3]

The Ladies' Aid Society continued its work of helping the war effort. A report issued by Emma M. Apple on April 23 told of a project where food was collected in the Shady Grove area and sent to the military hospital at Frederick. The collection consisted of rusk *(sweetened bread)*, butter, canned tomatoes and peaches, dried fruit, jelly, eggs, onions, and potatoes. In addition to the food, tracts and local papers were included. Another report, in early June, told of three boxes of hospital stores being sent to the Christian Commission in Philadelphia. Included were men's underclothing, cloth slings, pillow cases, lint, dried fruit, jelly, canned tomatoes and peaches, rice, and eight bottles of wine.

When the draft law went into effect the drain on manpower would surely create problems for farmers. Northern markets constantly increased the demand for food to feed the hundreds of thousands of men in the military establishment. Women, older men, and children supplied some of the labor needed but the nation's agricultural requirements could never have been met without improved farm machinery. Just as farm families rose to the challenge so did manufacturers. Greater production of mowers, reapers, mechanical rakes, cultivators, threshers, and grain drills led to harvests that far surpassed any previously known in the nation's history. By the end of the war enough food was being produced to, not only feed civilians and men in the armed forces, but excess quantitites were being exported to England and other parts of Europe.

The Greencastle company of Keller and Plum advertised in the May 19 edition of "The Pilot" an improved grain drill. This newly patented machine could be adjusted to not only plant grain but to spread fertilizer. It could be purchased at the firm's factory on South Carlisle Street, sometimes called Railroad Street by local residents.

Commission merchants advertised their services for securing the higher market prices for flour, wheat, rye, oats and corn. In 1863 there were two such firms operating in Greencastle - Schafhirt and Wunderlich and the C. W. Eyster Company whose local agent was J. R. Smith. The Eyster Warehouse was located on the corner of North Carlisle and North Street while the other had a "new and commodious" warehouse on South Carlisle Street in the same area where the railroad storage building was located. Schafhirt and Wunderlich also carried a line of coal, salt, plaster, fertilizer, and cement for local customers.

Despite the war, civic improvement was a constant concern of some Greencastle businessmen. On May 23 a meeting was held in the Union Hotel to consider forming a company to build a turnpike between Greencastle and Middleburg. This was the only major public road in the area that was not improved. Farmers in the Middleburg area were interested and willing to put money into the venture. An improved road from Hagerstown to the state line already existed and it was estimated that to continue it to Greencastle would require an investment of as much as $10,000. By year's end there was no movement on this project. [4]

Another need, considered to be increasingly essential, was to establish a local bank. It was agreed that the Greencastle area was a rich and growing agriculture district. Business growth over the past decade was said to have been without precedent and with improved rail facilities growth was predicted for the future. An earlier bank had failed in 1818 but economic conditions then were far different than those of 1863. People had to depend on Hagerstown and Chambersburg for banking services, an inconvenience of no little measure. If a bank were established in Greencastle, it was argued by "The Pilot," it would not only serve the local area but the milling region of Washington Township close to Antrim's Marsh district, and the rich lands of the Welsh Run settlement. "Besides the mechanics, merchants, and manufacturers of the neighboring towns would all find it convenient and profitable to patronize a bank here." Passage of the National Banking Act created still greater interest in McCrory's arguments but scarcity of ready cash among businessmen postponed action on such a project until better times. [5]

In keeping with the spirit of community improvement, the editor reminded borough officials, elected on May 5, of the paving and curbing ordinance, passed the year before. It had not been enforced to the degree expected of those interested in upgrading the busines part of town. This act provided for sidewalks on Baltimore and Carlisle Streets to be paved with brick, curbed with brick or stone, and to be ten feet wide. Walks along other streets were to have surfaces of brick, flat stones, or black gravel with curbs like those of the main streets. When owners neglected to meet these requirements the borough was to build the sidewalks and the owners charged the actual costs of construction plus a twenty percent levy beyond this expense. There was no immediate action taken by borough council. Later in the year James C. Austin constructed a row of houses on South East Street and he was praised for using a new material for side walks - patented cement. The Borough Council did not hesitate to add this kind of paving to its ordinance and by the end of the year more such pavements were to be found. [6]

The spring in the North was a long, cold, wet season. There was snow as late as March 31, but by the second week of April farmers were able to begin planting their grain in anticipation of still higher prices. Interest in growing flax and sorghum continued and Christian Hoover, a cigar maker, decided to attempt to grow tobacco on a piece of ground he rented from John Witmer. Hoover made cigars in the winter while in the summer he operated a brick yard. More sheep were being raised as wool prices kept improving. Sheep farmers were still plagued by killer dogs. In late February Robert McCleary, of the Clay Hill area, had nine sheep destroyed and a neighbor lost a similar number the same night. In both instances the animals were in barnyards when attacked by the dogs. [7]

Another peril to both farm and town people was the growing menace of horse thievery. The February 24 edition of "The Pilot" carried a lengthy story of a horse thief being chased from Mercersburg by Constable George Wolfe to Greencastle where a band of local men continued the pursuit out the Leitersburg Road. Finally the posse cornered the culprit in an out building on the Philip Overcash farm near the intersection with Ridge Road. By then the thief was identified as Joe Hooker - no relative of the general. While the pursuers waited for farmers to arrive with fire arms, Mr. Hooker was on his way, making an escape through a wooded portion of the farm. He had left the stolen horse near the building to let the posse believe he was hiding there. That same evening a singing school was held at Bushtown, about two miles across country from the Overcash farm. When the entertainment was finished, a Mr. Emmet of Funkstown who had attended the program, found his horse and buggy missing. Joe Hookeer had "borrowed" it for more important business than singing school.

In mid-April the culprit was arrested in Washington, where he was caught selling stolen horses, stealing them back, and re-marketing the animals to other customers. On April 17, Constable Wolfe went to the capital city and brought Mr. Hooker back to the county jail. By May 12 the prisoner had grown tired of jail life and along with a fellow inmate, Edward Byers of Greencastle, the two made their escape. The next night both escapees reached Greencastle, Byers went to his home on South Carlisle Street where Sheriff Samuel Brandt was waiting. While questioning his companion, Joe Hooker was across several lots from the Byers residence in a stable owned by John Wilhelm on South Street.

Just as Hooker was about to ride to freedom on one of the Wilhelm horses, he heard people approaching. Knowing this was no welcoming committee, the thief slipped quietly across nearby fields not far from the Williamsport Pike. As search parties combed the area in all directions, the thief had again disappeared into the darkness of the night. Once more this purloiner of horse flesh had found freedom. It was not the last he would make his presence known, but when the Confederate invasion engulfed the community his kind of work was taken over by foraging squads of the invaders. [8]

After the invasion seven weeks elapsed before Greencastle's newspaper re-appeared on July 28. It had not published since June 16, the day after Jenkins made his appearance. The first post-invasion edition gave a complete review of events that occurred throughout the period along with tributes to William Boyd and Ulric Dahlgren for their exploits during this trying time. McCrory apologized for the suspension of publication. The invasion, death in the family, "indisposition" of the principal typesetter, and prolonged absence of other employees "have further prevented us from issuing this number as soon as we desired." The inability of the owner to publish during this crucial time leaves a gap in the ongoing story of the period - a loss to history but apparently no great inconvenience to the town's citizens.

Thursday, August 6, was declared a National Thanksgiving Day by President Lincoln. Business places were closed and a special service was held in the Lutheran Church with the town's ministers participating. It was reported the church was filled with both town and country people. The invasion had hurt many residents in a variety of ways but everyone was now free from anxieties produced by the constant presence of enemy soldiers.

The following week another event helped brighten the spirits of the community. The 158th Regiment came home. This was the unit of nine month drafted militia that left the area back in November of 1863. Approximately eighty local men were part of this regiment. The only casualties suffered were death from typhoid fever. William Peterman, John and William Hollinger, and Samuel Hollabaugh of the area were among those who would never see their homes again.

The veterans got to Chambersburg on Saturday, August 8, and the following Wednesday arrived in Greencastle. Since no trains were running they were driven home in buggies and wagons which relatives, friends, and neighbors were able to muster from the area's limited horsepower and limited number of vehicles. The welcome celebration was sincere but not nearly as elaborate as the one given the 126th three months earlier. Scarcity of money and food brought limitations the community must have regretted. However, "The Pilot's" editor offered apologies for the meager recognition given these men. He did his best to compensate by writing a welcome home editorial of profuse tribute to the returning heroes.[9]

Some returned, others left for the war. Among the new units being raised was the 21st Pennsylvania Cavalry. This regiment was mainly composed of volunteers called up by Governor Curtin for six months service during the invasion. Six of its twelve companies were raised in Franklin County (*Companies D, H, I, K, L, and M*) the largest contingent of horse soldiers raised here. Men from the Green-castle-Antrim area were scattered throughout the ranks of the troopers, many of them veterans of the 126th and 158th Infantry regiments. The largest concentration of local men was to be found in Company K, generally called the Upton Company. This outfit was headed by Captain Robert Boyd and most of its other enlistees were from Peters and Montgomery Townships.

The regimental commander of the 21st was Col. William Boyd, recently a captain in the 1st New York "Lincoln Cavalry." The colonel had been released from the New York unit to organize his own regiment under a commission of Governor Curtin. At the time, Boyd and his wife were living at Chambersburg in a home on Federal Hill. Milton Cafferty, the cavalry sergeant wounded in the fighting at the Fleming house, had been given the rank of lieutenant and although still with the Lincoln Cavalry, he was now temporarily assigned the duty of getting volunteers to fill the ranks of Boyd's new regiment. [10]

On August 28 the first draft selection for men of the Greencastle area was held. Envelopes containing 487 names were placed in a revolving container and a blind-folded veteran drew the names of those who would represent the first local contingent of draftees. Names of men who had served earlier were excused. This wheel of fortune named 146, including twenty-two Negroes, who would be eligible for call to a three year term of service. Men who joined volunteer units from the county or elsewhere would be excused. [11]

The invasion's aftermath brought major problems for farmers, especially those whose holdings were along the main routes of the invaders. They saw their grain rotting and fields along the roads used by the Rebels had to be cleared of debris - dead horses, broken wagons, and caissons, plus other types of military paraphanalia. Lands near these highways, tramped down by thousands of men and horses, were next to impossible to plow. When it was, the soil broke into hugh clods and lumps which then had to be pulverized with axes and mallets. Fences had to be rebuilt. Most cattle and horses were gone and the task of gathering together what was left was the first order of business. Many rural families were short of food since their cellars, smoke houses, and chicken yards had been raided so often. They had to ask for credit at general stores and help from more fortunate friends and relatives who still had food left.

Those farmers who stayed and struggled to get things back to normal shared the few horses and wagons that were left to get the work done. In the areas not along the invasion's path fall planting got done but it was generally later than usual. In many cases th damaged fields along the roads did not get cultivated until spring. On some farms the middle fences used to separate fields were uprooted to provide extra rows when planting time did come.

Some families never did recover. They simply sold out, and in time, left to make new lives for themselves on western lands. The pages of area newspapers told of migrations to the West during the remaining war years and for decades beyond. Here they were able to begin again a kind of living they had known before the war.

The scarcity of horses continued. Some relief came when the government sold those no longer fit for military use. William Heyser recorded in his diary, of September 3, that he attended such a sale in Chambersburg. "All skin and bones, brought from $1 to $60. None would I take as a gift. Left in disgust." The local paper noted in late August that a few privately owned horses were coming to the area from Bedford County - "many of them very fine looking." [12]

As more horses became available thier owners were plagued by a renewal of theivery. As early as August 4 "The Pilot" reported the theft of three horses and this danger continued through the rest of the war. In September a Farmers' Association was organized in Washington Township to fight the menace. It consisted of men, who through cooperative efforts, planned to go after these thieves through a network aimed at detection, pursuit, and arrest of the criminals. "The Pilot" urged Antrim's farmers to follow this example. They apparently did not, yet there is little evidence that the Washington Township vigilantes were very successful in their efforts either. A month later it was reported that the theivery was rampant all along the border. "Nearly every night some farmer is missing one or more horses," said "The Pilot" in its September 1 edition.

Just as farmers faced numerous problems so did the town's businesses. Storekeepers' stocks, depleted by the "purchases by the Confederates," were reappearing on shelves by mid-August. Freight traffic was once again seen on the turnpike to Balimore and by the end of the month inventories seemed back to normal. Advertisements began to proclaim the recovery.

One problem for shopkeepers was the shortage of coins - particularly pennies and nickles. Merchants and businessmen, in the absence of these smaller coins, had to give their customers small articles of goods for change. This was not just a local problem. Larger city stores instituted a practice of using tokens representing certain money values. These metal disks, carrying the name of the firm and their value, were given instead of change. This was good for business since customers had to return with their tokens to make later purchases. Adding to the merchants' worries was a report in mid-September that counterfeit twenty-five cent currency stamps had appeared in Philadelphia. All business people were warned to be aware of this phony money. The local paper advised, "The general appearance of the note is bad and it an easily be detected by comparing it with the genuine " [13]

By early August the task of repairing the rail line between Greencastle and Chambersburg was well on its way. To keep the mail service intact the local postmaster, George Eby, at his own expense, carried letters and parcels to and from the county seat. At times this was irregular and full service was not resumed until September 15 when the road was sufficiently repaired to allow cars to run once again - the first time in twelve weeks. Renewed freight service meant warehouses would be in full operation. [14]

Jacob Hostetter, in an article years later, recalled this resurgence of commercial activity and how he, in cooperation with the town's commission merchants, started operating a system of privately owned freight cars. They ran between Greencastle and Baltimore, carrying to the city produce and grain and bringing back goods ordered by area merchants. At that time freight rates were so high and cars so scarce that the rail companies charged much less to haul privately owned cars than they did for the use of their own freighters.

These cars came in two sizes - four wheeled, about the size of a present day caboose and those with eight wheels, twice the size of the smaller ones. Cargoes of 8,500 pounds were hauled by the four wheelers and 18,000 by the larger ones. At this time there were no rail facilities in Waynesboro or Mercersburg and when a shipment arrived, merchants from these towns would come to Greencastle with their wagons and carry home loads of merchandise for their customers. This arrangement lasted until 1867 when the railroad companies began providing their own freight service. Business by the Greencastle entrepreneurs ended, but for nearly four years, their monopoly on freighting was an extremely prosperous enterprise. [15]

Business gradually improved but the community's health was a big worry to many. The passage of Lee's army left rural roads and town streets in deplorable condition. The turnpike companies were forced to make repairs from their own revenues. Township supervisors encouraged farmers, whose properties fronted roads, to clean up debris left by the invaders and to fill in holes and ruts where needed. Accumulated filth in and along rural water courses had to be removed. This, too, became the responsibility of the farmers.

Town authorities faced similar problems and local property owners were obliged to remove deposits of decaying vegetation, and enormous amounts of animal wastes left by the enemy's host of horses and thousands of cattle and sheep foragers had driven through the borough. In "The Pilot" of August 11, the editor urged councilmen to increase efforts to enforce ordinances that required citizens to "cause half the the street in front of their lots to be well scraped and cleaned, and the dirt to be immediately removed." Gutters were to be kept clean and free at all times from impure water. Fines of one dollar could be levied against those who failed to meet these requirements. The editor's concern for health conditions extended into the homes. He urged families to air their cellars and apply liberal coatings of whitewash to the walls and sprinkle basement floors with lime. The threat of contagion and epidemic was a constant fear.

Back in February McCrory had warned his readers, "There are some cases of smallpox in most of our neighboring towns. But, the terrible disease has not made its appearance here." Although vaccination had been accepted by some, the great body of people was still not convinced that vaccination was a legitimate way to combat this disease. Some objected to it on religious grounds or superstitions, with which a great number of people still lived, worked against acceptance of such a "new fangled idea." They were content to treat disease with home remedies such as one found in a day-book of the pre-war period. This concoction was labeled a "sure cure for smallpox and scarlet fever. - One grain of sulphate of zinc; one grain of foxglove; half a teaspoonful of sugar mixed with two tablespoonsful of water. When thoroughly mixed, add four ounces of water." There were no directions for administering the "remedy," but like similar concoctions it was probably given to the victim until he recovered or died. Varioloid, a mild form of smallpox, did strike the community in late January but it was reported in early March that the disease was rapidly abating and a few new cases were occurring. Such attitudes towards sickness were apparent again in August of 1863. Despite the editor's warnings there was sickness, not from smallpox, but fevers that rose from unsanitary conditions in the town. Impure drinking water and the proliferation of disease carrying flies undoubtedly were sources of the rising amount of illness. From mid-June to late August the paper reported thirty-seven deaths and in the August 25 issue the editor said, "We have lost many of our most useful citizens during the past few months. Not only the gray haired father and mother, but the light, the gay, the young and beautiful have left us forever." The latter observation was no exaggeration. Of those who died, twenty-five were children under the age of twelve. In a similar period the year before seventeen people died, twelve of them children. The invasion's toll had to be measured not only in farm and business losses but in this extraordinary increase in deaths, especially among children. The heat of summer would soon end and colder weather represented the best hope for stopping the sickness and the dying.

The fall season was not far off and work continued on improving water courses and the town's streets. A notice in early September indicated th slowness with which this work was proceeding. A shortage of manpower was the major drawback and men were urged to see Charles Hartman or other council members for employment. It was noted that if more workers could be found this important job could be completed before winter set in.

Schools were being readied for the coming term. An advertisement in the September 1 issue of the local paper showed the township needed twenty teachers to fill vacant positions. Samuel Lesher, the school district's secretary, placed this notice and stated that on September 12, the board would meet at the Franklin House to consider applicants. All teaching positions had been filled in Greencastle for the term that was scheduled to begin in both town and country on October 5. A new two room building had been erected on South East Street. Two other one room schools were on West Street, while a fourth was to be operated in the Fleming residence on North Carlisle Street.

On October 31 town and rural teachers met to form the Antrim Teachers' Institute. Meetings, planned for twice a month, were to be held in various schools of the area where experienced teachers would demonstrate methods for teaching the basic subjects. Officers of the Institute included Samuel H. Eby, President; Lemuel Snively, Secretary; and J. W. P. Reid, Treasurer. Editor McCrory praised this move to improve education - "Educate the young, for we want no more rebellions, and no further spread of vice and wickedness. But, first of all, the teacher himself must be educated, and that is what we want done." [16]

The editor's obsession with misbehavior of town boys was constant. At one time he editorialized on the way boys delighted in being noisy, rough, and troublesome. The constable was urged to take matters in hand and send the juveniles home to their mothers. He was outraged at seeing little fellows, aged five to ten, out at all hours. "Haven't parents time to think of the evils to which their children are exposed, by being out at late hours in company with older and worse boys?"

That misbehavior of the boys was a menace may have been exaggerated by the editor, but it seemed to be a phenomenon that developed after the invasion. There was no mention of this problem during the first six months of the year. Could this outbreak of "juvenile delinquency" have been another result of a time when chaos seemed to rule while the Confederates held the town from mid-June through early July? The Rebels took anything they wanted and went anywhere they cared to go without restraint and civilians got away with much when they felt they could. These were not the best examples of law and order. More importantly in many families normal home life had broken down while fathers or older brothers were serving in the military. With no male authority in the house discipline might be more relaxed. These explanations, however, do not erase the fact that the local editor was irritated by the youths' shenanigans. His crusade would continue but for the time being, it was the teachers who were expected to eliminate the "vice and wickedness" of their charges. [17]

Since the McDowell Academy had closed the year before, Joseph S. Loose decided to open a private school at his home on South East Street. It was to be known as the Greencastle Seminary for both girls and boys. A newspaper announcement told of a curriculum which would include all branches taught in a first class school. "Music and other ornamental branches will be taught by an experienced female teacher." A limited number of boarding students could be accommodated in the home of the principal, Mr. Loose. Classes were scheduled to start on the first Monday of October. [18]

The opening of schools was one of the many harbingers of autumn and approaching winter. Getting ready for cold weather was reflected in the paper's advertisements. J. W. Barr told the public of his full line of cooking, parlor, and nine plate stoves. Wood burning stoves were still in demand but more coal burners were being used each year. Lacquered coal buckets were also available for greater convenience and cleanliness. Heavy footwear was advertised by John Bert's establishment. In September his stock of newly acquired boots and shoes contained the latest styles. John's brother, George, specializing in custom made footwear and shoe repairing, operated his shop above the emporium on South Carlisle Street. The S. H. Prather store's notices told of ample stocks of fall and winter goods - wooden dressgoods, cloaking cloths, shawls, shirting flannels, stocking yarn, along with a full line of boots and shoes. John B. Byers announced the opening a new boot and shoe store on West Baltimore Street with a well stocked line of footwear for women, men, and children. Another business, the Wunderlich Millinery Shop, reminded the ladies of a newly received line from the city representing the latest styles in bonnets, hats, and trimming. A. W. Welsh, a dealer in hardware and cutlery, told of his generous supplies including those needed for the coming butchering season. Finally, portents of cold weather brought reminders from those selling patent medicines that good health could be preserved by liberal doses of Kunkel's Bitter Wine of Iron Tonic. Coughing, chills, and other signs of cold induced illnesses could be helped by laying in a supply of Coe's Cough Balsam. [19]

Hunting season had started and reports showed an abundance of quail, pheasants and rabbits. A notice, published in the September 29 issue of the "The Pilot" reminded hunters of laws protecting blue birds. Since there were no limits, the slaughter of game continued relentlessly. In early December, the paper commented, "The poor partridges suffer. It will not be long before all the birds are killed."

Families were beginning to lay in their supply of wood. Solomon Dome was the wood corder. He was supposed to see that families received the right amounts when they bought firewood. His office was in Lewis Cantner's tailor shop on South Carlisle Street. Benjamin Bert was the borough's assistant wood corder and his headquarters were located in the Haus and Bradley Tailor establishment on West Baltimore Street. [20]

By early October the war was still see-sawing back and forth with no end in sight. Lee and Meade were facing each other in Virginia but their forces had not engaged in any major battles. The fighting in Tennessee was slowly moving toward Federal occupation of the state. Occasional reports were heard of Federal cavalry headed by General William Averell, going against Imboden and Jenkins in the Shenandoah. Locally it was reported that a considerable portion of the recently recruited cavalry force headed by William Boyd was camped on the Witmer farm at Moss Spring.

Another local activity involving the war effort continued. This was the work of the Ladies Aid Society. On the evening of October 5 the Rev. John C. Bliss of Carlisle delivered an address in the German Reformed Church. Bliss told of successes by civilian groups, such as the Ladies Aid Society, in bringing comfort to the wounded. He had served with the Christian Commission during the Peninsula Campaign and subsequent fighting, helping to handle thousands of wounded. This was a fund raising event and about forty dollars were raised through sales of tickets by local storekeepers. Another account told of sending food to the wounded at Gettysburg. The shipment contained supplies of tomatoes, potatoes, grapes, apples, and peaches, plus nine dozen eggs, eight dozen doughnuts, twenty-five dozen rusks, nine jars of jelly, a crock of apple butter, a sack of dried fruit and six heads of cabbages. A contribution of twenty dollars was also sent to the Christian Commission. [21]

State elections were scheduled for October 13 and as the campaign moved toward election day there seemed to be a definite trend away from support for the war and Republican control of many states was in jeopardy. Despite victories at Gettysburg and Vicksburg there was a growing discontent over the conduct of the war. In many states, including Pennsylvania, resentment against the use of black troops and the draft was spreading. This feeling was nurtured and spread by political leaders in a part of the Democrat party still opposed to the war. It was this opposition from the Peace Democrats, that seemed to threaten Republican candidates all over the North.

Riots broke out in northern cities like Boston, Troy, and Newark, but the most serious uprising occurred in New York City where, in July, a thousand people were killed and wounded - the majority being black men, women, and children. Discontent in Pennsylvania's anthracite coal fields centered around opposition to the draft and the "Rich Man's War." A militant miners' organization, known as the Molly Maguires, led riots that brought property damage and loss of life in such towns as Pottsville, Mahanoy City, Shamokin, and Sunbury.

Amid this anti-war sentiment the Peace Democrats waged a vicious campaign against Republicans. Their speakers harangued voter rallies with anti-draft, anti-Negro, and stop-the-war speeches. But, the Republicans and those Democrats who favored the war came together to form the Union Party. Their rallies were filled with patriotic fervor and President Lincoln had published, throughout the North, a letter which denounced those who were attempting to divide the nation and give victory to the Confederacy.

Although in ill health, Pennsylvania's Governor Curtin ran for re-election. His opponent was George W. Woodward, a moderate Democrat and a justice of the state's Supreme Court, but his supporters mustered all the arguments against the war throughout the campaign. A disadvantage for Curtin came from the absence of a law that would have permitted soldiers in the field to cast absentee ballots. Other states had such laws but Pennsylvania's was still tied up in the intricacies of the Commonwealth's legislative processes. Soldiers were allowed to come home on furloughs to vote, but many Pennsylvanians were too far away in the western and Tennessee campaigns. Those closer were in Virginia but since large scale fighting could break out there at any moment few could be sent home. However, Secretary Stanton did what he could to furlough as many as possible.

Finally the voters cast their ballots and despite the apprehension of Lincoln and Republican leaders every Northern state except New Jersey went for Union candidates. Andrew Curtin, by a meager margin, was re-elected but the slimness of his majority did reflect widespread opposition to the draft and weariness with the war.

Pennsylvania' results showed Curtin with 269,496 votes while Woodward received 254,171. Franklin County's voters barely went for Curtin - 3,876 to 3,710 and the Greencastle-Antrim vote was only 483 to 464 for the governor. This narrow margin of nineteen votes showed the continued strength of those who earlier had been called the Breckenridge Democrats. [22]

Undoubtedly Curtin's low vote margin in the county came, in part, from dissatisfaction with the state militia in both 1863 and the year before. Business and farm losses suffered during 1862 and the Confederate invasion and retreat hurt the governor. Assurances were given that land owners would be paid for the use of their property for encampments and damages resulting from the presence of the militia in Franklin County, but this was a slow process. Discontent over the progress of the war and misgivings concerning the draft were other factors that affected Curtin's popularity in Franklin County.

A report of the State Board of Military Claims showed that by the end of 1863 a total of $498,536 represented the amount of back claims against the Commonwealth, but only $166,415 had been paid - $332,121 was still unsettled. By year's end $7,044 had been paid to Franklin County farmers. In the Greencastle area Jacob Shank of the Milnor area was paid $255; Adam B. Wingerd and Archibald Fleming received $515 each; and John Shank, who lived about a mile south of Greencastle along the Williamsport Pike, got $115 for damages. These settlements were probably for damages back in 1861. [23]

Settling claims was usually a long drawn out process sometimes made longer by court involvement and appeals. As late as February 16, 1864 "The Pilot" reported that Commissioners appointed to appraise damages resulting from Stuart's raid of 1862 were still adjudicating these losses. There had been a hundred claims in Adams County and over three hundred in Franklin and Fulton. Claims arising from damages from the presence of the Anderson or 15th Cavalry and state militia in 1862 were still to be heard. It was estimated that $1,250,000 would be required to cover the losses of that year. No estimate was reported for damages in 1863. What were called border claims were presented to the federal government to cover losses resulting from Confederate foraging and field or fence damages. For years these claims were submitted and resubmitted, with no results except unfulfilled promises by politicians. [24]

The only comment concerning the election by James McCrory was that he was gratified to see the extraordinary quietness that prevailed. "There was a larger vote polled than ever before; but like good citizens after executing their patriotic duty, most of the voters went quietly home and resumed their avocations." The editor had not taken sides prior to October 13 and in the election's aftermath he had to play it safe. There was little profit gained from congratulating the governor in a community of such closely divided loyalties. Anyhow McCrory was too busy running Greencastle. If he did not tell town council what to do, who would? Another job was to organize the farmers to catch horse thieves. Who else could do this? Above everything, who was going to see to all the details of the draft and other war measures? It was his duty to make sure the war was won.[25]

Within the week following the election the community was once again jolted into realizing that war was still not far from its borders. Word of another possible foray into the valley spread through the area on Monday, October 19. Cannonading had been heard on Sunday in southern Antrim and even in Greencastle. It was later learned that fighting with Imboden's forces had taken place near Charles Town now in the new state of West Virginia. *(It had been admitted to the Union on June 20, 1863.)* His forces were repulsed and the press assured the public that no raid was imminent. "The Pilot," in addition to giving this assurance reminded its readers that the area was better prepared than ever before. "General Couch's Department of the Susquehanna's soldiers were ready to repel the Rebels if ever they attempted to pass this way again." "Some guarantee!" was the likely comment heard throughout the region.

Despite the political hazards generated by the Draft Act, President Lincoln, on October 17, issued another call for 300,000 men. On the same day Governor Curtin announced Pennsylvania's quota to be 38,268. In keeping with federal regulations the governor's call outlined the inducements which would make volunteering more advantageous than waiting to be drafted. Enlistees would be assigned to Pennsylvania regiments. Veterans who volunteered would receive one month's pay in advance and a bounty plus premiums amounting to $402. Non-veterans would get a month's advance pay and $302 in bounty and premiums. Men were urged to go to the nearest recruiting and mustering office to take advantage of this offer. If the quotas were not met, deficiencies would result in municipalities paying penalties.

Greencastle's editor urged local men to take advantage of the monetary inducements and escape the draft. "There are so many who object to drafting who will now have an opportunity to enter the service by their own free will and choice, or encourage others to do so. The ranks of our armies will then be filled and we may look forward to a speedy termination of the war." Franklin County's quota was set at 1426 and by August, 313 men had gone into the service. This left a deficit of 1,103 that could be filled by volunteers or the draft after the January 5 deadline. Greencastle needed twenty-one to fill its quota while Antrim had to raise ninety-one. [26]

Enthusiasm for volunteering was somewhat less than "fair to middling." Week after week James McCrory urged, cajoled, goaded, prodded, and constantly held the carrot stick of all the extra money available if only local men would enlist. As the year approached its end he resorted to the community's sense of patriotism, its self pride, and past record of volunteering. Then in the final issue of the year, he once more reminded - "Those contemplating volunteering had better do it before January 5, else they may not get any of the liberal bounties that they will a week or month after this. Think of it." This was Mr. McCrory's final plea or warning. (Greencastle was now offering an additional fifty dollar bounty.) [27]

On October 2 a sad reminder of the price paid at Gettysburg was sent from the governor's office. This was in the form of a notice to families whose sons lay buried in different parts of the battle field. A national cemetery was being prepared by the several states interested in the proper burial of their deceased soldiers. "All the dead will be disinterred and the remains, placed in coffins and buried and the graves where marked or known will be carefully and permanently re-marked in this soldiers' cemetery." Families who intended to remove bodies to their home burial sites were urged to do this immediately. This notice appeared in "The Pilot" of October 20 and was signed by the official in charge, David Wills. Later issues of the paper told of arrangements being made for ceremonies to be held on November 19 when this National Cemetery would be dedicated. The Hon. Edward Everett was scheduled to deliver the principal oration. No mention was made of any other speakers for this occasion. People were reminded that all rooms in the hotels of the town were already engaged and that if local citizens were planning to attend they should take their own "provisions" with them.

An account of the dedication ceremonies appeared in the December 1 edition of "The Pilot." No mention was made of Everett's oration but President Lincoln's speech was printed without comment. The only other news of this event was that during the speechmaking - "a great number of persons had their pockets picked. Forty empty pocketbooks were found the next day at Hanover Junction." The press story that thievery was associated with the solemnity of the occasion appears to indicate an indiffernce to Abraham Lincoln's profound words. However, McCrory, was not alone. Throughout the nation other newspapers exhibited little more than passing interest in what the President said.

So there were pickpockets at Gettysburg. In Franklin County there still were horse theives, but just before Thanksgiving, news came that pleased all horse owners. Joe Hooker was caught again. This time he was arrested in Frederick and would be returned to the Chambersburg jail. His capture resulted from the work of four young men from the Greencastle area. The constant theft of horses in the region prompted this posse to go into the South Mountains to look for stolen animals. After searching and finding none, they went on to Frederick where they learned Hooker and his family were living. By cautious inquiries they found the thief's home. Then, along with local policemen, the house was surrounded and Mr. Hooker captured. Further detective work led the men to a farm where fourteen horses were stabled. Some were identified as property of farmers in Antrim Township. The owner of the farm was also arrested as an accomplice. It was later learned that other animals had been sold in Washington markets and that those rescued would have been taken to the capital city eventually.

The young men who took part in the discovery and arrests were not identified. They had to remain anonymous since it was believed members of Hooker's gang might even the score by violent means. This was a dangerous game and to get involved was to risk being severely hurt or killed. "The Pilot" reminded farmers to continue their vigilance for "doubtless Hooker's accomplices will continue this nefarious business." [28]

President Lincoln, on October 3, issued a proclamation calling for the observance of a day of Thanksgiving on the last Thursday of November. Although there had been days of thanks at various times through the war, this proclamation permanently established Thanksgiving as a holiday that has been celebrated ever since. November 26, 1863 was a day of solemnity in Greencastle. All businesses were closed and a service was held that forenoon at eleven o'clock in the Presbyterian Church. The Rev. J. W. Wightman delivered a sermon, said to have been "eloquent, powerful, and patriotic." Special music was provided by a choir with singers from all the town's churches. At the close of the ceremonies a special collection was taken by the Ladies Aid Society for the benefit of hospitalized soldiers and prisoners held in the South. One hundred and twelve dollars were raised in this manner. Editor McCrory commented - "The day was well observed; much better than usual on such occasions. Soberness and quiet prevailed. Poultry suffered considerable destruction." [29]

Christmas was coming and stores were advertising wares that would be suitable for the holidays. It was reported, "The windows of the shopkeepers are already filled with toys and fancy goods." Hostetter's grocery store, the only one of its kind in town, was ready to meet all cooking and baking needs of the season. Programs were planned by the various churches and fund raising activities of the Ladies Aid Society were scheduled, including four performances by the Philo Dramatic Association, a company of local young men, to be held in a hall in the A. L. Irwin store on East Baltimore Street. A special program was scheduled for Christmas morning in the lecture room of the German Reformed Church. It was also announced that a singing school was being conducted in the lecture room of the Presbyterian Church. The local editor urged public support for this venture. R. A. McClure, the school's leader, was described as a gentleman of more than ordinary musical ability readying the singers for the carol season.

Midst all this season of goodwill, glad tidings, songs of joy, and reasonable contentment, the town's boys were still giving McCrory fits. Just ten days before Christmas he complained of the crowding around the post office door every evening to the dismay and inconvenience of adults. "It usually requires the services of the constable to enforce order." Three days before the holiday of "good tidings to all men" it was reported, with an air of great satisfaction that crime does not pay. "On last Friday morning one or two juveniles were arraigned before Squire Kauffman, on charges of making noise and otherwise disturbing the peace and quiet of the Post Office. The lads were very penitent and made to pay some costs, reprimanded, and sent to school." It was also reported that someone was trying to frighten the town's children at night. Dressed as a "devil," he walked on stilts to give greater size to his image. This time the "devil received his due" when the boys "took it into their heads to stone the fellow off the streets." No one was arrested and the devil never appeared again in that particular way. The boys probably kept on throwing rocks at anything suspicious.

Despite "The Pilot" campaign to reform the boys, Christmas came at its appointed time and the rituals and customs that had been a part of the community's style of living for generations were faithfully observed: fashioning evergreen decorations and wreaths for windows and doorways; searching for holly and mistletoe for indoor arrangements; finding and cutting the right cedar or pine and gettig it into the house to be laced with home styled decorations; baking cookies, pies, and cakes; seeing to the gifts for the youngsters; preparing food ahead of time to be ready for the biggest meal of the year; attending the Christmas Eve services; lighting the windows' candles; caroling; and feasting for hours on that day of all days. All proceeded as usual. [30]

Christmas in many families was still filled with thoughts of those not present and of the ones who would never see home again, but the grief that gripped so many homes the year before was not present in 1863. No major battle had been fought just before the holiday as in 1862 at Fredericksburg.

"The Pilot" reported that Christmas was celebrated in a normal fashion and that the performances of the Philo Dramatic Association were well attended. Proceeds amounted to an estimated two hundred dollars for the four nights. The musical numbers and comedy sketches, based on Irish and Negro dialectal humor were praised by the critic, James McCrory. Some disorder from drunks in the audience was squelched on two occasions and the doorkeeper, ushers, and others were complimented on the manner in which the trouble makers were ejected. The paper also noted that, "Great numbers of people from the surrounding country came to town and tried to feel as happy as they could. Some of them, we dare say, hardly felt so gay the next morning." Obviously the hotel's were open, apparently serving their saloon clientele steadily throughout the holiday.

Mr. McCrory's reaction to the local state of intemperance was relentless. He called on the ladies of the community to use their influence and take a strong stand in favor of temperance. Something had to be done to roll back the tide of drunkenness and rowdyism. He not only struck out at public drinking but "fashionable" private imbibing in homes. Mercersburg was complimented for the steps taken there to kindle the "flame of temperance reform." The editor, in a column long editorial, warned of the consequences of New Year's debaucheries. He traced the pathway from a simple social drink to drunkenness, to moral depravity, and eventually the grave. He warned young men to beware of the seduction of the goblet of the drawing room brimmed with excitement and pleasure. "Who can suspect the serpent that lurks in the hospitality profered by the fairest hand? Yet scores on Friday (*New Year's Day*) will take their first step on the road to ruin in sipping wine or punch at the house of their fair friends." The final admonition followed - "Young man, if you are not already the slave of a fatal appetite, taste not, touch not, aught that can intoxicate, but resolve to commence the New Year with a deliberately formed resolution to live henceforth a life of Temperance and Virtue." [31]

That drunkenness was a social problem of major proportions

cannot be denied. It was a source of crime; it led to loss of wages, jobs, and the eventual breakdown of family life; it was the cause of ill health; and most certainly the origin of many sicknesses that led to premature deaths. However, drinking had been a part of the life of communities, such as Greencastle, since colonial times. Whiskey was found in practically every home. It was used for medicinal purposes to relieve the sick or injured members of the family - babies, children, and adults. Wine, cider, brandies, beer, or liquor were served at any number of gatherings - funerals, weddings, christenings, holidays, harvest times, barn raisings, and a host of other occasions - important and many not so important.

War times are always fraught with a decline in normal restraints. When men are far from home their inhibitions suffer and the constraints of family, church, and friends often break down in a totally changed environment. With thousands of soldiers encamped or on temporary duty in and near the town at various periods throughout the war their relaxation through drinking or drunkenness certainly had some influence on the youth of Greencastle and its rural area.

James W. McCrory's attempts to chase away "Demon Rum" by editorial comment might have sounded as a "voice crying in the wilderness" yet he did have support among the town's church people, especially the women and ministers. However, one tirade, one warning of the evil tenacles of the serpent, or one essay a year at holiday time would likely have little impact on his readers. Little progress was made during the war but before the century's end the temperance movement had given birth to the Women's Christian Temperance Union, the Anti-saloon League, and a Prohibition Political Party. Editorials like McCrory's did in the end, bear fruit, but for the year 1863 his words were as "seeds falling on barren soil."

Long before his advice on drinking, McCrory had warned the town's juveniles of the consequences they faced if the New Year was welcomed with its customary noise making. In the December 1 issue of "The Pilot" there appeared a warning that all should observe the borough's law which expressly forbade exploding torpedoes, fire crackers, fire balls, gun cotton, or any other exploding device including pistols, guns, or cannons in the public square, streets, or alleys. Persons caught in such acts or found to be keeping or selling these kinds of noise makers were subject to a fine of one dollar. Those inclined to welcome the New Year as it should be and always had been were likely saying, "We'll see about that." Further reflection might also have evokd the question, "Where could anyone get a cannon?"

As the year approached its end it is likely many people were saying that no newspaper man was about to tell them how to finish it off. What they had gone through over the past twelve months was enough to make most men turn to drink and who cared about noise for just one night. "Let'er rip; who cares; we've had enough of 1863, we'll get rid of her as fast as possible in anyway we can."

New Years Eve came and it must be assumed the old year was ushered out and the new brought in with the usual racket of guns and pistols. However, there was no report of any cannon firings. It also must be supposed that as much liquor or wine flowed as in prior years. The absence of further comment by the editor in subsequent issues would indicate this. If the celebration had been calm and peaceful he surely would have taken credit. There was no such assessment and there were no repots of anyone being arrested.

The calendar showed it was all over, but for many who lived then this year would never end. It would be an unforgotten time for the rest of their lives. Into the early decades of the next century they still recalled its anxieties and sorrows. When grandchildren asked about 1863 their elders might answer - "It was the year Rebels came or the time horses and cattle were taken." A common response was, "It was a time the war passed this way." Perhaps this was the best of all answers. It covered everything.

CHAPTER X

1864

Philadelphia's Inquirer called Greencastle the "Banner Town" of the state. It was the first to meet its draft quota of forty-nine men. James McCrory, as can be imagined, was "beside himself," but words did not fail him. In a column long article he told how the goal was achieved.

A committee of businessmen, composed of Jacob Pensinger, H. P. Prather, A. K. Schaffert, A. L. Irvin, Thomas Pawling, John Goetz, and John Wilhelm, who served as treasurer, raised enough money to pay the extra fifty dollar bonus to all who enlisted. This meant that non-veterans received, with the local and federal inducements, $352 and veterans $452 for signing up before being drafted. The achievement was praised by the editor as a supreme example of the town's patriotism, its liberality, and enterprise. That filling its quota was an example of the town's patriotism must have raised some eyebrows. Its liberality could also be questioned, but most certainly the manner in which volunteers were raised had to be characterized as enterprising. What the Greencastle leaders did was to enlist six non-resident Negroes to meet the draft requirements. These blacks were from Greene Township and reaction from this municipality was not long in coming.

In a letter to the Franklin Repository, two officials protested the invasion of "Africa," the black community of the township. Jacob Glass and Jacob Bollinger resented this intrusion into their jurisdiction and posed some very direct concerns. Referring to the Greencastle leaders who perpetrated this arrangement - "In the future this township expects them to look after the interests of the colored families of Africa---in educating their children and supplying their other wants." They also inferred that a bounty of fifty dollars was a miserly price to pay when other areas were offering high bounties - $100 to $150.

The Greencastle editor, in a three column reply, was quick to uphold the town's honor by arguing that the fifty dollar bonus was enough to attract volunteers in the early days of recruiting because other parts of the county had acted slowing in solving their draft shortages before the bounties for enlisting had risen. Greencastle had simply "jumped the gun" on other municipalities. It was now February, but would Greene be offering $150 if they had found substitutes earlier for fifty dollars? Because they had been dilatory, officials of their township were then in Chambersburg "offering large bounties to everyone willing to accept."

McCrory's defense also pointed out that men from both Antrim and Greencastle had enlisted in other areas, and there were no complaints. He also suggested that Greene Township had shown no interest in looking to "Africa" for men to serve in the draft. Now that Greencastle had set a precedent they were incensed. Finally the editor clarified the extent of Greencastle's involvement. "We enlisted six Africans. Four of them are single and are presumed to have no families to be provided for, at least no children to be educated. Of the two married recruits, we already have with us the family of one." His parting blast was - "All this thunder and lightning - all this is about the family of a solitary poor devil of an African who is now in the armies of the Republic.--The mountain labors; out pops a ridiculous mouse." [1]

Such bickering over means of filling quotas and the cost of buying men to go into the military service seems to make a mockery of the word "patriotism." These practices, plus provisions for paying three hundred dollars or securing substitutes to escape the draft, raise the obvious question of whether the whole process met the spirit of equality and the sharing of sacrifices "that this nation might live" so recently pronounced at Gettysburg by President Lincoln. Perhaps not, but these were the methods used to raise armies to save the Union. Abraham Lincoln may have seen their injustices but he was a pragmatic man. He would use any means at his disposal to give his generals the manpower required to quell the rebellion.

The only local note of dismay in this controversy came with news that Antrim had not met its required allotment. A meeting was held on January 23 at the Antrim school house, just beyond the town's eastern border on East Baltimore Street. Its purpose was to raise enough money to attract forty-eight more men to fill the remainder of its quota of ninety-seven. David Strite presided, F. B. Snively was made secretary and A. B. Wingerd served as treasurer. It was determined that the monetary offer to induce enlistments had to be higher than Greencastle's and that an extra bonus of a hundred dollars was necessary. The township was divided into four districts and committees were named to solicit residents for contributions.

McCrory noted - "While the meeting was in session, more than a hundred young men from the country, subject to the draft, were standing in the streets, some looking at the railroad cars or whatever else that attracted their attention. Others were running about from saloon to saloon. We ask them -- why did they not attend the meeting? It was for their benefit. Some of them are not deserving of the generous efforts made in their behalf. They can yet redeem their character." Even with the proffered bonus, twice that of Greencastle's, Antrim's young men still preferred the comforts of home.

Raising money for bonuses was a slow process. The committees labored faithfully, according to the editor, but "they have not met with the encouragement they should receive, why do persons refuse to contribute? Some are to be excused for they have not the means. To them our remarks do not apply. Some object to giving upon the grounds of being opposed to all war (*the plain sects*). Yet owners of lands and property along the border need protection. --Then why do they not contribute of their abundance? --If these persons refuse, there are others who will with more reason, refuse also. --What respect can they receive in the community where they are known? --and they will be known."

The editorial went on to chastise these recalcitrants - "They want the quota filled but they want their kind hearted, generous, and liberal neighbors to do the work and pay the neighbors. --Then who shall be drafted to fill the deficit? Not the men who have used their time and money to put soldiers in the army, --but those who have not contributed of their means must stand the draft. Honor, justice and sentiment demand it. --The case is clear. One of three things must be done: join the army, pay four hundred dollars after the draft (*this was the per capita penalty for unfilled quotas)* or a small portion of this sum now. Men of Antrim! Choose you this day."[2]

Near the end of February, Antrim's quota was nearly filled. Reports told of John Wallech being authorized to raise a full company for service in the heavy artillery and that another regiment of cavalry, the 22nd, was being re-organized. Recruits were also being sought by the signal corps. An epidemic of young boys, aged fourteen and fifteen, running off to enlist, was reported. Upon appeals to General Couch they have been "delivered up" to their parents.[3]

While the draft quotas were being met many men, already in the service, were re-enlisting. A news item of January 19 told of men of the 77th Pennsylvania Volunteer Infantry re-enlisting after three years of heavy fighting in Kentucky and Tennessee. Before going into their second term of service they would be given a thirty day furlough and the county's people were encouraged to extend a "warm welcome" to these heroes.

Another story told of the 21st Pennsylvania Cavalry participating in quelling the Molly Maguire uprising in the coal fields back in November. It had been stationed at Pottsville during the winter and throughout December and January they were active in hunting down draft resisters and deserters hiding in the mountains of the area. Unfamilarity with the country did not hinder the work of the Upton unit, however. Two hundred men were caught and turned over to state authorities. Although the term of service was about to expire, about one third of Company K had re-enlisted. The company's new commander was Captain Robert J. Boyd of Upton.[4]

Concern for meeting new draft demands was generated once again when it was announced that 500,000 men were to be taken for three years or for the war's duration. March 10 was the time set for this call and local officials began looking for volunteers to meet quotas being set for the various municipalities. The county's allotment was 1409. However, volunteers already in the service provided a credit of 825 leaving 584 men to raised. Antrim's allotment was 129 but a credit of eighty-two reduced its number to be drafted to forty-seven. Greencastle's quota of fifty-nine was already met by enlistments so no men would be taken from the borough. Re-enlistments in the 77th Infantry, the 21st and 22nd Cavalry had helped keep McCrory from going through a period of torment again.

Worries about conscription, meeting quotas, the safety of those already in the service and keeping teenagers from enlisting occupied some minds. However, everyone was subject to the harsh winter of January and February with its bitter cold and heavy snows. Firewood dealers kept busy supplying their customers but some home owners were criticized for allowing newly delivered piles of wood to remain on their front pavements. Days would elaspse before the fuel was stacked in back yards or in wood sheds. Home owners and renters were reminded of fines that could be levied if the sidewalks were not cleared.

Sleighing parties were popular and skating on the First Dam was reported to be excellent. This was one of two dams west of the town which held water from McCauley's Spring that ran the grist mill and the one that pulverized bones for fertilizer. The enterprising Jacob Hostetter expected to gain a later profit from the frigid weather by erecting an ice house back of his store. Ice could be cut from ponds or dams and stored for summer use or at least for its early months. Usually not enough could be stored to meet customers' needs through the entire warm weather season. However, with temperatures in late February dipping to as much as six below zero, thoughts of summer's warmth were of little concern to anyone.[5]

One note of satisfaction must have come to the local editor when, in the March 29 issue of "The Pilot", it was announced that Mrs. Elizabeth Wilhelm had decided to discontinue the sale of liquor at her hotel in Upton. In the future the business would be "conducted on temperance principles." McCrory said, "This is one good sign of temperance reform. May others be induced to follow this example." (*This did not happen. Throughout the remainder of the century such places in both Greencastle and Middleburg continued business as usual.*)

Greencastle was saddened by the death of Charles Hartman on February 10. He was sixty-four years of age and had been in ill health ever since the invasion, when Rebel foragers forced him to accompany them on foot through parts of Antrim to look for runaway Negroes. His obituary called him "one of our most esteemed citizens" and cited the many years of service he had given the borough as a councilman and chief burgess. As a leader in the German Reformed Church "he exemplified an unparallelled example of Christian living."

Although the weather kept most people indoors, reports of horse stealing continued. Accounts told of theives working in both Maryland and Pennsylvania areas along the Mason-Dixon Line. Federal officers were looking into the matter by seizing all horses believed to have been purchased for much less than their real value. Hopes were high that this kind of investigation might break up "this nefarious trade." Of one thing everyone was assured, Joe Hooker was no longer leading any gang of theives. In the January Quarter Session Court, he was sentenced to six years in the Eastern Penitentiary.

Another example of the "mills of justice grinding slowly but surely" came with the arrest, in Hagerstown, of a character named David Pretzman. Better known as "Cross-eyed," he was a Southern sympathizer who had accompanied the Rebels during the invasion. His chief contribution, during this time, was to ride through Greencastle's streets "breathing out fierce threatenings of slaughter against all Yankees he would meet" --scaring women and children off the streets into hiding to escape his curses. "Cross-eyed" was finally caught in his home town and taken on charges of being a Rebel spy. By late February he had been removed from circulation and placed in custody of officials at the Old Capitol Prison at Washington. [6]

After the holidays the singing school, conducted by R. A. McClure, was reactivated. Persons interested were urged to attend a meeting at the Presbyterian Church where plans for the coming spring season would be disclosed. "The Pilot" once more supported the work of McClure - "The best teacher we have had here for sometime." In addition to developing an adult chorus, McClure had been working with a choral group of sixty girls and boys. On February 8 they presented, in Irvin's Hall, an Oratorio - "The Palace of Industry". Designed to illustrate the "poetry of labor," these singers traced man's progression of work from that of children in the schoolroom to the labor of men and women in the various branches of industry. Beside the instruments used to support the chorus an anvil's ring ing sounds formed a part of the accompaniment. Real class had come to town.

The editor, so often critical of "juveniles," praised the work of the youngsters to the "high heavens." "They performed their parts, keeping time to the music, without making a single mistake and without seeming to be confused in the least." McCrory actually told his readers that most adult performances had never excelled the work of these young people.

A month later McClure's choir of men and women presented "The Cantata of Esther" an appropriate Lenten offering. Performed in the Presbyterian Church before a large audience the cantata was met with enthusiastic praise by everyone including the editor. Later in the "entertainment season" a male string band of limited numbers (*estimated to be three guitar players*) was heard in the nightly hours and McCrory waxed eloquently - "Deep in the silent night when all is quiet and still, these sounds are the sweetest nightcaps imaginable and the surest instrument of a sound sleep --- We can only say, play again boys, play often, play every night." Advertisements at the time pointed to George Goetz as the promoter of this string instrumentation. His fortunes rested on enticing young men and ladies into learning to play the Spanish guitar. He sold them and he could teach anyone with a musical ear to play marches, waltzes, gallopades, mazurkas, and to accompany the most recent ballads and war songs.[7]

While all these aesthetic happenings were enthralling the town's people the calendar pointed to the coming spring. No news yet broke the seeming reverie that prevailed. Major armies of both sides lay quietly facing each other with only minor skirmishes reported. However, during the second week of March the lull was rudely shattered when Ulric Dahlgren's death was announced. Again Greencastle's people mourned the loss of another soldier, one they had come to think of as their own. The March 8 issue of the local paper told of fighting near Richmond in which Dahlgren and his men were engaged, but it was assumed that he had been taken prisoner. By the following week his death was confirmed. It was reported, "The whole community laments the death of this gallant soldier." An editorial recalled the two occasions in early July of 1863 when he and his men intercepted Rebel squads and how, after being under the control of the Confederate forces, this young cavalryman brought hope to the beleagured people of the town.

General Kilpatrick's aborted raid on Richmond, which led to Dahlgren's death was the only foray of consequence at the time. The main armies in Virginia were still marking time and Sherman's forces had yet to move in Georgia. Ulysses S. Grant was given the rank of lieutenant general and by March 10 he was authorized to command all Federal armies. By then he was with General Meade in Virginia and his presence there could only mean that a compaign against Lee was to be expected and that fighting in the Shenandoah Valley might accompany such a move.

Occasional troop movements in and around Greencastle were reported in early March. The town was plagued from time to time by visits from these men who apparently were new recruits with plenty of bounty money to spend in local saloons. Their drunken behavior, including loud and profane language at all hours, was brought to General Couch's attention and the nuisance ended when additional provost guards were assigned to police the borough. [8]

All through the month reports of troop movements in the various eastern sectors were heard. From time to time there would be more than ordinary numbers of soldiers going through the area toward Virginia. On March 20 a special train passed through the town carrying recruits for the 21st Cavalry. It was also reported that General Franz Sigel was assembling a sizable body of men in the Martinsburg area. A week later a battallion of Pennsylvania's 22nd Cavalry came through, by rail, on their way to the mountain country of West Virginia.

These developments were constant omens that full scale fighting was imminent. Other happenings served to refresh memories of the previous year. Forty-one farms or portions of farmland in Antrim were listed for public sale on the first of April and in the late weeks of March through mid-April news accounts told of families moving out, hoping for a better life in the West. "Passenger trains are crowded every morning with passengers going to the West. Indeed there has not been such an emigration westward for many years."

Another reminder was the continuing horse shortage. "The Pilot" reported a sale of a string of horses of "the high in bone and low in flesh order." The prices were "corresponding to the quality of the stock." Despite this low opinion, farmers bought them. They were better than nothing. The army's insatiable need for horses left only those rejected by the military purchasers. [9]

Unusually heavy spring rains prevented farmers from getting in fields to ready the soil for planting. "The Pilot" of April 19, reported the Conococheague and its tributaries beyond their banks. Town homes found their cellars filled with water causing great inconvenience and loss of stored edibles. The editor commented - "Cellars have not for years been so deeply inundated."

When the rains ceased warmer weather followed and by late April and early May farmers were able to ready their fields for another growing season. Grain prices were holding at high levels with wheat quoted at a dollar sixty and corn at a high of a dollar five. Flour was selling for as much as eight dollars a barrel and hay was bringng twenty dollars a ton on local markets, but if farmers could get it to Washington military officials were paying as much as forty dollars.

More tobacco would be planted since Christian Hoover had demostrated the practicality of raising this crop the year before. On a two and a half acre plot he was able to harvest and cure nearly 5,000 pounds. It was viewed as a profitable venture by leading farmers at the time. Christian Lesher, the mill owner in the Marsh area specializing in producing sorghum syrup, was encouraging farmers to raise more "sugar cane." He issued a circular on the culture of this crop. It was reported that more farmers were expected to venture into this kind of farming. To overcome losses suffered during the invasion, increased numbers of sheep were being shipped into the area. John Ruthrauff told of selling five hundred head of a new breed, Coteswolds, during the winter. This animal produced all white and extra long fleece. It was larger than ordinary breeds and was said to be of value, not only for wool production, but for high quality mutton. [10]

The advent of warmer weather produced news of other community activities. Committees of ladies, clergymen, and business leaders were being organized to promote and participate in a giant fair to be held in Philadelphia during the first week of June to raise money for the Sanitary Commission. Residents of not only Pennsylvania but New Jersey and Delaware were to be part of this massive fund drive. The local committee was headed by the Rev. Breidenbaugh, with Dr. J. K. Davison as vice president. Col. D. W. Rowe was secretary and G. W. Ziegler served as treasurer. Circulars were distributed throughout the town and country telling people of the project. Farm produce, cured meat, canned food, usuable clothing, tools, and any other materials which could be auctioned or sold at the Fair were to be brought to the town warehouses. Money contributions could be sent to the treasurer. It was also reported that local craftsmen were busy making items to be donated. August Shirey was proudly showing a washstand made from white oak salvaged from discarded lumber when the railroad was rebuilt. Such an occasion was made for newly designed quilts by the ladies, specially decorated harness or horse collars by the leather workers, and iron or brass pieces fashioned by local foundry workers. [11]

Certain problems seemed to constantly torment the town fathers. Streets were hoplessly dirty, alleys filthy, and recent rains produced mud everywhere. Councilmen were urged to force property owners to clean the thoroughfares along their holdings and to stop them from throwing rubbish in alleys. With May's warmer weather, hogs were venturing further from home. Swine owners were warned that all hogs running at large in the borough could be caught and sold by town authorities with the proceeds going into the municipal treasury.

More moderate temperatures brought the town boys out, much to the consternation of the local editor. They were using the muddy streets as mock battle grounds and their principal missiles consisted of "mud balls" aimed at opposing "armies." In the course of battle their projectiles landed on porches, on windows, and occasionally on ladies' clothing or in their faces. The editor called for this to stop. "If the parents do not attend to it, let the constable." In the same spirit of mock warfare some of the more heroic "soldiers" ventured into the foraging business, also. It was noted - "A lot of rascally little boys got into a lady's garden on South Carlisle Street a few evenings ago and tore up a lot of vegetables." Once more the editor urged peace officers to "hunt them up and teach them a lesson."

In early May James McCrory assigned the responsibilities for editing "The Pilot" to William Reid. Under his direction the paper continued to indicate its concern for civic and business progress, but the new editor seemed to be less puritanical in his views with a hint of less concern for the moral life of its readers. [12]

The long awaited start of campaigning finally came, and when it did, war seemed to explode all over the South at the same time. On May 4, Grant, with Meade's Army of the Potomac, crossed the Rapidan River and moved into the Wilderness country against Lee's Army of Northern Virginia. Three days later Sherman's Army began its gigantic campaign in Georgia while the notorious Benjamin F. Butler commanded another army that was moving up the James River to attack the Confederate capital. The next several weeks brought reports of fighting on the Virginia fronts through war department releases and letters to families and the town paper. Word of the terrible losses in the Wilderness campaign caused anxieties in many local homes.

Day after day steamers from the Rappahannock kept coming into Washington to unload their cargoes of wounded and dead. Here they were delivered to waiting ambulances and hearses. Hospitals in the city were filled to overflowing while train after train pulled out of the depot with walking wounded going home to their families.

After one full month of fighting Grant's forces were within nine miles of Richmond getting there at the terrible cost of fifty-four thousand dead and wounded soldiers. Revulsion swept over the North as this carnage became known. The cigar smoking hero from the West was now called "The Butcher." Why would any President permit such a slaughter? Even within the Republican Party a move was started to dump Lincoln at the nominating convention, scheduled for June 7 in Baltimore. On May 31 a splinter group met in Cleveland and nominated John C. Fremont as their choice for the presidency. But Abraham Lincoln would not move from his initial confidence in Ulysses S. Grant. He was still convinced that if Lee's army was to be destroyed, this general was the one who could do it.

With ever mounting numbers of wounded the work of the Sanitary Commission became more crucial. Meetings continued to be held by the Ladies Aid Society and the committee promoting the Great Central Fair in Philadelphia. In a public gathering on May 14 it was decided to circularize the town and township to appeal for contributions and ministers were urged to notify their congregations of the need to "respond liberally to the demand made for the wounded and suffering heroes of our army."

It was noted later in the summer that the Philadelphia Fair raised more than a million dollars from the sale of home crafted objects and food. "Young girls acted as waitresses, sold flowers, served at the booths and exerted all their charms to add to the fund to help the soldiers." All over the North similar fairs were held in other large cities and when hostilities ceased the Sanitary Commission reported $4,924,480 had been collected in money and the value of supplies sent by home based chapters of aid societies amounted to fifteen million dollars. [13]

The severe fighting called for more surgeons. Dr. George W. Hewitt, who had come to town in February, joined other Pennsylvania physicians when called by the governor. He was assigned to work in a hospital at Fredericksburg. Other evidence of hostilities in Virginia came with reports of large numbers of deserters fleeing northward. In early May several soldiers of a New York regiment were caught in the South Mountains as they attempted to get home through the little used roads of the mountain timberland. Several natives acting as guides were also arrested. A later newspaper account told of four more deserters, one from the 21st Pennsylvania Cavalry and the others from New York units, breaking out of jail. When last heard it was thought the escapees were making their way to safety through the Amberson Valley region. Rewards of eighty dollars per man were being offered for their capture.

Civilians from Virginia were also fleeing into Pennsylvania. A party of twenty-four men were said to have fled into Adams County where they were employed at cutting timber. In mid June twenty-two women and children, families of some of these men, were able to get to Martinsburg by hauling the children in a wagon while the mothers walked. When they finally arrived in the Greencastle area the party was taken in by the Harry Mickley family of Upton where they were able to rest for several days before going on to join their husbands and fathers in Adams County. [14]

In Virginia the fighting continued as Grant made plans to lay siege to Petersburg. Further south Sherman's army was slowly advancing through Georgia, towards Atlanta. As the summer moved through June and into July the progress was slow but sure despite severe losses on both sides. Grant's and Sherman's campaigns generated widespread public concern but while the nation's eyes were focused on these sections, a campaign in the Shenandoah Valley, led by General Franz Sigel, ended in defeat at New Market, May 15. Sigel was demoted and David Hunter took over the forces in the valley. This campaign was of direct importance to the people of Maryland and southern Pennsylvania. It was from the Great Valley that raids and the 1863 invasion had brought destruction and terror into the Cumberland Valley.

Throughout May and early June Hunter's forces conducted a systematic campaign aimed at destroying the Shenandoah country's ability to sustain Confederate armies which had so often moved up and down the Valley at will. Beginning at Staunton Federal forces began the destruction of mills, iron furnaces, storehouses, granaries, farming equipment, and anything else that could supply the Southerners. The Virginia Military Institute was burned. The state governor's home was leveled by fire along with other plantation mansions and farm buildings. David Hunter became the most odious name in Virginia.

Finally General Lee sent Jubal Early's Corps from the main army at Richmond, to drive Hunter out of the Valley. Early struck the Union forces at Lynchburg and by June 19 Hunter had fled with his men westward across the Alleghenies into West Virginia, leaving the Valley with little or no opposition to Early's advancing legion of avengers.

With the conflict's end not in sight and the fighting never ceasing, the war machine demanded the draft quotas issued in March, to be satisfied in early June. Although Greencastle had no quota to meet, Antrim needed to furnish forty-five men. It was noted that of this number some had been drafted as often as three times and already had substitutes now in the service. The Solicitor General had ruled that payment of a three hundred dollar exemption or buying a substitute only protected a man from one call, leaving him liable to all future drafts. Others who had been exempted earlier because of physical disablilities were also liable if their names were called again. By June 9 it was announced that the county's quota of 1409 had been met.

This was hardly over before rumors began flying of another call being considered. "The Pilot" suggested that measures be taken immediately to recruit volunteers to fill any future quotas. "As we know from experience, that those who first begin a work of this kind are certain to accomplish a first. Would it not be well to call together the old organization and re-organize? We think it would be a wise and prudent thing to do. With all the trouble Antrim had in its attempts to meet quotas it might have been something they should consider." Perhaps Greene Township would also be interested in such an idea. [15]

Summer's advent brought word of more men and boys being killed, wounded, or captured and again their families were engulfed in grief or terrible anxiety. Yet despite these sorrows and worries, business was booming. Stores were advertising their latest wear for children, ladies, and men. A new retail establishment was announced by Samuel Hammill. Located on West Baltimore Street, he specialized in boots and shoes sold at "short profits." Hardware stores were offering new lines of farming and gardening implements along with home building and repair necessities.

Greencastle's agriculture and farm implement factories were flourishing. The editor in commenting on this prosperity said, "There is no town can vie with us in this respect. We supply this state and to a certain degree our neighboring states. Every piece of local workmanship taken to county or state fairs has always drawn a premium. Farmers cannot complain for want of agricultural conveniences." Commission merchants were advertising improved shipping arrangements and higher prices available in the New York markets. Merchandise and produce could be shipped directly with no freight transfers between Greencastle and the northern port city. Attempting to capitalize on the western migrations the Pennsylvania Railroad advertised new time tables for trains traveling to eastern cities and Pittsburgh. Accompanying this new schedule was an announcement of the Pittsburgh, Ft. Wayne, and Chicago line telling of three trains a day to Cleveland and Chicago. [16]

With prosperity at so many levels, the first step to establish a bank was taken by leaders of the business and farming community. On June 3 an organization certificate was signed to designate a financial center to be known as the First National Bank of Greencastle. Capital stock amounting to $100,000 had been raised by a hundred and thirteen shareholders - affluent businessmen and farmers of the area. The ones chosen to sign the certificate were representative of these groups - Samuel H. and Henry P. Prather, John G. Rowe, Jacob Hostetter, William Kreps, Charles W. Ruthfauff, Adam B. Wingerd, George Book, and Robert Boyd. The bank could not begin operating until the Comptroller of the Currency gave his approval, but this first step was the beginning. Greencastle would have a bank. No longer would business people need to depend on their strong boxes or banks in Chambersburg or Hagerstown. Despite the ever presence of war and the continuing possibility of more Confederate raids a decision had been made to provide financial services come what may. [17]

Of immediate importance was the slowness with which claims against the government were being paid. This concern brought a new kind of professional service to the area. Known as claims agents, they were available on a commission basis, to assist persons with problems such as collecting pensions, bounties, back militia pay, or bounty lands promised to those who had served in the military or heirs of deceased soldiers. Hastings Gehr, of Chambersburg, was available to help local residents who had these kinds of problems. [18]

Working class families had more money from higher wages but their incomes rarely stayed even with the rising cost of living. The new editor, commenting on this, recognized the sacrifices these families were making. "Laborers, mechanics, and families of small means are compelled to reduce still lower their now plain style of living." However, his solution did not lie in appealing for higher wages for these people. All he could suggest was that "families of small means" look for bargains to be found in the stores of those who advertised in his paper. Such generosity surely must have stirred the souls of those trying to make ends meet. [19]

War time's economy brought a prosperity not totally free of annoyances or threats to orderly business operations. In early June a potential danger came with reports of counterfeit twenty dollar bills being circulated in the county. The Franklin Repository told of faults that could be found in the bogus bills and warned business people to "mark the difference between the genuine and counterfeit closely to protect themselves from being victims." [20]

Another nuisance came in the form of night prowlers. "The Pilot" protested the freedom with which older boys and sometimes adults roamed the streets at all hours. "They generally salute with a vociferous shout or sometimes by projecting a stone, cautiously, so as to pass you and attract your attention. The business of these fellows is to visit gardens or hen roosts, and to start all the dogs in town barking." The editor told of being awakened one night by an unusual noise and upon looking to the street below he counted not less than ten canines exercising their right to howl at any hour they pleased. His solution was to establish a police force. The town was getting too big to depend on just a constable. [21]

Later in the month it was reported the town was at the mercy of theives specializing in stealing chickens, butter, eggs, and milk. The editor noted that one such thief had his headquarters in the basement of his home on West Baltimore Street. Others of this "dispicable class" trained their children in the ways of pilfering food which was brought home for their mothers to cook. "These parties are known and marked, and may climb the wrong post some night." If they wished to try the editor's chickens, he invited them with the promise "they might also get the pleasing sensation of one of Allen and Wheelock's pointed ticklers." He was ready to greet the visitors with a load of buckshot. No constable, no police force, it was time somebody put the thieves in their place. [22]

But it was not all work, accumulating profits, or ferreting out the town's mischief makers and crooks. Summertime was fun time for both the affluent as well as poor families. It was a time for picnics and fishing excursions. "The Pilot" reported young ladies and gentlemen of the town were generally taking advantage of the pleasant days with much pleasure in their innocent enjoyments. "Sow your wild oats today - tomorrow may demand a more serious duty." The only discordant note to such advice was found in a warning from M. M. McCauley who declared that anyone fishing or swimming or in any way trespassing on his lands along the Conococheague would be prosecuted. McCauley's property was no place to "sow wild oats."

Hostetter's ice brought welcome refreshment to townspeople during the hot summer days. Iced lemonade and homemade ice cream were now possible. Such a delicacy as ice cream had been available only in cold weather when ice could be found for home freezers outside the kitchen door. Now, through the enterprise of the town's grocer, there was "an abundant supply" of this winter's gift to the good old summertime. [23]

247

It was also noted that the Franklin House had been remodeled by its new owner, John H. Adams, who had purchased the hotel from Daniel Foreman. Later, Foreman and Daniel Gilds bought the Union Hotel from the heirs of Joseph Hollar who had died in March. Evidence of more tolerant views of the new editor came with his praise for the renovated Adams House - its newly furnished dining room with an excellent cuisine and the barroom. He was ecstatic when describing its array of offerings, served with utmost gentility - brandy, gin, whiskey, or for tastes more moderate - a sweetened cocktail, ice cold sherry, tame ale or foaming lager beer. For the really modest patron there also was lemonade. The toasts of the house, however, were champagne, bourbon, wine, cognac, and sweet Maderia eggnog. All were served in a newly paneled and frescoed saloon furnished with easy chairs and cushioned lounges. Such luxury the town had never known. Contrary to what would have been McCrory's reaction to such a center of debauchery, William Reid exhibited a genuine appreciation for this remarkable tribute to Bacchus. If the cup could lead to eternal damnation, as McCrory had strongly intimated, Reid was certainly encouraging his readers to travel that road with class and high style. Let the good times roll. [24]

Fourth of July was celebrated with a huge community picnic at Moss Spring. A committee, consisting of D. W. Rowe, J. M. Irvin, and S. H. Prather, arranged the program. There were speeches and Hamsher Clippinger, a government employee home for the holiday, organized a chorus to sing patriotic songs. Each family furnished its own food which was enjoyed to the accompaniment of band music. All stores and other businesses were closed and both town and township families enjoyed the celebration. The only discordant note in the whole affair was reported the following week. "Some low despicable person, with the soul of a mustard seed, stole the muslin cover off the band wagon." [25]

Far more dismaying than a stolen muslin was the news that spread across the North following Independence Day. Early had come out of the valley with an army of over 20,000 to enter Maryland and threaten Pennsylvania. Northern newspapers claimed he had twice this number. Governor Curtin, issuing another call to defend the state, asked for volunteers for a hundred days service. On July 6, General John McCausland, who had taken over Jenkin's command when he was mortally wounded at Cloyd's Mountain, took possession of Hagerstown and threatened to burn the town if $20,000 and specified clothing were not raised. Although the clothing demands were not totally met, the money was paid and the Confederates left.

News of a possible invasion was sent to Harrisburg by William Wilson, the telegrapher Greencastle first came to know in the summer of 1862. General Couch immediately warned local authorities to get word to farmers and business men of an impending raid. Scores of Negroes rushed out of Virginia and Maryland fleeing through the town toward Harrisburg. Storekeepers and commission merchants packed their merchandise and sidewalks were filled with boxes as owners waited for wagons to take their goods to the railroad where it could be hauled away to safety. At night the train finally came, and when the cars were filled it slowly moved toward Chambersburg.

A detachment of the 6th U. S. Cavalry, led by Lieutenant Hancock T. McLean, had been sent from Carlisle Barracks to Hagerstown. On July 6 they were forced back to Middleburg, where the small force was nearly surrounded by the numerically superior Confederates. From here they withdrew to Greencastle. A Confederate attack was expected at any time Taking every precaution, McLean put pickets out on every road. Detachments from the 14th Pennsylvania and 1st New York Cavalry also patrolled the roads along the Maryland border.

The next day a patrol sent to Middleburg reported "no more rebels this side of Hagerstown except a few horse thieves." Area residents heard heavy cannon fire coming from the direct of Frederick. This was Early's force trying to capture Maryland Heights, near Harpers Ferry. On the morning of July 8th McLean moved his entire force to Muttontown. While here, he tried to find horses to replace those that had been lost or worn out, but he reported Rebels had beaten him to the few that remained in the area. He also sent a request to his superiors for rations of food and whiskey for his men. That evening the detachment moved into Hagerstown which had been abandoned by the Rebels. The 6th Cavalry continued to patrol the area for enemy activity and when the threat of invasion seemed over, McLean and his men returned to Carlisle.[26]

In the meantime McCausland's force went on to Frederick where $200,000 was raised to save it from a threatened fiery fate. From there, Early's main body moved toward Washington and on July 9 met Lew Wallace's hastily formed division at the Battle of Monocacy. The Union force was defeated but Wallace delayed the enemy long enough to allow Grant to send reinforcements for the defense of the capital city. Early did get as far as the city's outskirts where on July 12, the President, who had gone to Fort Stevens to watch the fighting, narrowly escaped being hit by bullets from Rebel sharpshooters. When the Confederate leader saw the city was too strongly defended he left and within a matter of days his forces were back in the Shenandoah country.

When word came that Early was no longer a threat, farmers began bringing their animals home and business people returned with their stock. The newspaper reported "We had no idea before of the vast number of horses in this section of the county. There are thousands of them. *(Many were from Maryland farms.)* Skedaddlers and contrabands are back. Our country friends are busy cutting and hauling in their grain. With all the dry weather the wheat will be garnered without serious loss. The danger is over for the present and we hope it is over forever." The dateline for this article was Tuesday July 26 and by the end of the week this proved to be a forlorn hope.

On July 29 a force, again headed by McCausland, including Bradley Johnson's Maryland cavalry, crossed the Potomac at several points in the Clearspring area. When this news hit Greencastle panic reigned again. All through the afternoon business people hid their stocks while some were fortunate enough to ship merchandise to Philadelphia by rail. As dusk fell wagons from Hunter's command came through the town, going up the valley toward Carlisle. Along with the wagon train a thousand infantry and cavalry marched northward. Farmers again were taking their livestock in the same direction as fast as possible. [27]

William Fleming, Jr. later recalled these hours of turmoil and fright. He was just ten years old when he and his brother, Rankin, along with uncles, Archibald and Blair, started up the valley with their horses and cattle. "The road was crowded with farmers from both Maryland and Pennsylvania. We traveled all night stopping an hour at Shippensburg to water our stock and separate them from the other herds with which they had become so mixed that it appeared as one great drove. At two o'clock the caravan left Shippensburg and found shelter and pasture near Carlisle late the next day." [28]

When McCausland's movements were detected as early as July 27, Lieutenant McLean was again sent to Franklin County. Arriving in Greencastle, the next day, he and forty-four men proceeded to Mercersburg while a detachment led by Lieutenant Jones stayed in Greencastle to patrol roads in Antrim and Washington townships. However, the action was not to be in this part of the county.

McLean reported that his patrols extended out the Shimpstown road as far as the fordings at Clear Spring, McCoys, and Cherry Run. At three o'clock on the afternoon of July 29 he and his men were driven back from Shimpstown. A series of running encounters with the enemy continued all the way into Mercersburg. Before McCausland entered the town a final stand was taken by McLean's cavalry, but when a force of two hundred Rebels rushed them, they were forced to retreat to a position along the road to St. Thomas. [29]

The Rebel force of about 2,800 cavalry and four pieces of artillery started to arrive in Mercersburg around four o'clock in the afternoon and until eight that evening they continued passing through the town. Separate squads broke into stores emptying them of merchandise while money and other valuables were taken from residents. From Mercersburg the Confederates moved out the road towards Bridgeport (*Markes*) and at the farm of William Hoke a temporary encampment was made. After feeding their horses and waiting for stragglers the march continued through the night to the turnpike leading to Chambersburg. [30]

While McCausland's cavalry was moving through the western part of the county a diversionary force, led by Generals William L. Jacobson and John C. Vaughn, was moving on Hagerstown. Here they were met by Maryland cavalry led by Colonel Henry Cole. For three hours the opposing forces fought through the streets of the Maryland town. C. Armour Newcomer, a member of Cole's command, told of this affair. "We were forced back to the road leading to Greencastle. After being driven out of Hagerstown a short distance, what was our astonishment to find General William Averell's brigade drawn up in line; they did not engage the enemy as the Rebels halted on the northern edge of the town. Averell fell back to Greencastle and encamped there for the night." Cole's men eventually joined Averell and Newcomer was given leave to spend the night with his uncle, Jacob Newcomer, who ran a popular restaurant in Greencastle. The rest of the contingent found Averell's force of 2,500 men just north of the town along the road to Chambersburg. Here they set up their encampment about eight o'clock that evening. [31]

According to William Reid, Averell, who commanded a cavalry division in the Dept. of West Virginia, came to Greencastle by way of the Williamsport Pike in the late afternoon of July 29. He surveyed the town's southern limits, near the Cumberland Valley railroad's warehouse, apparently looking for a suitable place to station his men in case a Rebel force made an appearance. A body of state emergency men had been sent to the town by General Couch and they were resting on the Diamond and along Carlisle Street when the cavalry moved on to the Archibald Fleming farm. Here the Fleming residence became the general's headquarters and nearby fields served as the men's campsite. Three orderlies were stationed at the Greencastle telegraph office, operated by H. R. Fetterhoff, the town's photographer whose studio occupied the same building. D. C. Auginbaugh, a Hagerstown telegrapher, was with Fetterhoff at the time. [32]

Averell and his staff ate supper with the Fleming family and during the evening he and his officers studied a map of Franklin County which hung in the hallway of the house. Upon conferring

with William Fleming, Sr. who managed his father's farm, a route was determined that could get the cavalry to the east of Chambersburg where it might make contact with McCausland's force, thought to be following the same route Stuart took in 1862. Later the general and his staff left to rest in the open. The night air would be a relief from the heat they had suffered all through the day. The officers left the commander to himself as they went to join their men. [33]

Lieutenant McLean had kept General Couch informed of McCausland's progress and of the threat to Chambersburg. Courier after courier had been sent when the Rebel force headed east on the turnpike. Couch had come to the county seat when Early's army invaded Maryland and presented a danger to Pennsylvania. After this crisis subsided his forces were reduced to about a hundred and thirty-five soldiers - forty cavalrymen from the Carlisle Barracks, sixty members of the Patapsco Guards, and a detachment of the 1st New York Light Artillery with just two cannons. [34]

When the Commander of the Susquehanna Department heard Averell was at Greencastle, he probably felt, that McCausland could be turned back. Couch telegraphed him to come immediately and stop the Rebel advance. During the night two more messages were sent, the last arriving in Greencastle at three o'clock in the morning of July 30. The orderlies who carried the messages could not find their commander and no one at the camp could either. [35]

Thomas Bard, an assistant to the superintendent of the Cumberland Valley Railroad, had fled with William Wilson to Greencastle. When the Rebels came to Hagerstown they secured a handcar and pumped themselves to safety all through the afternoon of July 29. Bard was in the Greencastle telegraph office where Averell's orderlies received the messages they were unable to deliver. All through the night he saw the telegrams and there were no replies. Such failure to observe normal military courtesy disturbed Bard.

Since the three o'clock message told of Couch's preparations to leave Chambersburg, Bard decided to ride to the camp. Along the road he met the orderlies "riding leisurely towards Greencastle." Bard saw the latest telegram and when he learned the earlier messages had not been delivered he and the orderlies rushed back to camp. Within minutes they arrived and asked for the general. Still no one knew where he was and an officer joined in the search. Around four o'clock they found the commander asleep by the side of a fence. When Bard explained Couch's predicament and asked if he would go to his aid, Averell replied, "Tell Couch I'll be there in the morning."[36]

It was morning. Bard knew this and everyone in the camp knew this, but the cavalry's leader made no further move to show he was concerned about Couch or Chambersburg. Yet just nine miles away, nearly three thousand enemy soldiers lined the town's western hills waiting to take the place. Thomas Bard, standing in total disbelief, heard through the damp morning air the faint sound of a cannon firing. It was the report of a Union shell exploding among Rebels along the hills. This shot, which killed one and wounded several of McCausland's men, was the only resistance offered by the small army defending the town. Although Couch had assembled a local guard of about five hundred citizens he quickly saw that such an unorganized and poorly armed group would be useless. His only recourse was to desert the county seat as quickly as possible and within the hour he and his meager body of soldiers were on their way to Harrisburg.

In the dimness of early dawn, residents could see McCausland's men strung along the ridges looking down on Chambersburg. The invaders fired three shells into the place, damaging one building but injuring no one. Then about eight hundred men were ordered to leave the western heights and move into the alleys and streets of Chambersburg. The remainder stayed on the hills ready to rush to any point where resistance might develop. By six o'clock the town was at the complete mercy of General John McCausland.

Borough leaders were brought to Center Square where the demands were made. The town was to be burned if one hundred thousand dollars in gold or five hundred thousand in greenbacks was not raised. Local leaders assured McCausland and his staff that no such sum was available. All bank funds had been removed and there was nothing close to such an amount in the town. The court house bell was rung to get more citizens to the Square. They were to be told of the demands and the consequences if not met. Pleading with the Rebel leader caused no change in the original conditions and the order was given to start the burning. Barrels of kerosene were brought to the square from nearby stores. Here the soldiers soaked their torches and ignited them to begin carrying out their orders.

Few household belongings could be saved as houses were set afire. All over the center of town business buildings were soon ablaze. Before applying the torches many places were ransacked and valuables taken by the arsonists. Saloons were emptied and as drunken torchbearers approached homes to be fired, cries of women and children were ignored as they pleaded to be allowed to save keepsakes or valuable belongings. By ten o'clock all buildings and structures around the Square and as far as two blocks in all directions were burning. Well known landmarks such as the Court House, the Mansion House, the Chambersburg Bank, and Town Hall were in flames. Mills, the tannery, the brewery, and the paper mill were destroyed. The Academy building that had served as a hospital for both Union and Confederate wounded was burned to the ground. A. K. McClure's home and the Chambers house were reduced to ashes. [37]

Two buildings, purposefully saved, were the home of William Boyd and the Masonic Temple. When the officer in charge of the squad, about to fire Boyd's house, learned from Mrs. Boyd that she and her husband lived there, he ordered his men away with the explanation that the residence belonged to a gallant officer whose conduct during battle was always in the highest tradition of the military. The Masonic building, home of Chambersburg's George Washington Lodge, was saved when an officer, obviously a brother Mason, posted guards around the temple to make sure it was not harmed. This unknown Southerner allowed the precepts of Masonic fraternalism to take precedence over orders from his superiors. [38]

As officers and men continued to fire the buildings citizens constantly accused them of violating rules of civilized warfare. They were destroying a defenseless town. Those who bothered to defend their actions usually gave the official reason - upon orders from General Early they were firing Chambersburg in retaliation for what Hunter had done to the Shenandoah Valley. Sometimes the justification was based on the desire to avenge the vandalizing of Fredericksburg or more generally to even the score for the destruction of towns and cities in Northern Virginia.

McCausland left the blazing town at eleven o'clock and began traveling west towards St. Thomas and Fort Loudon. When the Rebels reached the mountain's side they could look down on a devastated Chambersburg. Clouds of smoke covered its part of the valley as the burning continued all through the day. The Confederates had done what their orders required with a resulting toll of two hundred and seventy-eight houses, factories, and business places destroyed; a hundred and seventy-three utility sheds and buildings in ashes; and ninety-eight barns and stables burned to the ground. The loss was estimated by a commission appointed by Governor Curtin to be $1,628,431 in real estate and personal property. Three thousand persons were said to be without homes. [39]

General Averell finally arrived about two o'clock in the afternoon. He had left the encampment near Greencastle and followed a road from Brown's Mill to one east of Marion that led to New Franklin. Near ten o'clock he arrived at the farm of Christian Lehman where the horses were fed. The Union cavalry then moved east through New Franklin to New Guilford (Duffield). From this hamlet they reached the Philadelphia Turnpike at Greenwood. [40]

J. Milton Snyder who lived in the New Franklin area recalled when Averell's men were there - "I distinctly remember that many of the soldiers were eager to march directly to the place and many were angry with their commander. The smoke and flames were leaping and rolling high in the heavens, shutting out the sun. — If Averell had marched to Chambersburg at once instead of eastwardly the beautiful town would have been saved." [41]

What might have been was irrelevant. What Averell did was to hurry his troops toward Chambersburg from Greenwood. Armour Newcomer in his account told of their approach and passage through the town - "When orders came to mount, every man in the command, including Cole's cavalry, was eager and anxious to avenge this act of incendiarism, but on our arrival in Chambersburg the enemy had gone. They had accomplished their hellish work and were retreating in the direction of the Potomac. Those of us, who were in the advance, went through the burning town, bending forward upon our horses' necks, as fast as our faithful steeds would carry us. We had no knowledge of the great destruction and devastation that we should witness and when we had once started it was necessary to continue through the burning streets. Houses on fire on both sides, it was no time to turn back and to stop was to be burned up; our poor horses were mad with fright. Each and everyone of us felt relieved when we got to the outer edge of the town. The atmosphere was stifling, with the smoke that settled over the earth like a pall. The citizens were gathered in groups; strong men with bowed heads; women wringing their hands; and the little children clinging to their mothers' dresses and everything." [42]

Out the turnpike the Union horsemen rushed to overtake McCausland. It was learned that he had crossed the mountain and from McConnellsburg had gone down Big Cove toward Hancock. Here an advance force ran into the Rebels but after a brief skirmish they escaped. Later the claim was made that this encounter saved Hancock from being burned. When the main Federal force came into the town it was joined by the 1st New York Cavalry that had been in the Smithsburg area when orders came to head west on the National Pike to help stop the retreating Confederates. Averell's troops followed McCausland into the mountains of West Virginia and by August 7 the Rebels were found near Moorefield.

In the early hours of the following morning, through a fog shrouded valley, the Union troops moved cautiously against their enemy, camped in a meadow along the south branch of the Potomac River. After crossing this rapidly flowing, stony bottomed stream, they entered a cornfield above the meadow land. Elements of the 1st New York and the 3rd West Viginia moved down on the Confederate camp. Upon reaching the edge of the cornfield they charged - firing, swinging their sabers, and yelling "to the full extent of their united capacity." The enemy broke and fled but the attackers gave no quarter. Within the hour McCausland's force was reduced by a hundred and fifty men killed or wounded, four hundred and fifty prisoners, four cannons, and all its wagons. This victory is said to have practically eliminated McCausland's brigade for the rest of the war. The Union cavalry lost thirty-six killed and wounded. [43]

BRIG. GEN. JOHN McCAUSLAND   U.S.A.M.H.I. — CARLISLE, PA.   GEN. WILLIAM AVERELL

Why Averell did not go to Couch's aid was never fully explained and in the minds of those who lived through this fiery hell nothing could be said to justify his failure to save Chambersburg. Available military records concerning this episode, however, do indicate a con stant concern of the War Department that McCausland's force might be part of another invasion that could endanger Baltimore or Washington. General Halleck was aware of this possible threat and as the War Department's Chief of Staff, he stood ready to halt any further moves toward the Baltimore-Washington region. Throughout the forenoon and afternoon of July 29 Couch was in touch with Averell and the cavalry leader was fully aware of the Rebel force approaching

Chambersburg. Yet Halleck was concerned that the passes through South Mountain be covered. His orders to Hunter, who was at Harpers Ferry, were all directed at McCausland to keep him from moving eastward. Hunter blocked South Mountain roads and sent more troops as far as Emmitsburg.

From Halleck down to Hunter and to Averell the paramount concern was to prevent McCausland from moving beyond South Mountain. It is true that Averell was responsible to Hunter and when his commanding officer was communicating with him the cavalry leader knew his concern was to prevent the Confederates from penetrating the area beyond the mountain. Yet Hunter had been out of touch with Averell after he had left Hagerstown. Telegraph lines were down and there had been no messages from Harpers Ferry since the day before.

However, Couch was in touch with Averell and there still is no explanation of why he never replied to telegrams that came from Chambersburg through the early morning hours of July 30. At the time it was inferred by many, including Thomas Bard, that when he found the general asleep along a fence row he was intoxicated - too stupified to understand the full extent of Chambersburg's plight and unable to fully comprehend the nature of Couch's predicament. However, this inference was never confirmed and was never the subject of a military inquiry. [44]

Couch had left Chambersburg after four o'clock on the morning of July 30. Later in the day a message from Averell reached him at Harrisburg. - "Your dispatches reporting the approach of enemy forces from Mercersburg were not received until 3:30 a.m. today. Vaughn, Jackson, and Imboden were on my front and Johnston and McCausland to my rear. At 4:30 McCausland set fire to the principal portion of Chambersburg. Marching as rapidly as possible leaving my infantry behind I placed my command between the enemy and Baltimore and advanced to attack the enemy retreating in the direction of St. Thomas." The message continued with a request that Couch send a train (*wagons*) with hard tack, coffee, and sugar for six days. It ended - "It was the intention of the enemy to burn Carlisle in retaliation for burning private homes by Hunter." [45]

There are certain obvious contradictions concerning the receipt of messages from Couch. The claim that he had forces on his front and back must be viewed with some doubts. That he placed his command "between the enemy and Baltimore" coincides with earlier orders. That Carlisle was to be McCausland's next target seems to be pure conjecture. This does no have any documentation in available records.

Averell's message to Couch could have been his way of covering himself in case of future inquiries. Yet he later served with Sheridan in the Shenandoah campaign, but in late September he was relieved of his command for lack of aggressiveness in pursuing Early. This charge might have been made by Couch after July 30 if he had been his commander.

Reaction to the tragedy of Chambersburg was immediate. Early in the morning of Sunday, July 31, people from the countryside poured into the burning town with food and other necessities - Greencastle ministers called upon their congregations to give money, food, and clothing for relief of their neighbors - a call that re-echoed throughout the other churches of the county. [46]

If William Fleming, Jr. could have told his fellow Presbyterians what he had seen they would have understood completely why help was needed. When the Flemings got their cattle to Carlisle, William and Rankin decided to come home. "The older ones tried to dissuade us but being homesick to see the old home town, we slipped away footing it to Greenvillage when we were overtaken by Colonel Thomas Fletcher and Mr. George Chambers who insisted upon my riding with them. My brother, Rankin, continued to walk. After leaving Greenvillage the great fire from the burning of Chambersburg was plainly visible illuminating the sky for miles. The road was filled with people hurrying from the burning town carrying bundles, clocks, chairs, and all manner of household effects, including cooking utensils. It was a most pitiful sight but a much sadder one was to follow. When we entered the burned town about six o'clock on the evening of the 30th we saw what had been about as fine a city or town as could be, now a mass of ruined homes almost depopulated. With Mr. Fletcher and Mr. Chambers I walked through the streets with houses burning on either side, the heat from which was almost unbearable. We finally reached Mr. Fletcher's home which had not been burned and I was one of more than fifty persons who, that night, occupied his house, a large majority of us finding rest on the floors.

"No boy was ever so eager to catch a glimpse of old Greencastle and when my brother and I, on the following evening, saw the church spires from the hill north of my grandfather Archibald Fleming's home where we met the most hearty welcome and a large feast for which we were ready." [47]

Such eye witness accounts did come to people and through the weeks that followed money was collected and sent, while carloads of furniture, clothing, bed clothes, cooking equipment, and food poured in from all over the valley. The warehouse of Wunderlich and Nead had escaped the fire and it was used to store food and articles brought to Chambersburg. Prices skyrocketed and most families were completely dependent upon donated necessities. Provisions were sent daily for several weeks by the military. Temporary housing was provided in homes not destroyed while the railroad company gave free transportation to those who left to live with friends and relatives in other parts of the state. The governor called a special session of the legislature and its members came to view the town's destruction. One hundred thousand dollars was appropriated for immediate relief. Later legislative action brought more financial help, but in the end only half of the losses were covered by the state.[48]

Sightseers came by the carload and generally offered little but sympathy. Northern newspapers sent reporters to cover the story through pictures and special articles. All except a few New York papers were sympathetic, but the New York journals could not understand why the town had not been defended by Pennsylvania troops. A great body of local people were pondering the same question.

BESORE COLLECTION   WEST MARKET STREET RUINS

One redeeming feature of the entire unhappy affair was that no one was killed. Compared to the sacking of Lawrence, Kansas on August 21 the year before, Chambersburg was fortunate. Not only did the renegade William Clarke Quantrill, acting in the name of the Confederacy, burn Lawrence to the ground but he and his gang of guerrillas killed a hundred and eighty men and boys - most of them shot down in cold blood while offering no resistance.

The week that followed the McCausland raid brought a flurry of military activity. Cavalry groups seemed to be everywhere as patrols covered the various main and rural roads leading into Maryland. Thursday, August 4, was declared a National fast-day and prayer services were held in the churches. The next day rumors spread - Rebels were concentrating again across the Potomac at Williamsport and guerilla bands were in the Welsh Run region looking for horses.

Eventually these stories subsided but the patrols continued. It was learned that a system of signal stations was being established to deal more effectively, in the future, with threats of invasion or raiding parties. This network would be able to notify military authorities much faster than in the past when the border was threatened. Greencastle was to serve as headquarters for the United States Signal Corps of the Department of the Susquehanna.

With news of McCausland's defeat and that the Signal Corps meant better protection a sense of relief spread throughout southern Pennsylvania. Stores, hotels, and other businesses, closed for nearly two weeks, resumed operations. Farmers began returning with their livestock and by the end of August practically every aspect of normal living had returned - that is all but one. At the end of July James McCrory announced his retirement. He would be missed for he had been associated with Greencastle's weekly as an editor or owner for nearly a decade. A fellow journalist, William Kreps, noted that McCrory had published "one of the brightest journals in southern Pennsylvania." The town was without a newspaper and for over a year's time Greencastle people had to depend on Chambersburg and Waynesboro journals for their local news. [49]

As August ended, the siege at Petersburg remained unchanged, Atlanta was still holding out against Sherman, but Mobile Bay had fallen. These campaigns were still eating away the North's manpower and draft calls were being announced again. This led to new volunteer regiments being organized for one year's service. Men from the county, including recruits from the Greencastle area, joined the 201st on August 29. Part of one company came out of Franklin County. the men were used for provost duty in Pennsylvania - hunting draft dodgers and deserters. During the first two weeks of September two more regiments were raised at Harrisburg. The first was the 205th in which a portion of one company was from the county. This unit saw fighting in the Petersburg campaign. The other, the 207th, with a company from Franklin, also saw action near Richmond.

The county's next volunteers came with the raising of a company inducted on September 16. Many veterans of other units were in this regiment - the 209th. Tobias Kauffman was its colonel and two of his staff came from the local region - Major John L. Richey of Mercersburg and Adjutant Andrew R. Davison from Greencastle. The regiment was taken to Virginia immediately and fought in the continuing seige of Petersburg. Except for local home guards and "Hundred Day" units, on call for temporary duty, Franklin County's Company D of the 209th was the last volunteer regiment with men from the area to be recruited. [50]

Atlanta fell on Friday, September 2. As Union forces from Pennsylvania fought through Georgia it was reported that the cry, "Remember Chambersburg" was sometimes heard as they went into skirmishes or full scale battls. When they saw Atlanta burning, some likely equated the smoke and flames devouring this ancient and proud city with the fires that leveled the small town in Pennsylvania. Most of them had probably never seen Chambersburg, but to many the scales of warfare were once again being balanced. [51]

The President declared Monday, September 5, a day of celebration for the victory in Georgia and the taking of Mobile. Local residents would have felt better if they had been able to celebrate a victory over Early's forces in the Shenandoah. Philip H. Sheridan had taken command of the armies in the Valley when he succeeded Hunter shortly after the burning of Chambersburg. As yet he had failed to gain any decisive advantage over "Old Jube."

Farmers did welcome the end of a long summer drought when rains came on the national day of celebration. Waynesboro's "Village Record" noted on September 5 the first rain for weeks. "The ground had become so dry and hard that some of our farmers almost despaired of getting their fields plowed." Then word came that Sheridan had soundly defeated Early at Winchester on September 19 and Fisher's Hill three days later. Such news, along with the rain, gave reason for heartfelt thanks and cause for real celebration.

Sheridan's campaign continued, through the fall and winter, with brutal fighting against Early's army. Guerrilla bands, including Mosby's Rangers, harrassed Union forces and both sides resorted to harsh reprisals against each other. The devastation of the Great Valley far surpassed the early destruction by Hunter and as it progressed, the Shenandoah country became what was described as a "vast moor' or a "barren desert." The boast that crows would have to carry their own food when crossing the valley was virtually true. Hundreds of families who lost their barns and farm buildings fled, many coming into the Cumberland Valley to live with relatives. This was true of many Mennonites and Dunkards who left their devastated farms to live with their brethren in Franklin and Cumberland counties or as far away as Lebanon or Lancaster.

While the people of the Shenandoah were suffering the agonies of total war, local residents began assessing results of a long, hot drought. Dry weather had obviously affected the corn crop, a major source of feed for farm animals and meal for both rural and town families. Tobacco and sorghum farming had not increased by any great extent so only the few who had ventured into this kind of agriculture were affected. Prices continued to hold for most farm products although through the winter beef prices rose to as much as sixteen cents a pound, butter reached fifty-five cents, and potatoes went as high as six dollars a bushel.

Owners of sawmills were reaping a harvest with increased lumber prices in the Chambersburg area. Rebuilding homes, factories, and business places went on through the fall and winter at as rapid a pace weather allowed. Heavy rains, sleet, and snow prevailed through much of the late fall and winter period. As a corallary to increased lumber costs, fire wood prices rose also. By late 1864 costs had risen to as much as seven dollars a cord. Coal, that before the war sold for three dollars a ton, eventually cost seven dollars. [52]

The signal station near Greencastle brought a slight stimulus to the town's economy. Its horses needed hay, oats, and bedding which local suppliers stood ready to sell. Hamilton Hartman, now in charge of his father's blacksmith shop, was a supplier of horse shoes, while various harness makers were called on for mending jobs or new accoutrements. Hotels welcomed members of the corps and officials who came to the station from time to time. Some of the men became regular patrons of both the dining rooms and bars of the town's hostelries. Many were also quite regular in attending church services when not on duty.

The first of October meant another school term and another hunting season - both opening with little fanfare. However, it also marked the beginning of intense campaigning for the presidental election. Lincoln was the sole Republican candidate. After the President was re-nominated at Baltimore in June, the other candidate, John C. Fremont eventually withdrew from the race. General George B. McClellan had been chosen by the Democrats at their Chicago convention on August 32. Their party's platform, among other things, called for peace "at the earliest possible moment." Throughout the summer few Republican leaders felt Lincoln could be re-elected, but when Atlanta fell and Sheridan began getting the better of Jubal Early his chances began to improve.

Republican and Democrat meetings were held in county towns throughout the month. A political rally, including a parade, was held in Greencastle on October 4. The Chambersburg band furnished music for this event but no record shows who the speakers were. Friday, October 28, a rally took place in Chambersburg with Vice-President Hamlin as the principal speaker. [53]

Some feeling of how men in the army viewed the coming election can be found in two letters to families living in the Greencastle area. Andrew Davison, Adjutant of Pennsylvania's 209th regiment, writing to his mother from the Bermuda Hundred near Richmond, gave his views. In a letter of October 14 he expressed hope that the Pennsylvania election went Republican. "I hope it went right as that will insure the defeat of McClelland. The Rebels in our front have been cheering for him for several days. If they want him elected I think every man in the North should endeavor to defeat him." [54]

Andrew was the son of Abraham S. Davison of Antrim Township. His younger brother, James, was with the 22nd Pennsylvania Cavalry at the time and his older brother, Joseph A., had served with the 6th Pennsylvania Reserves until mustered out in July with the rank of lieutenant-colonel. Later Joseph received a letter from a fellow officer written the day before the election. He was Calvin M. Hassler, who had been with Davison in the 6th Reserves. At the time, Hassler was stationed in he Adjutant-General's Office at Washington. His letter seemed to represent the prevalent opinion in the capital... "Well tomorrow will tell who is to be president for the next four years. I think Old Abe's chance is good. The Democrats here, for a while, were very sure of defeating him, but for the past few days are rather down in life. I think General McClellan has no chance. I hope old Franklin will cast a large majority for the Old Man." [55]

Lincoln won by carrying every state except Delaware, New Jersey, and Kentucky. Pennsylvania went to him by a margin of 20,081 votes - 296,389 to 276,308 for McClellan. Franklin's vote must have disappointed Calvin Hassler. Lincoln barely won with a 3,862 to 3,821 victory. Antrim and Greencastle's vote was close with 468 for Lincoln and 443 for the general. Of the twenty-two voting districts in the county, McClellan won thirteen. The rural vote did not go for Lincoln. For the first time servicemen exercised their franchise in a presidental election through absentee ballots and those from Franklin gave 346 to the President and 259 to McClelland. The soldiers' votes won the county for "Old Abe." [56]

Without doubt Lincoln was not as popular in Franklin County as he had been in 1860. This was certainly true in the Greencastle-Antrim community. His strength lay among the shop owners, store keepers, clerks, skilled craftsmen, and men of affluence. This decline in popularity ran parallel to the difficulties in meeting draft quotas in rural areas. Franklin County's people expressed their opposition to conscription through the ballot and not by violence.

It was no secret that keeping sons of some affluent families safe from war was costly. By modern monetary standards the payment of three hundred dollars for a draft exemption seems a small price to pay. Yet such an amount represented a year's pay for many farm workers or unskilled laborers. Since some well-to-do families had an abundance of sons this requirement could really hurt the family finances. Paving into a fund or paying directly for substitutes was costly too. By these practices each draft call meant that unless volunteers enlisted or veterans re-enlisted the men most likely to be taken were those who were unable to pay - usually low paid workers whose wage earning sons could ill afford to leave their families. That this pattern of securing exemptions continued to the war's end can be seen in Antrim's final call. The quota was seventy-one. Of this number, five paid the commutation fee; twenty-six furnished substitutes; thirty-seven were accepted (*drafted*); and three were awarded exemptions for physical reasons.

Another record indicates that sixty-one men in Greencastle escaped the draft by hiring substitutes or paying exemption money. This record was kept by one of the town's mothers whose son was already in the service. There may have been other lists but this lady's record was found long after her death by a grandchild who never revealed the names for fear of embarrassing members of these families. [57]

One household is known to have substituted a younger son for an older brother who was drafted. Whether this happened often is not known but it did in this instance. A Greencastle area family tells of their grandfather, who as a boy, lived in the Fayetteville area. When his older brother, John, was to be drafted, his father could not afford to lose him. He was too valuable as a worker. However, the solution lay right within the family. The father offered Emmanuel, the younger son, a hundred dollars if he would go as a substitute for his brother. He promised to pay him when he returned from the war. Emmanuel accepted the proposition and went off to fight for his country, his father, and his brother.

The only family recollection is that this young bounty soldier fought in Virginia where he suffered a knee wound. Upon returning to the homestead with a stiffened leg that impaired his usefulness as a farmer the father refused to pay the promised hundred dollars. In anger and with a hurt that lasted a lifetime, the youthful veteran came to Antrim Township, learned the blacksmith trade, and set up his shop along the Williamsport Turnpike where he prospered. His marriage to a local girl led to a family of seven children. Seventy-eight descendants, most still living in the Greencastle area, represent a highly respected legacy of this mistreated farm boy. Emmanuel never forgave his father and his posterity still point with disbelief to a man who would treat anyone, let alone his son, so cruelly.[58]

That the draft cost President Lincoln votes cannot be disputed. However, Union military records indicate that if the war's outcome had depended on conscripted soldiers the North could not have saved the Union. Approximately 250,000 men were affected. Of this number nearly 87,000 paid commutation fees, totalling $26,366,000. Out of the remainder only 46,347 went into the service - the rest furnished substitutes. Although the draft raised less than 150,000 men, its main effect was to encourage volunteers. From the war's beginning it was volunteer soldiers that fought the battles for four long years and in the end brought victory to the North.

After all of Pennsylvania's experiences with the draft, it only produced about 5,000 draftees and approximately 12,500 substitutes or bounty men. The remainder of the 362,000 soldiers, who came out of the Keystone State, were volunteers. From the war's beginning to its end they served enlistments varying from three months to three years - some of them re-enlisted as often as three times.[59]

With the election over, the people were assured the draft would continue. Abraham Lincoln had received a mandate to pursue the war to its end. A day of Thanksgiving was again declared for November 24. Greencastle celebrated with services in the German Reformed Church. In early December a call came from the Sanitary Commission for generous donations of food for a Christmas dinner for the thousands of wounded in military hospitals. The Ladies Aid Society responded by calling for contributions of money or non-perishable foods. [60]

The holidays were observed as always - Christmas with its customary activities and New Years celebrated in the traditional noise filled manner that both town and rural people had always known. Another dimension to this year's season came with an abundance of cold and snowy weather. Skating and sledding parties, sleighing, and bobsled straw rides with the usual house parties made the 1864 holidays one of the gayest in many years.

It was reported that barrels and boxes of turkeys, mince pies, cakes, fruit, doughnuts, and other assorted food were shipped into the hospitals. This Christmas was the most lavish ever experienced by the wounded veterans of the Virginia campaigns. While these men celebrated the holiday, for their comrades in ice and sleet covered trenches at Petersburg, it was celebration enough to find warmth from the cruel winter that surrounded them.

Yet news of victories in the South during this closing month of 1864 were celebrated all over the Union. On December 18 word came of George H. Thomas's Army of the Cumberland's victory near Nashville over John B. Hood's Army of Tennessee. Then on December 22, General Sherman sent another piece of good news to the President - "I beg to present you, as a Christmas gift, the city of Savannah with a hundred fifty heavy guns, plenty of ammunition, and also about 25,000 bales of cotton."

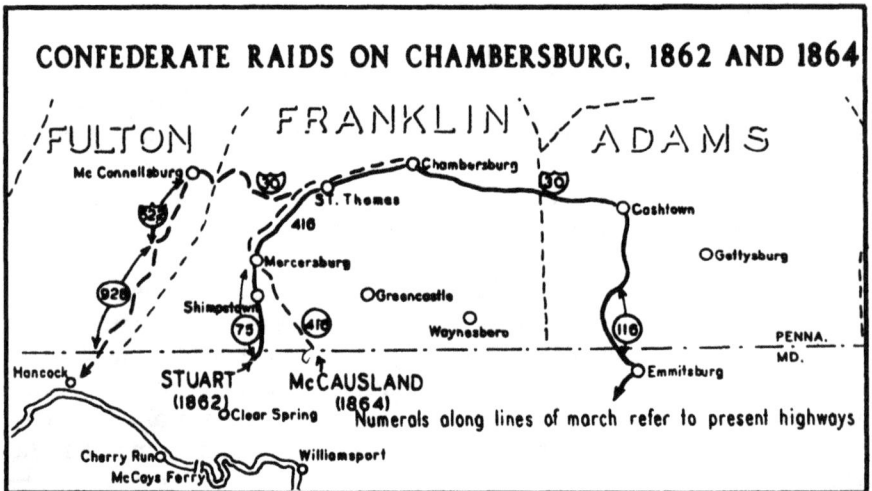

CONFEDERATE RAIDS ON CHAMBERSBURG, 1862 AND 1864

THE PENNSYLVANIA HISTORICAL AND MUSEUM COMMISSION   HARRISBURG, PA.

CHAPTER XI

THE SIGNAL CORPS

On August 17, 1864 the signal company assigned to the station at Greencastle arrived. The men went into their encampment on the McCauley farm west of town, and for approximately one year, its personnel monitored activity along the Potomac River and its environs. The camp was part of a network of stations that formed one of the early attempts at systematic signalling by using the technology available at the time.

Prior to June 27, 1860 the only form of signals used by the United States Army consisted of short range orders provided by drums or bugles. From this day forward the Signal Corps evolved, beginning with the appointment of Albert J. Myer, who with the rank of major, was authorized to establish a body of soldiers to serve as signalmen. Those elected were educated men, picked from volunteer regiments, and for three years the unit operated on an experimental basis. These men handled signal communications through a system that gradually evolved into a very important component of military operations.

Although the Confederates used semaphore signalling at the First Battle of Manassas, there was general opposition to the efforts of Major Myer and his men during the early part of the war. Much of the criticism leveled at this new part of the service came from older officers who viewed most innovations as wasteful, impractical pieces of "tomfoolery." Inter-departmental jealousies added more confusion and misunderstandings.

Finally, on March 3, 1863, an act of Congress officially created the Signal Corps and authorized its officers to range in rank from lieutenant to colonel. Enlisted men would have no rating beyond that of sergeant. Some stations were to be served with mounted patrols but this was not true of all camps. Through this legislation the Signal Corps grew over the remaining years of the conflict to a body of over three hundred officers and 2,500 enlisted men.

The corps established its stations in crucial areas of high elevations or when this was impossible, wooden towers or platforms were erected. From such vantage points messages were relayed by using flags, torches, rockets and flares. This was usually achieved with rapidity and accuracy except in bad weather. Rain, snow, or fog closed down the operations and long periods of inclement weather required greater reliance on horses to carry crucial messages to the nearest telegraph station.

An intricate system of codes involved use of several signal devices in various arm positions. Combinations of these positions stood for letters, phrases, or numbers. Flags, the most frequently used instruments, consisted of three basic color combinations - white with a red square in the center; black, visible in light rain or snow; and red with a white square, that could be seen against varied backgrounds. Colored lights or rockets were used at night with combinations of pre-arranged sets of signals. Messages were sent by signalmen with flags or lights as numbers were read to them by the officer in charge.

Since wigwagging flags or lights could be seen by anyone, including the enemy, messages were seldom sent in the "clear." Codes or ciphers of many complexities were used. A cipher device consisting of two concentric discs, one smaller than the other, was developed to correlate numbers with letters or phrases. Signalmen could turn the disc to a number to determine the code to be used. *(One such disc, from the records of the Greencastle station, can be seen at the National Archives.)* Certain words could represent phrases, sentences, or entire messages. The reports were then decoded by using a code book. Cipher messages were based on keys and the receiving signalman or officer, by knowing the correct key, could decipher the message immediately without the aid of a code book. Codes and ciphers were constantly changed to prevent enemy cryptographers from interpreting messages. [1]

There was no distinctive uniform for the Signal Corps until late in the war and many posts never did have men who wore the designated uniforms. Two characteristics of the official dress for enlisted men were short dark blue jackets and trousers. Not until 1864 were the corpsmen given an insignia - a device showing crossed flags which non-commissioned men wore on their sleeves and officers placed on their caps or hats. By November of that year Greencastle's troop wore this insignia. [2]

The Signal Corps came into its own during 1864 and before the war ended practically every military department embraced the new system of intelligence gathering and reporting. In the post-war era it continued to function, not only as an adjunct of the armed forces, but as a valuable aid to civilian life. Its observations of weather patterns and relaying such information to stations across the nation made the corps invaluable as an agency for forecasting weather. This continued until 1890 when responsibility for predicting weather was transferred

SIGNAL CORPS INSIGNIA   GIRTON COLLECTION

to the Department of Agriculture. [3]

Greencastle's newspaper noted that after the Battle of Gettysburg, a signal corps detachment camped near the town and in late August it moved on to Maryland Heights in the Harpers Ferry area. [4]   When the Signal Corps Detachment for the Department of the Susquehanna was organized, men from Adams, Cumberland, Dauphin, Franklin, and Perry counties quickly filled its ranks. Samuel H. Eby of Greencastle was one of the enlistees. He wrote - "The majority of the men were teachers, graduates of some college, or students in some institution of learning. A number of them came from Pennsylvania College, located in Gettysburg." A review of the roster of those assigned to the training camp shows that in addition to teachers and college men there were clerks, shoemakers, and coachmakers. The rolls also included a telegraph operator, confectioner, railway agent, boat builder, druggist, dentist, and one man identified only as a "gentleman." [5]

Initially the trainees were in a camp three and a half miles west of Chambersburg where they were armed and trained in cavalry and infantry procedures plus fundamentals of signalling with flags. James H. Montgomery of St. Thomas was one of this group. He was a thirty-three year old school teacher and had served as a captain of the village home guards. A diary kept by Montgomery shows the processes involved in becoming a member of the corps. He reported to the chief signal officer at the camp who administered an examination consisting of tests in orthography *(spelling)*, reading, writing, geography, grammar, and arithmetic. From seven o'clock until noon, Montgomery was involved with these tests and a physical examination. After this he and his fellow recruits were taken by train to Harrisburg where they were mustered into the service. In the evening he attended a performance at Brandt's City Hall and then returned to his camp. The next morning, after breakfast, the men were sworn into the service for a term of three years. This happened on February 11 and while in Harrisburg, they spent the remaining time in sightseeing or visiting men they knew in other camps near the city. Two days later the group returned to Chambersburg. Upon reaching the signal corps camp, Montgomery was given a certificate to show he was a member of the army. This he took to St. Thomas as evidence which permitted him to receive the township's bounty of one hundred dollars. Before returning to camp he spent the weekend with the family. On Monday morning he said goodbye to relatives and friends, but before going on to Chambersburg, he stopped at his school to bid farewell to the students. Upon arriving in the county seat the former teacher, along with other signalmen, boarded a train to Hagerstown. In a camp situated west of the town they were to receive more training under the direction of Captain H. Clay Snyder. The enlistees were now in separate camps. Some, including Samuel Eby, stayed at Chambersburg.

Not long after arriving at Hagerstown Snyder went to Harrisburg to get more men. Montgomery and his comrades were left to themselves with everything in confusion and nobody in charge. There were no rations, and their horses, with no forage, were left to wander freely in the camp, while the men stayed in town over night. Here they received supper and lodging at the "Byers Private Boarding House" for fifty cents. Adding to the discomfort of both men and horses was a constant snow fall.

Bitter cold weather, no rations, no uniforms (*the men were still in civilian attire*), and no officers to bring order out of the chaos continued throughout the week. On February 18 temperatures went to twelve below zero. On the same day food arrived. Now they had beef, pork, beans, rice, potatoes, coffee, sugar, salt and above all "fresh bread." One of the men volunteered and "cooked up" a good supper, but they still had to sleep at boarding houses. Many became ill to the point of being bedridden and all suffered from colds. Their only protection against the weather was hastily prepared wind breakers made from loose boards. They called the place "Camp Desolation," a fitting appelation from the descriptions given by Montgomery.

On Saturday, February 20, two things happened to bring some cheer to Montgomery. D. D. Fickes arrived in camp with a uniform he had ordered at White's clothing store in Chambersburg. The outfit cost him twenty-seven dollars, one quarter the bounty money he received for enlisting. The other happening was an order that directed the men to get ready to move back to Chambersburg.

Monday was a day of celebration. It was Washington's Birthday and cannon at Maryland Heights could be heard firing salutes to the nation's first president. Rice pudding with milk and sugar was a part of the noon meal - the camp's only way of recognizing the occasion. The next day they broke camp, said goodbye to their source of so much misery and marched into Hagerstown, and at three o'clock in the afternoon the troops boarded a train for Chambersburg. While in the process of leave taking it was learned why officers who had been assigned to Camp Desolation never arrived. Their terms had expired and they were no longer in the service when ordered to Hagerstown. Montgomery and his comrades had spent this week of complete disorder and discomfort because someone in the military's bureaucracy had mishandled the orders. In modern army parlance it was just another snafu - "situation normal, all fouled up" or words to that affect.

By the end of the week all were back in Franklin County, at a new camp, on lands owned by Josiah Allen - known as "Allen's Grove" - located along the road to St. Thomas, west of Chambersburg. Its water supply came from Back Creek which flowed through the farm. Before settling in at the new site, Montgomery was sent back to Hagerstown to make a final check on the deserted remains of their former camp. On returning he and his squad ate their noon meal at a hotel in Greencastle.

While in Camp Allen the men had many visitors, including parents, girl friends, wives, and children. Montgomery's family came down from St. Thomas and his youngsters joined the soldiers in singing familiar songs. Those men who lived not far from camp could also get occasional leaves to visit their homes. Under the command of Captain Snyder the whole contingent began to fit into a routine consisting principally of signal drill procedures. On Saturday, March 12, General Couch paid a surprise visit to see how the company was progressing. It was still cold, windy, and rainy causing much discomfort and illness. Montgomery's principal complaint was that Snyder spent too many hours away from camp - "His time appears to be entirely taken up by the ladies of Chambersburg."

A Bible class was organized and met in a nearby school house. Rev. Meade, a new recruit, was the teacher. Classes were held on Sundays and Montgomery, a religious man, encouraged his comrades to attend. Thursday, March 17, was St. Patrick's Day, yet since few, if any Irish Catholics were part of the camp, it is reasonable that no mention was made of a parade. But Snyder did order Montgomery to go to Brake's sawmill to secure lumber to reinforce the captain's tent. He returned with "228 ft. of boards and sixty-eight of scantling" purchased at a cost of four dollars and sixty cents. The big news of the day was an announcement that boxing gloves had arrived and from that day on the manly act of pugilism was to be part of the camp's recreation program. However, the start of this pastime was delayed. On March 25 the weather turned cold again and by the next morning six inches of snow lay on the drill grounds.

At a nearby post the 20th and 21st Pennsylvania Cavalry Regiments, stationed there before the signal corps arrived, held a review for Governor Curtin and General Couch on Thursday, March 31. On Friday the 20th left for the front and during the following week the signalmen moved to another camp site. Located on the Samuel Coble farm along the turnpike, it was nearer St. Thomas, with water still supplied by Back Creek.

The new camp also was closer to the Tuscarora Mountain and on April 12, Montgomery was sent with a detail to Mt. Parnell to establish a temporary signal station. This location could readily be seen by telescope from the Coble farm. When the squad finally cleared the underbrush and trees for direct sighting to the camp, it began raining. All through the night more rain fell and by morning a heavy mist enveloped the entire mountain making signalling impossible. Visibility was limited to less than a hundred yards, but by noon the fog lifted and for several hours flag communication was practiced. This was their first signalling experience and Captain Snyder was so pleased that three days later he sent the same squad to Casey's Knob on the mountain south of Mercersburg. The weather held and by horseback the trip to the Knob resulted in another signal site.[6]

On April 23 sixty-three of the signal trainees were sent to Cumberland, Maryland. It was noted that a hundred and thirty-five were being trained at the time. As Captain Snyder was putting his men through the rigorous training schedule he was probably unaware of charges about to be leveled against him. Provost officers came to camp on April 25 and placed him under arrest. Montgomery said there were rumors that Snyder was "engaged in the bounty business." Most men knew that, compared to being with Grant or Sherman, signal corps service was about as safe as being home with the family. It was good duty and was it possible that Snyder was hiking test results to place men who were unqualified? Did he accept money to place volunteers, who wanted to escape the draft? Such talk was probably circulating but these were not the charges made against the captain.

Records indicate that Snyder was tried for failure to keep adequate records and submit required reports. Lack of leadership ability was his biggest fault. If he was responsible for the chaos at "Camp Desolation" he certainly was no manager. His hearing was held on May 6 and a month later H. Clay Snyder was dismissed from the service. This whole affair does not ring true. The charges against him would usually mean censure, but not dismissal. No one will ever know if the entire affair was a "cover up" of more serious offenses. The record does not show this. [7]

On May 7 Lieutenant Amos M. Thayer replaced Snyder and the following week the men began seeing a more rigid schedule, occupying them from an early morning roll call at six o'clock until nine in the evening. For the next two months each day was spent drilling in weaponry, signal practice, care of horses, inspection, and dress parades. By June 26 the men were ready and Thayer was confident they could man signal posts effectively. Additional officers Lieutenants F. K. McClosky, G. W. Kennedy, and Michael Reymer, of Greencastle, had come during June. They would be assigned to stations in other sections of the Department's network.

LT. AMOS THAYER
U.S.A.M.H.I.

CPT. CLAY SNYDER

LT. MICHAEL REYMER
CARLISLE, PA.

The following day the entire detachment left Chambersburg. Those on horseback, led by Kennedy, went to Greencastle. Here the horses were fed and curried and the men ate their noon meal. The march continued into Maryland by side roads until evening when camp was made in a field of clover near Maugansville. Later that night the force moved into Hagerstown. Here they met a detail, headed by Thayer, that had traveled by train from Chambersburg.

The next day, Tuesday, June 28, their march continued down the Sharpsburg Pike to the Antietam area. Montgomery noted, as they passed over the battlefield - "At every stop the eye rests upon something to remind the traveler of that awful day of carnage. Now the old battlefield is covered with a golden harvest and better crops are seldom seen than abounds in Washington County." By the following evening the force arrived at Maryland Heights.

Samuel Eby wrote that upon arriving, "The corps was divided and signal stations established for miles along the Potomac." Members, not at signal posts, were assigned to scout duty in the Shenandoah Valley, around Charles Town, Shepherdstown, and Winchester, and through Frederick and Washington counties. The stations included one on Maryland Heights assigned to a Union force, headed by General Max Weber, and another at Fort Duncan, located up the Potomac about one and a half miles west of Harpers Ferry. Eby and his fellow signalmen apparently were not aware of the approaching army led by Jubal Early. When they reached the Harpers Ferry region, the Confederates had left Staunton and two days later were in Winchester having driven Franz Sigel's West Virginia Reserve Division before them at Leetown and Darkesville. The first indication of Confederates being nearby came on July 3 when sounds of cannon fire, from the direction of Martinsburg, continued through the early morning hours.

Thayer telegraphed Sigel's headquarters, near Martinsburg, to let the general know the signal corps was at Maryland Heights. If telegraph lines were cut he could still communicate with Washington by using the corps. A reply from Sigel's adjutant general told Thayer this would be unnecessary since the Union troops were withdrawing and the army was on its way to Shepherdstown.

The next morning, after Thayer learned Sigel had reached Shepherdstown, he again suggested that a signal line be established between his army and General Weber's camp, but the offer was declined. By eight o'clock word reached Maryland Heights that enemy troops were moving from Charles Town toward Harpers Ferry. Weber's pickets, located on Bolivar Heights, lying to the west of the Ferry, were notified to prepare for enemy advance skirmishes. They prepared themselves by getting off the Heights as fast as possible and fleeing into the town. The pickets willingly accepted a later order to cross the Potomac into Maryland. A signalman, Thomas J. Franklin, did stay and kept informing Weber's headquarters of the enemy's progress. Later, he too was ordered to cross the Potomac to safety.

By July 5, Sigel became aware of a strong Rebel force approaching Harpers Ferry. He concentrated his army along the Maryland side of the Potomac from Maryland Heights as far as Fort Duncan. This time he made use of the signalmen. His command post was located in the center of the line with a station there to communicate with either flank. By noon Thayer discovered that Early was moving his men up the Virginia side of the river and crossing into Maryland north of Sigel's defenses. They were being out flanked and Union troops were deployed to counter an attack which came the next day.

Early had decided to capture the Harpers Ferry garrison to keep its force from threatening his rear as he moved toward his objective. For four days, July 4-7, the Rebels probed the Union defenses only to find them too strong. Although Sigel had only 6,500 men of which two thirds were untried, green, and quickly raised hundred day militia, the Confederate leader saw that his opposition was too strongly fortified. Though his army numbered 20,000 there would be little achieved by mounting a full scale attack. It would be a needless waste of men and time since his goal still lay ahead. [8]

When the morning's early mists cleared on July 8 Sigel's men saw nothing but open countryside where the enemy had been the day before. The Rebels had vanished. Although a body of Federal cavalry caught sight of Early's rear guard the main part of the army was not be found. Throughout the morning signalmen and reconnaisance groups spent their time trying to find the Rebels. Then at noon General Sigel reported General Stahel's cavalry "has orders to follow the enemy's movements from Pleasant Valley toward Boonsborough. He is now engaged with them."

Later the main enemy force was spotted. After crossing the Catoctin range they were streaming through the Middletown Valley advancing on Frederick. The next day Early's force met Lew Wallace's hastily assembled army at the Monocacy River. Although momentarily stopped, the Confederates succeeded in pushing this Union force back toward Baltimore.

A temporary signal station on Catoctin mountain received word of this Union defeat. As reconnaisance continued the reason for Early's isolated thrust into Maryland might be revealed. What was his next move? Would he pursue Wallace, bypass Washington and go on to Baltimore or would he push on toward the capital? Was it possible that by now he felt he had over extended himself and the wise move would be to get back into the Shenandoah Valley?

An answer was not long in coming as reports told of the enemy moving straight ahead - down the road that led to the District of Columbia. It was clear now. They were on their way to take the prize for which the campaign was launched. The Federals now knew what the Southerners had in mind from the beginning. To capture or besiege Washington would relieve pressure of Richmond and possibly bring peace on the Confederacy's terms. These were the high stakes for which Early was gambling. He lost. He lost because the delay at Harpers Ferry and Wallace's show of force at Monocacy had disrupted his schedule. These two time consuming encounters had given Grant the time he needed to reinforce the city's defenses with units from the Richmond front. Washington was too strongly fortified. Now Early had only one alternative. He was forced to seek the safety of the Shenandoah country. By July 16 his army was in Berryville about ten miles east of Winchester - where just over a month before the campaign had been launched.

Later Thayer was authorized to place a post on Sugar Loaf Mountain, about fifteen miles south of Frederick, for surveillance over two crossings on the Potomac. Here the men stayed, without incident until July 14, when the station was taken over by a signal detail from the Department of West Virginia. Thayer's men returned to Harpers Ferry and re-established posts they had been operating before Early had interrupted them. [9]

SIGNALMAN MONTGOMERY
GIRTON COLLECTION

Montgomery's diary through the remainder of the month indicates no knowledge of McCausland's raid. At the time the men apparently knew nothing of the burning of Chambersburg. His entry of July 31 noted, "Rebs reported in Pennsylvania. Rumors a plenty but nothing reliable. Enemy appears to be moving on Cumberland." Not until the evening of August 1 did they learn that Chambersburg lay in ashes. "This is the first instance during the war in which a town offering no resistance has been deliberately destroyed." *(This lament does not indicate any remorse concerning the failure of the corps to provide intelligence which might have brought assistance to Couch. What had happened to all the patrols that Samuel Eby had mentioned?)*

On August 10 the men broke camp and, without horses, marched to Hagerstown. The next day they passed through Greencastle and on August 12 a camp was established west of Chambersburg "on the hill in the rear of the Fairgrounds." Montgomery noted the place was known as "Siberia." After all were settled Thayer with a small detail left for Harrisburg to find more horses. The following day everyone received two month's pay, less twenty-five cents - a deduction or "donation" for the Soldiers Rest Home in Washington. It was Saturday and many went to town to see the ruins. "All returned to camp depressed." The lieutenant came back on Monday with forty horses and Montgomery was issued a "bay, five years old, of good appearance and high mettle." On Wednesday, the men assigned to the Greencastle post, left camp by way of the Warm Spring Road and arrived at their destination later in the forenoon. It was located on a high elevation in a field owned by John McCauley. Here, off the left side of the turnpike to Mercersburg, about a half mile west of the town, is where the station was to operate. (*This would have been in the area now occupied by the Melrose and Greencastle Metal Works businesses.*) From this point an observer had a clear view of Casey's Knob which lay to the southwest in a direct line, about eleven miles away. Mt. Parnell was over twelve miles to the northwest. Since no forested elevation or higher hills interferred, telescopic sightings were possible on most days and torch type signals could be seen at night.

For their noon meal, the men rode to one of the town's hotels and then returned to camp. While marching out West Baltimore Street, Montgomery reported getting acquainted with a woman whom he described as a "she Devil in the person of Mrs. Mary Pence." Apparently she accosted the men in a most virulent manner, probably berating the horsemen whom she understood would be spending their time waving flags at each other while good men were fighting and dying to save the nation. Little did she know how important these flagmen might be in protecting her.

Thayer reported that the signal system's key station was at Greencastle. It could take signals from Parnell, but more important was the camp at Casey's Knob, sometimes called the North Mountain station. From there messages could be received or sent to a post on Fairview Mountain near Hancock. It, in turn, kept in touch with a station at Williamsport or one as far away as the Maryland Heights at Harpers Ferry. It was possible that this network could then contact signal systems covering both Maryland and the Shenandoah Valley.

The stations directly responsible to the Greencastle post commanded a view of approximately fifty miles along the Potomac where many fordings were available to Rebel raiding parties. By sightings of the signal posts or from messages relayed by patrols, reports of imminent Confederate raids were to be sent immediately to Greencastle, and from there telegraphed to Chambersburg or Harrisburg. The office of the Commander of the Department of the Susquehanna would be notified at all times of any suspicious enemy movements.

On August 20 six man teams were sent out to the various stations. These would alternate with others back at the Greencastle encampment every ten days. Later the assignments lasted much longer. Montgomery noted the next day that the post at Casey's was in working order. Since it was a Sunday "a great crowd of visitors came to the camp from Greencastle." The next week was filled with many work details. The weather was fine as the camp got its tents in place. A daily schedule called for reveille at half past five. Mounted guards left two hours later for the day's reconnaissance assignments, while the remaining men spent their time in cavalry drill and other training. Taps sounded at nine every evening. [10]

The camp was supplied with ample rations but through the months ahead the diary tells how men were invited into Greencastle homes from time to time. Montgomery did not take long to make himself known to the Koons family on North West Street. Just a week after his arrival he notes - "Had dinner of apple dumplings at Mr. Koons, all well." Hotel records tell of signalmen patronizing their dining rooms at frequent intervals. Later in the fall arrangements were made by Montgomery and several others to eat at the McCauley farm house. Camp rations were given the housewife who added vegetables and syrup to go with their bread. The McCauleys charged seventy-five cents for cooking and preparing the meal. The men referred to this as "a very nice kind of soldiering, while it lasts."

GREENCASTLE SIGNAL STATION   SKETCH BY MARK T. NOE

Friday, August 25, brought news of Rebel forces trying to cross the river at Williamsport and Hancock. The Confederates were "driven back at both places with considerable loss." The next week Montgomery was sent to Chambersburg to get a detail of horses shod. He noted "considerable building going on." On Wednesday Lieutenant Michael Reymer returned to camp after a leave of absence. The diary noted that on Sunday, September 4, a train, carrying seventy-two Rebel prisoners taken by Averell's men, passed through Greencastle. Averell was then with Sheridan in the Shenandoah. Monday brought news that Captain L. B. Norton was to replace Thayer as the Chief Signal Officer of the Department of the Susquehanna.

The rains of early September made camp life miserable. Tents did not repel the constant downpour and the men complained of being soaked to the skin. In this kind of weather a squad, including Montgomery, Reymer, and Samuel Eby, was ordered to Williamsport. Here they found no tents and all had to sleep with heavy rain drenching everyone. Most of the group came down with colds and on September 13 Eby became so ill that he was escorted to Greencastle by John Detrich, a signalman from Harrisburg. Norton came to Greencastle the next day but more important to the men at Williamsport - their tents finally arrived.

On the evening of September 18 a message flashed up the river to Williamsport by torch type signals. "General Grant at Harpers Ferry in consultation with General Sheridan. Look out for tomorrow. The entire army will move on the enemy. Averell's move today was but a ruse." This last part referred to action near Martinsburg. Cannonading had been heard from that direction during the day. The showdown was about to commence. "Little Phil" was ready to begin his campaign to purge the Shenandoah of its protector, Jubal Early.

Montgomery was part of a patrol detail the next day. Again heavy firing could be heard in the Martinsburg region. The patrol crossed the river and during the forenoon the men captured a Confederate deserter from the 22nd Georgia Regiment. He reported a gradual withdrawal of enemy forces. Later they learned of Sheridan's victory at Winchester. Montgomery's diary of September 20 noted the camp learned of the death of Confederate General Robert E. Rodes. He was killed in the fighting· at Winchester the day before. The Rebels were "still retreating south through the Valley."

Signal corps personnel apparently were privy to information which later became public. Two days went by, then it was learned that Sheridan had relieved Averell of his command and at about four o'clock in the afternoon the dejected cavalry leader was seen passing the camp on his way to Hagerstown. Subsequent information indicated that Averell was relieved for "lack of agressiveness." (*Many Chambersburg people, upon hearing this news, were probably saying, "We knew this since July 30."*)

Montgomery, on October 3, received a pass to visit his family. He wrote, "Old acquaintenances well and making money, everything sells at enormous prices." Upon his return to Greencastle, he noted the weather had turned extremely cold and stormy but camp operations were continuing despite the change. He and five other soldiers were appointed as clerks for the state elections, held Tuesday, October 11. "The polls opened at Captain Norton's office. Thirteen votes were cast." The same day Sergeant Anthony Fegethoff, from Georgetown, reported for duty. "He is a Prussian by birth and a Catholic priest by profession." Montgomery commented, "Thank God for my 'Know Nothing' sensibilities." This reference to the Know Nothing Party obviously reveals his anti-Catholic feelings. (*The Know Nothing Party was founded in 1849 as a secret political organization whose platform was based, in part, on resentment by native Americans against the rising tide of Roman Catholic immigrants from Europe.*)

Montgomery's penchant for secret organizations, motivated by his strong feelings for preserving America against, what he felt, were dangers to the nation, was also reflected in a later decision. On November 5 he reported attending and becoming a member of the Greencastle Chapter of the Union League. This was a covert political society designed for self protection and aiding the government in its struggle for the preservation of the Union. It was directed at ferreting out those suspected of pro-Southern sympathies and seeing that proper officials were notified of suspicious activities.

The state election results were not known until Thursday and Montgomery expressed satisfaction with the Republican victory. He noted that soldiers of Pennsylvania, for the first time, were considered "legal voters." The same day voting returns became known it was discovered that one of the station's men had deserted. "Ebbert ran away from camp on a drunk. Sergeant Neely and Private Detrich were ordered to bring him in." The pursuers evidently knew where to look for their man since they soon found him at Christman's Crossing on Back Creek about four miles from St. Thomas. The next day's diary revealed that Ebbert was severely punished - "yet he deserved it all." Another note indicated "Three hundred of Mosby's Guerillas crossed into Maryland last night but were quickly driven back." The signal network was apparently serving it's purpose well.

Montgomery expressed satisfaction with the camp's new leader.

The station by this time had taken on the appearance of a well organized permanent camp. Tents were described as being fifteen feet in length and eight feet wide. They had wooden floors and all were arranged in an orderly manner along a "pretty good" street.

Patrol parties were sent out daily and on October 19 Montgomery and four men were ordered to go on night patrol in the Mercersburg area - the road leading from Church Hill to Shimpstown; the road from Mercersburg to the mouth of Blair's Valley; and another from Cove Gap to Little Cove. Montgomery and two men were then to ride as far as McConnellsburg and "to make note of the number and situation of all pickets along that route." They left camp near six o'clock. It was a "very dark night" yet by eight o'clock they were in Mercersburg and by midnight Montgomery with another rider crossed the mountain on the turnpike to McConnellsburg. His only comment about this part of the reconnaissance mission was that it was a "very cool" trip. Upon the patrol's return, the next day, they found great excitement. Word arrived that Sheridan had struck Early's forces in the Great Valley with extraordinary results. Forty-three artillery pieces and twenty-five hundred prisoners were taken.

The patrol duty continued. Two nights later Montgomery and another man covered a different route. From Greencastle they rode to Waynesboro and completed a circuit by way of Leitersburg, Hagerstown, Chewsville, Cavetown, Smithtown (*Smithsburg*), Ringold, Waterloo, and back to Waynesboro. The assignment took the entire night, and upon arriving at Greencastle, Montgomery said he "went to bed to dream if not to rest. Am suffering some with pain on my breast." He had been in the saddle for fifty-one miles, riding most of the time through a cold rain. [11]

On Saturday, October 29, Montgomery noted the passage of a regiment of the state's emergency troops. These were men called into service during the time Early was threatening Washington. Sunday was spent on home leave and when he returned to camp later in the day, the diary noted the arrival of twenty men from an independent company of mounted infantry. They would be assigned to patrol duty. Official records indicate that Captain Norton had explained the need for such horsemen. His men, aside from signal duty, were required to cover areas in southern Franklin County and Maryland's Washington County which could not be observed by the "lookout" stations. If this was to continue he needed more men to prevent another Chambersburg disaster. No time was wasted. That night Montgomery took two newly arrived soldiers on patrol. It was not only regular duty but an exercise in training the recruits.

The following Tuesday, November 1, Norton was ordered to report to Bermuda Hundred for duty as a signal officer. Located on the Richmond Peninsula, this was where Benjamin F. Butler commanded the Department of Virginia and North Carolina. Butler's army, at the time, was part of Grant's forces besieging the Confederate capital. Official records show that Captain Norton was placed in charge of the entire Department's Signal Corps. Lieutenant Thayer replaced him after his departure. [12]

The next day was clear and pleasant as a contingent of men plastered walls of the "officers house." Montgomery made special note of a treat that evening at the McCauleys. They had "corn pone" for supper. By Friday the rain started again and scouting in a steady downpour became routine once more. Eight of the new men were sent to Williamsport and four to each of the other stations. Orders were given to the patrols to "arrest as deserters all soldiers traveling without papers." Gangs of deserters were roaming through parts of Franklin County. One such group was reported to be hiding near Quincy. [13] Patrols in that region were told to contact Government Detective Benchoff and advise him to be on the lookout for deserters who might try to vote in the November 8 election. Voting at the Greencastle camp proceeded despite the ever present rain and results gave Lincoln fifteen votes to McClellan's eight. Later in the day a report showed that four deserters were apprehended and turned over to Provost Marshall Eyster. Three horses taken from the deserters were retained at camp.

Saturday brought sudden excitement to Greencastle when it was learned that Harry Gilmore and his Maryland cavalry were reported to have crossed the Potomac at Sheperdstown with a force of fifty men. Most of the entire camp was ordered out and Montgomery, now a sergeant, was left with six men to run the signal station. Attempts to signal Casey's Knob went unanswered and a man was sent to determine why no signals were being received or replies sent by the mountain post. A company of mounted infantry with a section of artillery arrived to reinforce the area in case of trouble from Gilmore. In late afternoon Private Benedict, the signalman at Casey's was brought into camp and placed under arrest for neglecting his duty. Montgomery then noted that it had been snowing all day. It would seem that Benedict would have had difficulty seeing Greencastle signals. The snow was heavy and covered the valley. No record shows the outcome of charges against him.

Fear of another invasion or raid did not subside. On Tuesday, November 15, a dispatch came from Harrisburg. General Couch was now warning everyone to be ready for any kind of Rebel incursion.

CYRUS ALEXANDER
100 DAY CAVALRYMAN
PALM COLLECTION

SAMUEL EBY
SIGNALMAN
GIRTON COLLECTION

J. M. BENEDICT
SIGNALMAN
GIRTON COLLECTION

Citizens were urged to arm themselves and be prepared to protect their homes. Out of this concern a company of home guards was organized in Greencastle. Another was formed the following week and other towns followed. Three companies were raised in Chambersburg, while men of Waynesboro and Mercersburg filled two units in their towns. [14]

An attempted crossing at Hancock by a Confederate force was repulsed the day after Couch's message had been received. But fears still continued until heavy snows made troop movements practically impossible. Although the signal network brought warnings, men had to be ready to respond to them. Hopefully the home guard units could provide such a response. During this uncertain time, a Rebel deserter was arrested, but he aroused suspicions in Montgomery's mind. It was known that "deserters" sometimes were really enemy agents, planted beyond their lines to gather news and then return with important pieces of information for raiders waiting in West Virginia. He undoubtedly was turned over to the provost marshall.

The continued cold and rainy weather finally caught up with Montgomery. On Friday he secured sick leave and went home to St. Thomas after complaining of chest pains, first noticed in late October. However, he was back by Sunday but for several days his duty was limited to "taking care of the horses." The diary noted that the camp's officers dined with Montgomery and his friends at the McCauley home. Another entry told of the officers and their ladies going to Mt. Parnell to spend Thanksgiving.

On the weekend following the holiday six more deserters were apprehended. Montgomery and his friend Sergeant John Lesher made their tent more secure by erecting wooden walls around its exterior.

The diary noted, "Thus I am enabled to enjoy peace and quiet instead of the frolic and noise of the Sergeants' Quarters. Whiskey and cards are not to be indulged in our quarters. John has always been a more congenial companion than the others." Montgomery was a very religious man and many passages in his diary exhibited a concern for moral values which he supported with appropriate scripture. He and a few of his friends, when free, attended services in various Greencastle churches.

The camp was constantly aware of the fighting in the Shenandoah. The diary told of the anxieties when defeats were reported and the joy that followed word of victories. There was a confident feeling that Sheridan would eventually drive Early from the Valley. However, on November 29, a courier was sent from the Greencastle camp with orders for the small command of soldiers at Shimpstown to advance and double their pickets toward the river near Blair's Valley. A suspected Rebel raid failed to materialize and normalcy returned once more. [15]

Thayer's report to the Signal Bureau at Washington for the month of November told of ninety messages being transmitted and of the diligence exercised in requiring regular evening reports by stations to him. He also mentioned how the patrols were apprehending deserters and suspected spies. That additional men were responsible for improving this part of the station's assignment was also noted. [16]

Montgomery reported on December 1, the arrest of a man, thought to be a bounty jumper or deserter at Greencastle's Antrim House. Lieutenant McCloskey, who apprehended the culprit, brought to camp a young four year old mare, said to belong to the suspect, and turned the animal over to Montgomery for his use. The following day word came that General George Cadwalader had arrived in Chambersburg. He had been ordered to replace General Couch as head of the Department of the Susquehanna. Couch was assigned to duty with General George Thomas in Tennessee. [17]

During the first week of December, Lesher helped place a stove in the tent. "We now live cosy and at home," said Montgomery. Later he and Lesher went on patrol toward Waynesboro and on their return they stopped to visit Charlie and Will Kunkle who lived east of Greencastle. The same day an entry tells of "great preparations" being made for a concert the next evening at Irvin's Hall in Greencastle by the signal corps chorus. Officers and their ladies, plus men not on duty, attended the performance and all agreed it was a "perfect success." The following day Lieutenant Thayer went to Williamsport where Reymer was in charge. During the camp leader's absence the concert troupe went on a "general drunk."

Celebration of the troupe's success was rudely interrupted the next day when it was reported that a Greencastle gentleman was suspected of buying and selling government property. Under orders of Lieutenant McCloskey, Montgomery was sent into town where he informed Phineas Hollar of these charges and placed him under arrest. Sergeant Cutler and Private Hutchinson escorted the prisoner back to camp. Evidence of Hollar's illegal enterprise was found in his possession. This included a government issued bridle, a saddle blanket, two saddles, and two horses. Lieutenant Thayer in a later report told of Hollar approaching one of his men to persuade him and other soldiers to steal government property. They would be paid reasonable rates for the stolen goods according to Thayer's informant. The post's commander also said, "This man I am confident has been engaged in such illegal traffic for sometime and is also connected with the party dealing in government horses."

Hollar was a short term veteran, having joined the Pennsylvania's 6th Reserves on April 24, 1861. After only six month's service he was discharged on a surgeon's certificate, October 31. The closest he ever got to seeing action was in Baltimore on July 22. This was the time the 6th was on its way to Washington and William Kriner was accidentally wounded when another soldier slipped, fell, and his musket accidentally discharged.

Like others, Hollar had possibly seen how army material, which could be used by civilians, had a ready marketability. Unlike some who profited from such enterprises successfully, Phineas Hollar was caught. Montgomery did not tell of his fate, but he undoubtedly was turned over to the provost marshall for trial and possible imprisonment. [18]

Diary entries covering December continued to tell of the weather and the soldiers' attempts to cope with the bitter cold. Everybody was busy trying to keep snow from blowing into the tents. Walking was hazardous because of ice that also made riding patrol extremely dangerous. However, civilians and officers were enjoying sleighing and skating parties. Social activities also included three weddings in Greencastle, going to a singing school at Highland's Schoolhouse near Welsh Run and attending local dances.

On Christmas Day Montgomery worshipped at a service in Greencastle's Presbyterian Church where the Rev. J. W. Wightman preached. After this he returned to camp where everyone "sat around campfires and chatted and passed from tent to tent greeting each other with a "Merry Christmas." Two days later the men got into a snowball battle which nearly "ended in a fight." It was also noted that one signalman came to camp from Casey's with a bad case of frozen feet. On December 27 a detail served as an escort at the funeral of Andrew Scully, a member of Company K with the 21st Cavalry, who had been killed in the Virginia fighting. The next day the camp was alerted to be on the "lookout" for a Rebel spy, L. W. Loyd, who had escaped from the Guard House at Chambersburg. A complete description of the man had been received by telegraph. Montgomery was ordered to head a squad to look for the escapee "on the roads south of the Pittsburg Turnpike."

At the time, records indicate that between August, 1864 and July, 1865 nearly six hundred prisoners were temporarily kept in the Chambersburg compound before being transferred to other prisons. Most of those detained were Union deserters with only fifty classified as Confederates. Some of the inmates were local soldiers, arrested for offenses such as stealing, brawling, or drunkenness. Desertions during the fighting in Virginia were high. Many who were in the service as substitutes for drafted men were particularly susceptible to this urgent need to escape the dangers of battle. The high rate or run-a-way "bounty men" probably explained the excessive number of prisoners at Chamberburg. [19]

Holiday events included a sham battle between the Greencastle signalmen and Washington Township's militia or home guard. This affair, staged to show the military abilities of both groups, was held on December 31. [20] No outcome was noted by Montgomery. It could have ended like the concert troupe's celebration, with the opposing forces testing the libation qualities each side possessed. New Year's was spent at home by Montgomery. The weather continued to hamper work of the signal system. Heavy snow was again reported and one accident resulted in serious injuries to a patrol member. His horse slipped, fell on him, and dragged him for a distance before being rescued by members of the squad. Snow accumulated to such depths that rail transportation was indefinitely delayed. In this kind of weather, Montgomery told of attending his mother-in-law's funeral. She died in the State Asylum "where she had been committed for treatment of insanity caused by the recent Rebel burning of Chambersburg."

Other diary entries, beginning on January 17, tell of a ton of hay being purchased from David Hawbecker who lived in the Shady Grove area. Although the weather began to moderate, snow still covered the roads and sleighing continued. Montgomery and "most of the boys" on January 20 attended services at the Presbyterian Church but the principal news of the day came when word was received that a sleigh, assigned to Lieutenant Kennedy, was broken to pieces. The horse, frightened at something, panicked and ran away.

No injuries to man or beast were reported. The signalman's diary continues to tell of daily activities and the cold and snowy weather. On February 14 Lieutenant Thayer, who had been ill for several weeks, was relieved of duty. McClosky assumed command of the station.

A week later Lieutenant Reymer reported from the Williamsport camp that word had been received of a raid, the night before, on Cumberland. One hundred Rebels, led by the guerilla, Jesse McNeill, of West Virginia, had sneaked into the town. *(McNeill was an irregular in the invasion of 1863 who took many local blacks back into slavery.)* This time he captured Generals George Crook and Benjamin Kelley. Both were taken from their hotel beds and carried into the mountain country known so well to the raiders. Later accounts of this incident tell of only sixty-three men in McNeill's party. After escaping with their captives the guerilla band escorted Crook and Kelley through the mountains by seldom used back roads, into the Shenandoah Valley, and on to Harrisonburg. Here the men were taken, under heavy guard, by stage coach to Staunton. After a trip of 154 miles the Union officers were turned over to Jubal Early. Of further interest is the fact that McNeill's men missed two other hotel occupants in Cumberland. They were General James A. Garfield and Major William McKinley, both destined to serve as presidents of the United States.

From this point on, the news seemed to tell of few reverses for the Union cause. On March 2, McCloskey received word indicating "all quiet" in the Shenandoah and continued success of the Army of the Potomac. Through the remaining weeks of the war a few guerilla bands came into western Maryland threatening Pennsylvania, yet such forays were only nuisance raids. Later in the spring Captain William S. Stryker was given command of the local post. Montgomery was discharged on August 28, 1865. Records indicate that about this same time the Greencastle signal station was abandoned. For four years the countryside near the town had accommodated thousands of men. The camp on McCauley's farm, with its complement of perhaps forty signalmen, seemed to have blended well with the town's people. Its quiet passing from the local scene was a peaceful way to end Greencastle's experience with the military establishment. [21]

Signal Corps System
1864-65

Mr Parnell
X

Chambersburg
X

Mercersburg
X

Averell's
Hdq. July 29. 1864

Fleming
House

Signal
Corps

Greencastle

Caseys
Knob

Middleburg
(Muttontown)

Skirmish
July 6, 1864

Hancock
X

Fairview
Mtn.

Hagerstown
X

Potomac River

Williamsport

Harpers
Ferry
X

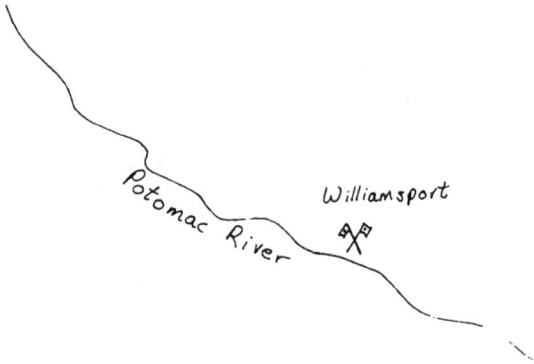

BY ANDREW BARBAZANES

288

CHAPTER XII

WHERE HAD ALL THE SOLDIERS GONE?

When Ulysses S. Grant was given command of the Union army, he developed a strategy that held the promise of final victory for the North. To fulfill this strategy, the Union had to smash two major Confederate armies. Of course there were other Southern forces beyond the Mississippi, in coastal fortifications, and in various local detachments, but only two really mattered. In the East was the formidable Army of Northern Virginia under Robert E. Lee and in the West stood the Army of Tennessee. Grant would establish this headquarters with General George G. Meade's Army of the Potomac, defeat Lee's army and take the Confederate capital at Richmond. While Grant and Lee maneuvered across Virginia, the Army of Tennessee, had to be dealt with in the western theater. Union forces, under Gen. William T. Sherman, would move to smash these Rebels, commanded by Joseph C. Johnston and march into the untouched Southern hinterland to Atlanta and beyond. This would then deprive the South of produce, livestock, and its manufacturing facilities.

Although Sherman's Army was primarily composed of midwesterners, eastern states also were represented. Among them were the 77th, 78th and 79th Pennsylvania Regiments. The 77th was organized for three year's service at camps in Chambersburg and Pittsburgh during the summer and fall of 1861. Although principally recruited from counties throughout the state Company A was from Franklin County. In October, 1861 Frederick S. Stumbaugh and Peter B. Housum, of the Chambersburg area, were chosen colonel and lieutenant colonel, respectively, of the regiment. A battery of guns, also attached to the 77th, was later detached from the regiment and became known as Independent Battery B.

Prior to moving to the front the regiment was assigned to a brigade composed of the 77th, 78th and 79th Pennsylvania Regiments under command of Brigadier General James S. Negley. Upon reaching camp in Kentucky the 77th was taken from Negley's brigade and throughout most of the war, this unit was part of a brigade composed of Indiana, Illinois, and Ohio regiments.

After fighting at Shiloh the regiment took part in the seige of Corinth, Mississippi. In September, 1862 it was transferred, first to Nashville, Tennessee, then to Louisville, Kentucky to assist in repelling Braxton Bragg's invasion of that state. Although the 77th did not take part in the bloody battle of Perryville, it was involved in skirmishes in support of the main body of the Union army. After the invasion of Kentucky the regiment moved back to the Nashville area until the opening of the winter campaign. By this time Col. Stumbaugh had resigned and Lt. Colonel Housum was placed in command.

On December 31 and January 1, 1863 the unit faced Bragg's army again at Murfreesboro or Stones River. Here the 77th was praised by General Rosecrans as the ". . . banner regiment at Stones River. They never broke their ranks." Casualties were heavy throughout the Union and Confederate ranks and the 77th was no exception. Lt. Col. Housum was killed as he led a counter attack to capture an enemy battery. James Craig and James Spangler also lost their lives in the fighting. Jackson Smith, John Walker, and Robert Kerr suffered wounds while Henry Trenary was declared missing. [1]

Among those treating the wounded was Dr. Victor Miller, a physician from Antrim Township, serving as assistant surgeon of the 78th Pennsylvania Volunteer Infantry. During the battle, while on the field engaged in dressing wounds of the commander of an Indiana regiment, he narrowly escaped injury when two enemy bullets cut through his coat. The exhaustion that followed the rigors of caring for the thousands of wounded soldiers at Stones River left him in a weakened condition which in turn led to his physical collapse. Because of this he was forced to resign and return to his practice in the township. [2]

On June 24, 1863, the 77th was engaged in heavy fighting at Liberty Gap, Tennessee. This was one of the first engagements in the summer campaign designed to drive Bragg out of Tennessee. The fighting was heavy and the regiment suffered many casualties. In September the men of the 77th took part in the Battle of Chickamauga. Here, General George H. Thomas became a national hero. Greencastle residents remembered this man, now called the "Rock of Chickamauga," as the colonel who led the first Union troops into the town in 1861 as part of Patterson's army. Confederate General John Bell Hood, who, with his Texans, camped south of Greencastle just four months earlier during the Gettysburg campaign, lost his leg in this encounter.

During the battle of September 19 the 77th advanced too far, making a charge which repulsed the Rebels but leaving the Pennsylvanians and the 79th Illinois, far ahead of the main Union line, with their flanks exposed. Other units were ordered to their support but it was too late. Just at dark a heavy Southern counterattack overran their position and catastrophe followed. Outnumbered more than two to one, and surrounded by the enemy, the men of the 77th fought bravely. Sergeant John W. Bryson, of Company A, killed Confederate General Preston Smith as that officer rode into the midst of the fighting. The Pennsylvanians also managed to kill two other members of Smith's staff before it was all over. Under cover of darkness some of the regiment's men got away but all of it's seven field officers and seventy men were taken prisoner along with the regimental colors. A few days later the unit retreated to Chattanooga where only eighty-four were left to answer roll calls. The 77th had gone into the Battle of Chickamauga with less than two hundred men and throughout the course of the struggle had suffered over fifty percent casualties.[3]

In the weeks that followed local news accounts told of the regiment's heavy losses. Captain Jesse R. Frey wrote to the Newville newspaper that only eight of his company (D) remained. Adam Goetz, of Greencastle, reported that his son, William (Independent Battery B), had received an arm wound and that he asked his father to let the parents of William and John Pensinger know their sons were still safe. A letter from Captain John Walker (Company A), of Waynesboro, published in the October 20, 1863 "Pilot" revealed more local casualties. One was Jacob Sites, of the Pine Hills west of Greencastle who had enlisted when only fifteen. He suffered a shoulder wound.

UNIDENTIFIED LOCAL SOLDIER
HENSON COLLECTION

In mid January of 1864 the 77th gave a thirty day furlough to those who desired to re-enlist. Despite the hardships they had been through, many refused to quit the war. "The Pilot," on January 19, reported "...almost to a man they re-enlisted for three more years." Independent Battery B saw eighty-two rejoin. When its men returned to action the regiment became part of Sherman's "host of liberators" in the campaign which coincided with Grant's thrust into Virginia. These men who had re-enlisted would now be part of the great struggle that would end the war. Seven local men who re-joined were destined to a share in the "grand strategy" for victory.

William Pensinger, of Greencastle, who had joined a second time, suffered no injuries during the entire war and when discharged he was a sergeant. His brother, John, also served a second enlistment without harm. William Goetz, who had already served one term in the artillery, re-enlisted on March 8, 1865, as an infantryman and came through to war's end unhurt. John Rowe served three years and signed up for another term. After surviving all the 77th's campaigns unharmed, while stationed in Texas after the war, he died on October 6, 1865. Jacob Poper, of Antrim Township, re-enlisted as an artilleryman and served until the end without incident.

With Sherman's army the regiment participated in the campaign against Atlanta. Names like Tunnel Hill, Rockyface Ridge, New Hope Church, Kenesaw Mountain, Chattahoochee River, and Peach Tree were fixed indelibly in the minds of all who fought and lived through the battles associated with the fighting to take Atlanta. By August the Confederates, under John Bell Hood (Joseph E. Johnston had been relieved of command in July), had been pushed back into the city limits. Heavy bombardments and strong infantry thrusts forced Hood to evacuate the city on September 1, 1864. However, the campaign had been costly. Numbered among thousands of casualties was A Company's commander, Captain John Walker, killed on August 5.

Shortly after the fall of Atlanta, Hood moved his army into Tennessee to threaten Sherman's line of communications. Sherman did not follow with his army. Instead he embarked upon his famous "March to the Sea" and sent the 4th and 23rd Corps, under General John M. Schofield, to reinforce General George H. Thomas at Nashville. Hood intercepted Schofield before he reached Nashville, at the town of Franklin, Tennessee. Here, on November 30, the Confederates lost many men during a frontal assault against entrenched Federal troops across an open area two miles long. Union losses were 2,326 men. Once again the 77th Pennsylvania found itself in desperate combat. Jacob Sites, who had recently been promoted to sergeant received his second wound of the war, was taken prisoner. He was not freed until April 28, 1865.

The 77th then took part in the battle of Nashville (December 15 and 16, 1864) where the enemy was completely routed. Union forces then pursued the remnants of Hood's army into Alabama. The regiment was one of the units which occasionally skirmished with the enemy's rear guard, until it reached Huntsville, where the pursuit was called off. Here the regiment remained until March of 1865 when it was transferred to eastern Tennessee. After Confederate units east of the Mississippi River had surrendered, the 77th was sent to Texas where some Rebels hoped to continue the war.[4]

The 78th Pennsylvania was at Nashville, also, and prior to that had participated in many of the major battles in the west. Most of its men were recruited in western Pennsylvania. However, a few were from the Cumberland Valley. Beyond Dr. Victor Miller, the only local man known to have served in this regiment was Samuel Showalter. A veteran of Company B, 126th Pennsylvania Infantry, he was either drafted or came in as a substitute late in the war, probably seeing no action in the Tennessee fighting. [5]

The 79th Regiment was raised in Lancaster County in early August of 1861. Only one local region man is thought to have served throughout the regiment's military active service. He was William M. Finfrock. Records indicate that he was from Fulton County but later lived in the Greencastle area.[6] Local men who later become members of the 79th were probably drafted or served as substitutes from February 22, 1865 until they were discharged between June and August the same year. They joined Sherman's army on its march from Savannah through the Carolinas. It is likely that the Greencastle area men became part of this army at Goldsboro, North Carolina on March 22 when records show the regiment received two hundred recruits. They arrived just three days after the last major engagement of the campaign, the Battle of Bentonville.

The 79th was dispatched to Martha's Vineyard and, while encamped in this coastal region of North Carolina, its men learned of General Joseph Johnston's army being defeated at Bentonville. *(Johnston had been reinstated as commander of the Army of Tennessee)*. The old nemesis of General Patterson in the Shenandoah Campaign of 1861 had suffered his final defeat. These last recruits were spared from violent death, wounds, or captivity. Yet none knew how long the war would last when they enlisted. Greencastle area soldiers among the two hundred latecomers were Pinkney G. Clary, James J. Hill, William Hollingshead, Jacob Harmony, Isaiah Martin, Daniel Pike, William H. Pope, George Rebok, Daniel Valentine, David Young, and George W. Poper. The first of these men to arrive home was James Hill, discharged on June 2 and the last was William Hollingshead, mustered out August 28, 1865. [7]

On May 4, 1864, while local soldiers with Sherman's army were preparing to leave Chattanooga and fight their way to Atlanta, another offensive was beginning in Virginia. The Army of the Potomac, still under the command of the hot tempered, yet competent George Gordon Meade of Pennsylvania, crossed the Rapidan River. Under the immediate direction of General Grant, this campaign against the Army of Northern Virginia would result in some of the bloodiest fighting of the war. The Army of the Potomac was now approximately 118,000 strong. Over eighty infantry, cavalry and artillery units from Pennsylvania were in this host of blue clad soldiers and Greencastle area men were with them in company strength or scattered through the ranks of at least fourteen regiments and batteries. Units containing concentrations of local soldiers included such regiments as the 2nd Heavy Artillery; the 6th and 12th Reserves; the 55th with Butler's Army of the James, and the 17th and 21st Cavalry. Even one of the famous "Bucktail" regiments, the 149th, contained some area soldiers. This account of the Army of the Potomac's advance towards Richmond and its battles has been gathered from the experiences of men in these outfits. Contemporary letters, newspaper accounts, official records and diaries, as well as stories recorded in later years, provide a glimpse into what was common to all.

One reason the Army of the Potomac was numerically strong at this time was because Grant had stripped the Washington defenses of heavy artillery. These regiments, organized to occupy the forts around Washington, had led a relative easy life, requiring practically no marching and only the remote chance of combat. Among these was the 2nd Pennsylvania Heavy Artillery, organized in January, 1862. Most of the local recruiting for this regiment had been done in the fall of 1862 under the direction of Lieutenant Benjamin F. Winger.

DETAIL OF BATTERY F — PA. HEAVIES   ALEXANDER COLLECTION

For two years the regiment had been in the Washington defenses and had even helped construct them. During this time its members lived in permanent barracks, with regular meals, life on the town, and hotel-like sleeping quarters. However, to their credit, scores of these Pennsylvanians defending the capital took "French leave" during Lee's invasion of 1863. They returned to their native state and joined the Army of the Potomac during its march to Gettysburg to defend their "homes and firesides." Their regimental history noted, "Many such men were killed, wounded or captured, and to this day some are marked on the records as "deserters," and, owing to that fact, those recorded as such in the roster at this time may be thus accounted for." [8]

On July 13, 1863, Lieutenant Winger was named "Acting Assistant Inspector General for First Brigade Defenses North of the Potomac." He continued in this capacity until the regiment left Washington on March 26, 1864, crossed the Potomac, occupied Forts Ethan Allen and Marcy, and proceeded to drill as infantry in preparation for the role they would play in Grant's move against the Confederates. By this time the popularity of the Washington defense units had drawn so many recruits that the 2nd Pennsylvania Heavy Artillery numbered over 3,600 men, making it the largest "regiment" in the Union army. Although regulations called for a thousand men per regiment, the average for infantry regiments in the spring of 1864 was less than five hundred. Beyond its unheard of size, the 2nd had a shortage of officers to manage this "mob" of relatively green troops who, within weeks, would take part in some of the greatest battles of the war. Fortunately the problem was solved when, on April 20, the artillerymen were divided into two regiments. A second unit, composed of the most recent recruits, was designated the Provisional 2nd Pennsylvania Heavy Artillery. These men, along with the 24th New York Cavalry (dismounted) and the 14th New York Heavy Artillery, were part of a "Provisional Brigade" attached to the IX Corps and were the first to leave for the front. The original 2nd Pennsylvania "Heavies" followed on May 27. [9]

Meanwhile, the green troops of the "Provisionals" were thrown into combat on May 5 when the Battle of the Wilderness began. For two days the armies battled each other in the rough wooded terrain near Chancellorsville, where local men had fought and died the previous year. Although the struggle involved many untried troops, older outfits such as the 6th and 12th Pennsylvania Reserves also saw combat in this first engagement of the campaign. Greatly reduced in number, compared to their former strength, these proud regiments, each with a company from Franklin County, would fight out the remaining weeks of their enlistment until mustered out in early June. Local men with the 149th Pennsylvania, one of the three famous "Bucktail Regiments," were in this fight also. [10]

Although the Wilderness was primarily an infantrymen's battle, cavalry was also involved. Among the horse soldiers was the 17th Pennsylvania Cavalry whose Company G was from the county and included many veterans of the 126th Pennsylvania Volunteers. The 17th had ridden to the left of the Union line, where it dismounted and fought off numerous Confederate attempts to turn the Northern flank. [11]

While the Wilderness fighting was in progress, Major General Benjamin F. Butler, commander of the Army of the James, had been ordered to advance up the James River and threaten Richmond from the southeast. His army of 40,000 included a number of Pennsylvania regiments. One was the 55th in which local men were serving. These soldiers had been stationed in the coastal regions of South Carolina near the town of Beaufort. Although many suffered from sea sickness during their transfer from South Carolina to Virginia and others fell victim to enemy guerillas near their new camp, a local soldier in the 55th wrote that "all the Greencastle boys are well and in fine spirits." [12] On May 4, Butler's force took City Point, a place between Richmond and Petersburg at the junction of the James and Appomattox Rivers. This became the Union's principal supply center during the campaign for Petersburg. However, within two weeks, a smaller Confederate force shut up the Army of the James, "as if it had been in a bottle strongly corked," in Bermuda Hundred, a loop formed by the

LT. COL. B. F. WINGER   MOLLUS MASS. AND BERT COLLECTIONS   LT. COL. JOSEPH DAVISON

winding James and Appomattox Rivers. Here Butler waited while, to the north, Lee's and Grant's armies fought it out. During Butler's move toward Richmond, the 55th suffered several hundred casualties, among them a local man, Jesse K. Norris who was wounded in both arms. [13]

On May 10 the Army of the Potomac again struck Lee who had now moved his forces out of the Wilderness and was entrenched at Spottsylvania. During the next 12 days several assaults were made upon the Rebel defenses. Union losses were high and so were those of the Confederates but Lee could not replace his manpower. Only Grant possessed this luxury. It was in this fighting that Greencastle's Joseph A. Davison, of the 6th Reserves, was cited for bravery for which he received the brevet rank of lieutenant colonel. He had been promoted to brevet major just days before in the Wilderness for similar acts of conduct.

By the end of the fighting at Spottsylvania the 6th had suffered thirteen killed, sixty-four wounded and nine missing. No casualties among Greencastle-Antrim men can be found in the Wilderness and Spottsylvania campaigns. However, the county's Company D had a number killed, wounded and missing. *(For a list of them the reader should refer to Bates' History of Pennsylvania Volunteers, Vol. I, p. 708-709.)* The regiment continued fighting and on May 22 it captured ninety men of A. P. Hill's Corps. On its very last day of service, May 30, the 6th was in the Battle of Bethesda Church. Here, with its ranks diminished to about one hundred and fifty men, the regiment captured over one hundred Rebel prisoners and killed over seventy with considerable losses. After three years of service, from its early weeks of training at Camp Biddle in Greencastle, through the major engagements of the Army of the Potomac, the 6th started for Harrisburg on June 1 and arrived in the state's capital the following Monday. By the weekend its soldiers were mustered out and, on June 15, Franklin County's survivors of this proud regiment finally came home. [14]

As news of these battles reached Greencastle, families whose fathers and sons were in the fighting anxiously waited for letters or casualty lists to learn if their loved ones were still alive. The local newspaper, reporting battle results throughout May, brought dismay to the community when it was learned that David Bowman's boys were victims. Bowman was a blacksmith who lived along the turnpike east of Shady Grove. His four sons were with Company E, 149th Pennsylvania, in the Wilderness fighting. Calvin, with severe wounds was hospitalized in Baltimore. *(A later issue would report his death.)* Upton, with gunshot wounds and a broken leg, was a prisoner of the

Rebels; Franklin was home recovering from a wound, and Davis was injured during a charge. Other reports told of Jonathan Pentz of the 12th U. S. Infantry receiving a hand wound; A. Jackson Cline, of the 148th Pennsylvania and Daniel Mowen of the 7th Maryland *(a number of local men joined Maryland regiments)* were also listed as wounded. John F. Byers, a draftee from Antrim Township, was killed while serving with Company B, 148th Pennsylvania. He had been in the service for less than a year. John Pike received notice that his son, Ferdinand, had been killed at Spottsylvania on May 11. He had been serving out his enlistment in the 93rd Pennsylvania.[15]

As the carnage continued, Grant ordered reinforcements to join the Army of the Potomac. On May 28th the original 2nd Pennsylvania Heavy Artillery arrived by boat at Port Royal, Virginia and was soon forced to march sixty miles to join the XVIII Corps. Under General Baldy Smith, this corps had been detached from Butler's Army of the James to support the Army of the Potomac. The 55th Pennsylvania was one of the regiments assigned to Smith's command.

Heavy artillerymen weren't the only troops Grant was converting into infantry. About the same time that the 2nd Pennsylvania was leaving for the front, the 21st Pennsylvania Cavalry was preparing for a similar experience. It had arrived in Washington on May 15 and was dismounted, armed and equipped as infantrymen. During the fall and winter of 1863-1864, most of the Franklin County companies had been sent to track deserters in the Pennsylvania coal fields, while the rest did duty fighting guerrilas in the Shenandoah near Harpers Ferry. In February, 1864, the regiment was re-organized at Chambersburg for three year's service with many original members and veterans of the 126th and 158th Pennsylvania Infantry re-enlisting. These men arrived at the front on June 2.[16]

In the race for possession of a crossroads known as Cold Harbor, just eight miles northeast of Richmond, Confederate cavalry won by a few hours. But in the afternoon on May 31, General Philip Sheridan's cavalry drove them out and held the crossing until relieved by the Federal VI Corps. Most of Sheridan's troopers were armed with the new Spencer repeating carbine, which made them formidable opponents against Confederate infantrymen armed with muzzleloaders. The 17th Pennsylvania Cavalry was one of these units and suffered severe losses, while helping to rout a Confederate attempt to turn the Union left flank. On the morning of June 1, Lee ordered an assault against the VI Corps in a bold attempt to seize the crossroads and roll up the exposed flank before Grant could reinforce it. Once again Union cavalry, such as the 17th Pennsylvania, did deadly work with their repeaters until relieved by infantry. The Confederates were repulsed and that afternoon the 55th Pennsylvania Infantry took part in the attack of Smith's XVIII Corps in an unsuccessful attempt to break the Southern lines. In several places, however, the Rebels were pushed back. The 55th managed to capture a line of rifle pits and take a large number of prisoners. Meanwhile, on the Union right, elements of Burnside's IX Corps, including the Provisional 2nd Pennsylvania Heavy Artillery, repulsed other Confederate attacks. [17]

Grant assumed the Confederates had been weakened so he planned an all out assuault for June 2. However, it had to be postponed until the next day because a corps got lost in the woods and swamps while moving to its assigned position. Lee's men, taking advantage of this fatal delay, entrenched themselves so that all approaches to their positions would be covered by a murderous fire. At 4:30 a.m. on June 3, over 40,000 Union troops began the attack on a two and a half mile front. Grant had hoped to crush the enemy but within an hour the outcome was decided. 7,000 men in blue lay scattered along the Rebel ramparts, half of them dead. The charge had failed and the Battle of Cold Harbor became another defeat for the Army of the Potomac. However, it would prove to be Lee's last major victory in the field. No other massive assaults were attempted by either army although the troops stayed in the trenches until June 12 with constant nerve wracking sharpshooting and skirmishing. From June 1-12 the Union losses totaled 12,700. Confederate losses were about 2,000.

The 21st Pennsylvania Cavalry got it's first taste of infantry fighting at this battle, losing over fifty men killed and wounded. Henry F. Charles, who had been in Greencastle in 1862 with the state's emergency troops, was now with Company C of the 21st. He told of his unit's experiences at Cold Harbor. "There had been fighting there two days before and the dead and wounded still lay on the field. We charged the rebel works next morning. We were successful in the middle, but the right and left ends were repulsed and we could not get back, so we lay among the dead of the day before. Our batteries protected us as good as they could and we fell back that night . . Some of the dead were bloated so bad that the buttons tore off their coats. All of us that had blankets took them to cover the dead next day and shoveled a little dirt over them and that is all the burial they got. It was too horrible for a human to behold and what we tell human ears cannot understand." [18]

Among the many casualties of the 21st was Colonel William Boyd, the regimental commander. He was struck on the side of the neck by a sharp-shooter's bullet but continued to direct his troops until nearly exhausted from loss of blood before he was taken from the field. Within weeks he was at his residence in Chambersburg convalesing from this wound that eventually led to his discharge. Others listed as wounded were Sergeant Kennedy Hood, J. Shultz, and George Pawling of the Greencastle area. [19]

One veteran of the 126th and now with the 21st was Christian Hager. At Cold Harbor Hager received wounds but was able to rejoin his outfit later and continued fighting. Another veteran, Jacob Lear, a blacksmith, in Company M, was wounded in the left leg by a rifle ball. It shattered the bone and Lear was sent home to recover. Other former members of the 126th now with the 21st were Henry Bartle, Abram Bowman, Jonas Freze, Isaiah Illginfritz, Simon Palmer, William Snively, Samuel Stickell and James Wilson. Henry White, who had escaped the Rebels twice at Antietam, and Upton Easton, later known as Greencastle's blind veteran, were also among the members of the 21st who remained unscathed in the battle. All escaped the carnage at Cold Harbor and continued to serve throughout the campaign. Two physicians from Greencastle, T. M. Kennedy and William H. King, helped care for the regiment's wounded. [20]

The 55th Pennsylvania lost nearly 140 men, killed or wounded, most of them during the attack of June 3. Greencastle men with the regiment were found in casualty lists as news came of this debacle. Sergeant William Shorts was killed and the town paper praised him for his heroism. He had served in the first company raised in Greencastle *(Company C, 2nd Pennsylvania.)* The paper's editor said, "There never was a truer patriot and a soldier. God comfort his afflicted parents." At the time William died, his brother, Henry, was wounded but by July 5 he was home recuperating. Another casualty, William Snodie, was wounded and placed in an army hospital in Washington. The 17th Cavalry suffered heavy losses also. Among the wounded was John Shockey, an area man, who died two days later. [21]

After Cold Harbor, the 17th was sent back to the Spottsylvania battlefield to look for wounded Union soldiers said to be in a state of neglect at a field hospital. This mission of mercy resulted in finding thirty-five men in a famished condition. Upon investigation the wounded were taken to another hospital for better treatment. [22]

The Provisional 2nd Pennsylvania Heavy Artillery was in the action at Cold Harbor on June 1 and 2 and lost heavily while repulsing several Confederate attacks. Some companies lost half their men in this carnage. Among the captured was Lieutenant D. M. Niswander of Welsh Run. The original 2nd Pennsylvania Heavy Artillery arrived on the field on June 5, but missed the major fighting. However, they served as pickets and were involved in several skirmishes that followed.[23] "The Pilot" continued to report on local casualties of Cold Harbor for the next month. William Mellinger, of the Middleburg area, with the 7th Maryland Infantry, was wounded.[24]

After Cold Harbor, Grant decided to move quickly to the south of Richmond to isolate the city and the defending troops by cutting the railroads which supplied it. To do this he would need to attack Petersburg, an important railway center, twenty-five miles south of the Rebel capital. On June 9 Butler's troops, in a half hearted attack, assaulted the defenses of Petersburg with no success. At the time only a few thousand Confederates, mostly a hastily organized force of old men and boys from the city, manned the defenses. During this fighting the Army of the Potomac secretly and hurriedly began assembling for its departure from Cold Harbor. On June 12 an army of over 100,000 men moved undetected out of the trenches. Lee was not aware of this movement until the following day. To accomplish this Grant had his engineers build a pontoon bridge across the 2,100 foot wide James River. It was "the longest continuous pontoon bridge ever used in war." By June 14 it was completed and the next day forward elements of the army stood before the undermanned trenches of Petersburg, earthworks first erected in 1862 as part of the defenses against McClellan's forces in the Peninsula Campaign.

Lee, under the impression that Grant was preparing another assault, moved from Cold Harbor to block the road to Richmond, a road the Union army had no intention of taking. His scouts still did not indicate Grant was moving south of the capital. Meanwhile, to divert Federal strength from his front, Lee dispatched General Jubal Early to drive David Hunter out of the Shenandoah Valley and then threaten the North. *(This was the campaign that enabled Early to extract tribute from Hagerstown and Frederick and threaten Washington.)*

On June 15 Baldy Smith led his XVIII Corps against the Petersburg defenses held by a meager force of some 4,000 Southerners under General P. G. T. Beauregard. This small army should never have stopped the Federals who numbered 18,000, but an abundance of ineptness — poor maps, faulty orders, lack of rations, and indecisive commanders, combined with the courage of the little band of defenders, saved the day for the Confederacy. Some of the Union regiments, however, were successful in capturing a few Confederate works. For example, the 55th Pennsylvania claimed credit for taking eighteen cannons and 400 prisoners. [25]

More Federal troops crossed the James and on June 16, another assault began which pushed Beauregard's forces from their outer entrenchments into fortifications to the rear. Finally, after continued appeals for help, Lee sent two divisions that recaptured the trenches sealing off Bermuda Hundred. Once again Union troops managed to take a number of Rebel positions, but with heavy losses.

The 2nd Pennsylvania Heavy Artillery entered the fighting on the 16th as part of Smith's Corps. Captain Nicholas Baggs of Battery D, wrote that when he and his men were ordered to the front it was nearly dusk. "Lieutenant B. F. Winger, who had been on detached duty at headquarters, joined the command, saying, 'Captain, I heard you were going into the fight and I want to be with you.' We moved out the woods towards a barn and wheat field. We could not see the rebels, but they saw us, and the firing both of rifles and cannon, was very hot . . . as it grew darker the intensity of the fire increased and we were ordered to lie down. As soon as the men got down they commenced throwing up breastworks with their tincups and bayonets . . . I do not know how near we got to the rebel works, but about 10 o'clock it was known that the rebels had retreated."[26]

Later, Winger told of officers ordering the men to stay in position and to keep their lines straight in spite of the bursting shells and solid shot coming into their ranks. "...the only thing to be done was to do a whole lot of good, hard swearing, and, with a corporal behind them, to prevent shirking, I gave orders to fix bayonets, and every fellow went into the charge with alacrity...the way they did their work proved them to be the bravest of the brave." One of the wounded in this fight was Corporal Benjamin Dougherty, a member of Battery L, from the local area. [27]

The fighting continued on the 17th. By then the Provisional 2nd Pennsylvania Heavy Artillery, which was with the IX Corps, had been forced to march to the front. Early that morning, the Provisionals formed a line of battle and advanced under heavy fire over a field the XVIII Corps had fought over the previous two days and on which many dead and wounded still lay. Enemy fire in this area was so heavy the regiment took cover behind a hill, where it remained until dark. At eight o'clock, the unit advanced across an open field under heavy Confederate rifle and musket fire, capturing the Rebel position along with many prisoners. The main Confederate line held, however, and the price was high in the Union ranks for what was gained. One brigade lost 840 out of 1,890 men in this assault.

Company A of the Provisionals went into the fight without a commissioned officer, all of them being sick or taken prisoner, so First Sergeant David H. Wolff, of Welsh Run was put in command.

Early in the engagement that evening, he was severely wounded in the arm and leg while trying to capture a Confederate flag. Then in the act of grasping the Rebel colors he received a wound in the stomach. As he was assisted to the rear he was again shot and this wound proved fatal. Less than one-third of the regiment was present for roll call the next morning. The day was spent burying the dead and bringing in the wounded. Among the dead was Private John Robinson of Greencastle. [28]

Grant ordered a general assault for the Union forces at 4 a.m. on June 18. These attacks continued throughout the day with bloody repulses as Lee, finally aware of Grant's true intentions, directed more troops to the aid of the Petersburg defenders. In this crucial fighting, men of the 2nd Pennsylvania Heavy Artillery overran Rebel positions, but the 55th Pennsylvania, which was supporting the heavies, suffered over fifty percent casualties and fell back. This left the artillerymen exposed to a murderous crossfire. The men, however, using tin plates and bayonets, dug in and held their ground under continuous enemy fire. Within fifteen minutes the 2nd lost over eighty men killed and wounded. Among the latter was Francis Hoffman of Battery H. He received a bullet wound in the left thigh — so severe that his leg was amputated almost to the hip. *(Contrary to the high percentage of fatalities from such operations, Hoffman survived, returned to Greencastle, and lived to a ripe old age.)* [29]

The 21st Pennsylvania Cavalry, still serving as infantry, also was in the midst of the action at Petersburg. One participant wrote, "If Cold Harbor was hard, the fight of the 18th of June was harder. We charged . . . the rebel fort . . . directly in front of us, at a distance of about one hundred and fifty yards. Here we found that we could go no farther. He who went beyond this, went to his grave. Four times were our colors shot down, and four times were they raised again." At this point the men dug in, having suffered over 90 casualties. Area casualties were heavy — Franklin Gamble, John McCormick, Henry Ruthrauff, wounded; Samuel Pike and George Shaffer killed, from Company K. [30]

The fighting of June 18 ended with the Confederates still holding the defenses around Petersburg. Opposite the Rebel entrenchments Union troops began occupying outer trenches they had taken and constructed their own network of fortifications to lead into the captured lines. About 50,000 men manned the Southern lines with Grant's force, of approximately 112,000, facing them. This dual defense system covered a distance of twenty-six miles, stretching from east of Richmond to the Jerusalem Plank Road south of Petersburg.

Sealing off Petersburg became the prime objective. To do this, Grant had to cut the rail lines and roads to the south of the city. In addition localized assaults designed to cut through the Confederate lines continued. Both of these tactics occupied the Federal forces through the summer and fall of 1864 until winter weather halted the operations.

On June 21 a Union force moved to threaten the Weldon Railroad. The next day two Confederate divisions attacked these troops and halted the operation. However, the following day, a cavalry unit reached the tracks and began destroying its rails. A counter attack forced them to withdraw. Although the Rebels saved their railroad, these engagements resulted in the Union getting control of the Jerusalem Plank Road, a major supply line for Petersburg's defenders. Pennsylvania's 21st Cavalry took part in this attempt to destroy the rail line. The regiment lost two men killed and three wounded. There were no casualties from the Franklin County companies. [31]

While this action was taking place, former coal miners in Pennsylvania's 48th Regiment led by Colonel Henry Pleasants, were planning to dig a mine under the Confederate defenses directly east of Petersburg. On June 25 they began this underground approach to the enemy's lines. Pleasants, a mining engineer, directed the entire operation, getting the tunnel angled properly, providing ventilation by air shafts, shoring up the mine, and laying explosives under the Confederate works. The miners not only dug a direct line to the Rebel trenches but tunneled lateraly at the end of the main line to run parallel to Confederate fortifications above. When finished this underground approach was 586 feet long. Four tons of black powder were placed to explode upwards through twenty feet of earth separating the mine from the entrenchments overhead.

At 4:45 on the morning of July 30 the massive charge was detonated. The earth trembled as an explosion threw men, horses, cannon, and other equipment into the air, leaving a crater nearly 170 feet long, 60 to 80 feet wide and 30 feet deep. Union troops advanced into this vast depression but failed to go further. By half past eight, 15,000 Federal soldiers had moved into the breach but had not gone beyond the crater. After the initial shock of the explosion, Lee's forces gathered to counter the attackers. Their batteries began shelling the men in this hugh cavity. Mortars were brought nearer and lobbed shell after shell into the mass of soldiers. General Edward Ferrero's division of Negroes, who had drilled for weeks for this assault, were held back. Belatedly, they were sent into the crater and, along with some white soldiers, they did advance beyond the devastated area. Finally Confederate infantry began a charge that forced everyone back into its depth's again and many retreated into their lines. General Meade ordered a withdrawal. Shortly after one o'clock the Battle of the Crater was over.

The Provisional 2nd Pennsylvania Heavy Artillery's men were said to be among the first to enter the crater and the last to leave. Comapny B's survivors always claimed they were the first. They went through this catastrophy and held out to the last, with many taken as prisoners after escape routes were cut off. Official records show the Provisionals had eleven killed, fifty-seven men and officers wounded, and a 118 captured.

The regimental historian wrote; "That the Provisional Regiment stood the brunt of the battle is without a doubt," and General Burnside, in his Conduct of the War says: "One regiment, the 2nd Pennsylvania Heavy Artillery, advanced some one hundred yards beyond the crater, but, not supported, fell back." One eyewitness wrote, "How any men escaped death in the crater is a mystery to me. Cannon on the right and left, and musketry in front, pouring in their deadly hail of iron and lead, seemed to cover every inch of ground therein." [32]

The outcome of this battle may have been different if Ferrero's Negroes had led the assault. However, Grant had deliberately held them back for fear that, if the attack failed, Radical Republicans in Washington would have accused him of using the blacks as "cannon fodder."

Although Negro soldiers were enlisted in northern states, notably Pennsylvania, New York and Massachusetts, they were not integrated into white regiments and many white officers and enlisted men resented the use of Negroes as soldiers. At first Negro recruitment was officially frowned upon by state and federal officials. However, Lincoln gave Presidential blessing to such endeavors in the Emancipation Proclamation of January 1, 1863. Thereafter, organization of black regiments developed in earnest. Although most of these men who entered the service were former slaves from liberated parts of the South, Pennsylvania led the northern states by furnishing 8,612 from June, 1863 to war's end. Approximately five hundred Negroes from Franklin County, including an undetermined number from the Greencastle area, were among these soldiers. [33]

For a northern state, however, Pennsylvania had lagged behind on matters concerning blacks. Indeed, as late as 1862, the state legislature had considered a bill to punish by fine and imprisonment any "colored" person coming into the state. Despite the Emancipation Proclamation, on February 6, 1863 Governor Curtin rejected a request by the noted black abolitionist, Frederick Douglas, to accept colored volunteers.

The reluctance of Pennsylvanians to accept Negroes was abated with Lee's invasion of 1863. Then all hands were needed to defend the state. On June 23, 1863, the first black recruits arrived at Camp William Penn near Philadelphia. By May of 1864, ten full colored regiments had been organized. [34]

The Greencastle area had at least five men from its colored community in the Richmond-Petersburg theater. Sergeant Timothy Anderson was with Company M, 2nd Regiment of Cavalry, U.S. Colored Troops. His outfit was stationed near Norfolk and later City Point, Virginia. Private Gilghman Cain served with Company I, 127th U.S. Colored Infantry. Privates Harrison Shipe and Meshac Smith of Company B, 45th U.S. Colored Infantry, took part in the final operations at Petersburg. Private Robert Henderson, of the 38th U.S. Colored Infantry, served in the Petersburg campaign and became part of Richmond's occupation force after it was evacuated. All of the above regiments were part of the Army of the James.

Three other local Negroes served in the Department of the Gulf and the Department of Florida. Private Robert Hill was in Company C of the 2nd Regiment, U.S. Colored Infantry. Privates George W. Lewis and John Smith served in Company C, 25th U.S. Colored Infantry. This regiment, recruited for the most part in Pennsylvania, spent most of its time in the defenses of Pensacola Harbor, Florida. Here the men were drilled as both infantrymen and heavy artillerymen, becoming quite proficient. In January, 1865, the unit played a limited supportive role in the Mobile Campaign. During the spring and summer of 1864, the men suffered terribly from scurvy and about 150 died. At one point four to six men were dying daily. This epidemic was due to a lack of proper rations. The officers in command appealed for better rations but did not receive them until the disease had run its course. With its depleted ranks the regiment was discharged in early December of 1865. [35]

The 25th's flag symbolized the meaning of the Civil War for all Negro soldiers. Painted by a black man in Philadelphia, the banner showed a Freedman in the foreground and as the shackles of bondage are falling from his ankles, he reaches for the musket and uniform of his country's defenders being handed to him by the Goddess of Liberty. [36]

Nearly 179,000 Negroes served in the armed forces of the Union. Approximately seventy-five percent (134,000) came from slave holding areas controlled by Union forces. Over 68,000 black soldiers died. 2,751 were killed in action while the remainder died of wounds or disease.

After the crater disaster, both sides dug in for a war of attrition. The seige of Petersburg would last for nearly nine more months. The Union continued to strike at the rail lines or roads leading to Petersburg and extend its entrenchments around the city. On August 18 a series of battles and skirmishes took place to sever the Weldon Railroad. Two days later the upper portion of the line was destroyed and trains could only get to a point twenty miles below besieged Petersburg. Pennsylvania's 21st Cavalry took part in this operation. Its losses were one killed and twenty-seven wounded, but all Franklin Countians came through this encounter unscathed. [37]

Not all the casualties were caused by battle at the seige of Petersburg. In August during a heavy rainstorm, a dam near the breastworks of the 2nd Pennsylvania Heavy Artillery, broke and washed away all the camp's equipment. Nearly two hundred soldiers in a nearby camp were not so lucky; they were caught in the sudden rise of the water and swept away. Many were seen floating down the current on logs, being unable to reach shore, and were carried to a railroad bridge, where, upon striking the stone abutments, became entangled in the jam of logs and either drowned or were crushed to death.

B. F. Winger, in a letter, referred to the flood and his experiences as follows: "A funny, yet sad thing occurred at the time of a big Virginia flood in the ravine in the rear of Fort Steadman, in 1864, where we had our main headquarters. Several sutlers' tents were in this ravine, and their whole stock was flooded down the stream towards the Appomattox. A number of cases of champagne were seen swimming along, and an old sailor jumped in and got a case. An old soldier failed, for, although a good swimmer, the swift current of the waters carried him down to the railroad bridge, where, being caught and fastened in the debris, he was drowned. During our service of three and a half years we did much hard and faithful duty; and yet we had with it some pleasant experiences, all of which we would not surrender for all the other experiences of our lives." [38]

About this time General Grant decided something had to be done about Jubal Early in the Shenandoah Valley. Throughout the war this area had served as a valuable supply source for the South — "The Breadbasket of the Confederacy" — and as a major avenue of approach for raids into the Cumberland Valley. After Early's Washington raid, Federal authorities established the Middle Military Division, Department of the Shenandoah. A new army, the Army of the Shenandoah, was formed from units taken from the Army of the Potomac, the Department of the Gulf, and the Army of West Virginia. Grant gave General Philip Sheridan this command with orders to destroy Early's army and devastate the Shenandoah region, thus eliminating this fertile area's capacity to feed Lee's army at Petersburg and provide subsistence to local guerillas.

Sheridan's forces marched up and down the valley, fighting and defeating Early at Winchester, September 19, 1864; Fisher's Hill, September 22; and Cedar Creek, October 19. The latter engagement was the last major military action in the Shenandoah. On March 2, 1865 the remainder of Early's force was annihilated at Waynesboro, Virginia. Besides Early, the Union forces also had to contend with Confederate guerillas such as John S. Mosby, who in September 1864, during a period of just a few weeks, killed, wounded or captured 1,200 Federals, took 1,600 horses, and 230 beef cattle. In retaliation and to hurt Lee's food supply, Sheridan burned homes, farms, mills, and factories throughout the valley. Summing up this devastation, Sheridan was credited with saying, "A crow would have had to carry its rations if it had flown across the valley."

Cavalry played an important role in the campaign and the 17th Pennsylvania was one of the participating regiments. Company G was recruited in Franklin County with membership largely from the Waynesboro area, and some from Greencastle. By 1864 over forty men from the Greencastle area were serving in the regiment.[39]

The 17th took part in most of the major engagements in the Valley and many local men saw heavy fighting. During the battle of Winchester, September 19, Jacob Potter *(a resident of Greencastle after the war)*, quartermaster sergeant of Company B, performed a heroic deed which later won for him promotion to lieutenant. In a charge upon the Southern rearguard, the enemy turned and made a strong attack against the Union cavalry, who were compelled to retreat. Sergeant Potter was surrounded by the Confederates who demanded his surrender. However, being well mounted, he cut his way through the enemy lines and made his escape.[40]

On September 30, a number of men from Company B were taken

prisoner by Mosby's guerillas while on patrol duty. The detail, consisting of Private John B. Mowrey, Emory F. Morganthall, Jacob Weiss and David Detrich, led by Sergeant David Royer, was ambushed and only Royer escaped. The prisoners were first sent to Andersonville and later transferred to Salisbury prison. Morganthall died while in captivity but the others were eventually paroled in late February of 1865. Disease took its toll, however after the war John B. Mowrey died at Mercersburg April 8, 1865. David C. Detrich, upon arriving in Greencastle on March 1, was taken to his home in the Canebrake area of Antrim Township. He had contracted typhoid, suffered from hernias, and his feet had been frost bitten while in prison. Detrich remained in poor health the rest of his life.[41]

Another Greencastle man, Private Daniel H. Frederick, of Company E was killed in action at Stevensons Depot on November 16 during an attack by Confederate guerillas.[42] Private Jacob Unger, Company G, of Upton, was captured at the battle of Gordonsville, while participating in a mounted assault against Confederate held earthworks. This Greencastle born husband and father of five, was a veteran of the 126th Volunteers who had been wounded at Chancellorsville. When captured, he was taken to Staunton and later to Libby Prison from which he was paroled in February, 1865. He received a month furlough, returned to the regiment and continued fighting until the war's end.[43]

After Gordonsville the 17th moved into permanent quarters near Winchester where it was employed in picket and scout duty. On December 31 the regiment was sent with its brigade to Lovettsville, in the Loudon Valley, "for the protection of the Baltimore & Ohio Railroad and for guarding the citizens against lawless bands that were constantly committing depredations." The 17th rejoined the Army of the Potomac in March, 1865, took part in the Appomattox Campaign and was mustered out June 16, 1865.[44]

Two other regiments that deserve mention are the 20th and 22nd Pennsylvania Cavalry. These two units with local men operated in the Maryland, Pennsylvania and Western Virginia areas. The 20th was organized in July, 1863 from volunteer companies raised during the invasion. On the 7th of July the regiment left Harrisburg and marched to Greencastle. From here it did scouting duty in Maryland in conjunction with elements of the 1st New York "Lincoln" Cavalry. Near Hagerstown they fought a skirmish with some of the Confederate rearguard, capturing a few prisoners and horses. From Greencastle, the regiment marched to Falling Waters where it picketed the shores of the Potomac for several weeks prior to being sent to a camp near Clear Spring. After being reorganized in August, seven companies of the 20th were detailed to guard the Baltimore and Ohio Railroad and to patrol the area between Berkeley Springs and Winchester. Also, five companies were sent to chase draft evaders in eastern Pennsylvania and did not rejoin the rest of the regiment for the rest of their enlistment. The regiment kept busy fighting Confederate guerillas in the mountains of western Virginia until December, when it was mustered out. However, in February, 1864 the unit was reorganized for three year's service. Upon taking the field, it reported to General Franz Sigel and took part in the battle of New Market, May 15. In June the 20th fought under General Hunter at Lynchburg and the next month did duty in the vicinity of Martinsburg and Harpers Ferry. From August to December, the men were at Halltown, West Virginia and Pleasant Valley and Cumberland, Maryland. Later they were attached to Sheridan's army and fought at Gordonsville and Waynesboro, where the last of Early's forces were crushed. The 20th took part in the Appomattox Campaign and then returned to the neighborhood of Washington, D.C. where it was consolidated with the 2nd Pennsylvania Cavalry, under the name of the 1st Provisional Cavalry. This unit was finally mustered out on July 13, 1865 at Clouds Mill, Virginia. [45]

The 22nd Pennsylvania Cavalry was formed by combining a battalion, known as the Ringgold Cavalry, with another battalion reorganized from a force of four companies that had been called out for six months, during Lee's advance into Pennsylvania. These units were raised primarily in Huntingdon, Bedford and Blair Counties. The Ringgold companies were from Washington County, Maryland. During Lee's invasion, elements of these outfits guarded fords of the Susquehanna, above and below Harrisburg, and patroled various roads leading into the Cumberland Valley. On July 20, 1863 they marched from Harrisburg to Chambersburg, camping at a site known as "Camp Ferry." Toward the end of August units were dispersed to Mercersburg, Bedford, Waynesboro and Greencastle for provost duty. In October the companies rendezvoused at Chambersburg where they received orders to march to Virginia. Later they were joined by the 21st Pennsylvania Cavalry, under Colonel William Boyd, south of Hagerstown. During the fall and winter the regiment did scouting duty near Harpers Ferry and in the Shenandoah Valley. The 22nd was mustered out and then reorganized for three year's service at Chambersburg in February, 1864. Here the Ringgold Battalion, which had been serving in West Virginia since 1862, was united with the other companies to finish the regimental organization. A number of Franklin County men joined at this time. They included Elias S. Troxell, who was major of the regiment and Thomas D. French, captain of Company L. James H. Davison, of Greencastle and a brother of Joseph, of the 6th Reserves, also became a sergeant in the same company. Until the regiment was mustered out on October 13, 1865 at Cumberland, Maryland, it served in the western Maryland and Virginia theater of war. The 22nd was with Averell at Greencastle during the burning of Chambersburg and at Moorefield, West Virginia on August 7, to avenge the burning. It also took part in many engagements during Sheridan's Valley Campaign. [46]

Since numerous cavalry outfits were in the Greencastle area, particularly after Lee's invasion and McCausland's raid, articles in "The Pilot" often recorded their presence. The January 12, 1864 issue told of an encampment of Company B, 21st Pennsylvania Cavalry at Moss Spring. When cold weather came the men had no winter quarters. Some found shelter at nearby farm houses while others were quartered in one of the town's school houses. The editor noted, "We have not witnessed a single case of disorder or insubordination among them since they have been here. Our people we are sure will not refuse them any kindness." Until the end of the war local residents continued to see cavalry move through the town to patrol the border.[47]

Back at Petersburg, fighting in late September at Peeble's Farm enabled Meade to extend his left flank for three miles further west. The 21st Cavalry took part in this action but with no casualties from Company K. While the fighting was going on around Peeble's Farm, Grant ordered a surprise attack against several important redoubts on the outer defenses of Richmond. Fort Harrison, an important link in this line was captured. The 55th Pennsylvania Infantry and 2nd Pennsylvania Heavy Artillery took part in this operation. *(In late August, the Provisional 2nd Pennsylvania, having lost significantly at the Crater and other actions, was disbanded and re-joined the original regiment.)* Corporal Henry Bricker, of Battery D, and Private John Repp, of Battery B, were wounded at Chaffin's Farm, one of the engagements in this operation, on September 29, 1864. With the assaults around Peeble's Farm and Fort Harrison over, Grant had still failed to capture either Petersburg or Richmond. However, the Union lines had been further extended and although the Confederates had held, each extension meant their lines became that much thinner. [48]

By now life in the trenches was more typical than going into battle. The great majority of the Army of the Potomac was occupied with camp routine or taking turns at picket duty when not in the fortifications. Josiah Shuman, Company I, of the 198th Pennsylvania Infantry, reported, in his diary, of army experience in and near the siege of Petersburg. Shuman, whose home was in Antrim Township, had enlisted on August 31 in the regiment raised in Philadelphia by

Colonel Horatio Sickel, an active Union supporter responsible for organizing earlier units. By September 24 the infantry had arrived at the Petersburg front and was stationed near the Weldon Railroad. The regiment's first experience was filled with drill, drill and more drill. [49]

Four days later Josiah was on guard detail when he experienced his first encounter with the "enemy." "First head louse caught and killed while on picket." The same day's entry told of one of his comrades shooting himself through the foot — an injury found among green troops more often than veterans. Anxieties built up when near the front and "accidents" occurred, often arising from extreme nervousness or loss of nerve. This sometimes ended in self inflicted wounds that could lead to a medical discharge.

The regiment moved into a "line of breastworks" on September 30 and spent the time, not in keeping their eyes on the Rebels, but in digging and shoring up the trenches. After several days of labor the men were glad to pull out and go to the rear. Here a tent camp had been erected. All felt safe since it was three quarters of a mile behind the lines. Beyond normal camp routine, nothing of importance happened until a dress parade was held on October 9. Earlier Josiah learned that the 21st Cavalry was no longer an infantry outfit. It had been remounted and ordered to General D. M. Gregg's division. Shuman would miss seeing some of his friends from Antrim because, as infantrymen, they had been among his camp neighbors.

On October 11, Pennsylvania men voted in the state election. The vote in Shuman's company went Republican twenty-three to three. Three days later the diary noted a man was shot for trying to desert to "the Rebel ranks." A promised visit of Secretary of War, Stanton, failed to materialize on the 17th and all the frenzied work put into "cleaning up" the camp had been wasted — another case of "hurry up and wait," but this time the wait was for nothing. Yet the day after Stanton failed to appear, General Meade and his staff did ride along the lines. [50]

On October 27 a battle at the Boydton Plank Road and a stream called Hatcher's Run took place about twelve miles southwest of Petersburg. This represented another Union attempt to extend its lines and halt the flow of supplies into the city. The fighting was heavy, and the Federals were forced to retire, with the cavalry holding the line until all infantry and artillery were out of the way. The horse soldiers were then forced to cut their way out that night. The 21st Pennsylvania took part in this action, suffering over forty casualties in killed, wounded and missing. Company K's casualties included Andrew Scully and Philip Gardner who later died of wounds; John M. Miller, George Swisher and Samuel Zumbro — all wounded, and William L. Smith who was taken prisoner and held until April 5, 1865. [51]

The threat of death in battle was not the only thing the men of the 21st and other regiments had to fear. It is estimated that approximately 224,580 Union soldiers died of disease. A case in point is the deaths of two Greencastle area men in the 21st Cavalry. Private William H. Shatzer enrolled in the regiment at Chambersburg on October 6, 1864 and was Company G's blacksmith. He contracted smallpox and died in the hospital at City Point, Virginia on May 9, 1865, one month after Lee's surrender.[52] Eighteen year old Albert Alexander and his brother John, thirty-two, joined Company K at Chambersburg in February 1864. In August, Albert contracted typhoid fever after he marched with the regiment through several swamps on the way to the Weldon Railroad. Since there was no regimental doctor available at the time, Albert was sent to a hospital in the rear. As his condition worsened he was soon transferred to an army hospital at Point Lookout, Maryland, where he died on September 26, 1864. [53]

Election day came on November 8 and Shuman's company voted — Lincoln 27 and 20 for "Little Mac." Many soldiers admired McClellan but they wanted to finish the job of bringing the Confederacy to its knees. Their faith in Grant and Lincoln far out weighed everything else. One officer claimed that the Army of the Potomac was never pluckier than when it voted by a big majority for Lincoln's re-election.

The day after the voting Josiah wrote that they were ordered to put up winter quarters — log huts, covered with canvas, and furnished with chimneys made of barrels. They not only built their own quarters, but had to erect those of the officers. On Thanksgiving Day, November 24, the chaplain read the President's Proclamation to the regiment and from that time through the early weeks of December the days were spent in routine picket duty, drill, inspections, and maneuvers.

Just before Christmas the regiment was moved to a new campsite where the men had to construct more huts. For many, Christmas Day was spent in this work. Josiah noted, "Some of the men worked till three o'clock when the axes were turned in. Preaching at 3 p.m." Christmas came on Sunday and the rest of the week was spent in finishing their quarters, helping to construct a church, and facilities for the officers. This continued until New Year's Eve when, despite rain and snow, guards had to quell troops all along the line who were welcoming the New Year with excessive firing of weapons.

The men seemed to take pride in building the church and parsonage for the chaplain. Josiah and his comrades worked through days of frigid weather to finish the job. Throughout his diary, he mentions attending services, church, or preaching. Religion appeared to be a sincere concern for this man, but he was not alone. Thousands like him on both sides of the conflict shared the same concern.

On January 13, seats were placed in the house of worship. The next day it was finished, to the great satisfaction of officers and men. Additional happiness the same day was indicated with the entry — "boots received from V. Kriner of Waynesboro." Two days later, Sunday, January 15, the church was dedicated with a sermon based on the familiar verse of Psalm 122 — "I was glad when they said unto me, let me go into the house of the Lord." That evening a chaplain from the 89th Pennsylvania conducted a second service. Josiah Shuman attended both. The following Thursday Shuman might have lost his religion and faith in his fellowman. He washed his shirt and drawers that morning and put them out to dry. By evening they were stolen. [54]

Another diary, kept by Jacob Finafrock, of Antrim Township, recounted experiences similar to those of Josiah Shuman. He had joined the 209th Pennsylvania Infantry in September. Finafrock's regiment, along with four others from the home state, came into the war later in the month. He was a corporal in Company D, commanded by Captain John L. Ritchey of Mercersburg. It was filled with men from Franklin County — many, including Finafrock, from Greencastle and Antrim. Another local soldier, Andrew Davison, was the adjutant. [55]

The regiment arrived at Bermuda Hundred and helped man the trenches there while the operations to capture Ft. Harrison were conducted in late September of 1864. Jacob and his comrades were abruptly introduced to the war when a Confederate shell killed two men and wounded two others standing near him in the trenches. His notes reflect the same routine that Shuman and thousands of others experienced. He described the monotony of life in the trenches, relieved at times during quiet periods when the men opposing each other carried on conversations, joined in singing famliar songs, and at times, exchanged tobacco, newspapers, and other items. Like Shuman, Finafrock and his fellow soldiers had to build winter huts, only he and his friends, Thomas Duffy, went "down at the river for brick" to be used in building their chimney.

Jacob Lear had returned to the 21st Cavalry after recovering from the wound he received at Cold Harbor. He and Christian Hager, also wounded in this battle, came to visit Finafrock on December 14 and three days before Christmas Finafrock wrote, "The boys got their boxes from home."

CPT. ROBERT J. BOYD   CO. K, 21st PA. CAVALRY   JACOB LEAR
STICKELL AND ALEXANDER COLLECTIONS

On January 31 Jacob wrote that he had seen Alexander Stevens, the Confederacy's Vice President.[56] This was the day Stevens, John A. Campbell, the Southern Assistant Secretary of War, and R. M. T. Hunter, former Secretary of State, came to discuss, with Lincoln and Secretary Seward, terms that might end the war. Grant, approached earlier, had contacted the President and established the day for the conference.

When carriages, carrying the three Confederate dignitaries, came through the Petersburg lines, a tremendous cheer rose from soldiers of both sides. Stevens and his companions walked across "no man's land," were seated in ambulances provided by General Grant and taken to meet the President and the Secretary of State. They talked but by day's end the Confederate officials went back through the lines and the war continued. Lincoln had refused to discuss ending the war on terms that could have preserved the Confederacy. Hope for peace vanished and the killing and wounding of thousands more would continue.

On February 5 Josiah Shuman took part in the battle at Hatcher's Run. Two other times Union forces had fought here to strengthen their grip on Petersburg. Again the 21st Cavalry was there with

Gregg's division. It saw little action but Shuman's regiment got into heavy fighting. He escaped unhurt as Union forces lost 2,300 men. However, this battle enabled them to cut off another section of road leading to the city. Four days later Josiah's regiment moved again and on February 14 he and his comrades began building new housing facilities. As this work continued he noted that on the 27th the men received four month's pay and he got the first installment on his government bounty.

Through the month of March Josiah indicated all was quiet in the trenches and his time was spent writing letters to family and friends. He also had an "ambrotype" taken by one of the many photographers following the army and on the evening of the 17th a horse race was held in camp. Then on March 25 he wrote, "Our lines attacked by the Rebs." His unit was held in reserve at what became the Battle of Fort Stedman. This was an attempt to break through the Union defenses. The attack began at four o'clock in the morning but four hours later Lee ordered a withdrawal after taking heavy losses. Later Meade's forces counter-attacked and the day's fighting resulted in Confederate casualties of nearly 5,000 men. The Union lost over 2,000 dead, wounded, and missing. One of this battle's casualties was George W. Garling of Antrim Township. He had been drafted and placed in Company D of the Pennsylvania's 100th Regiment on February 22. With barely a month's experience, this untried unit was thrown into this fighting. Garling was wounded in the left elbow.[57]

The fighting on March 25 represented a desperate attempt by General Lee to break through the Federal lines and move his army of less than 50,000 men to the Southside Railroad, the only one at Petersburg still held by the Confederates. His hope was to carry the defenders of the city to the Richmond and Danville rail line. Here he could haul his small army southward to join Joseph Johnston's forces, retreating from Sherman in North Carolina. Bringing these two armies together was Lee's only hope. He had to get to Johnston and he began to gather food and ammunition and waited for clear weather. Torrential rains had been falling for several days making all roads impassable. By March 31 the rain ended and preliminary fighting began at new places like Dinwiddie Court House, White Oak Road, and again on familiar ground near Hatcher's Run. No local casualties were reported.

This fighting brought the month to a close. By then the Confederacy was nearly bled dry. Little was left except a fast dying, proud spirit. The Shenandoah had been under complete Union control since Early's army was crushed at Cedar Creek and its remnants overwhelmed in subsequent engagements. Sheridan and his men were now back at Petersburg. Sherman's army, moving north since leaving Savannah in January, was now getting closer and closer to Virginia while Union forces were completing their final operations in the Mobile region.

Nearly a million men in the various Union armies stood ready to crush the remnants of the once formidable forces of the Confederacy now numbering 100,000 men. In the confei ence on January 31, Stevens and his companions learned there would be no peace except through unconditional surrender. Jefferson Davis knew this. Robert E. Lee knew this and his adversaries would never rest until the war ended on their terms.

On April 1, Lee ordered General Pickett to "Hold Five Forks at all hazards." This was a key position, to the west, which would enable him to move the remainder of the Army of Northern Virginia out of Petersburg. Although well entrenched, Pickett's men, outnumbered more than two to one, were quickly overcome and Lee's army was nearly surrounded.

The 17th Cavalry took part in the charge upon the Confederate works and suffered severe casualties. Two members of Company G, Lieutenant Henry G. Bonebrake of Waynesboro, and Private William Cummings of Greencastle, were among the first to leap over the breastworks at one point. Seeing a Confederate color bearer, Bone-brake rushed to his side, grasped his colors and demanded his surrender. A hand to hand struggle followed and he succeeded in capturing the flag. Lieutenant Bonebrake's distinguished and meritorious act won him the Congressional Medal of Honor, the only Franklin County resident to ever have that honor. Andrew Baker of Greencastle and a member of the 17th, was wounded and Daniel Miller, another county man with the same regiment, was killed. [58]

Josiah Shuman told of his regiment going to the left side of the line, and that evening taking part in the final phases of the battle, capturing many of the 3,200 prisoners taken from Pickett's command. The 21st Cavalry, posted on the Union's left flank, did not get into the fighting. [59]

Throughout the night following Five Forks, Union artillery continued shelling the Rebel earthworks and the city itself. Grant's intention was to mount a wide massive attack to overwhelm remaining resistance and take Petersburg. A heavy fog delayed his forces, but by seven o'clock on this Sunday morning, the assault began. As Federal troops swept forward the Rebel lines folded. A. P. Hill, one of Lee's remaining capable generals, was killed. As news of the Union success reached Richmond, the Confederacy's government leaders began leaving the capital. By mid-day Petersburg was completely encircled, the west bank of the Appomattox River was in Union hands and near nightfall Lee began organizing the remnants of his army to abandon the city. By eight o'clock that evening the enemy's retreat was under way. The Rebels moved through the night with Amelia Court House designated as the gathering place for what was left of the Army of Northern Virginia.

Pennsylvania's 55th took part in this fighting but no local soldiers were reported as casualties. The regiment was in a sector where Confederate fortifications, manned by a small number of men, delayed the Union advance. This allowed the main army time to retreat. Later the 55th was the first regiment to occupy Fort Baldwin, one of these works. [60]

Josiah Shuman told how his regiment "started about eleven o'clock and marched to the South Side Railroad. Finding no enemy, we marched towards Petersburg and encamped for the night about 9 to 10 miles south of the Petersburg." The 17th had a spirited engagement with the enemy and succeeded in driving them back. Local cavalrymen went through this assault with no losses. [61]

Grant, ready for the "coup de grace," ordered the assault on Lee's remaining entrenchments to start early the next morning. As early as three o'clock he received word the trenches were empty and an hour later the Army of the Potomac marched into Petersburg. By eight o'clock the city of Richmond officially surrendered. President Lincoln had come to the front and after consultations with Grant and Sherman, who had come to Virginia by sea, he met with Grant alone in Richmond. They talked for over an hour and the President returned to City Point. Both men knew the end was just a matter of days and the terms to be offered Lee were, in all likelihood, reviewed at this meeting.

Josiah Shuman apparently was too far away to hear the great shout and cheers of the Union forces when they saw the abandoned trenches. His diary simply said, "marched all day towards the Danville Railroad." Lieutenant Bonebrake noted that the 17th "met with little opposition, encamped near the Appomattox. A large number of straggling Rebels were picked up along the road. A number of abandoned wagons and caissons of the enemy were destroyed on the road." Lee's little army could stop for nothing. It was hurrying to Amelia Court House where rations and ammunition awaited them. [62]

The following day, April 4, just after eight in the morning, the retreating Rebels reached the Court House. Here they found munitions but no food. The 17th, later that night, ran into the Confederates and a "brief skirmish" followed. Many of Lee's men had not eaten since leaving Petersburg. After the minor fight with the cavalry they settled down for the night, hoping for rations the next day. When he found no supplies, Lee turned toward Farmville hoping to get rations he had ordered sent from Lynchburg by rail. The same day, April 5, Bonebrake noted that detachments of the 17th picked up nearly a thousand Rebels, "also some artillery and several hundred wagons." The 21st was involved in an attack on an enemy wagon train that yielded more cannon. Two hundred wagons were destroyed and nine hundred mules taken. [63]

SGT. THOMAS DUFFY   209th REGIMENT   SGT. JACOB A. FINAFROCK
ERVIN COLLECTION

The next day Shuman wrote, "Started on our march toward the Appomattox Court House. Encamped for the night at half past eight." Bonebrake recorded the results of the battle with the fleeing Rebels fought at Sayler's Creek. Forces of Ewell and R. H. Anderson became separated from the main body and in the end the Federals captured 6,000 Confederates, including nine generals. One of the captives was Richard S. Ewell, the one legged general who triumphantly rode up the Cumberland Valley in the 1863 invasion — "sic transit gloria" (so passes away the glory.) From this day on the cavalry kept up a running battle with the retreating Rebel army. [64]

319

Friday, April 7, saw Josiah Shuman's regiment marching from six in the morning to nine o'clock that evening to get to Prince Edward's Court House. Here they bivouacked for the night. During this time the 2nd Pennsylvania Heavy Artillery, now part of General Edward Ferreo's division, was sent to Petersburg for guard duty in the fallen city. The 21st Cavalry ran into trouble in a "sharp and . . . disasterous fight at Farmville" where it lost some prisoners. [65] At Farmville the remaining men of Lee's army finally received rations. The same day Grant wrote General Lee to suggest that he surrender and stop the unnecessary loss of more lives. Lee's answer came the next day. His reply also indicated the hopelessness of his situation, but before "considering the proposition" Lee asked for "the terms you will offer" for the surrender of the Army of Northern Virginia.

Lieutenant Bonebrake, on April 8, wrote, "Cavalry Corps and the 24th Infantry Corps made connection at Prospect Station. Cavalry marched to Appomattox Station, there Custer captured three trains of cars, about forty pieces of artillery, and a large portion of the enemy's train, together with prisoners." Josiah Shuman's day was uneventful, a fitting prelude to what happened the next day. [66]

On Palm Sunday, April 9, 1865, Robert E. Lee surrendered to Ulysses S. Grant. The two commanding generals met in the home of Wilmer McLean at Appomattox Court House. Lee and an aide met Grant, accompanied by his staff and several major commanders. It was afternoon and when preliminary greetings were finished, the Union general reviewed the terms President Lincoln had given him — officers and men to be paroled, arms and military supplies to be turned over with no other conditions except total surrender. Grant did agree to allow the Southerners to keep their horses and feed Lee's army. The Union leader had prepared the surrender document and Lee wrote his acceptance of the terms.

It was between three thirty and four o'clock that afternoon that Corporal Joseph R. Davison, of the 21st Cavalry, saw the white hair-ed man in a gray dress uniform leave the McLean house. He had been Sheridan's dispatch bearer that day and had accompanied the general to this important meeting[67] Josiah Shuman's diary entry for April 9 was simple and to the point — "The Rebs were entirely sur-rounded by the Union troops and General Lee surrendered his whole force, consisting of 35,000 troops." (Lee really had less than 30,000 men left.) Lieutenant Jacob Bonebrake was equally anti-climactic — "he surrendered his entire forces. This evening the prisoners taken from us were returned." Jacob Finafrock, still with his regiment at Petersburg, said, "In the evening we had the dispatch read to us that Lee had surrendered his army and there was great cheering."[68]

Fighting between the Army of the Potomac and the Army of Northern Virginia was finished. Other armies were still facing each other in the South but as word reached them the war ended there too. Grant, later in the afternoon, ordered the news telegraphed to Washington. That evening the President arrived from his visit to the front and found the city celebrating. All over the North the news brought bonfires, ringing church bells, impromptu parades, and a great amount of drinking and rowdyism. Soldiers at the front celebrated too. Flags waved, bands played, and the air seemed to be continuously filled with hats, knapsacks, and any other paraphernalia that hands could find. Cannon roared, men cheered and sang, they danced and hugged each other. It was over. This terrible tragedy was finally done and no more soldiers killed in action would be reported by hometown newspapers even though many months would pass before all the boys were home to stay.

CHAPTER XIII

PEACE

News of the Army of Northern Virginia's surrender swept through the Cumberland Valley on Palm Sunday evening and celebrations erupted everywhere. People streamed onto the streets and rural people hurried into the nearest town as sounds of bells and gun fire filled the air while bonfires lighted the heavens everywhere. Impromptu parades led by bands or singing throngs filled the thoroughfares. Soldiers stationed near the county seat joined in the processions, while Greencastle's townspeople marched up and down the borough streets.

As the processions showed signs of losing momentum local orators climbed the nearest bench, porch, or tree stump to renew the crowd's enthusiasm and extol the greatness of Lincoln, Grant, his officers, and the noble soldiers who had fought and died to bring the victory. The "Valley Spirit" reported that A. K. McClure was the principal speaker during the county seat's celebration and ministers everywhere offered thanks for the Divine Power that finally brought an end to hostilities. The paper reported that celebrations continued through the night and on into the next day when a full military parade and ceremony was held. It included a two hundred gun salute to the Army of the Potomac and General Grant in honor of their "glorious victory." [1]

Captain Stryker of the local Signal Corps detachment asked General Cadwalader for just one cannon to provide a salute with appropriate ceremonies in Greencastle. The records do not show that any such weapon was delivered. A rifle salute was probably substituted. [2]

Chambersburg had the distinction of holding two parades on successive days. The day before Lee surrendered, Dr. George Kauffman, J. Porter Brown, and D. M. Eiker arrived in the county seat on the noon train. These were the last of the men who had gone to Hagerstown on July 6, 1863 to see a battle between the retreating Rebels and Meade's pursuing army. They were arrested, sent to the infamous Salisbury Prison in North Carolina, eventually escaped and finally made their way back home. The returnees were met at the train depot and escorted to their homes by the town band and a host of welcoming citizens, with the musicians "discoursing some of its choiciest music along the route." [3]

When news of Lee's surrender reached Mercersburg, Dr. Creigh told of church bells ringing, stores closing, and guns being fired to salute the occasion. His diary voiced the hope of the nation — "May this rebellion have received its death blow." The Reverend Henry Harbaugh wrote that when the glad news arrived the bells rang for an hour. Seminary students raised the flag on Old Main while the boys sang the "Star Spangled Banner" from its cupola. [4]

Harrisburg's "Daily Telegraph" of April 12 invited farm people and others living in the Cumberland Valley to come to the state capital to join in a celebration the following Saturday. The "Valley Spirit" told of raising — "A beautiful Union pole surmounted by the stars and stripes on West Market Street, opposite the residence of John M. McDowell on Friday last (April 14). As the flag was being run up and given to the breeze the hazzahing from the crowd that surrounded the pole made the welkin ring again. The pole was erected in honor of our recent great victory and fall of the Rebel capital." [5]

The county seat's flag raising took place as President Lincoln prepared to attend the performance, "Our American Cousin," playing at Ford's Theater. He and Mrs. Lincoln had left for the theater at half past eight that evening. When the president's party, including Miss Clara Harris and Major H. R. Rathbone, entered the box over the stage, the audience interrupted the play by standing and cheering the President. Greencastle's Hamsher Clippinger was in the audience and joined in this happy reception given the Chief Executive. As the applause ended the play continued. Shortly after ten o'clock John Wilkes Booth shot Mr. Lincoln. [6]

Of special interest to Franklin County people was the fact that Captain Theodore McGowan, of Chambersburg, was sitting on a stool in the aisle near the door of the President's box when the assassination occurred. The New York Tribune of April 16 published a statement given by McGowan which "may be relied on as a correct version of the assassination." The captain told how he and his friend, Lieutenant Crawford, had arrived at the theater just after the entrance of Mr. and Mrs. Lincoln and their guests. He and Crawford were unable to obtain seats and had procured camp stools to sit in the aisle about five feet from Lincoln's box. "Sometime later I was disturbed in my seat by the approach of a man who desired to pass up the aisle. Giving him room by bending my chair forward, he passed me and stepped one step down upon the level below me."

McGowan saw the man select a visiting card from his pocket and give it to an attendant who apparently recognized him. A few minutes later, the same man entered a door of the lobby leading to the box and the door closed behind him. "How long I watched the play after his entering I do not know. It was perhaps two or three minutes, possibly four. The house was perfectly still, the large audience listening to dialogue between Florence Trenchard and May Meredity, when the sharp report of a pistol rang through the house."

There followed the familiar description of the assassin leaping to the stage. "As he leaped he cried distinctly the motto of Virginia, 'Sic semper tyrannies.' In an instant the man disappeared behind the side scene." The captain then described him — "He was a gentlemanly looking person — —. He seemed for a moment or two to survey the house with the deliberation of an habitue of the theater."[7]

The following morning the President died. Later in the forenoon, at eleven o'clock, Andrew Johnson took the oath of office. The nation had a new president and the government proceeded. Cavalrymen swept through southern Maryland and northern Virginia as they searched for the fleeing killer and the nation was filled with disbelief. How could such a thing have happened? Rage mixed with sorrow swept across the land as the American people mourned the loss of the leader who had finally brought an end to the war. Area events scheduled to continue celebrating Grant's victory were cancelled and church services took their place as people all over the nation flocked to their sanctuaries for memorial sermons and prayers.

Chambersburg's "Valley Spirit" told of the President's death on April 15. "The news spread with great rapidity causing universal

HARPER'S WEEKLY   THE ASSASSINATION   APRIL 28, 1865

gloom and sorrow. The Chief Burgess at once passed a recommendation that all businesses be suspended and that the bells be tolled from eleven o'clock for the rest of the day. In the evening a meeting of citizens was held in the Methodist Church at which arrangements were made to give a fitting expression to the public sentiment at this great national calamity. The several churches on the Sabbath were clothed in sable and the services were of the most solemn and imposing character. All the sufferings of our citizens since the outbreak of the Rebellion are as nothing compared with this last crushing affliction by which the whole nation suffers." Similar services were held in churches throughout the county and signs of mourning — churches, homes and business places draped in black and flags at half mast — seemed to dominate the entire local region. [8]

Lincoln's death brought not only sorrow but violence in many parts of the country. Grief turned to retaliation against suspected pro-Southerners. Mobs chasing Rebel sympathizers were reported in many northern town and cities. Copperheads were forced to hide in their homes or police stations. There were reports of soldiers in city streets shooting and killing radicals who had foolishly exulted over the death of the President. In Baltimore two photographers were mobbed when it was learned they had pictures of Booth. In Troy, New York, a man from Rochester in a state of drunkeness remarked that Lincoln should have been shot four years before. His life was spared from a mob only by the timely arrival of police who jailed him. Many towns or cities witnessed pro-Southerners riding rails or being tarred and feathered and chased beyond the municipal limits. [9]

News of the assassination added to an already tense atmosphere that existed in southern Pennsylvania and its bordering states. Rebel "bushwhackers" continued to raid and rob in West Virginia and Maryland and on April 27, Captain Stryker, of the Signal Corps, requested twenty mounted infantry for temporary duty to protect one of his signal stations (Casey's Knob or Fairview) from a "projected raid in order to capture horses and stores." [10]

In the South Mountains a gang of deserters, said to number as many as thirty, harassed the people of the Quincy area. Stories of this gang robbing the region of chickens, bacon, saddles, and other materials were reported. Beyond this criminal activity the deserters were said to have threatened to burn the homes of Union families. [11]

There were also reports of copperheads burning barns and other property of Union men in nearby Fulton County. (Anti-government feeling there was evident as early as September, 1862, when a company of Independent Infantry, which had been in the Middleburg area was *sent to Fulton County for provost duty. On February 2, 1863, while arresting deserters in the mountans, Lieutenant Eben W. Ford was killed).* [12]

McConnellsburg's paper "The Fulton Democrat" quoted the "Bedfored Gazette" in its issue of April 14. An editorial indicated that with the war over "the beginning of Democratic ascendency was not far off." The end of war meant the Republicans would no longer have a cause with which to elect their candidates. The Democratic South would be back in the fold and once more could dominate the nation's legislative and executive branches.

As resentment over Lincoln's death mounted against many Democrats, the Bedford journal changed its tune. Its May 5 issue's editorial, headed "Who are Traitors," warned fellow Democrats to obey all laws and "respect and support all in authority." *(This was excellent advice since Southern Democracy did not rise as rapidly as the April 14 editorial suggested.)*

Known pro-Southerners or those suspected of harboring sympathies for the South became targets of local Unionists. J. D. Reamer, a Waynesboro business man, went to the county jail and asked to be incarcerted for his own protection. In early March he had confidentially informed a customer that he heard — $100,000 was being raised to "secure the assassination of President Lincoln." The man feared for his life when this became known. [13]

A story, dated April 16, told of a group of men breaking into the office of a Westminster newspaper, "The Democrat," smashing its printing press and burning type, paper, and furniture in the street. This Maryland town's editor was accused of making derogatory remarks about the late President. [14] The Waynesboro "Village Record" of May 12 told of a Vigilance Committee being formed in Maryland's Washington County to "drive all ex-Rebels out of the county."

Later in the summer the "Hagerstown Herald" carried a story about a character well known to Franklin County residents. Clagett Fitzhugh and his friend, George Shearer, "put up at the City Hotel" on July 29. When they registered their names "in large letters . . . Major George Shearer, Confederate States Army, Captain C. Fitzhugh, ditto," they were promptly waited upon by "members of the Vigilance Committee and required to get up and dust." In early August it was reported that Fitzhugh visited a Colonel Hughes, who lived "just outside of Hagerstown." Some Maryland veterans heard of the visitor and decided to call at Hughes's home, also. Upon seeing the approaching crowd Clagett quickly departed through a nearby cornfield. [15]

Amid the grief and outrage that enveloped the North, rumors of all kinds concerning the whereabouts of Booth and his accomplices were rampant. People were caught up in an atmosphere of suspicion and strangers in towns were viewed with distrust from the time they came until they departed.

Harrisburg's "Patriot and Union" of April 17 reported that Laura Keane and two actors, of the troupe that was playing at Ford's Theater the night of the assassination, were arrested that afternoon at the Harrisburg railroad station by Lieutenant Charles Gresh of the state's 17th Cavalry. It was claimed that "one of the troupe's confession has led to the belief that he is an important witness." The next day's paper reported a man had been arrested in Greensburg. It was thought he was Booth in disguise. Then on April 20 the same journal said the assassin had been spotted in Reading.

As violence or threats against those suspected of having pro-Southern feelings continued the great body of Americans followed news accounts of the funeral arrangements for the martyred President. The final honors began with a service during the forenoon of April 19 in the East Room of the White House. Here family members, President Johnson and Cabinet officers; military leaders; members of Congress; the diplomatic corps; relatives; and aides to the President heard the reading of scripture, appropriate remarks, and prayers. Then at two o'clock the casket was readied for the first of many processions to follow.

From the White House the coffin was placed in a huge hearse drawn by six white horses. Church bells of Washington, Georgetown and Alexandria began to toll; guns from fortresses around the city boomed their salutes; and with bands playing traditional dirges, the procession began its long journey up Pennsylvania Avenue to the Capitol. The line of march was headed by a body of Negro soldiers. Then came the hearse followed by a riderless horse; military and government officials; foreign dignataries and Congressional leaders — slowly moving to the drums' measured cadence. Others joined the sorrow ladened march as it moved forward. Wounded veterans from city hospitals, some on crutches, followed their Commander-In-Chief while thousands of blacks joined the procession that also included endless delegations from churches, fire companies, states, cities, and lodges that had come from all over the nation.

Upon reaching the Capitol the body was placed in the Rotunda on a catafalque where a brief prayer service was held. At ten o'clock the next morning a deluge of people began streaming by the bier. All day long they passed until the doors were closed at midnight. Twenty-five thousand citizens paid their final respects to the slain President.

Again, the ever present Hamsher Clippinger was there and as he moved by the casket he was successful in snatching a sprig of box-wood, part of the greenery at the base of the catafalque. *(It remains to this day in the home of one of his descendants.)* [16]

Before sunup the next morning the casket was closed and with Grant, the Cabinet, and an Illinois delegation, the coffin was taken to the funeral train. The body of Willie Lincoln, who had died on February 20, 1862, had been disinterred and placed in a coffin next to that of his father. This was Friday, April 22, seven days after his death, when Abraham Lincoln began the long, long journey that would take him home for the last time.

With bells tolling and guns resounding through the morning air the Baltimore and Ohio funeral train of eight coaches, swathed in black, began pulling out of the station between two long lines of soldiers from regiments stationed in the city. A pilot engine ran ahead to see that the track was clear. The first stop was Baltimore where the coffin was placed in the Exchange Building. Between

BESORE COLLECTION   PROCESSION TO THE RAILROAD STATION

eleven that morning and two in the afternoon, ten thousand people viewed the remains, before the body was returned to the station for the next leg of its journey.

Up into Pennsylvania the train moved through the countryside where an almost constant line of people waited along the tracks to get a glimpse of the funeral coach. Town houses and farm dwellings were sheathed in black and local bands assembled to present their sad salutes as the train slowly moved along. Be eight thirty the coffin was in the State House at Harrisburg. Two companies of mounted infantry from the 201st Pennsylvania Volunteers along with Battery A New York Artillery were ordered from Chambersburg to serve in the escort which accompanied the President's body from the depot to the State House. [17]

Through heavy rains people of Franklin County joined others from the Cumberland Valley as they journeyed by rail or horsedrawn carriages to view Lincoln's remains. When the State House doors closed at midnight, thousands of Pennsylvanians waited through the night to chance seeing the President when the building was again opened at seven o'clock the next morning. However, as the cortege left at noon vast numbers still had not seen their fallen leader.

Again, all along the right of way, country people stood with heads bared as the train moved toward Philadelphia. Some may have noticed Thaddeus Stevens standing on a rock near the tracks outside Lancaster. Here this man, who disliked Lincoln with a passion, solemnly raised his hat when the train passed. As the locomotive slowed to a crawl the procession moved into the town where thousands crowded around the depot. On the outskirts of this mass of mourners sat James Buchanan in his carriage. His eyes followed the creeping train carrying his fallen successor as it faded into the distance making its way to Philadelphia, where on April 22, a massive parade, consisting of eleven divisions, escorted the body to Independence Hall for public viewing. Throughout the evening until midnight thousands pushed their way past the casket and the next morning more were ready after waiting all night. On through the Sabbath they continued to view the remains and not until two o'clock the following morning was the body removed to resume its funereal pilgrimmage to New York City. [18]

New York's reception surpassed all previous ones. Thousands lined the streets and avenues as the body was paraded to City Hall. Booming cannons, pounding bells, choral groups, and a host of bands accompanied the procession that included floats carrying tableaus, banners, and floral arrangements. Again thousands moved past the open coffin for twenty-four hours and when it was closed at noon,

Tuesday, April 25, three hundred thousand were still in line. Then at four o'clock that afternoon the train left for Albany. All along the route there was no end of people, bands, choirs, and flower arrangements. From the state's capital the excursion continued to Buffalo; then down into the Ohio country; through Indiana, and finally Illinois — every town and city along the way trying to out do all others. What started as a solemn tribute to the dead Lincoln had become an extravaganza rivalling any spectacle known before or since. Chicago surpassed all others. The "Tribune" boasted that New York's tribute was but one fourth of the Windy City's.

Finally the last ceremonies were held in Springfield after the prairie people viewed their beloved son for the last time as he lay in the State Capitol's House of Representatives. At ten o'clock in the forenoon of Thursday, May 4, a final service was held and the bodies of Willie Lincoln and his father were buried in Oak Ridge Cemetery, a wooded area two miles beyond Springfield. It was finished. The long black journey had ended.

Seven million people had seen the train and one and a half million had actually viewed the body. This sixteen hundred mile procession, lasting seventeen days, had mounted an hysteria that gripped the entire North. It had provided Northerners an opportunity to directly participate in the last rites for the man who had preserved the nation. More importantly it gave Republican leaders a vast base of emotional support for a program to punish the South. Abraham Lincoln's plans to bind up the wounds and reunite the nation would never happen because of those who saw the future only through avenging eyes. The assassination brought sadness not only to the North but to many people of the South who saw in Lincoln their best hope for a peace devoid of harsh retribution — a hope not to be realized. [19]

In the weeks that followed elements of the Confederacy's armed forces gradually surrendered to Union military authorities. While this was happening the President of the Confederacy, along with members of his government, continued to flee from pursuers. Jefferson Davis held the last meeting with his cabinet on April 24 at Charlotte, North Carolina and continued to travel southward. On April 26, John Wilkes Booth was shot and killed on the farm of Richard Garrett, in Virginia. Others involved in the plot to kill Lincoln were eventually taken into custody, tried, found guilty, hanged or sentenced to long prison terms. While this was happening President Johnson offered a reward for the capture of Davis for inciting the murder of Lincoln.

Finally on May 10, at Irwinsville, Georgia, Davis and his wife, along with several other officials, were taken into custody by Federal troops. *(Among the units in this area, looking for Davis, was the Pennsylvania 7th Cavalry. It was reported that Michael Bushey, brother of Dr. Franklin Bushey of Greencastle, was a member of this regiment which assisted in hunting down the fugitive President of the Southern Confederacy.)* [20]Davis was taken to Macon and later transferred to Fort Monroe in Virginia where he was imprisoned. Never brought to trial, the Southern leader was said to have maintained a dignified bearing throughout his captivity until he was released two years later on May 13, 1867.

On the day Davis was captured, President Johnson proclaimed armed resistance at an end, however, fragments of opposition from Missouri to Texas *(Trans-Mississippi Theater)* were still causing trouble. Also, many Confederates were attempting to escape to Mexico where they hoped to join Maximilian's forces and possibly continue the struggle from there. *(Taking advantage of the Civil War, Napoleon III of France had established Austrian Archduke Maximilian as Emperor of Mexico and sent French troops — including elements of the Foreign Legion — to support him. During the war Napoleon III ignored U.S. demands that French troops be evacuated. In May, 1865 Sheridan forces concentrated along the Rio Grande, while in June, General Schofield was sent to Europe to persuade Napoleon to get out of Mexico. General Sherman was then sent on a mission to Juarez, the Mexican revolutionary leader, as a gesture of recognition. Napoleon withdrew his troops in May, 1866 leaving Maximillian to be overthrown and executed.)* [21] On May 17, Philip Sheridan moved to the Rio Grande with his force of 50,000 veterans, to deal with these problems and to supervise reconstruction in that area. Many local men were part of this force.

Most Confederates in the Trans-Mississippi area laid down their arms by mid-summer. Among the exiles were Jubal Early and John McCausland — names well known to the people of Franklin County. Early went to Mexico but became disenchanted with Maximilian, the puppet ruler. When hopes of gathering support to keep the war going disappeared he went to Canada. Although he considered emigrating to New Zealand, Early eventually returned to Lynchburg, practiced law, and wrote his highly opinionated memoirs of the war. Later, he served as president of the Southern Historical Society. Jubal Anderson Early died, an unrepentant believer in the right of the Southern Cause, on March 2, 1894. He was seventy-eight years of age. John McCausland escaped capture, went to England and later Mexico, where he served the Maxmilian government as a surveyor. He returned to the United States and spent the remainder of his life on a farm in West Virginia until his death in 1928. [22]

Through the week after Lee's surrender Union soldiers were involved with the many details connected with war's aftermath. Josiah Shuman's outfit was busy receiving and storing Rebel arms. Henry Bonebrake told of gathering supplies and the 2nd Pennsylvania Heavy Artillery was stationed in the Petersburg sector where contingents of homeward bound Southerners took a final look at the trenches in which they had fought and where so many of their comrades died. Then when word of the President's assassination reached Petersburg's encampments, men of the Heavy Artillery Regiment were posted along the roads of the area to possibly intercept John Wilkes Booth. It was reported that the assassin was coming through that part of Virginia in an attempt to reach safety in the lower Southern states. Memorial services were held in the various camps to honor the fallen leader. The following week soldiers were given badges to honor their deceased Commander-In-Chief. [23]

Lieutenant Bonebrake, by April 18, was in Washington and he noted that he was able to view Lincoln's remains at the Capitol. He described the immense crowd that poured through the Rotunda to see, for the last time, their President. Bonebrake, also, stood with thousands of others as the body was taken to the Baltimore and Ohio station. The Lieutenant was given leave and collected three month's pay ($374.33) before continuing his homeward journey. His leave lasted until May 22 but within a month's time he and his comrades of the 17th Cavalry were mustered out. On the evening of June 24 he arrived in Greencastle and took the omnibus to Waynesboro where he was greeted by old friends and "was glad to share the enjoyments of civil life with them again." [24]

This experience was shared by thousands of others as the volunteer units were mustered out after the May 23-24 Grand Review of the Army of the Potomac and Sherman's Army. Josiah Shuman was discharged with his regiment on June 12 at Camp Cadwalader in Philadelphia. He reached his home in Antrim Township the following day. [25]

On July 8 the 21st Pennsylvania Cavalry was relieved of duty after spending its final days in the Lynchburg region. Like many families on both sides of the war, parents often failed to recognize their sons when they arrived home. This was true of John H. Dulebohn as he approached his homestead between Welsh Run and Greencastle. John was barely twenty years of age when he joined Company K of the 21st in the summer of 1864. Now, nearly a year later, lean and scrawny with a heavy beard, his mother did not recognize her boy when he came to the kitchen door, opened it, and walked in, "Who are you?" she asked, hurrying to the back porch to call her husband. Running into the house from a nearby field, the farmer stopped at the door, needed no second look as he shouted, "Mother, don't you know your own son?" For the rest of the day there was no more field work. The family was all together again. It was a time to celebrate.[26]

Throughout the remainder of the year men came home and by early October most units containing local soldiers were back in Franklin County. However, some of the regiments sent to Texas were not discharged until the early months of the following year. This was true of the 38th United States Colored Infantry in which Robert B. Henderson, of Greencastle, served. It was March 2, 1866 before he was mustered out. [27]

Men of the 77th Pennsylvania, sent to Texas in early August of 1865, were stationed in the vicinity of Victoria approximately a hundred and fifty miles southwest of Galveston. Here they stayed for three months and in that time many Pennsylvanians who had survived battles from Shiloh through the Nashville campaign died of fever. On December 5 the regiment received orders to return to its native state and on January 16, 1866 this proud body of veterans reached Philadelphia. Two days later they were in Harrisburg waiting for a train to take them home. When Franklin's Company A was mustered out it contained only seventy officers and men. In 1861, when first formed, the Company had eighty-four enlistees, however, over the war years of service it accumulated a roster of two hundred and twenty. Forty-seven were killed on distant fields of battle, or captured and placed in prison camps where many died, while others were discharged earlier because of wounds or illnesses. [28]

Pennsylvania's 2nd Heavy Artillery did not get home until after being discharged at City Point in late January of 1866. When Lee surrendered, this regiment and New York's 170th formed an occupying army at Petersburg under the command of Colonel Benjamin F. Winger. Later the force became one of the units responsible for "reconstructing" Virginia. [29]

Bringing the seceded states back into the Union according to President Johnson's plan began with granting amnesty to all who had participated in the rebellion except certain high ranking Confederate military and governmental officials. Military governors were appointed to supervise reconstruction procedures for each state. Constitutional conventions were held and after they ratified the Thirteenth Amendment *(freeing all slaves)* the states were to be readmitted to the Union upon approval by Congress.

This procedure was strongly opposed by those Republicans who advocated more severe requirements. However, the Johnson Plan held force until after the Congressional election of 1866, when enough new Republicans were elected to reconstruct the South in a manner that would reduce the power of re-established southern states and give Negroes the right to vote, have public schools for black children, allow former slaves to own farm land, and eliminate vagrancy laws which were being used to turn unemployed blacks back into a form of slavery. The Republicans who favored this harsher reconstruction policy were known as the Radicals.

In the meantime the President was going ahead with his less harsh reconstruction plan. Colonel Winger was the military governor responsible for administering the Johnson Plan in south central Virginia. His territory consisted of nine counties with headquarters at Burkeville Junction of Nottoway County. When the job was completed Winger and his men were mustered out. By January 29 he and the local soldiers who had served with him were back in their Franklin County homes. [30]

As Southern armies surrendered, their men returned to a land lying in ruins. With the exception of West Virginia, Maryland and south central Pennsylvania the war in the Eastern Theater had been fought almost entirely in the Confederate states. Factories, warehouses, and business places were destroyed. Its railway system was practically non-existent. Although a vast agriculture area before the war, lack of tools, labor, seed, and transportation had combined to limit food production. Foraging troops of both the North and the South had stripped whole areas of food. Feed shortages had curtailed beef and pork production and a lack of salt prevented that which was produced from being preserved. By war's end there was widespread malnutrition and actual starvation.

Shortages were not limited to food. As the war progressed practically everything needed for normal living was in scarce supply. By 1865 women were using drapes and carpets to clothe themselves and their children. Shoes gradually disappeared and footwear made from animal skins, wood, and even leather from bookbindings was commonly seen. Drug shortages and a lack of physicians added to the general misery and a high death rate among civilians. The shortages led to inflation, profiteering, and a rapid depreciation of Confederate paper money. By the end of the conflict flour was selling for over a thousand dollars a barrel and bacon cost as much as twenty dollars a pound.

Into such a homeland the Confederacy's veterans returned. Thousands became refugees while many, with their families, fled to the West hoping to find farmland on which to start over again. Most, however, remained and gradually put together what little was left to rebuild their businesses or farms and plantations. Negroes, now free, were used as laborers and along with their former owners they helped to bring economic life back to the Southland.

Unlike Southern veterans the soldiers of the North returned to homes untouched by war and most people were better clothed, sheltered, and fed than before the conflict. Many ex-soldiers had responsibilities to families they left behind and their immediate concern was to return to their former employment or similar jobs. Some saw adventure ahead either in the cities or the West. However, the great majority were so happy to be finished with military life, that to be home with friends and family satisfied them for the rest of their lives.

Within months after war's end and on through the years that followed those veterans, whose homes were in the metropolitan areas of the nation, found business and industry unable to provide enough jobs to accommodate all the ex-soldiers. Early in the war the federal government had given pensions to the wounded, widows and orphans and dependent mothers of those men killed or those who died while in the service. No federal or state laws existed to provide hospital care for disabled veterans and there was no legislation to guarantee employment to ex-soldiers.

All across the land, from Wisconsin to New York, the plight of jobless veterans became a matter of public concern. Charitable organizations raised money to benefit the unemployed of the cities, employment bureaus were established, and newspapers began to call for government action to establish programs to ease the problem. In April, 1866, President Johnson issued orders to give veterans preference in filling civil service jobs. Thousands of ex-soldiers poured into Washington for government work but it is estimated that perhaps one in a hundred was lucky enough to find such employment. Before the year ended various veterans groups began forming to press politicians for relief. Finally a bounty measure was passed by Congress in August of 1866 — a stop gap measure designed to quiet the rising chorus calling for help. However, in the end, the great body of unemployed gradually found work in the expanding economy that came from business and industrial growth by 1870.

Lack of employment apparently was no major problem in Franklin County or the rest of the Valley area. There were jobs in growing industries and on the farms. The railroad company required laborers. Clerks and sales representatives were needed in a variety of businesses and industries. For those who wanted a farm of their own the Homestead Act gave preference to veterans if they met the law's requirements for gaining title to the hundred and sixty acre grants. For those who had some financial backing there were opportunities in neighboring Maryland. Waynesboro's "Village Record" of May 26 announced that farms in the Free State could be bought for as little as eight dollars an acre. [31]

Local business progress was reflected in the establishment of the First National Bank of Greencastle when its organizers received

authorization from the Comptroller of Currency. Although this official document was dated April 28, 1865, directors were elected on March 4 since assurance of the Comptroller's approval had been received earlier. Men chosen to serve on the first board of directors represented major elements of the area's economic structure — agriculture, merchandising, and industry. Jesse Craig, J. C. McLanathan, Jacob Shook, Melchi Snively, John Wilhelm, A. B. Wingerd, and John Ruthrauff, were leading farmers. Samuel Bradley and Jacob B. Crowell were manufacturers, while John Rowe and George W. Ziegler were merchants. McLanahan served the eleven member body as president and received an annual salary of one hundred dollars.

The First National began operating in a house, owned by William C. Kreps, on the west side of North Carlisle Street two lots north of the site of the present building. Business was conducted in the front and back parlors with L. H. Fletcher serving as cashier. His salary was $1,000 a year and Kreps received an annual rent of $125 for the use of his facilities.

Five years after the bank began business the three storied building, which still stands as the main portion of its present day operation, was erected. The contract to build this brick structure was awarded to the E. O. Bias firm of Chambersburg on March 5, 1869 at a cost of $4,600. Business was conducted in the portion of the building located at the corner of the Diamond and North Carlisle Street. The remainder of the new facility became rented rooms for retail stores and offices.

For years the only bank in the county was located in Chambersburg. In February of 1864 Waynesboro's First National started operations, taking the place of the earlier Waynesboro Savings Fund

Society. Later in 1865 another financial operation came to Chambersburg when the Franklin County Bank was organized. Colonel J. C. Austin of Greencastle and Colonel James G. Elder of St. Thomas, were leaders in establishing this newest institution. The fast growth of banks is perhaps the best indication of the general prosperity that had developed in south central Pennsylvania during the war.[32]

Business also was booming for the Cumberland Valley Railroad. Early in the year it began a major program of rebuilding the tracks damaged during the war. The company's Chambersburg shop was rebuilt and all timbered bridges were replaced with wrought iron structures. On July 28 it was announced that three passenger trains would make daily runs between Hagerstown and Harrisburg to "accomodate the large and constantly, increasing travel through the Cumberland Valley." By the end of the year the company reported an all time gross revenue of approximately $300,000, yielding an eight percent dividend for its stockholders.[33]

In October Waynesboro people received an improved transportation service to connect their town with Greencastle. Wolfersberger and Stoner put a new bus on the mail line that met the Cumberland Valley's trains. The vehicle was said to have "spring seats, handsomely cushioned and much more comfortable than the former one."[34]

Out of the ashes, that followed McCausland's raid, Chambersburg was still busy rebuilding its businesses and factories. In another year its economy would be close to the prosperity the town knew before the Rebels came. Throughout the rest of the county prosperity flourished. Waynesboro's Frick Company was expanding its business. In addition to grain, drills, threshers, and steam engines, by 1866, boilers and saw mills had become part of its line.[35]

In Greencastle J. B. Crowell and William H. Davison were operating a firm on South Cedar Lane. This partnership had grown over the war years by mergers and purchases. When peace came the business included a foundry engaged in making plows, stoves, and farm bells; a mill which manufactured doors, sashes, blinds and other lumber products; and a plant where corn shellers and grain drills were produced. This industrial complex, which eventually became the sole property of Crowell, was the largest employer in the Greencastle area. Another manufacturer of grain drills was John Fisher whose shop was on East North Street. Stiffel's tan yard, on North Cedar Lane, recovered from losses to the Confederates in 1863, was reported to be a very busy place. There were shops that built wagons and other horsedrawn vehicles, while skilled craftsmen continued to make hats, boots, shoes, and men's clothing. Rural artisan were still fashioning farm implements such as sickles, scythes, grain cradles, shaking forks, and grain rakes while Antrim's water powered mills continued serving local needs and city markets with flour, animal feed, cornmeal, and lumber. [36]

After a hard winter filled with snows that lay for weeks, spring brought adequate time for planting and showers that made the Valley one vast sea of green, stretching from mountain to mountain. Throughout the first week of the Lincoln funeral train's westward journey there was rain in eastern Pennsylvania. Late June and early July brought one of the richest wheat harvests on record and through the remainder of the summer showers nurtured the fields that eventually gave area farmers a bountiful corn crop. [37]

Interest in growing hemp did not last. In fact by war's end practically none was being produced. Tobacco cultivation seemed to be limited to only a few farmers, including Christian Hoover. After the war Hoover discontinued tobacco farming, gave up the cigar making business, and went into brickmaking on a full time basis. A resurgence of sorghum growing continued for several years beyond the war, but as sugar and molasses became available this crop disappeared, also. [38]

Although the years following the war brought continued farm prosperity the perennial problem of horse stealing persisted. News accounts told of the same patterns of thievery in the Pennsylvania border areas continuing. Although the average value of horses dropped from a high of $185.00 during the last year of the war to $57.50 in 1867, farmers could ill afford these losses when they occurred. [39]

As war-time emergencies passed, Antrim's farmers returned to the traditional patterns they knew before the conflict. However, an early evidence of specialized farming came in the post-war years when Jacob Stover's son, Mitchell, developed a field devoted solely to apples and peaches. This was the first orchard of this kind in the township. His concern for specialization also led to dairy farming and house to house milk deliveries in Greencastle. [40]

Peace time brought few changes in the retail businesses of Greencastle. Jacob Hostetter's prosperous enterprise continued and in 1865 he and William Reid formed a partnership to operate a grocery store in Waynesboro. The town's weekly announced on August 11 that the new business would carry, not only a complete line of groceries, but, queensware, glassware, tobacco, cigars, and sundries. Hostetter's "Greencastle Wagon" was also delivering watermelons and cantaloupes every week during the month. Later, in November, fresh fish and oysters were available. Hostetter's rail freight cars were bringing not only extensive profits in the wholesale business but through his retail outlets in both Greencastle and Waynesboro.[41]

The only major changes in Greencastle's business structure occurred in the town's newspaper ownership and the proprietorship of the Antrim House. When James McCrory discontinued "The Pilot" in July of 1864 there was no immediate sale, but by August, 1865, Robert and William Crooks had bought the paper and William A. Reid served as its editor. It was a short lived ownership for within a year's time the brothers sold the business to the Rev. John R. Gaff who changed the journal's name to the "Valley Echo." Reid left his job as editor and returned to the grocery business when he purchased Hostetter's share in the Waynesboro store and ran it as his own.[42]

In 1867 Thomas Pawling sold his hotel to Jacob L. Detrich of the Canebrake area. The new owner was a veteran having served as a second lieutenant in the 1st Regiment of Pennsylvania Light Artillery. At the time the business was prospering but Pawling was caught up in public opinion sweeping America — the future was in the West.

(Horace Greely had advised young Americans — "The best business you can get into you will find on your father's farm or in his workshop. If you have no family or friends to aid you, and no prospect opened to you there, turn your face to the great West, and there build up a home and a future.")

Thousands of veterans were heeding this advice yet Pawling, no longer a young man, saw his future in Greely's wise counsel. His mother died in 1864 and her estate had been settled. His children were grown, so at the age of forty-six, he and his wife, Malinda, left Greencastle in 1870 to take up lands in Pottowotamie County, Kansas, where they lived the remainder of their lives. Tom Pawling died in 1904. He lived to be eighty years of age, but never was he a bigger man, a greater hero, than in 1863 when he fought the Confederates, right there in Greencastle. His daring escapades during the invasion and the retreat of the hospital train left his mark on the town's history for all time.[43]

Pawling was not alone, other local men left their homes to find a new life for themselves and their families in the West. Many were veterans who, over the decades following the war, continued to migrate to the newer states along the Mississippi and lands extending to the towering Rockies. Getting land under provisions of the Homestead Act did not mean that it was free with no obligation to the government. A grant of a hundred and sixty acres became the grantee's after he had occupied and begun cultivating it over a five year period. This required hard work especially in the heavy grass areas that defied early type plows. Yet, with improved machinery, within twenty years after the war this undeveloped part of America became the bread basket of the nation.

Beyond the hard work, the Plains Indians presented another problem for the early homesteaders. Following the war the government took measures to roundup the war-like tribes, push them onto reservations, and station army units at strategic points to control them. Many tribes, such as the Sioux, refused to submit to the U. S. Government and the Indian wars that followed continued for nearly two decades, culminating at the Battle of Wounded Knee in 1890. This ended the last major Indian threat and the homesteaders were free to work the rich prairie soil while the once proud tribes languished in their compounds, as wards of the United States Government.

Of the soldiers who continued in the military at western posts after the Civil War, two officers were from Franklin County. One was David H. Brotherton, a Waynesboro native whose family came from Antrim Township. A graduate of West Point, class of 1854, he first served in Texas as a second lieutenant and was later attached to a military reconnoissance unit to determine a route for the Southern Pacific Railroad. When the Civil War came he was engaged in a campaign to destroy the power of the Navajos. Throughout the war with the South he served in New Mexico. For gallant and meritorious service in the Battle of Valverde, where the Rebels defeated a Union force, he was awarded the brevet-major rank. Until 1879 Brotherton was on frontier duty ranging from Texas to Montana.

In 1881, while post commander at Fort Buford in the Dakota Territory, he received Sitting Bull's rifle as a symbol of his tribe's surrender. With him were forty-five men, sixty-seven women, and seventy-three children — pitiful survivors of the once proud warriors who had destroyed Custer and his command, at the battle of Little Big Horn in 1876. This capitulation resulted from negotiations led by Major Brotherton in which the tribesmen were persuaded to return to the lands reserved for them. They had fled to Canade to escape the wrath of the U. S. Army but homesickness and starvation had brought them back. The harsh winters of the northern plains severely affected Brotherton's health and he was forced to retire due to disability. He retired, with the rank of lieutenant colonel, April 14, 1884 and died in his home town of Waynesboro, September 17, 1889 in his fifty-eighth year. [44]

The other Indian fighter from the area was David Stewart Gordon, whose home was in Antrim's Browns Mill community. Born in 1832, he lived there until 1857 when he moved to Leavenworth, Kansas. The early days of the Civil War found him in the Frontier Guard, a group that later served as Lincoln's personal body guard at the White House. Gordon became a second lieutenant in the 2nd United States Cavalry on April 26, 1861 and took part in early fighting at Fairfax Court House. At the first Battle of Manassas he served as aide-de-camp to General E. D. Keyes. When his horse was killed he was captured and spent thirteen months in Confederate prisons. After being released, Lieutenant Gordon fought with the Army of the Potomac throughout the war. At Gettysburg he was awarded the rank of brevet major for gallant and meritorious service.

After the war Gordon remained with the 2nd Cavalry and was stationed on the western frontier. He won the rank of lieutenant colonel for gallant service against Indians in fighting at Miner's Delight, Wyoming March 4, 1870. By 1892 he had risen to the rank of colonel and commanded the 6th United States Cavalry. During the Chicago Pullman Strike of July and August, 1884, his regiment was part of the army President Grover Cleveland ordered to enforce a Supreme Court injunction against workers who had called for a nationwide stoppage of rail traffic. Gordon's last command was at Fort Myers, Virginia. After his retirement, in 1896, he lived to be ninety-eight years of age, dying on January 27, 1930 in Takoma Park, Maryland. At the time he was holding the rank of brigadier general.[45]

Michael Bushey, brother of Dr. Franklin Bushey, although not in the army after the war, was believed to have been a casualty in the Indian wars. In 1867 he married Rebecca Klink of Newville and four years later the couple moved to Newton, Jasper County, Iowa. In the spring of 1880 he left his Iowa home to look for better ways to make a living in Colorado. Michael reached his destination near the end of the month, and on or about June 1, in an ambush near Sangachi, Bushey was killed by a shot in the back. His body was left by the roadside while his wagon, horses, and supplies were said to have been taken by Indians. Clothing, false teeth, boots, and other items were returned to his family for verification. As a tribute to his brother, Dr. Bushey erected a monument in the Cedar Hill Cemetery with the inscription, "Killed by Indians." Rebecca returned to Newville in the 1890's and died there in 1896. [46]

Michael Bushey lost his life by following a dream of a more prosperous life in the West. Hundreds like him met a similar fate but there were hundreds of thousands whose dreams did come true. Among the many veterans who left the Greencastle area, five stand out as examples of the successful life that could be found in the West. They were Andrew Davison of the 126th and the 209th; Cyrus Kennedy who was with the United States Signal Corps; Joseph Holman of the 126th and a Mississippi River flotilla; Scott Snively who served with the 126th and the New York 13th Cavalry; and Joseph Strickler of the 2nd Pennsylvania Volunteer Infantry. These men may not have been typical but what they became in later years exemplifies the pioneer spirit that went into the opening of the new lands.

Davison took title to Homestead lands and eventually became the cashier of the First National Bank of Brownville, Nebraska. Kennedy acquired lands in Fulton County, Illinois and became a successful farmer in that part of the state. Holman had a unique and varied career. He first went to Ohio and eventually settled in Michigan. He worked at a variety of callings — storekeeper, carpenter, millwright, and bridge builder but at the age of forty-one became an attorney and practiced law in his home community of Rochester, Michigan. He also served as a legislator in the state's House of Representatives where he was recognized as one of its most able speakers. Newspapers of the day referred to him as the "Orator of the House."[47]

After teaching for several years in Antrim's schools, Scott Snively, in 1874, moved to Arkoe, Missouri, where he eventually served in the state legislature. In 1893, after a cyclone destroyed their home, he and his family moved to Sheridan County, Wyoming. Here Scott continued farming and dealing in livestock. Again he became a political figure, serving in the state's General Assembly, from 1902 to 1908, where he was elected Speaker of the House during his last term. His kind lived hard and long. He died at the age of eighty-eight in 1931. [48]

Joseph Strickler, a first lieutenant in the 2nd Pennsylvania Volunteers, went into the retail business in Greencastle after the war. He was a man of unusual talent with experience in the building trades. At the time the First National Bank building was being considered he was employed to design the structure and its clock tower. Shortly after its completion, he migrated to Nemaha County, Nebraska where he acquired a land grant, went into farming, and remained in the West the remainder of his days. [49]

The great majority of veterans returned to their home towns and villages or rural homes to carry on the work they left when they enlisted or were drafted. Those who had families and the ones who eventually married settled down and established homes, raised families, continued to go to church, saw that their children went to school, voted, and paid their taxes. Some joined the Grand Army of the Republic and, maybe, a fraternal society. For the most part they formed the basic, sound, majority of citizenry in their communities.

Exceptions to such a life style varied. Some became active leaders in their home areas through political connections, by virtue of additional education, or because they possessed inherent leadership qualities. Many, while in the service had acquired a desire for a life beyond the ordinary. They had associated with others from other sections of the nation and came to share their dreams. These were the men who became energizers of social forces that brought better living conditions into their home communities. Changes that came after the war affecting government at various levels undoubtedly reflected the influence of such men. They also brought new ideas for improving business and enriching leisure time for their friends and neighbors.

Of the nineteen charter members of Greencastle's Mount Pisgah Masonic Lodge, organized in 1869, eleven were veterans. The Independent Order of Odd Fellows, revived in 1876, had nine charter members — all ex-soldiers. Returning soldiers became enthusiastic supporters of Greencastle's Town Hall, as a center for lectures, home talent shows, traveling theatrical groups, choral organizations, socials, dances, and community dinners or suppers. Some ran for local, county, and state offices. They taught school, became leaders in business and farming, and studied to become preachers, lawyers, or doctors. [50]

Captain Robert Boyd returned to Upton, continued in the retailing business, served as a county commissioner and was the village postmaster for many years. Dr. Henry Chritzman came back to Welsh Run to practice medicine and in 1884 he was elected to the General Assembly. Samuel Eby taught school, became the principal of Greencastle's schools, was elected County School Superintendent in 1875 and 1878 and later became the Citizen Bank's first cashier. Joseph Davison, the popular officer in the 6th Reserves, became a warehouse manager. He was never a strong man after the Peninsula Campaign and this led to his death in 1879. At the time he was a leader in numerous church and community activities. [51]

Although not a veteran, Dr. George R. Kauffman had spent two years in a Confederate prison. Upon his return he continued his medical studies at the Bellvue Medical College in New York, and upon graduation returned to practice medicine in the Browns Mill community. Frederick Klinefelter, a member of the 126th, became a Lutheran minister and came back, in 1872, to serve the local congregation. Jacob Lear resumed his blacksmith business in Shady Grove and for several years taught in Antrim's schools. Dr. Victor Miller practiced medicine in the Mason-Dixon area and served as county coroner from 1864 to 1866. [52]

Colonel D. Watson Rowe studied law, practiced in Greencastle, and served the county as its presiding judge for twenty-one years. George Snively, of the 17th Cavalry, went west to Nodaway County, Missouri, farmed for two years and came home to operate the family homestead in the Shady Grove area. Jacob Snively, who was with the 21st Cavalry, returned to his farm, became active in Republican politics, and served as a county commissioner. [53]

Henry Strickler, wounded at Fredericksburg, served as the county's Register and Recorder from 1863 to 1866, was appointed the United States "storekeeper of internal revenue," and later served as a deputy collector for the Internal Revenue Service. Colonel Benjamin F. Winger became an attorney and newspaper publisher. He owned the "Valley Echo" from 1867 to 1876, sold it and established a second weekly called the "Greencastle Press." George F. Ziegler, of the 126th, after completing his studies at Amherst and Princeton Seminary, returned to his home town to establish a private school. It became one of the area's leading educational institutions providing a classical education for the young men and women of the town and surrounding communities. [54]

The soldiers, whose diaries helped to tell this story continued to live in their home areas after the war. Henry Bonebrake became a postmaster in Waynesboro, Jacob Finafrock farmed in Antrim, became an authority on fruit growing, and was later employed by a Philadelphia fruit processing firm. Josiah Shuman taught for many years in Antrim's schools. [55]

Greencastle and Antrim also attracted veterans who came and lived there after the war. They returned to the area because while in local encampments they saw opportunities for making a living for their families. Some

GROSH COLLECTION
HENRY WHITE
THE OLD WARRIOR

344

came from Maryland, Ohio, and other parts of Pennsylvania. There was a German born immigrant and an Englishman, both veterans, who came to live in Greencastle. Then there were young men who, while stationed in the area, fell in love with local girls. One of these was Henry White. When his company of the 21st Cavalry was encamped in the community young White, whose home was in Adams County, fell in love with Elnora Koontz, who lived with her parents on North West Street. When peace came the soldier returned and married Elnora. Four girls and three boys were born to the couple and the former soldier supported his family as a coach painter and trimmer. He later worked for J. B. Crowell as foreman of the company's paint shop. The children, Sallie, Maude, Genevieve, Lenora, Clifford K., Claude and John grew to adulthood in Greencastle. However, all except Clifford Kinsley, left the town to seek their fortunes elsewhere. He became a popular barber and lightning rod dealer. In later years strong ties with the Republican Party led to his serving two terms as a Director of the Poor in Franklin County and still later employment as an inspector for a state licensing agency. Of all Henry's and Elnora's children, C. K. was the one best known and loved by his home town people. [56]

Another cavalryman from Adams County, with the 21st, was Samuel Musselman. While in the Greencastle area, Samuel met a young lady named Sarah, the daughter of the Rev. John and Sara Eshleman who lived on a farm in the southern part of Antrim Township. After the war young Musselman married Sarah and four children — Andrew, Christian, Charlotte, and Sarah — were born to the couple. Their offspring have given the area leadership in church work, government, agriculture, and business enterprises for several generations. At present there are approximately seventy-two men, women and children who trace their ancestry to a cavalryman who fell in love with a preacher's daughter so many years ago. [57]

The most romantic tale of young love occurred in the Browns Mill area. During the retreat from Gettysburg some Confederates were following the Cumberland Valley tracks that ran parallel to the Chambersburg Pike as the wagon train was retreating into Maryland. Joseph Heayd's farm lay along the rail line and as these soldiers were passing the farm house Mrs. Heayd was taking bread from the outdoor oven. When she saw them looking eagerly at the fresh loaves she invited them to come to the back porch to eat some of the warm bread with apple butter. The Heayd girls helped serve the hungry Southerners. One of them was Lee Rhodes of Louisiana and when his eyes met those of the oldest daughter, Allie, he saw a thing of beauty that swept aside all the tragic ugliness war had brought into his young life.

Lee Rhodes never forgot this moment and Allie remembered, too. When the war was over the Southerner came back. A courtship followed and two years after their first encounter Lee and Allie were married. The couple lived with the bride's parents and when the Heayds died Lee Rhodes became the owner of the farm. Three boys and four girls were born to the couple and the family continued to live there until near the turn of the century when they moved to Greencastle. The sons left the community, but the daughters stayed with their parents on South Washington Street until they died — the father in 1902 and the mother in 1908. Carrie, Mary, Estella, and Pearl, the Rhodes girls, continued to live in Greencastle. Carrie became a nurse while the others were teachers who taught in both town and rural schools, touching the lives of the community's children for at least three decades. [58]

Throughout this era Antrim continued educating its young people in one and two room schools. However, in the post-war period log buildings were replaced with brick and weather boarded structures. Their popularity as centers for singing schools, spelling bees, and social gatherings continued and by the early 1900's the township had twenty-eight school houses. Greencastle, in 1868, erected a school house, large enough to contan elementary and grammar school classes on what had been the Methodist graveyard, at the corner of East Franklin and South Washington streets. The one and two room log schools that had dotted the town for so many years were closed and the town's children used this building through the remainder of the century.

The decade following the war saw similar developments in the county's major towns. This same period brought the beginnings of secondary education also. Chambersburg's first high school graduation was held in 1870. Waynesboro began a secondary program the same year and Greencastle's high school began in 1875. Three years later Mercersburg conducted its first high school classes. [59]

Hundreds of former slaves had fled into Franklin County and other border regions of Pennsylvania during the war years and the Greencastle area had its share of contrabands coming from Virginia through the Shenandoah Valley and its eastern regions in the final year of war. Perhaps the longest journey for any slave was from Tennessee to Greencastle. The one who held this record was Samuel Rankin who, as a boy, became a follower of Sherman's army as it crossed Georgia and continued through the Carolinas into Virginia. After the Grand Review Rankin eventually made his way to Greencastle. Although some of the blacks returned to their home regions after the war others, including Rankin, stayed in their new found homes. The illiteracy found among this considerable body of Negroes became a concern of the church people of the community. To teach these former slaves to read and write local churches established Mission Sunday Schools. [60]

George F. Ziegler was the promoter of this kind of school in the Presbyterian Church. J. C. McLanahan served as superintendent of the classes and Moses Anderson, an educated Negro and a member of the congregation, was the assistant superintendent. Fifteen men and women of the church volunteered to teach the classes. Yearly registration for this instruction ranged from twenty-five to sixty-two and continued for seven years beyond war's end. After a new church building was erected in 1872 to replace the earlier African Methodist Episcopal Church, this kind of teaching continued in the former slaves' own house of worship.

(Moses Anderson, the assistant superintendent, was the father of Matthew Anderson who later served Philadelphia's Berean Presbyterian Church as its pastor. He was the first Negro to be graduated from Princeton Theological Seminary, class of 1877, and ordained by the Carlisle Presbytery the following year. In 1880 he became the pastor of the Philadelphia church, a charge he held for forty-eight years. His work to help Negro youth of the city by developing a program of industrial training brought him nationwide recognition. He also was instrumental in establishing the Berean Building and Loan Association to help families of his race to own their own homes. When he died in 1928, at the age of eighty-two, Matthew Anderson was known throughout America as one of the nation's leading Negro religious and educational leaders.) [61]

Peace not only brought changes in local education but in municipal affairs too. Borough Council renamed the town's principal side streets within two years after the war. For nearly ninety years they had carried names indicating their direction from the main streets. They were given names by which they are known today — Washington, Jefferson, Franklin and Madison. The street called East Second was called Allison to honor the town's founder, and South Second was renamed Dahlgren. It was the town's tribute to Ulric Dahlgren the young cavalry leader who brought hope to local people with his exploits against the Confederates during the Gettysburg campaign. [62]

Behavior of the town's boys and others apparently had not improved since the days of Editor McCrory's concern. An ordinance was passed to punish those found guilty of "breaking or injuring street lamps or lamp posts." Also, there were enactments to prohibit "disorderly conduct . . . and assembling to obstruct streets and pavements." Playing ball and throwing stones on the streets or center square were not allowed and congregating at the railroad station, located where the Citizens Bank now stands, were punishable by fines. [63]

Fire prevention was a dominant theme of ordinance in the period. There were laws detailing specifications for constructing chimneys, the storage of kerosene and gunpowder in stores, and controlling the sale of gunpowder. It could not be sold by artificial light — candles or oil lamps. (Sounds sensible enough.) [64]

As the bank building was constructed, a group of civic minded businessmen suggested placing a town clock on its roof. The board of directors agreed, $1,800 was raised through private subscriptions, and the clock tower was erected. Upon its completion, in 1872, Town Council agreed to assume responsibility for maintaining the tower and its timepiece. [65]

Greencastle seemed to be in the midst of a building boom. First there was the new school house, then the bank building, and in 1870 a Town Hall was built. This was another three story brick edifice located at the corner of East Baltimore and South Washington streets. It was financed by a company of seven local investors — Jacob Pensinger, John Wilhelm, Jacob Deardorff, J. C. McLanahan, James Crunkleton, Addison Imbrie, and Dr. J. K. Davison. At street level the building provided rooms for offices and retail businesses. The top floor was available for lodge meetings and band rehearsals. An auditorium on the second floor had accomodations for dramatic productions, dances, lectures, concerts, and other occasions of community interest. For nearly fifty years it served as the town's chief entertainment center.

The town hall concept was new to Greencastle. However, Chambersburg and Waynesboro had such buildings before the war. Chambersburg's Franklin Hall, on the northeast corner of the Public Square, was destroyed by the fire of 1864 and in its place a similar building, known as Repository Hall, was erected. It was a three storied structure with storerooms on the first floor, an auditorium on the second and lodge rooms at the top level. Waynesboro had its Town Hall on the southeast corner of Center Square. It was a two storied structure with a community hall on the second floor. The first floor housed the fire company and a general store. A feature, not found in other such county buildings, was a cupola which housed the town clock. [66]

AN EARLY BASEBALL GAME

Although these halls afforded convenient accomodations for entertainment, traditional pastimes continued. People still found pleasure in picnicking, church socials, quilting parties, husking bees, singing schools, barn dances, and parties for special occasions throughout the year, while traditional winter sports — sledding and skating never lost their popularity. Farm fairs became a big attraction in the post war years and community wide picnics and patriotic holiday celebrations drew large crowds. Shooting matches, horse racing, and wrestling continued to test the prowess of their male participants.

A new game began to create interest. It was called baseball, a kind of contest that soldiers learned while in their camps. Before the post war decade ended there were organized teams in many parts of the county. The earliest baseball games in Greencastle were played on a lot at the southeast corner where East Franklin Street met South Allison, but not until 1868 were there organized teams. Records of the time show that two games were played in August when Greencastle's "Kangaroos" hosted the Waynesboro "First Nationals." The local team won the game by a score of 80 to 37. A later contest resulted in a 52-46 victory for Waynesboro. In a game two years later between Gettysburg and Waynesboro, Gettysburg won by a score of 55-22 and this struggle lasted only seven innings. Progress in learning the game's skills was slow indeed. *(The early version of the game contained several differences from today's national pastime. Players had no gloves; pitchers threw the ball underhanded; the catcher stood at a distance back of the batter in order to catch the ball on its first bounce; and base runners could be put out by being hit with a thrown ball. Contests often lasted between four and five hours and the high scores by both sides indicated the loose type of play that marked these early contests.)* [67]

Although traveling tent shows and circuses had been playing the North during the war, few ventured into the border areas for obvious reasons. The "Metropolitan Circus," headed by M. J. Robinson, a well known circus name in later years, was scheduled for Greencastle on Friday, July 29, 1864, but McCausland's raid forced the show's cancellation. However, 1865's summer was filled with an abundance of this kind of entertainment. As early as April 5 the Viva Lanvied troupe played in Greencastle. On August 15, I. I. Dorial's company came to town and the following day "Deery's Great World Circus" appeared in Waynesboro. Perhaps the biggest attraction of the summer came with the arrival of the "Bailey and Company Circus and Menagerie" in Greencastle for two performances on August 31. For the remainder of the 1800's and into the early decades of the new century, tent show performers and circus troupes continued to entertain the people of small town America. [68]

Another kind of entertainment that soldiers learned to appreciate in the service was band music. During the war there was only one such musical organization in the county — the Chambersburg Brass Band. However, the post war years found such musical groups in practically every village and principal town of the county. Greencastle's town hall, as early as 1875, provided a rehearsal room for such a local organization. Early bands sponsored special events — picnics, festivals, and concerts as money raising projects. In 1865

ELROD COLLECTION   MILITIA BAND — PICTURE TAKEN IN CHAMBERSBURG

Chambersburg's Cornet Band placed a notice in area newspapers announcing a Picnic Excursion from Chambersburg to Browns Mill on Wednesday, August 16. The picnic, with games and concert music, was to run from half past eight in the morning until seven that evening. Transportation was available on the Cumberland Valley line. [69]

Peace and prosperity erased the memories of war for many, but a sad remnant of the war for some families came with an announcement in September 1865 — "All applications for transportation to and from Virginia for the removal of the dead bodies of Pennsylvania soldiers for burial within the state should be addressed to Colonel Charles F. F. Gregg, Chief of Transportation, Harrisburg, Pa."[70]

After those battles within reasonable transport distance, hundreds of parents or wives had gone by horse drawn vehicles or rail to find the bodies of sons or husbands killed in action. Newspapers carried stories of such pilgrimages following the battles at Antietam and Gettysburg. When death occurred in engagements too far from home, most burials became permanent and the bodies of Southern and Northern soldiers still lie in cemeteries on battlefields where they fell.

Residents of the Greencastle area who lived along roads leading out of Maryland saw the sad procession of relatives hauling their dead to homes in Pennsylvania after the Battle of Antietam. On one occasion a father and mother, in a horse drawn wagon, stopped at a farm home just north of Middleburg. They sought permission to bury their son on the farmer's premises until winter came. The decomposed body of their boy created such a stench that they could go no further. With colder weather, the parents returned, disinterred the dead soldier and took him to his final resting place. Robert Johnston told his children of helping people from Virginia find their son's body after the war. The soldier had died during the retreat from Gettysburg and his remains were buried along the Williamsport Pike in the vicinity of the Johnston farm. [71]

Greencastle area families availed themselves of the state's offer to pay transportation costs to bring bodies of their sons home from battlefields near and beyond the Rappahannock River. George Missavy's family was one of these. Money was raised by the townspeople to help defray expenses of Isaiah Illginfritz who volunteered to go to Chancellorsville and recover the body. He had been in the fighting when Missavy and Simon Rupley were wounded. Within a few hours both died and he knew where they were buried.

In mid-March, 1866 Illginfritz traveled to Chancellorsville and returned with Missavy's remains on Friday, March 23. The funeral was held in the Reformed Church on the following Sunday afternoon. After the service, conducted by the Rev. T. G. Apple, a procession formed with former comrades of the 126th serving as pallbearers. As bells of the town's churches tolled, the funeral march, headed by a band playing a solemn dirge, moved slowly down Baltimore Street to the Diamond and south on Carlisle Street to the church graveyard. The local paper commented — "The number in attendance was unusually large — so large that the spacious church was completely filled, and numbers were unable to procure seats . . . The deceased stood high in the estimation of those who were personally acquainted with him." His parents and sisters would have liked that.

Remains of the other local soldier who died at Chancellorsville, Simon Rupley, were brought back to Greencastle two months later. Isaiah Illginfritz again went to the battlefield to recover and return with the skeletal remnants. On May 17, 1866 Simon Rupley was buried in the Reformed graveyard with ceremonies similar to those that honored George Missavy. *(After the Cedar Hill Cemetery was established, in 1870, many bodies buried in local church plots were reinterred there. Today the graves of Missavy and Rupley can be found in this burial ground.)* [72] *(See Appendix)*

As the first year of peace approached its end Pennsylvania's Governor, Andrew G. Curtin, was doing what he could to ease the pain and sorrow that gripped so many families. He not only was responsible for the state's role in helping to get the bodies of deceased soldiers returned to their loved ones, but he was instrumental in initiating programs to care for orphans of these men. Homes for such children were established in Philadelphia, Lancaster, Pittsburgh, Mount Joy, Quakertown, and Orangeville. This concern laid the foundation for the later establishment of the Pennsylvania Soldiers' Orphan Industrial School, in 1895, at Scotland, four miles north of Chambersburg. [73]

Equality for all soldiers, regardless of race, was demonstrated in late October. The "Village Record" of October 27, 1865 carried an item announcing the State Comptroller had ruled that all colored volunteers should be placed on the same footing as white soldiers in regard to bounties and paymasters were instructed to pay them accordingly. This refers to a hundred dollar bounty the Governor had secured for volunteer soldiers who had been or were being discharged.

Andrew Curtin had been an early advocate of the Thirteenth Amendment which would abolish slavery. Pennsylvania, as early as

February 4, had approved this proposal. Near the close of the year, on December 18, William H. Seward, Secretary of State, announced that the Amendment had become law of the land: that "neither slavery nor involuntary servitude, except as punishment for a crime can exist in the United States or any area under its jurisdiction."

It was a proper way for the year to end. The Amendment surely served as a fitting tribute to the memory of the martyred President and all who gave of themselves — "The living and the dead —" to the cause that "gave this nation a new birth of freedom."

CHAPTER XIV

THE G.A.R.

The promise of freedom for Negroes and the additional amendments to implement this freedom, the Fourteenth, to give them citizenship and the Fifteenth — to guarantee them rights, became involved in the political struggles that followed the war. Veterans were caught up in the ongoing fight by Radical Republicans to dominate their party and to reduce the Democrats to a minority party henceforth and forevermore.

Early in the war Nathaniel Hawthorne went to Washington for inspiration to place into words his thoughts concerning the crusade to preserve the nation. Instead he left the city with a broad skepticism of how the war was being conducted. This beloved writer, who had described the beauty and agony of human experience, and searched for the mysteries of men's souls, found little promise of a future that would make America proud. Instead of unselfish devotion to the cause of justice and freedom, Hawthorne saw a capital filled with politically appointed officers using every available means to secure undeserved military advancement. He envisioned a government, for decades ahead, dominated by men of high military rank and a succession of "bullet headed" generals being elected to the presidency. These observations were made in 1862 and that his concerns often became reality is a matter of history. Characterizing every president, with military experience, who served through the decades beyond the war as "bullet headed" maybe too strong, but it was certainly true that Civil War veterans dominated much government at all levels until the end of the century. [1]

Between 1867 and 1903 there were eight governors in Pennsylvania and all except one, Robert E. Pattison, were veterans — five of them commissioned officers. John W. Geary, Andrew Curtin's successor, was the governor with the highest military rank, a brigadier general. Serving two terms, he provided leadership that led to the Constitution of 1873 which brought changes to Pennsylvania's government needed to make it more responsive to the will of the people. Geary also advocated improved education for the state's children through better qualified teachers, implemented by legislation to promote tax supported high schools, and to build state normal schools. John Geary would have been given high grades by Nathaniel Hawthorne. [2]

Of the national legislators who represented the county from 1866 to 1900, most were Civil War veterans. One of these was the colorful Thaddeus Mahon who had served in the 126th Infantry Regiment and the 21st Cavalry. In 1866 he was elected Clerk of the County Courts. As a Republican he was named to the state legislature in 1871 and elected in 1872. Four years later he ran for the United States House of Representatives but was defeated by his Democratic opponent W. S. Stenger, who won by a scant majority of twenty-five votes. Stenger was the owner of Chambersburg's "Valley Spirit."

Mahon left the political arena until 1888 when he ran for the county's judgeship. Again he suffered defeat, this time at the hands of John Stewart, another veteran of the 126th. Four years later he was elected to the nation's House of Representatives and for thirteen years he continued to serve the Legislative District of which Franklin County was a part. This long tenure was attributed to continued support from the many G.A.R. posts in the area he represented. Advocacy of improved pensions for veterans and his constant introduction of border claims made him invincible. His critics chastised him for this political ploy. It impressed his constituents but in his heart he knew the claims had no chance of being passed. The claims were designed to reimburse property owners for losses suffered from the Stuart and McCausland raids and Lee's 1863 invasion. For decades Mahon went through the motions of introducing claims exceeding a million dollars but never succeeded in getting one cent for the claimants. One county historian wrote, at a later time, "He offered his bill regularly each session in the Congress and just as often it was defeated or not taken out of committee. Mr. Mahon either died or was finally defeated and nothing more has ever been heard of the Border Claims." Actually the congressman retired for health reasons during his seventh term.

His biography shows that he was responsible for improving pension claims of eighteen hundred of his constituents. As a Republican he was a strong supporter of tariff legislation, an advocate of improved rural mail service, and a leader in extending railroads in the Cumberland Valley. Mahon was prominent in the G.A.R. and Loyal Legion. Nathaniel Hawthorne might have given him a below average political rating, but to the veterans, he was their champion — one hundred percent of the time. [3]

Of the state legislators from Franklin County between 1865 and 1900 at least half were veterans. This same ratio held for all county offices and practically every federally appointed officer in the county was a veteran. This political dominance by the former soldiers undoubtedly came from the loyalty people felt they deserved but most of all it emerged from the unity former soldiers eventually developed. [4]

Many veteran organizations came into being when the war was finished. Early ones were generally limited to commissioned officers such as the Military Order of the Loyal Legion of the United States — a prestigious body similar to the Society of Cincinnati formed by Revolutionary War officers. The first group for all soldiers was the Soldiers' and Sailors' National Union League. This had been preceeded by groups limited to particular armies like the Society of the Army of Tennessee or the Society of the Army of the Potomac.

But the organization that outlasted them all, the Grand Army of the Republic, proved to be the most powerful. Its origin rose from the desire to help needy veterans and widows. Men were "starving for want of work, widows of slain soldiers were begging for work and the lowest kind of work to feed themselves and their children and find clothing to cover their nakedness." The G.A.R. aimed at those who stayed at home and escaped the rigors and dangers of war who now were finding reasons to deny jobs to ex-soldiers and assistance to widows and their children.

The Grand Army of the Republic was said to have been the brainchild of Dr. B. F. Stephenson of Springfield, Illinois. Early in 1866 he communicated with many of his former comrades and finally a meeting was called for July 12 — a year and three months beyond the day Lee surrendered. Stephenson's idea was embraced with enthusiasm. Those who met on that day in July went back to their home districts and by year's end, Illinois had 40,000 veterans enrolled in posts all over the state. Other groups, on hearing of this phenomenal growth, got in touch with the Springfield leaders and departments (statewide organizational areas) were started all over the nation.

Pennsylvania's department came into existence January 16, 1867, the twelfth to be recognized in the nation. Annual conventions, known as national encampments, began at Indianapolis on November 20, 1866 and Pennsylvania was host to the second gathering, at Philadelphia the following year. [5]

Greencastle's first G.A.R. Post was organized sometime after the state department was started, but it never succeeded in creating an interest necessary to sustain a membership of operational size. It was named for the cavalry leader, Ulric Dahlgren.

That many early G.A.R. posts collapsed can be seen in how membership fell within the first decade following the war. In Pennsylvania two thirds of the earlier posts had been abandoned by 1872. Political leaders who had used veterans' organizations, including the G.A.R., had achieved their ends. This was particularly true in

Congress where after the election of 1866, the Radical Republicans were solidly in control and able to alter the direction of President Johnson's plans for reconstructing the South. *(From then on the Congressional plan was aimed at making citizens of Negroes and establishing state governments that recognized their needs.)* Veterans, feeling they had been used, dropped memberships. It was also true as ex-soldiers, found jobs, married, and began raising families, they lost interest.

Many felt the early G.A.R. organization was modeled too much along lines they had learned to dislike while in the service — rigid supervision, regular inspection of posts, and decisions of higher officers and national encampments being treated as orders which were to be obeyed implicitly. There were suspicions of how the dues money was being spent by higher officers. Local posts wondered why they had to buy supplies — badges, ritual manuals, and other paraphernalia from headquarters and nowhere else. [6]

It is assumed that the early Greencastle post was one of those that fell by the wayside along with the many others during the early post-war years. However, between 1876 and 1890 the veterans reorganized. A rebirth of interest saw the low enrollment of 1875 *(about 25,000)* rise to more than 400,000 by 1890. This renaissance came from energetic recruitment campaigns, concern for pensions as veterans became older, enthusiasm for organizing women's auxiliary groups, and the continued need for homes for aged veterans and schools for children of ex-soldiers. One important self serving agency, that published the National Tribune — the national capital's largest pension agent firm — used its publication to beat the drums for veteran unity to achieve benefits from the government.

This revival of interest was also attributed to the leadership of Paul Van Dervoort of Nebraska, who served as commander, 1883-84, and Robert B. Beath, a Philadelphian, who served as the national leader the following year. These men were responsible for bringing a new spirit into the organization. They traveled all over the North, visiting encampments, giving instructions on how to generate enthusiasm for recruitment drives. Their leadership was said to have brought a greater sense of mission to the G.A.R. as they spelled out the nationwide plight of veterans and families of deceased soldiers.

It was under Van Dervoort that the auxiliary group known as the National Women's Relief Corps was organized with Mrs. Florence Barker, of Malden Massachusetts, as its first president and Mrs. Kate B. Sherwood of Toledo, Ohio as senior vice-president. Mrs. Sherwood gained national fame as an author and poet who extolled the work of both women and veterans as they worked to help those in need.[7]

During this period of intense recruitment, Franklin County's permanent G.A.R. posts were organized. Waynesboro's Post 287 was established September 22, 1882. It was named for Captain John E. Walker who was killed near Atlanta, August 5, 1864. He was a member of the 77th Pennsylvania Volunteers. Chambersburg came next with Post 309, organized on February 21, 1883 and named for Lieutenant Colonel P. B. Housum, also of the 77th Regiment, who died of wounds suffered at Stones River, on January 1, 1863. Greencastle's Post 438, organized May 12, 1884, was named for Corporal William H. Rihl *(misspelled Rhial)*, of the 1st New York Cavalry, who was killed at the Fleming farm June 22, 1863. Mercersburg's Post 497, honored the memory of Captain J. P. McCullough, of the 126th and the Pennsylvania 209th, who died at Petersburg, April 2, 1865. Fayetteville's Steven's Post 317, organized April 3, 1883, was named for Alanson J. Stevens, nephew of Thaddeus Stevens, who was killed at Chickamauga. [8]

The Corporal Rhial Post had thirty charter members with Joseph R. Davison serving as Commander. Senior Vice Commander was Jacob S. Snively; Junior Commander, M. W. Kisecker; Adjutant, C. H. Fulweiler; and Chaplain, Rev. J. Y. Shannon, of the Methodist church. The new organization's first activity was that of sponsoring

LEGION POST 373 COLLECTION   G.A.R. MISSPELLED BADGES

the annual Decoration Day observance. This holiday was started by General John A. Logan who proclaimed May 30, 1868 as Memorial Day. Logan called on posts throughout the nation to observe it with appropriate ceremonies to honor the dead who had served the Union cause. [9]

In Greencastle the earliest Decoration Day programs were conducted by the Knights of Pythias. Milton A. Embick, a local veteran and later a state assemblyman, contributed an account of the first such occasion in a letter to the May 23, 1905 edition of the Echo Pilot. "I am carried back to the first official Decoration Day under the auspices of the Knights of Pythias Lodge, when Colonel Joe Davison, as chairman of a committee, selected William Patton, M. D. Reymer, and the writer as the orators; comrade Reymer for the Reformed graveyard, Patton for the Cemetery, and the writer for the Lutheran graveyard." Although available records reveal nothing more of this observance, it occurred after 1870 since this was the year the Cedar Hill Cemetery started. Mr. Embick's letter indicates that they continued for some time before the G.A.R. accepted the responsibility. It should be noted that throughout the early decades of the local post's existence May 30 was always referred to as "Decoration Day."

The first observance conducted by the Corporal Rhial Post was held on May 30, 1884. Commander Davison appointed committees to make the proper arrangements: Music — James Moorehead and William Brenizer; Invitations — C. H. Fulweiler, William Snyder, J. Boggs Byers, E. B. Carpenter, and Frank Hoffman; Marking graves — Hoffman and Carpenter. The membership declined on invitation of Reno Post No. 4 of Hagerstown to participate in decoration services at Antietam. They would be too busy with their own program.[10]

Although there is no account of this first Decoration Day observance a later record *(1886)* indicates the procedure usually followed. Two comrades, under orders from the Post Commander, marched to the Moss Spring graveyard to decorate veterans' graves and returned to headquarters at the Town Hall. When they returned the post would gather on the Square and march with the City Band in front of the post members. The procession, which also included Greencastle's American Steam Fire Engine Company and the Junior Order Band, would then march around the town to the different cemeteries to decorate graves of deceased veterans. The marchers then proceeded west on Baltimore Street to Cedar Hill Cemetery for ceremonies conducted by ministers of the town. The program in 1886 began with a prayer by the Rev. J. C. Brown of the Methodist church. The Lutheran pastor, Frederick Klinefelter, gave a patriotic address and the ceremony closed with a prayer by the United Brethren minister, J. B.

Weidler. [11]

Post headquarters was in the Knights of Honor room at the Town Hall. For this an annual rent of thirty-five dollars was paid. Money for rent and other post needs came from dues, set at two and a half dollars a year, and fund raising affairs. At first, meetings were held twice a month but by September of the first year it was agreed to meet monthly. At a meeting of June 24, 1884 the post decided to take part in Franklin County's Centennial Parade to be held in Chambersburg. [12]

By any scale for evaluating human endeavor this Centennial celebration was the greatest in county history. It began at ten o'clock on Monday, September 8, with a parade. H. G. Bonebrake, Commander of Waynesboro's Walker Post, was marshall of the first division, composed solely of G.A.R. posts in the county. Area bands in this section included those from Welsh Run, Shady Grove, Clay Hill, and Greencastle. In all, there were fourteen bands and three drum corps participating in the procession. Greencastle's fire company was there with all other firemen of the county and practically every known lodge — Odd Fellows, Knights of Pythias, Red Men, and other secret societies all dressed in their various regalia. Horse drawn floats, carrying over a hundred girls and boys, were found throughout the procession — many with banners carrying temperance messages. One thousand and eighty-three people were in the line of march, most in uniform, and at least five thousand spectators lined the streets to see this spectacular event.

The day ended with another parade — a Carnival of History. Horse drawn wagons, carrying tableaus portraying phases of American history, moved along selected streets illuminated by lanterns of many patterns and colors. A special feature, six electric lights generated by the Cumberland Valley Railroad Company, created an extra brilliance along Market and Main streets. About a hundred and seventy-five actors, dressed in costumes required for each tableau, took part in this extravaganza. Nothing like it had ever been seen in Franklin County.

The next day brought another parade. This one saw representatives from all the governmental bodies of the county, with displays showing the industry found throughout the region. There were more bands and drum corps accompanying floats depicting historic scenes from various parts of the county. There were wagons displaying merchandise and products from rural areas. Hundreds of horsemen and walkers, carrying banners, extolled their towns and townships. Four thousand persons were in this gigantic spectacle and an estimated fifteen thousand people came to witness the pageantry of this massive procession. The day ended with an elaborate fireworks display at East Point. Nothing before or since ever equalled this two day celebration. [13]

The Corporal Rhial Post ended the year by choosing new officers on December 26. Davison continued as the commander while George Arendt and George Anderson were elected to the senior and junior vice commands. Quartermaster was G. B. Snively, Sergeant-at-Arms — Dr. Franklin A. Bushey, and Jasper Sheely was named chaplain. Boggs Byers became officer of the day and E. B. Carpenter, officer of the guard. At this meeting Commander Davison and C. H. Fulweiler were appointed to represent the post as delegates to the Grand Encampment. [14]

A proposal to hold a "campfire" on April 9 to commemorate the twentieth anniversary of Lee's surrender was voted down at the March 29, 1885 meeting. However, the members did agree to solicit funds to erect a monument as a memorial to Corporal Rhial. J. R. Davison, B. F. Winger, William Snyder, Jasper Sheely, Mathias Kisecker, Dr. Bushey, and C. H. Fulweiler were named to serve as a fund raising committee.

Plans for the 1885 Decoration Day were made at the May 22 meeting. The post had agreed, earlier, to participate in this year's Antietam program. This meant the local ceremony would be held early in the day, before the journey to Sharpsburg. Arrangements for the Greencastle celebration called for Colonel B. F. Winger to be the "Orator of the Day," and flowers were to be delivered to the Town Hall on the afternoon of May 27. Post members were to report at six in the morning on May 30 and the memorial service was scheduled to begin at seven thirty. All participants in the procession were to wear white gloves and carry canes.

After these ceremonies, members of Post 438 proceeded by rail to Hagerstown and on to Sharpsburg by horse drawn buses. The City Band accompanied the veterans. No mention is made of the program at Antietam, but at the June 26 meeting a motion to chastise a member for "conduct unbecoming an officer and a gentleman while attending Memorial Services at Antietam" was adopted. The offender was J. Boggs Byers and it was ordered that he "be severely reprimanded by the commander at the July 31 meeting." The nature of his misconduct is not recorded, but it can be assumed that Boggs may have reinforced himself too lavishly from the "cup of good fellowship."

Whether Comrade Byers was properly reprimanded is unclear. Before he could be brought to judgement the post became engulfed in details to properly express its sorrow over the death of Ulysses S. Grant. He died on July 23 and at a special meeting, held the next day, plans were made to memorialize the dead leader. A committee was appointed to draft appropriate resolutions. It was decided that all members wear a piece of black crepe or ribbon on the left breast "until after the funeral of our deceased comrade, General Grant." The post room would be draped for thirty days and a committee was formed to request business places of Greencastle and Antrim to close during the funeral services. Also, businessmen were asked to drape their establishments during the period of mourning. Plans were made to hold a memorial service on Saturday, August 8, in Town Hall for veterans, their families, and the public in general. The final decision called for publication in the local paper a Resolution of Respect approved by the post members. It was also to become a part of the official minutes.

The resolution reflected the literary talents of the committee's chairman, Dr. Franklin A. Bushey, and the proper order of the encomiums were likely suggested by B. F. Winger and William Snyder, the other committee members. No praise was spared for the departed hero. He was equated with George Washington, constantly referred to as the sole savior of the Republic, and a President who stood far beyond and above all his predecessors after the nation's founding father. The final paragraph left no doubt as to his eternal destiny.

"The grim reaper has thus gleaned a bounteous harvest. The silver cord that bound us together has been snapt asunder. Our ranks are broken, one leader has fallen. Clouds gather quickly over us. In the dark hour of our solitude a ray of sunlight streams out from the throne of God, lighting up with ineffable radiance the form and face of our dead comrade. Calm, serene, beautiful even in death he will be ever a grand inspiration. Farewell dear comrade, rest in peace for evermore."

This glowing tribute, written in a familiar style of the day, Victorian prose with effusive praise, emerged as the handiwork of Dr. Bushey. History would not be as kind to the fallen general and former president as the good doctor and his comrades who ratified the Resolutions of Respect, but its sincerity could never be challenged. Since Ulysess Simpson Grant was their military hero and fellow comrade, not only in war but in the Grand Army of the Republic, he deserved every single word of praise they gave him.

The memorial service for Comrade Grant was held as scheduled, Saturday afternoon, August 8, in the Town Hall's auditorium. It was noted that the occasion was a community wide observance, including the Rhial Post, together with the Town Council and citizens of both Greencastle and Antrim. Business places were closed from one to five o'clock and the hall was filled to capacity. The program follows: Prayer, Dirge by Band, Record of Deceased Comrade Grant by Adjutant, Roll on Muffled Drums, Responsive Reading by Members of G.A.R. Post, Dirge by Choir, Reading of Scripture, Dirge by Band, Addresses by Rev. F. Klinefelter — General A. B. Sharpe of Carlisle — Rev. Weidler and others, Music by Band, Responsive Reading by Post, Dirge by Choir, Benediction.

When the mourning period was finished the post returned to regular business. It was decided that proceeds of an earlier benefit program, a Bell Ringer Group, be placed in the general treasury. On October 30 the members were treated to a program by Comrade Kaiser of Stevens Post, Fayetteville and his "inevitable accordeon." They voted a donation of two dollars to Kaiser to help him buy a magic lantern to "enable him to gain a livlihood." For the members enlightenment, Comrades Amos Miller and Mathias Kisecker presented a set of the Bates History of the War to the post.[15]

Plans continued in the new year for the monument to honor Corporal Rhial. On February 26, 1886, it was announced that forty dollars had been raised for the project through a lecture by the Hon. Hiram Price of Washington, D.C. At the same meeting members resolved to honor the memory of Lieutenant George W. Kennedy of Pennsylvania's 21st Cavalry. He had recently died and a period of thirty days' mourning was placed in effect. Colonel William Boyd, of the Pottsville Post 23, sent a copy of the recently published book "Boots and Saddles" — a history of the 1st New York "Lincoln" Cavalry by James H. Stevenson.

Subsequent meetings in March and April revealed that William Fleming's family had agreed to donate land for the Rhial monument. The post accepted the plot and entered into a 999 year lease agreement with the Flemings. It was also decided that the remains of the cavalryman would be disinterred and re-buried at the site where he died.

Decoration Day services were held according to plans on May 30. That evening, members of the post joined in a memorial service held at the Lutheran Church. The Rev. J. D. Hunter delivered a sermon on the theme, "The Soldier's Duty."

At the June 18 meeting arrangements were made for reinterrment of the remains of Corporal Rhial on June 22 at the Fleming farm site. A guard of honor was named — William Brenizer, _____ Davis, Simon Palmer, Jacob Poper, Adam Jacobs, Upton Easton, James Moorehead, _____ Wentling, _____Swisher, Daniel Hellane, Theodore Koontz, and W. F. Patton. Pallbearers were to be Charles Shirey, Samuel Eby, Jacob Snively, Samuel Showalter, _____ Speck, William Stickel, and Philip Ruthrauff.

Two days before the ceremony, the coffin containing the remains was taken from the Lutheran graveyard by the undertakers, Jeremiah Detrich and his son, William. Large crowds gathered at Detrichs and G.A.R. members were posted to control the many curious people looking for souvenirs of this special occasion. Into a new coffin, made by the undertakers, the remains were placed and on the appointed day, the ceremony proceeded as planned. A long procession accompanied a horse drawn hearse flanked by the pallbearers. In the line of march from the Lutheran Church to the Fleming farm, were local officials, officers and members of the post, other veterans, and a host of townspeople. One account said this occasion brought "one of the largest crowds, — that has ever visited the town."

The Rev. Cyrus Cort, of the Reformed Church, was the principal speaker. He spoke of the nation's obligation to honor its heroic dead and declared the spot where the cavalryman fell as "holy ground." Appropriate thanks to the Fleming family for their grant of land and to the local G.A.R. post for their efforts were given — "cease not in your efforts until a monument, as lasting as the grand mountains that look down in majesty upon us, shall mark this sacred spot and fitly crown your endeavors. God bless you and prosper the work in which you are now enlisted. Amen." The Rev. T. J. Shannon gave a response to the address on behalf of his comrades in the local post. Then Rev. Frederick Klinefelter offered a prayer and Dr. Crawford, of Chambersburg, provided graveside remarks. A twelve gun salute followed to close the ceremonies.

When the rites were finished, the crowd, estimated at 2,000, adjourned to the Spielman Park, also called Spielman's Grove, located on the northern edge of Greencastle in what is today the Jerome R. King Playground. For years it was the town's most popular summer recreation area. Here Dr. Chritzman presided over another program which included an address by a Dr. Hall of Altoona who had been a member of the cavalry squad that was ambushed when Rhial was killed. The cavalrymen's leader, William Boyd, was also present.[16]

The monument was not placed at the new grave site until the next year. Prior to this it was disclosed that the post had been spelling the corporal's name incorrectly. This was discovered sometime in January, 1887 and the February 4 meeting's minutes show a motion to change the spelling of the name to Rihl and that the post's name correspond to the name on the monument. For nearly three years the veterans had been misspelling the cavalryman's name. The earlier spelling was on a company roll kept by Captain James H. Stevenson. However, other records found in Albany and Washington, including the muster and payrolls of the regiment, contained the correct spelling. Finding this error in time was important since the design to be used by the stone cutters carried the spelling — Rhial.

BESORE COLLECTION
THE YOUNG DR. FRANKLIN BUSHEY

The post had not yet raised enough money to pay for the monument but at the last minute Comrade Dr. H. G. Chritzman, a member of the State Legislature, introduced a bill calling for an appropriation of five hundred dollars to be allocated to the memorial fund. The bill passed and plans continued to erect the granite memorial and dedicate it on June 22, 1887.

At its May 6 meeting it was announced that Dr. Bushey was to be the principal speaker at the unveiling of the monument. Spielman Park would be used for the exercises and a committee was named to decorate it — S. S. Easton, Theodore Koontz, Upton Easton, and Simon Palmer. The guard of honor would be W. F. Patton, Jacob Unger, _____ Davis, and Jacob Poper. [17]

The years that followed saw the post meetings generally occupied with routine matters. But from time to time there was other business. The members had to decide whether they would participate in activities sponsored by other posts. A popular pastime was the "camp fire" held locally or in neighboring towns. These occasions attracted veterans from all over the county and sometimes Hagerstown. They provided a chance for fellowship through ample refreshments, singing war songs, and the simple pleasure of sitting around and exchanging wartime tales — some tall ones and others still taller. It was claimed that as time passed and the war receded in memories, some veterans seemed to get braver with each passing year as they recalled their military exploits.

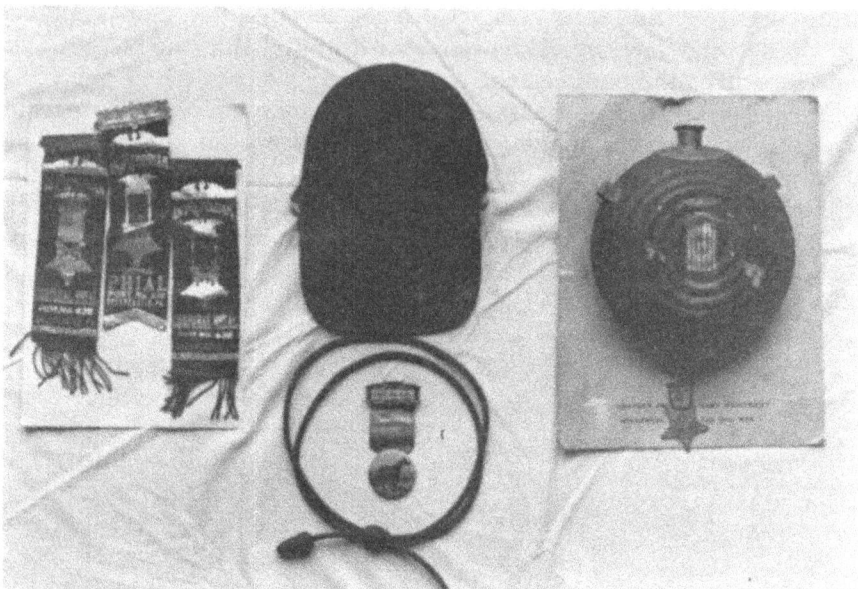

MORE G.A.R. MEMORABILIA

There were other forms of entertainment. A G.A.R. Picnic for all county posts was held at Mont Alto in the spring of 1887. There were excursions to battlefields and illustrated talks were given by visiting veterans at post meetings. Sometimes a fellow veteran would invite the post members to his home or a town restaurant for refreshments following a regular meeting. Gifts in the form of battlefield relics were presented from time to time and on February 17, 1888 D. Watson Rowe sent twenty copies of his "History of the Hundred and Twenty-Sixth Regiment." At a later meeting, Jacob Finafrock presented the post with a new flag.

Solicitations for contributions to various projects usually brought donations from the post treasury or through collections taken at meetings. When former Commander of the G.A.R., Senator John Logan, died, a fund was started by the National Tribune to erect a monument in Washington to honor the founder of Decoration Day. This was accomplished through a nationwide campaign and today's Logan Circle's equestrain statue stands as the result. G.A.R. Post 483's contribution to this project reflected a somewhat restrained feeling toward Senator Logan's importance. The members contributed one dollar. [18]

On May 15, 1891 the post ordered that a draft of ten dollars be paid to a fellow veteran, John R. Stickel — "To assist him in making up his loss sustained, losing his crops and barn by lightning." At another time the members gave assistance to the widow of a veteran and pledged their help in securing a pension for her. In 1893 the Post encouraged contributions to a fund to help pay for a marker on Chambersburg's Center Square — an appropriate addition to the Veteran's Memorial erected in 1878. [19]

In November, 1894 state G.A.R. Headquarters instructed the local post inspection officers to investigate an alarming situation in the schools of the area. Antrim Township had twenty-nine schools with only six possessing an "American flag floating over them." Twenty-three school houses had no flag. At the November 16 meeting this matter was brought to the attention of the members. There is no record of how it was resolved.

Interest in helping those in need continued. On September 14, 1894 the post members petitioned the Soldiers' Orphans School at Chester to admit the children of John Williams, a deceased Negro veteran. The school was filled at the time and the appeal was filed for future consideration. [20]

Improving Decoration Day observances continued to be a constant concern of the G.A.R. leaders. After state military authorities notified the post that guns were not available for drill, honor guard, or parade purposes, it was agreed to purchase them and after 1889 any appearance was always accompanied by a firing squad. In 1891 fife and drum music became part of the May 30 rituals. On March 15, 1895, Post 438 approved a resolution to support a bill before the Legislature to prohibit the sale of intoxicating drinks on Decoration Day. The members also invited the Greencastle school principal, Professor W. D. Smiley, to have a chorus sing appropriate "patriotic airs" and lead in singing the National Anthem at the May 30 ceremony. In June 1896 the Rihl Post agreed to purchase one hundred and fifty markers for the graves of deceased veterans. A year before, the post bought a lot in the Cedar Hill Cemetery for deceased indigent comrades. [21]

The local G.A.R. members were not quiet where the interests of veterans were involved. At its November 1, 1889 meeting the following resolution was adopted: "Whereas — The survivors of the Second Maryland Rebel Regiment have erected on the Battlefield of Gettysburg within four feet of the Monument erected by a loyal Maryland Regiment, a monument commemorating the disloyal deeds of said rebel regiment.

"Whereas — There is every indication that other Rebel organizations and regiments will, if permitted, follow the example and then undertake to make treason honorable, "Therefore — Be it resolved that Corporal Rihl Post No. 438, Department of Pennsylvania G.A.R., composed of men who gave their best services in defense of the flag and many of whom shed their blood on the Battlefield of Gettysburg, desire to enter this solemn protest against this sacrilige and most emphatically denounce any such intrusion by traitors upon sacred soil and ask that the Gettysburg Battlefield Association, the chairman of which is our worthy Governor James H. Beaver, Governor of the Commonwealth, cause the said rebel monument to be removed and express orders given that no more of that nation's be erected." [22]

No response from the governor was noted, but in subsequent years the acceptance of memorials for Confederate units and officers continued. Despite stong opinions of posts like Greencastle's, an attitude of reconciliation gradually replaced such feelings. Other factors entered into this matter of appeasing both Northern and Southern veterans where battlefields were concerned. As rail transportation improved, visits to battle sites became the targets of excursion promoters and commercial interests naturally followed. Eventually it was a matter of economics to promote the valor of soldiers and leaders of both sides in order to attract visitors. Monument companies, stone cutters, and sculptors rejoiced at the booming business such reconciliation brought and artists found a new kind of employment in recreating panoramic battle scenes.

Commercial advantages were also found in other areas. The end of Reconstruction brought renewed interest in Confederate heroes. The Lost Cause became a theme for Southern writers and former officers of Confederate armies were in demand as northern newspapers began to feature articles written by them. A. K. McClure, Andrew Curtin's right hand man throughout the North-South struggle, was one of these. He had started the "Philadelphia Times" in 1877 and through his exploitation of the war, he built his journal into the city's second largest daily. His "Annals of the Civil War" featured articles by former military leaders, many of them former Southern officers. General John Imboden wrote of the Shenandoah campaigns and McClure ran his "Fire, Sword, and Halter" in serial form. Another author, John E. Cooke, whose writing brought a romanticism to the Southern cause, was featured and the enterprising McClure secured General James Longstreet to contribute to the "Annals" series. [23]

Records of the local G.A.R. post reveal nothing concerning the members' feelings about popularizing the Southerners or the rampant commercialization of the war in which they fought and saw so many of their comrades die. They must have realized that the Grand Army of the Republic, also, was subject to the inticements of the market place. There were companies that promoted the sale of flags, hats, uniforms, badges, post regalia, and other items that no veteran's organization should be without. Music publishers were constantly advancing their latest scores suitable for special occasions, including the most popular songs for the traditional May 30 observances. Publications of national headquarters contained advertisements promoting the commercial houses where these items could be purchased. It is doubtful that the Corporal Rihl Post set any record of extravagance when it came to buying much of the paraphernalia that was offered. [24]

Another proposal they refused to accept was an invitation to establish an Auxiliary for the post. A letter from Lizzie Carpenter, Installing Officer of the Woman's Relief Corps, issued such an invitation in 1896. There was no immediate or later response to Lizzie's entreaty. The post continued as an all-male sanctuary. [25]

Without doubt the erection of the Corporal Rihl monument was the post's most outstanding and longest remembered contribution to the community. Through the remainder of the century records of Post 438 reveal no exceptional activity. New members were admitted, some dropped out, while others died. By 1900 a record shows the roster consisted of just thirty members — the same number as that of the charter membership. Available post records indicate that, over the years of its existence, a total of eighty-two veterans belonged at one time or another. Since some reports were not readily accessible a conservative estimate would put this figure at approximately a hundred men who held membership. Estimates of the number of veterans living in the Greencastle area in the post-war period run as high as four hundred. Accordingly the Rihl Post attracted approximately twenty-

LEGION POST 373 COLLECTION
REUNION MEMENTO

five percent of those eligible for membership during its lifetime.[26]

The Greencastle post's membership had never reached its full potential, but its ratio of members to available veterans was not unique. This was true throughout the nation and by 1900 the trend was towards still lower enrollments. The enthusiasm generated by Commander Van Dervoort, more than a decade earlier, had lost its momentum. In its peak year, 1890, the organization's membership rose to 409,487 but by 1900 it had declined to 276,662. By this time the G.A.R.'s political clout of earlier years was beginning to diminish. At one time the powerful veterans organization was referred to as "Generally All Republicans," but the G.O.P. was now more involved with issues beyond meeting demands for pensions and other legislation affecting veterans. Also, many ex-soldiers were becoming indifferent. They had secured what was thought to be a good pension program through the Act of 1890 and having accomplished this they let their membership lapse. [27]

The rise and fall of membership revealed another development which Post 438 came to have within its ranks — veterans who were not natives of the Greencastle area. One was Milton Ewers a salesman from Ohio who decided he wanted to join the local group. Another was William Birkmeyer, a native of Germany, who served in the Union cause and listed his occupation as "peddlar." John Ware, an Englishman who described himself as a "butler," became a member. There is no explanation of his local employment. Where did he practice his butlership? William Palmer, a cooper hoping to find better opportunity to ply his trade, moved his family into the Shady Grove area from Maryland and became a member in 1887.[28]

As the Corporal Rihl Post entered the new century the majority of members would have been in their mid fifties with the older comrades near the age of sixty-five. However, age did not dampen their zeal for protecting the rights and well being of veterans. At the May 4, 1900 meeting they objected to the appointment of a non-veteran to a county committee responsible for burying deceased ex-soldiers who were wards of the county. In 1903 they protested the erection of a monument at Hanover to commemorate the "first battle in Pennsylvania." This honor belonged to the Greencastle area and if there were any state monies for such a marker it should be given to the local post. Its members would see that it was located near the Corporal Rihl monument. [29]

On September 14, 1901 President William McKinley was assassinated. When word reached Greencastle the Corporal Rihl Post immediately went into a special session. Following general orders from the G.A.R. Commander-in-Chief, Ell Torrance, of Minneapolis, local headquarters and colors were appropriately draped. All officers were ordered to wear the usual badge of mourning at public occasions for sixty days. Post 438 also published, in local papers, a resolution of grief at the death of Comrade McKinley. [30]

On January 6, 1902 the Liberty Bell, on its way to the Charleston Exposition, came to Greencastle. Post Commander Samuel Eby urged all members to be on hand for this exceptional occasion. The town newspaper, the "Echo Pilot," told of the event in its January 9 edition — "The largest crowd which has been seen in Greencastle since the Civil War assembled on the streets Monday afternoon to greet the passage of the Liberty Bell. All morning the farmers of Antrim Township were coming into the town and when the Bell arrived the crowd was estimated at over 4,000 people. Promptly at 2:50, amid the ringing of bells and blowing of *(shop)* whistles, the long train of Pullman cars, drawn by two engines, drew into town and stopped with the open car upon which the Bell stood, in the middle of the Square. There was no cheering, but the silence of the immense crowd was most impressive, and more eloquent of their feelings, than any more boisterous greeting could have been.

"From the passenger station *(at the corner of North Carlisle and Madison streets — now a residence)* to the Square both sides of the street were lined with school children, each carrying pieces of pine and many flags. As the train stopped they took up a line of march, past the Bell, headed by the Junior Order of United American Mechanics Band, and as they passed the pine was thrown upon the Bell. Although the march was rapid, and each got but a glimpse of the Bell, almost fifteen minutes was occupied by these school children. Among them were not only the Greencastle schools, in full force, but Clay Hill, Broadway, and the Upton schools, each in a body, were present, and many students from other schools in the surrounding country."

This brief march included not only children. The local firemen, with their 1741 Rescue Fire Engine, were in the procession along with the procession along with the Rescue Hose Bugle Corps, the all-Negro Willow Spring Band, and the G.A.R. Drum Corps. The only other organized body in the parade was the Corporal Rihl Post. The editor commented — "These veterans who, in their later generation, represent the same principles for which the Bell stands, turned out in full strength." Sam Eby would have been proud.

Before the train continued its journey, speeches were made by J.

Hampton Moore, Philadelphia's treasurer, and the city's Mayor Ashbridge. Their remarks were followed by a distribution of souvenirs for the children. The editor said, "Probably no child went away without some keepsake to impress the memory of the day upon its mind."

Later in the year plans for Greencastle's first Old Boys Reunion were being made. It was to be held in August and the G.A.R. Post arranged to welcome veterans who returned for this occasion. Philip E. Baer, the promoter of this reunion, had gained national prominence as a concert artist and on his tours through the western cities he met many former Greencastle residents. Through him this celebration was scheduled as an opportunity for these sons of the local area to meet and relive some of their boyhood happiness in the old home town. Between fifty and sixty came home and from August 10, for ten days, events were scheduled for their entertainment. These included a chicken dinner in the Town Hall; a picnic at Sandy Hollow, a favorite swimming hole along the Conococheague; a minstrel show; and speeches with band concerts on the Diamond. Of the men who returned, some were former soldiers and they took the opportunity to meet with their comrades in a session of the G.A.R. Post.[31]

The Old Boys Reunion marked the beginning of what became Greencastle's Triennial Old Home Week celebration. In 1905 the second homecoming was celebrated and for the next decade Civil War veterans participated in many scheduled events. Part of the 1908 Old Home Week was a Reunion of the 126th Regiment with headquarters in Town Hall. The veterans had Friday, August 21 to themselves. No other event was scheduled. From ten thirty to twelve the time was devoted to business and election of officers. After lunch and through the rest of the afternoon there were speeches by Company A's First Lieutenant John Stewart, a State Supreme Court Justice; Samuel Niccolls, the regiment's first chaplain; Representative Thad Mahon; Rev. Clay McCauley, the young lieutenant captured at Chancellorsville — a Presbyterian minister; and Colonel D. Watson Rowe. The speech making was followed by a March of the Battalion accompanied by the Wayne Band; Roll Call, by Company; and a Dress Parade. After supper the evening hours were spent in a campfire where recollections were shared by all.

The 1911 Old Home Week included a picnic for veterans organized by the Corporal Rihl Post. This was the last scheduled event in which Civil War veterans formally participated. However, they continued to take part in regional G.A.R. ceremonies and campfires in nearby towns. [32]

Despite the post's reduced participation in community activities, there was no diminution of effort to keep the citizenry alerted to observance of the annual Decoration Day. By 1900 post records were calling it Memorial Day but for at least another generation the earlier name continued to be used by many. On through the early years of the new century, the membership declined, decimated as time took its unalterable toll. But the survivors insisted on reminding people of their duty to remember the cause for which they had fought and to honor those soldiers who had gone to their final rest.

Memorial Day services still held to earlier procedures, including the parade to Cedar Hill and speakers with local backgrounds. Expanding community involvement in the day's program continued. This began when the schools were first invited. In 1902 the post invited the band from the Scotland Orphans School and the year that followed, Sunday School classes participated. [33]

The fiftieth anniversary of the Battle of Gettysburg was remembered by elaborate ceremonies and reenactment of the battle. Local veterans and members of Post 438 who attended this important occasion, July 1-3, 1913, met not only comrades who had been part of this gigantic battle but veterans of the Confederate divisions who had fought in vain on the open fields and ridges now filled with memorials honoring both the victors and the vanquished.

Post records indicate that by this time there were fewer conventions or ceremonies in which local veterans participated. In earlier years post commanders usually attended state and national encampments and many members took part in reunions of their regiments. There were occasions when the state furnished transportation to dedication services for Pennsylvania monuments on distant battlefields or Confederate prisons but few local veterans availed themselves of these free trips. Jeremiah Hollinger, of the Rihl Post, did have the distinction of serving as an aid-de-camp on Milton A. Embick's staff at the unveiling services of two state monuments dedicated on May 10, 1909 at Petersburg. Embick was Secretary of the Pennsylvania Monument Commission at the time. [34]

Recollections of Gettysburg's celebration had barely subsided when word reached Greencastle that D. Watson Rowe was ill and within a week's time the town's veterans and older residents were saddened to hear of his death on July 15. Like so many others of his generation he, too, had answered the final roll call. The Colonel of the 126th Regiment had died in his seventy-sixth year and G.A.R. posts all over the county went into a period of mourning. Veterans of the old regiment saw to that.

Judge Rowe was buried in his home town's cemetery on July 17. It was a very simple burial. There were no military ceremonies. Services were held in his Chambersburg home at the corner of Second and Market Streets. By train the body was brought to Greencastle and from Center Square the funeral cortege moved westward to Cedar Hill where final graveside services were held.

The day Judge Rowe was buried, the 10th United States Cavalry was encamped at Moss Spring. This was a regiment of Negro horse soldiers that had earned a reputation as the Fighting Tenth. It had fought against the Indians of the Southwest and in the Spanish-American War. Although it did not receive publicity, this regiment, along with Theodore Roosevelt's Rough Riders, had fought and helped win the Battle of San Juan Hill. Consisting of 750 soldiers, with thirty-four white officers, the regiment was on its way, from Fort Ethan Allen in Vermont, to Winchester for special maneuvers.[35]

Memories of the Civil War surely must have swept through the minds of veterans and older people over this period in July of 1913. The Gettysburg anniversary would have caused remembrances of the invasion, the passage of the hospital train, and incidents associated with its retreat. D. Watson Rowe's death certainly rekindled memories of the 126th battle losses and the joyful homecoming, and the 10th Cavalry camping at Moss Spring would have reminded those who had lived in the 1860's of the times this camp site was used by both Federal and Confederate armies. Most of all the passage of a half century stood as a grim reminder to those veterans who remained that time was a luxury that should be savored every day of their lives.

WELCH COLLECTION
INSPECTING THE MONUMENT

Each Memorial Day that came and passed saw additions to the names of the dead honored the year before. New graves lay decorated as taps sounded across Cedar Hill at the yearly ceremony. By the end of the first World War, Post 438's membership gradually lessened but those who remained still stood tall and proud as they carried on the tradition that began with them. Among the proudest was Dr. Franklin A. Bushey. As long as he lived no one in his presence ever forgot what he stood for.

The custom of holding a service in one of the town's churches the

374

Sunday before Memorial Day was still a part of the tradition the G.A.R. held as sacred. No matter how small the membership, the Rihl Post continued to attend these services. Dr. Bushey, that towering, lean, ramrod erect veteran who lived on and on, never missed one of these — just as he rarely missed a post meeting except for medical emergencies and there was never a Memorial Day program without him.

Comrade Bushey was a proud man with strong opinions on matters related to the Civil War, the veterans and their role in saving the Union, or the Grand Army of the Republic. At one of these church services during the post World War I period a newly arrived minister, somewhat younger than the veterans, delivered the sermon. In the course of his remarks the preacher referred to the post members as "old and feeble veterans of the Civil War." This went beyond the threshold of the doctor's sense of propriety. Although past the allotted age of three score and ten, this proud veteran rose from his pew and left the service. Those in the congregation, near his exit, were not too amazed to hear him say, "Damned if any preacher is going to call me feeble." The sound of his cane accompanying his descent of the church's front stairway, along with appropriate mutterings, was heard by the ushers until he reached the coolness of the springtime evening beyond the sanctuary's portals. [36]

Such an incident only served to increase the doctor's dedication to the veterans' cause and when he saw injustice he continued to fight to overcome the wrong. As late as 1921 he was not insensitive to the needs of those who were too old to work and deserved improved benefits to cope with the wartime inflation that continued into the first World War's aftermath. The Corporal Rihl Post, although diminished to perhaps a dozen members, took up this cause for all veterans and the widows of their dead comrades. At its meeting of September 16 the post approved a resolution to be sent to Senators Boise Penrose and P. C. Knox and Representative Benjamin E. Focht. "We are honorably discharged survivors of the bloodiest war in the history of this nation. We are self-respecting law abiding, loyal Americans. We represent the entire Civil War soldier interests in this section of this great Valley. We gave our young manhood and strength to the preservation of this Government. We are all old, and no longer able to labor and require needed assistance. We respectfully request your aid in securing the speedy passage by Congress of the Morgan Bill granting $72 per month to every honorably discharged veteran of the Civil War and $50 per month to every veteran's widow." The resolution was signed Franklin A. Bushey, Commander and J. A. Hollinger, Adjutant. [37]

Time was running out for most of them but if at all possible they wanted what they felt they deserved. Sharing in this desire to help the Civil War soldiers was a new generation of veterans, those of the first World War. On September 29, 1919 fifteen of them met to form what became the Frank L. Carbaugh Post No. 373 of the American Legion. Its early meeting place was the G.A.R. Post headquarters located in a small store room at the corner of East Franklin and South Carlisle Streets. Through the years the Corporal Rihl Post had been at many different places — Town Hall, the Odd Fellows Hall, the First National Bank building, Dr. Bushey's home, and finally the storeroom which now served both veteran groups.

The Carbaugh post was chartered in 1920 and from then on Memorial Day became a joint venture but the G.A.R. still dominated the ceremonies. It was their day and the Legion would have to wait. The 1921 program was an example. Both groups were in the parade that formed on South Carlisle Street. Of the Rihl Post, those who were able still marched and the remainder were hauled in motor cars. Along with the Shady Grove and the Junior Order bands, the veterans and other dignitaries marched to Cedar Hill for the traditional ceremonies.

Shady Grove's band rendered an appropriate number. The Rev. H. B. Burkholder gave the invocation and Jeremiah Hollinger followed with a reading of John Logan's first Memorial Day address. Dr. Bushey presented the official address and three readings — by Samuel Eby, David M. Nisewander, and Thomas Gordon followed. Then a prayer was offered by the Rev. W. Morgan Cross. While the Junior Order Band played a dirge the Civil War veterans decorated graves of their departed comrades. With this finished the program continued with a selection by the Shady Grove Band's male quartet. The Hon. Norman L. Bonebrake, prominent Chambersurg attorney, delivered the memorial oration. Only after these ceremonies did the Amercan Legion have a part. Its members marched to the grave of Comrade Harold E. Pentz and after a brief service, terminated with a salute by the post's firing squad, the Legionaires returned to the principal program which ended with the singing of "America," a benediction, and sounding of "Taps." [38]

Gradually this service became the obligation of the Legion veterans and by the end of the decade Memorial Day was primarily their responsibility. Perhaps the last occasion in which the G.A.R. had full responsibility was in 1923. The following year saw the beginning of the end of the Corporal Rihl's leadership. Samuel Eby, in his eighty-sixth year, died on February 23, 1924 and for the first and only time a woman became an officer in this all male establishment. The last

ECHO PILOT REPRINT   ONE OF THE LAST G.A.R. MEMORIAL DAYS   MAY 30, 1963
THOMAS GORDON — FLAG BEARER, S. H. EBY AND DR. F. A. BUSHEY. WILLIAM HOLLINSHEAD, HARRY McGAUGHEY, JOSIAH SHUMAN, JASPER SHEELEY, JEREMIAH HOLLINGER. OTHERS UNIDENTIFIED.

minutes, those of the March 2 meeting, show that Miss Grace Eby was duly elected quartermaster as a replacement for her father. Then on June 26, 1924, at the age of eighty-three, the old warrior, Franklin A. Bushey, passed to his eternal reward. The commander was dead and with him the post died too. Through the years that followed the remaining comrades followed him until there was only one survivor. On May 24, 1931 the annual Memorial Service was held in the Reformed Church with John W. Singer, the only Civil War veteran attending.

This old soldier, a retired auctioneer, lived at his home on East Baltimore Street. Singer was a veteran of the 97th Regiment Pennsylvania Volunteers. He entered the service in 1864 at the age of eighteen as a substitute for a draftee and saw action at Petersburg and in the North Carolina fighting that led to Joseph Johnston's surrender to Sherman.

Upon his discharge in September of 1865, Singer returned to his home in Washington Township. After marrying Susan Young the couple moved to the Greencastle community where they lived the rest of their lives. Susan died in 1925 and eight years later, on February 6, John W. Singer passed from the earthly scene. His death marked the end of that long blue line that began its march to war seventy-two years before. His passing erased the last living memory of those from the area who left their homes and families to preserve the Union. The few non-veterans who remembered something of these years of conflict would soon be gone too and over the decades that followed the curtain of time gradually closed on much of this sad episode in the nation's history. [39]

Corporal Rihl Post 438 before its demise passed its torch to the American Legion Post 373. The records — minutes, correspondence, resolutions, reports, newspaper clippings, and other papers still remain in the Legion's custody. The post's limited library of Civil War books and pamphlets, along with certain regalia and other paraphernalia, have been preserved by the Carbaugh Post. Last, but most importantly, the Legionaries preserved the tradition of Memorial Day. After the Second World War the newly formed Harry D. Zeigler Post of the Veterans of Foreign Wars joined in continuing a custom that had its origin in the grief and heartaches of all those whose sons had died in the war that passed this way more than a century before.

APPENDIX I

From Jacob Hoke's Reminiscences of War

THE ROLL OF HONOR; OR THE NAMES OF THOSE WHO FIRST FLEW TO THE RESCUE OF THEIR IMPERILLED COUNTRY FROM FRANKLIN COUNTY.

The Chambers Artillery, after arriving at Camp Curtin, near Harrisburg, was divided into two companies, Lieut. Doebler taking command of the second company formed. These two companies, with one other, composed mostly of men from Greencastle and St. Thomas and under command of J. G. Elder, were attached to the Second Regiment Pennsylvania Volunteers. F. S. Stumbaugh, Esq., of our town, was made Colonel of this regiment; _____ Irwin, of _____, Lieut. Colonel; Jas. S. Given, of West Chester, Major; Isaac S. Waterburry, of Harrisburg, Ad'jt. General; D. Watson Rowe, Serg't. Major; Isadore A. Stumbaugh, Quarter Master Serg't; John A. King, M.D., Acting Asst. Surgeon.

The names and residences of the persons composing these three companies, are as follows:

LIST OF CO. A, 2ND REGT. PENNA. VOLUNTEERS.

Capt. Peter B. Housum, Chambersburg
1st Lieut., George Stitzell, Chambersburg
2nd Lieut., K. Shannon Taylor, Chambersburg
1st Sergt., Thomas G. Cochran, Chambersburg
2nd Sergt., Sam'l McDowell, Chambersburg
3rd Sergt., Adam Smith, Chambersburg
4th Sergt., Bruce Lambert, Chambersburg
1st Corporal, Allison McDowell, Chambersburg
2nd Corporal, Thomas Myers, Chambersburg
3rd Corporal, John F. Snyder, Chambersburg
4th Corporal, Jno. F. Pensinger, Chambersburg

PRIVATES — *Chambersburg*

Justina McGuigan
Josephus Senseny
Alexander Flack
John F. Metz
George S. Houser
James C. Sample
R. B. Fisher
Jacob W. Miles
John C. Gerbie
Thomas W. Merklein
Robert F. McCurdy
Frederick Shinefield
Richard Hardin
John W. Jones
John C. Hullinger
John King
Geo. J. Ludwig
Jacob Lutz
Geo. S. Eyster
Abraham A. Huber
David W. Newman

Peter Danner
James Shuman
Lewis Monath
Francis Donovan
Ephraim Finetrock
George Goetman
Peter Myers
Edmund Ferry
Thomas Durborow
Wm. Harmony
Ernest Causler
Allison Whitstone
Edgar D. Washabaugh
Janus E. Cook
Franklin Yeager
John A. Seiders
Samuel A. Stouffer
James Aughinbaugh
Frank Fortesene
Harry Fortesene
Lewis Fisher

Chambersburg (Con't.)
Edward Kline
Frederick Batner
John F. Peiffer
Greenvillage
John Gaff
Franklin D. Ditzlear
Daniel Shatzler
David Wallace
New Franklin
Henry Hannagan
Waynesboro
John E. Walker
John N. Hullinger
Fayetteville
Sylvester Weldy

Walter B. Crawford
Jeremiah Burkholder
Caledonia Iron Works
Alexander J. Stevens
Newville
Wm. B. Over
John B. Johnston
Wm. D. Cobaugh
John P. Wagner
James C. Eckenrode
Jonas B. Huntsberger
McConnellsburg
David Hoke
Ed. E. Fairweather
John H. Neely

LIST OF CO. B, 2ND REGT. PENNA. VOLUNTEERS.

Captain, John Doebler, Chambersburg
1st Lieut., George Miles, Chambersburg
2nd Lieut., Geo. W. Welsh, Chambersburg
1st Sergt., Benjamin Rnodes, Chambersburg
2nd Sergt., Peter Ackerman, Chambersburg
3rd Sergt., Joseph Thomas, Chambersburg
4th Sergt., George Cook, Chambersburg
1st Corpl., Henry Melvin, Chambersburg
2nd Corpl., Alexander C. Landis, Chambersburg
3rd Corpl., Henry McCauley, Shippensburg
4th Corpl., Porter J. Brown, Chambersburg

PRIVATES — *Chambersburg*
Hamilton Spence
Theophilus Stratton
James Ridgley
Jeremiah Smith
Peter Dorty
John Elser
Samuel K. Snively
Franklin Gipe
Michael Harmony
Edward Monath
Wm. Fentiman
Emanuel H. Forney
Samuel Uglow
James Borland
Isaac S. Noel
(Honorably discharged)
Charles Jones
I. A. Stumbaugh
(Transferred to Col's. Staff)
John Hicks
John H. Frederick
Hugh Brotherton
Dennis Riley
John J. Hershberger

Jacob Jones
Wm. Henneberger
Robert Smith
Wm. Eaker
John King
Charles Shanebrook
Frank Kline
Geo. W. Baker
Robert W. Moore
Jacob W. Smith
James McGeehan
John Fisher
P. A. J. Snider
Harrison Hutton
Adolphus McGuigan
John S. White
Wm. T. Smith
Peter Snider
John Stoner
Quincy
Harrison Seabrooks
John W. Bryson
Wm. H. Pence

John Pence
Geo. Seabrooks
Newville
Samuel Hardy
Isaac Hardy
Scotland
Lanson Coleman
Greenwood
Jeremiah Perri
Fayetteville
Wm. T. Hazlett
Mercersburg
Martin Louman
George W. Daley
David L. Hoffman
Loudon
Alexander McCurdy

McConnellsburg
Alexander Prosser
Samuel Shoemaker
Strasburg
Walker Shearer
Springville Lancaster Co.
J. H. Martin
Fairviewtownship, York County
Peter Corden
Edgar Wolf
(Honorably discharged)
Alexandria, Huntingdon County
Edgar G. McLaughlin
New York
Julius C. Ladd
Poland
John Swuninski

LIST OF CO. C, 2ND REGT. PENNA. VOLUNTEERS

Captain, J. G. Elder, St. Thomas
1st Lieut., J. B. Strickler, Greencastle
2nd Lieut., Jacob West, St. Thomas
Q. M. Sergt., T. J. Reilly, Greencastle
1st Sergt., W. B. Shirk, Greencastle
2nd Sergt., G. H. Miller, Greencastle

3rd Sergt., Jacob Snyder, Loudon
4th Sergt., G. A. Pool, Greencastle
1st Corpl., T. J. Koonse, Greencastle
2nd Corpl., Christian Burkholder, Loudon
3rd Corpl., Thomas Hill, St. Thomas
4th Corpl., David C. Shaffer, Greencastle

PRIVATES — *Greencastle*
Edwin P. Byers
Geo. Bence
Charles Byers
Cor. Barnhisel
John B. Byers
Wm. Byers
Geo. Bush
James B. Comins
Emanuel Carpenter
James Gaff
David Hess
John F. Koonse
John H. Logue
Geo. F. Missavey
John A. Marshal
Jessie K. Norris
Miller H. Pensinger
Samuel H. Prather
John E. Pool
John G. Rowe
Abraham H. Shealy
Emanuel F. Shatzer
Wm. Shorts
David Tracy
Jacob Watson

Joseph Wildern
Wm. A. Weyant
Wm. A. Wildern
Leander B. Zook
Waynesboro
Joel Haffly
Jacob H. Funk
Cyrus Gossert
Henry Grabill
John Mickle
David Morehead
St. Thomas
Samuel Antrim
Jacob Detrich
John Ferry
Wm. A. Hosler
Jeremiah Martin
Samuel Bennecker
Geo. Sulavan
Alexander Speer
Wm. H. Snow
George Vorler
Marion
George Butts
John H. Stickel

Upton
  Thomas Dayley
  John Doubleman
  Joseph Stoner
Mercersburg
  David E. Hays
  John S. King
  John Shatzer
Chambersburg
  Christian Miller
Cashtown
  Simon Rupert

Loudon
  John H. Unger
  James McElrea
  Henry M. Spidle
Gettysburg
  Wm. G. Little
  Geo. Little
Leitersburg, Md.
  Martin Morgan
  Wm. A. Cassatt

APPENDIX II

Patterson's Army Organization

From Jacob Hoke's Reminiscences of War

First Division — Brev. Maj.-Gen. George Cadwallader commanding, consisting of First, Third and Fourth Brigades.

First Brigade — Col. George H. Thomas, Second United States Cavalry, commanding, consisting of four companies United States Cavalry, and First Philadelphia City Troop, Capt. James; battalion of artillery and infantry, Capt. Doubleday; First Rhode Island Regiment and battery, Col. Burnside; Sixth Pennsylvania Regiment, Col. Nagle; Twenty-first Pennsylvania Regiment, Col. Ballier; Twenty-third Pennsylvania Regiment, Co. Dare.

Third Brigade — Brig.-Gen. E. C. Williams commanding, consisting of Seventh Regiment Pennsylvania Volunteers, Col. Irwin; Eighth Regiment Pennsylvania Volunteers, Col. Emly; Tenth Regiment, Pennsylvania Volunteers, Col. Meredith; Twentieth Regiment, Scott Legion, Col. Gray.

Fourth Brigade — Col. D. S. Miles, United States Infantry, commanding, consisting of Second and Third United States Infantry, Maj. Sheppard; Ninth Pennsylvania, Col. Longenecker; Thirteenth Pennsylvania, Col. Rowley; Sixteenth Pennsylvania, Col. Zeigle.

Second Division — Maj.-Gen. Wm. H. Keim, commanding, consisting of the Second and Fifth Brigades.

Second Brigade — Brig.-Gen. G. C. Wyncoop, commanding, consisting of First Pennsylvania, Col. Yohe; Second Pennsylvania, Col. Stumbaugh; Third Pennsylvania, Col. Minier; Twenty-fourth Pennsylvania Regiment, Col. Owens.

Fifth Brigade — Brig.-Gen. J. S. Negley, commanding, consisting of First Wisconsin, Col. Starkweather; Fourth Connecticut, Col. Woodhouse, Eleventh Pennsylvania, Col. Jarrett; Fourteenth Pennsylvania, Col. Johnson; Fifthteenth Pennsylvania, Col. Oakford.

APPENDIX III

From Greencastle's "The Pilot" — August 12, 1862

Roll of Honor — Below we present the Muster Roll of the first Greencastle Company. This is an array of names, of which we are all justly proud. The members are young, but they are active, energetic, and intelligent. Some changes of officers have been made since the company left here, on the 6th inst.; it was them commanded by Capt. D. W. Rowe, (since chosen Major of the Regiment), 1st Lieut. A. R. Davison, and 2nd Lieut., J. W. P. Reid. The election of officers consequent upon the promotion of their Captain, was favorably received by every one, and grace the most perfect satisfaction to every member of the Company:

OFFICERS

Captain, Andrew R. Davison
First Lieutenant, John G. Rowe
Second Lieutenant, John W. P. Reid
First Sergeant, William Snyder
Second Sergeant, John H. Logue
Third Sergeant
Fourth Sergeant, Simon W. Rupley
Fifth Sergeant, Henry Strickler

First Corporal, Emanuel Hawbecker
Second Corporal, William C. Byers
Third Corporal, Scott K. Snively
Fourth Corporal, Thomas Daily
Fifth Corporal, John M. D. Detrich
Sixth Corporal, Joshua K. Hood
Seventh Corporal, George F. Missavy
Eighth Corporal, David W. Buchanan

MUSICIANS

John H. Byers   William Snodie
Wagoner — George W. Bartle

PRIVATES

Appenzeller, David K.
Alexander, George W.
Bert, Adam C.
Bemisderfer, John S.
Beck, William H.
Byers, John B.
Barr, James W.
Bartle, Henry
Byers, George M.
Bushey, Calvin
Brown, John M.C.
Buchanan, James II
Baughman, Cyrus
Cleverstone, Daniel D.
Crooks, William W.
Colby, George
Donothan, James H.
Davison, John B.
Daniels, William
Eachus, James C.
Eyler, George W.
Ferry, John W.
Fry, Charles M.
Fry, Jonas M.
Gardner, Philip L.
Gordon, James C. R.
Gordon, Jeremiah C.

Hollar, J. Wilson
Hammel, Albertus K.
Hollman, Joseph
Hyssong, Jeremiah G.
Ilginfritz, Isaiah
Kreps, Michael H.
Kunkel Charles H.
Kuhn, John W.
Keims, William T.
Lear, Jacob
Lowe, John
Lowe, Philip C.F.
Laughlin, Henry
Moorehead, James C.
Marshal, John H.
Mowers, Samuel
Mitchell, James
Newcomer, Charles H.
Palmer, John
Parker, William H.
Palmer, Samuel
Potter, George H.
Palmer, Charles H.
Pensinger, Lazarus
Pool, Jacob W.
Palmer, Simon
Pensinger, David N.
Pawling, George W.

Pentz David
Robinson, John
Reymer, Michael D.
Rule, David
Rupert, William T.
Ritter, David McF.
Ritter, Jacob
Reneker, Samuel
Shook, George W.
Salmon, James
Shirey, James
Stoner, Joel
Shirey, Charles H.

Snively, William H.
Shoafle, Amos J.
Stoner, Joseph C.
Spidel, Henry M.
Shatzer, Joseph
Unger, Jacob A.
Valentine, Gilbert
Winkfield, Jacob
Wiser, Reuben
Wilders, William
Wagner, John M.
Zeigler, G. Frederick
Zimmerman, Andrew

OFFICERS OF COMPANY B

Captain, William H. Davison, Franklin county
First Lieutenant, Henry M. Hoke, Fulton county
Second Lieutenant, James Pott, Fulton county
First Sergeant, Henry S. Wishart, Fulton county
Second Sergeant, I. Y. Atherton, Franklin county
Third Sergeant, John B. Lesher, Fulton county
Fourth Sergeant, Joseph Myers, Franklin county
Fifth Sergeant, J. L. P. Detrich, Franklin county
First Corporal, L. W. Speilman, Franklin county
Second Corporal, S. D. Anderson, Fulton county
Third Corporal, W. H. Weyant, Franklin county
Fourth Corporal, J. H. Swisher, Fulton county
Fifth Corporal, William Orth, Fulton county
Sixth Corporal, C. G. Glenn, Franklin county
Seventh Corporal, Peter Wesner, Franklin county
Eighth Corporal, Jas. Cummins, Franklin county

DRUMMER
John S. Bush, Franklin county

FIFER
Jared Irwin, Fulton county

AMBULANCE DRIVER
James S. Hoke, Fulton county

Privates in Co. B, 126th Reg., from Franklin County

Abbott Thomas J
Allabaugh S G
Baker Andrew
Bernhisel Reid W
Brunner George
Bowman Abram
Bowman Jonathan
Cleary Thomas J
Cleary James O
Conrad Moses
Crunkilton Robert
Chambers Thomas J
Felteberger John
Forman John M
Gossart S E
Greenawalt Jacob

Hager C C
Jacobs Adam
Kissecker M W
Lininger Reuben
Long Philip
Long William
Missavy John
Martin Lazarus
Peddicord Charles W
Peddicord John M
Ruthrauff Henry
Shrader George
Sleighter Amos
Shatzer Joseph
Stine John
Showalter Samuel

Wilson James
Witherspoon D C

Wilders James
Young Carlton

Privates in Co. B, 126th Reg., from Fulton County

Boener Adam
Barnett Joseph E
Clevenger A
Denisar Daniel
Deaver Jesse A
Edwards John
Finney William
Glenn George W
Glenn Andrew
Glass Daniel
Gordon David
Grove William A
Grove Emanuel
Gossert Samuel C
Hoopengarner A
Kendall J F
Keith Wilson R
Kelso D W
Lindsay J Mc
Litten Richmond
Lamberson D A

Logan William C
Moore William H
Mellott Norris
Mellott George W
Oliver John
Pittman B F
Parlett John
Richardson A C
Salkeld S W
Sterrett M. Nead
Smith William D
Tritle Luthur D
Tritle Jacob M
Traux William
Taylor John
Unger William P
Unger Samuel
Walker William
Wright Paul F
Woy James H
Woodcock W W

APPENDIX IV

REYMER'S POEM

Greencastle's weekly paper featured occasional poems written sometimes by the editors or readers. One of the most prolific contributors to "The Pilot" was Michael D. Reymer. While with the 126th, he became a member of the provo marshall's staff and apparently had plenty of spare time to compose lengthy accounts of the regiment's experiences. Mostly in prose form, he reported to the Greencastle paper, but after the Battle of Fredericksburg he contributed a poem entitled "The Charge of Tyler's Brave Brigade." It appeared in the February 24, 1863 edition.

THE CHARGE OF TYLER'S BRAVE BRIGADE

Lay the dead in hundreds,
   Scattered o'er the plain,
Groaned and shrieked the wounded,
   More num'rous than the slain.
Marye's crest is still unscaled —
   There still the Rebs remain.
Thrice charged the Union army —
   Thrice were their efforts vain.

Shall night her ebon curtains drop,
   And hide these scenes of woe
Sure blood enough already
   Has shed the murd'rous foe!
Not yet! Still another order!
   With twilights dark'ning shade, —
"Charge the works — the first brigade!"
   This order Humphrey made.

"Forward boys" — the bugle sounds!
A line is formed, and onward bounds
To death, or still more painful wounds —
    Tyler's brave brigade.
Hills to the right of them,
Hills to the left of them,
Hills in the front of them,
    Cannon-crowned all.

Vollied and thundered,
    These weapons of hell.
Shrieked in succession
    The murderous shell.
Whistled the minnie ball,
Whistled — brave victims fall,
Whistled, shrieked, thundered all,
    These weapons of hell.

Into the valley of death,
    For some one had blundered;
Charged Tyler's brave brigade —
    Brave sixteen hundred.
Bravely did they charge, and well.
    Spectators wondered.
Bravely stood the shrieking shell,
Stood, though half their number fell —
    Brave sixteen hundred.

No ancient field of battle
    Can boast more honored dead:
No man e'er fought more bravely —
    No soldiers better led.
Hearts that swelled with country's love,
Hearts as true as God above,
Hearts, nor death nor fear could move
    Tyler's brave brigade.

"When can their glory fade!
Oh the wild charge they made,
    All the world wondered.
Honor the charge they made."
Honor Tyler's brigade,
    Brave sixteen hundred.

APPENDIX V

THE FLAG WAVING GIRL

The story of General George Pickett's gallantry towards the flag waving girl on North Carlisle Street during the invasion of 1863 fired a controversy that stretched into the early decades of the next century. The first recollection of this event was noted in remarks made at the Gettysburg Reunion of 1887, by Colonel William Aylett of Pickett's division. The colonel recalled the flag waving incident in a speech prepared for the occasion. "Why the bravest woman I ever saw was a Pennsylvania girl who defied Pickett's whole division as we marched through the little town called Greencastle. She had a United States flag as an apron which she defiantly waved up and down as our columns passed by her and dared us to take it from her." The colonel continued to describe Pickett's chivalry and how his regiment presented arms and cheered him with a "good old fashioned rebel yell."

The "Harrisburg Telegram" became interested in Aylett's story and put a reporter on it to discover the identity of the "bravest woman" the colonel had ever seen. He talked to Robert E. Garrett, of Baltimore, who was an officer in the Fourth Alabama regiment, a part of Pickett's division. He recalled the girl waving the flag and described her as "dark haired with a dark complexion." He also located the house on North Carlisle Street where she lived.

Then an affadavit, dated September 17, 1887, was received from John Boyd of Company K of the Fifty Seventh Virginia Volunteers. His unit had camped south of the town the night before Pickett's men marched through Greencastle. Boyd identified the girl as Dolly Harris, whose father, James, was a cabinet maker. The Virginian had

PICKETT SALUTES THE FLAG

known the Harris family before the war and had received permission from his commander, General Armistead, to visit them prior to resuming the march the next morning. He was with Dolly and her parents when Pickett's division began passing the Harris home and remembered the entire incident. "An earlier officer had told her to take off the flag apron. Dolly replied, "Not for you or any of your men." He raised his hat and passed on. Boyd's statement continued, "The next I remember well, was General Pickett and his staff. As they passed Dolly waved the stars and stripes at them. General Pickett saluted her and the boys all along the line gave her one of the old rebel yells."

A later affadavit was given the "Telegram" by Dolly's mother which agreed with the incident described by the former Confederates. Then the newspaper sent a representative to Waynesboro to interview the woman who was Dolly Harris before her marriage to John R. Lesher. By then, September of 1887, she was the mother of four sons and two daughters. Her husband was a veteran and received a pension. Mrs. Lesher related the Pickett incident and her story coincided with what Colonel Aylett and the other soldiers had said.

But the October 15, 1891 issue of Greencastle's "Valley Echo" carried an account of Pickett and the flag waving incident along with the tribute given the Greencastle girl by Colonel Aylett four years earlier. At the time Charles W. Gaff was editor of the town's weekly and he identified the local heroine as Sadie Smith, daughter of J. R. Smith, one of the town's commission merchants during the war years. The Smiths lived about a block beyond the Harris home. Gaff's promotion of Sadie Smith included a poem that depicted her as a relentless foe of the Rebels; that every soul in Greencastle went into hiding when Pickett's division appeared; and that she alone stood in the path of the invaders hurling accusations of disloyalty — "defiant in the army's track."

Could there have been two flag waving maidens? If there were, General Pickett saw only one. This was established when McClure's Magazine began publishing, in serial form, the letters he had written to his fiancee, LaSalle Corbell, during the war. He married his beloved "Sallie" after the war and she had saved each "billet doux."

General Pickett died in 1875 and sometime after his death Samuel S. McClure secured the rights to print the letters. His magazine began publication in 1893 and within a short time the letters began to appear in print under the title "Heart of a Soldier." One of the missives told of the march through Greencastle and the flag waving incident. He wrote that while he and his men were passing a "vine bowered home, a young girl rushed out on the porch and waved a United States flag. Then, either fearing that it might be taken from her or finding it too large and unwieldy, she fastened it around her as an apron, and taking hold of it on each side, and waving it in defiance, called out with all the strength of her girlish voice and all the courage of her brave young heart; 'Traitors — traitors — traitors come and take this flag, the man of you who dares!'

"Knowing that many of my men were from a section of the country which had been within the enemy lines, and fearing lest some might forget their manhood, I took off my hat and bowed to her, saluted her flag and then turned, facing the men who felt and saw my spoken order. And don't you know that they were all Virginians and didn't forget it, and that almost every man lifted his cap and cheered the little maiden who, though she kept waving her flag, ceased calling us traitors, till, finally letting it drop in front of her, she cried out: 'Oh I wish — I wish I had a rebel flag — I'd wave that too.' "

Pickett continued his letter by telling his fiancee that the Greencastle Yankee girl reminded him of her. His closing observation was "we left the little girl standing there with the flag gathered up in her arms, as if too scared to be waved, now that even the enemy had done it reverance." The general's letter adds only one ingredient to the story. He identified the home as one that was "vine bowered." He left no name or a description of the girl. Those who knew Dolly Harris agreed with Robert Garrett's description. She was dark haired with a dark complexion.

Although the "Harrisburg Telegram" was satisfied that its investigation had established beyond question that it was Dolly Harris, Editor Gaff continued to maintain the heroine was Sadie Smith and for years Alfred Smith, her brother, insisted that it was his sister that Pickett and Aylett had written and talked about. Mr. Smith, affectionately known as "Bones," took every opportunity at his disposal to continue arguing that the honor belonged to his sister but as the years passed fewer and fewer people seemed to care.

However, C. C. Kauffman was not about to let the matter rest. His Progressive News of November 29, 1912 carried a headline in half inch letters "The Honor Justly Belongs to Dolly Harris." He then proceeded to cover his paper's front page and at least half of a continuing page with the "Harrisburg Telegram" documentation of September, 1887. For all intents the matter was settled and Mr. Kauffman would hear no more of any other heroine. Henceforth and forevermore it was Dolly Harris.

Yet the poets would not let the matter rest. For at least half a century poems appeared in veteran's journals, magazines, and local papers. The first, of course, appeared in the "Valley Echo" of October 15, 1891. It is assumed that Mr. Gaff was the author.

HEROIC SADIE SMITH

From Fredericksburg and Chancellorsville
    Lee's victory flushed brigades
Rush into Shenandoah's vale
    From Northern battle raids.
Nor are they hindered anywhere
    By Union horse or foot
Though wild Potomac hurls her flood
    Across their daring route.

Milroy, McReynolds, Kelley flee,
    And Maryland is bared
To shock and Rebel heel and hoof —
    Defenseless, unprepared.
Greencastle reached by Pickett's men,
    On Pennsylvania soil,
Sets Northern hearts abeat with fear
    And loyal blood aboil.

Deserted streets and empty homes
    Proclaim the dreadful fear,
While e'en the bravest doubtless feel
    When conquering hosts appear.
Yet one though fear may blanch her cheek
    Stands firm, nor does she feel
Like yielding, spirit crushed and awed,
    At flash of Southern steel.

Her face was fair — for goddess fit,
    Her form — the sculptors mould,
And what she was in soul and race
    Her every feature told.
Yet neither form nor feature was
    Her most commanding grace,
For spirit high and courage bold
    To such yield never place.

Defiant in the army's track
    She stood, nor yielded way —
Proud-poised before the tramping hosts
    Like wounded doe at bay.
Alone? 'Tis surely courage mad
    Her friends, and where were they?
At clank of hoof and tramp of foot
    They trembling slunk away.

A thousand pairs of soldier eyes
    Were fastened on her now;
Nor less to them her beauty was
    For crimson-mantled brow.
Nor less indeed befitting seemed
    The garb she had devised;
The stars and stripes — her count
    An apron improvised.

Though hurrying toward Gettysburg,
    For conquest and for fame
To fullest halt these dust-brown ranks
    Before the maiden came.
Saluted where she stood
    Surrendered! Yes indeed!
More conquered now than afterward
    They were by gallant Meade.

Who is this fair Semiramus —
    This new Joan of Arc?
Her rightful place on history's page
    We fain at last would mark.
No mists surround her origin
    We know her kin and kith
Nor sounding titles aught could add
    To loyal Sadie Smith.

What, though, for fun and banter
    Some little chaffing tried,
Suggesting that a soldier brave
    Bespoke her for his bride.
At this she caught her apron-flag
    And flaunting it on high,
With crimson cheek and curling lip,
    Flung at them this reply:

"While clouds of dark disloyalty
    Hang sullen o'er my land
He freely must this flag accept
    Who e'er would claim my hand!"
And one more bold — less manly though —
    Requested ardent drink;
"A good supply of meade," she said
    "Is hereabout, I think."

To these replies, — so apt, so brave —
    The ranks sent back a cheer
And Pickett, with salute adieu,
    Passed on and left her here.
Left her in proud possession of
    This well-defended field,
Not much adverse to such a foe
    In gallantry to yield.

For daughters brave like this fair maid
    America gives thanks,
Depending on them more for peace
    Than on her armied ranks.
May Heaven multiply to us
    Their number o'er and o'er,
And God bestow upon us peace
    Unbroken evermore.

She honors, too, those gallant men
    Who hush the battle's rage
To offer at the hero's shrine
    Some simple, worthy pledge.
With Pickett's and with Aylett's then
    We'll write fair Sadie's name —
Heroic trio, blazoned high
    Upon the scroll of fame.

GREENCASTLE JENNY — A BALLAD OF '63

In the November, 1913 edition of the magazine known as the "Confederate Veteran," there appeared a poem by Helen Gray Cone, a professor of English literature at Hunter College. Its title brought into the controversy a third name, — "Jenny." The poem was called "Greencastle Jenny — A Ballad of '63." Every girl in town seemed to be getting into the act. However, the author apparently did not know of the local controversy or if she did know she was not about to be drawn into it. The first stanza of the "Ballad" explains that she "was a slip of a girl — we'll call her Jenny." Thus the identity is fictitious, but the story seems to be the same.

On Greencastle's streets was a stream of steel
    From the slanting muskets the soldiers bore,
And the scarred earth trembled and shook to feel
    The tramp and rumble of Longstreet's Corps.
The bands were blaring "The Bonny Blue Flag,"
    And the banners they bore were a motley many,
And watching the gray column wind and drag
    Was a slip of a girl — we'll call her Jenny.

Pickett's Virginians were marching through,
    Supple as steel and brown as leather,
Rusty and dusty of hat and shoe,
    Wonted to war and hunger and weather.
Fearless, peerless, an army's pride —
    Better soldiers the world saw never —
Marching away through the sweet Junetide
    To death and disaster — and fame forever.

A slip of a girl (what matter her name?)
    With her cheeks aflame and her lips a-quiver
As she stood and gazed with a loyal shame
    At the steady flow of the steely river,
Till a storm grew black in the hazel eyes
    Time had not tamed nor a lover sighed for,
And she ran and girded her, apronwise,
    With the flag she loved and her brother died for.

Out of the doorway they saw her start
    (Pickett's Virginians were marching through),
The hot little foolish hero heart
    Armored with stars on their field of blue.
Clutching the folds of red and white,
    Stood she and bearded those ranks of theirs,
Shouting shrilly with all her might:
    "Come and take it, the man that dares!"

Rose from the ranks a rippling cheer;
　　Pickett saluted, his bold eyes beaming,
Doffing his hat like a cavalier,
　　His tawny locks in the warm breeze streaming.
Fierce little Jenny, her courage fell
　　As she heard the sound of the friendly laughter,
And Greencastle's street gave forth the yell
　　That Gettysburg slope heard again soon after.

So they cheered for the flag they fought
　　With the sturdy pride of the stubborn fighter,
Loving the brave as brave men ought,
　　And never a finger was raised to fright her.
And so they marched, though they knew it not,
　　Through the sweet green roads to the shock infernal,
To the hell of the shell and the plunging shot —
　　And a fame that has left them a name eternal.

And she felt, as she hid her burning face,
　　There had hid at the root of her childish daring
A trust in the men of her own brave race
　　And a secret faith in the foe's forbearing.
And she sobbed and sobbed till the rumbling gun
　　And the rhythmic tread of the marching men
Were a memory only, and day was done.
　　And the stars were out in the blue again.

Thank God that the day of the sword is done,
And the stars are out in the blue again.

THE BRAVEST GIRL IN TOWN

In the same era W. W. Jacobs, assumed to be a resident of the Waynesboro area, wrote the poem, "The Bravest Girl in Town." He identifies the young lady as Dolly Harris and seems to follow the evidence developed by the Harrisburg Journal.

　　　You may write of heroes on land or sea,
　　　And of knights and deeds of chivalry,
　　　Brave men who struck at tyrants laws,
　　　And martyrs who fell in Freedom's cause
　　　Of warriors who fought for wrong or right
　　　Clad in their armor grim or bright

2. But here is a maiden, young and fair
　　With her rosy cheeks and jet black hair;
　　Her only weapon, that piercing dart,
　　A Union-loving and contrite heart
　　At the trampling sound of Picketts command,
　　She rushed to the front and took her stand.

3. She donned her apron, the "Flag of the Free,"
　　And stood on the sidewalk defiantly.
　　"Take this flag if you dare!" said she,
　　Flaunting the emblem of Liberty;
　　While twice ten thousand Southern men
　　There marching by our heroine then.

4. Struck by her courage and bravery rare,
   Take that flag, — there was none would dare.
   But General Pickett in admiration,
   Doffed his hat in salutation.
   And twice ten thousand Southern troops
   Presented arms with cheers and whoops.

5. Then to the maiden brave and true,
   To Dolly Harris, they bade adieu.
   While still she waved the "Stripes and Stars."
   To the passing troops with their "Stars and Bars."
   Still firm as a Roman sentry there,
   Stood the maiden, loyal, true, and fair.

6. To Barbara Fritchie and Elizabeth —
   Are written deeds of glory and fame.
   And unto Greencastles bravest maid
   Be a word of praise and honor and right
   That may shine forever bright.

DOLLIE HARRIS AT GREENCASTLE

Next came a poetic rendition by J. Howard West. It appeared in a publication — "The Veteran's Campfire" under the heading "Martial Recitations, Heroic, Pathetic, and Humorous." The verses carried the title "Dollie Harris at Greencastle." How Mr. West identified his heroine may never be known. C. C. Kauffman must have applauded Mr. West's effort as well as that of Mr. Jacobs.

For two long days the ranks in gray
　Had surged past town and farm;
Lee was upon his northward way!
　With hot and wild alarm,
Across the Susquehanna pressed
　In endless caravan,
Those who with eyes devoid of rest,
　From shadowing terrors ran.

The breathless farmer with his stock
　In dust-enveloped ranks;
The hapless contrabands who flock
　To seek its Pisgah banks;
The merchant in tumultuous haste
　To save what wealth he can;
With fancies wild of land laid waste
　Clan rushes after clan.

The sweetest valley 'neath the sun
　Is rent with war's alarms,
As from the fields already won,
　The gleaming Southern arms
Press on in solid miles of steel;
　Then flows from gate to gate,
From town to town the trembling peal
　Of mingled fear and hate.

At length battalions all controlled
　By one great master mind,
Swift toward one common hub are rolled,
　The foe in blue to find;
At last of all the grand array,
　With steady, martial tread,
Five thousand veterans clad in gray
　With Pickett at their head.

For hours they poured in mass along,
　No coward men are they,
That soon 'mid shrapnel's shrieking song
　Shall join the ensanguined fray!
Along the quiet village streets
　They came. Without command
Aghast at what their vision greets,
　One impulse checked the band:

Aye, proudly, bravely stood she there,
　Among the mighty throng.
"God bless her!" was the muttered prayer
　Of many a soldier strong,
Whose moistened eye bespoke the love
　Still in his heart concealed
For the flag that floats our land above,
　Which that moment had revealed.

With one accord Virginia's sons,
   Whose valor oft had flamed
"Mid bursting shells and heated guns,
   In thrilling words exclaimed:
"Three hearty cheers the fearless maid
   Has won by bravery;
The flag in which she is arrayed
   We'll greet with three times three!"

Our flag now waves o'er all our land;
   No shock of war's alarms,
Nor hostile raid, nor flaming brand,
   Nor frantic call to arms
Disturb this peaceful valley fair,
   With heavenly bounty blessed;
From former foeman comes the prayer,
   With fervent lips expressed:

God bless the maiden fair and sweet;
   Let still the flag of love,
When oft in unison we meet,
   Soar blue and gray above;
Cursed be for aye the heart or hand
   That mars its stars or fame,
Whilst rings forever through the land
   Brave Dollie Harris' name.

DOLLY HARRIS

Another literary effort, entitled "Dolly Harris," was written by George W. Kettoman, the south mountain bard, of Highfield, Md.

The heroine is depicted as an extremely hostily young woman, hiding a dagger in the folds of the flag and ready to defend Old Glory to the end.

Twas on a sunny day in June
And wearing through the afternoon,
That General Pickett, under Lee,
Led up his Southern Chivalry
Through old Greencastle's loyal town,
And "stars and bars' and bayonets shone,
When out ran Dolly Harris true
Wrapped in the old red, white and blue,
One hand lay hidden in a fold
And clasped a dagger in its hold,
'Come, tear this from my loins,' she said —
'The wretch that dares it — he is dead!
Vile traitors to your father's trust,
You should long since bit the dust.
Your whole cur'ed army I defy,
And I shall scorn you till I die!'

She flung back her tangled hair,
Her eyes put on an angry glare;
The pendant portion of her flag
She shook and sneered the 'rebel rag.'
Louder she shouted in her wrath,
'Why do you seem to shun my path?
Come take the flag you have betrayed, —
'Halt,' said the Southern general. 'Halt!
Return salute for such assault!
Present arms! She's a noble maid,
A true American, ' he said,
Five thousand rifles glittered clear,
Five thousand men sent up a cheer
For her, the bravest of the brave.
Unawed by prison cell or grave.

THE LITTLE GREENCASTLE GIRL

There may have been other poetic treatments of the flag waving incident but the final verse in this anthology is that of Moody Rock, a well known teacher in the schools of Montgomery Township. It appeared in the Mercersburg Journal of May, 1928. This was the same year that Pickett's letters to LaSalle Corbell appeared in book form under the title, "Soldier of the South." Mr. Rock may have been inspired by the general's letter which described the Greencastle encounter with Dolly Harris. Note: Mrs John Lesher (Dolly Harris) died February 17, 1906 and was buried in Chambersburg's Cedar Grove Cemetery on February 21, 1906 with military honors by officers of the Housum G.A.R. Post.

Up the valley with pipe and drum
The ranks of the invaders boisterously come,
Through Greencastle one day in June,
Marching in rhythm to a Southern Tune.
In endless lines these ranks of gray
Through Antrim's metropolis vend their way.
What troops are these to draw such attention
Who later in history get special mention?
Who march along with such precision,
Pickett's Division — Pride of the Old Dominion,
Inbred with spirit to conquer or die
As many did on the Third of July,
Flower of manhood — gallantly lead
By Pettigrew, Kemper and Armistead
But suddenly the ranks falter and stumble
The song of "Dixie" becomes a mumble
By the vine bowered home as they pass
Stands waving Old Glory, a lass,
Parents and friends fearing at heart
Lest by this act, trouble should start.
Call, "Traitirs" — Come and take
This flag your sires struggled to make.
Pickett visioning a Southern Beauty
Rides forward and does his duty.
Lest forgetting manhood they should dare
Accept the challenge of the maiden fair
Bows and salutes the flag of the free
Which stands for virtue and liberty
Showed his chivalry and saved the day.
From what might have been a disgraceful fray
The maiden respecting such manly virtue
Wished she might wave their flag too.
Forward they march to the edge of town
Where they encamped as sun went down,
The maiden and Pickett both are gone
But virtue and fame of their deed lives on.

APPENDIX VI

MONTEREY FIGHTING

From History of Franklin County — Warner, Beers — 1887

Rouzerville, Penn., October 12, 1886

Mr. J. Fraise Richard,

    Dear Sir: Your favor of the 11th inst. received, and questions answered as far as I can remember. I lived at that time at Fountain Dale, Adams Co., Penna., two miles east of Monterey Springs, on the turnpike leading to Emmittsburg. I found out through a man by the name of James Embley, who came to my place and told me that Lee's wagon train was retreating by way of the Furnace road, a mountain road leading from Fairfield to the turnpike, coming on the pike at the toll-gate near Monterey Springs. That was on Saturday afternoon, about 2 o'clock, July 4, 1863, as near as I can remember.

When I found out that Lee's wagon train was retreating, I mounted a horse and started to inform our cavalry, which I supposed would be at Emmittsburg. But two miles below my place I came to the Yankee pickets, and with them was one of Kilpattick's scouts that I was well acquainted with. I told him of the wagon train retreating: he sent me to Gen. Custer, and Custer sent me to Gen. Kilpatrick. At that time they were just planting a cannon to shell the rebels on McMullin's Hill. When I informed Gen. Kilpatrick he ordered an advance at once to Monterey. I rode with the General as far as my farm, two miles east of Monterey. Just before getting to my place we met a little girl that had just left Monterey. She knew me, and told me to tell the soldiers not to go to Monterey, as the rebels had planted the pike full of cannons in front of Monterey and would kill all the soldiers when they got there. Kilpatrick laughed and remarked that they kept no account of cannons, as they just rode over them. When I got to the gate that goes into my farm I told the General I lived there, and would stop; but he requested me to go with them to Monterey and see the fun; so I went with him. We ran against the rebel pickets at Clermont, a quarter of a mile east of Monterey. It was then getting dark in the evening. After passing Clermont about 150 yards the rebels fired three or four shots with grape and canister, and then pulled up their battery and retreated. I don't think they killed any of Kilpatrick's men with the battery, as they fired too soon, and the grape and canister went over our men's heads; but it made some of our men retreat, and caused a great deal of confusion. I told Kilpatrick if he would dismount a regiment and go down through the edge of the woods, he could flank them and capture the battery. He did so but they had retreated by the time our men got to Monterey.

Kilpatrick asked me which way I thought the wagon train was going, and where I supposed they would strike the river. I told him they could go by Smithsburg and Boonsboro, and cross the river at Sharpsburg, or go by Leitersburg and Hagerstown and cross at Williamsport. He asked me if there was any road that I knew of that I could take a regiment and head off that wagon train. I told him there was. That I could take them by Mount Zion and then down the Raven Rock Hollow and strike Smithsburg, and if they had not taken that road, we could cross to Leitersburg and there we would strike them for certain. It was the 1st Vermont regiment, commanded by Colonel Preston that I was with. When we got to Smithsburg we found everything quiet, as the Rebels had taken the Leitersburg road. The Colonel asked me what was to be done now, as there were no Rebels there. I told him we would find plenty of them before daylight, as we must strike them as Leitersburg. We got to Leitersburg about daybreak on Sunday morning, finding the road crowded with Rebels, cattle, horses, wagons, etc.

The regiment I was with captured a great many prisoners, cattle, horses, etc., and destroyed the wagon train from Leitersburg back to Ringgold. There they met the remainder of Kilpatrick's cavalry. They had destroyed the wagon train from Monterey to Ringgold, a distance of six miles, and from Ringgold to Leitersburg, a distance of three miles more, making nine miles of wagon train captured or burned or destroyed by cutting off wagon tongues and cutting spokes in wheels. I am not able to say how much, if any, of the wagon train was destroyed between Leitersburg and Hagerstown, as I went only as far as Leitersburg with the 1st Vermont regiment, when it divided, part going toward Hagerstown, and part toward Ringgold. I went with the part that went toward Ringgold, as that was on my way home. I left them about 8 o'clock on Sunday morning, and started home by way of Ringgold.

Before I got to Ringgold I was taken by Kilpatrick's pickets. They took me for a Rebel, and all I could say would not change their opinion, as they would not believe anything I said. They took me to the schoolhouse as Ringgold, where the officers had their headquarters; but as soon as the officers saw me they recognized me, having seen me with Kilpatrick the evening before. After leaving Ringgold on my way home, on going up a bill near the farm of George Harbaugh, when I got to the top of the hill the Rebels were coming up the other side. I saw them when I was about 100 yards from them; turned my horse and rode slowly until I got down the hill far enough that they could not see me. Then I ran my horse to the foot of the hill and left the road and got in the woods and got away from them. I kept the woods until I came to the Germantown road, near the Germantown schoolhouse; then took a near cut through the swamp and came out on the Sabillasville road, near Monterey; but the Rebel pickets were stationed near Monterey at a turn in the lane. They saw me first, and had dismounted and gone around the turn of the lane. I could not see them for a very large cherry tree that stood at the corner of the lane. They let me ride up within about sixty yards of them, when four of them stepped around the turn of the lane and told me to halt. There was an orchard on the left side of the road and a high post fence on each side. I knew my horse could not jump the fence, and I did not dare to turn him and go back, as it was a straight lane for a quarter of a mile and they would have easily hit me if I had made the attempt. One of them called to me to dismount, and, as I was near the orchard fence, I "dismounted" over the fence and did some good running from that to the Pine Swamp, about one-fourth of a mile. They shot four times at me, but missed me. I heard the balls whistle over my head, as it was down hill and they shot over me. I lost my horse, saddle and bridle. I was in the swamp only a few minutes until they were there; but as the bushes were very thick, I soon got away from them and kept the woods until I got home, two miles from there. It was then two or three o'clock on Sunday afternoon. I was at home only a few minutes when I saw the Rebel cavalry coming to my house. They took a near cut from Clermont, and came down the old road. They saw me at the same time I saw them. I passed in my front door and out my back door.

My orchard runs right back of my house, and one of my horses was standing under an apple tree near the house. I mounted the horse and got to the mountain before they were aware that I was not in the house. They searched the house from garret to cellar, and told my wife if they found me they would hang me to the first tree they came to. When I got to the mountain I made a halter out of hickory bark, and saved the horse in that way, as they did not find him. I kept myself hid until after the retreat of Lee's army, but lost three horses and nine head of cattle by being away. I have given you the facts as near as I can remember.

Yours very respectfully,
C. H. BUHRMAN

Clermont, Penn., November 23, 1886.
Prof. J. Fraise Richard,

Dear Sir — In answer to your letter concerning the capture of Lee's wagon train by Gen. Kilpatrick on the night of July 4, and morning of the 5th, 1863, I beg to say I remember it very distinctly.

My father rented Monterey Springs from Mr. Samuel Buhrman and kept the house from April, 1861, to April, 1866. Monterey being on the turnpike, at the top of South Mountain is the main crossing in the southeastern part of Franklin County, Penn., and was resorted to in times of rebel invasions by not only many persons of Washington and Antrim Townships of this county, but by many from Washington County, Maryland, and the Valley of Virginia. At this place, in times of danger, pickets were always placed from the Monterey House to the western side of the mountain to give notice if the rebels were approaching.

At the times of the battle of Gettysburg a large number of people were here anxiously awaiting news from the field of carnage, which could be seen from the adjacent hills. On the afternoon of July 4, a company of rebel cavalry came to Monterey from the tollgate, about half a mile on the western side, where the old Furnace road intersects the turnpike, over which roads the train was passing. After staying an hour or longer they left, and soon a rebel battery came from the same direction and placed a cannon on the turnpike between the house and barn. Another party was stationed farther east where the Clermont house now is and the pike commences to descend the mountain.

They kept all the persons at the Monterey as prisoners, placing a guard over them at the house. They gave my nephew, Willie Waddell, and myself privilege to go wherever we wished, to look after things, but required us to report every fifteen minutes to Sergt. Grabill, who was stationed at the front door of the house. About dusk I saw a great deal of commotion among them and asked some of the soldiers what was going on. "Oh nothing! Just you report to Sergt. Grabill," was the reply. I came to the house and asked Willie Waddell whether he knew what was going on. "Yes" said he, "I just came down from the observatory on the top of the house and could hear the Union troops coming up the mountain."

Very soon the cannonading commenced, but did not last long. The rebels hitched horses to their cannon and went toward the tollgate on a run, Sergt. Grabill not waiting for any one to report to him. One of the first men I met after the arrival of the Union troops was Gen. Custer, who, after questioning me, called Gen. Kilpatrick standing near. Gen. Kilpatrick asked me the distance to the foot of the mountain on the western side and whether troops could march on both sides of the turnpike. I told him they could as far as the tollgate. He immediately ordered a cannon to be placed in front of the Monterey house to throw shells after the retreating rebels. At the same time he ordered a regiment to march after them. The officer in command said he could not go while they were throwing shell in the rear of his men. Kilpatrick said, "Yes you can," and at the same directed the officer in charge of the cannon to throw his shells high so that there would be no danger in the Union troops. The rebels returned the fire for a time from the neighborhood of the tollgate, but when the Union troops approached they ceased.

Kilpatrick inquired of me whether there was any other road by which he could get to the foot of the mountain. I informed him of the Mount Zion road to Smithsburg and Leitersburg, the distance to the former place being eight miles, to the latter eleven. He then asked me whether I knew of any one acquainted with the road who would go as a guide. I had seen Mr. C. H. Buhrman with the soldiers when they came to Monterey. I said, "Mr. Buhrman is the man for you." Mr. Buhrman being called up, Gen. Kilpatrick asked him whether he knew the Mount Zion road to Smithsburg and Leitersburg, and whether he could find it such a dark night; if so, whether he would go as a guide for a regiment. Mr. Buhrman said he knew the road well, could find it no matter how dark the night, and would go as a guide.

Calling Col. Preston, Gen. Kilpatrick informed him that Mr. Buhrman would act as his guide. Soon the tramping of horses began through mud and rain in one of the darkest nights I ever knew. As soon as Col. Preston had started, Gen. Kilpatrick ordered a lieutenant, with James McCulloh as guide to go past the Benchoff farm to the old Furnace road to cut off that portion of the train between the Gum Spring and the turnpike, which added one and a half miles more to the part already attacked and from which they brought from seventy-five to one hundred prisoners to Monterey. The cannonading continued for several hours as our troops were descending the western side of the mountain. By day light on Sunday morning, July 5, Gen. Kilpatrick, with all his troops and prisoners except a few who were too badly wounded to be moved, had left Monterey. One of these wounded died soon after.

I never knew any one to direct movement so rapidly as Gen. Kilpatrick did that night, nor men so eager to follow as were the Union soldiers. There never was a greater victory under such adverse circumstances with the loss of so small a number of men.

Respectfully yours   DAVID MILLER

APPENDIX VII

The following is a list of "Emergency" Regiments known to have camped in the Greencastle area; taken from the July 28th and August 4, 1863 issues of "The Pilot." Additional information including company rosters may be found in **History of Pennsylvania Volunteers 1861-5** by Samuel P. Bates pp. 1222-1341.

Camped near Rankins Mill the week of July 14 —
        26th Regiment — Colonel William W. Jennings
        50th Regiment — Colonel Emlen Franklin
Passed through Greencastle on July 27 — 47th Regiment — Colonel James
Wickersham Camped at Tobias Woods the week of July 28
        Colonel James Nagle's Brigade —
        35th Regiment, Colonel Henry B. M'Kean
        37th Regiment, Colonel John Trout
        38th Regiment, Colonel Melchior H. Horn
        39th Regiment, Colonel James H. Campbell
        41st Regiment, Colonel Edward R. Mayer
        45th Regiment, Colonel _____ Wheeler
Camped at Moss Spring the week of July 28 —
        Colonel Brisbain's Brigade
        28th Regiment — Colonel James Chamberlin
        32nd Regiment "Philadelphia Blues" — Colonel Charles S. Smith
        33rd Regiment "Philadelphia Greys" — Colonel William W. Taylor

APPENDIX VIII

Burial of George Missavy

The most solemn and impressive scene that has taken place in our town for some time past occurred on Sabbath last. The occasion was the re-interment of Corp. George Missavy, formerly a member of Capt. A. R. Davison's company of the 126th Regt. Pa. Vol. Inf. He was wounded in the battle of Chancellorsville on the 3rd of May, 1863, and died in a field hospital the next morning, and was buried on the Battle-field. Last week out citizens raised sufficient funds to have his remains brought home and Mr. Isaih Ilgenfritz volunteered to recover the remains as he was present at his burial and knew where his grave was. After an absence of a few days Mr. Ilginfritz returned on Friday evening last, having been successful in finding the grave and procuring the body. When the remains arrived they were taken to the Cabinet shop of Gen. Detrich and placed in a beautiful finished coffin which was in waiting. Sabbath afternoon at two o'clock, a procession was formed at the shop and preceded by the pall bearers, composed entirely of young men who were his former companions in arms, bore the remains to the German Reformed church. The coffin beautifully festooned with our National colors was placed in front of the altar, and Rev. T. G. Apple delivered an appropriate address. He spoke of the noble duty the community performed in gathering the remains of our fallen heroes from the obscure graves they occupied and giving them christian burial where friends and kindred sleep, and where living friends and kindred can visit their tombs. He beautifully compared our National cemeteries to the sun, and the tombs of martyr's for the preservation of our Union scattered as they are in almost every city and hamlet burial ground, to bright sparkling stars that penetrate the gloom of saddened hearts and cheer up mourning friends. After his address was concluded and a prayer offered, the procession reformed and proceeded to the Reformed burial ground, where the remains were placed in their last resting place; the procession was preceded by the band, which played a solemn dirge with muffled instruments.

The number in attendance was unusually large — so large that the spacious chuch was completely filled, and numbers were unable to procure seats. With an unblemished character, kind and generous disposition, the deceased stood high in the estimation of those who were personally acquainted with him.

Valley Echo — March 27, 1866

FOOTNOTES

(For Complete Names of Sources and Repositories Refer to Bibliography)

CHAPTER I

1. W. P. Conrad, *Conococheague*, pp. 12-23; *Echo Pilot*, Oct. 19, 1939.

2. *Atlas of Franklin County, Pennsylvania*, pp. 7, 9; *Greencastle Map of 1853*, BLC: *Echo Pilot*, Mar. 23, 1905; Samuel P. Bates and J. Fraise Richard, *History of Franklin County, Pennsylvania*, pp. 700-37.

3. W. P. Conrad, "The Coachman's Horn is Heard No More," KHSP, V XVIII, pp.99-123; The Lazarus Wingerd Day Book 1802-1868, Conrad Collection, *The Record Herald*, Mar. 13, 1947; *The Echo Pilot*, Sept. 22, 1949.

4. Wingerd Daybook; *Echo Pilot*, Mar. 23, 1905, Sept. 22, 1949; Conrad, *Conococheague*, pp. 123-24.

5. *Echo Pilot*, Mar. 23, 1905, Sept. 22, 1949; Conrad, *Conocoheague*, pp. 207-15.

6. Clement Easton, *The Growth of Southern Civilization 1790-1860*, pp. 197-8.

7. *County Atlas*, pp. 7, 9, 57; *Farm Scenes: The Early Years in Cumberland County*, p. 7.

8. Stevenson Whitcomb Fletcher, *Pennsylvania Agriculture and Country Life 1640-1840*. pp.107-16. Talks with older residents throughout the years, confirm that this system was practiced in the Greencastle-Antrim area.

9. *Echo Pilot*, Mar. 23, 1905; Bates and Richard, op. cit., pp. 700-37; *County Atlas*, pp. 7, 9, 57.

10. *Echo Pilot*, Mar. 23, 1905. There was a $5.00 fine for killing rabbits, and certain birds out of season. *Pilot*, Sept. 29, 1863, Mar. 15, 1864.

11. *County Atlas*, pp. 7, 9, *Echo Pilot*, Nov. 29, 1962; Conrad, *Conochocheague*, pp. 22-23.

12. Conrad, "Coachman's Horn," pp. 97-98.

13. Bates and Richard, op. cit., pp. 543-44, 546-50; Conrad, *Conococheague*, pp. 132-37; W. P. Conrad, *Franklin County School Superintendents*, p. 1

14. Conrad, *School Superintendents*, pp. 1-3; Conrad, *Conococheague*, pp. 145-52; U. L. Gordy "The Old Browns Mill School," KHSP, V. XI, pp. 344-52; *County Altas*, p. 57.

15. U.S. Bureau of the Census; *Historical Statistics of the United States: Colonial Times to 1957*. p. 24; *Echo Pilot*, Mar. 23, 1905; Ambrose Watts Thrush, *Medical Men of Franklin County 1750-1925;* pp. 209-35; Conrad, *Conococheague*, pp. 157-61.

16. Fletcher, op. cit. pp. 433-75; Russel W. Gilbert, *A Picture of the Pennsylvania Germans*, pp. 61-68; I. H. M'Cauley, *Historical Sketch of Franklin County, Pennsylvania*, pp. 58-63; Bates and Richard, op. cit, pp. 324-29.

CHAPTER II

1. J. G. Randall and David Donald, *The Civil War and Reconstruction*, p. 61; Stevenson W. Fletcher, *Pennsylvania Agriculture and Country Life 1640-1840*, pp. 116-19; Ira Berlin, *Slaves Without Masters*, pp. 21-24; Samuel P. Bates and J. Fraise Richard, *History of Franklin County, Pennsylvania*, pp. 319-21. Just to the South, in Washington County, Maryland, there were 1,435 slaves as late as 1860. However, this number soon dwindled since it was easy to escape into Pennsylvania. J. C. Thomas Williams, *A History of Washington County, Maryland*, p. 457.

2. Larry Gara, *The Liberty Line: The Legend of the Underground Railroad*, p. 46.

3. Bates and Richard, op. cit., pp. 320-21.

4. Jonathan Katz, *Resistance at Christiana*, pp. 92-103, 247-98.

5. John F. Coleman, *The Disruption of the Pennsylvania Democracy: 1848-1860*, pp. 81-101; Bates and Richard, op. cit., pp. 736-37.

6. C. W. Cremer, "Historical Incidents Connected with Waynesboro and Franklin County," KHSP, V. IX, p. 360; Virginia Ott Stake, *John Brown in Chambersburg*, pp. 35, 54.

7. Randall and Donald, op. cit., pp. 127-41; William H. Egle, ed., *Andrew Gregg Curtin: His Life and Services*, p.37.

8. J. L. Finafrock, "Biographical Sketches," *Franklin County School Annual*, Nov. 1917, p. 42.

9. Coleman, op. cit., pp. 177-78; *Record Herald*, Mar. 13, 1947; *Daily Mail*, July 1, 1978.

10. Randall and Donald, op. cit., pp. 126-41.

11. Jacob Hoke, *Reminiscences of the War*, pp. 7-8; *Record Herald*, Mar. 13, 1947. This list of subscribers was given to the Kittochtinny Historical Society by Mrs. Jacob Shrader in 1935. Mrs. Jeanette Nelson provided the authors with a copy of it.

12. Hoke, op. cit., pp. 10, 11.

CHAPTER III

1. *B & L*, V. I, pp. 7-25; Harold R. Manakee, Maryland in the Civil War, pp. 30-38; Samuel P. Bates, *History of Pennsylvania Volunteers*, 1861-65, V. I. pp. 3-8; *Valley Spirit*, June 1, 1861.

2. Thomas, J. C. Williams, *A History of Washington County, Maryland*, p. 307; *B & L*, V. I, pp. 7-25; Jacob Hoke, *Reminiscenses of the War*, p. 9. Area residents would have found even less comfort from the knowledge that on April 3, 1861, over ten men registered at the Washington House Hotel in Hagerstown signing CSA beside their names. Many of them were from states such as Alabama, Mississippi and Louisiana. The purpose of this gathering is still a mystery. Washington House Register Apirl 3, 1861, Western Maryland Room, Washington County Free Library, Hagerstown Maryland.

3. *Valley Spirit*, May 1, 1861; Williams, op. cit., p. 307; Hoke, *Reminiscenses*, p. 9.

4. Edward George Evertt, "Pennsylvania's Mobilization for War, 1860-1861," Ph.D. dissertation, University of Pittsburgh, (1950), pp. 72, 124; Thomas G. Tousey, Military History of Carlisle and Carlisle Barracks, pp. 222-23.

5. Tousey, op. cit., p. 220; Everett, op. cit., p. 73.

6. *Record Herald*, Mar. 13, 1947.

7. *Dispatch*, May 31, 1861.

8. Ibid., Sept. 17, 1861.

9. Ibid., Aug. 20, 23, 30, Sept. 20, 1861; *Echo Pilot*, Mar. 23, 1905.

10. *Dispatch*, May 21, 1861; *New York Herald*, May 25, 1861; Frank Moore, ed., *The Rebellion Record*, V. I, Diary of Events, p. 77.

11. "Some History Connected with Enoch Brown School," *Franklin County School Annual*, Nov., 1919, p. 32.

12. Robert Patterson, *A Narrative of the Campaign in the Valley of the Shenandoah in 1861*, pp. 26-27; William C. Davis, *Battle at Bull Run*, pp. 4-8.

13. Everett, op. cit., p. 72; Bates, *Pennsylvania Volunteers*, V. I, p.23.

14. Everett, op. cit, pp. 64-65; Frederick P. Todd, *American Military Equipage 1851-1872*, (3 Volumes), V. III, pp. 605-11; Randy Hackenburg, "The Columbia Guards - Danville Volunteer Infantry 1817-1861; "Masters Thesis, Bloomsburg State College (1975), pp. 8-13. For a brief overview of the pre-war state militia, see also, Bruce S. Bazelon and John B. B. Trussell, *Defending the Commonwealth: Catalogue of the Militia Exhibit at the William Penn Memorial Museum, Harrisburg, Pennsylvania*.

15. Bates, *Pennsylvania Volunteers*, V. I, p. 241; *History of the First Troop Philadelphia City Cavalry*, pp. 60-61.

16. Samuel P. Bates and J. Fraise Richard, *History of Franklin County, Pennsylvania*, pp. 235-49. The Military traditions of the Detrich family are traced in C. M. Deatrich's *The Drummer Boy of the Conococheague*.

17. *Valley Spirit*, May 8, 1861; Joseph E. Walker, "Path Valley's Washington Blues in the Civil War," KHSP, V. XIII, pp. 373-74.

18. William H. Egle, ed., *Andrew Gregg Curtin: His Life and Services*, p. 212.

19. Ibid.

20. Ibid, pp. 227-28; Todd, op. cit., p. 687, John Severn and Frederick P. Todd, "1st Regiment Rhode Island Detached Militia, 1861," plate #103, MUA, The Company of Military Historians; Bates, *Pennsylvania Volunteers*, V. I, pp. 13, 14, 86, 185; Circular, Hdq. 1st Div. Williamsport, Md. June 26, 1861, signed by Captain Thomas H. Neill, Cadwalader Coll., HSP; Calvin Pardee to father, June 11, 1861, Pardee - Robison Family Coll., USMHI, *Dispatch*, June 7, 1861.

21. *Dispatch*, June 4, 20, 1861; Todd, op. cit., p. 681; Bates, *Pennsylvania Volunteers*, V. I, p. 185; Severin and Todd, Loc. cit. Samples of gray material proposed to make uniforms for state forces can be found today in Record Group 19, "Department of Military Affairs, Office of the QMG, Proposals, Contracts and Bonds" at the Pennsylvania Historical and Museum Commission's Archives Division in Harrisburg. Michael J. Winey, "Pennsylvanians in Gray" *Military Images Magazine* V. IV (July-Aug. 1982), pp. 16-23.

22. Todd, op. cit. V. I, pp. 45-50; J. L. Martel, "Les Zouaves," *Campaigns*, V. II, (Jan.-Feb., 1977), p. 32; Bates, op. cit., p. 210; Gen. Cadwalader to Gov. Curtin, June 30, 1861, Cadwalader Coll., HSP; *Dispatch*, Aug. 5, Oct. 11, 1861.

23. Hoke, Reminiscenses, p. 13.

24. Ibid., pp. 14-15.

25. Ibid., pp. 13-14. Various issues of the *Dispatch* for May and June, are the main references for sickness in the camps. See also, A. M. Stewart, *Camp, March and Battlefield*, pp. 7-8.

26. *Dispatch*, May 31, 1861.

27. Ibid., Aug. 20, 1861.

28. Ibid., June 14, 1861.

29. "Report of the Commissary General of the Commonwealth of Pennsylvania for the Year 1861." *Reports of the Heads of Departments* ... pp. 5-11.

30. Hoke, *Reminiscenses*, p. 15.

31. O. R., V. II, pp. 657-8.

32. Ibid., p. 658; *Dispatch*, June 4, 1861.

33. Hoke, *Reminiscenses*, p. 16.

34. O. R., V. II., p. 661; Bates, *Pennsylvania Volunteers*, V. I, pp. 106-07.

35. O. R., V. II., pp. 669-70.

36. Harold B. Simpson, *Cry Commanche, 1855-1861*, pp. 167-70.

37. O. R., V. II., p. 669; Bates, *Pennsylvania Volunteers*, V. I., p. 194; *Echo Pilot*, Mar. 23, 1905; *B & L*, V. I., p. 49.

38. *Valley Spirit*, June 12, 1861; Bates, *Pennsylvania Volunteers*, V. I., p. 96; "The Civil War Military Record of Peter Augustus Filbert," p. 4, HCWRTC, USAMHI. One account tells of a camp 3 miles south of Greencastle, called Camp Lee. Letter from K. G. Metzger, June 15, 1861, Camp Riley, HCWRT, USAMHI.

39. O. R., V. II., p. 670.

40. Fitz John Porter to F. C. Williams, Chambersburg, June 9, 1861, Department of Pennsylvania, RG. 393, NA.

41. *B & L*, V. I., p. 124.

42. Filbert, p. 4. HCWRTC, Pardee Letter, June 11, 1861, Pardee-Robison Family Coll., USAMHI.

43. *Dispatch*, June 21, 1861.

44. Charges against Major John E. Wynkoop, Camp Wingerd, Greencastle. June 13, 1861, Cadwalader Coll., HSP.

45. *Dispatch*, June 11, July 9, 1861.

46. *Dispatch*, June 14, 1861; F. Stansbury Haydon, *Aeronautics in the Union and Confederate Armies*, V. I. pp. 46-47; Augustus Woodbury, *A Narrative of the Campaign of the First Rhode Island Regiment*, pp. 59-60.

47. O. R., V. II, pp. 678-9.

48. Cadwalader to Porter, Greencastle, June 12, 1861, Special Orders No. 4 and 5, Greencastle, June 14, 1861, Cadwalader coll, HSP; Pardee letter, Loc. cit., Bates, V. I., pp. 32, 96; *Dispatch*, June 21, 1861; OR. V. II, p. 679.

49. Williams, op. cit., p. 309.

50. Ibid., p. 313; *Dispatch*, June 18, 1861.

51. Maynard J. Shier, "The Battle of Falling Waters," *CWTI*, V, XV. (Feb. 1977), p. 17; see also, Jeffry D. Wert, "Johnson vs. Patterson," *CWTI*, V. XVII (Dec. 1978), p. 5.

52. Patterson, op. cit. pp. 52-57; Davis, op. cit., pp. 148-151.

53. Bates and Richard, op. cit., p. 340; Bates *Pennsylvania Volunteers*, V. I., pp. 692-701, 708-09.

54. *Valley Spirit*, July 30, 1861; *Dispatch*, Aug. 20, 1861; Bates and Richard, op. cit., p. 343.

55. *Dispatch*, Aug. 20, 30, 1861.

56. Williams, op. cit., pp. 318-19.

57. *Dispatch*, Sept. 3, 1861.

58. Albert Castel, "The Guerrilla War 1861-1865," Special issue *CWTI*, Oct. 1974, pp. 7, 9.

59. Bates and Richard, op. cit., pp. 341-42.

60. E. B. Long, *The Civil War Day by Day;* p. 121; Manakee, op. cit., pp. 47-61.

CHAPTER IV

1. Robert Tanner, *Stonewall in the Valley*, pp. 62-64, 69-77; E. B. Long, *The Civil War Day by Day*, pp. 157-58; *Dispatch*, Jan. 7, 1862.

2. Paul W. Gates, *Agriculture and the Civil War*, pp. 158-75, 244; *Record Herald*, Mar. 13, 1947.

3. Gates, op. cit., pp. 154-55; *Echo Pilot*, Aug. 4, 1938, Nov. 29, 1962; *Valley Spirit*, Sept. 10, 1862.

4. W. P. Conrad, *Conococheague*, p. 151.

5. *Valley Spirit*, Apr. 2, 1862.

6. Samuel P. Bates, *History of Pennsylvania Volunteers*, 1861-65, V. II, p. 986; *Dispatch*, Apr. 22, 25, May 2, 1862.

7. Bates, *Pennsylvania Volunteers*, V. I, pp. 692-93, V. III, pp. 411-412; Samuel P. Bates and J. Fraise Richard, *History of Franklin County, Pennsylvania*, pp. 340-43.

8. *Valley Spirit*, Sept. 10, 1862.

9. Bates and Richard, op. cit., pp. 342-44.

10. James Murfin, *The Gleam of Bayonets*, pp. 68, 113, 159; OR, V. XIX, pt. 2, pp. 169, 590-91; *Echo-Pilot*, Sept. 20, 1962; Bates, *Pennsylvania Volunteers*, V. V, pp. 1147-48; Jacob Hoke, *Reminiscenses of the War*, pp. 22-23; J. D. Edmiston Turner. "Civil War Days in Mercersburg," KHSP, V. XII, pp. 30-31.

11. Henry Kyd Douglas, *I Rode With Stonewall*, p. 151; Murfin, op. cit., pp. 66-67, 159.

12. OR, V. XIX, pt. 1, p. 810, pt. 2, pp. 267-68; Thomas J. C. Williams, *History of Frederick County, Maryland*, V. II, pp. 824-25; Robert Krick, *Lee's Colonels*, p. 59; John M. Koehnlein, *"Zion: City of Our God. A History of the Evangelical Lutheran Congregation of Greencastle."* (unpublished paper - Evangelical Lutheran Church, Greencastle, Pa.) On Sept. 12, 1862, scouts of the 15th Pennsylvania Cavalry reported that Col Brien, (spelled Brinn in Union dispatches) "is said to have been making exceeding merry at his house about one-half mile South from the State Line, and he is guarded by some 500 cavalry." Charles H. Kirk, *History of the Fifteenth Pennsylvania Volunteer Cavalry*, p. 642.

13. *Valley Spirit,* Sept. 10, 1862, p. 5

14. William H. Egle, Ed., *Andrew Gregg Curtin,* pp. 344-53.

15. James Stamatelos and Michael J. Winey, "15th Pennsylvania Volunteer Cavalry Regiment," plate #413, MUA, The Company of Military Historians; OR, V. XIX, pt. 2, pp. 247-303; Suzanne Colton Wilson, *Column South with the Fifteenth Pennsylvania Cavalry,* pp. 13-23; Kirk, op. cit., pp. 18, 30-34, 41-49, 56, 60-61, 65-66, 640-47; Egle, op. cit; pp. 349-53. A telegram from Palmer to A. K. McClure, dated Greencastle, Sept. 12, 1862, closed with the promise to leave "three men in citizens clothing in Greencastle" if his forces were forced to retire to Chambersburg. Kirk, op. cit. p. 641.

16. Egle, op. cit., pp. 349.

17. William M. Luff, "March of the Cavalry from Harpers Ferry, September 14, 1862," *MOLLUS- ILL.,* V. II, pp. 33-48; John W. Mies, "Breakout at Harpers Ferry," *CWH,* V. II, (June, 1956) pp. 21-28; John F. McCormick, "The Harpers Ferry Skedaddlers," *CWTI,* V. XIV (Dec., 1975) pp. 32-39.

18. One of the prisoners, Captain Francis W. Dawson, wrote that upon arrival in Greencastle; "My horse was taken from me … and ridden off by a dirty-looking cavalrymen." After a short time in confinement, Dawson was back with the Army of Northern Virginia in time for the invasion of Pennsylvania in June 1863. He recalled; "It was some satisfaction for me to pass once more through Greencastle, where I had been bedeviled by both men and women when taken there … the year before." Francis W. Dawson, *Reminiscenses of Confederate Service 1861-1865,* pp. 65-66, 92; Wilson, op. cit. p. 18; Charles Carleton Coffin, *The Boys of '61,* p. 114; Hoke, op. cit., pp. 23-24; Figures vary on how much booty and how many Confederates were captured. S. B. Pettengill stated that "thirty to forty head of fat young steers" were taken. S. B. Pettengill, *The College Cavaliers,* pp. 84-85; General Julius White puts the figures rather high with 97 wagons and 600 men captured, *B & L,* V. II, p. 613; Most reports by participants estimate from 40 to 75 wagons and 200-300 prisoners taken. See Henry Norton, *A Sketch of the 8th New York Cavalry,* pp. 11-12. See also, OR, V. XIX, pt. 2 p. 305.

19. Luff, op. cit., p. 46; Pettengill, op. cit., pp. 85, 89, 90.

20. "Report of the Quartermaster General of the Commonwealth of Pennsylvania for the year 1862," *Reports of the Heads of Departments* … p. 5; Pettengill, op. cit., p. 86; Bates, *Pennsylvania Volunteers,* V. V., pp. 1147-48; Edward J. Nichols, *Toward Gettysburg: A Biography of General John F. Reynolds,* pp. 123-33.

21. The Civil War Record of Henry F. Charles 1862-1865, pp. 5-8; Boyer Coll., USAMHI. The Moss Spring site was known as "Camp Rest." Jerold E. Rowe, "The Civil War Diary of John T. Lewis," *Camp Chase Gazette,* pp. 13-14, Oct. 1980; Another camp just South of town was designated "Camp McCormick." *Eleven Days in the Militia During the War of the Rebellion, Being a Journal of the "Emergency" Campaign of 1862* - by a Militiaman, p. 48.

22. Nichols, op. cit., pp. 134

23. Local newspapers reported, "Almost incessant cannonading has been heard south of here during the past several days." *Record Herald,* Mar. 13, 1947; Nichols, op. cit., pp. 134-39; Gov. Curtin arrived in Hagerstown around 1 p.m., Sept. 18, 1862. OR, V. XIX, pt. 2, pp. 329, 333. George Edgar Turner, *Victory Rode the Rails,* pp. 215.-16; Paul J. Weshaeffer, *History of the Cumberland Valley Railroad 1835-1919.* pp. 68-79.

24. John B. Hege, *Marion and Environments,* p. 44; Henry F. Charles wrote - "The farmers were very liberal with their provisions. Some came with cloth baskets of bread, pies, cakes, apple butter and anything they could provide. They did not come to sell but to give the food to us. But there were three regiments of us and they could not give enough food." Charles War Record, Boyer Coll. USAMHI.

25. Bates, V. V., p. 1148. Although the "Emergency" men didn't take part in the Battle of Antietam, some exchanged shots with Confederate cavalry while on the picket line near Williamsport on Sept. 21, 1862. Some men did manage to shoot themselves and at one point, one regiment almost fired on another mistaking them for Confederates. On Sunday evening, Sept. 21, the people of Greencastle were startled to hear heavy rifle fire toward Middleburg. This was merely several militia units returning from Maryland who had been ordered to discharge their weapons, "which had been loaded for the rebels." Nichols, op. cit., pp. 37-38, 45-46, 135.

26. *B & L,* V. II, pp. 598-600; Henry White obituary, Kathleen Grosh Coll., Greencastle, Pa. Bates and Richard, op. cit., pp. 339-40, 342.

27. Accounts by Palmer and his men indicate some skirmishing occurred on the southern edge of Antrim Township during the Maryland Campaign. Kirk, op. cit., pp. 60-61, 641-47; Wilson, op. cit., pp. 14, 22; aside from the 15th cavalry and "Emergency" troops, home guard units from towns around the county volunteered to guard major area roads. Hoke, op. cit., p. 23; Turner, op. cit., p. 31. A telegram to Palmer from the state's assistant Adjutant General, states

that cavalry companies from Waynesboro and Mercersburg were ordered to report to Chambersburg for "sabres and ammunition." Kirk, op. cit., p. 647. 938 men from Franklin County served with the "Emergency" forces. Bates and Richard, op. cit., pp. 354-355.

28   *Echo Pilot*, Sept. 20, 1962.

29.   William S. Bowers, ed. "The William Heyser Diary," KSHP, V. XVI, pp. 54-55; Hoke, op. cit., pp. 27-28.

30.   Hoke, op. cit., pp. 28-33; Turner, op. cit., p. 33.

31.   *Pilot*, Feb. 10, Feb. 17, 1863; *Kauffman's Progressive News*, July 9, 1915; Kirk, op. cit., pp. 59-61.

32.   Bates and Richard, op. cit., p. 735; George W. Ward, *History of the Second Pennsylvania Veteran Heavy Artillery from 1861-1866*, pp. 23-24.

33.   Bates, *Pennsylvania Volunteers*, V. IV, pp. 834-50; Bates and Richard, op. cit., pp. 349-50.

34.   Bowers, op. cit., p. 57.

35.   *"Report of the Commissary General of the Commonwealth of Pennsylvania for the Year 1862,"* pp. 3-7; *"Report of the Quartermaster General of the Commonwealth of Pennsylvania for the Year 1862,"* pp. 3-8; *Reports of the Heads of Departments* ...

36.   Lazarus Wingerd Daybook; Gates, op. cit., pp. 129-247.

CHAPTER V

1.   David Watson Rowe, *A Sketch of the 126th Regiment Pennsylvania Volunteers*, pp. 5-7.

2.   Ibid., pp. 7-8; William H. Groninger, "Lincoln's Visit to Antietam Battlefield," *National Tribune*, Apr. 7, 1927, p. 5.

3.   Rowe, op. cit., pp. 8-13, 53-89; Groninger, "Lincoln's Visit", p. 5.

4.   Groninger, "Lincoln's Visit," p. 5.

5.   Rowe, op. cit., pp. 12-13; Samuel P. Bates, *History of Pennsylvania Volunteers, 1861-5;* V. IV, p. 128.

6.   William H. Groninger, "With General Burnside at Fredericksburg," *National Tribune*, Apr. 1, 1926, p. 5.

7.   Rowe, op. cit., pp. 13-15; Groninger, "Lincoln's Visit," p. 5.

8.   "Civil War Letters From Two Brothers," *The Yale Review*, V. XVIII. Sept., 1928, No. 1, p. 154 (hereafter cited as Welsh Letters).

9.   Rowe, op. cit., p. 15; Major Francis E. Pierce, "A Letter from Fredericksburg,"*CWTI*, V. 1. Dec., 1962, pp. 7-9, 28-29.

10.   Rowe, op. cit., pp. 15-24.

11.   *Welsh Letters*, pp. 157-59.

12.   Rowe, op. cit., pp. 41-88; W. P. Conrad, *Conococheague*, pp. 37-38.

13.   *Pilot*, Feb., 23, 1863, p. 1.

14.   Charles Hartman Diary 1862-1863; Philip Schaff Library, LTS.

15.   Stephen B. Oates, *With Malice Toward None*. pp. 327-33; Rowe, op. cit., pp. 21-26; *Welsh Letters*, pp. 159-60.

16.   Rowe, op. cit., p. 27.

17.   Oates, op. cit., pp. 345-49.

18.   Bates, *Pennsylvania Volunteers*, V. IV, pp. 1002-1003.

19.   Rowe, op. cit., pp. 32-37.

20. Clay MacCauley, "From Chancellorsville to Libby Prison, "MOLLUS - Minn. V. I. pp. 186-90.

21. *Pilot,* June 9, 1863.

22. Rowe, op. cit., pp. 35, 51-52.

23. Oates, op. cit., pp. 347-48.

24. Hartman Diary, 1863; Philip Schaff Library, LTS. Pension file of George and John Missavy, 126th Pennsylvania Regiment, RG. 15, NA.

25. *Pilot,* May 12, 19, 26, 1863; Rowe, op. cit., pp. 37-38.

26. Rev. J. D. Edmiston Turner, "Civil War Days in Mercersburg, KHSP, V. XII, pp. 33-34.

CHAPTER VI

1. *Pilot,* July 28, 1863; *New York Herald,* July 12, 1863; Jacob Hoke, *Reminiscences of the War,* p. 34; Samuel P. Bates and J. Fraise Richard, *History of Franklin County, Pennsylvania,* p. 726.

2. *Pilot,* July 28, 1863; Herman Schuricht, "Jenkins Brigade in the Gettysburg Campaign," SHSP, V. XXIV, pp. 339-40.

3. *Pilot,* July 28, 1863; *Philadelphia Inquirer,* June 16, 1863.

4. Jacob Hoke, *The Great Invasion,* pp. 110-111; Wilbur S. Nye, *Here Come the Rebels,* pp. 252-53.

5. Nye, op. cit., pp. 142-43.

6. *Pilot,* July 28, 1863; Hoke, *Invasion,* pp. 108-109, 158-60; Nye, op. cit., pp. 138-40.

7. Story told to Charles Bert by his grandfather.

8. M. Jacobs, *Notes on the Rebel Invasion of Maryland and Pennsylvania and the Battle of Gettysburg,* pp. 3-5; *Pilot,* July 28, 1863; Hoke, *Invasion,* p. 108; *New York Herald,* June 20, 1863.

9. Hoke, *Invasion,* p. 111; *OR,* V. XXVII, pt. 3, p. 914.

10. Jacobs, op. cit., pp. 4-5; *Pilot,* July 28, 1863.

11. *Pilot,* July 23, 1863, Hoke, *Invasion,* pp. 96, 111-13.

12. *Pilot,* July 28, 1863.

13. Hoke, *Invasion,* p. 113; Edwin B. Coddington, *The Gettysburg Campaign,* p. 162. Traditional local story told to W. P. Conrad.

14. Mary A. Laughlin and Grace E. Laughlin Hykes, *History of the Prather, Shank, Royer, Laughlin Families,* p. 15.

15. *Echo Pilot,* Sept. 22, 1949.

16. *Echo Pilot,* Nov. 22, 1962.

17. Christian S. Stouffer and Mary Zarger Stouffer, *Zarger-Zarker Genealogy,* pp. 104-05.

18. *Pilot,* July 28, 1863.

19. *Pilot,* Aug. 11, 1863; Coddington, op. cit., pp. 174-75; "General R. E. Rodes' Report of The Battle of Gettysburg," SHSP, V. II, p. 143.

20. Story told to Mr. Ralph Horst, Henry B. Hege's grandson. W. P. Conrad, *Conococheague,* pp. 39-41; Hoke, *Invasion,* p. 176; J. D. Edmiston Turner, "Civil War Days in Mercersburg," KHSP, V. XII, p. 36, Nye, op. cit., pp. 254-55.

21. *Pilot,* July 28, 1863.

22. Nye, op. cit., p. 307.

23. Bell I. Wiley, *The Life of Johnny Reb,* p. 120.

24. Nye, op. cit., pp. 60-65, 149-62, 212-21; Coddington, op. cit., pp. 134-52.

25. Nye, op. cit., pp. 236-50; Hoke, *Invasion*, pp. 120-23.

26. William H. Beach, *The First New York (Lincoln) Cavalry*, pp. 248-50. An account of the skirmish was written by W. A. Reed and originally appeared in the June 22, 1886 issue of the *Greencastle Press*. This story was reprinted in a pamphlet titled "Death of Corporal Rihl" and was distributed by the Citizens National Bank in Sept., 1963; *Pilot*, July 28, 1863; *Echo Pilot*, Mar. 23, 1905; Hoke, *Invasion*, pp. 123-27; The story of cannoneer Miller appears in the *Echo Pilot*, Aug. 8, 1929 and *Franklin Repository*, Jan. 1, 1980. Details are sketchy. *The Record Herald* of June 22, 1961, reprinted an article by A. A. Arnold. He claimed to have shot Corporal Rihl, however, this story is rather dubious. His account has Rihl leading the patrol at a gallop and pointing a pistol at Arnold and his comrades at the moment of his death.

27. Beach, op. cit., pp. 249-50; Frederick H. Dyer, *A Compendium of the War of the Rebellion*, V. II, pp. 1367-68; *The Public Opinion;* May 30, 1913.

28. Hoke, *Invasion*, pp. 128-30.

29. Charles Hartman Diary, 1863., Philip Schaff Library, LTS.

30. Manley Wade Wellman, *Rebel Boast*, p. 117; L. Leon, *Diary of a Tar Heel Confederate Soldier*, p. 32.

31. Wellman, op. cit., pp. 117.

32. *Pilot*, July 28, 1863.

33. Rodes' Report, p. 143.

34. Isaac Trimble, "The Battle of Gettysburg," SHSP, V. XXVI, p. 119.

35. Rodes' Report, p. 143, *Pilot*, July 28, 1863.

36. Ibid; Hoke, *Invasion*, p. 132.

37. *Pilot*, July 28, 1863; Hotchkiss Diary, June 22-24, 1863, Hotchkiss Papers, LC.

38. *Pilot*, July 28, 1863; *Record Herald*, Nov. 16, 1979; Payment order to Jeremiah Detrich from 1st Lieutenant S. M. Moore, Acting A.A.G., Rodes Division, Detrich Coll., Greencastle, Pa.

39. Leon, op. cit., p. 32

40. Hotchkiss, op. cit., June 23, 1863.

41. Samuel Grove Sollenberger and Grace Hege, *Jacob Grove and Elizabeth Lesher Grove* Family, pp. 6-7.

42. Conrad, *Conococheague*, p. 41.

43. Hotchkiss, Diary, June 22-24, 1863, Hotchkiss Papers, LC, Hoke, *Invasion*, p. 138; Nye, op cit., p. 268.

44. This story was provided by Henry Strickler's granddaughter, Mrs. Helen Welch, Greencastle, Pa.

45. Schuricht, op. cit., p. 342.

46. *B & L*, V. III, pp. 437-39; James I. Robertson, Jr., *The Stonewall Brigade* pp. 12-17.

47. Nye, op. cit., p. 282; Hoke, *Invasion*, pp. 147-53, 170, 183-90.

48. Samuel Firebaugh Diary, p. 1, Wayland Coll., The Winchester-Frederick County Historical Society.

49. Jedediah Hotchkiss to Sara Hotchkiss, June 24, 1863, Letter Books, Hotchkiss Papers, LC, *Pilot*, July 28, 1863.

50. Hoke, *Invasion*, pp. 136-38; Nye, op. cit., p. 308.

51. *Record Herald*, Sept. 28, 1959; *Kauffmans Progressive News*, Nov. 29, 1912; Arthur Crew Inman, ed., *Soldier of the South: General Pickett's War Letters to His Wife*, pp. 43-45.

52. D. Augustus Dickert, *History of Kershaws Brigade*, p. 230.

53. Nye, op. cit., p. 20; Hoke, *Invasion;* p. 167. Jacob Hoke described Lee at Chambersburg on June 26th: "General Lee, as he sat on his horse that day in the public square ... looked every inch a soldier. He was at that time about fifty-two years of age, stoutly built, of medium height, hair strongly mixed with gray, and a rough, gray beard. He wore the usual Confederate gray, with some little ornamentation about the collar of his coat. His hat was a soft black without ornament other than a military cord around the crown."

54. Ibid, pp. 162-67.

55. Charles Minor Blackford, ed., *Letters From Lee's Army,* p. 183.

56. J. G. DeRoulhac Hamilton, ed., *The Papers of Randolph Abbott Shotwell,* V. I., pp. 490-91.

57. *Record Herald,* Nov. 16, 1979.

58. Hamilton, op. cit., pp. 491-92.

59. *Battles and Leaders,* V. III, pp. 437-40; *Pilot,* July 28, 1863; E. P. Alexander with Headquarters, 1st Corps, June 26, 1863. E. P. Alexander Coll., SHC, UNC; William Miller Owen, *In Camp and Battle with the Washington Artillery of New Orleans,* pp. 240-41.

60. Ella Lonn, *Foreigners in the Confederacy,* pp. 30-31; Harry H. Hall, *A Johnny Reb Band from Salem,* p. 42.

61. *Pilot,* July 28, 1863; Harold B. Simpson, *Hood's Texas Brigade* pp. 251-53.

62. Simpson, op. cit., pp. 254-55. This may have been the Allison house, just South of the present site of Corning Glass.

63. Harold B. Simpson, *Gaines Mill to Appomattox,* p. 133.

64. J. B. Polley, "Hood's Texans in Pennsylvania," Confederate Veteran, V. IV, Nov. 1896, pp. 377-79.

65. Captain W. C. Ward, "Incidents and Personal Experiences on the Battlefield at Gettysburg," Confederate Veteran, V. VIII, Aug., 1900, p. 345.

66. Walter Lord, ed., *The Fremantle Diary,* pp. 190-91

67. Story handed down to Sara Hade's granddaughter, Mrs. Mary Elden, Waynesboro, Pa.

68. Lord, op. cit., pp. 186-87.

69. *Pilot,* July 28, 1863; Lafayette McClaws to wife, Emily - June 28th, 1863, (unpublished letter) Lafayette McClaw's Papers, SHC, UNC.

70. Hoke, *Invasion,* pp. 215-258.

71. Ibid.

72. OR, V. XXVII, pt. 3, pp. 947-48.

CHAPTER VII

1. Mark M. Boatner, *The Civil War Dictionary,* p. 218; Frank Moore, ed., *The Rebellion Record,* V. VII, Diary of Events, p. 21; Rear-Admiral Dahlgren, *Memoir of Ulrich Dahlgren,* p. 160; Hugh Scott, "Philadelphia's Versatile Admiral," *Today ... The Philadelphia Inquirer Sunday Magazine,* Apr. 9, 1961, pp. 48-49.

2   *Kauffmans Progressive News,* Mar. 11, 1921. This issue contains several first hand accounts of the raid and also a letter from Dahlgren's mother.

3. Ibid.; *Mercersburg Journal,* July 17, 1863.

4. *Kauffmans Progressive News,* Mar. 11, 1921; Jacob Hoke, *Reminiscenses of the War,* p. 56.

5. Col. Edward A. Palfrey, "Some of the Secret History of Gettysburg," SHSP, V. VIII, pp. 521-26.

6. Hoke, op. cit., p. 56.

7. E. P. Alexander, Memoirs, p. 49, SHC, UNC.

8. Dahlgren, op. cit., pp. 162-63; Rev. S. L. Gracey, *Annals of the Sixth Pennsylvania Cavalry*, pp. 189-90; Samuel P. Bates, *History of Pennsylvania Volunteers, 1861-5*, V. II, pp. .741, 748; *Pilot*, July 28, 1863.

9. McHenry, Howard, *Recollections of a Maryland Confederate Soldier and Staff Officer*, pp. 209-12.

10. *Public Opinion*, May 30, 1913.

11. *Pilot*, July 28, 1863.

12. Gracy, op. cit., p. 189; Hoke, op. cit., p. 56.

13. Dahlgren, op. cit., p. 165.

14. Ibid., pp. 166-77; Gracey, op. cit., pp. 189-92.

15. Dahlgren, op. cit., pp. 175-76; Morris Fradin, "Curious Burial for a Hero's Leg," *The Hagerstown Cracker Barrel*, Nov. 1972, p. 10-12.

16. Donald J. Sobol, *Two Flags Flying*, pp. 153-56.

17. *Echo Pilot*, Aug. 9, 1917; *Kauffman's Progressive News*, Feb. 25, 1921.

18. *Kauffmans Progressive News*, Mar. 11, 1921; *The Herald Mail*, Mar. 10, 1955; Fradin, op. cit., p. 11.

19. Kendall Banning, *Annapolis Today*, p. 180.

CHAPTER VIII

1. Samuel P. Bates and J. Fraise Richard, *History of Franklin County, Pennsylvania*, pp. 339-40, 342, 350.

2. Ibid., pp. 730-31.

3. Glenn R. Cordell, *Shaking the Cordell Family Tree*, p. 103.

4. Jacob Hoke, *The Great Invasion*, p. 508.

5. W. P. Conrad, *Conococheague*, p. 34.

6. Hoke, *Invasion*, pp. 508-19.

7. *B & L*, V. III, pp. 420-29; Hoke, *Invasion*, pp. 493-507. Contrary to other accounts, Mrs. Mary Alice Fleming, of Greencastle, recalled years later that some citizens of the town aided the wounded and that there was no evidence of bitterness. *Echo Pilot*, Sept. 7, 1939.

8. I. Norvel Baker Diary, pp. 2-3, CWTIC, USAMHI.

9. *B & L*, V. III, pp. 420-29; Hoke, *Invasion*, pp. 493-507.

10. Hoke, *Invasion*, pp. 493-97.

11. Conrad, op. cit., p. 41.

12. Henry Omwake, *Papers and Addresses*, pp. 181-86.

13. Hoke, *Invasion*, pp. 499-502.

14. Ibid., pp. 502-03.

15. Harry H. Hall, *A Johnny Reb Band from Salem*, p. 54.

16. J. G. DeRoulhac Hamilton, ed., *The Papers of Randolph Abbott Shotwell*, p. 33.

17. Hoke, *Invasion*, p. 504.

18. *B & L*, V. III, p. 425.

19. I. Norvel Baker Diary, pp. 2-3, CWTIC, USAMHI.

20. S. L. Gracey, *Annals of the Sixth Pennsylvania Cavalry*, pp. 189-90. Pawling's role in these actions are pointed out in the *Pilot*, July 28, 1863. and *Kauffmans Progressive News*, Feb. 25, 1921.

21. *B & L*, V. III, p. 425; Jennings Cropper Wise, *The Long Arm of Lee*, V. II, pp. 698-99.

22. OR, V. XXVII, pt. II, p. 280; J. D. Edmiston Turner, "Civil War Days in Mercersburg," KHSP, V. XII, p. 36; Hoke, *Invasion*, pp. 504-507.

23. *Echo Pilot*, Mar. 23, 1905.

24. *Pilot*, July 28, 1863, p. 3.

25. Bates and Richard, op. cit., p. 349; John B. Hege, *Marion and Environments*, pp. 54-55.

26. Omwake, op. cit., pp. 185-86.

27. *Pilot*, July 28, 1863.

28. Edwin B. Coddington, *The Gettysburg Campaign*, pp. 553-54, 558-62; Bates, *Pennsylvania Volunteers*, V. IV, pp. 834-35.

29. Walter Lord, ed., *The Fremantle Diary*, p. 220; Hoke, *Invasion*, pp. 452-54.

30. Bates and Richard, op. cit., p. 382.

31. OR, V. XXVII, pt. 1, p. 994, pt. 2, pp. 309, 322.

32. OR, V. XXVII, pt. 3, p. 623.

33. Coddington, op. cit., pp. 565-72; John W. Schildt, *Roads from Gettysburg*, pp. 139-42.

34. OR, V. XXVII, pt. 3, p. 694; James H. Stevenson, *Boots and Saddles*, pp. 206, 215.

35. Jacob Hoke, *Reminiscenses of the War*, pp. 140-65.

36. *OR*, V. XXVII, pt. 3, p. 634; *Pilot*, Aug. 4, 1863; Wilbur S. Nye, *Here Come The Rebels, p. 302.*

37. Coddington, op. cit., pp. 560-61; Benjamin M. Nead, *Waynesboro Centennial History*, pp. 248-49.

38. "History of the 23rd Regiment National Guard, State of New York." (unpublished manuscript), pp. 78-80; Powers Coll. U.S. AMHI.

39. Coddington, op. cit., pp. 561-63.

40. *OR*, V, XXVII, pt. 3, p. 697.

41. *Pilot*, July 28, 1863, p. 2.

42. William Bowers ed., "The William Heyser Diary", KHSP, V. XVI, pp. 84-85.

43. *Pilot*, July 28, 1863.

44. *OR*, V. XXVII, pt. 3, p. 758.

45. *Pilot*, Aug. 4, 1863.

46. *Pilot*, Aug. 4, 1863, p. 2

47. *Pilot*, Aug. 4, 1863, p. 3.

48. Jerold E. Rowe, "The Civil War Diary of John T. Lewis, Jr.", *Camp Chase Gazette*, Oct. 1980, pp. 13-15.

49. Pinkerton letter, Mary Elden Coll., Waynesboro, Pa.

50. *Pilot*, Jan. 5, 1864.

CHAPTER IX

1. William S. Bowers, ed., "William Heyser Diary," KHSP, V. XVI, p. 64; *Pilot*, Feb. 10, 1863.

2. *Pilot*, Mar. 17, 1863.

3. Ibid., Feb. 10, 1863.

4. Ibid., Apr. 28, May 19, 1863.

5. W. P. Conrad, *Conococheague*, p. 220; *Pilot*, Apr. 21, 1863.

6. *Pilot*, Mar. 3, May 12, Nov. 17, 1863.

7. Bowers, op. cit., pp. 66-67; *Pilot*, Nov. 24, 1863; Samuel P. Bates and J. Fraise Richard, *History of Franklin County, Pennsylvania*, pp. 714-15.

8. *Pilot*, Apr. 21, May 19, 1863.

9. Ibid., Aug. 11, 18, 1863.

10. Samuel P. Bates, *History of Pennsylvania Volunteers 1861-65*, V. V, p. 77, Cemetery List, *Pilot*, Aug. 4, 18, 25, 1863.

11. *Pilot*, Sept. 1, 1863.

12. *Pilot*, Aug. 4, 11, 18, 25, Sept. 1, Nov. 17, 24, 1863; Bowers, op. cit., p. 85.

13. *Pilot*, Sept. 15, 1863. A token from a New York City saloon was found in the Moss Spring area in 1979.

14. *Pilot*, Aug. 4, Sept. 1, 15, 1863.

15. Ibid., Dec. 29, 1863; *Echo Pilot*, Mar. 23, 1905.

16. Lazarus Wingerd Daybook; *Pilot*, Feb. 3, 1863.

17. *Pilot*, Dec. 1, 8, 1863.

18. Ibid., Sept. 29, 1863.

19. Ibid., Sept. 1, 29, Nov. 17, 1863.

20. Ibid., Sept. 15, 29, 1863.

21. Ibid., Sept. 29, Oct. 6, 1863.

22. Ibid., Oct. 13, 20, Nov. 10, 17, 1863; William H. Egle, ed., *Andrew Gregg Curtin*, pp. 160-61.

23. "Report of the Board of Military Claims, made to the Legislature of Pennsylvania, for the year 1863." *Reports of the Heads of Departments* ... V. II, pp. 140, 142.

24. *Pilot*, Feb. 16, 1864, p. 2.

25. *Pilot*, Oct. 20, 1863.

26. Ibid., Nov. 10, 17, 1863.

27. Ibid., Dec. 29, 1863.

28. Ibid., Nov. 24, 1863.

29. Ibid. Dec. 1, 1863.

30. Ibid., Dec. 8, 15, 22, 29, 1863.

31. Ibid., Dec. 29, 1863.

CHAPTER X

1. *Pilot*, Jan. 5, Feb. 16, 1864.

2. Ibid., Jan. 26, Feb. 2, 1864.

3. Ibid., Feb. 23, 1864.

4. Ibid., Jan. 19, 1864.

5. Ibid., Feb. 23, Mar. 1, 8, May 3, 1864.

6. Ibid., Feb. 2, 16, 23, 1864.

7. Ibid., Jan 5, Feb. 2, Mar. 8, 15, 22, 1864.

8. Ibid., Feb. 23, Mar. 22, 1864.

9. Ibid., Mar. 1, 22, 29, Apr. 5, 1864.

10. Ibid., May 3, 10, 17, 24, 1864.

11. Ibid., May 10, 17, 24, 1864.

12. Ibid.

13. Ibid., May 24, 1864; Francis Trevelyan Miller, ed., *The Photographic History of the Civil War*, V. VII, pp. 329, 340.

14. *Pilot*, Apr. 5, May 3, 31, June 7, 21, 1864. Newspaper accounts throughout late 1863 and 1864, tell of both Union and Confederate deserters in the area.

15. Ibid., June 7, 14, 1864.

16. Ibid., June 7, 14, 28, 1864.

17. W. P. Conrad, *Conococheague*, pp. 220-21.

18. *Pilot*, June 28, 1864.

19. Ibid.

20. Ibid., June 14, 1864.

21. Ibid., June 21, 1864.

22. Ibid, June 28, 1864.

23. Ibid., June 7, 14, 28, 1864.

24. Ibid., Apr. 5, June 28, 1864.

25. Ibid., June 28, July 5, 1864.

26. Ibid., July 26, 1864; William H. Egle, ed., *Andrew Gregg Curtin*, pp. 174-78; Jacob Hoke, *Reminiscences of the War*, pp. 102-103. On July 9, General Couch informed Secretary of War Stanton that his total force in the Cumberland Valley consisted of "about 130 cavalry, 200 infantry and 4 pieces of artillery." OR; V. XXXVII, pt. 1, pp. 336-41, pt. 2, p. 150.

27. The July 26 issue of the *Pilot* also carried this interesting story: "Major General Franz Sigel passed through this place in the morning train of cars on last Monday, on his way to Harrisburg - Quite a crowd collected around the cars to get a glimpse of the old war horse." Sigel, an incompetent political general, had led a Union Army to defeat that spring at New Market. By late July he had been relieved of duty for "Lack of aggression." Mark M. Boatner, *The Civil War Dictionary*, p. 761; Jacob Hoke described this force of 1,000 as "stragglers ... weary, hungry and greatly demoralized." Hoke, *Reminiscences*, pp. 110-111.

28. *Echo Pilot*, Mar. 23, 1905.

29. OR, V. XXXVII, pt. 1, pp. 341-42.

30. J. D. Edmiston Turner, *Civil War Days in Mercersburg*, KHSP, V. XII pp. 37-38.

31. Egle, op. cit., pp. 179-80; C. Armour Newcomer, *Coles Cavalry*, pp. 142-45.

32. Hoke, *Reminiscences*, p. 192.

33. Ibid.

34. OR, V XXXVII, pt. 1, pp. 336-37.

35. Hoke, *Reminiscences,* pp. 134-35.

36. Ibid., pp. 133-34.

37. Hoke's *Reminiscences* contains numerous eyewitness accounts, both Northern and Southern, of the burning. See pp. 112-31, 202-204.

38. Harry Gilmor, *Four Years in the Saddle,* pp. 210-211; Samuel P. Bates and J. Fraise Richard, *History of Franklin County, Pennsylvania,* p. 476.

39. Hoke, *Reminiscences,* pp. 135-40.

40. Ibid., p. 135.

41. Ibid.

42. Newcomer, op. cit., pp. 146-48.

43. Hoke, *Reminiscences,* p. 130; William H. Beach, *The First New York (Lincoln) Cavalry,* pp. 402-10.

44. Local tradition holds that Averell was too drunk to take command that day. Hoke, *Reminiscences,* p. 134.

45. OR, V. XXXVII, pt. 2, p. 515.

46. Hoke, *Reminiscences,* pp. 128-29.

47. *Echo Pilot,* Mar. 23, 1905.

48. Hoke, *Reminiscences,* pp. 126-31, 135-40.

49. *Pilot,* July 26, 1864.

50. Bates and Richard, op. cit., p. 353.

51. Hoke points out that Ringgold, Georgia was burned partly in retaliation for the destruction of Chambersburg: "During General Sherman's campaign through that State, Ringgold was captured with a considerable amount of Confederate stores ... General Geary who was in command in that place, was ordered by General Sherman to burn whatever of the supplies they could not bring away and then evacuate the place. Whether Sherman's order contemplated the destruction of the whole town, I cannot say, but General Geary gave it that interpretation and the whole place was laid in ruins. General Geary's command was composed in part of Pennsylvanians, and to the cry of 'retaliation for Chambersburg' they applied the torch." (Geary later became Governor of Pennsylvania) Hoke, *Reminiscences, p. 193.*

52. Paul W. Gates, Agriculture and the Civil War, passim; Lazarus Wingerd Daybook.

53. James H. Montgomery Diary, p. 62, C. W. Misc. Coll. USAMHI; Adams House Register, Ervin Coll., Greencastle, Pa.

54. Davison Letters, Bert Coll., Greencastle, Pa.

55. Ibid.

56. *Valley Spirit,* Nov. 30, Dec. 21, 1864.

57. This information was passed on in a 1935 letter to the Kittochtinny Historical Society by Mrs. Jacob Shrader of Greencastle, Pa.

58. Story related by Mrs. Blanche Barr, Greencastle, Pa.

59. Egle, op. cit., pp. 242-55.

CHAPTER XI

1. Jack Coggins, *Arms and Equipment of the Civil War,* pp. 106-107; Frederick P. Todd, *American Military Equipage, 1851-1872,* V. II, p. 399, Mark M. Boatner, *The Civil War Dictionary,* pp. 576-77.

2. Todd, op. cit., pp. 399-401.

3. Robert M. Utley, *Frontier Regulars - The United States Army and the Indian: 1866-1890*, p. 28.

4. *Pilot,* Sept. 15, 1863.

5. J. Willard Brown, *The Signal Corps, U.S.A. in the War of the Rebellion*, p. 671; Letters Received, 1864 R-Y, Descriptive List, RG 111, NA.

6. Brown, op. cit., pp. 671-73; *Historical Data Concerning St. Thomas Township*, p. 17; James H. Montgomery Diary, pp. 1-18, C. W. Misc. Coll., USAMHI.

7. Special Orders 104 and 111, May 6, 14, 1864, Hdq. Dept. of Susquehanna; Letters Received R-4, RG 111, NA; Montgomery Diary, p. 23, C. W. Misc. Coll., USAMHI.

8. Brown, op. cit., pp. 671-77; Captain Amos M. Thayer, Military Histories of Officers, RG 111, NA; Montgomery Diary, pp. 24-33, C. W. Misc. Coll., USAMHI; Charles W. Snell, "Harpers Ferry Repels an Attack and Becomes the Major Base of Operations for Sheridans Army, July 4, 1864 to July 27, 1865." Research Project No. HF 98D, Harpers Ferry National Historical Park, pp. 13-29.

9. Snell, op. cit., p. 29-33; Brown, op. cit., pp. 676-77.

10. Montgomery Diary, pp. 43-48, C. W. Misc. Coll., USAMHI; Brown, op. cit., pp. 677-78; Reports of operations, Capt. Amos Thayer to Chief Signal Officer, Aug. 31, 1864, RG 111, NA.

11. Montgomery Diary, pp. 44-63, C. W. Misc. Coll, USAMHI; Captain L. B. Norton, Military Histories of Officers, RG 111, NA. The main Signal Corps camp of instruction was located at Georgetown, D.C.

12. Montgomery Diary, pp. 63-64, C. W. Misc. Coll., USAMHI; Reports of operations, Captain L. B. Norton to Captain S. M. Eaton, Oct. 31, 1864, RG 111, NA.

13. Montgomery Diary, p. 63, C. W. Misc. Coll., USAMHI. These gangs continued to operate until the end of the war. See *Village Record,* March 31 and Apr. 7, 1865.

14. Montgomery Diary, pp. 64-67, C. W. Misc. Coll., USAMHI: *Village Record,* Nov. 18, 25, 1864; O.R., V. XLIII, pt. 2, pp. 635-36.

15. Montgomery Diary, pp. 68-70; C. W. Misc. Coll., USAMHI.

16. Reports of Operations, Lt. Amos Thayer to Captain H. R. Clum, Nov. 30, 1864. RG 111, NA.

17. Montgomery Diary, p. 72, C. W. Misc. Coll., USAMHI; *Village Record,* Dec. 2, 1864; O.R. V. XLIII, pt. 2, pp. 662-63.

18. Montgomery Diary, pp. 72-74, C. W. Misc. Coll., USAMHI, Telegrams Sent, Lt. Amos Thayer to Major John L. Shultze, RG 393, NA; Samuel P. Bates, *History of Pennsylvania Volunteers 1861-65*, V. I., p. 708.

19. Montgomery Diary, pp. 76-84, C. W. Misc. Coll., USAMHI: List of Prisoners, Juniata District and Post of Chambersburg, Aug., 1864 - July, 1865, Department of Susquehanna, RG 393, NA.

20. *Village Record,* Dec. 16, 1864.

21. Montgomery Diary, pp. 90-100, C. W. Misc. Coll., USAMHI. Telegrams Sent, Major John Morgan to Lt. Francis McClosky, Greencastle, Feb. 21, 1865, Department of Susquehanna, RG 393, NA.

CHAPTER XII

1. Samuel P. Bates, *History of Pennsylvania Volunteers 1861.-65*, V. II, pp. 985-1113; Cemetery List.

2. Samuel P. Bates and J. Fraise Richard, *History of Franklin County, Pennsylvania*, p. 721.

3. John Obreiter, *The Seventy-Seventh Pennsylvania at Shiloh: History of the Seventy-Seventh Pennsylvania Volunteers*, pp. 115-36.

4. *Pilot,* Oct. 6, 1863; *Echo Pilot,* Feb. 14, 1963; Bates, *Pennsylvania Volunteers,* V. II, pp. 989-997; Obreiter, op. cit., pp. 136-86.

5. Cemetery List.

6. Ibid.

7. Bates, *Pennsylvania Volunteers*, V. II, pp. 1108-1113.

8. *B & L*, V. IV, pp. 179-82. George W. Ward, *History of the Second Pennsylvania Veteran Heavy Artillery*, pp. 29-30.

9. Ward, op. cit., pp. 31-47.

10. Bates and Richard, op. cit., pp. 339-40, Cemetery List.

11. Bates, *Pennsylvania Volunteers*, V. IV, pp. 1005, 1025-28.

12. Bates, *Pennsylvania Volunteers*, V. II, pp. 176-78; *Pilot*, May 24, 1864.

13. *Pilot*, May 10, 1864.

14. Compiled Service Record of Joseph Davison, RG 94, NA; Bates and Richard, op. cit., pp. 692-701, 708; Bates *Pennsylvania Volunteers*, V. I, pp. 692-701; *Pilot*, June 14, 1864.

15. *Pilot*, May 24, 31, June 7, 14, 1864.

16. Ward, op. cit., p. 48-55; Bates, *Pennsylvania Volunteers*, V. V., pp. 77-78.

17. Bates, *Pennsylvania Volunteers*, V. II, p. 178, V. IV, p. 1005; Mark M. Boatner, *The Civil War Dictionary*, pp. 162-65; Ward, op. cit., pp. 181-88.

18. Boatner, op. cit., Bates, *Pennsylvania Volunteers*, V. V, pp. 77-78; The Civil War Record of Henry F. Charles, 1862-1865, pp. 16-17, Boyer Coll., USAMHI.

19. Bates, *Pennsylvania Volunteers*, p. 78; *Pilot*, June 21, 1864.

20. *Pilot*, June 21, 1864; Bates and Richard, op. cit., p. 719; Bates, *Pennsylvania Volunteers*, V. V, pp. 97-127.

21. Bates, *Pennsylvania Volunteers*, V. II, p. 178; *Pilot*, June 14, 21, July 5, 1864.

22. Bates, *Pennsylvania Volunteers*, V. IV, p. 1005.

23. Ward, op. cit., pp. 56-61, 181-88; *Pilot*, June 21, 1864. Niswander served 9 months in Rebel prisons - first at Libby Prison in Richmond then at prisons in Macon and Savannah, Ga. With the approach of Sherman's forces through Georgia, he was transferred to Charleston then Columbia, S.C. Finally, he was sent to Charlotte, N.C. where he was exchanged in Feb., 1865. After the war he served as commander of Corporal Rihl Post #438, GAR in Greencastle. This information was obtained from the Niswander grave marker at the Church of the Brethren Cemetery in Welsh Run.

24. *Pilot*, June 21, 1864.

25. Bates, *Pennsylvania Volunteers*, V. II, pp. 178-79; Richard Wayne Lykes, *Campaign for Petersburg*, pp. 1-12.

26. Ward, op. cit., p. 65.

27. Ibid., p. 66; *Pilot*, July 5, 1864.

28. Ward, op. cit., pp. 189-91; *Village Record*, July 22, 1864; Cemetery List.

29. Ward, op. cit., p. 67; Bates, *Pennsylvania Volunteers*, V. II, p. 179; Francis Hoffman pension and service, Harold Hoffman collection.

30. Bates, *Pennsylvania Volunteers*, V. V, p. 78, 119-21; *Pilot*, July 5, 1864.

31. Lykes, op. cit., pp. 16-18; Bates, *Pennsylvania Volunteers*, V. V, p. 79.

32. Lykes, op. cit., pp. 24-33.

33. James I. Robertson, Jr., *Negro Soldiers in the Civil War* (CWTI Reprint), p. 11; Bates and Richard, op. cit., p. 355.

34. Benjamin Quarles, *The Negro in the Civil War*, pp. 186-87.

35. Cemetery List; Compiled Service Records of Timothy Anderson, 2nd U.S. Colored Cavalry, Tilghman Cain, 127th U.S. Colored Infantry, RG 94, NA; Bates, *Pennsylvania Volunteers*, V. V, pp. 1026-27, 1106, 1125; Frederick H. Dyer,

A *Compendium of the War of the Rebellion,* V. II., pp. 1723, 1730.

36. Bates, *Pennsylvania Volunteers,* V. V, pp. 1026-27.

37. Ibid, p. 79.

38. Ward, op. cit., pp. 96-97.

39. Boatner, op. cit., pp. 549, 743-45; Bates, *Pennsylvania Volunteers,* V. IV, pp. 1025-28; T. W. Bean, *The Roll of Honor of the 17th Pennsylvania Cavalry,* passim.

40. H. P. Moyer, *History of the Seventeenth Regiment Pennsylvania Volunteer Cavalry,* p. 408.

41. Rachel Minick, "Company G, 17th Pennsylvania Cavalry," unpublished paper presented before the Kittochtinny Historical Society.

42. Cemetery List.

43. Minick op. cit.

44. Bates, *Pennsylvania Volunteers,* V. IV, pp. 1008-09.

45. Ibid., V. V, pp. 32-35.

46. Samuel Clarke Farrar, *The Twenty Second Pennsylvania Cavalry,* pp. 176-77; Bates *Pennsylvania Volunteers,* V V, pp. 170-73; Bates and Richard, op. cit., pp. 352-53, 707.

47. *Pilot,* Jan. 12, 1864, p. 2.

48. Ward, op, cit., pp. 106-23. The definitive work on this operation is Dr. Richard J. Sommers, *Richmond Redeemed.*

49. Bates, *Pennsylvania Volunteers,* V. V, p. 404; *Civil War Diary of Josiah Shuman,* typed copy in the possession of Mrs. Hazel Eshleman, Hagerstown, Md., p. 1.

50. Shuman Diary, p. 1.

51. Bates, *Pennsylvania Volunteers,* V. V, pp. 79, 119-21.

52. Compiled Service Record of William H. Shatzer, 21st Pennsylvania Cavalry, RG 94, NA.

53. Pension File of Albert Alexander, 21st Pennsylvania Cavalry, RG 15, NA.

54. Shuman Diary, pp. 2-4.

55. Bates and Richard, op. cit., p. 353.

56. *Jacob Finafrock Diary* -Erwin collection, Sept. 29, Oct. 31, Dec. 14, 1864, Jan. 31, 1865.

57. Shuman Diary, pp. 5-6; *Echo Pilot,* Feb. 14, 1963.

58. Moyer, op. cit., pp. 155-56; Bean, op. cit.

59. Shuman Diary, p. 6.

60. Bates, *Pennsylvania Volunteers,* V. II, pp. 180-81.

61. Shuman Diary, p. 6; Bates, *Pennsylvania Volunteers,* V. V, pp. 1008-09.

62. Shuman Diary, p. 6; Lt. Henry G. Bonebrake Diary, Alexander Collection, Apr. 3, 1865.

63. Bates, *Pennsylvania Volunteers,* V. V, pp. 80, 1008-09.

64. Shuman Diary, p. 6; Bonebrake Diary, Apr. 6, 1865.

65. Shuman Diary, p. 6; Ward, op. cit., pp. 138-39; Bates, *Pennsylvania Volunteers,* pp. 1008-09.

66. Bonebrake Diary, Apr. 8, 1865; Shuman Diary, p. 6.

67. Bates and Richard, op. cit., p. 709; Shuman Diary, p. 6.

68. Shuman Diary p. 6; Bonebrake Diary, Apr. 9, 1865; Finafrock Diary, Apr. 9, 1865.

CHAPTER XIII

1. *Valley Spirit*, Apr. 11, 1865; General Order #46, April 10, Telegram Sent, RG 111, NA.

2. Captain W. L. Stryker to Lt. W. A. Adams, Apr. 15, 1865, Greencastle, Telegrams Sent. RG 111, NA.

3. *Valley Spirit*, Apr. 11, 1865.

4. J. D. Edmiston Turner, "Civil War Days in Mercersburg," KHSP, V. XII, p. 40; *Old Mercersburg*, p. 162.

5. *Valley Spirit*, Apr. 11, 1865.

6. Story told to Clippinger's granddaughter, Mrs. Mary Elden, of Waynesboro, Pa.

7. Charles R. Nicklas, "He Was There: The Story of Colonel Theodore McGowan," KSHP, V. XV, pp. 89-93.

8. *Valley Spirit*, Apr. 18, 1865.

9. Lloyd Lewis, *Myths After Lincoln*, pp. 58-60.

10. Captain W. L. Stryker to Major Morgan at Chambersburg, Apr. 27, 1865, RG 111, NA.

11. *Village Record*, Mar. 31, Apr. 7, 1865.

12. Ibid., Mar. 24, 1865; Samuel P. Bates, *History of Pennsylvania Volunteers, 1861-65*, V. V, p. 922.

13. *Village Record*, Apr. 21, 1865.

14. Ibid., Apr. 26, 1865.

15. Ibid., Aug. 4, 11, 1865.

16. Lewis, op. cit. pp. 111-15.

17. *Patriot and Union*, Apr. 21, 1865.

18. Lewis, op. cit., pp. 117-19.

19. Ibid., pp. 120-30.

20. *Franklin Repository*, Jan 1, 1890; E. B. Long, *The Civil War Day by Day*, pp. 687-691.

21. Mark M. Boatner, *The Civil War Dictionary*, p. 521.

22. Ibid., pp. 255, 523-24; Andrew F. Rolle, *The Lost Cause*, pp. 119, 123-24.

23. George W. Ward, *History of the Second Pennsylvania Veteran Heavy Artillery*, pp. 139-40; *Civil War Diary of Josiah Shuman*, p. 7; *Henry Bonebrake Diary*, Apr. 12, 1865.

24. *Bonebrake Diary*, Apr. 18, June 24, 1865.

25. *Shuman Diary*, p. 8.

26. Story related by John Dulebohn's grandson, Paul Hollinger of Waynesboro, Pa.

27. Compiled Service Record of Robert B. Henderson, 38th U.S. Colored Infantry, RG 94, NA.

28. Samuel L. Daihl, "1865 - Our Johnnies Come Marching Home," KHSP, V. XV, pp. 130-35.

29. Ward, op. cit., pp. 143-46.

30. Ibid., p. 141.

31. Paul J. Weshaeffer, *History of the Cumberland Valley Railroad, 1835-1919*, p. 85; Jacob H. Stoner, "George Frick, Father of Waynesboro Industry," KHSP, V. XII, pp. 59-60; W. P. Conrad, *Conococheague*, pp. 43-47.

32. *Village Record*, Mar. 17, 1865; *County History*, pp. 465, 531, 551; Conrad, *Conococheague*, p. 220.

33. Westhaeffer, op. cit., p. 85; *Village Record*, July 28, 1865.

34. *Village Record*, Nov. 3, 1865.

35. Samuel P. Bates and J. Fraise Richard, *History of Franklin County, Pennsylvania*, p. 532.

36. Conrad, *Conococheague*, pp. 43-46, 49-50.

37. *Village Record*, May 26, 1865.

38. Bates and Richard, op. cit., p. 715.

39. *Valley Spirit*, Apr. 18, 1865.

40. Conrad, *Conococheague*, p. 46.

41. *Village Record*, Mar. 24, May 26, Aug. 11, Nov. 3, 1865.

42. *Village Record*, Aug. 18, 1865.

43. W. P. Conrad, "The Coachman's Horn is Heard No More," KHSP, V. XVII, p. 117.

44. Bates and Richard, op. cit., pp. 936-37; Robert M. Utley, *Frontier Regulars; The United States Army and the Indian, 1886-1890*, p. 288; George W. Cullum, *Biographical Register of the Officers and Graduates of the U.S. Military Academy*, pp. 601-602; Francis B. Heitman, *Historical Register and Dictionary of the United States Army*, p. 250.

45 Compiled Service Record of Brig. General David S. Gordon, 3157, Appointments, Commission and Personal Branch, RG 94, NA.

46. Pension file of Michael Bushey, 7th Pennsylvania Cavalry, RG 15, NA; *Franklin Repository*, Jan. 1, 1890.

47. Bates and Richard, op. cit., pp. 707, 717; The information on Joseph Holman was provided by Mrs. Eleanor Lyon of Livonia, Michigan.

48. John Graham Palmer, "The Evolution of a Challenge," KHSP, V. XIII, pp. 256-57.

49. Bates and Richard, op. cit., p. 733.

50. Ibid., pp. 551-52; Conrad, *Conococheague*, pp. 48-49; Conrad, "Coachman's Horn,", pp. 112-14.

51. Bates and Richard, op. cit., pp. 707-08, 854, 873; W. P. Conrad, *Franklin County School Superintendents*, p. 9.

52. Bates and Richard, op. cit., pp. 715-16, 718-19, 721.

53. *Public Opinion*, July 16, 1913; Bates and Richard, op. cit., pp. 680-82, 730-32.

54. Bates and Richard, op. cit., pp. 732-36; Conrad, *Conococheague*, p. 152.

55. Information provided by Mr. and Mrs. Richard Ervin, Greencastle, Pa.

56. Information provided by Mrs. Kathleen Grosh, Greencastle, Pa.

57. Information provided by Mr. Paul Musselman, Greencastle, Pa.

58. *Echo Pilot*, Nov. 22, 1962.

59. Conrad, *School Superintendents*, p. 8.

60. Samuel Houston Rankin, obituary, provided by John T. Conrad, III, Greencastle, Pa.

61. William A. Reid, *Narrative of the History of the Presbyterian Sabbath School of Greencastle, Pa.*, p. 17. W. P. Conrad, *Conococheague*, p. 137; John Graham Palmer "The Evolution of a Challenge," KHSP, V. XIII, pp. 162-63.

62. D. G. Beers, *Atlas of Franklin County,* Pennsylvania, p. 9.

63. W. P. Conrad, *A Town Grows in Antrim,* p. 3.

64. Ibid. p. 9.

65. A good account of the bank's founding is the pamphlet by G. Fred Ziegler, *History of the First National Bank.*

66. Bates and Richard, op. cit., pp. 551; Conrad, *School Superintendents,* p. 9; *Record Herald,* Mar. 13, 1947.

67. Conrad, *Conococheague,* op. cit., p. 187; *Record Herald,* Mar. 13, 1947.

68. *Pilot,* July 26, 1864; *Village Record,* Aug. 11, 1865; Conrad, "Coachman's Horn," p. 109.

69. *Village Record,* Aug. 11, 1865.

70. Ibid., Sept. 29, 1865.

71. Stories related to W. P. Conrad by Nelson Leckron, State Line, Pa. and Robert L. Johnston, (deceased), Greencastle, Pa.

72. Carl E. Robinson, *Necrology of Franklin County, Pennsylvania.* A copy of the Missavy obituary in the possession of W. P. Conrad.

73. The Scotland School is still in operation today.

CHAPTER XIV

1. Mary R. Dearing, *Veterans in Politics,* pp. 1-6.

2. Arthur D. Graeff, *The History of Pennsylvania,* pp. 298-99; A. J. White Hutton, "John White Geary," KHSP, V. XIII, pp. 451-61.

3. George O. Seilhamer, *Biographical Annals of Franklin County, Pennsylvania,* pp. 158-60; Jacob H. Stoner, *Historical Papers,* p. 524. The "border claims" have not been forgotten. The following appeared in the Jan. 30, 1982 issue of the Chambersburg *Public Opinion:* "R. Budd Dwyer, treasurer of Pennsylvania, had a suggestion for Franklin County residents looking for restitution of Civil War losses in his message at this month's courthouse dedication. The county submitted a claim in 1872 for $809.55 for destruction of the old courthouse by Confederate forces, he said. The claim was signed by the governor, but the federal government never authorized payment. Such approval would be a great windfall to Chambersburg since the issue 'pertains to Franklin County more than any other county in Pennsylvania,' said Dwyer. He called it a cause for persons interested in lobbying in Washington. Anyone care to propose federal approval to these days of budget-cutting."

4. This is an estimate based on biographical data provided in Samuel P. Bates and J. Fraise Richard, *History of Franklin County, Pennsylvania.*

5. Wallace Evins Davis, *Patriotism on Parade,* pp. 28-43; Paul F. Mottelay and T. Campbell-Copeland, ed., *The Soldier in Our Civil War,* V. 11, pp. 390-92.

6. Davis, op. cit., pp. 33-36; *Kauffmans Progressive News,* Feb. 25, 1921.

7. Davis, op. cit., pp. 35-40.

8. Bates and Richard, op. cit., pp. 481-82, 529, 534-35, 553, 603-04.

9. Ibid., p. 553.

10. *Minute book,* p. 3, G.A.R. Coll., Greencastle, Pa.

11. Ibid., p. 39.

12. Ibid., pp. 6-7.

13. Bates and Richard, op. cit., pp. 433-42.

14. *Minute Book,* p. 15, G.A.R. Coll., Greencastle, Pa.

15. Ibid., pp. 18-29; *Grant Memorial Service Program,* G.A.R. Coll., Greencastle, Pa. D. Z. Shook of Greencastle attend-

ed Grant's funeral in New York City. *Echo Pilot*, Mar. 7, 1963.

16. *Minute Book*, pp. 33-42, G.A.R. Coll., Greencastle, Pa.; *Echo Pilot*, June 20, 1963; Rev. Cyrus Cort, *Corporal Rihl Dedicatory Services*, pp. 96-101.

17. *Minute Book*, pp. 52, 55, 58, G.A.R. Coll., Greencastle, Pa.

18. Ibid., pp. 61, 62, 69, 71, 75. 76.

19. Ibid., pp. 137, 172.

20. Ibid., pp. 193, 194, 198.

21. Ibid., pp. 97, 131, 205, 207, 212, 221; Letter from Adjutant General to Post 438 Commander, August 19, 1889, G.A.R. Coll., Greencastle, Pa.

22. *Minute Book*, pp. 106-07. G.A.R. Coll., Greencastle, Pa.

23. Many veterans visited the battlefields when they were well up in years. In 1927, Clinton Gordon, accompanied by his son, Ross, visited Fredericksburg Battlefield, where he had fought 64 years earlier. *Echo Pilot*, Nov. 3, 1927; Thomas L. Connelly, *The Marble Man*, pp. 69-71.

24. Miscellaneous advertisements, G.A.R. Coll., Greencastle, Pa.

25. Woman's Relief Corps Letter, Aug. 25, 1896, G.A.R. Coll., Greencastle, Pa.

26. Adjutant Reports, G.A.R. Coll., Greencastle, Pa. Calculations of Robert Meck, Veterans Affairs Director, Franklin County, Pa.

27. Dearing, op. cit., pp. 496-97.

28. Birkmeyer, Ewers, and Palmer applications for membership, Adjutant's Report, June, 1895, G.A.R. Coll., Greencastle, Pa.

29. *Minute Book*, pp. 258, 288, G.A.R. Coll., Greencastle, Pa.

30. General Orders No. 1, Headquarters Grand Army of the Republic, Sept. 23, 1901, G.A.R. Coll., Greencastle, Pa.

31. *Echo Pilot*, Jan. 9, 1902, Aug. 4, 1977; W. P. Conrad, *Conococheague*, pp. 196-206.

32. *Echo Pilot*, Aug. 20, 1908, Aug. 10, 1911; *Official Program* - 1908 Old Home Week, Helen Welch Coll., Greencastle, Pa.

33. *Minute Book*, p. 283. G.A.R. Coll., Greencastle, Pa.

34. *Public Opinion*, June 19, 1913; see also Lt. Col. Lewis E. Beitler, ed., *Fiftieth Anniversary of the Battle of Gettysburg;* Milton A. Embich, ed., *Military History of the Third Division, Ninth Corps Army of the Potomac*, p. 72.

35. *Public Opinion*, July 16 & 17, 1913.

36. *Echo Pilot*, May 30, 1963.

37. Post Resolution, Sept. 16, 1921, G.A.R. Coll., Greencastle, Pa.

38. *Public Opinion*, Mar. 28, 1941; Conrad, op. cit., pp. 66-67; *1921 Memorial Day Program*, G.A.R. Coll., Greencastle, Pa.

39. *Minute Book*, p. 362, G.A.R. Coll., Greencastle, Pa. *Egan Scrapbook #3*, Besore Coll., Greencastle, Pa., Singer obituary, provided by Mrs. Pauline Maxwell, Waynesboro, Pa.

BIBLIOGRAPHY

LIST OF ABBREVIATIONS

BLC: Besore Library Collection.

B & L: Battles and Leaders of the Civil War.

Cemetery List: Refers to Civil War Burial List of Franklin County Office of Veterans Affairs.

CWTI: Civil War Times Illustrated.

CWTI Coll: Civil War Times Illustrated Collection, U.S. Army Military History Institute.

CW Misc. Coll: Civil War Miscellaneous Collection, U.S. Army Military History Institute.

G.A.R. Coll: Records of Corporal Rihl Post 438, Grand Army of the Republic, Greencastle, PA.

HCWRT Coll: Harrisburg Civil War Roundtable Collection, U.S. Army Military History Institute.

HSP: Historical Society of Pennsylvania.

KHSP: *Kittochtinny Historial Society Papers.*

LC: Library of Congress.

NA: National Archives.

OR: *War of the Rebellion: A Compilation of the Official Records of the Union and Confederate Armies.*

RG: Refers to Record Groups in the National Archives.

SHC: Southern Historical Collection, University of North Carolina.

SHSP: *Southern Historical Society Papers.*

USAMHI: U.S. Army Military History Institute.

MANUSCRIPTS

BESORE LIBRARY COLLECTION
> Egan Scrapbook.
> List of men drafted from Antrim Township, February 22, 1865.
> Greencastle Map of 1853.

FRANKLIN COUNTY OFFICE OF VETERANS AFFAIRS
> Civil War Burial List

HISTORICAL SOCIETY OF PENNSYLVANIA (HSP)
> Cadwalader, George Coll.

LIBRARY OF CONGRESS (LC)
> Hotchkiss, Jedediah Papers.
> > War Diary, June 15, 1861-December 23, 1865.
> > Letter Book, June 27, 1861-November 14, 1864.

NATIONAL ARCHIVES (NA)
> Record Group 15: Records of the Veterans Administration
> > Union Pension Files.
> Record Group 94: The Adjutant General's Office
> > Compiled Union Service Records.
> Record Group 111: Office of the Chief Signal Officer
> > Letters Received 1864.
> > Military Histories of Officers.
> > Telegrams Sent 1864-1865.
> > Reports of Operations 1864-1865.
> Record Group 393: United States Army Continental Commands, 1821-1920
> > Department of Pennsylvania Papers.
> > Department of Susquehanna Papers.

PHILIP SCHAFF LIBRARY, LANCASTER THEOLOGICAL SEMINARY (LTS)
> Hartman, Charles Diary, 1862-1863.

SOUTHERN HISTORICAL COLLECTION, UNIVERSITY OF NORTH CAROLINA (SHC)
> Alexander, Edward Porter. Coll.
> > Memoirs
> McClaws, Lafayette. Papers
> > Letters 1863.

THE WINCHESTER-FREDERICK COUNTY (VA) HISTORICAL SOCIETY
> Wayland Collection
> > Firebaugh, Samuel Diary, September 25, 1862-March 3, 1864.

U.S. ARMY MILITARY HISTORY INSTITUTE
    Boyer, Ronald Coll.
        Bilighous, H. A. Diary, September, 1862.
        Charles, Henry F. Memoirs, 1862-1865.
    Civil War Miscellaneous Coll.
        Montgomery, James H. Diary
    Civil War Times Illustrated Coll.
        Craig, Samuel E. Memoirs of Civil War and Reconstruction.
        Baker, I. Norvel Diary, 1861-65.
    Pardee-Robison Family Coll.
        Pardee, Calvin Letters - 1861.
    Harrisburg Civil War Round Table Coll.
        Filbert, Peter Augustus, The Civil War Military Record
        Metzger, K. G. Letters, 1861.
    Powers, Kenneth H. Coll.
        "History of the 23rd Regiment, National Guard, State of New York." (Unpublished manuscript), 1937.

WESTERN MARYLAND ROOM, WASHINGTON COUNTY FREE LIBRARY, HAGERSTOWN, MARYLAND
    Washington House Register, 1858-1861.

PRIVATE COLLECTIONS

CHARLES BERT COLLECTION, Greencastle, PA.
    Davison, Joseph A., Letters 1861-65.

FRANK L. CARBAUGH AMERICAN LEGION POST 373, Greencastle, PA.
    Records of Corporal Rihl Post 438, Grand Army of the Republic, Greencastle, PA
    (G.A.R. Coll.)
        Minute Book
        Adjutant Records
        Miscellaneous Records and Correspondence

W. P. CONRAD COLLECTION, Greencastle, PA.
    The Lazarus Wingerd Day Book, 1802-1862.

MARY DETRICH COLLECTION, Greencastle, PA.
    Payment order to Jeremiah Detrich from 1st Lieutenant S. M. Moore, Acting A.A.G., Rodes Division.

MARY ELDEN COLLECTION, Waynesboro, PA.
    H. W. Pinkerton to Mrs. Sarah Hade Letter, August 6th, 1863.

MR. AND MRS. RICHARD ERVIN COLLECTION, Greencastle, PA.
    Copy of Adams House Register
    Finafrock, Jacob Diary

MRS. HAZEL ESHLEMAN COLLECTION, Hagerstown, MD.
    Shuman, Josiah Civil War Diary.

KATHLEEN GROSH COLLECTION, Greencastle, PA.
    Henry White Papers.

HAROLD HOFFMAN COLLECTION, Greencastle, PA.
    Hoffman, Francis, Pension and Service Records.

MINNICH-MILLER FUNERAL HOME, Greencastle, PA.
    Detrich Burial Records.

DISSERTATIONS AND THESES

EVERETT, EDWARD GEORGE. "Pennsylvania's Mobilization for War, 1860-1861."
    Ph.D. dissertation, University of Pittsburgh, 1950.

GILBERT, BETTYE. "The People of the Cumberland Valley in the Gettysburg Campaign."
    B. A. Thesis, Gettysburg College, 1963.

HACKENBURG, RANDY. "The Columbia Guards - Danville Volunteer Infantry 1817-1861."
    M. A. Thesis, Bloomsburg State College, 1975.

NEWSPAPERS

Chambersburg, PA — *Dispatch.*
Chambersburg, PA — *Franklin Repository.*
Chambersburg, PA — *Public Opinion.*
Chambersburg, PA — *Valley Spirit.*
Detroit *Daily Tribune.*
Greencastle, PA — *Echo-Pilot.*
Greencastle, PA — *Kauffmans Progressive News.*
Greencastle, PA — *The Pilot.*
Greencastle, PA — *Valley Echo.*
Hagerstown, MD — *Herald Mail.*
Harrisburg *Daily Telegraph.*
Harrisburg *Patriot and Union.*
Mercersburg Journal.
National Tribune.
New York *Herald.*
Philadelphia *Inquirer.*
The Fulton Democrat.
Valley News Echo - Monthly Civil War Newspaper published 1959-1965 by the Potomac Edison Co.,
   Hagerstown, MD.
Waynesboro, PA — *Record Herald.*
Waynesboro, PA — *Village Record.*

ARTICLES, BOOKS, AND PAMPHLETS
OFFICIAL DOCUMENTS

Annual Report of the Adjutant General of the State of Rhode Island, for the Year 1865. Providence. Providence Press
   Company. 1866.

"Report of the Board of Military Claims, made to the Legislature of Pennsylvania, for the Year 1863." Ex. Doc. *Reports
   of the Heads of Departments Transmitted to the Governor of Pennsylvania in Pursuance of Law for the Financial Year
   Ending November, 1863.* Vol. II Harrisburg. Singley and Myers State Printers. 1864.

"Report of the Commissary General of the Commonwealth of Pennsylvania for the Year 1861." Ex. Doc. *Reports of the
   Heads of Departments, Transmitted to the Governor in Pursuance of Law for the Financial Year Ending November
   30, 1861, together with the Report of the Superintendent of Common Schools.* Harrisburg. A. Boyd Hamilton, State
   Printer, 1861.

"Report of the Commissary General, of the Commonwealth of Pennsylvania, for the Year 1862." Ex. Doc. *Reports of the
   Heads of Departments, Transmitted to the Governor in Pursuance of Law for the Financial Year Ending November
   30, 1862, together with the Report of the Superintendent of Common Schools.* Harrisburg. Singerly and Myers, State
   Printer, 1863.

"Report of the Quartermaster General of the Commonwealth of Pennsylvania, for the Year 1862." Ex. Doc. *Reports of the
   Heads of Departments, Transmitted to the Governor in Pursuance of law for the Financial Year Ending November
   30, 1862, together with the Report of the Superintendent of Commons Schools.* Harrisburg. Singerly and Myers, State
   Printer, 1863.

The War of the Rebellion: A Compilation of the Official Records of the Union and Confederate Armies. Washington, D.C.
   U.S. Government Printing Office, 1880-1901.

LOCAL AND REGIONAL STUDIES

Atlas of Franklin County, Pennsylvania. Philadelphia. Pomeroy and Beers, 1868.

Bates, Samuel P. and Richard, J. Fraise. *History of Franklin County, Pennsylvania.* Chicago. Warner, Beers and
   Co., 1887

Beitler, Lewis E., ed. *Fiftieth Anniversary of the Battle of Gettysburg.* Harrisburg, PA. Wm. Stanley Ray, State
   Printer. 1914.

Bi-Centennial Committee; *Historial Data Concerning St. Thomas Township: 1734-1934.* St. Thomas, PA. August 1,
   2, 3, 4, 1934.

Coleman, John F.; *The Disruption of the Pennsylvania Democracy 1848-1860.* Harrisburg, PA. The Pennsylvania

Historical and Museum Commission. 1975.

Conrad, W. P. *A Town Grows in Antrim*, Greencastle, PA Graphic Universal, Inc. 1977. Conrad, W. P. *Conococheague: A History of the Greencastle-Antrim Community: 1736-1971*.

Robson and Kaye, Inc. Chambersburg, PA. 1971.

Conrad, W. P. *Franklin County School Superintendents*. Greencastle, PA. Graphics Universal, Inc. 1977.

Conrad, W. P. "The Coachman's Horn is Heard No More." *The Kittochtinny Historical Society Papers*. (KHSP), Vol. XVII, pp. 93-123.

Conrad, W. P. *The Greenmount Story*.

Cordell, Glenn R. *Shaking the Cordell Family Tree*. Chambersburg, PA. Craft Press, Inc. 1977.

Cort, Cyrus, ed. *Enoch Brown Sesqui-Centennial Memorial Services August 4, 1914 ... with Appendix: Corporal Rihl Dedicatory Services, June 22, 1886*. Reading, PA. I. M. Beaver, Printer, 1915.

Cremer, C. W. "Historical Incidents Connected with Waynesboro and Franklin County." *The Kittochtinny Historical Society Papers*. (KHSP), Vol. IX.

Deatrich, C. M. *The Drummer Boy of the Conococheague*.

Eaton, Clement. *The Growth of Southern Civilization: 1790-1860*. New York. Harper and Row. 1961.

Farm Scenes: The Early Years in Cumberland County. Carlisle, PA. The Cumberland County Historical Society and the Hamilton Library Association. 1977.

Finafrock, J. L. "Biographical Sketches." *Franklin County School Annual*, November, 1917. pp. 4-62.

Fletcher, Stevenson Whitcomb. *Pennsylvania Agriculture and Country Life. 1640-1840*. Harrisburg. Commonwealth of Pennsylvania Historical and Museum Commission. 1971.

Garling, Paul E. *The Garling Family from 1751-1953*. Chambersburg, PA. Kerr Printing Co. 1954.

Gilbert, Russell Wieder. *A Picture of the Pennsylvania Germans*. Gettysburg. The Pennsylvania Historical Association. 1971.

Gordy, U. L. "The Old Browns Mill School." *The Kittochtinny Historical Society Papers*, (KHSP) Vol. XI. pp. 333-364.

Graeff, Arthur D. *The History of Pennsylvania*. Philadelphia. John C. Winston Co. 1945.

Hege, Grace; Sollenberger, Samuel Grove. *Jacob Grove and Elizabeth Lesher Grove Family*. 1974.

Hege, John B. *Marion and Environments: Franklin County, PA Historical and Reminiscent*.

Hoke, Jacob *Reminiscenses of the War; or Incidents Which Transpired in and about Chambersburg*. Chambersburg, M. A. Foltz. 1884.

Koehnlein, John M. "Zion: City of Our God. A History of the Evangelical Lutheran Congregation of Greencastle." (Unpublished paper - Evangelical Lutheran Church, Greencastle, PA)

Laughlin and Hykes. *A History of the Prather, Shank, Royer, Laughlin Families*.

M'Cauley, I. H. *Historical Sketch of Franklin County, Pennsylvania*. Chambersburg, PA. John M. Pomeroy. 1877.

Manakee, Harold R. *Maryland in the Civil War*. Balitmore. Garamond Pridemark Press. 1961.

Nead, Matthias Benjamin. *Waynesboro 1797-1900 Centennial History*. Harrisburg, PA. Harrisburg Publishing Co. 1900.

Old Home Week Committee. *Official Program: Old Home Week Celebration, Greencastle, PA, August 17-22. 1908*.

Old Mercersburg. Williamsport, PA. Grit Publishing Co. 1949.

Omwake, Henry. *Papers and Addresses*. Harrisburg. 1912.

Reid, William A. *Narrative of the History of the Presbyterian Sabbath School of Greencastle, PA*. Greencastle. Press Printing House. 1885.

Robinson, Carl. *"Necrology of Franklin County, Pennsylvania*.

Robinson, Carl E.; Strite, Amos W. *Strite Family History*. 1963.

Seilhamer, George O. *Biographical Annals of Franklin County, Pennsylvania*. Chicago. The Genealogical Publishing Co. 1905.

"Some History Connected with Enoch Brown School," *Franklin County School Annual*, November, 1919. pp. 28-32.

Stake, Virginia Ott. *John Brown in Chambersburg*. Chambersburg, PA. Franklin County Heritage, Inc. 1977.

Stoner, Jacob H. "George Frick, Father of Waynesboro Industry." *Kittochtinny Historical Society Papers*. (KHSP), Vol. XII, pp. 51-70.

Stoner, Jacob H. *Historical Papers, Franklin County and the Cumberland Valley Pennsylvania*. Chambersburg, PA. The Craft Press, Inc.

Stouffer, Christian S.; Stouffer, Mary Zarger. *Zarger-Zarker Genealogy*. Pottstown, PA. Smale's Printery. 1974.

The Omwakes of Indian Spring Farm. Cincinnatti, OH. 1926.

Thrush, Ambrose Watts. *Medical Men of Franklin County*. By the author. Chambersburg, PA. 1929.

Tousey, Thomas G. *Military History of Carlisle and Carlisle Barracks*. Richmond, Virginia. The Dietz Press. 1939.

Westhaeffer, Paul J. *History of the Cumberland Valley Railroad 1835-1919*. Ephrata, Pa. Science Press. 1979.

Williams, T.J.C. *History of Frederick County, Maryland. Vol. II*. Baltimore. L. R. Titsworth & Co. 1910.

Williams, Thomas J. C. *A History of Washington County, Maryland*. John M. Runk and L. R. Titsworth. 1906.

Ziegler, G. Fred. *A Brief History of the First National Bank* - Booklet published by the bank in 1964.

AUTOBIOGRAPHIES, BIOGRAPHIES, DIARIES, LETTERS, MEMOIRS, AND PERSONAL NARRATIVES

Battles and Leaders of the Civil War (B & L) 4 Vols. New York. The Century Company. 1887.

Blackford III, Charles Minor, ed. *Letters From Lee's Army: or Memoirs of Life In and Out of the Army in Virginia During the War Between the States*. New York. Charles Scribner's Sons. 1947.

Bowers, William S. ed. "The William Heyser Diary," *Kittochtinny Historical Society Papers* (KHSP) pp. 1-96.

Catton, Bruce. *U.S. Grant and the American Military Tradition*. New York. Grosset & Dunlap. 1954.

"Civil War Letters From Two Brothers," *The Yale Review*, Vol. XVIII, September, 1928. pp. 148-161.

Coffin, Charles Carleton. *The Boys of '61: or, Four Years of Fighting*. Boston. Estes and Lauriat. 1883.

Connelly, Thomas L. *The Marble Man, Robert E. Lee and His Image in American Society*. Baton Rouge. Louisiana State University Press. 1977.

Cullum, George W. *Biographical Register of the Officers and Graduates of the U.S. Military Academy at West Point, N.Y. from its Establishment in 1802 to 1890 with the Early History of the United States Military Academy*, Vol. II. Boston and New York. Houghton Mifflin and Company, 1891.

Dahlgren, Rear-Admiral. *Memoir of Ulric Dahlgren*. Philadelphia. J. B. Lippincott & Co. 1872.

Dawson, Francis W. Capt. C.S.A. *Reminiscenses of Confederate Service, 1861-1865*. Charleston, S.C. The News and Courier Book Presses. 1882.

Douglas, Henry Kyd. *I Rode With Stonewall*. Chapel Hill, N.C. Fawcett Publications, Inc. 1940.

Egle, William H. ed. *Andrew Gregg Curtin: His Life and Services*. Philadelphia. Avil Printing Co. 1895.

Fradin, Morris. "Curious Burial for A Hero's Leg," *The Hagerstown Cracker Barrel*, November, 1972, pp. 10-12.

Freeman, Douglas Southall. *Lee's Lieutenants*. Vols. I, II, III. New York. Charles Scribner's Sons. 1944.

Gannett, Michael R. ed. "Twelve Letters From Altoona, June-July, 1863." *Pennsylvania History*, Vol. XLVII, No. 1 (January 1980) pp. 38-56.

Gilmor, Harry. *Four Years in the Saddle*. New York. Harper & Brothers. 1866.

Groninger, William H. "Lincoln's Visit to Antietam Battlefield." *National Tribune*, April 7, 1927, p. 5.

Hamilton, J. G. De Roulhac; Cameron, Rebecca, eds. *The Papers of Randolph Abbott Shotwell*. Vols. I, II. Raleigh. The North Carolina Historical Commission. 1931.

Heitman, Francis B. *Historical Register and Dictionary of the United States Army, from its organization, September 29, 1789 to March 2, 1903*. Vol. I. Washington. Government Printing Office. 1903.

Howard, McHenry. *Recollections of a Maryland Confederate Soldier and Staff Officer under Johnston, Jackson and Lee*. Morningside Bookshop. 1975.

Hutton, A. J. White. "John White Geary," *Kittochtinny Historical Society Papers* (KHSP), Vol. XIII, pp. 451-461.

Inman, Arthur Crew, ed. *Soldier of the South: General Pickett's War Letters to His Wife*. Boston. Houghton Mifflin Co. 1928.

Jones, Virgil Carrington. *Gray Ghosts and Rebel Raiders*. New York. Henry Holt and Company. 1956.

Jones, Virgil Carrington. *Ranger Mosby*. Chapel Hill. The University of North Carolina Press. 1944.

Krick, Robert K. *Lee's Colonels*. Dayton, Ohio. Morningside Press. 1919.

Leon, L. *Diary of a Tar Heel Confederate Soldier*. Charlotte, N.C. Stone Publishing Company. 1913.

Lewis, Lloyd. *Myths After Lincoln*. New York. Press of the Readers Club. 1941.

Lord, Walter. *The Fremantle Diary*. Boston. Little, Brown and Company. 1954.

MacCauley, Clay. "From Chancellorsville to Libby Prison." Glimpses of a Nation's Struggle. A series of Papers Read Before the Minnesota Commandery of the Military Order of the Loyal Legion of the United States. St. Paul. St. Paul Book and Stationery Co. 1887.

MacCauley, Clay. "Through Chancellorsville, Into and Out of Libby Prison." Personal Narratives Sixth Series, No. 7. Soldiers and Sailors Historical Society of Rhode Island. Providence. 1904.

McKim, Randolph H. *A Soldier's Recollections, Leaves from the Diary of a Young Confederate*. London. 1910.

Moore, Frank, ed. *Rebellion Record: A Diary of American Events with Documents, Narratives, Illustrative Incidents, Poetry, etc.* 11 Vols. and Supplement. New York. 1861-1868.

Nichols, Edward J. *Toward Gettysburg: A Biography of General John F. Reynolds*. The Pennsylvania State University Press. 1958.

Nicklas, Charles R. "He Was There: The Story of Colonel Theodore McGowan," *Kittochtinny Historical Society Papers*. Vol. XV, pp. 89-95.

Oates, Stephen B. *With Malice Toward None: The Life of Abraham Lincoln*. New York. Harper & Row. 1977.

Pierce, Francis E. "A Letter from Fredericksburg." Civil War Times Illustrated (CWTI), Vol. I. December, 1962, pp. 6-9, 28-30.

Patterson, Robert. *A Narrative of the Campaign in the Valley of the Shenandoah in 1861*. Philadelphia. Sherman & Co. Printers. 1865.

Rowe, Jerold E. ed. "The Civil War Diary of John T. Lewis," *Camp Chase Gazette*, October, 1980, pp. 13-15.

Scott, Hugh. "Philadelphia's Versatile Admiral," *Today ... The Philadelphia Inquirer Sunday Magazine*, April 9, 1961, pp. 48-49.

Stewart, A. M. *Camp, March and Battle-Field; or, Three Years and a Half with the Army of the Potomac*. Philadelphia. Jas. B. Rodgers. 1865.

Snow, Richard F. "Belle Boyd." *American Heritage* Vol. XXXI (Feb.-Mar., 1980), pp. 94-95.

Thomas, Wilbur. *General George H. Thomas: The Indomitable Warrior*. New York. Exposition Press. 1964.

Turner, J. D. Edmiston, ed. "Civil War Days in Mercersburg, as related in the Diary of the Rev. Thomas Creigh, D.D. August 1, 1862-July 20, 1865." *Kittochtinny Historical Society Papers* (KSHP), pp. 29-49.

CAMPAIGN AND BATTLE NARRATIVES

Bill, Alfred Hoyt; Johnson, James Ralph; Millhollen, Hirst Dillon. Horseman: *Blue and Gray.* New York. Oxford University Press. 1960.

Castel, Albert. "The Guerrilla War 1861-1865." Special Issue Civil War Times Illustrated. (Oct., 1974.)

Catton, Bruce. *A Stillness at Appomattox.* Garden City, N.Y. Doubleday & Co., Inc. 1953.

Coddington, Edwin B. *The Gettysburg Campaign.* Dayton, Ohio. Morningside Bookshop. 1979.

Cullen, Joseph P. *Richmond National Battlefield Park Virginia.* Washington, D.C. United States Department of the Interior. 1961.

Davis, William C. *Battle at Bull Run.* Baton Rouge. Louisiana State University Press. 1977.

Death of Corporal Rihl. Pamphlet distributed by the Citizens National Bank of Greencastle, September, 1963.

Eleven Days in the Militia During the War of the Rebellion; Being a Journal of the "Emergency" Campaign of 1862. By a Militiaman. Collins Printer. Philadelphia. 1883.

"General R. E. Rodes' Report of the Battle of Gettysburg," *Southern Historical Society Papers,* Vol. II, (July to December, 1876.

Groninger, William H. "With General Burnside at Fredericksburg, " *National Tribune,* April 1, 1926.

Hoke, Jacob. *The Great Invasion.* New York. Thomas Yoseloff.

Jacobs, M. *Notes on the Rebel Invasion of Maryland and Pennsylvania and the Battle of Gettysburg July 1st, 2nd and 3rd, 1863.* Gettysburg, PA. The Times Printing House. 1909.

Luff, William M. "March of the Cavalry from Harper's Ferry, September 14, 1862." Military Essays and Recollections. Papers read before the Commandery of the State of Illinois, Military Order of the Loyal Legion of the United States. Vol. II, pp. 33-48. Published by Order of the Commandery. Chicago. A. C. McClurg and Co. 1894.

Lykes, Richard Wayne. *Campaign for Petersburg.* U.S. Department of the Interior, U.S. Government Printing Office, Washington, D.C. 1970.

McCormick, John F. "The Harpers Ferry Skedaddlers," Civil War Times Illustrated (CWTI), Vol. XIV (Dec., 1975), pp. 32-39.

Mies, John W. "Breakout at Harpers Ferry," Civil War History (CWH), Vol. II, (June, 1956) pp. 21-28.

Mitchell, Joseph B. *Decisive Battles of the Civil War.* Greenwich, Conn. Fawcett Publications, Inc. 1955.

Murfin, James V. *The Gleam of Bayonets: The Battle of Antietam and the Maryland Campaign of 1862.* New York. Thomas Yoseloff. 1965.

Nye, Wilbur Sturtevant. *Here Come the Rebels!* Baton Rouge. Louisiana State University Press. 1965.

Palfrey, Edward A. "Some of the Secret History of Gettysburg," *Southern Historical Society Papers,* SHSP, Vol. VIII, pp. 521-26.

Polley, J. B. "Hood's Texans in Pennsylvania," *Confederate Veteran,* Vol. IV, November, 1896, pp. 377-79.

Schildt, John W. *Roads from Gettysburg.* Chewsville, MD. John W. Schildt. 1979.

Schildt, John W. *Roads to Gettysburg.* Parsons, W.VA. McClain Printing Company. 1978.

Schuricht, Herman. "Jenkins Brigade in the Gettysburg Campaign," *Southern Historical Society Papers,* SHSP, Vol. XXIV, pp. 339-350.

Shier, Maynard J. "The Battle of Falling Waters," Civil War Times Illustrated. Vol. XI. (February, 1977), pp. 16-26.

Snell, Charles W. *"Harpers Ferry Repels an Attack and Becomes the Major Base of Operations for Sheridan's Army, July 4, 1864, to July 27, 1865.* (A Report on the Federal Fortifications at Harpers Ferry, W.VA. January 1, 1864, to July, 1865, to accompany "Map IV-Harper's Ferry, W.VA., July 4, 1864-April 9, 1865," date January 15, 1950) Harpers

Ferry National Monument, Research Project No. HF-98D, January 21, 1960.

Sommers, Richard J. *Richmond Redeemed: The Siege at Petersburg.* Garden City, N.Y. Doublday & Co., Inc. 1981.

Stewart, George R. *Pickett's Charge.* Boston. Houghton Mifflin Co. 1959.

Tanner, Robert G. *Stonewall in the Valley: Thomas J. 'Stonewall' Jackson's Shenandoah Valley Campaign, Spring 1862.* Garden City, N.Y. Doubleday & Co., Inc. 1976.

Trimble, Isaac. "The Battle of Gettysburg," *Southern Historical Society Papers,* SHSP, Vol. XXVI. pp. 116-128.

Tucker, Glenn, *Chickamauga: Bloody Battle in the West.* Dayton, OH. Morningside Bookshop Press. 1976.

Ward, W. C. "Incidents and Personal Experiences on the Battlefield at Gettysburg," *Confederate Veteran,* Vol. VIII, August, 1900, pp. 345-49.

Wert, Jeffry D. "Johnston vs. Patterson," Civil War Times Illustrated. Vol. XVII. (December, 1978). pp. 4-11, 41-44.

Woodbury, Augustus. *A Narrative of the Campaign of the First Rhode Island Regiment, in the Spring and Summer of 1861.* Providence. Sidneys Rider. 1862.

UNIT HISTORIES

UNION

Bates, Samuel P. *History of Pennsylvania Volunteers, 1861-5.* 5 Vols. Harrisburg. B. Singerly. 1871.

Bazelon, Bruce S. and Trussell, John B. B. *Defending the Commonwealth: Catalogue of the Militia Exhibit at the William Penn Memorial Museum, Harrisburg, Pennsylvania.* Providence, RI. Mowbray Company. 1980.

Beach, William H. *The First New York (Lincoln) Cavalry: From April 19, 1861 to July 7, 1865.* New York. The Lincoln Cavalry Association. 1902.

Bean, T.W. *The Roll of Honor of the 17th Pennsylvania Cavalry.* Philadelphia. James Claxton. 1865.

Brown, J. Willard. *The Signal Corps, U.S.A. in the War of the Rebellion.* Boston. U.S. Veteran Signal Corps Association. 1896.

Corliss, Augustus W. *History of the 7th Squadron RI Cavalry.* Yarmouth, Maine. Old Times Office. 1879.

Daihl, Samuel L. "1865-Our Johnnies Come Marching Home," *Kittochtinny Historical Society Papers,* (KHSP), Vol. XV. pp. 128-136.

Dyer, Frederick H. *A Compendium of the War of the Rebellion.* 2 Vols. Dayton, OH. Morningside Press, 1979.

Embick, Milton A. ed. *Military History of the Third Division, Ninth Corps, Army of the Potomac.* C. E. Aughinbaugh, Printer to the State of Pennsylvania, 1913.

Farrar, Samuel Clarke. *The Twenty-Second Pennsylvania Cavalry and the Ringgold Battalion: 1861-1865.* Pittsburgh, PA. Published under the auspices of the Twenty-Second Pennsylvania Ringgold Cavalry Association. 1911.

Gracey, Rev. S. L. *Annals of the Sixth Pennsylvania Cavalry.* E. H. Butler & Co. 1868.

History of the First Troop Philadelphia City Cavalry. From its Organization November 17th, 1774 to its Centennial Anniversary November 17th, 1874. Trenton-Princeton.

History of the Twenty-Third Pennsylvania Volunteer Infantry: Birney's Zouaves. Survivors Association Twenty-Third Regiment Pennsylvania Volunteers. Philadelphia, 1903.

Kirk, Charles H. *History of the Fifteenth Pennsylvania Volunteer Cavalry.* Philadelphia. 1906.

Latta, James W. *History of the First Regiment Infantry National Guard of Pennsylvania (Gray Reserves) 1861-1911.* Philadelphia. J. B. Lippincott Co. 1912.

Martel, J. L. "Les Zouaves," *Campaigns,* Vol. II, (Jan.-Feb., 1977), pp. 32-34, 54.

Minick, Rachel, "Company G, 17th Pennsylvania Cavalry." (Unpublished Paper presented before the Kittochtinny Historical Society.

Moyer, H. P. *History of the Seventeenth Regiment Pennsylvania Volunteer Cavalry or One Hundred and Sixty-Second in the Line of Pennsylvania Volunteer Regiments: War to Suppress the Rebellion, 1861-1865.* Moyer.

Newcomer, C. Armour. *Cole's Cavalry or Three Years in the Saddle in the Shenandoah Valley.* Freeport, N.Y. Books for Libraries Press. 1970.

Norton, Henry. *A Sketch of the 8th N.Y. Cavalry, Unwritten History of the Rebellion.* Norwich, N.Y. 1888.

Norton, Henry. *Deed of Daring, or History of the Eighth N.Y. Volunteer Cavalry.* Norwich, N.Y. Chenango Telegraph Printing House. 1889.

Obretier, John. *The Seventy-Seventh Pennsylvania at Shiloh: History of the Seventy-Seventh Pennsylvania Volunteers.* Harrisburg, PA Harrisburg Publishing Co. State Printers. 1905.

Pettengill, Samuel B. *The College Cavaliers.* Chicago. H. McAllister & Co. 1883.

Robertson, James I. Jr. *Negro Soldiers in the Civil War.* Gettysburg, PA. Reprinted from Civil War Times. 1969.

Rowe, David Watson. *A Sketch of the 126th Regiment Pennsylvania Volunteers.* Chambersburg, PA. Cook & Hays. 1869.

Severn, John and Todd; Frederick P. "1st Regiment Rhode Island Detached Militia, 1861," Plate #103., Military Uniforms in America Series (MUA), The Company of Military Historians.

Simpson, Harold B. *Cry Comanche: The 2nd U.S. Cavalry in Texas, 1855-1861.* Hillsboro, Texas, Hill Junior College Press. 1979.

Stamatelos, James and Winey, Michael J. "15th Pennsylvania Volunteer Cavalry Regiment," Plate #413, Military Uniforms in America Series (MUA), The Company of Military Historians.

Starr, Stephen Z. *The Union Cavalry in the Civil War.* Vol. I. Baton Rouge. Louisiana State University Press.

Stevenson, James H. *"Boots and Saddles." A History of the First Volunteer Cavalry of the War. Known as the First New York (Lincoln) Cavalry, and also as The Sabre Regiment. Its Organization, Campaigns and Battles.* Harrisburg. Patriot Publishing Co. 1879.

Walker, Edward A. *Our First Year of Army Life.* An Anniversary Address, delivered to the First Regiment of Connecticut Volunteer Heavy Artillery, at their camp near Gaines' Mills, VA, June, 1862, by the Chaplain of the Regiment. New Haven. Thomas J. Stafford. 1862.

Walker, Joseph E. "Path Valley's Washington Blues in the Civil War." Kittochtinny Historical Society Papers (KHSP), V. XIII, pp. 373-88.

Ward, George W. *History of the Second Pennsylvania Veteran. Heavy Artillery: (112th Regiment Pennsylvania Volunteers) From 1861 to 1866, including the Provisional Second Penn's Heavy Artillery.* Philadelphia. George W. Ward, Printer. 1904.

Wilson, Suzanne Colton, ed. *Column South with the Fifteenth Pennsylvania Cavalry.* Flagstaff. J. F. Colton & Co. 1960.

Winey, Michael J. "Pennsylvanians in Gray," Military Images Magazine. Vol. IV. (July-August, 1982), pp. 16-23.

CONFEDERATE

Caldwell, J. F. F. *The History of a Brigade of South Carolina Known First as "Greggs" and Subsequently as McGowan's Brigade.* Philadelphia. 1866.

Dickert, D. Augustus. *History of Kershaw's Brigade.* Dayton, OH. Morningside Press. 1976.

Goldsborough, W. W. *The Maryland Line in the Confederate Army 1861-1865.*

Hall, Harry A. *A Johnny Reb Band from Salem: The Pride of Tarheelia.* Raleigh. The North Carolina Confederate Centennial Commission. 1963.

Owen, William Miller, *In Camp and Battle with the Washington Artillery of New Orleans.* Boston. Ticknor & Co. 1885.

Polley, J. B. *Hood's Texas Brigade: Its Marches, Its Battles, Its Achievements.* New York. The Neale Publishing Company. 1910.

Robertson, James I. Jr. *The Stonewall Brigade.* Baton Rouge. Louisiana State University Press. 1963.

Simpson, Harold B. *Gaines' Mill to Appomattox: Waco & McLennan County in Hood's Texas Brigade.* Waco, Texas. Texian Press. 1963.

Simpson, Harold B. *Hood's Texas Brigade in Poetry and Song*. Hillsboro, Texas. Hill Junior College Press. 1968.

Simpson, Harold B. *Hood's Texas Brigade: Lee's Grenadier Guard*. Waco, Texas, Texian Press. 1970.

Wellman, Manly Wade. *Rebel Boast: First at Bethel--Last at Appomattox*. New York. Henry Holt & Company. 1956.

Wise, Jennings Cropper. *The Long Arm of Lee or the History of the Artillery of the Army of Northern Virginia*. Vol. II. Lynchburg, VA. J. P. Bell Company, Inc. 1915.

MISCELLANEOUS WORKS

Banning, Kendall *Annapolis Today*. U.S. Naval Institute. 1945.

Barney, William L. *The Road to Secession*. New York. Praeger Publishers. 1972.

Berlin, Ira. *Slaves Without Masters: The Free Negro in the Antebellum South*. New York. Pantheon Books, Division of Random House. 1975.

Boatner, Mark Mayo III. *The Civil War Dictionary*. New York. David McKay Company. 1959.

Brownlee, James Henry. *Martial Recitations Heroic, Pathetic, and Humorous for the Veteran's Camp Fire*. Chicago-New York. The Werner Co.

Coggins, Jack. *Arms and Equipment of the Civil War*. Garden City, N.Y. Doubleday & Co. 1962.

Davies, Walker E. *Patriotism on Parade, the Story of Veterans and Hereditary Organization in America, 1783-1900*. Cambridge, Mass. Harvard University Press. 1955.

Dearing, Mary R. *Veterans in Politics; the Story of the G.A.R.* Baton Rouge. Louisiana State University Press. 1952.

Gara, Larry. *The Liberty Line: The Legend of the Underground Railroad*. Lexington, KY. University of Kentucky Press. 1961.

Gates, Paul W. *Agriculture and the Civil War*. New York. Alfred A. Knopf. 1965.

Haydon, F. Stansbury. *Aeronautics in the Union and Confederate Armies*. Vol. I Baltimore. The Johns Hopkins Press. 1941.

Katz, Jonathan. *Resistance at Christiana*. New York. Thomas Y. Crowell Co. 1974.

Long, E. B. *The Civil War Day by Day: An Almanac, 1861-1865*. Garden City, N.Y. Doubleday and Company, Inc. 1971.

Lonn, Ella. *Foreigners in the Confederacy*. Chapel Hill. The University of North Carolina Press. 1940.

Lord, Francis A. *They Fought for the Union*.

Lord, Francis A; Wise, Arthur. *Uniforms of the Civil War*. New York. Thomas Yoseloff. 1970.

Miller, Francis T. ed. *The Photographic History of the Civil War*. New York. Thomas Yoseloff. 1957.

Mittelay, Paul F. and Copeland-Campbell, T. *The Soldier in Our Civil War*. Vol. II. New York. J. H. Brown Publishing Co. 1885.

Quarles, Benjamin. *The Negro in the Civil War*. Boston. Little, Brown and Co. 1953.

Randall, J. G. and Donald, David. *The Civil War and Reconstruction*. Boston. D.C. Heath and Co. 1961.

Rolle, Andrew F. *The Lost Cause: The Confederate Exodus to Mexico*. University of Oklahoma Press. Norman, Oklahoma. 1965.

Sobol, Donald J. *Two Flags Flying*. New York. Platt and Munk. 1960.

Todd, Frederick P. *American Military Equipage: 1851-1872*. Providence, RI. The Company of Military Historians. 1974. 3 Vols.

Turner, George Edgar, *Victory Rode the Rails: The Strategic Place of the Railroads*. Indianapolis. The Bobbs-Merrill Co., Inc. 1953.

Utley, Robert M. *Frontier Regulars: The United States Army and the Indian, 1866-1890*. New York. Macmillan Publishing Co., Inc. 1973.

Wiley, Bell Irvin. *The Life of Johnny Reb*. Garden City. N.Y. Doubleday & Co., Inc. 1971.

PHOTOGRAPHS

Ted Alexander, Greencastle, PA
Besore Library, Greencastle, PA
Mary Detrich, Greencastle, PA
Robert Donohue, Chambersburg, PA
Mark Elrod, Gaithersburg, MD

Mrs. John A. Girton, Williamsport, PA
Kathleen Grosh, Greencastle, PA
U.S. Army Military History Institute-MOLLUS Coll.
Ronn Palm, Kittaning, PA
Catherine Stickell, Greencastle, PA

RESOURCE PERSONS

We wish to recognize the following persons who have contributed information from their family records.

GREENCASTLE-ANTRIM AREA

Bill Amos
Vada Angle
Andrew Barbuzanes
Isabell Barnes
Blanche Barr
Mr. and Mrs. Edward Beard
Charles W. Bert
Tom Bohon
Mike Bowers
Eleanora Briggs
Helen Burkholder
Adam Byers
Frank Cantrell
John T. Conrad III
William Cole
Lillian Colletta
John Craig

Karen Craig
Glen Cump
Mabel Davis
Mary Detrich
Mr. and Mrs. Richard Ervin
Dorothy Gordon
Dorothy Gift
Mr. and Mrs. Glen Grosh
Joseph Hensen, Sr.
Robert Johnston (Deceased)
Earl Leckron
Nelson Leckron
Ivan Martin
Melody Mentzer
Aaron Meyers
H. Norman Meyers
Marvin Miller

Bill Moore
Frank Mowen
Ray Mowen, Jr.
Paul Musselman
Jeannette Nelson
Clayton Phipps (Deceased)
Eric Pittman
Lance "Lover" Roscoe
Arabelle T. Shaffer
Elmer Shatzer
Tom Shook
Catherine A. Stickell
Garth Weeks
Wendy Weeks
Helen K. Welch
Stella Wingert
Edward Zarger

WAYNESBORO AREA

Ray Barnhart
Larry Calimer
Mrs. Fred Easton
Lillian Good

Paul Hollinger
Nancy Mace
Pauline Maxwell
Robert Meck

Earl Shatzer
George Shatzer

CHAMBERSBURG AREA

Robert Donohue
Patricia Farrell
Janet Gabler

Aaron Hartman
Ralph B. Horst
Ruth Keller

Mrs. Curtis Lawyer
Charles P. Schaff

OTHER AREAS

Dr. Charles W. Bert, Jr. Norman OK

Mr. and Mrs. G. H. Bricker, Philip Schaff Library, Lancaster Theological Seminary, Lancaster, PA.

Dr. Thomas Brumbaugh, Vanderbilt University, Nashville, TN.

Ed. Campbell, Harrisburg, PA.

Joseph Conrad, Mercersburg, PA.

Michael Conrad, Carlisle, PA.

Dennis Frye, Harpers Ferry National Historical Park, Harpers Ferry, WV.

Kathleen Georg, Gettysburg National Military Park, Gettysburg, PA.

John Geschwindt, Government Publications Section, State Library of Pennsylvania, Harrisburg, PA.

Mrs. John Girton, Williamsport, PA.

Les Jensen, Museum of the Confederacy, Richmond, VA.

Bettye Gilbert Kramer, Manchester, CN.

Robert Krick, Fredericksburg-Spotsylvania National Military Park, Fredericksburg, VA.

Mrs. Donald E. Lyon, Livonia, MI.

Robert Mason, Newspaper Room, State Library of Pennsylvania, Harrisburg, PA.

Hayes E. Pentz, Leola, PA.

Louis F. Ravco, Newspaper Room, State Library of Pennsylvania, Harrisburg, PA.

John W. Schildt, Chewsville, MD.

John Shelly, Division of Archives and Manuscripts, Pennsylvania Historical and Museum Commission, Harrisburg, PA.

Richard A. Shrader, University of North Carolina, Chapel Hill, NC.

Montgomery Shroyer, Westminister, MD.

Harold B. Simpson, Hill Junior College, Hillsboro, TX.

Roger Sturcke, Woodbridge, PA.

Mrs. A. K. Williamson, Hemet, CA.

INDEX

434

Spotsylvania Court House — 182
Sprague, Gov. William — 58
Springfield, Illinois — 355
St. James, MD — 79
St. Thomas, PA — 37, 87, 90, 101, 250, 251,
    269-272, 280, 283
Stanton, Sec. Edward — 94, 143, 168, 170, 180, 183,
    205, 312
Staunton, VA — 244, 274, 309
Stahel, Gen. Julius — 275
Steiger, George — 90
Stenger, W. S. — 355
Stephenson, Dr. B. F. — 355
Steuart's Brigade — 154, 155
Stevens, Alexander — 315, 317
Stevens, John — 161, 162, 163
Stevens Post — 363
Stevens, Thaddeus — 155, 329
Stevenson, Capt. James H. — 363, 365
Stevenson's Depot — 309
Steward, Adj. John — 101
Steward, Judge John — 355, 372
Stewart, Jack — 165
Stickell, Jonathan — 71
Stickell, John R. — 64, 367
Stickell, Samuel — 149, 300
Stickell, William — 364
Stiffel, Andrew — 5, 149, 152, 337
Stitzel, Capt. George — 64, 72
Stine, Henry — 71
Stine, Rev. I. J. — 92-94
Stoodard, G. E. — 185
Stone, Henry — 71
Stoneman, Gen. George — 118, 171
Stoner, Samuel — 5
Stones River Battle — 290
Stonewall Brigade — 154
Stover, Jacob — 14, 55, 158, 338
Stover, John — 71
Stover, Mitchell — 338
Strasburg, PA — 37
Streets - Greencastle — 2, 347
Street Lights — 7
Strickler, Sgt. Henry — 114, 154, 344
Strickler, Joseph — 114, 342
Strite, David — 14, 235
Strite, Isaac — 141
Stryker, Capt. William A. — 287, 322
Stuart, Gen. J.E.B. — 29, 61, 88-92, 94, 118, 132,
    134, 168, 171, 200, 201, 252
Stuart's Raid — 89-94
Stumbaugh, Col. Frederick — 71, 289, 290
Sugar Loaf Mountain — 276
Sumner, Gen. Edward — 106
Sunday School Classes — 373
Susquehanna River — 74, 143, 155, 168, 310
Swisher, George — 313
Swisher, Jacob — 114
Swisher, — 364
Swuninski, John — 37

T

Takoma Park, MD — 341
Taylor's Heights — 106
Temperance Movement — 21, 22, 231, 232, 237
Tennessee — 204
Tennessee Campaign — 140, 224, 284, 290
Texas Brigade — 87

Texas 5th Regiment — 161
Thanksgiving — 96, 217, 229, 265, 313
Thayer, Lt. Amos M. — 273, 275-277, 284-287
Thomas, Gen. George H. — 46, 52, 54, 58, 244,
    266,290
Thomas, Gen. Lorenzo — 205
Thompson, J. Edgar — 77
Tiotter, Tom — 152
Tobacco Farming — 241, 338
Tobias, John — 208, 209
Torrence, Com. Eli — 371
Town Clock — 348
Trade — 8, 9
Trans-Mississippi Theater — 331
Tremont, PA — 211
Trenary, Henry — 290
Treichel, Capt. — 176
Trimble, Gen. Isaac — 150
Troxell, Maj. Elias S. — 310
Tunnel Hill Battle — 292
Turnpikes — 7, 8
Turner, Nat — 27
Turner's Gap Battle — 87
Turner's Gap, MD — 87, 199
Tyler, Gen. Erastus — 101-105, 114-117, 173

U

Underground R. R. — 26
Unger, Jacob — 309, 365
Union Hotel — 6, 28, 174, 214, 248
Union League — 128, 280
Union Mills, MD — 168
Union Party — 31
Union Volunteers — 47
United Brethren Church — 17, 359
United States Arsenal — 39
United States Colored —
    2nd Cavalry — 55, 306, 341
    2nd Infantry — 306
    10th Cavalry — 374
    25th Infantry — 306
    38th Infantry — 306, 333
    45th Infantry — 306
    127th Infantry — 306
United States Ford — 123
United States —
    1st Artillery — 55
    2nd Cavalry — 55
    6th Cavalry — 249
    8th Infantry — 55
United States Light House Board — 188
United States Marines — 29
United States Naval Academy — 185
Upton, PA — 9, 16, 37, 244, 309
Upton Company — 218, 237, 343

V

Valentine, Daniel — 293
Valley Echo — 339, 344
Valley Spirit — 70, 76, 322-324, 355
Valverde Battle — 340
VanDervoot, Paul — 357, 370
Vaughn, Gen. John C. — 251, 257
Veteran's Memorial Square — 367
Vicksburg Siege — 130, 266
Vicksburg Surrender — 202

444

MAP INDEX

ILLUSTRATIONS

ERRATA

I. Corrections and additions to content matter.

p. 84 — Last paragraph, fourth line: ". . . over 26,000 . . ." — ". . . over 23,000 . . ."

p. 89 — Last paragraph, fifth line: ". . . upon reaching the Pennsylvania shore. . ." — ". . . upon reaching the Maryland shore. . ."

p. 115 — Second paragraph: General Robert Ransom's Brigade was not in the Gettysburg Campaign, having been transferred to North Carolina prior to it. General Lafayette McLaws commanded a division not a brigade.

p. 132 — First paragraph: Most of Jenkin's men were recruited in southwestern Virginia and what is now West Virginia. These units had not served with Turner Ashby or Stonewall Jackson as previously stated. Rather, they had been involved in operations in West Virginia prior to the Gettysburg Campaign.

p. 167 — Fourth paragraph, tenth and eleventh lines: The source for Fitzhugh Lee's Brigade being in Greencastle was "The Pilot." Actually, Fitzhugh Lee was with Stuart's Cavalry near Rockville, Md. on June 28. Lee's Cavalry Brigade did pass through the town on the retreat. The editor, no doubt, was referring to the cavalry brigades of Jones and Robertson, which brought up the rear of Lee's invasion force.

p. 169 — Map: This map fails to show the movement of Early's Division through Waynesboro to Greenwood.

p. 187 — First paragraph: The casualties at Gettysburg totalled over 47,000 not 50,000 as stated.

p. 205 — Third paragraph, first line: Lorenzo Thomas was not State Adjutant General but rather Adjutant General of the United States Army.

p. 266 — Map: The map shows McCausland's force taking present day Route 416 to Mercersburg in 1864. Actually, his main force followed the same route as Stuart in 1862 (Route 75). A diversionary force under Major Harry Gilmor moved east on the National Road and joined McCausland at Mercersburg via 416.

p. 275 — Second paragraph, seventh line: Early's force numbered probably no more than 14,000 men.

p. 275 — Fourth paragraph: After crossing the South Mountain Range, not the Catoctin Range, Early advanced across the Middletown Valley. He would cross the Catoctin Range prior to entering Frederick.

p. 310 — Second paragraph, sixth line: "Washington County, Pennsylvania."

p. 317 — Fourth paragraph: Another Medal of Honor winner, Thaddeus S. Smith, Co. E, 6th Pennsylvania Reserves claimed Franklin County as his place of birth. Smith won the Medal for helping to storm a Confederate held log cabin near Devils Den at Gettysburg on July 2, 1863. Smith's Franklin County roots are confusing. His compiled service record at the National Archives (Record Group 94) lists his place of birth as "Cumberland, Pa." His furlough papers indicate his home was Mechanicsburg, Pa. The only mention of Franklin County are his enlistment papers into the 191st Pennsylvania in 1864, listing his place of birth as Franklin County.

p. 345 — Last paragraph: The Lee Rhodes story is full of the material that of which legends are made. However, researching beyond local legend, the authors have found that William Lee Rhodes was born in Frederick County, Md. June 25, 1840 and lived there prior to the outbreak of the war. In 1861 he joined the 1st Maryland Infantry (Confederate). He was wounded in the foot at Gettysburg and later in the war was a Captain in the 8th Virginia Cavalry. After the war he moved to Greencastle to work as a clerk for his brother, C. C. Rhodes, a local businessman. He married Barbara Hade, not Allie Heayed, perhaps in 1867 or 1879 (his obituary reads 1829, an obvious typo.) This information was found in the *Echo Pilot* February 20, 1902 and compiled Service Record, National Archives, Record Group 94.

II. Typographical and Spelling Errors.

p. 23 — First paragraph, sixth line: "Surrounding"

p. 68, 75, 250 and 309 — "Clearspring, MD." — "Clear Spring, MD."

p. 104 — Last paragraph, sixth line: "Loudoun"

p. 154 — Fifth paragraph, third line: "Steuart"

p. 155 — Fourth paragraph, fifth line: "flour"

p. 216 — Second paragraph, sixteenth line: "Hooker"

p. 218 — Fifth paragraph, fourth line: "the"

p. 230 — Fourth paragraph, sixth line: "getting"

p. 251 — Second paragraph, third line: "Generals William L. *Jackson*"

p. 298 — Third paragraph, first line: ". . . were not . . ."

p. 339 — Fourth paragraph, first line: "Greeley"

p. 393 — Middle of page — George W. Kettoman, the "South Mountain Bard"

III. Corrections to Picture Credits and Captions.

p. 31 — *History of Franklin County, Pennsylvania*

p. 76 — *Valley News Echo*

p. 77 — *History of the 15th Pennsylvania Volunteer Cavalry*

p. 94 — Beard - Greenawalt collection

p. 102 — *History of Franklin County, Pennsylvania*

p. 109 — *Battles and Leaders of the Civil War*

p. 133 — USAMHI

p. 145 — *Medical Men of Franklin County*

p. 148 — Caption: "Confederates Destroying A Railroad."

p. 151 — Detrich Collection

p. 177 — *Recollections of a Maryland Confederate.*

p. 194 — *Battles and Leaders of the Civil War*

p. 200 — *History of Franklin County, Pennsylvania.*

p. 252 — *History of Franklin County, Pennsylvania.*

p. 259 — *Miller's Photographic History.*

p. 273 — *The Signal Corps, U.S.A. in the War of the Rebellion*

p. 294 — *History of the Second Pennsylvania Veteran Heavy Artillery.*

p. 315 — Stickell and Donoho Collections.

p. 338 — *History of Franklin County, Pennsylvania.*

p. 365 — *Medical Men of Franklin County.*

p. 369 — Alexander Collection

IV. Corrections to Footnotes and Bibliography

p. 406 — Footnote 26, fifth line: Franklin Repository, January 1, 1890.

p. 407 — Footnote 69: McLaws.

p. 420 — Southern Historical Collection: McLaws.

p. 423 — Conrad citations at top of page should be separated as they are two different works. *Conococheague* was published by the Greencastle-Antrim School District in cooperation with the Lilian Besore Memorial Library, 1971.

p. 426 — Hoke, Jacob — *The Great Invasion.* New York. Thomas Yoseloff, 1959.

p. 428 — Moyer, H. P. *History of the Seventeenth Pennsylvania Volunteer Cavalry or One Hundred and Sixty Second in the Line of Pennsylvania Volunteer Regiments: War to Suppress the Rebellion 1861-1865.* Lebanon, Pa. Sowers Printing. 1911

p. 429 — Miscellaneous Works: Lord, Francis A. *They Fought for the Union.* New York. Bonanza Books. 1960.

p. 430 — Photographs: Mr. and Mrs. Edward Beard, Greencastle, Pa.

p. 430 — Resource Persons: Mr. and Mrs. Barry Thomas, Greencastle, Pa.

p. 431 — 9th name down: Louis F. Rauco.